# The Wheels of Friend

## BOOK 1
A WORLDWIDE BICYCLE JOURNEY

## ERIC NORLAND

**AUTHOR OF** *FROM FOUR ROYAL PERSIAN STARS TO JESUS AND THE SUN.*
**AUTHOR OF** *HAPPY'S WORLD*

**THE WHEELS OF FRIEND**
**A WORLDWIDE BICYCLE JOURNEY**

*Copyright © 2020 Eric Norland.*

*All rights reserved. No part of this book may be used or reproduced by any means, graphic, electronic, or mechanical, including photocopying, recording, taping or by any information storage retrieval system without the written permission of the author except in the case of brief quotations embodied in critical articles and reviews.*

*iUniverse books may be ordered through booksellers or by contacting:*

*iUniverse*
*1663 Liberty Drive*
*Bloomington, IN 47403*
*www.iuniverse.com*
*1-800-Authors (1-800-288-4677)*

*Because of the dynamic nature of the Internet, any web addresses or links contained in this book may have changed since publication and may no longer be valid. The views expressed in this work are solely those of the author and do not necessarily reflect the views of the publisher, and the publisher hereby disclaims any responsibility for them.*

*Any people depicted in stock imagery provided by Getty Images are models,*
*and such images are being used for illustrative purposes only.*
*Certain stock imagery © Getty Images.*

*ISBN: 978-1-5320-9821-5 (sc)*
*ISBN: 978-1-5320-9828-4 (e)*

*Library of Congress Control Number: 2020905609*

*Print information available on the last page.*

*iUniverse rev. date: 04/23/2020*

# Contents

| | |
|---|---|
| Chapter 1 | 1 |
| Chapter 2 | 67 |
| Chapter 3 | 113 |
| Chapter 4 | 135 |
| Chapter 5 | 153 |
| Chapter 6 | 167 |
| Chapter 7 | 189 |
| Chapter 8 | 217 |
| Chapter 9 | 229 |
| Chapter 10 | 261 |
| Chapter 11 | 271 |
| Chapter 12 | 297 |
| Chapter 13 | 307 |
| Chapter 14 | 359 |
| Chapter 15 | 395 |
| Chapter 16 | 413 |
| Chapter 17 | 421 |
| Chapter 18 | 439 |

**Friday July 1st, 1983** dawned foggy and cool in Santa Barbara, California when the alarm went off at 7:30am. My bed was warm and comfortable and instinctively the blankets were pulled up higher while rolling over in an attempt to drift back to sleep. I'd slept well, but wasn't leaping out of bed. There was no desire to do anything, even though this was the day that I'd planned for so long. After many months of preparation, everything was ready to go, but an incentive seemed missing, and a total lack of motivation had drifted in. There was this feeling of being at the very bottom of a very high mountain, without hope of making the first beginning steps up the climb, let alone to reach the top. Reluctantly, I was consoling with defeat, but wishing for immediate victory.

The pillow felt snugly soft, as seconds ticked past, then minutes were lost cuddling fluffy blankets and lying still. I was caught between two worlds, one of which was to get going, the other was to forget about the whole thing. Frustration came, then fear, anxiety, and almost tears. Why am I doing this and what am I doing this for? I felt stuck.

Shear willpower pushed the first blanket off and a glimmer of hope helped peel off the next and out of the bed reached one intrepid foot toward the floor, then another. When they made contact the journey around the world had begun.

I trudged toward the shower, as an unexplained destiny pushed me. Inside brewed a turmoil of perplexing emotions and feelings. What was to be gained over what was there to lose? Surely it seemed more logical to just give up. I could easily head for the beach today. But my mind was set on doing this. Now it was a matter of following through.

It was this headstrong determination, which, in the last few weeks, had caused co-workers to question the seriousness of my proposed journey. The questions they asked were often discouraging. "What will you do if you run out of money, or what if you have no place to go, or what if you are robbed or what about this or that?" They flooded me with 'what if's'. Yet the question I asked myself was - why me? I saw others falling in love, earning good incomes and becoming established in positions or starting families. On the contrary, I was tearing down all those ties and avoiding relationships. Mine was a kind of divine intervention to be alone and too try and be independent. I could hardly concentrate on anything, as my mind focused on the constant dream of around the world travel. Feeling obscured by the realization that the motivator that got me to this point was now like that alarm going off, it was time for a new unknown to reveal what was yet to come.

    I stepped into the shower and turned a fearful face into the hot spray to drive away the sleepy anxiety. It doused my awakening mind and kindled the senses of what was about to be done. In another hour I would begin pedaling my way eastward, toward New York. I would be **out there** on my own, severed from every security. The pulsating shower blurred my senses. How did I ever get to this point?

### *It started back in the summer of 1978.*

*I'd just graduated from college, was 23 years of age and had started a new job. My dad said, "If you want to live at home, you'll have to start paying rent." This gave me some incentive to move out and thus I began renting a room in a house with two other guys in Duluth, Minnesota.*

*The house was owned by Howard, a dirt bike riding friend. He was interested in renting it out for a year while working in Florida, selling insurance.*

*My friends, Gordy, Mark and Gary expressed an interest in living there. We were all dirt bikers, and decided to pool our resources and rent out the place. At the last minute Gary had to cancel, so Mark, Gordy and I, moved into the Regent Street house in August of 1978.*

*The first thing that became apparent was my new roommates and I hardly knew each other. Though we'd lived in the same part of town, and rode dirt bikes together, we were not real close. We knew each other's names, and I'd known Gordy from church, but really we were strangers at first. What we had in common was each of us wanting an inexpensive place to live.*

*This was our first experience at living away from home. Everything in our youthful eyes was novel and fun. We were suddenly released from the bonds of our parents. It soon became like the movie Animal House, because of all the zaniness that went on there. We were adolescents charged with the energy of youth, exploring life to the hilt. We were simpletons of excitement. Each of us acted like giggle pusses encapsulated into our own little dramas. Like a play, our acts were unfolding and leading to some final performance, where big changes would yet come.*

*We put on many Saturday night parties. They were social gatherings of friends, with drinking of beer and occasionally passing a joint. Eight track tapes played music by Stykx, Rush and The Little River Band on Gordy's 200 watt stereo. This created an atmosphere of partiesville, with lively discussions and new acquaintances.*

*As time went on word must have spread amongst friends, that we had good parties. In the next few months, they became bigger and wilder. It was at one of those gatherings that something happened which ultimately propelled me in the direction of a bicycle journey around the world.*

## From the shower into a bike journey

I stepped out of the shower, as butterflies fluttered to life in my stomach while eating a running breakfast, packing clothing away and stuffing items into garbage bags. By 8:30am, my trusty car, nicknamed the Hotel Gordini, was loaded up with all earthly belongings as well as other keepsakes ready for storage, while I was traveling on the journey.

Ken, who had allowed me to stay in his house that last week, followed me in his small pickup truck, as we drove south through Montecido and Carpenteria, along the coastline of the Ventura Highway, to Joe Beth's house in Ventura. It was a memorable drive. My car was fully packed so heavily that I feared the tires would go flat. On this final ride, I hurriedly played my favorite cassette tapes. Songs like Christopher Cross'- Sailing, and Bob Dylan's- Idiot Wind -off the album 'Blood on the Tracks.' I frantically hastened to hear them one last time, as the morning sun shone above the Channel Islands, illuminating the frothing, tumbling surf on the coastline of the blue Pacific Ocean. Doubts about why I was going on this journey frequently interspersed between positive thoughts; that I was really going to go forward with this adventure. I'd get these death-griping-fearful thoughts and then sudden bursts of freedom. As I neared my destination at Joe Beth's house, I had last minute fearful thoughts that flooded me within. They were nearly shouting at me to cancel this whole adventure before it even started. They challenged me to change my mind, but I felt set on a course that seemed stubbornly predestined.

I parked the Hotel Gordini in Joe Beth's garage and covered it with a tarp. I gave her the keys and talked a few things over with her about what to do should I never return. Then I said, "I'll see you in about nine months." Her words were encouraging, "Do not to worry about anything, just have a good trip." We shook hands, embraced and said goodbye.

On the return trip to Santa Barbara in Ken's little pickup, he calmly talked in a Louisiana accent about his job. He was concerned that the company we'd both worked for these last two years was moving to Minnesota. "I'm not sure I'd get along well in Minnesota, with all that snow and cold," he said with his Alabama accent. He admitted to me his marriage was on the rocks. He had a drinking problem and liked doing drugs. His was such a tangled web, I couldn't tell him that I secretly knew of another co-worker who'd slept with his wife. It was better to just be nice, and say goodbye.

As his truck strained to climb the final steep hill toward his house I noticed that he downshifted and it worried me. Could I ride my fully loaded bike and equipment up similar grades? Doubts about my own capabilities once again teased my mind. Will my knees hold out? There were more thoughts about backing out of this bike trip. Will I have enough strength to do this crazy feat? Suddenly I was weak and very tired. I wanted to go back to bed.

Back at Ken's house, I changed into cycling shorts, put on my homemade yellow t-shirt saying FRIEND and then readied the bike and equipment. What a strange sensation it was to think that now my only possessions were this heavily loaded bicycle and these simple belongings. I felt almost naked, embarrassed, revealed and downright foolish, while rolling the wiggling bike out of the garage.

Ken's wife, Kitti and their sons Dennis and Michael stood woefully looking at me, preparing for my departure. There was a last minute scramble to fill my water bottles and then I said some very heartfelt good-byes to them. Kitti said to me, "I admire you for what you are doing," and gave me a hug. Her boobs pushed against my chest. Ken said, "Watch out for those wild women." We shook a dampened handshake. I was kind of choked up. They had helped me so much these last few months. I was forever indebted to them. With one last thank you, I pushed off, looking down at my yellow t-shirt and the hand painted name of my bike FRIEND. This is the journey I'd soon be on.

## The Beginning

I pushed off with my left foot and coasted away, fumbling, missing the pedal, unable to get my left shoe into the stirrup. They all let out a hearty laugh. "Sure you don't want to stay a little longer?" said Ken. "No, but thanks," I rasply said, as I placed the shoe onto the pedal, turned around, took a good long look back and gave a big wave. I was off, this was my journeys beginning.

They stood behind me, getting smaller as I coasted down the street past fine Santa Barbara hillside homes toward the city center. I felt exhilarated, but with a silent panic, as the wind whistled in my face, there was a fragrant smell of flowers that dizzied me. The bike picked up speed and chiseled through the morning fog. I was shocked at the amount of weight the bike was carrying while rounding a curve. I had never known it to be this heavy. The front wheel started to wobble severely and for a moment I lost control, I panicked and was forced to jam on the brakes and come to a screeching stop. My feet crunched the ground. I stopped and thought maybe this wasn't going to work and the whole bike journey should be called off. I could just turn around and walk the bike back up the hill. Instead I nervously fumbled with the pannier bags and readjusted the weight on the bike. It was the only option available. Resuming the downhill stretch, the wobble was less, but it was still there, and I thought I would just have to try and live with it. I felt so green to this mode of transportation, and at times sheepish with the attention it drew. People driving by would look at me with such amusement. I felt like a fool, standing out like a spectacle. But this sudden notoriety was short-lived, as soon the busy streets of downtown Santa Barbara were behind me, giving way to more rural settings. I turned right, saying goodbye to the last convenience store and began the long and grueling climb up 2000 foot high San Marcos Pass. A road sign ahead read; <u>Bicycles Prohibited</u>, but I pedaled past it and continued pedaling like a madman as the road narrowed and the grade steepened. It was a sticky morning because of the thick mountain fog and I continued until it became unbearably hot from the rigorous physical workout. I took off my shirt and was pedaling like crazy but seemingly getting nowhere. Had, I been in my car, I'd already be twenty miles down the road. It was very frustrating and for an angry moment I cried out, "Why am I doing this to myself?" I wanted to go back and suck on a cold drink and sit upon the beach. But I knew that would be an easy escape. This would be my baptism to fire and my initiation to bicycle touring in the most brutal sense.

I was about halfway up when the fog burned off and behind was a spectacular view of the Santa Barbara airport and the endless blue Pacific Ocean. It was only a backdrop to my agony, as I was now in the lowest gear and lugging along, with salty sweat dripping upon my burning eyes. A fear set in that the chain would snap, that the wheels would burst, that the frame would give way under this strain.

I soon became overheated and feared my heart would burst out from my chest. Is this whole thing insane? I questioned myself, my intentions. "I'm just one little exhausted heart trying to move all of this f_ _ _ gear." Many stops were made along that grade to catch a breath and to allow motor homes, which I coined 'road monsters,' too pass. Their wide breadth and slow travel seemed as if they would run over and gobble me up.

The asphalt shoulder was only a foot wide and sometimes that's all there was to prevent my going over an embankment of several hundred feet. With each step, all my capabilities were contested to maintain strength, balance and stamina. After two hours of pedaling, there was one final long steep up hill grade. Each pedal was utter agony, I strained and struggled to use whatever power was available. By zigzagging back and forth on the whole lane and in the lowest gear I finally made it to the top of San Marcos Pass. Some people watched me as I pedaled even harder to get up to the small store, located on the right side. I was dying for a cold drink and finally came to a stop and sat down huffing and puffing, trying desperately to catch each breath as my heart threatened to come out of my chest. I nearly collapsed.

I went into the small store and bought a drink. A very cold orange juice was engorged down my dry throat and it pierced but soothed this hollow stomach with each swallow. My face was beet-red, like a man fresh out of a sauna. My head was pounding and heart doing the beat of a disco dancer.

Looking back down the grade I thought, San Marcos Pass you were brutal. "But someday," I said aloud, "I will avenge you by coasting down your monstrous grade shouting obscenities with up-raised arms." Then I dreamed how someday I'd ride victoriously into Santa Barbara and cross the finish line ribbon, as a brass band played. The song would be; 'Oh When the Saints come Marching in.' There would be pretty girls running to embrace me and I'd drink champagne. After that, I'd be finished with travel and with this hair brained adventure.

I scoffed at my delusional thoughts as a toothless man approached and asked, "Where ya headin?" "San Francisco," I answered. "Whew! San Francisco, wow! That is too far to go on a bike!" he said while shaking his head and saying "no way," which revealed his wrinkled face and long gray hairs. He walked away from me, still shaking his head and saying, "No way!"

From the top of San Marcos Pass I coasted downhill heading north along a fine stretch of highway for the next three miles. This was fun, freewheeling along at breathtaking speeds over Cold Springs Canyon Bridge and past Lake Cachuma. I gripped the handlebars firmly to prevent the bike from wobbling. Oh, what a heavenly joy ride this was. I was free! This bicycle journey seemed like such a breeze!

But the picnic soon ended as the grueling pedaling resumed, up and over more rolling hills. By noon the fog had burned away and I pedaled under the fierce Southern California sun. I was soon overheated and felt weak and stopped to eat lunch and rest, on the roadside. My arms and legs turned to rubber. A while later, I continued on, struggling over more parched yellow hills toward Santa Ynez and Solvang. Frequent stops were made to ease my nervously shaking legs and this faint feeling in my head. At one point I got under a bridge, to get out of the sun and catch my breath.

I passed through Solvang and saw tourists gawking at me and my clumsy looking bike. Some asked where I was headed. When I acknowledged, they smirked at such a notion of biking to San Francisco.

The sun was murderously hot at 6pm while riding into Los Alamos. I'd gone as far as I could, probably about 70 miles, and was very hungry and in need of a cold drink. There was a small restaurant, which I entered into, walking like a man wearing concrete boots. I plopped down and ordered the most quantity of food for the cheapest price from the menu. I wolfed down a plate of spaghetti, while gazing in a hazy daze at several cute waitresses. Every morsel of food on the plate was devoured and then washed down with several glasses of chocolate milk, which made the meal expensive. I dreaded the thought of spending six dollars for every meal.

Before leaving the restaurant, I cleaned up thoroughly by standing in the urinal, holding the lever down and splashing water over my sticky body until sufficiently clean. I soaped up and continued, but was startled when a woman walked in on me during the midst of my bath. She said "humf" and did a good job of ignoring me, then headed straight into a stall and closed the door. I wiped off my body with a t-shirt, redressed and made a quick exit to avoid any further embarrassment. That was my first exposure to a unisex washroom!

After dinner I pedaled over to a campground which cost an exuberant $9 to stay the night. The manager, who was a short, curly haired elderly woman could sense I was economizing. "Go next door to the Exxon station, there's a young man living behind it. He'll let you stay in his yard for less," she said. I went over there and knocked on the front door of the small house and the young man was real nice and said, "Sure your welcome to pitch your tent over under the oak tree, enjoy yourself." I asked him, "Can I pay yah?" "No, no," he exclaimed, while waving his hands.

I put up my tent and got inside while the sun was setting at the end of my first day on the road. I was sore, tired, sunburned and wondering about what tomorrow would bring. I drifted off to sleep hoping a miracle would happen, that tomorrow would never come and make me ride that bike anymore. I started thinking back about those silly days.

### *Recollections of Regent Street*

*Our animal house was on the upper side of Regent Street near 42nd Ave East. It was a quaint little four-bedroom bungalow, two bedrooms up and two down. Howard, the owner, rented it to us for $275 per month. During our stay at the house it was up for sale, but since the economy was pretty bad, few people came around to look at it. The three of us each had our own bedroom and we remodeled one downstairs bedroom into a party room with a bar. We called it the "freak out room." I painted blacklight murals onto the wall that looked like Close Encounters of the Third Kind. Another wall had a galaxy and then 'stars' were splattered on the ceiling. I enjoyed astronomy, and had studied the subject at the university. Here was a place to express that interest. We had a blacklight set up and there was a flashing strobe light in the room as well and a few speakers hooked up to the stereo. That room became the collecting spot for our Saturday night parties. Often times it was wall to wall with young people dancing to songs like My Sharrona and Cat Scratch Fever. I felt gifted to be living in our animal house, as this was a dream come true for my existentialism of youth.*

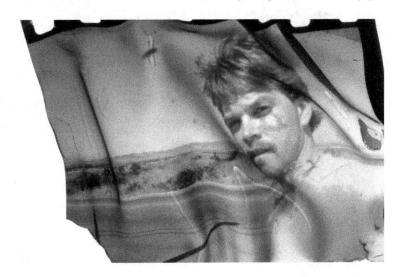

## Saturday July 2nd

At 6:30 I awoke with my body aching at every move. It seemed impossible to get things packed up. Things just didn't fit into my panniers like they did yesterday. I finally was ready to go by 7am and was soon struggling to get the bike underway. It seemed very heavy and ungainly. I decided to leave highway 101 and travel along less traveled highway #166. While traffic was much quieter, it was also much slower going. The road zig zagged and slowed my northward progress. Every crack in the road was jarring to the bones. After passing through the small Mexican town of Guadalupe and downing a couple of Cokes, I felt lightheaded and wondered if a sickness was coming on. The road passed through gorgeous groves of fragrant eucalyptus trees. The color of the landscape was wonderful. At times the sunlight and the leaves reminded me of fall back home. I wanted to give up, pull over and set up camp. The thought of taking a couple of days to rest entered my mind. But this driving force kept me pedaling on. I counted the slow passing miles in agonizing disappointment. It was torturous just to see how hard won each mile was. It was better to not even look at the pedometer. I wondered how I would ever get anywhere at this speed. The monotony was overwhelming. I pondered adding knitting or model building to my 'activities' while pedaling along at this slow pace. Finally I saw the wondrous ocean lapping against Centennial Rock off of Pismo Beach. It was great to enter that town and revisit the place again. I recalled when I first past through here in 1981 and how I'd slept in my car on the beach. I chuckled when recalling how tongue-tied I was when meeting a fine young gal in a bikini.

From Pismo, the route continued up freeway 101, struggling against menacing headwinds that beleaguered me, but was still making pretty good time.

Especially troublesome became a very steep grade called Santa Margarita hill. This high hill has a 1500-foot incline which is long and straight with one sweeping left turn. Traffic was heavy and it sounded like thunder from the roar of so many vehicles. It was midmorning and because of the heat I'd taken my shirt off and draped it across my back like a cape, clasping it up front with a wire tie. It worked fine for keeping the hot sun off my back, and allowed air to circulate over my sunburned shoulders.

I pedaled hard near the roads edge, while straining to maintain a straight course even in the lowest gear. A large semi-trailer truck, or should I say a road monster, down shifted behind me and then crept by with its huge tires rolling perilously close. The hot, thick, black diesel exhaust pelted me, nearly robbing me of breath, from its sickening stench. Then his huge semi trailer, which was loaded with steel crept to my left, dangerously close to my pumping leg. Suddenly a gust of wind flipped my draped shirt, over my helmet and over my face, blinding my view! Only a few inches away to my left were the crunching truck tires rolling past! To my right was a deep rocky ditch. I could only go straight! Every possible effort was applied to keep a steady course. It was pure pilotage, for if I swerved only inches off the path I'd be crushed by the trailer tires or wrecked in the ditch. It was lucky for me to have practiced aircraft instrument flight training! I stayed on course by maintaining a certain distance from the pavements edge by looking straight down at the roadbed, directly between my pumping legs. This was accomplished without missing a stroke nor stumbling. Finally the truck passed and the t- shirt was brushed off of my face.

Around 4:30 I stopped into the small town of San Miguel to buy groceries. There, I met a young couple riding a bicycle built for two. They had cycled down from Vancouver in 3 weeks time and offered some advice about where to look for a place to stay tonight. "There's a nice wayside rest south of King City," he said. After a few minutes of conversation my cycling resumed northward.

I was making good time on this lovely afternoon, even though feeling tired and annoyed by the whining sounds of passing cars and dodging a litter of tire parts and animal carcasses. My greatest problem at this time was an aching butt from the hard, edgy bicycle seat. It seemed each time that I pedaled it hurt worse. I tried hard to take my mind off of the agony, but it was hard to do. It was easier for my thoughts to drift back to Julie.

### *The lady who changed my world*

*She was a nice looking brunette who often dropped by our Regent Street house and its party like disposition. This mysterious young lady had fine features, she was shapely and well endowed. Her hair was long and straight. She came by to chat and to see what was happening. Her name was Julie. Despite being 18 years of age, she seemed so liberated and so much older and wiser then her age. With a disposition of confidence, she was independently minded and had the courage to casually drift in and visit with 'the guys.' I didn't know who she was for some time, but our conversations were easy enough to generate. She knew about art, spoke the language of an artist and liked music. She teased my senses, enticed my thoughts, I was reawakened by her...*

## *Once again heading up toward Paso Robles*

As the day was getting late, my legs ached as I dodged many dead rabbits while pedaling up the fine shoulder of freeway #101. I was nearly exhausted and feared collapse when in the distance appeared the grassy roadside rest area that the two Vancouver cyclists had mentioned. It looked like a mirage. It was so inviting. Every pedal I made was hurting me, just to get there, sometimes it felt like forever. I coasted in and claimed a picnic table like a man does a couch.

As the sun set behind the Coast Range, a very refreshing shower was enjoyed by jumping over the lawn sprinkler. There were some kids laughing at my silly behavior. I cooked a dinner of macaroni and cheese while people looked oddly at me. I ignored them, inhaled my dinner while seated at this fine picnic table, all the while watching the passing traffic and the gorgeous purplish California twilight.

When bedtime came, the bike was locked up to the picnic table at this fine grassy spot, which offered comfort to lay out my sleeping bag under the stars and provided a good watch over my equipment. This seemed the perfect end to a pretty good day.

### *A surprise in the night.*

At about 9 p.m. I dozed off to a deep sleep and was dreaming of all the wonderful little trickles of thought that cross ones mind. Suddenly it was raining. Raining I thought? I looked up and could see the stars. My watch said 11:30. I was drenched with buckets of water and aroused out of my delirium to hear the sound of a sprinkler system. I jumped to my feet naked as a bean sprout, while a gush of rain hit my body. With sleeping bag at my knees, as if in a gunny sac race, I hopped over and dove onto the sprinkler as it rotated and sprayed me again and again. I compressed the sprinkler and it blasted me once more in the face. Then I felt underneath the metal plate and stopped the turning nozzle by aiming the sprayer away from me. Soon thereafter another nozzle was blasting me from another position and like a mad man tore up a clump of sod with bare hands and stuffed the clumps into the spraying menace to divert its spray. Finally after clogging up six of the troublemakers, I went back to sleep soaking wet, my watch said it was 12:45am. I was too tired to care, as thoughts came rushing in before slumber.

### *Oh how I loved machines*

*Machines were a big part of my life. I loved anything that was mechanical and went fast. I enjoyed tinkering with them and the challenge of getting more performance out of them. It was something that started when I was a kid. Even as a boy I was good at fiddling with the carburetors on my dads lawn mowers, snow blowers or the neighbors snowmobiles. The real challenge was to try and get a little more performance out of engines. When it came to working on engines I was a natural. I had this ability to "feel" what was wrong with a machine. There were many times when our neighbor, Mr. Luther or Steve down the street would ask me to fix their snowmobile or lawnmower. When I did, it usually ran better. I really had a gift for this. I just turned the correct screw and it felt and sounded right. It was an intuition, not a love affair, but machines and I clicked. I got a natural high when driving fast on machines and thrived on it. Eventually that led into snowmobile racing and then to racing motorcycles. I even tried racing a car on the ice of St. Louis Bay. This interest in machines led to my pursuit of a private pilot license. I was truly hooked on machines and this romance was deeply rooted in my world.*

**The morning of Sunday July 3** treated me to a purplish sky at 5am. I ate, cleaned up and was underway by 5:30. I wanted to get an early start on the headwinds and therefore rode at a good steady pace across an open plain. The cool morning air had a flowery smell except for a frequent bad whiff from the many dead rabbits along the roadside. At a fast pace I made good time and by 10am, was already 55 miles down the road. My rear hurt so badly that I'd improvised a thicker seat cushion from some foam found along the roadside.

So many thoughts passed through my head while pedaling. There were songs, sayings and the recollections of people that I know and love. I thought of those that I'm angry at and those I love. There was time to just think of the world in general. Traveling such as this was good for deliberation. Immersed in my thoughts, I was just a little past San Ardo, passing a farm when I heard a crackling sound. Then I saw a fire leaping to my right, with high flames along the roadside near some low slung electric wires. It appeared to be an electrical fire. I pedaled like mad to get farther up the road and told a farmer about the fire, but he was Hispanic and spoke only broken English. Yet, he understood what I was excited about when I pointed to the flames and I then made a hand gesture of a telephone to my ear and said, "policee, policee," and made a siren like sound. He nodded and said "see, see" then rushed over to call for help. There was nothing more I could do and continued north as a firetruck screamed by headed for the inferno.

Later in the day I was riding past some guys who were sunbathing in the back yard of their house. As I pedaled past they got up and came running over toward me while hollering. "Hey buddy come here! Come here! Hey come back," said a black fellow. There was a fence between us and I thought this was odd that they seemed so joyous to see me, so I slowed down a bit to converse, but did not stop. They all laughed as I waved my arm and said, "I'm running for governor." I kept pedaling and was wondering who they were. I was even more surprised to see a sign that read; San Lucas Prison Yard and Correction Facility.

Later that afternoon while straining against a strong headwind on a wide open chaparral plain I was surprised to see Bob and Mary waiting for me up ahead beside their motorcycle. They said they had been heading south on highway 101 and saw me going north and then turned around to come back and wish me well. Mary said, "How are you doing? Geez-I didn't really think you were going to do this!" I was breathlessly tired when I said, "Well here I'am." How, I pondered in my thoughts, could I discuss whether I was actually going to do this - when I obviously was! Mary gave me that look which made me feel like she was pissed off at me and that I was doing something wrong, just like she did when she was my boss. But then her face changed and she lit up with a proud smile, perhaps realizing she no longer had any right to over power me. "Well have fun," said Mary with a laugh. "Drop us a post card," said Bob. They gave me some cookies and wished me well as I pedaled off. That final meeting of ours had some kind of an ironic twist. I was glad to leave the both of them on friendly terms.

I rode until 2:30pm and then cruised into Salinas, which seemed to be a very sprawled out community. I was extremely tired and it was real hot outside. I wanted to find a McDonald's, but it took me half an hour to do so. I was exhausted. I ordered two Big Macs, a large fries and a large Coke and sat down to gorge myself. Immediately after devouring them, I fell asleep with my head upon the tray. Twenty minutes had passed before being awakened by an attendant who wondered if I needed a doctor. My muscles were very sore and I was delirious and near exhaustion. I had the 1000 yard stare that soldiers have in combat. I was so tired it took all my strength to get out to my bike. It took even more to get on it. But amazingly my strength returned shortly thereafter and I rode another 30 miles, over some very long down hills on the road to Gilroy. By the time I arrived in Gilroy my butt was so raw that I had to pedal standing up and lift it up every mile and let out a scream. By now it was early evening and I stopped for a cold drink at a 7-11 store and called my sister Nancy who lived in the San Francisco area. She said she wanted to come and pick me up because she said the directions were difficult for me to follow. It took her an hour before she arrived and then again that long for us to get back to her home. I did not realize that she lived 70 miles from where I had called!. Nonetheless I was very thankful for her picking me up, as I doubted whether I could ride another mile.

We drove north on that very busy and fast freeway, through San Jose and up some canyons to my sisters apartment. I met her husband Chuck and had an enjoyable dinner. It was a gorgeous evening and we talked until 11pm. I was so tired it didn't take long to crash into a deep sleep.

## *My roommates at the animal house*

*Gordy was one of my roomates. I'd classify him as the guru of mechanically inclined, race savy techno-know it alls. Our admiration of each other grew after we had a snowmobile race that took place on the east end of Skyline Drive. It was under a blanket of stars on a cold winter's night when we met at the starting line of the Seventh Bridge. We started in a standing racers position, feet back, arms outstretched and blasted off. Our engines roared to life and it was a neck 'n' neck contest, side by side, wide open throttles along a two mile long corridor. His machine was a modified 440 Ski Doo Blizzard and mine a stock Polaris 340TX. In this race, they were perfectly matched. The lead went back and forth. In one moment his lights would shine on my backside and then mine on his. In another it was just that whining, high speed sound of our machines, side by side, in perfect mechanical harmony, and the two of us racers straining to get the edge over the other. The contest could have ended in a wreck, as the curves came up fast, but instead we ended in a tie, our thick gloves touching high fives and helmets reflecting our excitement. After that race, we became friendly competitors, each in love with his favorite brand of machines.*

*Even before living at Regent Street, I knew who Gordy was through some humorous blunder. Once, I was in the church service and Reverend Kunkel was giving a sermon, when all of us overheard a CB radio on the church speakers. It was Gordy. He said, "Hey Squirrel (Marks nickname) where the hell are you?" I then heard Mark say, "I'm going to go into the outhouse, where are you?" Gordy then said, "I'm screwing around with my radio just outside of the church in my truck"*

*That is when Gordy's mother abruptly stood up in the church service and headed outside to tell him to stop his talking on the radio. I overheard her say, "Gordy!"*

*I got to know Gordy even better after our nearly catastrophic boating incident near Isle Royale. Gordy had a big cabin cruiser and invited Mark, Gary and I to join him on the 15 mile ride across to the Isle Royale. We spent a week skirting around the Lake Superior island fishing for trout. The incident occurred on the boat ride back to Grand Portage in dense fog. We were going along at full throttle, eager to get back, with visibility at about 200 feet. I was the navigator, busily watching the compass, checking the charts and trying to keep an eye out. Gordy was driving. Suddenly out of the fog appeared a fast moving ship heading toward us, but slightly to the left. It zipped past on the left side and immediately disappeared into the fog. "Wow! That was the Voyageur!" we all shouted in unison. We then hit its wake. If we'd collided with that big passenger ship, we'd have been gonners. After that incident, we were all bonded like comrades.*

*Gordy worked for a major snowmobile distributor and made a decent income, yet played every bit the part of a country hick and underdog. He raced dirt bikes, and so did I, we were competitors at heart and in love with our racing machines. I'd made a motocross course up at Champion Fields for us to practice on and he was my toughest competitor. We had many a race up at the Lakeview Ski Chalet track that went up and down and around the landing and ski hill. It would get so dusty there, that our faces would cover with it. On a separate occasion I once saw Gordy drive into the woods at 50 mph on an enduro bike and flip over a log. We all laughed. It was comical the way his feet went up into the air, I could see the bottoms of his boots, and they faced backwards. We laughed like idiots. Another time he went up a very steep hill and at the top let go of his Can Am, laughing like a fool as he sat in the dirt while his dirt bike crashed into the woods. Oh how we loved to ride our dirt bikes.*

*That same 'go for it' passion which he had for riding was also how he applied himself to the pursuit of chasing women. He had a way to set them at ease, to find something of interest in them and yet to flirt heavily with them. I admired that skill that he had.*

*Everyone who met Gordy liked him. Physically, he had this well defined double chin that when he smiled revealed his happy go lucky, wide grin, and ever so white teeth. His voice was deep and would even overpower the volume on his 100 watt stereo as he played again and again the eight-track-tapes of Rush or The Little River Band. One night I'd had a few too many beers and was crashed out on my bed upstairs, when he cranked up the volume so high that my bed not only vibrated, it felt like it was spinning. It was like sleeping upon a paint shaker. All the while Gordy was shouting, "Yahoo! Yahoo!" as he released those thunderous blasts from songs by the latest Styx eight track. Gordy was always easy to feed. Cooking supper for him was simply a pizza in the oven and a can of green beans or corn heated up on the stove burner.*

## July 4th, 1983

The fourth of July dawned and was spent relaxing near the swimming pool playing a guitar and soothing my very sore muscles. Because of my raw crotch, I walked like a man who'd ridden a horse a long distance. My appetite was awesome and therefore good food and several quarts of chocolate milk were consumed. Time was spent repairing the bike, reorganizing my bags, finding a journal to write my diaries. Nancy let me use her tent, which was much lighter than mine. In the evening we went to Concord to watch a fireworks presentation and afterwards I sat up until 1am playing the guitar and thinking about my trip.

## Tuesday July 5th

I repaired the rear tire which was found flat this morning. I also taped a large roll of foam rubber around the seat for x-tra derriere padding. Nancy drove me around to several bike shops from which at one, I purchased toe clips for the pedals. We then rode the B.A.R.T. into San Francisco.

The ride upon this fast train was novel, and the city has an exciting look to it from the trains vantage point. Nancy and I got along very well. We are close even though living far apart. I find she is such a fantastic sister and can only express my gratitude to her by saying thanks for being so wonderful. Nancy and her husband Chuck, and I drove over to cousin Jody's house and met her husband Jim. My cousin Justin was there and we had a warm and joyous reunion. I love all these people very much and was pleased that they gave me such support to accomplish my feat. I felt they were with me in spirit. We ate pizza and talked of a zillion things, but especially of interest was the fascinating subject about the "queers" of San Francisco. It seems as though everyone living here gets involved in this topic because they all have jokes to tell about the gays. I know little about who they are, but knew a few jokes as well and delighted in telling them. We drove back to Nancy's condo and after a little discussion I was again feeling a sense of apprehension and that strange loneliness as the night waned.

## Wednesday July 6th

Awoke at 5 a.m. on this and though Nancy invited me to stay longer and questioned whether I really should continue the journey, she saw my driving force and drove me to the Golden Gate Bridge.

I kiddingly called it the Golden Crate Bridge because of my nervousness to cross it.

Nancy had made me a lunch, which included a sandwich and a peach. We took a few pictures, hugged, said goodbye as she wept a little and I was soon off and waving as I left. Crossing the Golden Gate was an exhilarating experience. The view in every direction was stunning. Especially dizzying was the look down to the turbid and nauseating waters below. A bike lane on the bridge made the traverse pleasant and quick. Once across I rejoined the car traffic which was very heavy and fast.

I rode along the right side lane of highway 101 and at times there was no shoulder for me so the danger of passing trucks was ever present. It was a real test of concentration because the traffic was very fast and it was also noisy. On one steep downhill a truck sped past and missed my arm by inches. I rode as fast as I could in order to get off this roller coaster highway. It was a long ride and my butt and ankles began to hurt. I stopped only a couple of times to catch my breath and rest my sore rear. Finally the dangerous road that had skirted the north side of the bay was gladly exited for some more rural settings.

By noon headway was made into Napa, an area famous for it's delicious wines. I sat in a park in the cute little town and ate my sisters tender loving lunch there and then was onward toward Mount Vaca. I labored up the very steep grades, past orchards of fruit trees and vineyards. Finally, after much effort the reward of backing off the pedals came as I made it to the top of the 2000 foot pass. The road crossed a saddle and then started a gradual descent, winding its way through chaparral mountains which were gruelling because many times the road went up- up and up. By 4pm, all of my muscles started to hurt.

I was descending down one very steep and fast downhill and was just beginning to pull my goggles down over my eyes when a bee struck me directly in the eye with such a force that it jabbed its stinger deep and stung me terribly. I was momentarily blinded by the pain but on this fast ride had to maintain control of the bicycle. With one good eye I blearily steered the course until the hill bottomed out and I could safely pull over.

In agony, from the immense stinging pain, my eye immediately began to swell. I felt sickly but determined to continue. Remounting the bike, went only a few hundred feet of pedaling and feared falling off the bike from dizziness. I pulled over and found a spot to lay along the roadside and there slept for 15 minutes.

Groggy from the bee sting I pedaled onward in the late afternoon sun and made way into a campground which had a sign posted that asked $6 per night to camp. "The heck with that!" I said aloud, my eye aching like a toothache. I continued on down the road and pedaled into a small town named Winters. There I bought some food as anyone who looked at me seemed shocked at my swollen face. I looked like a criminal, or a guy who'd been given a black eye.

With a bag of food, I pedaled over to the city park to cook my dinner. A young man named Mike came by to say hello. I explained the bee sting and he was sympathetic. He told me he knew of a safe spot to camp the night. I hurriedly finished my meal and he led me to this creek bed on the outskirts of town. Though I was suspicious of his intentions and wondered if he would rob me, I thanked him as the sun was setting like a reddish fireball. After erecting the tent on the creek bed, I got inside and scribbled these notes in my journal - "Tonight I am afraid. I had difficulty getting over today's mountains and my route ahead will lead over mountains that are three times the height I've yet gone over. I wonder if it is possible? My success depends on going over them. For that reason I am fearful. Tonight my eye is swollen and the pain adds to my terribly sore muscles." I closed the book and thought of my predicament. My tent was in a creek bed, what if it rained hard? Would somebody sneak up on me and let me have it?" I slipped into slumber…

## *Mark and his friends*

*My other roommate at the animal house was Mark. He was pretty much down to earth and level headed in comparison to Gordy. He was mellow and had arts and crafts friends coming and going to our place. While he was easy going, he too loved snowmobiles and dirt bikes, and was often gutsy in the way he rode them. He knew them inside and out, but could let go of that infatuation. For the most part he liked hand made beauty, collecting arrowheads and the simple get-togetherness of people. His girlfriend, Susan was frequently at our house and together they introduced me to many new acquaintances. Ours was a meeting place for the young at heart. With so many new faces coming and going there was an interesting mix of personalities, but there was one of Marks friends who would impact me more than the others. She was the catalyst, the key inspiration to my venture around the world. She would laugh at the quarrels Mark and Gordy had. Their ongoing dispute was something I was learning, and would avoid as time progressed.*

*Mark and Gordy had a long going feud, from childhood years, that they were always trying to settle. Mark liked to amusingly say, "I don't get mad, I get even." They were always doing this to each other. Each consequence was more extreme than the previous.*

*One time Mark tucked a bag of dead minnows under Gordy's mattress. Gordy found them about a week later, stinking to high heaven. Just about that same time Mark brought home an injured rabbit. It had fallen off a cliff.*

*We tried to nurse it back to health, but it died in the bathtub. I laid it to final rest in the trash can. About one month later something smelled awful bad upstairs. Mark searched through his stuff and found that 'ripe rabbit' upstair, near his bedroom and inside his jewelers oven. Gordy chuckled, it was as good as him taking the blame. There were many other incidents, and I learned not to tread on their grounds lest there be some redemption against me.*

## Thursday July 7th

After a good nights rest I awoke at 5:15, in the morning. By 6am I'd left Winters and rode north on highway 505, which was poorly marked and kept me in suspense for many miles, wondering if I was on the right road. My eye was badly swollen shut and it hurt, but I felt pretty good and kept up a good pace. With a good tail wind the pace was all the more easy and enjoyable. I was hungry and pulled into the small town of Dunnigan and entered a grocery store. As soon as entering it the woman behind the counter gasped and put her hands over her mouth and said, "My lord what happened to your eye?" I told her, "I was stung by a bee," but knew she didn't believe me. It looked more like somebody gave me a black eye. She said she was allergic to bees and was glad it did not happen to her. I bought some bananas and then headed down interstate #5 heading north toward Redding.

The interstate was smooth and my pace was good and I made real good time. About 25 miles had passed when with great surprise I heard a siren behind and looked around to see red lights flashing from atop a California Highway Patrol (CHP) squad car. He was pulling me over! I stopped and he stopped and then I rode up and leaned the bike against his back bumper. The officer stepped out and told me in a slow steady voice, "It is against the law to ride a bicycle on the interstate, son, and I'm going to have to give you a ticket." He looked at my eye and my equipment and must have thought I was a fugitive. He started writing up a ticket after looking at my drivers license. He then asked me, "When can you appear in court?" I told him, "I'm planning on going around the world and it will take me about nine months." He sighed and said, "That won't work out very well with the judge." He shook his head in no-no-no fashion and then ripped up the ticket and said he would let me off with a warning, but before I left he pointed a finger at me and said, "Don't let me ever see you on this freeway again!" He followed me until I turned off on the next exit.

I then pedaled along a bumpy highway which closely followed the interstate. The countryside here was beautiful with many ranches scattered here and there and occasional large oak trees upon the open plain. There were mountains bordering both sides of this long valley. The ride was enjoyable under the hot sun and I was entertained by many crop dusting airplanes flying low over big farmers fields. On one occasion a plane flew right over my head and then sprayed, immersing me in a mist of chemicals. I held my breath so as not to breathe the stuff and soon was upwind and gasped wildly for air.

There were a variety of crops along this route, like olives, grapes, almonds and apples. It appeared to be a prosperous place to live. Just when things were going well, I heard a 'boing' sound come from the rear wheel and it started a horrible wobble. I looked over the trouble and found a spoke had broken. I had never changed a spoke and so stopped into the town of Orland to repair it. A fellow at a hardware store told me of a motorcycle shop, because there was no bike shop here. I pedaled over there and was graciously helped by a kind man named Tom. Tom was a great guy and he owned a beautiful store. He helped me so much to pull the rear sprocket hub off and replaced the broken spoke. I vowed to send him a card from Minnesota as he would take no payment for his efforts.

Passing by were more farms and ranches with large eucalyptus trees gracing the yards. The day was wearing thin when I wheeled into the nice little town of Corning and found a grass covered park to sit and cook my dinner. Two young boys about the age of 12 came walking by and asked me where I was going. I told them I was going to Minnesota, but that distance did not phase them. Then they asked me where I'd come from and when I said, "I rode all the way from Santa Barbara," they were amazed and said, "Wow your crazy to ride all the way from Santa Barbara." After eating I pedaled the bike past freshly mowed lawns, which reminded me of Minnesota, and pedaled north. After a few miles has passed I dashed into an almond orchard to set up camp and to avoid being noticed. I went down through the rows of trees until finding a secluded spot to set camp. Darkness fell quickly and this spot became extremely spooky. Small animals darted here and there. They made noises, shuffling about, leaves crunching. I was glad to have the security of my tent and slipped into dreams…

# ERIC NORLAND

## *A fixer of machines*

*While living at the animal house, I was employed as a mechanic at a small engine repair shop called Pike Lake Service Center. It was the service building for a local hardware store. The shop was across the freeway from the store. I was a small engine mechanic, who fixed lawnmowers, snowblowers and other machines in this trade.*

*What led me into this job was a strange twist of fate. A neighbor named Dale was the manager of the shop and he told me he needed mechanical help and if I were interested to come in and he'd pay me cash. So, I started working there part time in June of 1978, just after graduating from college. After only one month of employment, I was starting to know my way around and we were real busy, with a long line of lawnmowers waiting to be fixed, the little white service tags waving in the wind. More and more work was pouring in, when suddenly Dale flew into a rage. He'd just gotten off the phone and started throwing grease rags onto the floor and shouting that he was fed up with this place and its low pay and with the boss and maddeningly stomped into the bathroom, washed his hands, dried them on a towel dispenser and said, "I quit!" He put on his sweater and madder than a hornet abruptly left the shop, never to return. I was surprised and dumbfounded.*

*I was thrown into a strange situation. The shop was full of work to be done but now seemed destined to close. The boss, who's name was Dexter, put an ad in the local classifieds saying that he was looking for someone to fill Dales position. I read the ad the day it came out and was disappointed because he never talked to me about filling it. I did not have any formal training in this field, but figured, what the heck, I should go for it. On Monday, I told Dexter that I'd like to have a shot at doing Dales job. I was familiar with the operation of the shop and was pretty good at fixing machines, I had a knack for doing that. Dexter said he would give me a try, thus I became the new manager and mechanic at the service center. One day I'm wearing greasy clothes and the next a blue uniform with my name on it.*

*It was thrilling to be working a 'position' and to have the trust of the boss. I enjoyed helping the general public, as they entrusted me with their machines, and I was challenged to make them well again. The customers would come back to pick them up and I'd ring up a sale on the old cash register. It was adorned in a gold case and had big numbers pop up when the keys were pressed. It felt so much like being in a real honest-to-goodness business.*

## South of Redding
## Friday July 8th

It was a hot sticky night and my sleeping bag was much too warm. I peeled myself from it on this morning of as my watch read 5:15. I quietly packed up everything, to avoid being seen camping here in an almond orchard. Signs were posted warning trespassers from stealing almonds. It was such a temptation, I picked up a few and stuffed them into pockets.

Pedaling down the fine paved road on this very fragrant and pleasant morning I went into the pretty little town of Vina. There was a nice little park nearby and I cleaned up there and sat down to eat. While doing this a police car patrolled back and forth past me many times. The officer looked at me suspiciously and it was no wonder, as my swollen left eye was much worse and I looked every bit like a crook.

The ride north along highway 99 was pleasantly passed with thoughts and songs continuously circulating through my head. Especially prevalent was Bob Dylan song called "Idiot wind." It inspired me to pedal harder while singing the song aloud-

> *"Idiot wind, blowin every time you move your mouth,*
> *blowin down the backroads heading south,*
> *idiot wind, blowin every time you move your teeth,*
> *you're an idiot babe, It's a wonder that you still know how to breathe."*

The song rallyed me, and I thought of the bondage I felt working under Mary. Now the sound of gears churning and chain wringing and tires upon pavement added to this audio mix. I beheld in the distance the backdrop of a clear blue sky and beautiful Mt. Shasta protruding above the horizon in a purplish-pink color capped with white snow. I rode on toward the impressive sight of a perfectly shaped volcano, singing like a madman.

It was nearing noon while riding into Redding on a nice wide stretch of highway. I was viciously attacked by redwing blackbirds which dove down upon me and on several occasions forced me to duck else be hooked by their beaks or talons. I rather loved the excitement and egged them on.

The sun shone brightly above and I zipped thru busy traffic, past modern businesses and pulled into a newly paved parking lot of a McDonald's. Inside I met two other young male cyclists from San Jose. They both made the observation that people were much friendlier up here than in their hometown. They had stories to tell about their ride over the Sierra's to Reno, then to the snowfields of Mt. Lassen and now to Redding. These young men were real go getters. One of them was recently in a bad bike accident. He told me the gorry details of getting hit by a car and it was surprising he was back riding again after such a bad crash. They were heading toward the ocean, through some rugged country. I was impressed.

After filling my water bottles at a convenience store I exited the fine city of Redding and headed northeast on interstate #299 towards the Cascade mountains. There were a great many bums, hobos and vagrants hitchhiking and walking along this road. A highway patrolman bellered at me over his loudspeaker, "Cyclist make the next exit!" I did so fearing trouble with them and took a terrible detour road on a zig zag route which went many miles through rough construction but only came back onto the end of the interstate a half mile from where I exited. I cursed the whole while but was soon heading into higher country on highway #299. It was still very hot and sunny, but occasionally there were cool breezes circulating down from the mountainside. The hot sun beat upon my darkened shoulders as I made a real hard ride uphill until arriving in the small town of Round Mountain.

It was around 6 p.m. and while riding past a community club I noticed a sign saying, "ALL YOU CAN EAT-$4." I cruised up to a large tent set up in a parking lot. Upon walking inside, many people turned around to look in wonder at my bicycle attire and sweaty appearance. They then went back to their conversations and eating. After buying a meal ticket, I joined the chow line and soon was devouring a delicious meal of chop suey. It was very tasty and filling, so I went back for seconds. Nobody said a word to me while I ate. They all acted as though they were kind of shy or did not want to bother me. But when I walked outside and over to my bike, they seemed to stop eating or talking to look and see what I was up to. As I flung my leg over the seat, a fat fellow came up and said, "Good luck boy." I pushed off and started pedaling away and turned around and was amazed to see a large group of spectators who had stepped out from the tent. When I waved to them, they waved back and cheered loudly. It was an exhilarating moment.

With a full belly I really wanted to stop someplace and relax, but the mountain road steepened and I continued up this hard climb. A series of steep switchbacks greeted my little enthusiasm and whilst concentrating on pushing the pedals I was greatly alarmed to see how the sky was darkening with the threat of a rain storm. A fast wind swept up behind me and suddenly it began to pour down with rain. I pedaled like a madman as the tires swooshed and flung aside streams of water that was gushing down the road. A tremendous flash of lightning lit up the road like a flashbulb and was soon followed by a kaa-boom that nearly knocked me off the bike! "Wow!" I excitingly said. I recalled how long it had been since I heard a good thunderstorm. Santa Barbara hardly ever had such phenomena. I set a hard and desperate pace for the rest area, which was four miles up the road. The mountain grade kept steepening while I was becoming soaked to the bone. I pedaled like all hell until finally, to my surprise and joy, the rain quit as quickly as it had come. Finally I pulled into the beautiful rest area with its large coniferous trees swaying high above the brushless forest, just in time to witness a magnificent sunset. I stopped to catch my breath and sit on a picnic table. No sooner had I sat down when a car drove up and a young boy jumped out and asked me if I had ridden up that mountain on that bicycle. "Yes," I said adding, "And I rode it all the way from Santa Barbara." His eyes went wide with surprise and he said, "Your nuts! You rode all the way from Santa Barbara? Yah -your- nuts!-nuts-nuts-nuts!" he said over again and again while pointing a finger at me. His mom grabbed him by the arm and led him back to the car. "Nuts, nuts, nuts," the boy repeated by sticking his head out the car window as they drove away. I cupped my hands round my mouth like a megaphone and shouted back to him, "You'll probably do this someday!"

The night was calm and cool, a switch from all the heat of previous nights. My tent was pitched under pines with a soft bed of needles as a mattress. It was a very beautiful and romantic spot. Oh how I wished for something like a lost maiden, but realized the odds were next to none.

## Love of machines at the Animal House

*While living at the animal house my life revolved around machines. Both Gordy and Mark worked at motorcycle and snowmobile related businesses, so we had lots to talk about. We worked on machines until late in the night in the garage, which was behind the house. That place was a flurry of activity. Gordy started 'moonlighting' by repairing snowmobiles out of the garage. People were always coming and going, talking about machines. There seemed no job to big or to small. One cold winter night my Datsun 240Z blew a head gasket. I fit the car into the garage and took the head off the engine. A torpedo heater helped keep me warm. Later that night I became very sick, shaking and feverish. Was it from the diesel fumes of the torpedo heater or was it the flu bug? It took several days to recuperate and repair the engine.*

*I was real sick of those troubles with that Datsun. It was nickel and diming me to death. I sold it not only because of the endless problems, but also because the seats didn't recline and bought one that did, a brand new Renault Gordini from Archers Import Motors. This added to my list of machines. I had lots of toys, along with my new car there were a couple of motorcycles, a snowmobile and a go-cart. To add to my mechanical fray was my pursuit of a private pilots license.*

*We would gather in the garage talking 'shop' about our machines. Somebody would always have one boot up on the bumper and greasy fingers into the engine of something. That was about the only subject we ever talked about. Typical conversations revolved around our mechanical problems, from carburetors to the latest racing products. Of course when the ladies stopped by to say hi that kind of talk bored the heck out of them, especially Julie, she often said, "there is something wrong with you guys."*

## Saturday July 9th

Birds were singing on the morning of announcing the dawn. I was heading out by 6:30am. The bike felt heavy and progress was slow at first and my moral was low while passing through the deep evergreen tree landscape of mountain forests on this morning. I felt better after speeding down a couple of three-mile long hills. I coasted down a wonderful long grade under the morning sun, which illuminated a glorious landscape below a clear blue sky while entering the town of Burney around 9am. This touristy town has an old western look to it as the buildings have false facades and the shops were full of souvenirs and postcards. I bought a few and sat down to write and send them off to mom and dad.

Heading northeast out of town, the road went past ski hills with snow covering the slopes. This stretch of road could be likened to a roller coaster as up and down I went. It was enjoyable cycling though very tiresome. The scenery was becoming sparsely vegetated and noticeably dryer and my water intake increased. On a steep hill I stood up to bare upon the pedals and while doing so the pedal toe clip connected with the front fender bracket causing the fender to burst into many pieces. I trimmed the splintered plastic fender and continued for only a few hundred feet where I met two cyclists from Minnesota whom said they had left St. Paul four weeks previous. We had a friendly chat and exchanged information about road conditions. I shook their hands, wished them well and gave them some candies.

It was a grueling route over many passes until finally crossing a grassy plain and pulling into the very small town of Nubeiber at 1:30pm. I was very tired, weak and in need of food. I went into the store, but they did not have any food I liked, except a box of macaroni and cheese, which I bought and then cooked on the front porch of the store. While doing so a little boy came over and was real interested and friendly to me, as are most folks in this area. My belly was satisfied after wolfing down the hot cuisine. An hour later I was resuming the ride down the road.

It is a psychological effort as much as a physical one to bicycle up a mountain pass. Looking up ahead and seeing a long steep incline is demoralizing. I found the best medicine was to concentrate on the first twenty feet ahead, in order to nullify the enormity of it all. Adlin Pass was one such road as it tested my limits to arrive at the top of the 5188 foot summit. It is such an exhilarating feeling to reach the top of a pass. Perhaps not so much because of the achievement but moreso because of the exhilarating ride down the other side. I zipped down and struggled up another. After doing this up and down mountain climbing for the last thirty-four miles in three and a half hours it really wore me out.

I rode into Canby at 6pm as long shadows crept over the town. I was road-weary and wanted to go no further. There was a little country store where I purchased some food. While packing the food into my panniers a young boy approached and asked me, "Where do you think your going?" I said "Minnesota," at which he responded "Minnesota, It'll take you a year!" He kept shaking a definite NO with his head, which flicked his blonde hair out from under his baseball cap and into his eyes. He then said, "You'll never make it! Where's your TV?" I then responded, "Well you'll never make it if you keep talking like that and besides TV is for little kids." He lifted his chin up and looked over my shoulder and said "Well you'll never make it." I returned "I'll bet someday you'd like to do a bike trip like this." His eyes lit up and he blurted out, "Yes I would!" I flung my leg over the cross bar and coasted off with the sun against my back. It was as if I was Shane in that old Alan Ladd western movie. The boy stood on the street shouting to me, "Hope you make it mister, hope you make it, goodbye!"

I had not gone more than two hundred feet before spotting a picnic spot in the backyard of the fire hall. Across the street was a Union 76 station where I went to ask about staying the night at the fire hall. By lucky coincidence the mechanic was also the town's chief fire warden. I asked him about camping there for the night and he said, "Go ahead and pitch your tent and spend the night there if you'd like. Use the water from the spigot in the back of the building." "Much obliged," I said thanking him and coasting across the street. The green grass was a welcome sight and the picnic table a perfect place to enjoy my dinner. While eating a flock of Canadian geese flew over my head at a very low altitude in a perfect "V" formation. This place had typical small town sounds of barking dogs, kids playing and a distant lawnmower. They were comforting and peaceful as darkness brought an end to the day.

### *Events at the animal house*

*Some of the activities that went on at the animal house were hilarious. It was not unusual to see a motorcycle parked in the living room. On one occasion we drove motorcycles inside the house and spun the tires on the kitchen floor, leaving black 'donut' shapes upon it. There were often engine parts in the sink, instead of dirty dishes. On the dining room table sat a twin cylinder snowmobile engine (which we used as a center piece) that sat on top of oil soaked girly magazines. One night we were all sitting around when someone decided to start that engine up. We put a little gas into the carburetor and pulled the starter rope and the engine roared to life and immediately fell onto the floor spinning around until it sputtered out of gas and died, leaving a haze of blue smoke throughout the house.*

*On another occasion Mark and I made a shooting gallery down the basement to shoot 22's. It seemed like a good place to practice until Gordy became wild upstairs with his pistol and made us all run for cover as he was shooting through the living room floor toward the basement. So we 'shot back' (not at him) a few rounds, and then dashed for cover as he returned a couple more.*

*Yet another episode was when we had a bottle rocket fight. Gordy stood out on the sidewalk shooting rockets toward the house at Mark and I upstairs. We shot back until a bottle rocket exploded the window and broken glass fell all over.*

*Gordy's girlfriend, Sue, left some cats with us for a couple of weeks. We blew pot smoke into their faces and they got so stoned they climbed the up the fireplace brickwork.*

*We once had a contest to run around the house naked at midnight. I was the first one to go, but just after I did the ladies showed up. Gordy was dating Sue and Mark had his Susan and the ladies egged us on to run around the house once more. We were too shy and that ended that. But out of this joshing Mark was given the nickname; Marcus Erectionis for his immediacy of becoming aroused. Gordy also required some kidding and I gave him the nickname, Gordonger. As for me they would say "Eracker" and how they came up with that I do not know, other than my keen eye for well shaped ladies. Those were but some of the activities that gave the place an animal house like atmosphere.*

## Sunday July 10<sup>th</sup>.

I'd slept real good and awoke to a beautiful morning twilight. My watch shown 5:30am while I was packing up the tent and enjoying the sight of more geese flying over my head and making for the horizon. I packed everything into its proper place and sat down to feast on a cinnamon roll and juice before hitting the road. Canby is placed on a slight downhill grade to the east and I was sad to say goodbye to such a nice little town. A pleasant downhill ride was ensued for many miles and therefore kept up at a good pace. The air was cool and refreshing and I pondered how ideal of a way this was to start the day. There were green fields and large lonely hardwood trees scattered here and there upon dome shaped hills. The smell in the air was green leaves and grass and evergreens combined. The scenery was reminiscent of that which is scattered throughout much of California, only it was much greener here. Eighteen miles later I rolled into Alturas at 8:30am. I bought a gallon of fuel for the cook stove from a store and it cost $3.00. After filling my containers I realized there was more than half of the container yet remaining. I asked the store keeper if he'd like the remaining amount and he said, "Sure, and I'll give you a $1.50 for it." I was thankful for his kindness and realized that he did something that would never happen in a big city.

    Somewhere around the town of Davis Creek I pedaled along a flat plain and looked up ahead to see a very big bull was standing in the ditch eating grass. Upon approaching the old bull he became terribly spooked and ran in front of me from the left and then trotted gayly down the road. I thought he would cross and continue but instead he abruptly stopped dead center in the road and looked at me. I hit the brakes and faced a standoff with the big creature. I shouted at the top of my lungs, "Get out of the way!" But the behemoth stood his ground and looked ready to charge. I picked up a small rock and tossed it at him and by lucky chance it beamed him right between the horns. He suddenly kicked up his hind legs and ran off into the pasture, kicking again and again as he made his quick retreat.

**Welcome to Oregon** read the sign in New Pine Creek. This was a milestone for my journey and therefore worthy of taking several photos.

I bought some goods and pedaled crossed the Oregon border at 1pm and reveled at distant Mt. Shasta towering high above the horizon. It had a beautiful pinkish white hue against a vivid blue sky. I watched this beautiful spectacle of light while pedaling alongside of Goose Lake for a good many miles. Head winds off the lake caused me to strain into the pedals and lower my head against the wind. The terrain was much drier and there was far less vegetation. It was a welcome sight to see trees and ride into the nice town of Lakeview. I bought some fresh food and cold drink and then found a shady spot to sit and eat. After an hours lunch break I left the pleasant town and hit the open road against strong headwinds which were aptly cursed at all the while.

The landscape became even drier, a yellow color, and it was hotter. The hills were marked with sagebrush and high chaparral. On a flat desert stretch of road I heard and felt the rear wheel break a spoke. I turned the bike over and tried to disassemble the wheel. A passing truck knocked it over onto me. I tried to repair the problem but did not have the proper tool to get the hub off. I started pushing the bike until seeing a long driveway and what appeared to be a ranch at the end. One would not expect to see anyone living there. I probably would have passed through this area and figured it was uninhabited had it not been for this problem. After walking the bike up the long drive to the house, I looked around a bit before finding the owner. He was a quiet man, with gray hair and said his name was Mr. Schultz. I asked him if I might use his vise to take off the rear hub. He showed me an air compressor and tools that I could use to remove the back sprocket. While we worked on the hub he told me he had moved out here from the San Fernando and Woodland Hills area of Los Angeles. That was 11 years ago. He said he was having such severe respiratory problems from the L.A. air that he thought he would surely die there. He reminisced of a bike he had made in his youth from scrap parts at the dump. When I told him my bike cost $600 he nearly flipped. Once we put my bike back to together he demanded I take some of his water. "It's the best water from anywhere." He said as he pumped from a hand pump over the well. I gladly filled my canteens with this pure water. He was truly a kind man in a land so barren and I gave many thanks to this very kind Mr. Schultz.

Continuing along the chaparral valley surrounded with rocky hills, I strode across an open area with my legs pumping like a steam engine until the one store town of Valley Falls. I purchased an ice cold Pepsi and guzzled it down my dry throat. Immediately after leaving the shade trees of town, the countryside turned desert dry and the road forked. There were no signs telling me which road to take. I guessed the road to the right and headed that way, feeling distressed. The road skirted around alkali lake beds and undrinkable waters like those of Lake Albert, which were sparkling under the golden afternoon sun. The blue waters looked deceivingly refreshing, but I dared not put a foot in those acrid waters. The heat was extreme and the air very dry. I rationed my water, but could have drunk gallons. I was concerned about finding a rest area that was represented on the map, as it showed it not being too far north of the lake.

As the sun lowered in the sky, the hills never seemed to end, in height as well as length. I went up and down, up and down. Though my map suggested another rest area south of Wagon Tire, there was no rest area in sight. The sun was setting in a frenzy of colors as I went over one hard hill after another. This long exhausting day was getting late and my frustration at its peak. I was pedaling as hard as possible up a very long steep grade and feeling sorry for myself, wondering why I was in this situation, then it again struck me, how I got to this point in my life.

### *The crucial moment*

*It was at one of our animal house Saturday night parties, while we were having a beer and talking shop with the guys, that the catalyst for my journey occurred. The music was thumping away, and the living room was full of young guys and gals drinking. We were all stuffed onto the couch. On one side of me sat Gordy and on the other was Julie. Somehow the conversation was about each of our aspirations. She said, "So what do you want to do with your life?" I told her, "I'd like to be an artist and to paint art works with true meanings." Then I enlightened her about my other love. "I also like astronomy, and a couple of years ago did a series of blacklight paintings for the UMD planetarium." This led into a discussion about the universe. "Perhaps the exploration of space will provide new ways of looking at the earth as a lonely little planet in space. This is all that we have, the earth is everything to us." That in turn made me reflect about the state of Soviet-U.S. relations, which were in 1979 very bad, and our countries attitude about Russians being our enemy. "The general opinion of Americans is to nuke Russians into oblivion. I often question that viewpoint and wonder who would really win WW3 if we destroyed the planet with a nuclear war? I feel like I have to do something. What's the use of destroying earth just to fight a nuclear war with Russia? It seems to me that we do not understand the Russians and that is the reason we fear them as much as they fear us. What needs to be done is to go over there and get to know them," I said, taking a short chug of some beer.*

*Julie listened intently, but looked like she could see right through me. She guzzled her beer, leaned forward, smiled slightly and said loudly with beer breath, "Over the past months, I have seen and heard you talk of your obsession with machines. It is pretty obvious that is the only thing on your mind. I've heard all of you guys brag about how fast, how cool, how nice your machines are. Now here you are telling me about the universe, world peace and the Russians." Her voice turned steelic when she said, <u>"It's strange how you studied art and talk about art and about making peace with the Russians, and yet you dig machines so much.</u> I think **YOU LOVE MACHINES MORE THAN YOU LOVE PEOPLE!"** She stood up, quickly stomped down her beer upon the coffee table, sending foam into the air, and she walked away.*

*I wasn't real sure she was serious. But as the evening progressed it sunk in. The words were there, they were ringing in my head. They hit home, she was right.*

Under this darkening sky, I pedaled tortuously hard to get to the summit of this pass as Julie's words again rang in my brain. The sun had set, a hot wind was blowing, I was so thirsty and hungry, but I pedaled hard to get up this long grade. Just as I crested the top I pedaled in cadence to what Julie had said to me.

*"YOU LOVE MACHINES MORE THAN YOU LOVE PEOPLE!"*
*"YOU LOVE MACHINES MORE THAN YOU LOVE PEOPLE!"*
*"YOU LOVE MACHINES MORE THAN YOU LOVE PEOPLE!"*

Finally I made it to the top, backed off the pedals, coasted, and felt my heart drumming as the hot evening air blasted my face. I smelled the dry grass and arid dirt. There it was, the rest area! Dimly visible in the amber distance I could see it about two miles downhill in front of me.

I felt choked up to recollect what Julie had said. I knew it was the reason that I was here. I coasted along at about 50 miles per hour and was quiet with myself. Then I started to sing and shout "Yahoo! Yahoo!" as I zipped down the road while the purple sky of twilight began to twinkle with stars. I sang happily, then grew silent for fear somebody would hear me.

In the last two and a half hours I'd traveled 26 miles over grueling hills. It was past 8pm and I was delighted to arrive at the rest area. There was a large yellow water tank made of plastic which was nearly empty, but provided just enough water to wipe the sticky salt off my body. I cooked dinner and practically inhaled my fried hamburger and potatoes. While setting the tent, a coyote howled from the surrounding hills. It was a beautiful, warm evening with stars as companions, and a happy end to a hardy day. I laid there listening to the yipping in harmony from coyotes and whizzing orchestra from the crickets, gently entertaining me asleep.

## <u>YOU LOVE MACHINES MORE THAN YOU LOVE PEOPLE!"</u>

*I did not react very much to her outburst. What could I say? But it was like a slap in the face. I pretended to brush it off, yet it was a powerful blow to me. One that would come back and haunt me for the following days, nights, weeks and months until I fully realized it was like a dagger that ripped at my love for machines, revealing this great heap of junk inside my empty soul.*

*Did I really love machines more than I loved people? For months afterward I looked at my confused world that I'd lost myself in. It was like a black cloud hung over me at all times. I kept trying to rekindle that excitement of material things like my car, snowmobile and motorcycle but I became disillusioned by them, as if they preyed on me. In some ways a curse had been cast on my love for machines and I searched for a way of shaking it. I felt an inner calling to resolve my problem, to leave the old boy behind and to fill it in with someone new. But these things could not be had quickly until I grew out of this boyish phase. I knew something needed to be done, yet I was unsure how to go about doing it.*

## Monday July 11th

Camp was broke at 6am and then headed northward across big dry valleys on this morning of Monday. The hills have a rather sensuous look to them and could be likened to a woman's naked body, especially her bare bottom. I watched herds of antelope bound off in the morning sun. My presence was quiet enough to sneak up rather close before spooking them. The rough road became a big concern, as the cracks were one severe jolt after another. I swore my teeth fillings would come loose. Large gaps spanning across the road sent shock waves through my body and I wondered if the bike could hold up to such a beating. I leaned back and attempted to redistribute my body weight to the rear and to jump each crack prior to hitting them. It seemed to work.

At 10am I passed through a very deserted landscape to arrive at the town of Wagontire. The town is made up of only a bar, which also serves as a general store. While inside buying some snacks, I met a fellow who was seriously considering whether to buy the place. I noticed that he was much friendlier than the owners, who never smiled nor said thank you to me for buying goods from their store.

After leaving Wagontire the road turned northeastward and took me up and down barren hills. My moral was low and the same old tune recurs in my head. I tried to think of something else, but it kept bringing me back to that tune. Twenty eight miles later I arrived at the intersection of highway #20 and the town of Riley. Since it was noon, I ate lunch and had a Drumstick ice cream cone, during which a nice little dog came over to me and wagged his tail for a snack. I finally gave in and gave him the last of my cone. He reminded me of my old dog, Andy, and touched me deeply with those memories.

I continued eastward and was alone to my thoughts. While pedaling down the highway, well over on 'my side' of the road, a big truck went passed so damn close it nearly knocked me off the road. I flipped him off with a stick finger and shouted a few hundred obscene words. I wondered if he understood how much work it was to cycle across this horrid road. There were huge holes and cracks to avoid. I questioned how much effort it must be for a trucker to turn his wheel half an inch to go around me. Some of them are so inconsiderate!

My progress, considering all the circumstances, was very good as I stopped into a rest area on the west side of Burns at 2pm for a breather. It was real hot out. I then arrived at Burns at 3:30. There was a little thrift shop, where I bought a wrench that fit perfectly to tighten my front wheel bearings. Had I bought it from a bike shop it would have cost me $12, but this little store carried it for only .50 cents.

My map showed a rest area symbol, which looked, like a good location to stay the night. It required a 25 mile ride across a long valley. To the north I could see jagged edges of several mountains that looked intimidatingly hot and dry. They would be in the Malheur National Forest. A long steep grade demanded my lowest gear and extra muscle power to get up and over. As the sun was beginning to wane I made it to Stinkwater Pass rest area at 7:30. While coming out of the men's room I met a very nice fellow named Mr. Berg whom was a native Minnesotan and now lived in Sweet Home, Oregon. At the age of 80 years old he was very keen and open enough to be interested in my travels. He had a few stories to tell me of his days of youth. He still enjoyed getting out to travel the country. The thing that I thought was so great about him was he was very philosophical. He said to me, "You got to do those things you like to do because that's what you were put here for."

Later in the evening I met two young women who were traveling around America by car. They were from Illinois and their names were Philamena and Wilmaphena. These two adventurous ladies were school teachers and they were out exploring the small towns of America on their summer vacation. We had a good conversation as they invited me to have a seat in their car to talk and watch stars. We talked about our own observations of the cultural changes within America. The night sped away with all this fellowship and I soon returned to my tent for sleep.

## Tuesday July 12th

Awoke at 5:30 after a restless night perhaps because of the altitude. Packed up and made good time along a rough road heading northeast.

There was an excellent tailwind helping me out immensely and even pushing me up the hills. I was again thinking of that same tune in my head and was singing it aloud. The song is called <u>By the time I get to Phoenix</u>, and the melody came readily to mind, but I had trouble remembering the exact words. While I was bellering out the song an airplane suddenly flew low right over my head and then made a perfect landing on the highway in front of me. The pilot taxied the plane up a long driveway, to a house and I pondered what a good way that was to get around this country. Shortly thereafter I arrived at the one-store-town of Juntura. I stopped into the store and bought an ice cream cone. The woman who served me was very rough looking and certainly not very friendly. She looked like someone fresh out of a Hollywood wild western movie. I thought-how interesting-those western movies have people who look like they really do look.

It was early in the afternoon and already the heat was becoming nearly unbearable. I was pedaling up a steep climb alongside some rusty colored hills and to my pleasure saw a road sign which read, 'SPRING 500 FEET.' I counted each of those feet and arrived at the site. There was a path to my right, above which towered a high hill, at the base of which was a footpath leading up to a spigot. From it was flowing the most beautiful ice cold drinking water I'd seen since Mr. Smith's. I guzzled it down, washed up and then topped up all my water bottles. A car drove up and I met a nice young couple from the town of Homeland. They reminded me of my old animal house friends, Gordy and Sue. I also met a group of women from Brainerd, Minnesota and talking to them sort of cheered me up, but still my moral was low. Perhaps it was because of my low energy or perhaps it was because of my very sore butt. There was also a constant pain between the shoulder blades of my upper back, which sent sharp pains into my neck. It was a hot day, around 100 degrees and rather humid, the kind of weather that makes one feel tired. I continued on regardless and made it to the town of Vale at 2:30 and then onward to arrive in Ontario at 5:30, feeling very tired, weary, hot and dying for a cold drink.

Refreshed after a quart of cold orange juice I crossed the border into Idaho and continued on to the town of Fruitland at which I decided to keep going until the town of New Plymouth. It was there where a thorn in my tire forced me to pull off the highway into a parking lot to patch the tube. During my tire repair a policeman pulled up to have a look at what I was doing. I asked him if it was OK for me to sleep in the park. "Yes" he said. As I stood there talking to him many young boys gathered around and took great interest in my journey. They knew the officer well and we all had a most vivid conversation. After repairing the tire, I pedaled over to a pay phone from which I called my parents. All was OK with them. They were quite surprised to hear of the progress I was making. I then went to the town park and set camp. Just before climbing into the tent, a police car drove past and he saw me. It was a nice feeling to know that they were there to watch over me.

## Wednesday July 13th

After an uneventful evening I awoke at 5am on and was underway by 6am. The air was cool and there was little wind in the early morning. This helped me to go 23 miles until arriving at the town of Caldwell at 8:30. I drank a quart of orange juice at a 7-11 and then headed south along I-84.

Everything was going well until I heard a loud BANG! come from the rear wheel, which immediately began to wobble and rub against the frame. Once again a spoke had broken and sent the wheel into an 'S' shape. I pushed the bike for a ways and stopped under an overpass to repair the broken wheel, but my wrench was not large enough to take off the rear hub. Across the highway, I noticed there was a trucker who was cleaning out a cattle truck in a large gravel parking lot. I jumped over the highway dividers and walked over to ask the fellow if I could borrow a wrench. As I approached he was busy spraying the cattle carrier out with a hose and suddenly I was sprayed with a putrid blast of water, which flung gobs of cow shit on my face and body. I knew it was an accident and brushed it off as best I could. I went up and asked the guy, "Could I borrow a wrench to repair my bike." He said very nonchalantly, "Sure thing, just look in the cab, behind the seat and take what you need." I found a big wrench and returned back to the bike to spend an hour doing the repair, during which trucks would blast by. On one occurrence a trucks wind gust blew the bike over upon me, much to my disgust. Once everything was done, I ran back and gave the wrench back to the trucker, who was very nonchalant. Once again I was off pedaling into the hot sun.

At noon I cycled into Boise and found a bike shop where I purchased a dozen new spokes as well as an expensive rear hub removal tool. After buying the parts, I went back to the bike thinking about ways to reinforce the rear spokes. It dawned on me that back in my motocross racing days we would tie our spokes with wire, where they crossed. I sat down and wound a piece of light wire around each spoke at the point where it intersected another spoke. Hoping this would brace the spokes and help redistribute the shock to prevent spoke breakage, I rode off encouraged at how it seemed to sturdy up the back wheel and reduce wheel flexing.

With spoke problems temporarily resolved, I now had an even graver problem. It was the heat. This was hot, real hot, about 105 degrees. Riding in the blasting sunshine I could feel it burning my skin. It was hard to maintain my energy level and not pass out. To stay cool I sprayed myself with water and draped towels over my face like an Arab. It was hard to focus on the road and many times I felt dizzy. It took all I had to concentrate, to stay on the road and to keep pace. At every overpass I stopped to cool down. In one instance there was a car in the northbound lane with its hood up and steam coming out of the engine. The driver was a black man and he was looking at the car saying, "Shit man, shit." I had to pull over and lay down on a slab of shady concrete in an attempt to cool down. The black man drank from a can of Coke and then shouted to me, "Hey bro do you have some extra water for my car?" "No I don't, sorry." I said. I was damned if I'd give him my precious last few drops of water for his car. I truly wanted at that moment to drink all my water, but I had to conserve it in order to make it the next fifty miles.

I got back on the pedals and headed south into a blazing sun that made me dizzy and nauseous not only from the heat but also from the smell of diesel trucks. Some trucks went past and smelled like lumber and others like chickens. I could smell cigarette smoke from some passing cars. Smelling the air was a novel way of entertaining myself. In the extreme heat it helped keep me alert. Still it was important to stop every half hour to rest and sip on a drink. At another overpass I was so overwhelmed with heat and fatigue that I slept for twenty minutes on a slab of concrete. My pace was very slow across this desert wasteland. I figured out every five minutes, I would go about one mile. To confirm this I would time between little green mileposts, which had numbers written upon them, however I did not know from where the number had started counting. It was agonizing to see how slowly they were moving by. I would try to think of something else to pass the time, but it was pure torture and misery at this snails pace.

### *Goodbye to the animal house*

*In the late summer of 1979 we were informed by the owner that the animal house would be sold. We talked about finding another place, but soon each of us would go our separate ways. Gordy got married to Sue, even though I once slammed the screen door in her face and said, "I wouldn't do to my worst enemy what you do to my good friend Gordy." Mark was engaged to his Susan and though they seemed so opposite, they got along harmoniously. I moved out and rented a room at Tom's house. I had met Tom during the previous years parties at the animal house.*

*Tom had long curly blonde hair and wore round wire rimmed glasses. He had all the characteristics of a 60's pot smoker, but he, like me, loved machines. He worked at a small engine shop and was especially into fixing single cylinder engines with crankshaft problems. There was much more about Tom, he was rather comical at times, a great story teller, an apparent recluse and an authority on just about everything. He especially got into subjects I knew little about, like the fifth dimension, the mafia and Big Brothers watchful eyes always seeing everything we do. He often talked about snuffing out someone he didn't like. That's what made him scary. You could not tell with Tom, where he crossed the line.*

As the Idaho sun beat down on me like sharp nails, I finally made it into the town of Mountain Home at 5:30pm. This small town was indeed a welcome sight. I was exhausted and out of focus as I rode down the casual main street. My body was depleted and felt drunk with fatigue. I went directly to a small store and bought some groceries and a cold drink which was rapidly gulped down.

After shopping, I searched for the city park, which, as usual, was directly in the middle of town. Once there, I met some other cyclists who were setting up camp to spend the night. There names were Andy, Eric, and Roger and they were from Rhode Island and New York. We were headed in opposite directions. This was there fifth week on the road from New York. They were headed for Seattle. With our common mode of travel as a common bond, we became immediate friends and had much to talk about. We shared similar stories of adventure on the road. They especially liked telling the story of how they had to fight off clouds of mosquito's at the 11,000 foot level of Grand Teton Pass. Once they learned of my travel itinerary, Andy gave me his mom's phone number and address in Syracuse New York and promised me that if I came by he would surely let me stay at his place. That evening, our conversation under the large oak trees flew past very quickly as we exchanged snacks, stories and soon it was time for bed. I especially enjoyed sampling there 'gorp' mix of peanuts, raisins and M&M's.

Since they only had one small tent for the three of them I offered to ease there cramped conditions by inviting Eric to sleep in my tent. This he did, and it was rather humorous because whenever somebody would say, "Hey Eric" we would both answer, "Yah?"

During the night I awoke to hear the wind begin to blow. I did not know from which direction it was coming. I dreaded fighting a headwind. After tossing to and fro in worry, I fell asleep.

### Thursday July 14th

The morning heralded its arrival with a howling wind. I awoke at 5am after a night spent tossing and turning because of the uncomfortable heat. Eric elected to cook pancakes for everyone and we all feasted together on the thick and rich, but delicious cakes. The wind was blowing strong, and it appeared to be coming out of the northwest. Andy said to me, "Hey Eric, You'll sail today man!" We separated after shaking hands and saying good luck. I wished them the very best as they were heading off into that horrid wind.

Andy was right about me sailing, for that I did. I'd left Mountain Home at 8am and went down Interstate #84 at an effortless pace. As I sped down the freeway, a large truck seemed to slow behind my left side. I was then hit in the helmet with a bag of M&M's. It sent them scattering in every direction. I pondered if I should stop and pick them up, but kept on. The truck kept going. I think it was "given to me in good intention," but just a bad throw.

By noon I had nearly coasted all the ways into Twin Falls, a distance of 77 miles, which computed out to an average speed of almost 20 miles per hour! Desiring to get a burger for lunch, I pedaled across the Snake River Canyon bridge, which gave an impressive sight of the deep gorge below and abruptly got a flat tire on the grid iron walkway of the bridge. After fixing the puncture in that aggravating wind, I rode into town and ate at a McDonald's. There, a chance meeting occurred with a cute young lady and we had an "initiating conversation" while munching on our fast food cuisine and watching a brown dust storm approaching from the west. Realizing that I must get going to beat the storm, I finished my meal, said goodbye to the young lady and went back outside. Oh how I wanted to stay and talk more with her. But the storm alarmed me.

I noticed that the temperature had dropped several degrees and that the wind had picked up even more strength. To cycle back to the interstate was an enormous fight against a terribly strong crosswind and headwind. I feared being blown off of the bridge into the Snake River Canyon. It was five miles of utter agony, but once making a right turn right onto I-84 I was back sailing with the wind. At times the wind blew so strong that I could actually keep pace with the cars! I discovered that once reaching the speed of approximately 40 mph the bike would retain that speed without much pedaling. People in cars would smile and laugh at me as I rode beside them. I stopped and experimented in the making of a sail from my towel and a stick, but it was crudely built and soon fell apart.

Moving along at such a high speed presented new problems. I'd have to keep constant vigilance to avoid hitting objects as they would surely have destroyed my wheel and caused a crash. I kept a vigilant watch on the road for it was littered with large truck tires. It was common to see these shredded tires lying on the sides of the roadway. They took on strange forms. Some looked like corpses while others reminded me of fossils from a dinosaurs grave yard.

The map showed a roadside rest area appearing to be just a short ways south of the intersection of highway 86 and 84, which goes to Salt Lake City. After traveling seven miles there was finally a rest area but it was not the one I had intended for. Realizing that this was not the rest area I wanted to go to, I figured it was getting late and that this would have to do as the storm was still blowing. The rest area had sprinklers which I made darn sure were jammed with sticks to keep them from spraying my tent during the night. Nestled in for the evening a great exhilaration overcame me while calculating 120 miles had been traversed on this day with the help of that tremendous tailwind.

## Friday July 15th

Awoke at 6am on to hear a howling wind slapping against the tent. The fight was soon on, against a nasty headwind while pedaling back up that seven miles of road. Finally returning to I-84, I was once again heading east and had not gone more than a couple of miles before seeing the rest area that I intended to stay at. What a waste of energy! I had once again been foiled by the map and the lack of road signs!

The road gradually swung northeast and slowly climbed uphill, past rocky outcrops which overlooked vistas of the Snake River. With a good tailwind to my advantage, I had traveled 63 miles to arrive in Pocatello at noon, where observation was made of thick black smoke belching from a coal processing plant with a most sickening smell. I stopped into a supermarket, bought some goods and while eating outside met some folks interested in my travels. After talking to them a few extra moments were spent writing post cards and sipping on a extra big Coke that they had bought for me. After returning to the road I felt great and was cycling like crazy down highway #15, singing the national anthem and experiencing a rushing sensation from the caffeine and sugar buzz by that large Coke- or had they slipped something in my drink?

After passing through the town of Blackfoot I exited the interstate and took highway #91 in order to get off of the noisy and impersonal interstate. The landscape transformed into a mixture of river beds and rolling hills splattered with green trees. While enjoying the scenery a storm rapidly approached as if from knowhere. I was so tired that I took a nap for 15 minutes under an oak tree, while the rain fell. Refreshed after the siesta, the sky cleared again while making way into Idaho Falls at 5pm. During my grocery shopping, it again rained and this brought into the air the most wonderful aromatic smell of grass and pavement.

After traveling this day for 116 miles, I was tired yet wanted to get a little further out of the city to camp. Continuing down a fine paved shoulder of highway my guard was dropped as I looked up at an airplane flying low overhead. Just as I looked down to the road a jagged, broken pop bottle caught my attention directly in front of me but it was to late to avoid. "Woosh!" went the tire which immediately flattened. The glass was so sharp that it sliced the tire in half. I installed a replacement tire and tube, but shortly thereafter that tube also went flat. Pressing on, enough air could be pumped into the tire to go several miles along before repeating the procedure. Exiting off the highway, I went down a gravel road and found a park near a lake. As darkness set in I continued trying to fix the troublesome tube. The patches would not stick, and no matter what was tried the tube would not hold air. Frustrated and weary I laid my sleeping bag out under the stars, but shortly after midnight it began to rain and a quick and hasty effort to put up the tent was required. Finally under shelter, I thought of my predicament. Would I have to call it quits because of tire problems? I rolled in and out of slumber…remembering my past romance.

## *The lady of my dreams*

*Not long after moving out of the animal house a new friendship emerged from the acquaintances made there. She was a friend of Julie's, and Sue, Gordy's wife. Her name was Molly. She was a beautiful 20 year old Mediterranean looking woman, brought up in Lakeside. She was very shapely and elegant, a lady of a young mans dreams. But she had a handicap. She had a shrill voice, which may have left others the impression that she was a bimbo, but she was not. She was sharp and interested in life. I was so much a boy and she so much a girl, though we were both in our adult forms, exercising our youthful desires.*

*It was a lovely winter of 1980, getting to know Molly and doing things with her. In February I took a week off and flew down to Phoenix to visit my sister. This was a test to see how I did away from home and how I liked travel and at seeing parts of the southwest.*

*I returned and started a new job at Norco. It looked like a more promising future than what Pike Lake Service Center had to offer. I told Dexter that I was leaving because I would be involved in the repairs of more complex machinery and that was what I wanted, not because I was mad at him. He was pretty glum about the whole idea. He tried to offer me more money but that wouldn't keep me. Until the day I left he acted as if I'd betrayed him.*

*I started to notice a waning of our romance in the spring. Molly told me, "Your really not my type." It was blunt, and I tried to shrug it off, but should have known the early warning signs. I was still head over heels for her. Then early in the month of May, Molly went to Florida with an ex-boyfriend. She didn't tell me she was going, I heard it from her sister and then received a letter from her. After that, I fell apart. It did not make sense to me. After four months of dating, our relationship was at an end. Maybe I got too serious and was blinded, but she wanted to be free and went her way. I was devastated.*

*The hit song of that year was called "Lost in love," and the radio station played it constantly. That song was like the dentists drill on an abscessed tooth. It seemed to be directed at my soul and added to my total abyss of loneliness and intangible feelings. I was perplexed and so very alone with know one to turn to.*

## Saturday July 16th

The morning started off at "Camp Frustration" trying to get a patch to stick to the tube. The next dilemma was the challenge of getting the tube into the tire and on the wheel without pinching the tube. After trying several attempts without much success, I was ready to heave the bike and gear into the lake. This tube repair should be such an easy task, but was giving me many problems. Finally the tire held air and I was back on the main road. I hadn't even gone one mile when, "BANG" went the front tube again. While fixing the tube, a truck went past and blew the bike over and it landed on top of me. I was madder than a wet cat. Picked the bike up and spun it around a couple of times like a hula hoop and was going to throw it down the road and then stomp on it, but a little voice in my head said, "better not do that." Instead I set it down gently, and took a short walk. After a lucky tube fix, I was again heading north. The tire continually went soft, requiring pumping enough times to arrive at the small town of Rexburg, where a new tube was purchased. Believing all my problems would be solved, I was shocked when the new tube went flat on me in only 5 miles! By noon I'd had five flats and was hardly 35 miles down the road!

Even though my anger was near its peak I still took notice of the Grand Teton Mountains off to my right in starkly beautiful splendor. They were a stunning and impressive sight of purple valleys and snow covered peaks jutting high up into the blue sky. Expansive green meadows greeted me with grasses gracefully bending over in a warm and gentle wind. Continuing northward the road began a very steep incline as it entered into Targhee National Forest.

It was on that steep incline that my trip almost came to an end. I was halfway up the 10%grade when the front tire became mushy and went flat. I stopped to repair it and due to the grades steepness everything wanted to roll downhill. I laid down a roll of tape, but it rolled off and so I ran after it in pursuit. The same thing happened with the helmet. I caught it and walked back up to the bike which had fallen over in the wind. I again turned it over and was working on the tube when it fell over on me. I really wanted to end the trip right there and then! I picked up the bike and was near to tossing it over a guard rail and into a ravine. I swung it around like 'Snap the Whip' and shouted "Damn worthless cheap junk!" I hollered at the height of my lungs before gaining my wits and setting it down and taking another short walk. I cooled down and prayed that the tire problems would hold until Yellowstone, where I vowed to buy the best tubes and tires available.

Back underway, a good steady stride was made while traversing a beautiful green valley whose meadows were coated with white and yellow flowers alongside rumbling clear blue rivers. The sun shone and puffy white clouds added to give this a feeling of paradise. The road was so lovely that I hardly fretted when two more flat tires occured. More prayers were said while sewing up one very big gash and then pleading with 'FRIEND' to please get me to Yellowstone. Along the route, many stops were made to pump air into the tires. The tubes were so filled with patches that they were beginning to look like a quilt. On a long straight stretch the rear tire went flat and another tire and tube were installed. For the moment my conviction was to enjoy the lovely pine trees, grassy meadows, mountains with snow on top and air so exceptionally fresh. Even the noise and smell from the cars and trucks passing by was tolerated.

Now the road steepened like a ski jump while heading up Targhee Pass. The traffic was bad and progress was slow but steady until finally cresting the 7072 foot pass. A large sign said I was on the Continental Divide. It made my head dizzy to think I'd made it this far. The sign also told about Indian Chief Joseph using this route to escape conflict with chasing federal troops in the late 1890's.

As a rule the hills out west are exceedingly slow to bicycle up, but fast and fun to come down. This one followed the rule. I sped down the east side of the divide at 50 miles an hour for a distance of ten miles. This was an exhilarating way to cool down after that sweaty uphill ride. The ride was as fast as possible in hopes of getting to a bike shop before they'd close at 6 'o' clock. I rolled into West Yellowstone just in the nick of time to get directions and find the shop.

It was a wonderful bike shop with many items that lit up my eyes, but were beyond my budget. I did buy two new tires, made by Specialized and called 'Expedition' along with a couple of tubes and a inner tub puncture preventative which was called 'a tube saver.' The day was wearing thin and I was feeling very tired but glad to attain one of the last campsights at the campground. One has no choice but to stay at a campground in Yellowstone because it is unlawful to camp anywhere else - especially since several hikers had recently been killed by grizzly bears.

A badly needed shower was taken, my first one in 10 days and it was a glorious refreshment. After dinner, I walked around town to enjoy the yellow-stained log buildings and smell the air thick with wood smoke. I stopped into a bar and met two Aussies inside who were nice fellows, easy going and adventurous and who asked me if I wanted to, "Have a go at a drinking contest." I declined there invitation after a couple of beers. I slipped out into the moonlit night to walk back to camp eager for shuteye after eight flat tires on this day.

## Sunday morning of the 17th of July

Awoke at 6:30 and installed the new tires and tubes. Between the tube and the tire were placed a tube-saver, which is a nonperforating plastic strip, to help prevent punctures. With this added insurance a new confidence overcame me to put an end to flat tires. After taking a little time to clean up the bike and to organize equipment, I was underway at 9:30. While passing through West Yellowstone, I stopped to buy supplies and met many other bikers, tourists and backpackers, all of whom seemed to be enjoying a leisure pace. It was no wonder everyone was so happy as it was a fine morning, and while heading for Madison Junction I noticed the lovely evergreen trees and flowers as well as gushing mountain streams.

Along the ride I met cyclists Joni and her younger brother Skip whom had started their journey in Spokane and were riding to Virginia. We rode to Old Faithful at a fast pace stopping frequently to enjoy looking at the hot springs and mud pots. Joni was a competent and strong rider and somewhat of a Tom boy. We watched Old Faithful geyser blow at 2pm and then rode to Grants Village on Yellowstone Lake. During the day's ride we'd crossed the Continental Divide a couple of times and therefore were very hungry and ate a good supper at the campground. We shared the same campsite and pitched tents nearby. As the sun was setting Joni and I sat on a picnic table. I listened to Joni's tales about biking and camping as she loves the out of doors and sporting activities. She was hardy and yet beautiful and pleasant to be with. I was enjoying every moment of her company until a scruffy traveling cyclist came by who had long hair, a beard and a foul smell. He began asking me a zillion questions about my travels. He was like a sticky fly that I could not shake and soon Joni said she was calling it a night. Finally he left. I think he was sent by god to keep me from getting to know Joni further, because he sure blew my chances.

I laid in my bed and recalled how it was such an inspirational and eventful day. I wrote a poem about it.

>The snow capped mountains
>The icy trickling streams
>The thundering rivers
>Ever so magnificant
>In all their glory
>Seem as if they are
>Edible to the senses.

## Monday July 18th

Morning announced its arrival to the sound of birds singing and ravens cawing. I packed up the tent as Joni and Skip rolled out of there's in time for a few parting words. I said goodbye to them and then was on my way to Grants Village. I arrived at 6:30am and bought some supplies. While touring past the steaming hot geysers of Lake Yellowstone, which looked so pretty but smelled so bad, I was thinking about finding a place to camp and to sit and enjoy the beauty. The lake has utter tranquility even though everywhere one goes it smells foul like rotten eggs. It was a perfect morning with a blue sky and not a cloud in sight. Many ducks swam and flew over the lake. The highway snaked alongside of the north-side of the scenic lake. I was very thankful to be riding a bicycle, as it was the perfect way to thoroughly enjoy this fine morning and the right speed to take in all of the sights. At 8:30am I arrived in Lake Village and met ranger Jamie Hollowai, who told me if I needed a place to stay in Cody, that I could call her friend, Gail. She wrote the name on a slip of paper and handed it to me. The entire transaction lasted no more than a minute before I was off. Continuing along the lake shore I stopped to watch a big bull moose in a swamp. Then a little farther I observed a bison in a field. The great aspect to this park is the abundance of wildlife and the opportunity to see them moving unafraid in there native habitat.

Soon a treacherous climb was initiated up Sylvan Pass. It is not a very wide road and huge motor homes with long trailers would drive by and force me off. "Next time bring your house," I shouted to one driver. He probably didn't hear me - let alone see me. At my snails pace there was plenty of time to enjoy the warm sunshine and blue sky reflecting upon crystal clear lakes surrounded with evergreen trees. At 11:00a.m, I crested the saddle of Sylvan Pass, at 8,520 feet. People were having snowball fights while others wrestled in the white snow gasping for breath.

Before pushing off I checked my brakes and was lucky to have done so as the road below looked unbelievably steep. I was quickly in the midst of the most exhilarating ride yet. Heading down the east slope of the Rockies, was such a rapid descent that the brakes had to be applied all the way, as hard as I could compress them, to keep down my speed. One section of the road was very bumpy and there appeared a sharp left turn with a big whoop-dee-do in the road. I stood up and shifted my weight to the back of the bike, just enough to allow it to soar into the air! In short time there was another sharp left turn which I had to muscle the bike around or else slide over a thousand foot cliff. The bike responded to my every command along this thrilling descent.

After 15 miles of downhill the road flattened out and entered a dry rocky valley. The temperature began to rise and soon it was necessary to take off my shirt. I passed a clear mountain stream and stopped to plunge into it and bathe. This cooled me down, but within 10 miles I was dry and once again very hot. The pedals were spinning and my legs were pumping as this man and his machine crossed a mighty canyon walled in with high crags. Soon the terrain along highway #14 opened up into high plains desert with expansive valleys and long stretches of open road. Many miles had passed by and hunger pangs were increasing, therefore I was overjoyed to see a restaurant in the middle of nowhere. There was not another place to eat for fifty miles. I pulled up to the door step and gazed up at a log building darkened from seasons of weather. The building had a strong wood smell and a glorious ranch style charm. Inside the conditions were pleasant as it was air conditioned. Waitress's scurried here and there. I ordered a grilled cheese sandwich that cost me six dollars along with a cold drink which cost me a buck. Aside from the high prices the place was a step into the past as I noticed once again the old western-movie-faces on these people and a distinct drawl to their speech. I finished up, returned to the hot outside and met three other cyclists arriving at the restaurant. We struck up a conversation and I found out their names were Ken, Ken and Mark. They had started their journey from Seattle and were heading back home to New York. I wished them well and was soon off across a great expanse of arrid land heading east for Cody.

The ride to Cody was pleasant but my strength was contested against a steady wind. I pedaled past the waters of Buffalo Bill Reservoir, which was of high contrast to the dry surrounding countryside. Finally arriving in Cody, the green grass was a welcome sight and I made way to a grocery store. While buying provisions, I again met up with the three cyclists who had started from Seattle. We agreed to find a park in which we could cook dinner, eat and camp. We found a nice park and were in the midst of cooking our food, when the sheriff drove up and said, "Sorry fellows you cannot camp in the park." We acknowledged him and his warning and since none of us had anyplace to stay, I offered to call Gail, who I was referred to me by the ranger I'd met in Yellowstone. I called her impromptu and told her who I was and who told me of her and then asked her if we all could stay at her house. Even over the phone she sounded like a very effervescent gal and said we could all come over. We finished our meal and pedaled over to find Gail's house. I was about to knock on the door when we met her on this surprise visit. Gail was a very hardy woman and extremely hospitable. She gave us all a cold drink and popcorn and a lot of friendly company. We sat up until midnight talking about each of our great adventures before retiring for the night upon the floor.

### Tuesday July 19th

I awoke at 5 a.m. and plopped around trying to get my New York friends stirring, but they were very pokey and I was anxious to get underway. We said our thank you's and goodbyes to Gail at 6:30 and were off. The "New Yawkers" set a blistering pace that I could not keep up with. On a long flat plain they proceeded to leave me in the dust as my bike carried far more weight and was hence much slower. I watched them get farther away from me, until they looked very small. Yet, fifty miles down the road I met them in the little adobe town of Greybull at a grocery store.

They smiled at me and said, "We'll see you later." Then they pedaled eastward. I was struck how little gratitude they had for me after all the help I'd given them the last night.

Heading east on highway 14, the road passed into a valley and then began a very steep switchback ascent up a sheer canyon wall. Slowly I began working my way up the steep slope of the west side of the Bighorn Mountains. The climb was incredible and defeating to look up ahead. One notices switchbacks going back and forth for as far as the eye can see. But there was no way around it other than hitching or quitting which I was determined not to do. At high noon my assault on this mountain began under a hot sun and a temperature of 90 degrees. I labored hard under my heavy load and drank so much water that I had to stop and ask a motor home owner if I could get a refill for my water jugs. His wife kindly filled my bottles with the coldest water I'd ever drank. It gave me a cold rush, like ice cream does. Around 3 '0' clock I caught a glimpse of the New Yawkers up in front and continued my pursuit up the slopes closing in on the guys up ahead. A bike race was underway! Soon I caught up with them at a rest area, where a fountain refreshed my thirst. After a short rest I took off ahead of them, but not very far as when I was looking back I saw them mount their saddles.

Our competition for the summit became a battle of gritting teeth and putting all we had into the pedals. A close watch was kept on how far behind they were from me at each turn. They were gaining and so it was necessary to pour on the coal. Shifting of the gears could only be done one gear up or down on the setting. We stayed an equal ways apart for quite some time. Greater gain was made for me when it was real steep, because my bike had such low gears. But when it flattened out they rapidly moved up on me. On one steep uphill incline a biker going downhill whizzed past me and shouted, "Your going the wrong way," as he raised a fist and flew by. Shortly after, another downhill biker followed and shouted, "The summit is a long ways away." This added a demoralized feeling and it was tempting me to give it up when I saw a sign that said "SUMMIT 1000 FEET."

Now the New Yawkers were moving up real close. The last stretch was very steep and as much beef as I could give went into the pedals. I was getting so very tired, then suddenly a thundercloud boiled over the slope ahead of us and a mighty gust of wind blasted up from behind and gave me a boost. "Yahoo," I shouted as the wind thrust me, yes blew me up the last five hundred feet to arrive at the summit ahead of them!

It had taken me nearly six hours to reach the 8,950 foot summit of Granite Pass. As suddenly as I arrived the clouds burst open and it began to pour down with rain. A couple moments later the New Yawkers pulled up, cheering and we all were yahoooing and jumping about together.

I felt as if a true sense of victory had been won for me and FRIEND. In one respect it was our first point of bonding. We overcame them, even though my baggage was twice the weight of theirs. Yet we all rejoiced and laughed and danced at the top like jolly good friends. From there the road flattened out and we coasted along under a pouring rain with a blasting wind behind us pushing us effortlessly as we free wheeled across the flat meadows for nearly ten miles without hardly a pedal. The road started a slow descent down the east side of the mountain and as it was late before we decided to camp for the night in a picnic area next to a small pub. They went inside for a beer, but I stayed behind to avoid the expense. It got me to start recollecting about Tom.

### *Living with a drug dealer*

*After a couple of months of living at Tom's house I realized he was a drug dealer and a junkie. He smoked, drank, snorted and swallowed anything he could that would get him high. For kicks he drank NyQuil till he slurred his words and passed out. He sold cocaine and pot. No wonder he was always very paranoid. Whenever he heard a car door slam outside, he'd peep open the curtains to have a look outside. He kept a loaded rifle at his bedside and his dog was a big red haired retriever named Gus who claimed his own chair. Sitting down in his chair meant you would be covered with dog hair. In fact the whole house was infested with dog hair. When an ambulance or firetruck went past the house, Gus would howl in unison with the wailing siren. One memorable night was when a spotlight shone through my window and slowly moved across the wall of my room. I slid off my bed and laid flat on the floor fearful that someone would shoot into the window. The spotlights came from two cars-one in the front and the other in the rear of the house. Old Gus was growling and soon thereafter the cars left and I saw one of them was a police car. It was then that I understood that the cops were watching Tom.*

*Some nights Tom would have party's that lasted all night long. In the morning, I'd come out of my bedroom and find people crashed out with empty tequila bottles and marijuana roaches laying everywhere. One morning the phone rang and I hollered up to Tom to answer it, but even after several tries he did not respond. I started walking up the stairway and when I got about half way up, I heard Tom chamber a round into his 30-30. He said; "Don't you never come up those stairs again." Tom was getting darker and more sinister the longer I stayed there. After that incident I was fed up with his terror and soon moved out.*

## Wednesday July 20th

Dawned foggy and cool. At 6am I was packing up my things as the Yawkers were barely sturring. We all had such sore muscles that whenever anyone moved there was a groaning sound to accompany it. We agreed to meet in Buffalo at the end of this day and with that I said so long to them.

I headed downhill on this overcast morning and had not gone even a mile when it was necessary to hit the brakes hard as a cow moose and a calf walked out onto the road in front of me. I stopped to give way to them and fortunate that I did, as a bull moose came charging out of the woods, all bent for hell. In a tense moment, I thought he might charge, but I shouted in a baritone voice, "Hey! get out of here!" and they all jumped across the road and were off crashing into the brush.

Another mile or so down the grade stood a sign which read; "STEEP GRADE 9 MILES." My speed increased greatly going down that slope and as I rounded a bend there were several cattle on the road. Screech went my brakes and the noise was enough to startle the cattle into running off.

On another curve a geology class on a field trip from Wyoming University was looking at a geologic formation on the roadside as I approached at a high speed. I felt a rush of adrenaline and shouted with my thumb up in the air, "Purely geologic!" They all stopped whatever they were doing and everybody applauded, whistled and laughed as I zipped by.

It was a wonderful 25minute downhill ride and more pedaling to get into the town of Sheridan. I bought some fresh food for lunch and there met a guy who was originally from California and was once an avid surfer. He informed me where the post office was, as I needed to get rid of some excess baggage. Six pounds of clothing and shoes were mailed to my parents in Minnesota.

Now enjoying a much lighter load and more spacious panniers, I headed south against strong headwinds with agonizingly aching muscles. Hill after hill on highway #87 to Buffalo drained all my energy. The sun reappeared from the clouds around 3pm and this added intense heat to the high humidity. Exhausted and bone dry for a cold drink I rode into Buffalo and went straight to a 7-11 store where I bought a quart of orange juice and went outside to sit under a tree to guzzle it down. I was spent, barely able to talk.

While sitting there four other cycling travelers pedaled up and I met Rick, Dee dee, Judy and Jon who were from California. We went in search of a camp and along the way met up with the New Yawkers. All of us pitched in $2.35 each to get a group campsite. With this many people in our camp we had quite an active and boisterous time setting tents and getting to know one another. It was a good deal of fun until it started to rain and everyone sought shelter from the storm.

Awakening early, I got packed up and was underway before anyone else did on this **Thursday July 21st**. By 6:15 Buffalo was already behind me and a series of long uphills and slow downhills were presumed heading east across interstate #90. This high plains Wyoming desert is mostly flat country with sagebrush and occasional trees skirting dry river bottoms. Dead rabbits and rattle snakes littered the road side. I couldn't resist a souvenir of a rattle snake rattle and therefore cut one off from a big dead snake. It was a rather unexciting ride along a monotonous route so I thought about all of the wild land out here in America. Oh how easy it would be for someone to come out here and get lost. If a person wanted to do so they could come here and not see another soul for weeks. Why is it then that everybody collects in big cities? My answer was because they probably want money and not wide open space.

Many things were hashed over and theorized during those seventy miles of pedaling which brought me into the town of Gillette at 11:30.

## ERIC NORLAND

### *Summer of 1980*

*The summer of 1980 I rented out a room in a house owned by Tony. He was a trusting and easy going guy. I'd met Tony at the bars and we shared an interest in chasing girls and talking about hunting and trout fishing. Living at Tony's house was a positive experience because it gave me the space that I needed to make my plans. One of the things I liked about it there was that the house was near the woods. I had enough room to do art on a table set up downstairs in the laundry room. I recall working on a painting the night that John Lennon was murdered. It struck me how quickly life comes to an end and how I must do what I can to make things happen in my own life before time runs out. There was a sad feeling in the air. Because of the economy, sales were down and layoffs loomed. People did not have the money to fix their equipment and so they would come in and expect it fixed for nothing. Unemployed or retired old men shuffled through the shop looking for someone to BS with, which I always felt was somewhat of a obligation for me because it seemed so callous to ignore them. It drove Jim, the boss, crazy. I realized how much I wished I had the time to talk to those men, but it was against the rules, this I understood, but it still hurt me to see them needing someone to talk with. Jim was a good salesman, but he was not mechanically inclined at all. He constantly harped at us mechanics about sweeping the floor and keeping the place clean. He'd put away our tools even while we were in the middle of a job, which added to the madness in the air.*

*One of the guys I worked with was a 17 year old named Steve. He was a high school dropout and a rock 'n roll fanatic. He smoked pot like some people do cigarettes. He was a rebel that lacked motivation, yet he was very honest and I talked to him often. He wasn't afraid to speak out and to say what he felt. He thought of me as an educated man and that I didn't belong in a dump like this. I tried to encourage him to go back to school and to wear condoms because he was always screwing around with his girlfriend. When it came to work he was a lazy cat. He was always goofing off and didn't care about doing things right. I wasn't surprised when Vern, the general manager, fired him because of this. Still, his rebelliousness influenced me in many ways.*

*I was upset to see Steve go. But times were tough and Vern was a good guy and I liked him. I trusted Vern and he trusted me and we got along just great. He often times asked me what I was going to do with my life and he encouraged me to do it now before it was too late.*

After a short lunch the road was again resumed heading east toward Moorcroft. The next thirty miles rolled by on this hot and dry afternoon with further thoughts about why people accumulate in big cities. Perhaps they do not enjoy the rural living or are afraid to strike out and carve a home out on the land. Mostly the reason is probably economic. Most people have to live in the city because it is the only place they can find food, clothing and shelter. It seemed to me to be too bad, because such beauty and natural adventure awaits those who live in the country.

The miles had passed and soon arrival was made in the one street town of Moorcroft. Eager for a cold drink, I discovered a drive-in at the edge of town and shortly thereafter was sucking on a chocolate malt while talking to a young boy named Tracy. He was a fun loving, talkative and a rather knowledgeable boy. This boy gave straight and honest answers, which I considered to be like my own Midwestern values. Not being an ethnologist, but observant of people, it was there at that drive-in, about 58 miles west of the South Dakota border that I realized I was standing on a dividing line between the west and the Midwest. It felt good to realize that I was getting closer to my homeland and after a couple of ice waters, which were downed as though they were my last, a search was started to find the town park and camp for the night. While doing so a side road was taken and I became temporarily lost while searching to get back onto the main road.

I just happened past a Pizza Hut restaurant and saw some bicycles outside and noticed they belonged to the New Yawkers. They were inside waving at me to come in and join them. I went inside and met up again with Ken, Ken and Mark. We then saw Deedee, Rick, John and Judy drive up on their bikes. United again, we all ate pizza together and drank several pitchers of beer from which and I became somewhat inebriated. Our talk turned jovial as we attempted to recite the words to the Beverly Hillbilly's theme song and also to Gilligans Island. Riding back to the park was a blast as all of us were carefree and driving crazy from the beer. We camped in the town park and clumped our cluster of tents into a neat ring of celebration until nodding off around 10:30pm.

## Friday July 22nd

I awoke everyone who was still asleep in their tents at 5am on the morning of by singing aloud the tune to "The Beverly Hillbillies". There were a few chuckles from the tents, but everyone was slow in getting up, so I bid them farewell and left on my own at 6:15. The ride progressed over the last of the long slow hills of eastern Wyoming. A light sprinkling rain started but this was not so bad as it was a welcome relief from the heat. Off in the distance I could see the Black Hills jutting up above the flat plain. Far behind me I could see a string of cyclists, which were sure to be my accomplices. Without any wind I made good time across the open plain and therefore arrived in Newcastle at 10:30 where I sat to eat and talk with Dee and Rick till noon. They are both easy going people and interested in the lifestyle of traveling by bicycle.

We rode off together over the steep grades of the Black Hills. These hills could be compared to a camels back as they rise and fall with such rapidity that one feels as if riding upon a roller coaster. At 1pm we crossed the state line into South Dakota and by 2pm were halfway to Custer. Feeling more comfortable with all of my cycling companions, I enjoyed their comradery and was beginning to relax around them.

On one particularly steep grade I was leading the way uphill as Rick and Dee dee were directly behind. I stood up to exert additional effort upon the pedals and abruptly let loose a very loud and obnoxious fart. We all laughed hysterically and in such disorder that we nearly crashed- just as a big truck zoomed past blasting his horn and missing us by inches. This caused us to get a hold of our composure, and return to our senses.

The traffic on the hilly road was very dangerous as long strings of cars zoomed by inches away. Finally after much danger we made it into Custer at 4pm and were all very tired and saddle sore. While eating a dinner of fried ham and potatoes I showed the Yawkers a newspaper clipping from the start of my journey. They said they liked what I was doing. The evening flew by with enjoyable conversation and it was such a beautiful starlit night that we all slept under the stars on a mowed lawn, nearby to each other.

Around 1am, I was in a deep sleep and was dreaming when I became aware of a dog barking. The barking went on for a long time and I thought it was in my dream but soon realized it was not, as this big dog walked around us and yapped as if to no end. He stood about 50 feet away and barked continuously for a long period of time. At first I ignored the beast but realizing we were all close to a garbage can, I believed that was the reason he was barking. My patience was wearing thin and was about to get up and tell the dog off when I heard Mark say, "The first one to shut that dog up gets a big handful of my gorp." I jumped up and cussed and threw rocks at the dog till he ran off. I then crawled back into the sleeping bag as everyone in the group gave a big cheer and a round of applause.

## Saturday July 23rd

We awoke at 5:15am and headed off by 6:30am on the road. Mark gave me my handful of gorp and then everyone split up and went in their own direction so I headed over to see the Crazy Horse monument. This mountain was being carved to resemble the Indian chief upon his horse. He was the leader at the battle of the Little Bighorn. This carving project was obviously making slow progress and everywhere about the sight were donation boxes to help folks donate to help complete the cause. It was inspiring for me to see an artist take a dream of such magnitude and work it into reality.

In comparison to Crazy Horse, one cannot help but gaze in wonder at the awesome sight of the carved faces on Mt.Rushmore. I felt my patriotism rise to this overall theme of gung ho USA. Yet I was puzzled to some extent that the Crazy Horse memorial was so incomplete and how that project was troubled with financial woes. It becomes obvious that the Mt. Rushmore monument did not share the same fate, since it was completed back in the 1920's. It could be presumed the Indians were dealt an injustice or were prejudiced against for lack of any memorial to them. More prevalent is the fact that the Black Hills have always been sacred to the Indians. They believed this to be the center of their holy world. The white man was obviously expressing his dominance over this hallowed ground by placing the carved faces of U.S. Presidents there. It makes one ponder whether liberty, justice and freedom for all is correctly portrayed here.

A long and very fast downhill marked the departure from the Black Hills and was enjoyed down to the tourist town of Keystone. From there a series of uphills and downhills were attacked all the way to the final downhill into Rapid City. This large city based at the northern foothills of the Black Hills was pleasant and modern. At a large supermarket I met up with my cycling friends whom had stopped to buy lunch. In four or five short days I felt great fondness for all of them and it was difficult to let go and again be on my solo way. They had planned to spend the night here and to see a movie, but my schedule was such that I needed to continue. I said goodbye to each of them, we shook hands and it was sad to do so.

I was ready to pedal off from them when a passage from Bob Dylan's song-'Idiot Wind' came to mind. I blurted it out to all the group in a Dylan like voice, *"Down the highways-down the tracks-down the road to ecstasy I followed you beneath the stars, hounded by your memory and all your blazing glory!"* At which they all laughed and John said to me; "There is something very brogue about you, just what is your ancestry?" At which I responded, "I'm a link in the chain, influenced by Bob Dylan and travelin on a bicycle."

There is an emptiness, which occurs when returning to the silence of solo travel after being around comrades and conversation. I did not mind the quiet, in fact it was exhilarating, but still there is a vacuum that needs to be filled with thoughts, observations or songs to distract the physical strain and tedium of this method of travel.

The afternoon was passed under a hot sun as I skirted scenery reminiscent of a geology trip to the Badlands while in college. This reminded me of some of the bluffs and pastures I'd once explored for fossils. I recalled how we found a mammoth leg bone lying in a field and pondered taking it, but decided against it.

It was good to see familiar ground again. I made way into the tourist town of Wall at 6:30pm and was very tired and hungry. I had ridden 104 miles and was eager to stop. Wall Drug is advertised for hundreds of miles in these parts about their pure, fresh and free drinking water. I was dry as a sand flea and went directly to the store to fill my canteen with the fresh water. Disappointment greeted me as I was handed a small paper cup that provided only a quick swallow.

All the shops were stuffed with tourists buying ashtrays and other nick-nacs. They appeared to be decadent and complained about this or that while slurping on obscenely huge ice cream cones. I headed for the grocery store and bought some food and went to a picnic area. There was a family party going on with much laughter and teasing of each other. I could tell these jolly folk were definitely Midwesterners. One of the most noticeable Midwestern characteristic was that every one of them was talking at once. Also they had a sarcasm toward each other and were talking about stories from there past. This was something I did not detect in California.

It was getting late and I was lulled to sleep reminiscing of my youth, when I was a child in the upstairs of my grandparents house listening to the voices of my parents, grandparents, uncles and aunties downstairs socializing. This provided me a heartwarming and relaxing effect.

## Sunday July 24th

The morning of was wet and drizzly and I was underway at 7:45 pedaling through the town of Wall when a sudden rain storm forced me to scurry for shelter at a gas station to slip on my rain parka. A man asked me, "What do you do when it rains?" I responded, "I get wet," at which he laughed. I headed eastward on the large shoulder of interstate 90 and soon the rain stopped and the headwinds picked up, but I continued on.

A few hours later the rain clouds had all passed and warm sunshine and golden fields of grain waved in the wind. I stopped to hang the wet tent over a guard railing and to snack on delicious cinnamon Pop Tarts. The Great Plains gives one a feeling of easy breathing and each gasp fills the lungs with a piece of the endless and expansive openness of land touching the sky. From the perspective of a bicycle traveler these plains seem to swallow the rider into its vastness, for it is awesome and there are few prominent landforms to judge distance. I would look off to the horizon and note my position in relation to distant hills, but still feel miniscule and hardly moving. Time passed slower and tranquility set in. In all it was a good place to see but difficult not to feel the boredom of landscape.

## *Why I left Duluth*

*Norco Outdoors repair shop was such a dismal place to be. It was a large steel building with giant girders spanning the ceiling. In the winter it was drafty and had long icicles hanging from the walls. Nearby were the speakers of my stereo system. The radio station constantly played the hit song of the year "Lost in love." It made me feel dreadfully sad.*

*I wanted to see more of life than the dreary view through the windows of that big cold shop. I knew there was so much more to the world and yet wondered how to get out and see it. It was not as though I wasn't physically able, it's just that I was not sure how to go about doing it. I needed to make a plan and then make my move.*

*There I was, a 26-year-old man who's lifestyle revolved around partying. I drank socially a couple of times a week and pot was always around to add a thrill. I was not hooked on it, like some heavy users. Just one or two little puffs once in awhile was enough. I found it burned my lungs and made me feel drifty. I limited its use. Drugs were everywhere in the early 80's, at almost every gathering, so sampling of cocaine and speed occurred, but they were very hard on the body, and then there was unhappy with drawls.*

*I was doing so many activities that seemed a waste of time. Like going disco dancing, drinking on Sunday afternoons and bar hoping on weekday nights.*

*Those were the activities that my friends wanted to do and I felt pressured to do them. I knew I should be doing something else and wanted a change.*

*With my college degree in fine art, I thought how sad to not find a job that has something to do with it. Watercolor painting helped replenish that need and God knows I tried to sell them at galleries, but times were tough and some did not sell while others sold real slow. It made me feel unwanted and unsaleable. It also made me wonder what economic good my artistic skills were. This added to my restlessness and made me desire to go somewhere to rediscover who I was and develop a new artistic philosophy.*

The day had been passing pleasantly on my eastward ride down the fine shoulder of I-90, and while approaching the town of Murdo, as the sun beat on my back at around 5pm, I was startled by a bicycle rider who'd come up from behind me. The rider carried no baggage, was shy and rather introverted and did not offer much to initiate conversation. He seemed to be more or less riding alongside of me to pace himself. I was pushing hard and was tired after riding 95 miles, but still felt it my nature to talk to him. I asked him if he knew of places I might camp in Murdo and where I might find a grocery store. He told me there were places I could go. We did not have a whole lot to talk about and I was just about to leave him when he said, "Why not come stay at my house." He told me his name was Carl and he told me his address. He escorted me to a grocery store and with groceries strapped atop my rear bags, we rode over to his place.

Carl lived in a very nice split entry house and once inside I met his brother Joe, and his mother, Elaine. She was a wonderful woman, warm, cordial and she most kindly invited me for supper. I ate a vegetarian dinner of eggs and noodles with sauce and it was delicious. We then had hot fudge sundaes for dessert. All throughout the occasion they were much interested in my stories, and I in theirs, especially Joe was a very talkative and colorful chap. After dinner I reveled in a badly needed shower and then Elaine treated me to a visit of the town museum. The Murdo Musuem was full of old cars, bicycles and motorcycles, one of which was owned by Elvis Presley.

Elaine was a great woman, and wherever she went there was great respect given to her by all. She told me her husband had once owned the Chevrolet dealership in town and how it was such a thriving business. A large picture window was pointed out to me as once being smashed from the weight of seven feet of snow that fell during a blizzard. Her stories were mixed with friendship, hardship and joys of life at that dealership and how they all sadly reminded her of her husband, who had since passed away.

We returned back to her home and it was nearing midnight when she made a thick and delicious chocolate malt for me. I then helped her do the dishes as we talked some more. She placed some food out on the table which I could eat for breakfast and told me she had a bed made for me downstairs. She then showed me to the bedroom. Just before saying goodnight she asked me in a direct way, "You are a Christian, aren't you?" I did not hesitate long in my response, for I thought to do so would possibly jeopordize my sleeping in this fine bed. "Yes," I said. She returned with, "Then God and the Lord be with you." At which I said, "Thanks I can use all the help I can get." I thought hers was a trick question and wondered why it had to be asked at this moment.

## Monday July 25th

I could have slept for years in that comfortable bed, but instead was up at 5am after a glorious night sleep. It was a sunny morning. I ate a hardy breakfast and then said goodbye to this kind family. They had been so trusting to me and very giving. After leaving the town of Murdo I had good riding for the first hour of the morning as the wind blew out of the south and helped my effort. Then it changed to a strong left crosswind and then became a headwind. I struggled and cursed at the wind and kept repeating to myself; "The going gets harder the closer you get." There was time to think about Elaines question to me of whether I was a Christian. Why it was asked at that final moment I wondered. Had I answered "no" would the door have been opened for me to leave? It made me question how deep ones faith is that they will only help out those of like religion.

My internal debate went on while struggling against a headwind until arriving at the town of Reliance. I turned north and rode toward the Missouri River, who's large lazy blue waters were crossed at Fort Thompson, on Big Bend Damn. From there I entered the Crow Creek Indian reservation and as it was lunch time stopped at a general store on the reservation and bought a soda and then sat down to eat on a picnic table. Two giggling Indian boys came by and said "hi" and stared at me for some time. I said "Hi" back and went about eating and looking at the map. The boys soon left and a fat Indian woman looking weary and appearing hung-over came by and sat down. She said, "Do you always stop in Indian Reservations?" I responded, "No this is the first time I have ever been in an Indian Reservation." She listened intently while looking at me with sullen eyes and said, "Do you realize you are a white man and that this is an Indian Reservation?" At which I returned, "I am cool with Indians, as a matter of fact, I have a little Indian blood in me." "Well," she said, "You have a lot of guts!" I said back, "No lots of beans, that's what it takes to ride one of these things." Pointing to the bike. We talked a little more and I had a feeling like she wanted to either get amorous with me or else cause a fight. After finishing my meal I politely tipped my hat and was back on the road.

The pavement passed by underneath my tires while heading north across golden prairies occassionally littered with junked cars. Just prior to leaving the reservation I saw a young Indian boy riding bareback upon a horse. He held a stick in his hand and used it to tag the horses rear while galloping along through the golden grass. Though he was on a hill and about one thousand feet to my left, we raced along in an exciting way as some mystic energy flowed between us. The boy held his stick high and turned the horse back recapturing an image in my mind I'd seen from some old western movie. I recalled my very good friend, Kim.

## *A Good friend helps me*

*Kim inspired me many times with his stories of travel while in the Navy. Kim's nickname was Duck, and he was given that name because he once lived in the town of Blackduck, in Northern Minnesota. Duck had sailed with the Navy to many of the biggest cities of the orient and therefore talked often of places like Hong Kong, Singapore and Manila. Duck had some pretty good stories to tell. They were mostly about beautiful islands and the women he met on them. He found Navy life a real bummer, in fact his favorite saying was F.T.N., (F _ _ k The Navy) but what I sensed most from his stories were that he cherished those memories as his very own. His stories were treasures of real life drama and I began thinking how I'd like to have a few stories of my own. I remember the previous summer, when Duck and I were on a canoe trip in the Boundary Waters. While sitting around the campfire I was talking about how I wanted to go out and see the world. Duck said to me in an assertive voice and a pointed finger, "Eric just go!" Those words stuck in my head and were of great encouragement. I knew I wasn't ready to go on a big adventure quite yet. I did not have the street sense or the confidence to be out traveling the world. What I needed was a stepping stone toward that goal.*

*Taking karate at the local high school gymnasium helped improve my confidence. I worked my way up toward achieving a first degree belt and started to feel pretty good about using karate. One day I put it to use on this guy named Bob who often times hung around work because he was unemployed. He was the husband of Kathy who was our secretary. Bob was poking a few fake punches at me and so I gave him a fake karate kick into the stomach. Had I done it hard he probably would have backed off, instead it made him mad and he wrestled me to the ground. We tossed around in the parts room until the boss walked by and we broke it up. That experience deflated my karate ego and taught me not to get overzealous about using it improperly.*

Around 5pm I rode into a small South Dakota town with a high water tower called Highmore. It was real sunny and hot out and I saw an out door swimming pool and was permitted to use the adjacent shower. After a thorough cleaning on this fine day, progress was made into a supermarket where goods were bought for supper.

I cooked and ate hamburger and potatoes for supper at the town park and afterward enjoyed my latest craze in foods which are frozen strawberries in a sweet syrup that are sold in little cartons like milk is. A phone call was then made to my folks and they were told all is well and I updated them on all that had occurred since our last visit. Returning back to the camp I was pleased to meet an attractive young lady named Denise from Kentucky who was riding a bike across America with ten other members of a youth group. She was not very pleased with such a large group of people in her party. We had a nice chat before she was called off to her tent, by a group leader. The people in this town were very nice. The girls are wholesome, honest, friendly, not pretentious and are very cute. Even the police officers were very pleasant. It made me feel good to be here and ushered a peaceful sleep into my presence.

With the morning sun of **Tuesday July 26th** rising like a piece of molten steel, I straddled the bike and said goodbye to Denise. It was a surprise when she said, "You have beautiful blue eyes." I must have blushed for words escaped me as I waved and was off. The wind had blown hard all night long and now was coming out of the south. I headed east out of Highmore into a strong crosswind but upon making it to the town of Miller turned north and had a grand time blowing down the road with the wind behind me. It was great to be racing along and in one hour time had gone 23 miles. However, the fun ended when the road returned to heading east and for the rest of the day a savage crosswind was against me. I had the most disgusting attitude of my journey yet because of that wind. I cursed it many times and was flipping it off with a straight up middle finger and swearing blatantly. It was very interesting how I started to blame everything on the wind. I blamed myself as a failure and as a stupid idiot, because the wind was blasting me. I would pray and make attempts to divert my mind from the agony of the pushing wind, but this was to no avail. In one moment of optimism the wind would switch into my favor then all of a sudden it would gust against me with such force and nearly bring me to a halt. It was as though everything I had done in my life up to this point didn't matter-right now I was beaten by the wind. But I pushed on against it though I was sore, tired and sometimes felt like falling off the bike from exhaustion. The heat was intense and it was hard to breath. The minutes ticked by slowly -the miles even slower. I kept repeating to myself, "The closer you are, the harder it gets." The bike was acting up and getting harder to shift. It was taking a beating on rough gravel roads and the strain against strong winds. Through all this misery I still found the grass lands to be beautiful and found artistry in this area. The pedaling had a rythym that could rock a baby to sleep, I drifted into thoughts...

### *The Decision to leave my home town*

*One night after the bars closed down, I was driving home, to my room in Tony's house, I was alone and it dawned on me how many times I had done this; going to the bars to meet girls, with the hope that I'd find one that was right. Dancing, drinking and trying to put on a false sense of bravado. Then driving home alone. It made me depressed to think of ever doing it again. I looked at the moon over Lake Superior and made up my mind to take the first step and move out of Duluth in preparation of a grand adventure. I needed some kind of grand adventure in my life, before I could settle down. But first, I needed to leave my hometown.*

Many miles had passed, I was controlling on auto pilot, but the thoughts were elsewhere as I was cycling with enthusiasm on highway #212 and felt great encouragement when the next towns water tower was seen sticking up high above the landscape. Soon I entered the town of Clark at 6pm and was very tired and weary but glad to find people so wonderful. Once again the girls were cute and friendly and this added to make me feel good inside. I took a shower at a public pool and set camp in the local park. With great enthusiasm the journal was filled out with the explicit observation; "Tomorrow maybe I'll make it to Minnesota!"

## Wednesday July 27

A rain storm pelted down against the tent on this morning. At 5:30 the deliberation was made whether to stay in the tent till it stopped or leave. I packed up everything under a nearby shelter while it rained very hard. After the rain slowed down, I departed the town and proceeded to bound and bump along 22 miles of gravel road enroute to Watertown. This was a particularly bad stretch of road with washboards that threatened to tear the bike to pieces. At times the thin tires sunk in the soft dirt nearly stopping me immediately. Many times I stopped to lift the bike from its premature grave. Much of the ride was spent dodging large stones on the road as well as those that shot at me with high velocity from passing cars. At one point I saw a road crew and asked a workman, "How much more gravel is there ahead?" He responded "Ten more miles," and laughed with his head tilted back. About ten miles had passed and no end to the gravel was evident. I saw some more road crews and shouted to them, "This is the most terrible road in South Dakota!" They all looked at me with great surprise. Finally the gravel finished and the blacktop again resumed. There was a gang of workers standing by the roadside and I pointed backwards and burst out, "That road sucks!" They all seemed shocked at my intensity of emotion so I hollered out, "Fix that road! Fix that road!"

Watertown was a welcome respite and lunch was inhaled at the towns MacDonald's. I then went to a bike shop where the owner sold me the only can of chain lubricant he had in the repair shop. He instructed me to go to his mother's house and to use her hose to clean the grime off my bike. I went there and was warmly greeted by his mother and a plate of cookies, before doing the dirty job. With extreme gratitude to her kindness, the journey was resumed and not far out of town met up with two young guys who were from Switzerland on a trans-America bike trip heading west. After wishing them well the ride was continued.

I could tell I was going down a gradual descent from the Dakota plains to the level of Minnesota before arriving at the border at 1:40pm. I was whooping and hollering upon seeing a sign that said, "Welcome to Minnesota." A young girl eating a sandwich came down her driveway to see what all my ruckus was about. She gave me the rest of her sandwich and took my photograph alongside of the sign and then ran to her house and returned with an ice-cold lemonade. I thanked her immeasurably and then rode a short distance to see a covey of quail thunder into flight and minutes later heard the sound of gushing water coming out of an artesian well. I stopped as there flowed from the pipe ice cold water which I immediately splashed on my face. All these occurrences were such a welcome sight that I felt truly incredible to be back in my home state.

Headway was made under a hot sun and high humidity toward the town of Montevideo some twenty miles away. Along the way I met a touring cyclist and was surprised to discover she was a woman traveling solo from Boston. She said she was heading west as far as conditions warranted. Leaving her with goodwill, my next concern became the large trucks which were thundering past on this stretch of highway called 212. The road had no shoulder and many times when they would pass I would dive for the ditch, for fear they would run over me.

Arrival in the town of Montevideo at 5:30pm was heralded with the observation of children playing on the sidewalks and in yards. It was obvious that kids are kids here, unlike in Southern

California, where they grow up too quick and resort to egotistical actions and bad manners. After buying some food and heading for a park to cook my dinner, I met an elderly man, who was very kind and straightforward as Minnesota folk generally are. "Where are you going?" he inquired. "You're not running away from something are you?" We had a short discussion and then he went along his way. My comparison was again made to Southern California, where I did not find adults as relaxed and old-age-wise nor as cordial to younger people.

I hung around the park this evening and waited for the right time to set up my tent. I had an anxiety about staying here. There was mention in town of a murder which occurred recently. I felt a fear, but was to tired to let it hinder me. Every twig snapping was detected, I dozed off listening.

### *Time to move on*

*In January of 1981 I'd had it with working at Norco. They were talking about closing down, because business was very bad. Everywhere I looked were the long gray shadows of winter to add to my dreariness. I'd had many falling outs with girls and this continuous gnawing desire to move out of town. The weather reminded me of the hard decision I needed to make. The cold and snow, the tough times in Duluth, the national economy slumped to near depression and the hurt I still had in my love life. Everywhere I looked was gloom. Businesses were closing down, unemployment was high and I had this sinking feeling like I'd been in this city too long. Every street was trodden and well known. Every view reminded me of a previous experience. Love was impossible to find and nothing seemed new.*

*Friends were getting married, settling into their good paying jobs, buying new cars as well as homes and expecting children. The pressure for me to conform was extraordinary. My parents wondered why I wasn't following suit. Whenever I was around them, it seemed as if nothing else but getting married and finding a good job mattered. I felt the pressure all the time and it added more worries. I could not envision myself getting married or settling down or working an office job. I could not talk to them about my dreams or about this force that was drawing me away, avoiding me of commitment and causing me to withdraw and to search within myself to find an answer to who I was and why I was here. Only in my close friend named Kim could I confide with about these troubling emotions. He sensed and acknowledged that like I did, that it was time to move on.*

## Thursday July 28th

I awoke in the tent on the hot, muggy, mosquito infested morning. It was foggy outside and the bugs were thick as molasses and unlike any I have yet experienced on my journey. I threw my tent and pack upon the bike and headed for town to properly repack them. I started the ride at 6am and was soon dripping wet from the fog and heavy dew. Apprehension and excitement were high while riding into Willmar at 10am, as my relatives live not far from this town.

Shortly thereafter while heading down a stretch of highway, I saw a car approaching and could see that the driver was my Auntie Kathy. She saw me with great surprise and pulled over to talk along the shoulder of the road. She invited me to supper for this evening and then we parted ways.

Soon I arrived in the town of Atwater where my Uncle Jim and family live. It was about 10:30am and I felt positive to be able to find the turnoff to there farm, but instead never saw it and continued on highway #12 all the way to Grove City. This is the town where my mother was raised and her parents had lived most of there life. I called grandma Larson from Grove City and told her my situation of wanting to visit Uncle Jim in Atwater. She informed me of which road to take and so I pedaled back five miles to Atwater and found the right road to their farm.

They were all waiting for me as I pedaled down the long road and I was greeted very warmly yet in a low key, unrushed and very hospitable manner. I talked to my Uncle Jim and Aunt Sharlene and cousins Tom, Debbie and Jamie while gorging on tons of food. They kept putting more food in front of me until finally I was stuffed. We sat around visiting and they asked me many questions. My uncle called the Willmar newspaper and in a short time a reporter arrived to do an interview about my bicycle trip thus far. She thought I was super man to do such a feat. Yet I wasn't so absolute on the amazement of my own actions. I figured this was something that anybody could do. I was happy for the presses interest and flattered with the publicity but a little unnerved at thinking of becoming overconfident and seeing the journey flop. After the reporter took a few photographs I headed east about four miles along a gravel road and stopped into my uncle Garys farm.

Uncle Gary is a jolly, happy go lucky guy with several teeth missing alongside of other ones capped with gold. He comes across as warm, honest and delightful. My Aunt Kathy kept shaking her head in amazement at my "daring" journey and she said I had a lot of "guts." She too was feeding me many goodies and cold drinks. Soon my grandma Larson arrived and we sat down to a delicious lunch. Amazingly I still had room to feed my face again despite all the feasting.

I was adamant about riding my bike to grandmas rather than have her give me a ride there. She led the way in her big Chrysler so I would not get lost. I could hardly keep up to her. Fortunately she would stop and wait for me. One thing I noticed was that the farm country looked a lot different on a bike. The landscape moves by slower, making it harder to recognize familiar landmarks. Finally we arrived at the farm at which I cleaned up and sat back to talk to grandma. She was so hearty, robust and a hard working woman. She talked in an old country folk accent with high pitches in her voice and loud laughter. She reminisced about her hard working past, of the barn dances and of milking cows, feeding chickens and hogs. She told me people used to say about her, "Get out of her way or shell run you over." I believed it as she was still that same way.

At supper time we drove over to uncle Garys and ate a fantastic dinner prepared by Kathy. Even after all the food I'd eaten today, I still ate more than any one else there did. Whatever I put in my mouth seemed to be falling into a bottomless pit. I had lost 15 pounds on my journey from California and the way I was eating now would soon gain it back. That was the last thing on my mind, for everyone laughed when I told them of my taking a bath in a toilet and washing up in a urinal. Overall, there was warmth and humor abounding in our conversation and the evening slipped away until I was yawning from exhaustion. It was late when grandma and I drove back to her farm. I stood for awhile outside and enjoyed seeing the stars shining bright overhead on this warm evening and noted that the farm looked upkept, clean and orderly, despite her living alone, as grandpa Larson laid in a coma in the nursing home. It was such a pleasure to see these familar sights, visited since my youth that when I slipped into sleep were filled with nostalgic memories of days gone by.

The farm has certain sounds to start the day. Like the roosters, beginning to crow while it is still dark, and the doves, wooing there song of the day, and the sound of a distant tractor working a field. I awoke at 7:30 on this **Friday July 29th** morning after having slept hard but still felt groggy for awhile. My breakfast with grandma was that of Post Toasties and toast. She had more stories to tell me about everything in her life and was very keen to recall her past. She holds little back from telling me about grandpa, about the early years on the farm and how hard they worked. I enjoyed talking with her, yet knew my time to depart neared.

At 9am Kathy and Gary came over and more stories were told. Soon a reporter named Leanne from the Litchfield Herald came over and interviewed me. She asked me questions like, "Does your grandma think you are crazy? Did you do weird things in high school?" At the time my focus was more about the lack of communication our nation has with the Russians and how I'd like to try to make friends and gain an understanding of their culture. I told her my trip was to reach out to them. Leanne was continually interested in me and so I talked about my interests ranging from world people to religion (or lack of it) and other planetary topics. After a long talk I felt like saying no more and the interview ended.

It was nearing noon when I started riding away from grandmas. We'd said our farewells and hugged and I pedaled down the long driveway, knowing each bush, each fence post, each pebble on the drive, as they were my own. I turned left and headed east on the gravel country road. It was a bright sunny day and turning back to the farm, I could see everyone waving from the front of the house until they were out of sight. The blacktop was resumed heading north toward Painesville. I picked up the pace, got into a rythym, it felt good to be on the road, seeing the scenery, smelling the smells, I drifted into more thoughts…

### *It was time to go*

*Working that last year at Norco did not bring me to the mechanics mecca. I did not find fulfillment and was becoming more disenchanted with fixing machines in drafty garages under dim lights, with dirty hands and the breathing of internal combustion engine fumes. This was not what I wanted to do and the dissension grew within me until I realized I had to get out.*

*There was a sad feeling in the air. Because of the economy, sales were way down and layoffs were always being threatened. People did not have the money to fix their machines and so they would come in and expect it fixed for nothing. Unemployed or retired old men shuffled through the shop looking for someone to BS with, which I always felt was somewhat of a obligation for me because it seemed so callous to ignore them. It drove Jim, the boss, crazy. I realized how much I wished I had the time to talk to those men, but it was against the rules, this I understood, but it still hurt me to see them needing someone to talk with. Jim, the owner, was a good salesman, but he was not mechanically inclined at all. He constantly harped at us mechanics about sweeping the floor and keeping the place clean. He'd put away our tools even while we were in the middle of a job, which added to the madness in the air.*

*The third week in January, I walked into Jim's office and handed him my termination letter and said quite nervously, "I'm going to be leaving here in two weeks." He was surprised to hear this but understood and desired to help me make a smooth transition. As soon as I walked away from him a new sensation stirred in me, one unlike I'd ever known before. I was going on a journey and the gears were now in motion!*

# THE WHEELS OF FRIEND

*On the night before my last day at Norco, I wrote a poem about this feeling.*

*Tomorrow morning rises*
*And starts me another day*
*I'll prepare the same as always*
*But it will be a special way*
*For it has been one year on this job*
*And now time to move on*
*To look for a better living*
*And work that compels me to stay on*
*Now I think tomorrow*
*Is a final day till freedom*
*But truly its only intermission*
*On my journey and flight*
*As I sit here and think*
*It's my jobs last night.*

*It was my final day at Norco and Jim took me out to lunch and we talked about what I planned to do. He was encouraging me and sincere about wishing me the best, and he even bought one of my paintings for $75. He was so kind, so optimistic, I had to reshape my opinion of him.*

I had pedaled about ten miles north on highway #4, when an exciting event happened. As I made my way along the road I saw a man walking from the left side of the highway across to his truck parked on the right side. I passed by and said "How do you do?" he said "rotten". I chuckled and kept pedaling onward and heard some dogs barking at a house on the left side of the road. I saw several dogs racing across the long stretch of yard at full stride, coming directly for me! They were loud and aggressive and mean looking. The lead dog, was a golden retriever that seemed to be the instigator of this surprise attack. They came so fast, I thought of grabbing a weapon and my water bottle came to mind, so I reached for it. At the same instant a southbound car was rapidly approaching my direction. I didn't hardly get my water bottle aimed at the dog, when the car came to my side and hit that darn dog ran directly with the front bumper. It happened only a few inches to my left. The driver could have swerved but he would have hit me. Instead he slammed on the brakes and Whaack! that dog went flying threw the air and then skidding down the pavement. The dog let out a blood curdling whine and went spinning around and around down the highway. He cried and nipped at his back legs. His dog buddies sat on the roadside watching me while their wounded leader lay howling. Their ears dropped, tails went between legs and they retreated. Then the injured dog got up and ran, somewhat hurt and limping, but quickly darted along a ditch and into the grass.

A short distance later another dog chased me down the road but I out-ran this fellow. The remainder of the day was uneventful and I pedaled through the town of St. Cloud, crossed the Mississippi and went a total of 83 miles past all these familiar sights until arriving in the town of Milaca.

My camp was made near a swollen river in tall grass. I had spent the night killing a few and listening to all the other mosquito's whinning outside. They sounded like a siren.

## Saturday July 30th,

When I awoke at 5am I dreaded leaving the safety of the tent. But I had to. The mosquito's engulfed me so bad that I kept my mouth closed while tossing bags into compartments and strapping whatever on the bike for a hasty retreat. The bungee cords wrapped around the rear wheel. I grabbed to relieve them from this mess. The mosquitoes gorged on me. They left welts all over my body, even my lower back and buttocks. I went to the safety of a large parking lot at a grocery store to repack everything.

The day started off partly cloudy but soon it started raining at 9am. I pushed along in the swooshing drizzle and was rewarded with the sight of a deer crossing the road before me. I turned north and made way into the town of Hinckley at 10am under a heavy rain, then a half hour later passed through the town of Sandstone in a down pour. The rain I thought would hasten my arrival into Duluth until the evening. Yet the journey was progressing well despite the dreariness of it. There is a sense of meditation that comes from riding in the rain.

### *My plan to leave takes shape*

*The plan was to pack everything into my Renault and to drive across the country to California. I would sleep in the car at night and drive by day. It was early February and so I put two sleeping bags together for warmth.*

*When I told my parents about my adventure they were very concerned. They did not understand what this big idea was all about and wondered where I was going. I could only say, "I'm heading out west," because it upset them if I spoke about moving to California. They had this concept that California was such a terrible place to live. They thought of it as smog, earthquakes and people like Charles Manson everywhere. I didn't want to scare them so I said I'd go to Phoenix and visit my sister Nancy. Like any good Midwestern parent, they were mostly concerned about when I was coming back home. I had no answer for that nor for all the multitude of other questions. Yet, they saw that my desire to try something new was sincere. My father took our family out to dinner at the Chinese Lantern restaurant a couple of nights before departure. They gave me a hug and well wishes, but inside I felt like such a loser and wondered if this was a big mistake.*

I had ridden about 20 miles and was in a good mood while stopping in Moose Lake at 12:30pm for lunch under a shelter in the town park.

The forests of the northland were a welcome annunciation that I was nearing my homeland. The aroma of balsam and aspen filled the air. The roads took on a distinct tunnel like effect on account of the thick woods. I passed through Jay Cooke State Park in the late afternoon sunshine and caught occasional smells of distant Lake Superior. One might describe them likened to that of a supermarkets freezer odor. Anticipation increased as I readied to see my hometown of Duluth. The uphills in Jay Cooke Park wore me out and I was getting real tired, but the downhills were long and fun. I kept a good pace through Gary and across Duluth's West End and at 5pm stopped to call my folks from a Hardees on 38th Ave West. They were surprised to hear from me and said they would be waiting when I arrived. A voice inside my head said, "Eat or be beat," and so I wolfed down a burger.

I called the Duluth newspaper but no one was available to come and see my entry into Duluth. This was somewhat of a let down. While I pedaled further into Duluth I was not fired up like I should have been. I stopped to take my picture but my camera stopped working from the rain. I coasted down to the Aerial Bridge where I was asked by someone where I was coming from. When I told them where, I heard a shrill, "California?" Said one person, continuing, "Wow! I thought maybe you were bicycling up from Minneapolis!"

I headed through downtown Duluth, toward Lester Park for my parents home feeling kind of low since I had no reception-no acceptance-upon my return to the city. I could just as well have been invisible. Where were my friends? Duluth had always done that to me. More introspective.

## *Leaving Duluth*

*On the night before leaving Duluth, Tony and I had a party at his house. We got very drunk. Few things are clearly remembered about that night other than playing frizbee out in the snow with Gordy and Sue. Then some young ladies arrived and wouldn't you know it, they pleaded with me to stay in town. The next thing I remember was heaving into the bathroom sink, unable to find the toilet.*

*Come morning, I awoke with a terrible hangover but was eager to start a new day and a new adventure. I loaded the car and took one last look around the house for anything that may have been forgotten. Then I went out the front door and started up the car. After sitting there for a moment or two I shut it off and went back inside and sat down on the sofa a few more minutes to ponder what I was doing. Was I crazy? I thought about how Tony had offered me a job at his insurance business, and whether I should have a change of heart and go for that job instead of doing this. He said I could make up to $35,000 a year. I pondered at the thought of making that kind of money and walked into my empty bedroom. I almost cried, I wanted to stay here. "Come on, let's go," I said aloud to myself and walked out the front door. It was a very eirey feeling to lock that door and drop the key into the mailslot and to know that from now on I could not go back in. Now there was only one direction to go, and that was down the road.*

*The car was so full of stuff there was hardly room to sit. I turned the key, the engine revved to life and we rolled down streets that I'd driven on so many times before that I knew every crack in the road. But I was off and now they seemed entirely new. At first it was so exciting that I was shouting "alright" at every intersection and was shaking the steering wheel and waving. The freeway took me right past Norco. I raised a clenched fist and a single finger extruded into the heavens. As I exited the city on the interstate my mood became a little more somber. I wrote down the following poem.*

*Away from Duluth I go*
*Towards a land I don't know*
*Watching the city slip by*
*Cruising down I-35, feeling kind of high*
*A zillion imprints of this place on my mind*
*All those years I feel were kind*
*Just had to get out on my own*
*To find out if I'd truly grown*
*I zip down the freeway*
*And I see Norco coming my way*
*So I lay on the horn and flip the bird*
*And curse from my mouth a filthy word*
*That place got to me in a bad rap*
*I felt like I was inside a big trap*
*The car climbs up the hillside*
*And I turn around to watch*
*That damn old bridge and lake*
*Escape my catch*
*For a moment I feel sorry, then glad*
*And silence overwhelms me as it leaves my view*
*I hope it's a coming of something new.*

Then, I was jostled out of my memory just before passing Northland Country Club. I heard a beep-beep and saw my dad drive by. He did a 'u' turn and stopped and took pictures of me. He said, "Suppers waiting and there's champagne." Now my pace quickened. At the bottom of 60th Avenue East I decided to sprint the last six blocks uphill. At the top there was mom and dad with the neighbors; Fred and Dorothy waiting for me with hand shakes and hugs. I couldn't have been feeling any better. Soon my sister Cyndi and her husband Rick and daughter Erin came over. They watched me eat and eat and eat great food like fresh blueberry malts and burgers. There was mail to catch up on and talk and stories to be told. The moments were euphoric but the night swept by and I was tired. Alas I laid upon my old bed and dozed off into this absolute ecstasy.

**Sunday July 31st, 1983**
My sleep that night was like eating candy, that I couldn't get enough of. It was so good to awake refreshed at 7:30am on I got things in order and drove up to my sister Cyndi's. There was a strong northwest wind blowing and in many ways I was glad not to be riding this day on my bike. What a striking contrast it was to drive a car. The speed was exhilarating and almost hallucinatingly fast. All of Cyndi's family was asleep, and after awakening them I was treated to a grand meal of blueberry pancakes, bacon and eggs and melted cheese on Pita bread. There was much talk about my journey, yet I felt they could not relate to it. It was to far out of their realm of experiences.

I drove over to upper Woodland and stopped by my friend Steve's house and met his roommate, and fellow classmate; Jim. We discussed all the latest happenings. I felt isolated in a sense as I could only reflect on what had occurred to me as of late and how I saw things. They dwelled more upon those good old high school days and the years following.

I drove to my parents cabin noticing that Minnesota is so fantastically beautiful compared to all the other places I'd traveled through. The day was spent sitting around much of the time. My dad, Rick and I went fishing. Dad was very reflective of the time 15 years ago when we caught a big 9 pound walleye down in one corner of the bay after several days of wind blowing down into it. This day had much the same characteristics and I said, "Why don't we try that again?" We caught 3 walleyes this time in much the same pattern. I caught a crappie and Rick caught one northern. We watched as many rain clouds built along the horizon beneath beautiful blooming cumulas clouds. We went waterskiing which I hadn't forgot how to do but was admittedly rusty in my technique. Went swimming and took a sauna followed by a brisk jump into the lake. At 10pm I started to get very tired and went to bed at 11pm. Sleep again was wonderful.

## Monday Aug 1, 1983.

It was a beautiful morning at the cabin. The sky was clear blue and it was sunny and warm. There was sparkling sunlight reflecting off the calm water. I ate a big meal of pancakes with blueberries. My hunger was almost unsatisfiable. I thought to myself that I must do something to control this appetite. I called the Duluth News Tribune and they said they would send a reporter named Jennifer out to talk with me at 10am the following day. For exercise I ran several miles up to the corner of Island Lake Inn, feeling stiff as an old man. Then went swimming, still feeling stiff and tired. It was as if my body was suffering from exhaustion. I ate a big supper of BBQ ribs, fresh fish, two of which dad had just caught. It was becoming easier to enjoy Minnesota more now as it returned to me that this is my home and much more.

## Tuesday August 2,1983

This would be a day of meetings, starting off in the morning with the Tribune's reporter showing up with a photographer. We sat in the living room of my folks home and talked about the journey. I felt she did not grasp the true meanings of my journey. Perhaps I was not clear. She did not think it was a big deal what I was doing. We went down by the lake and took some pictures. Mom came by and we went down to the shoreline, skipped some rocks and talked.

I talked to Glenn. He was doing very well at M.W.A.P. We discussed world responsibilities and earth science as related to astronomy. After a good supper, I went to Gordy and Sues. I loved their place. We watched slides and saw a big thunderstorm with lots of lightning approach and then bombard us. It had been a long time since seeing such a storm. What a welcome it was to be back in the Midwest.

## Wednesday August 3

I knew I was asking for trouble when I went shopping with mom on this day. She's a shopper and so this day was spent standing around the shops wondering where the hell she was. Actually, aside from following her here and there, it turned out to be an ok experience. My time was spent looking at camping things. Later that day I went downtown on my motorcycle and looked at tents. On the way home I stopped by my dads office and met all the guys he works with. Everyone was so busy. That evening I motorcycled up to the Sunset Bar to watch Steve, Dave, Rick and Lou play in a softball game. After the game we put down some beers and B.S.'d. Steve talked a great deal about his bachelors sex life. With so many beers in my tank I was cautious but carefree on this dark nights ride home.

### Thursday Aug. 4th

It was sunny and hot this morning when I stepped outside to do some repair work on my bike. That task accomplished I mailed many post cards to friends whom I'd met along the way, and from California.

I ordered a one man tube tent from J.C. Penney for $28. They said it would arrive next week.

I pedaled down to park point and spent time hanging around the beach. Then rode up to eat supper at the London Road MacDonald's.

I headed back downtown to partake of the first event of our 10 year high school class reunion. Then went to the waterfront where an excursion boat awaited us. I saw faces I hadn't seen for so long. A typical question asked me by other classmates went like this. "Hi-Eric? Is that you? Your looking great! What are you doing now? You what? You Rode a bike from California? Wow-oh-ah me? I'm still living in Duluth, not quite as exciting as you or Colleen or Bob." Meeting old friends after so many years was like visiting a scenic spot not seen in a long while. You fall in love with it at first, then look the place over again and again until finally feeling it is time to move on. Yet how I love all of them. I cherish these people and felt so comfortable around them. We talked and compared notes. I know how much they propeled me to do things. The girls looked great. Old romances came back to life. Then it was time to go home.

I pedaled the seven miles home along Superior Street in the cities darkness and it was absolutely great. My little headlight shone my way as stars glittered above. It was so pleasant out and peaceful. Upon my arrival home I looked through the mail and found several Newspaper articles written about me. One came from Wilmar and the other from Litchfield.

They were fantastic.

### Friday August 5th

I had such a good time on the boat ride last night that when I got up the morning of I looked forward to the next nights events.

In bare feet I walked out onto the grass of the backyard under a warming sun and picked a colander of raspberries. Mom called from the cabin to see how everything was and while eating breakfast Kim called and said he would be coming over shortly. He soon arrived and we went shopping in Superior, where I bought a bright yellow two piece rain suit. A short while later we stopped by Park Point and saw classmate Phil Hammer. Together we walked down to the beach and soon met other classmates Paul, Lee and Steve. One of them had brought a fine boat which we boarded and sped out to our old swimming spot along the north shore. What a great time it was swimming and water skiing. Phil looked every bit the pro as he would slalom ski and jump the wake real high up in the air. Kim gave it a try as well but wiped out badly into the chilly waters of Lake Superior. I decided to pass on water skiing as to go behind this 50mph boat might jeopardize my already weary legs.

I ate dinner at Kim's house, rejoined his wife Barb and little boy Todd, who was quite a hell raiser!. Soon we got dressed for our reunion. I rode with Don Montgomery and headed off to the Hotel Duluth. Once again there were all these wonderfully familiar faces, each very eager to tell of their past 10 years. All of us bonded by virtue of our common pasts.

I realize how much I love all these people. It was a thrill to be dancing and talking with my X- heart throb named Janet. How she looked so good! She told me how she had such a crush on me, which was something I never really knew. It became so hot in the hotel and we were so close all of us, and so energetic that our garments became soaked with perspiration. No wonder we drove like excited young fools down to Park Point. Driving fast and feeling young, partying on the beach, some guys went skinny dipping. Steve met Karen while I talked to Tom Archer of his racing experience. What perseverance he has. I talked to Barb Fox and to Jolane, the pure as gold personality I admire and love so much. We stayed up until almost 4a.m. Yawns escorted us home as up came the rising sun. Even when we all agreed it was the best fun we ever shared, there was a sadness that it could not last forever.

# THE WHEELS OF FRIEND

**Sat. Aug. 7th.**
Again I picked a full colander of raspberries on the fine morning I rode my trusty bike down to Park Point and then up and over the hill to the mall area, only to return back to downtown and watch the Duluth Folk Festival. I swam, slept and sunned on the beach. There was lots of choice looking chicks visiting the beach. On the way back home I stopped by Gary's house and he was looking good. I talked with his dad named Dave. He was an x-cop and when we were teenagers he was always on top of us about not drinking. Now, ten years later he was very sharp to question my trips intentions, in fact he was kind of insulting. "What are you gonna do over there in na- na land if you get thrown into jail?" he said. I laughing responded, "Call you!" At which he swung a fake punch past my chin. Now we watched Dave as he could hardly choose which pair of stockings to wear. He reached for white ones, then browns, then a brown and white. We recalled "the peaches story" which happened back in 1972, when Gary got caught for being drunk. Gary was throwing up into a bowl of popcorn and his parents came home. Gary's mom said, "What's wrong with you?" Gary said, "I ate to many peaches." Dave said, "The hell you did-your drunk!" On another occasion Gary got caught by his dad after finding Gary asleep with a snowmobile helmet on. That got us all in trouble. "When your dad is a cop, he gets to the bottom of things." We all laughed at these stories.

Again my classmates met down at the arena at 7:30p.m. We ate a lousy dinner. I was seeing more faces from my past. We talked and laughed and were interested in each other. Joe Berini arose to the microphone and gave a touching speech. After awhile the music started. Unfortunately it was too loud to talk. Tom Archer had lots to say about his racing. Reed Byers told me where to go and what to do in Europe. I wanted to talk to these friends, but became annoyed because the music was so loud and the air so smoky. I kept thinking how I would like to be outside in the quiet and the fresh air. I danced with Barb Fox and Karla. Then I sat with Don Montgomery, who comically talked about his old Ford van. I laughed so hard. His way of putting things was so beautiful. Later on we all come over to my house where I made popcorn, raspberry daiquiris and we sat up till 3am talking.

On the morning of **Sunday Aug. 8th,** I went down to Gary's with Steve. We went to Perkins for brunch. Gary's dad Dave showed up. We had much conversation and heated argument with Dave about rape. I don't know how these subjects arose but we sure went at it.

We went back to Morris's house and boy was it hot outside. The mercury tipped 105F in Duluth! We sat down in the basement to stay cool and talked about our good old days. Then it was time for goodbyes once again. They come so fast. Gary had to head home to Osh Kosh. We embraced and said good luck.

Steve and I went up to the "secret spot" and jumped into the lake holding hands in a symbolic gest for our friendship. Wow that was Lake Superior! It was icy cold. A true shock to the system. We sat on the big glacially scraped rocks and talked about girls and our relationships with them, which were mostly fleeting and non committal. We went to my house and cooked a dinner of sweet corn and pizza. Afterward we walked down to the river where we saw girls go walking past. We swam in the big deeps and talked to these cute girls on the bridge. It was beautiful outside, the sun was setting and twinkling stars shone. Kim came down. We were together again. Just the three of us. Like the old days we sat around and talked. We kidded Steve about his huge vein. What fun we had together. We watched the northern lights. Then walked over to my house and threw apples in the backyard. Kim and I talked until late in the night. I was once again becoming sentimental. I felt the time for me to leave was coming. And I didn't feel like leaving home. I loved it here. My life was here. So often I turned to see another memory. My friends were so dear to me. We hung onto each other. This was most difficult for me to handle. I planned to leave Monday Aug 16th. It would be an exciting, but sad day. I vowed to keep to my plan and looked forward to those new horizons.

**Monday Aug. 9th,** started off getting a few odds and ends done until a chef I once worked with named Roger stopped by. He was a big greasy fellow who's eyes bulge out when he talked, and he loved to talk, talk and talk. Together he and I went up to visit the Youngblom's. We talked to Neil, Cristy, Dusty and Arlon. I talked to Keely over the telephone. We talked of old times in the restaurant business. I told them about my life over the past 3 years. They listened intently. I felt I'd been through some difficult times but it was almost more difficult telling it now. I said goodbye to them and shook off Roger else my voice would hoarse. Still there was enough energy left in me to go out that night with Steve and Jim to Grandmas Saloon.

### Tuesday Aug.10th

On I pedaled down to meet Jim. We stopped by Stewarts to browse for shoes and then headed out another 40 blocks to Twin Ports Cyclery. Dennis, the owner said he'd give me 10% off on his shoes. So he went down from $30.00 to $20.00 Then he said he'd match the $19.00 price I told him I saw at Stewart's. Then he finally went down to $17.95 and I was happy to get the price cut. From there Jim and I separated and I rode up steep Mesabi Ave and stopped by Kim's house. We talked well into the afternoon. I then stopped by the Planetarium and chatted with my good friend Glenn, the new director. I showed him slides of my bike travels thus far and we exchanged plans to one day meet again.

That night I went to Chuckee Cheese with my parents. It was a fun pizza restaurant for kids and adults. Later, I played the guitar at the house and awoke late in the night to hear a terrific thunder boomer rocking the house.

### Wed. Aug.11th

I went visiting to Keely's house where I met Chris her husband and their kids–Samera and Chelon. We talked alot. Keely looked good with her long blond hair and tanned body. She thanked me for the "thumbs up to love" plaque I gave her for her wedding years ago. Continuing my rounds of visiting old girl friends, I then went to Kathy's house to see her. She still was very pretty, but smoked alot. Tim and Rich were her sons names. We talked about us, our good old days and her latest tragedy which was when her dog had to be put to sleep. We embraced many times and I felt the rebounding of our old friendship. She told me, "Up until now I've always thought of you as a boy, but now I look at you and see you've become a man." She said that many times, as if the thought needed repeating. Admittedly it made me feel wonderful. She still defiantly said she wanted to divorce her husband, but she always said that, yet admitted she never would.

### Thursday Aug.12th

On this morning I was busy calling the Polish and Russian embassies to inquire about visas for traveling in those countries. It was all in vain as they could not help me. They did say it might take several months to do the paperwork. I also called my bank in California. Then I went down and made out a site draft as they will send money to my Duluth bank for a charge of $20.00 to wire the money. That pissed me off! The day was spent driving around and doing many errands. In the evening I went out for a walk and scared some girls walking up the sidewalk. They were cute though and very nice to talk too. Later I watched the Perseid meteor shower.

## Friday August 13th

The morning started off on the phone trying to gain more information about traveling in Russia. It sounded like there was absolutely no chance to bike in the U.S.S.R. or Poland. I called Washington D.C. and then New York City. It was a waste of time. I talked to Jolane over the phone and she invited me to come to her house for lunch.

What a lovely lady Jolane is, a dream, a goddess of pure gold. She made bratwurst and fried zuchini, talked about my travel plans and told me about her last travel adventure around the globe. In many ways it scared me on what lay ahead. India sounds bad, with bad roads, thieves, murder and the dreaded Kyber Pass. We stepped out onto the deck to look at her travel photos. They were beautiful pictures of places she and John had been and lovely ones of her as well! We drank lemonade in the hot sun while enjoying her backyard view of beautiful Lake Superior and the city of Duluth. There was something like love and a little bit of fortune telling and wise words slipping between us. She's like an arc angel fulfilling my inquiry of travel and also like a prophet. The sunshine illiuminated her profile, tanned legs slim and curves that made movements like arcing maddonas. Her hair, bleached blonde from the sun, curly on the long parts and tinted on the upper parts. At times I saw such intense beauty that I couldn't describe how radiant a magic it was. Every word was intense from her lips that blew each word my way in perfect pronunciation. I found it like a dream.

It was hard to leave her. To say goodbye. We have something. It's always been there. Perhaps a similar vibe, a travel bug, perhaps more. I found it so hard to go. I gave her a hug that wouldn't stop until we saw each other again. She told me these wise words, "Eric no matter what hardships and hassles you go through, this experience will be the greatest memory you will have for the rest of your life."

## Sat. Aug. 13th

I drove up to the cabin in the morning with a box of peaches for mom was eager to can. We ate lunch out there and I headed back to town, where I stopped by Kim's and drove to my parent's house. We backpacked up to Skyline Drive. Our route hiked through the backwoods and then up Amity Creek. These boulders on the creek bed I knew well since childhood.

We met two hefty chicks at the swimming hole called, "Keep Smiling." One was cute and I would have chased her around had she similar feelings. She did not.

Kim and hiked up to the campsite and spent the evening at our old favorite spot. It's a rock bluff at the pinnacle of a ridge, with a lookout cradled between weathered old spruce trees.

That night we had a vivid conversation about this journey of mine. Kim told me, "Take good care of yourself Eric, because I don't want to loose a friend like you." It was a beautiful warm night and the first night of many to come in my new tent.

### Sunday Aug 14

In the morning we hiked down to the river and took a swim. Stopped at another swimming hole called 'the big deeps' and jumped off what is known as the 'tower' into the cool water below. We reminisced about our good old days. Then we drove down to Park Point and swam and threw around a Frisbee. We had a delicious supper of B-B-Q steak and cottage fries at his house and then capped it off with Barb's home made blueberry pie.

### Monday, Aug 15

The final day before my departure arrived foggy and I spent time preparing and working on my bike. Kim stopped by and wished me his best. Sometimes I felt like I was going to a funeral. My own maybe! Everyone asked me many questions about my trip, my bike, money, how long, etc. I went to the bank and picked up $3000 in American Express Traveler Checks.

I stopped by our neighbors, the Gilbertson's before supper. Vern said; "Russians treat people like horses." Interesting comment. His wife kind of rolled her eyes at my adventure. It was too uncomfortable a journey for her to think about.

I had a big dinner at home with mom and dad and my sister Cindy and her husband Rick. Their daughter Erin was there too. We all went out for a walk after supper. Along that walk I saw my good friend Gary Frey and he wished me well. Then Steve and Jim came over and we sat around and talked about everything from freeways to biking to Russia. Little girl Samantha Smith was on TV. She said; "Russians are no different than us".

The hour was late, it was time for bed, I was real anxious to get underway and yet felt a danger. I was not really very happy to go, but then good-byes are never any fun. I prayed for a good trip. I was sad to see my home left behind. That night while laying in wait of sleep, a hail of memories that have occurred to me in this house raced through my mind. Then I became further anxious with the big adventure ahead and whether this, or that, or everything was truly ready. It became too much for me. I just said to myself, forget about it. Each journey begins with a footstep.

### Tuesday Aug. 16

I awoke at 6:25am and could hear mom and dad downstairs. They had the radio on KDAL. I got showered and felt sad. The time had come to go. My vacation was becoming a memory already. I ate a hardy breakfast of bacon, omelet, 3 blueberry muffins, orange juice and a couple of cinnamon rolls. Then got things packed onto the bike. One last look was made around the house. We took pictures in the morning sunshine. First it was mom and I. Then dad and I. Then mom and dad. We said our good-byes. I felt sort of choked up. I wished them the best of health and they wished me the best of luck and I was ready to head off into another adventure.

## Chapter 2

**August 17, 1983**

The bike slowly picked up speed as it coasted down 60th Ave East. I headed away from home, away from mom and dad, who stood together, wishing me well, waving and smiling delightfully in front of their yellow house. It was a sunny and pleasant morning. I passed the Luther family, standing at the edge of their driveway, and said "take care" whilst they waved and said "good luck Eric, bye, bye" in unison as I passed. Then I was by myself, alone to the bike's whizzing gears and the smooth downhill, in the cool morning air. I coasted past the homes of the Weatherbys, the Berglunds, the Udisons and had a sudden flashback.

This was so much like a dream I had back in June, in which, in a similar scenario, I found myself saying, "Goodbye home-goodbye Duluth-goodbye mom and dad." I could 'see' this same scene as was in that dream. Now, as then, I had to do like the dream and repeat exactly those words. When I did, it gave me shivers up my spine as the dream and the reality merged. The one difference was that the dream was very frightening, as if I was about to fall off a cliff. In reality this was more exciting.

I turned west on London Road, on this astonishingly beautiful sunny morning, as Lake Superior sparkled like blue emeralds and the sky was a brilliant blue. At about 45th Ave. East, dad passed me on his way to work and honked. I held my arm up as if to reach out to grasp him, then quietly said, "Bye dad."

I was approaching downtown and saw a wonderful view of the lake and decided to pull over to take one last photo of the Ariel Bridge. To my surprise, right across the street, there stood dad, Ray Joki and John Hinzmann standing on the curb in front of the Kitchi Gammi Club, waving at me. They jaunted over and we all posed for photos while shaking hands, joshing and exchanging well wishes.

Our good-byes finalized, I maneuvered the bike through downtown Duluth, watching my eflection in the big shop windows, then turned south at the Depot to head along bumpy and heavily rutted Railroad Street. I wondered if the trip would end here, with a broken bike frame, exploded wheels, or burst tires. The road was that rough. I progressed south on Garfield and began pedaling upon the approach for the Duluth High Bridge. A man in a truck pulled up to me, waved his arm backward and said," No you can't do that." I pedaled like mad and did it anyway, riding past him and up the steep grade of the bridge. A crew of workman on the approach watched me slowly make way to the top. Then- wow what a view it was from up there! It was like being in an airplane. I could see the dazzling water far below, ore ships here and there and glimpses of the city on the hillside. Yet, I treaded carefully, for dangers lurked, as wide expansion slots on the roadway could easily have swallowed my front tire and flipped me. As I went over each slot, I could see the water below. I aimed my course exactly over each steel rib of each slot. I had to steer precisely while at the same time riding like hell to avoid the stampede of traffic.

I was going pretty fast on the downhill side toward the city of Superior when suddenly a man far ahead stepped out on the roadway motioning his raised arms for me to stop. I would have shot past him, but recognized his face, as surprisingly it turned out to be a childhood friend of mine, Tim Harkonen. We talked awhile, shook hands, wished each other good luck and farewell.

From there, I turned east and followed highway #53 through Superior. It was a pretty uneventful ride, except when I panicked for having to ride back a few miles into Superior to find drinking water because I forgot to fill my water bottles. I continued on through town along the nice shoulder and then turned eastward on highway # 2. The rythym of the road reminded me of the last time I left Duluth in February of 1981.

### *Moving to California in 1981*

*As the car rolled south from Duluth on Interstate 35, I listened to my favorite cassette tapes and drove the four hours to Grandma Larson's farm at Grove City. We visited, ate some chile and I called home to tell mom that all was well. Grandma had confidence in my journey out west and patted me on the back saying, "You'll be alright." She stood on the front steps of her house, waving until I started the car, then she went back inside to keep warm.*

*I then drove to Uncle Jim Quello's farm and he gave me a solid handshake but forwarned me of the evils in big cities. From there it was to uncle Gary's. They are all farmers, and to them this was an interesting venture to go on, but it was also very risky. Perhaps a little too risky they thought, but none the less they gave me plenty of advice. After being well warned of all the dangers out in the world it was time for goodbyes. Midwesterners say goodbyes at least three times before they actually go. Auntie Kathy and Uncle Gary said a final goodbye and I drove down their long drive, watching auntie Kathy standing on her front steps waving goodbye to me until I could see her no more.*

*The next stop was to the nursing home in Litchfield, where my Grandpa Larson laid paralyzed and in a coma. The motorcycle accident he had was very severe. He had been hit broadside by a car and flew hundreds of feet down the freeway. Two nurses were in the following car and they saved his life by doing CPR. That was three years ago. He was such a great man, but now at the age of 75 reduced to blobs of absence. I walked to his bedside and talked to him. His eyes opened, but seemed expressionless until I mentioned that I was on my way to Arizona. Then he coughed wildly and phlegm came oozing out of his trachea. I was shocked to think that he may be conscious under this paralytic state. I talked some more to him and looked at this pitiful sight. Then I sat on a chair to await the end of his coughing. In some way I had a prayerful thought. I pondered how it would be to end his misery. I knew I had a 22 rifle in my car. For a fleeting moment it crossed my mind. Oh how he may have welcomed an end to his misery. It was almost as if he was saying 'grandson do it.' But I reflected on this horror and on life in prison and the devastation to my family. My disdain for killing anything ended further thought. I had to get going and said goodbye to Grandpa Larson. There was no further reaction from him. He was in a vegetative state.*

*A sad and heavy snow was falling while enroute to Minneapolis. The traffic picked up speed, I was on an unknown road with curves. I was lucky to have a car with excellent traction, else I'd have been in the trees.*

*The weather delayed my arrival to my childhood friend Alan's apartment in The Twin Cities. We had grown up in the same neighborhood and chummed around in high school. He was a lawyer now and yet for such loftiness of profession, had a down to earth disposition. Alan was one of those unique characters you'd expect to read about in the TV tabloids. He's dark and handsome and had this passion to get right in there, to mix in with the drama of city life. When we were teenagers he loved to pester the bum's in the alleys, the drunks on First Street, to push their buttons. We once rolled tires down the steepest avenues in Duluth, even right past the police department. But he was a humanist too, when it came to bailing a buddy out of jail, consoling about women, or tossing eggs, Al was there. This seems ironical today because he was now in such a respectable field.*

*I arrived at Al's apartment and we chatted just a little while, he had to get up early for a trial, I noticed all of his books on a bookshelf, and before I fell fast asleep on his couch, wished I had read as many and longed to spend a few days here to read some of them.*

*In the morning I said goodbye to Al. He was dressed so formally to go to work. His success was evident, I felt like such an aimless drifter. "Goodluck Eric, bye bye, watch out for those California women," he said in a giggly way.*

*I'd no sooner gone two miles when the car broke a belt while driving through The Twin Cities. I nearly thought of going back to Alan's, but realized I was on my own, I had to do this myself. To go back home would be defeat. I found a Renault dealer and bought the belt and fixed it myself on this cold winters day. My hands were black from the greasy job. I cleaned them best I could and headed south along the interstate.*

*Passing through busy suburbs and farm towns, then crossing the Iowa border, I kept thinking the car would break down at any minute. I made way into Des Moines and headed for a supermarket.*

*Supper was cooked on my single burner Coleman stove, just outside of my car door, at a Shopping Mall. I'd open the car door and flip the burger and stir the potatoes, then close the door to stay warm. This was my second night away from Duluth, and the first for sleeping in my car. The temperature was right around zero but with double sleeping bags, I was plenty warm. Sleeping on the reclined front seat worked well as a bed and seemed comfortable enough, except that a heavy frost that covered the inside of the car by morning.*

## Heading east in Northern Wisconsin

I was getting back into the routine of cross country cycling, dodging holes and debris, smelling the aromas, but I felt out of shape from my two week hiatus. By the time I arrived in Poplar, about 40 miles had passed, I was ready for a break. I stopped to stretch and look at the Bong Memorial, which has a WWII fighter aircraft, a P38, on a pedestal, it was like the one flown by hometown ace Major Richard Bong, who shot down 42 Japanese aircraft. I was marveling at the old plane when a very cute, curvaceous blond haired teenage girl wearing a red tank top and blue jean shorts walked past. My god she was so beautiful that I wished to marry her then and there just for her looks. We shyly smiled at each other. "Nice airplane," I said. It was my genuine love of aircraft, which probably hindered my rogue desires. The gal raised her eyebrows, wished me well and continued on her way as I did likewise, somewhat regrettably.

I continued heading east along highway #2 toward more small towns. At such a slow pace there were several Norman Rockwell type sights to observe. Take for instance the car in front of a garage with a hood up and men gathered around with a leg up on the bumper, drinking beers, each trying to tell-an-even-better-story than the next. There was also an old tavern outside of Iron River, tilting and forlorn, with alder growing inside where patrons once sat.

The distance between towns while riding a bicycle seemed greater by far than remembered in past road trips while seated in a car. The hills that I recalled as being little, now became a real challenge and always seemed much steeper.

When I finally rode into Ashland, the day was getting late. My butt hurt. It started to rain a bit. I dragged myself up to a Dairy Queen and stopped for a chocolate malt. Energy somewhat replenished, I went to eat at Hardees.

After supper, I spent some time seeking a free place to camp and met another solo bike traveler. We met, his name was Bill, he was traversing the Lake Superior circle route. He told me of a campground, so we pedaled there, a few miles down the road, as darkness crept in. We exchanged stories and hit the hay. In all it was a good first days ride of about 85 miles traveled and I spent $4.50.

It rained steadily for much of the night. I felt wet in my new tube tent and upon awakening at :30am discovered that the fly was not all the way up. It was a rainy, drizzly morning this **Wednesday Aug. 18th.**

I said goodbye to Bill and pedaled eastward and listened to my little radio, strapped on top of my handle bar bag. Lunch was devoured in Wakefield where I met two other bikers. One fellow was from Los Angeles, and his name was Greg, while the other was from Seattle and his name was Toby. We exchanged similar experiences and feelings about cycling especially our, "Sore butts!" We separated and while still within site, I nearly crashed on the loose gravel of the shoulder while trying to avoid a large truck.

Much of this ride was spent thinking about being a singer-songwriter, and thinking about Ellen. She was a real nice young lady whom I'd the opportunity to meet in Santa Barbara. I always felt fortunate to have met her. I went to a small dance on the hillside of Santa Barbara back in 1982. She was there with her sister, who was very good looking, but Ellen had personality and a twinkle in her eye. I liked that glow and wanted to get to know her more. The trouble was my Midwestern ways probably were not par with her California girl high esteems. I was kind of a step down for her. I did not let that hinder our meetings over the year and tried to deepen our relationship.

### This got me to recollecting about how I got to California in 1981.

*It was exciting to be heading down the road with nothing to do but drive and watch scenery. I felt unsure of my future and what lay ahead. I played over and over this cassette with Ray Orbison's song "Crying" sung by Don McLean. It made me feel homesick and alone, because I was on an enthusiastic bummer while driving the long snow covered expanses in Iowa. I knew as long as my wheels kept turning and the car was heading west, I would be fine and the homesick feelings would eventually pass.*

*I slept a night in my car, outside a drive-up motel, in the wood-smoke-filled-city of Denver. I felt like I was back in Duluth, and wanted to leave this dreary place.*

*The next day I headed westward up into the mountains and rolled into Vail around noon. Vail was beautiful with its ski lodges and fine hotels complete with jacuzzi hot tubs outside. Renting a room was too expensive for me, but I did not mind enjoying some of the comforts of the lodge. I'd hang around the spacious fireplace area to get warmed up and then when supper time came, dinner was cooked outside my car, over the cookstove, at the base of a ski run while I was seated in the car.*

*Around eight o'clock in the evening it was time to get cleaned up. I jumped over the snow covered fence and soaked in the bubbling heat of an outdoor jacuzzi behind a hotel. With the stars above and the crisp mountain air, this hot tub was a grand way to bathe. I lathered up with a bar of soap and at one point made comical gestures with my frozen white hair, while looking at my reflection in the big dark windows of the hotel. After several minutes of clowning, sticking my feet up in the air, I noticed cigarettes flickering behind those windows and then could see the faint faces of people seated at a bar, and others at dining tables smiling and watching my antics. They must have had quite a chuckle at my frolic in the tub, especially when I made a hasty leap over the fence in my underwear and dashed off into the winter night.*

*The evening was still young and Vail was one of those places with lots to do, so I went to a disco and was really stomping the floor with my waffle bottomed leather half boots as they played 'My Sharona.' I loved that song. That is when I met a young lady named Chris from Wisconsin. We danced till the wee hours, when the bar closed. I was invited over to her place. The night could have been spent on her couch, but there was more fun yet to do.*

*Chris wanted me to stick around a couple more days, but we were as two trains passing in the night. I headed west in the morning in a blizzard. Oh how I cried to go back, to spend some time with Chris. I asked her to come with me. But she said she didn't know me. I just thought it wouldn't work. I drove through the blizzard on highway #6 and often could not even see the road. Finally it went downhill into Grand Junction. I kept thinking I should go back to Vail. I really wanted to, but I was driven westward.*

*I drove up Colorado National Monument as the late day sun illuminated everything in a orange hue. The rock walls were awesome and painterly. I slept a cold night in the car. A ranger drove by late, and asked me if I was ok. He invited me in for coffee in the morning.*

## Cycling into Michigan

I made headway into a small town called Bruce Crossing at 5pm and there ate supper. Rode over to a wayside rest and swam in a river and washed up as it was warm and the sun was setting. Later a beautiful half moon appeared and except for the bugs, it was a lovely campsite. Darkness set into my spooky camping spot and thoughts about bears visiting me took over. In my tent I calculated traveling 97 miles and spending $6.70 today.

### *On the Utah road in 1981*

*I wasn't a coffee drinker, and passed on meeting the ranger, thus continued westward. After leaving Colorado it became an enchanting drive across Utah. I loved the landscape. While listening to Joni Mitchells album, Hiejra, I thought her songs of coyotes, the drone of flying engines and driving down some freeway were appropriate. At a wayside rest I met some fellows riding in a Suburban. This guy gave me a a joint and said "Enjoy." As the vehicle was about to drive away he was seated in the front passenger seat and made a gesture like a stage coach driver would to mush and whip his horses and off they went. Now the landscape was even more remarkable along highway #70 up and over some passes to #89 where I headed west on highway 50 and crossed over into Nevada as the day was getting late. This was an entrancing landscape, with far flat distances through valleys and wave after wave of mountains. That night I stayed in Ely Nevada.*

*On the sixth day of my oddessey I arrived in Reno and toured the casinos. With the night getting late, I returned to my car, which was parked in a large lot behind a casino. I put some towels up on the windows to block the bright casino lights. Then crawled into my sleeping bag and fell soundly asleep. About two o'clock in the morning I was awakened by the sound of someone knocking on my window. "Open up," said the policeman with his hand on his pistol. Spotlights from the tops of police cars shined on me from three directions. "Step out of the car", said an officer with a stern voice, continuing; "With your hands above your head." I tried to tell him I couldn't because I was in my underwear, but he insisted. I stepped out and put on my vest. They chuckled, "Got any hidden bazooka's?" he asked me. "No" I said. Two officers frisked me while the third ran a check on my drivers license. They asked me what a kid from Minnesota was doing out here. I said I was going to San Francisco. This one officer said, "San Francisco is a very rough place, they'll chew you up out there." He told me to get out of town before he wrote me a ticket. I thankfully obliged, and left.*

## Smelled a bear last night
## Thursday Aug.18th

Cars were beeping there horns periodically during the night and I wondered why. I awoke at 6am, packed up and was off on the hazy morning. I'd gone about a mile down the road in the cool morning air when suddenly a black bear bolted across the road, from a dark woods, right in front of me at a high speed. He never even saw me. I thought I could 'smell' a bear last night.

Later, around 9 a.m., I saw another cyclist far behind me. I didn't feel like riding with anyone who would not keep pace with me and also didn't feel much like talking. For nearly five miles he chased me over hill and across flats before nearing enough that I thought it polite to slow down and say hello. I met the most solemn biker yet. His name was Franklin and it turns out he was a M.D.- a doctor. He was from Topeka, Kansas, a nice person, humble and interested in nature. While we pedaled along he told me that he'd gone through many camping experiences in the Sierra's and the Adirondacks. "Now," he said, "I'm heading out trying to see more to life than what's presented before the doctors chair." At lunch we stopped, talked and exchanged food. The picnic area had a natural spring with deliciously cold water bubbling out of the ground near Kenton.

A nice downhill preceded our entry into Marquette at 4:30 on that hot, sticky day. We bought some groceries and headed east of town where sandy beaches were enjoyed as well as a Lake Superior swim. We cooked dinner, ate and lounged. There was no wind, the air was hot and heavy when we cycled off in search for a campsite.

We found a secluded and rather wild setting near some railroad tracks. In the dark we pitched our tents as distant lightning lit up the sky. Soon a few rain drops fell. While I laid in my shelter a tent pole broke and my tent sagged. I propped it up with my packs and helmet. The rain fell hard and leaks were created where anything touched the tent. Then the lightning flashed and thunder boomed and it stormed like crazy while I held the tent up with one arm. Finally it eased off to a light rain. It seemed the worst was over and the coast was clear. Then a distant rumble and haunting sound of a distant train horn could be heard. It became louder. I knew we were camped close to the tracks. It seemed that train would devour us.

What a frightening sound as that train bore down on us. It thundered past and roared by, pulling a long line of cars that clanked, squeeled and growled until disappearing into the inky blackness. "Hey Franklin, you ok?" I shouted. "Oh yeah, just fine," he said relievingly.

## Friday Aug. 19th

We awoke at 6:30am and packed up and rode together in the rain. Since it was very hot and sticky, we pulled over often to flap the air and to have a good long drink. Once we stopped for a morning swim and another time stopped to eat ice cream. Then sadly, we had to part ways as Franklin wanted to go north to Picturesque Rocks and I south. I had found Franklin a good riding companion. We shook hands and parted. I watched him over my shoulder, get smaller and smaller into the horizon. On my own again.

### *From San Francisco to Southern Cal*

*After a few days staying with my cousins; Jody and Justin in San Francisco, I was back on the road heading south along the California coast, enjoying the Pacific surf and sunshine along the way.*

*Santa Barbara's fragrant beauty caught my eye with its Spanish style buildings and pleasant beaches loaded with beautiful girls. I stayed there for the night. Since it was my first night in town I decided to visit a few bars. I walked into a country western bar named-The Texas Chile Factory and sat down for a beer. While sitting at the bar this fellow named David struck up a conversation with me. He bragged about his father being a millionaire and showed me the label on his pants and said they were very expensive and he wore nothing but the most expensive and the best.*

*He told me he had an airplane and a BMW. He said he lived in a nice house with a mountain view that had lots of extra rooms. He offered me a bed to sleep on if I wanted to stay the night at his house. I was partly impressed by all his talk of wealth, but mostly looking forward to sleeping in a bed for the night. He then told me he was a little short on cash and asked me, "Could you lend me twenty bucks? I'll pay you back tomorrow double what you lend me today." I lent him the money and then he invited me to ride in his B.M.W. on a tour of the town. This we did, ripping down the streets of Santa Barbara in his fine car with the stereo blasting while passing a sensimelia joint back and forth. We went to Peppers and Hobie Bakers, which are night clubs that demand a $5.00 dollar cover charge to get in. David started drinking like a fish and pretty soon the money I loaned him was spent. He asked me for some more money but I wouldn't give any more to him so we drove back to The Texas Chile Factory.*

*He went straight into the bar and I went out to check on my car. I found a light on in the car and the door slightly ajar. When I looked inside everything was gone. I'd been ripped off by thieves! Luckily they did not get my travelers checks in the glovebox, but nearly everything else was gone, including my electric razor- and I had never shaved without an electric razor!*

*I went back inside and found David and told him what had happened. He didn't seem to care and was playing pool while I called the police. A squad car came and the lady police officer took finger prints and had me file a report before leaving. I went back into the bar and caught a glimpse of David going out the front door. So I went out the back door and got into my car and drove after him. I tried to get him to pull over so I could ask him if I could stay the night at his place. He drove like a madman up the twisting grade of San Marcos pass. I flashed my lights at him until he finally stopped. I shouted to him, "Hey David, remember me, can I still stay the night at your place?" "Yah dude, just follow me," he said in his southern Cal accent. He took off and drove well over ninety miles per hour up and over the pass and then downhill along that dangerously curving road. Fog hindered my view and I soon lost him somewhere around Santa Ynez. I pulled over to sleep the night near a house under construction. It was cold out and I did not have any sleeping bag or jacket. All I had was a tent in the trunk. So I bundled that around me to keep warm in the cold mountain night.*

## A funny event while cycling in Manistique

I pedaled down 45 miles of uninhabited woodlands toward Manistique. It was a nice road with little traffic but real hot out and I drank lots of water and had very sore feet. I maintained a good pace and came into town at 4:30pm and stopped to drink down a huge Coke...Aahh! I went into a drug store to look at paperback books and cool off within the air-conditioned store. I was browsing, when the checkout girl at the counter started screaming. I looked up to see a bat was flying and wiggling next to the cash register. "Mom," she said, "There's a bat in here!" Her mom was in the back of the store behind the pharmacy counter and hailed back, "Your kidding me!" At which the young gal returned, "Mom, I don't kid about these things." Her mom said, "Get somebody to help you!" She looked at me. "Say young man," she said continuing. "You can have that book your reading if you move that bat out of here." It was flying around when I scooped it into my helmet and let it loose out the front door. But the darn bat turned around and would have flown back into the store had I not waved enthusiastically at it with my arms. A woman who wanted to come into the store at that moment was screaming hysterically.

Soon the incident was over, the bat flew off and the woman on the sidewalk and the young gal behind the counter regained composure. The lady behind the pharmacy desk came up to me and said, "I want to thank you and keep my word. You can have that book! Thank you!" I thanked her and walked out with a paperback called, 'Wise Quotations from Famous People throughout Human History.'

Continuing along my way I cruised into a Ramada Inn campground to have a look around. While checking out the camp a fellow invited me to share a campsite with he and his wife who were in a motor home. It was wonderful because I had access to a shower and a pool and it only cost me a couple of bucks. All total I'd spent $8.30 for the entire day.

## Saturday Aug 20<sup>th</sup>

My stay behind the Ramada Inn was a very pleasant one and after saying thanks to my neighbors I was on the road at 7 a.m. About half an hour passed when I found a rest area and there cooked a good breakfast of blueberry pancakes. It was a cool, clear and sunny day.

I had a nice tailwind, stopping often to observe the beautiful scenery of Lake Michigan's northern shores and the sandy beaches and blue water. I met a nice elderly woman storeowner in the town of Gulliver. She told me tales of catching 30 pound northern's through the ice. It was her easy going, not hurried demeanor which was most noticeable.

Back on the road, I listened to the radio for entertainment and made faces at cars for kicks. When an army convoy approached me and passed by I saluted and then gave them the peace symbol. The soldiers smiled and waved. At one point Paul Harvey was on the radio talking about stress. He said, "When the mother in law visits, men suddenly catch colds." I laughed at that. People driving past looked at me like I was nuts.

Along my route I was well received by inquisitive people who were shocked to hear that I rode all the way from California. One kind woman gave me a large bottle of fresh orange juice, which I guzzled down in a few miles. Upon pedaling into St. Ignas at 4 p.m., I met two young girls from Pontiac. They, like myself, were sight seeing this neat town which is over 300 years old. They advised me to eat at a Big Boy restaurant which I then did. After supper I asked a police officer if he could tell me where a campground was. He did and I pedaled into the campground and passed a group of ten bikers setting up tents. They were mostly young people, teenage guys and gals and one woman chaperon. We exchanged greetings and when they found out I was on a Trans-U.S.A., tour they invited me into camp. What an enthusiastic bunch! They then invited me to go along with them on an excursion boat ride. We went down to the fine looking boat and went out on the straits of Mackinaw. We passed under the Mackinaw Bridge and it was a breathtaking sight under a fabulously starlit night.

When we returned to the campground I was treated to pudding, chocolate bars, pop and snacks. We told stories and joshed and stayed up till 1 a.m., talking. One very exuberant fellow named Jack was a talkaholic. He always had cute young gals with him so I tolerated his mouth to be near them. Finally the group leader Mary came over and ordered them to leave me alone. She really praised me and talked highly of my feats, though I felt she made me into someone I was not.

A slight fog cast hazy shadows in the early morning sun on the morning of **Sunday Aug. 21st**. I departed St. Ignace after saying farewell to my bike friends. They were all great kids. I rode down to the Mackinaw Bridge, which I was not allowed to bike across, and the bridge supervisor asked me, "Are you the guy who wants a ride over the bridge." "Yes," I responded and asked, "How much will it cost." He said, "One dollar." I then responded, "Well, can I try to find a ride?" He said, "You'd better make up your mind-what will it be?" He seemed very bold. "I'll take the ride," I said.

We loaded up the bike and I sat in the pickup's front seat while this elderly gent proceeded to tell me how tough it was to pay the bills and put two kids through college. We talked at length about stress and money and traveling, which he knew something about as he was a former Great Lakes deckhand. We shook hands at the end of the bridge and I was off.

Throughout the day, I frequently stopped to pick up aluminum beer cans as they have a 10 cent refundable value for each can. I found twenty of them and turned them in for $2 at a store. Later that afternoon, a dark rainstorm started to blow in behind me, thus I raced along, bought groceries then sped down the road until luckily finding a covered picnic shelter at a place called Long Lake. Then all hell broke loose. It rained, thundered and blew hard for an hour. After it passed, I cooked supper and met several campers who became somewhat of a nuisance while I tried to eat and socialize, for they afterward stayed until dark, before I finally had some peace.

### *Tracking down a con artist in Santa Ynez in Feb. 1981*

*In the morning I telephoned David's father who said that he had disowned his son because he was such a bad kid. He told me where I might find him, and he wished me good luck and then hung-up.*

## THE WHEELS OF FRIEND

*I drove to the airport and found David there. He was pretty surprised to see me walk in. I asked him why he ditched me and he made up some excuse. I asked him about the money I loaned him last night and he said he could not repay me. I pursued him further about the money until he finally handed over $7.50 and asked if he could keep the rest for lunch and dinner because he didn't have any money. He said he would pay me back if I came by next Friday. I vowed to come back and get the rest of my money but I never did because the whole affair just bummed me out. It gave me a pretty negative attitude about Santa Barbara and was my first ever experience of meeting a con man.*

*In need of replacing the stolen items, I went to a Sears's store to buy a sleeping bag and met this red haired guy who was also looking at sleeping bags. We struck up a conversation and I learned his name was Ken, and he told me if I wanted a job I could come work for him at his concrete business. I told him I wanted to travel around the southwest and that I might return and take him up on the offer. He said I was welcome anytime.*

*I left Santa Barbara and drove down to Los Angeles, and hung around Laguna for a few days. I tried to see if I felt good about L.A. and whether I wanted to live there. But it was too crowded and everyone seemed like a fake, so I headed south for San Diego.*

*After a few nights I drove east to Phoenix and stayed with my sister Nancy in Arizona. Phoenix had the personality of a Midwest city and I wanted something different. After one month with her I made up my mind Phoenix wasn't for me and decided to head back for Santa Barbara.*

*It was March of 1981, and at first sight it was good to be back in Santa Barbara. I liked the small town feeling and the mountains and the sea. Ken gave me a job with his concrete business and I worked with him for two weeks. He let me stay in his apartment for one week. It was during that week at which time President Reagan was shot and wounded and we watched it happen on TV.*

*While I helped Ken I also applied for other jobs and was fortunate to get a job at Browne Corporation working as a draftsman. It was a real 40 hour a week job with a very modern looking company. The front office had nice looking women and people in general were friendly. The company had positive energy and optimism. They even had a company softball team which was exemplified by winning the season championship.*

*Mary was my manager and she taught me a great deal about drafting. At first she was working part time at Browne in addition to working at a computer resume business on the side. Mary would come in to check on me in the morning, give me an assignment, and then she would come back the next day. She always talked about quitting and wanted to do something else. For a 22 year old woman, she acted as if she'd been through it all. She dated the chief engineer Bob, who was a nice fellow, very smart and though he had a fiery temper, he was very intelligent and communicative around the company. They were such a sweet couple and it felt good to be working in this pleasant surroundings.*

## Cycling in Michigan

### Monday August 22nd

No sooner had I awoke when a man came by and struck up a conversation. He kept talking to me and made it hard for me to go. I was packing up and talking to him. It was the morning and not until 7:30 a.m. before I could leave Long Lake and the gabby camper.

A couple hours later I stopped in Alpena and browsed in a bookstore. I was not very welcome there. People looked at me suspiciously as if I was a tramp. Now I sensed a change of attitude around here. It was almost like when I would get close to Los Angeles.

Today I was riding down through a forest and looked at my chest to see I'd lost my necklace which had "Live, love, laugh" on it. This kind of bummed me out.

There was plenty of nice lake shore scenery to enjoy on this ride along the western shore of Lake Huron.

I arrived in Tawas City at 5:30pm and two guys gave me some misinformation, telling me the wrong way to go, and where a store was. They had a bad look in their eyes. I could feel the tension in this town.

There were lots of Detroit people here creating this. Perhaps this was their vacation spot.

I went into a grocery store and got a armful of food. The check-out girl said, "Take me with you," when I told her I was going around the world. I said, "Come on." She laughed.

I met a girl named Lacy on the beach just as the full moon was rising over the lake on a very pleasant evening. Set up camp in the bushes and listened for intruders.

### Tuesday August 23rd

I awoke to a pretty morning and rode down the Lake Huron coast. Picked up aluminum cans along the way, collecting 15 by noon. I stopped at a Schwinn dealer in Bay City and he looked at my bike and said the rear hub was dirty. The hub was sticking each time pedaling pressure was taken off. I bought some chain lube from him and then went across the street and bought a chocolate malt. It was mmm so good.

Further down I stopped at a grocery store and traded my cans in. An interested woman asked me about my trip. When I told her she seemed not to believe me. I stopped in Richville where a guy at a gas station asked where I was from. "Golly willickers," he said continuing. "How old a man are you?" He was amazed at my ride. I was passing a golf course and hollered to some golfers, "Now comes Miller time!"

One of them hollered back "I'll drink to that."

I met a kid, about 12 years old, riding a bike with one front tire that was literally shot. It had a bullet hole in the front rim. The front tire was held together with only the cord. The bike had no brakes. He followed me along like I was Mother Goose. I didn't even talk very much to him. He just kept following and talking. I made it to a roadside rest at 5:45pm and worked on the bike while he helped. I cooked and offered him supper but he wasn't interested in eating. I set up my tent and he helped. He even stood guard by my bike while I took a swim in the lake. What a good kid he was. I couldn't figure his intentions, other than that I was just someone new for him to talk to. He finally left in the dark. Then another guy walked by and began talking to me. He spilled his guts out about his misfortunes. He'd lost his wife and 11 year old son and now was losing his job. "Michigan is going downhill," he said. One thing I have noticed was that prices were more expensive here than anywhere I'd been yet.

As I readied to go asleep I thought about fear, and scribbled down a few lines.

Fear is the living realization that what is happening to us is beyond our control. As early as mans beginning he has tried to escape any acts which instill in him that nervous tension called fear. Fear can upset or dissatisfy our lives. The fear of attack was avoided by seeking shelter, making weaponry or congregating in groups for safety. To avoid hunger they stockpiled and harvested goods. And today the challenge is the fear of going broke or losing a job. We all wish we could win a million dollars. And we all want that perfect job. Both are solutions to a fear that is very difficult to coral. Therefore it is the realization that fear exists and not to achieve its end that is of importance. No matter when we live we must live with fear. The first aspect is to understand the fear and then to ask what is the worst that can happen to me? If the worst does happen, then what is the next to worst, until I resolve my dilemma in the best possible way. Once the best choices are known, one can now live with fear, because one knows what to do if it should occur.

## Wednesday Aug. 24th

I left camp at 8am after gorging myself with food. My appetite was growing enormously, but mostly for junk food. I especially liked to eat sugar coated cinnamon Pop-tarts. Each one had about three hundred calories and I would eat four of them.

I vowed to try and look into other alternatives. I rode steady until 11am and entered into the town of Sanduski. I went into a bookstore and had a great talk with the owner. He had a guitar and I strummed a few chords. The owner seemed like he wanted to get out and travel like me.

It was amazing how terrific the gals looked in this town. Admittedly I was very horny and though I smiled and said hi to them all I had no opportunity to converse. Continuing on, the truck traffic was horrible and I continually was being sucked into their awful drafts. This vacuum occurs when the big semis pass as I ride alongside. Their pull is very powerful. The only thing to do is to overcompensate by leaning and steering away each time at the right moment. The only trouble is that as soon as the truck is past there is a big blast of wind followed by a wake. My overcompensation would nearly throw me off the saddle. Several times I had to drop off a 2 inch road slab onto the shoulders loose grave.

At noon I stopped at a wayside rest and pigged out on peanut butter and jelly sandwiches.

Afterward I pedaled past a bad car accident. It was a Jeep hit broadside. There were people trapped in the car and an emergency crew was extracting them.

I pedaled into Port Huron at 5 p.m., and mistakenly rode 2 miles beyond my exit, that's a lot of extra pedaling. Before leaving Michigan and entering Canada, I cashed in my $1.20 worth in cans.

I went up to a gate thinking it was the customs agent and started to tell him my travel intentions. The guy looked dumbfounded. He turned out to be a liquor store worker and this was the stores shipment outlet. He pointed me the way to customs.

I walked the bike over a bridge enjoying the view of Lake St. Clair and was well aware that soon I would be passing Canadian customs. I also knew I had a little bit of pot in a film cassette in my panniers. I usually kept it in my billfold compartment but I thought that would be the first place they'd look. So I tucked it in with the tire repair bag. When I arrived, customs asked me for my I.D., then if I'd ever been rejected from Canada. "No," I said.

Then this agent wearing an official cap asked me into his office. He said, "Eric, I want to know how much money you have with you." I choked, not knowing why he asked that. I replied, "Well, aahh, I have $3000 in travelers checks." From behind his desk he said, "Well I asked you in here because I didn't want to talk about it out there. Now how much will you spend in Canada?" He said. I responded, "About $40." "Ok," he said. "Fine. Take this to the inspection officer." So I took the slip and went outside to him.

The inspector kicked two of my pannier bags and said, "I want to see what's in here." One of them had my stuff. I opened the first bag and he went through everything thoroughly. He discovered some tea and immediately said, "What's this?" "Tea." I said. He smelled it and was satisfied. Then he went to the rear pack, exactly where I'd hidden the stuff. "Let's see what's in these," he ordered. "Ok," I said opening the zipper. He looked at my hands as I pulled the tire repair kit bag out. That bag had a spare tube in it, a box with patches and the film container of pot. While I pulled the tube out with one hand, the other hand held the bag and I used my thumb to withhold the container of pot. It was close to plopping out. But, he never saw the container, it stayed far enough inside the bag. I placed everything on the ground for his inspection. Tire irons, extra tube and patch kit. All he had to do was lift up that bag and I'd be in trouble.

At the same time, he went through another zipper and pulled out a greasy rag and got grease on his hands. Cursing, he turned around, glanced over the tire kit and said, "All right you can go." I was nervous, excited, relieved and scared all in the same moment.

I departed so quickly I left the pockets half open, with stuff hanging out and took off. God what a relief. I stopped at a shopping mall and looked at the cute chicks. Sarnia had many interesting people. Later I found a ball field to camp at.

## Thursday Aug, 25th

It was still hot and sticky on the morning when I left camp at 7:30am and rode east along a nice road with no shoulders. It was a joy to observe slight differences from the States in this part of Canada. A little bit more politeness, a change of produce and new road signs.

I made it into London at noon. A big dog came out from the bushes and would have taken my leg off, but I got my bike between us and made plenty of noise. I talked to a cute chick at a shopping mall. The price was cheap enough for me to buy a cantaloupe, ice cream and bananas. Which I ate. While passing through downtown I stopped for a red light and observed next to me a truck running without a driver. It was really burning the blues. I reached in and shut it off, then started to leave as the fellow came out and got back in with a big question mark on his face. There were plenty of cute girls in this town. One asked me if I had a place to stay. The afternoon was still early so I continued on to Woodstock where I then ate dinner in a park. A guy named Bob came over and talked with me while I ate. We had a good talk about work, women and cars. I was somewhat annoyed, it seems I can't have any privacy. Bob left and then I met Mary Jane who sat down to chat. We were soon accompanied by her crazy boyfriend who talked about Spanish fly in the local water. As darkness fell I pedaled around in search of a campsite. All total this day I'd traveled 95 miles.

## Friday Aug 26th

I spent the night in the town of Woodstock in a playground behind a housing project. It was another hot, sticky night. I rode out of town at 7am traveling nice country roads. Stopped for breakfast at 10am and watched road construction under progress. As I traveled closer to the city of Niagara the roads became worse. Soon they were gravel with big pot holes. There is a saying which frequently would go through my mind. "The closer you get the harder it gets." The road pounded away at me and my bike, often rattling the thing like a jack hammer.

Finally I made way into Niagara at 5 p.m. I bought groceries and went down by the falls to cook a bag of sweet and sour pork with noodles. To compliment my feast I also had fresh orange juice and yogurt. What a beautiful evening it was. The shear drop of Niagara Falls thundering down that narrow canyon is a rewarding sight. It almost seems to be leaping like a diver on a high swan dive. Lovers leap had lots of romantic lovers strolling around.

After sunset, I rode up through town and on a small street saw a gal on a street corner wearing a miniskirt. I asked her if she might know a place I could camp for the night. She told me she would show me a spot. Her name was Marilyn. My goodness, I was looking at the prettiest woman I'd seen in a long while. Wowwy, she wore short, tight red pants, white tube top and had beautiful blonde hair and what legs. We talked a lot as I walked with her and pushed the bike. She was 18 years old and told me that she had a hard childhood. "My father was abusive my mother was a drunk," she said stoically. It was ironic, she was so gorgeous on the outside but so tough within. Marilyn was kind enough to show me a field of tall grass and trees in the midst of town, that she thought would be safe for me to camp the night. I thanked her.

Before leaving me she told me she would come see me about 11 p.m. I was so excited about it, that I gave myself a thorough water-bottle-bath. I set up my tent and waited there in great anticipation of seeing her. My imagination went wild. I struggled to stay awake and finally gave up.

Then at midnight I heard someone nearby and she said, "Eric?" I nearly leaped out and embraced her. She walked up and my heart was racing but then went numb when seeing she was with a guy. "This is Arty, my boyfriend," she said. We met and talked, but I was so disappointed, my fire was doused. Admittedly, I had such lustful thoughts that night I couldn't hardly sleep.

It had been a hot, sticky night and now I was greeted with misty fog on the morning of **Sat. Aug 27th**. I went downtown and bought some food and then pedaled over to gaze at the great falls while chowing down. Later, while passing through U.S. customs, the customs agent asked me about my bike and my trip. He sounded like he wanted to go along! I met 3 guys, from Pennsylvania, who had ridden their bikes from out west. They told me they were tired of talking to non-bikers about their ride, so we shared a few bike stories. I headed back down the road, thinking about those early days in Santa Barbara.

## *Getting a 'real' job*

*My first year at Browne was kind of rough. I had to pay the job agency $180 each month for the first four months to pay for my job position. In addition I had $180 car payments and this kept my spending to a minimum. One way to save money was by sleeping in my car every night. It wasn't that I couldn't afford an apartment, though admittedly they were expensive. I felt the challenge of new lifestyles and the freedom it allowed. The experiences*

*I was learning by being out on the street were interesting to me. By sleeping in my car every night I started to know the art of car camping. I'd found a couple of good spots to park. One was in a campground near the ocean and the other was in a residential area. The ocean made so much noise at night that I had trouble sleeping near it. In addition, two freight trains went by that place, one at midnight and the other around five in the morning. The noise was enough to wake the dead. So I opted for a residential area because of a much better quality of sleep. The police came by now and then and shined spotlights at my car, but I laid down below the windows and so they never did see me.*

*After about 6 months of working at the company, a coworker named Joyce, who worked in purchasing, found out I was sleeping in my car and said to me, "I've always noticed your clothes are so well pressed and clean, how can you do that and sleep in a car?" I told her I arranged things very carefully in the trunk to keep them neat. She then asked where I got cleaned up and where I'd go to the bathroom. "In the park bathhouse," I said. People were always so amazed at my lifestyle of sleeping in the car. Others soon found out about it and before long they had coined my car the nickname," The Hotel Gordini," and the name stuck ever since.*

*I'd usually cook my dinner down at the campground in Carpinteria. It was right at the end of Linden Avenue on the beach. The view from the campground was lovely when the sun was setting over the ocean and reflected amber hues upon the mountains. Daily, I would meet all kinds of characters at this place as it was the crossroads for vagrants and transients. Some people came by for a day or two while others stayed around longer.*

*On one occasion I was cooking my dinner when a van pulled up and out stepped a tall shirtless blond fellow wearing a straw cowboy hat. This guy had a bottle of beer in his hand and talked loud enough for anyone within five hundred feet to hear him. He had a couple of friends nearby and they walked over underneath a big tree to puff on some weed. When he talked it sounded like this, "I is impossibleeze the falling leaves under big treeze", he shouted it aloud and my initial impression was that he was obnoxious. He walked with a loping gait and had a truly athletic body. It was apparent he was extremely well coordinated by the way he'd run out to catch a frizbee. Once the frizbee landed near my table and he came over my way and with big smiling white teeth said, "What's cookin in the shmeggy?" "Just the usual grub." I said. He laughed outloud and said, "grub, nobody calls food grub, it's shmeggy!" I could smell beer from his breath as he picked up the frizbee and flung it back to his pals. I decided to play with his poetic speech and said, "Grub in my stomach, shmeggy in yours, either way would you like to try my horesdouvers." He laughed with his head way back and exclaimed to me, "That's cool, that's cool, your a poet that don't know it and can't show it cause he just blowed it." He reached out a thumbs up handshake and said he was the Desert Dog or otherwise Randy. He said he was from Wisconsin. Being that we were both midwesterners we hit it off immediately. Randy would be one of the characters I came to know as a friend over the years in Carpinteria.*

*Then there were the two Australians I met at the campground. They were traveling around America and sleeping in their car. I got a kick out of their Aussie accents and their stories. Their names were James and Dave. They sure liked to drink beer and get loaded. I loaned Dave twenty dollars cause he said he was short on cash. He paid me back a week later. One day James and Dave and I went to a soccer tournament and we were sitting in the bleachers and I felt sickly as everything turned pink. I went to a toilet and ralphed from both ends. Then I went and laid in my car as everything was spinning. The Aussies found me laying down and said, "Bloody hell man are you alright." I returned with, "It's your Fosters beer I drank last night." Actually it probably was a case of food poisoning.*

*Later that afternoon I showed the Aussies how to make a few quick bucks by picking up aluminum cans along the beach We collected a couple of sacks and made enough cash to buy us all dinner. The Aussies got a kick out of doing this even though they said." It's a bloody horrible job."*

## Into New York state

I started riding eastward across New York state on highway #31, through small towns on this very hot day, stopping frequently to refill my water bottles. This was an opportunity to talk to the local folks.

While riding along the highway I saw a fair in progress along the roadside and pulled over to take a rest, and have a drink. I noticed a fellow motioning me to come over. He introduced himself as Larry and insisted I join him and the crowd of others. "What's the occasion for this celebration," I asked. He said, "This is the Fisher-Price Company's annual picnic. Now please come have a cold drink and eat some food." So I ate 2 cobs of corn, a bratwurst, a hamburger, potato salad, popcorn and drank a beer. It was all so mmm good. A band was playing, folks were arm wrestling. They were all easy going, fun loving people and even took pictures of me for their albums and company newspaper. Afterward I was so full and slightly drunk such that I could hardly ride.

I made way to Brockport and asked a girl for directions to a camping area. She snubbed me and told me to go ask the Police department. I actually went there but nobody was around. I rode down a street lined with elm trees and saw a gal sitting on the front steps of a big house. I asked her for directions to a campground and she told me directions but then as we talked a bit more she said, "Why don't you come on in." I discovered her name was Mary. She was cute, dark haired, an Italian- American college student. We talked excitedly about my trip. She was very interested in bike travel. Then I learned that she had traveled around Greece the previous summer by bike. While we talked and looked at her photos of travel, she cooked me corn on the cob, made me a sandwich and gave me a beer. She was looking more beautiful by the moment and I was thinking gosh, here I am with this gal in this big house and nobody else was around, oh how my thoughts reeled. We were having a wonderful talk when someone knocked at the door. "Hi," said this voice. "I was just passing by and saw your bike all loaded up outside and thought maybe you were traveling across America by bike." "Yes I am," I said. "Mind if I come in," he responded. He also was a trans-U.S.A. bicycle rider who had started out from California.

His name was Bill and truly appeared a nerdy, stinky cyclist. "Where are you staying tonight," he said. "I'll find a place," I said. "Mind if I tag along," he said. I grimaced.

We talked about our travels. Mary then invited us to a party. We each showered and then went to Lake Ontario for the party. There were lots of college kids milling around the fine cabin next to the big lake. Mary and I went out on the lake in a rubber raft. Later while inside I tried to play guitar but it did not sound right. We stopped at a bar on the way back, but did not stay. While returning in the car, Bill slept and snored like a bear. I sat next to Mary and my head spun when our elbows touched. Back at her house I massaged her back and felt my temperature rise, but moves were too hard to make especially with Bill around. Mary said we could stay at her house for the night. I was glad because it was well past one in the morning. I slept on the floor in the kitchen, wishing she'd come down and trip over me.

I awoke at 8:30 and ate toast. Got cleaned and packed my stuff on Sunday, the **28th of Aug.** Mary came down, looking good, and cooked breakfast for Bill and I. She was kind enough to invite me to visit her on Long Island when I get there in a week. At 11 a.m. I was ready to leave and was given a wonderful goodbye kiss from Mary before going. I followed canals through the lumpy New York countryside, passing through Rochester which was deserted on account of the day. This made for pleasurable biking in the big city. Along the way I stopped often to talk and eat.

In Clyde I bought groceries and then continued my ride to Savannah where I ate supper in a ball field. There I met Roger, another touring cyclist who had ridden his bike from Los Angeles, with Bill nonetheless! "Where is Bill," he asked me when finding out I'd spent the previous night with him. "I don't know where he went," I said. "He just took off this morning," I continued. After eating we rode down country roads in fog and darkness toward a campground that Roger suggested we stay at. The stars were out and there was much to talk about. We went over some tall hills and rocketed down backsides at a frightening pace. I was glad he had such a good light. Finally we found the campsite and crashed out in our tents.

## Monday. Aug 29th

I awoke to a foggy, sticky, misty morning and took a shower and then Roger and I pedaled for Syracuse. The landscape was changing. There were many small hills. The buildings were older in design and historical in content. We stopped at a bakery and gorged ourselves on pastry and I gulped a cold pop, unlike Roger, who was a devoted coffee drinker. Afterward we rode into a very hilly section and while going up a steep grade, Rogers chain jammed and then tore a link. I helped him repair it with my chain link extractor. We continued on and Roger dropped back behind me a ways.

I saw a cat sneaking across the road and quietly I rolled right up to it and then hissed. That cat jumped clear off the ground and hightailed off the road! I turned around and saw the shaking cat on the roadside. I dismounted and held out a hand and made friends with the little feline, even petting the pretty cat, after my devious deed.

Roger and I rode into the city of Syracuse at noon and then after exchanging names, parted ways. I rode to Liverpool and there called Andy, whom I'd met out in Idaho. He was glad to hear from me and then rode down to meet me while I sipped merrily on an ice cold drink. It was good to see him once again. We went to his folk's nice house and there I met his pal Tom.

Andy told me he would soon start a job with I.B.M. in their chemical engineering department. Tom worked for the Patent Office.

After eating some munchies we took a bus to the local New York State Fair. At this annual fair we saw many fabulous exhibits on building construction and livestock. They had monster cows, hairy horses and colorful poultry. I egged the roosters to cock-a-doodle-do and then to fight by blowing on them. We ate a great dinner at the fair and feasted our eyes on all of the cute girls. We took rides on wild spinning wheels. On one of them I thought for sure I would loose me camera/money bag.

It was getting late when we took a bus back into town and sat in downtown Syracuse waiting for a transfer. I thought how much I would like to live like Dragons Lair, an adventurer, and then again how much I wanted to be an artist. We were just about ready to step off the bus when I checked my bag and found my wallet missing. I ran back into the bus and fortunately found it under my seat.

We arrived at Andy's house after midnight and I talked to his mom about my travel plans. She is the co-owner of a travel agency. It annoyed me to no end how I couldn't find information on where and what I was going to do. Perhaps that would only be found out via first hand experience. Anyway she helped me with some ideas, but I still had to arrange a plane ride to London. I ate a delicious bowl of peaches and then slept on the living room floor. I rocked to sleep thinking of those roosters crowing and those pigs feeding and listened to Andy's mom tell him how he would live the next year of his life, what kind of shoes he would need etc.

## Tuesday Aug. 30

It was a good night's sleep and a nice morning and I worked on my bike for a while and then called People's Express for a plane ticket. They had to search for many days advance for an opening or a cancellation. Finally she found me an opening on Sept. 12th. I called Ellie Roth, the travel agent, and she needed more information. So I called People's back and got my demands for a reservation and then called Ellie back and got my ticket for $149.

Shortly after noon, Andy and I rode to the travel agents house where I picked up my ticket. Andy's mom took me out to lunch, and then she dropped me off at her house and we said our good-byes. We shook hands and I thanked Andy for all of his kindness.

I rode off at 1:30pm. Feeling rather guilty about lazing about for the last day and therefore rode hard until arriving at the town of Ilion at 6:30pm. There I bought groceries and went to a marina to cook supper. I rode on in the rain and stopped at a grocery store where an old man came over to bug me by telling me his life story. He talked like a god-damn-old-pump-squeaked. "You know I can tell you something," he would start off. I couldn't believe how long I took all his jibberish. I felt like a well that was being shouted into. I couldn't do a damn thing with him hassling me. Oh well it was back to humanity for me. I pitched my tent and totaled up 60 miles traveled, $3 spent and the airline ticket cost me $152.

## Wed. Aug 31st

I had about an inch of water inside the tent sides in the morning. The seams must have leaked. I stayed pretty dry considering that it had rained hard. It was as I rode through the Mohawk valley, a scenic river valley where the legendary Indian tribe thrived. There were many old settlements to be seen. As I rode along the road I thought of a song and pulled over to write it down when an elderly man riding a bike pulled up to me and asked, "Is everything Ok?" "Yes," I responded continuing, "I'm writing a song." He raised his eyebrows and was off. I tried to catch up with him but he was very fast even though he must have been 60 years old.

## *Born Again!*

*During my stay in the Santa Barbara area, I would take mini trips on weekends to check out the area.*

*One Saturday morning I drove to Ojai, and then headed north up highway 33 into the valleys of the Sierra Madre mountains towards Bakersfield. I slept the night on top of Pine Mountain and in the morning headed down the east side to the San Joaquin valley town called Taft. I went looking for a church service and soon found a congregation waiting in line to go into a Baptist church. The sun beat hot upon my back as I entered the church. I found a place to sit near the middle of the congregation. During the service the minister said that anyone who would like to be born again could come up front and do so. I was spiritually withdrawn and curious about this ritual of being born again. I truly did want to experience more about God and so I went up to the front of the congregation with six other people. The minister said a few words of wisdom and then asked each of us if we would accept the Lord as our personal savior. He held his hand on my head and had me repeat a few words and then touched me with a drop of water and said, "Go yee now in peace and seek the truth for with the water are yee born again." We recited a little prayer and the audience applauded and everyone was real nice to me for fifteen minutes afterward. Then the minister came by and treated me like he felt sorry for me and he wanted to know if I would join his congregation. I told him my situation, where I lived and all, and he told me if I wanted I could come back again to join the church. With great enthusiasm I returned to Santa Barbara as a born again Christian.*

*I started going to church regularly on Sundays. I did not know which church to join so I tried different ones each week. Some Sundays I'd go to church two times, even three! Each church had a little different way of putting things than the next church which I found to be a curious phenomena.*

*Santa Barbara had many churches and I began to notice one thing that was repeated at each one I visited. The first time I'd go to a new church it felt good to anonymously sit back and listen to what the message was all about. I did not feel like I was expected of much, not expected to leave much of an offering in the plate. Then on the second visit people noticed me and welcomed me as if they knew me and treated me very hospitably. Around the third visit I could sense people were getting ticked off at me because I was not joining there church. What was I doing here? Then as time went on people would contest me on how true my belief as a Christian was. They'd ask me if I knew the story of Jacobs coat or something like that and when I did not know the answer, the allegations flew that I wasn't a good Christian. I also felt more pressure to put more cash into the offering plate. It's sort of a game church people play. Sometimes, upon my third visit, the feeling was downright hostile. At one church the members raised their hands and non members raised theirs and as a non member, I watched people turn around and sneer at me. It all seemed a mind game to me after awhile.*

*One Sunday morning I got Randy to go to church with me. It was a cute little old white Lutheran church in Carpinteria. We sat down right in the middle of the congregation, along side of some elderly folks. The minister came in and read a prayer about giving more tithings to the church. He likened it to increasing your investment in the kingdom of heaven. Then he had us sing a song about the end of the world being near. As we held up the hymnbook to sing along, Randy said aloud to me, "These words would make great lyrics for a rock song." Many people sitting nearby heard him and they frowned. The minister got up to the pulpit and gave his sermon and it was titled; <u>Leave all your money in a will to the church.</u> Randy and I listened intently as the minister told the congregation why and how they should sign a will to have all there money given to his church. The minister continued to give more emphasis on how the church needs their money, why god likes people who give the church money and so on. All of a sudden, Randy stood up and said aloud, "What a bunch of crap!" I heard a few gasps from those in the congregation and the minister stopped his sermon. Randy turned around to me and said, "Eric are you coming?" I said, "I'm right behind you," and we headed for the door. Grannies wearing thick spectacles watched us with open mouths as we walked out the door.*

*After that I became very disillusioned with the religion they were preaching in these churches and did not ever go back again. I changed from being a 'born again' to being a born skeptic.*

## Crossing the Hudson River

The rain started to fall as I cruised through the town of Schenectady. In Troy a guy tried to run me off the road in a pickup truck. I passed him at a red light and let him know I wasn't pleased with his actions. At another red light some kids at the crosswalk asked me if I was running away from home. I said. "Yah, all the way from California." They said. "What are you doing in Troy?" I said, "I heard this was where the best people in the world lived." They laughed with toothless grins.

I crossed over the mighty Hudson River, wondering how polluted it was here, as it looked clean. I then went up a steep hill to the town of Cropseyville and found a store for groceries and stopped at a bike shop. From there, I traveled up a twisting country road. Not a single car passed me. It was getting dark when I snuck into an empty campground in Grafton Lakes State Park and selected a site by a lake. Around midnight I was awakened by party goers with loud music and hoped they would not come near to me.

There was a touch of fall in the air on the morning of Thursday Sept 1st. I packed up my bike as fog rolled across the lake. It reminded me of the B.W.C.A. I rode up into the mountains and sped down exciting grades. These mountains were gorgeous, green and round. At one point a dog chased me and since I was going uphill and could not outrun him I stopped, but he kept coming. I laid the bike down, stood my ground and yelled. He took off.

The state line was crossed into Massachusetts at 10a.m. and I arrived in the quaint town of North Adams. I climbed up a steep mountain grade, stopping frequently, for the beauty was eye opening. While coming down the opposite side I noticed a truck up ahead run a stop sign and then start a turn right in front of me. Luckily I anticipated his move and swerved and missed him by five feet. I turned around and flipped the old cogger the middle finger.

A stop was made in the town of Greenfield near a school to air out my damp tent. A middle aged woman wearing an apron walked over, said, "Hello," and handed me a plate of homemade O'Henry bars. She said, "My son is also a biker, and I know others have done nice things to him. Just leave the plate there and I'll pick it up once your gone." I thanked her. The bars were delicious and I was thankful for her kindness.

I rode down a long gentle road and turned my radio on. They played Bob Dylan's song 'Like a Rolling Stone.' That truly fired me up. I was pedaling like a prize fighter, singing aloud- *"How does it feel? To be on your own, a complete unknown, no direction home, just like a Rolling Stone!"* The trees seemed to be like my huge audience, the feeling euphoric and even psychedelic. I felt a total union of life.

Later, a very pretty calm and clear lake named Lake Ervine was to irresistible to pass up as a campsite. I selected a nice spot, listened to Worchester on the radio, and was mildly amused at a girl who was out swimming on the lake screaming at her friends to come join her. They never did, she swam back to shore.

## Friday, Sept. 2nd

I had a real nice camp for the night near the lake shore of Laurel Lake. The morning of was foggy as it started out. I had good roads and low traffic along the route and passed through many small towns like Barre and Daxton, all of which were old. I started to notice more statues of memorabilia and famous individuals from the past. Around noon I was passing through the city of Worcester. I toured the town and checked out many of the old landmarks. The road continued north and then as it headed east I found more apple orchards, which were too irresistible to pass up without snitching an apple.

While at a convenience store getting a can of pop, I talked to a guy who had just returned from Europe. He traveled around there by car. He said he wanted to go back. This gave me some encouragement.

I got tired as the day went on, mostly from the hilly terrain. In Waltham I found a park and pulled over for a break. I again heard on the radio the Bob Dylan song, Like a Rolling Stone, and that fired me up, this time pedaling enthusiastically up to Prospect Hill Park, which overlooked Boston. It looked like my best bet for camping overnight.

I rode back down to Boston and called Roger, whom I'd met while on the road, and he said it wasn't to cool for me to come stay with him. "It's kind of like a human circus here," he said. I then stopped at a tackle store to talk to a man about purchasing a tent pole to replace mine. He told me, "Go out and cut the branch off an oak tree in the woods."

I ate a reasonably priced smorgasbord dinner at a supermarket and met Lucille while leaving the store on the way up to the park. She told me she had recently returned from Europe and enjoyed the change of pace. I tried in vain to talk more to her, she must have found me unusual, and had to go.

Pedaling back up the grade to Prospect Hill Park I found a good place to camp in the bushes and hid my bike. I climbed up an old fire tower to witness a fabulous view of Boston in the night. While up there I could see a police car come up the road and he spot lit everything, including my position, but did not see me hiding up on the tower. I went back down and set up my tent in a special little spot and climbed into my humble abode.

### *One year of living in a car in California*

*After a year of living in the Hotel Gordini, I really started to get a crook in my neck. During the Santa Barbara winter, it was the rainy season, and the sun roof on the Hotel Gordini was leaking pretty bad and I looked for better living conditions. The answer to my prayer came from Dick, one of the guys I worked with. Dick had an eight foot long pickup truck camper sitting up on block, out in the parking lot at Browne. I asked him if I could move into it. The camper was rather Spartan, a bunk, a table and not high enough for me to stand up in. Yet I considered it quite a luxury compared with the Hotel Gordini. Trouble was that Dick had used it as a kennel for his dog and so the place was infested with fleas. I tried to clean it out with bleach, but still they persisted.*

## Boston in the morning
## Saturday Sept. 3

I was up early as the first of many joggers came up the hill and stretched on the morning I rode down into Boston and toured the streets, stopping frequently to see statues and sights. Amongst the most unusual was a man who laid sleeping atop a grave, with a gravestone at his head, in a graveyard from the 1700's. Much to my surprise I met John and Judy, whom I had cycled with in Wyoming, at the crowded city square. We talked about what had occurred since departing. While we stood there chatting a beggar, dressed shabbily with his fly wide open, came over and asked me for some money. He then left and we continued talking. Then he came by again and drunkenly asked for money. So I told him, "Hey get a job-everyone else in America has to-so beat it!" And he stood there in shock. "Beat it." I said. He stumbled backward and promptly took off. John and Judy and a friend were shocked at my actions. I guess I was a little bit as well. The road has a way of hardening one, and for the moment I didn't sympathize with that beggar. I rode to Bunker Hill and was interested to read all the details of the historic battle. It really wasn't a big battle, more like a skirmish.

I went down and saw Old Ironside, the U.S.S Constitution, and took a tour on board the ship. I enjoyed Boston's old world charm, but traffic was offensive and thus was overjoyed to head out of town. I almost was mowed off the road when I swerved to avoid a chuckhole. The driver nearly got me with his door. The people drove like crazy there. My reception by the people wasn't much better. Once, I stopped at a gas station to refill my water bottle and was hastily greeted by the clerk but got water anyway.

Occasionally the Atlantic Ocean was in sight while riding down the coast. I met Jeff, another cyclist who had traveled from Salt Lake City and was in the Peace Corps. Since he was staying with friends who had no room to lodge me for the night, he showed me a spot to camp on a point near Minot Lighthouse. Afterward, I dove into the Atlantic Ocean, helmet shoes, bike and all. This was to acknowledge my having traveled coast to coast on a bicycle.

I cooked dinner on a park bench near the beach and met Bob a biker from Long Island. I also met Christine. She was an attractive gal whom talked with me till dark. A cop sat and watched us converse but I didn't give a fuck about him since I did no wrong. We went to a pub and she told me about the history of Minot Lighthouse. "The light says I love you when it flashes," she said.

Then she told me a story about a lighthouse near Cape Cod where lovers visit. Christine had a great laugh, bought me a beer, and I wanted to know more about her, but I became so tired sleep was more precious than the chase. We separated and I rode up to the private property leading to Minot Lighthouse and lifted my bike over a chain. Then I walked the bike up the wet grass and darkest trail I've yet gone up. There I saw an old watch tower, once used as a lookout for German U-boats, and set my camp under its spooky figure. It did not matter, as sleep came fast to this weary traveler.

### *Moving up in living conditions in California*

*In the spring of 1982 I bought a ten foot camper trailer for $800.00. It was small but the inside was rather well finished. There was a sink, a stove and a refrigerator but no shower and no toilet. It pulled easily behind my car.*

*I soon started finding really great places to park along the streets of Santa Barbara. Now having a place big enough to invite guests over, I sent out flyers around work and to friends announcing my housewarming beach party at the camper. I went to the liquor store and bought seventy dollars worth of booze and beer and made up a huge vat of chile. I'd also made a large bag full of popcorn and bought some apple and cherry pies. My guests were mostly the people from work and we had a very boisterous and spirited night along the sands of East Beach. The party got a little out of hand around midnight, with everyone ending up swimming in the ocean. In the morning the camper had two inches of sand on the carpeting and the worst part was the sand smelled heavily of urine. The folks at Browne thought of my beach party as quite a sensation and soon coined my camper the nick name; "The Tilton Hilton."*

*I parked the Tilton Hilton along a dead end street, high on a hill overlooking Santa Barbara's city beach. On a nice day, the beach was filled with suntanned ladies wearing swimsuits that covered as much as spaghetti noodles. Being that I was a young and single man, I had opportunities to entertain ladies in my palace on the hill, though it was more infrequent than I'd liked, and still stayed clear of any serious relationships.*

*By now, I was beginning to learn alot about street living and felt more confident about being in that environment. These were wonderful times as I had a steady job and a place to live with a most beautiful view of the Pacific Ocean. With prosperity in my favor I resumed taking flying lessons and was still depositing money in the bank.*

*The weather was generally mild in Santa Barbara, so riding a motorcycle was great transportation.*

*There was one night when a terrific storm blew in and the rain fell and the winds blew so strong that I thought it would blow The Tilton Hilton over a cliff. Each time the wind gusted, the camper leaned and it sounded like hell run wild. A river roared underneath the camper with such ferocity and volume that it picked up and moved the camper several feet down the street.*

## Sunday Sept 4, 1983.

I explored the old observation tower which I had slept near by the coast of the Atlantic on a rainy night. It had an eerier Macabre sense to it. As if a lone monolith lying watch over the sea. Made my breakfast of a grilled cheese sandwich and rode down to town. I stayed on country roads until Plymouth. In Scituate I stopped for an ice cream bar which I craved. A policeman who had watched me the previous night was there and he helped me with directions. Plymouth Rock was bustling with tourists. The Mayflower ship was there and I boarded and looked over the vessel. It is a wonder they could travel as many people on that ship across the ocean.

I looked at Plymouth Rock with '1620' chiseled on it. I saw an old gravestone and it told how the family had died of sickness. This really struck me as to how much suffering those people went through. They were certainly in need of Gods help with the way they came to this land. They came late in October and had a real hard time surviving the first winter. The Indians really helped them out. It's almost a romantic story, but also one full of Americanism. The devotion to freedom and hard work to get done what is needed.

I sat back for an hour and wrote post cards on this very hot day. Then rode down across the Sandwich Bridge into Cape Cod. The landscape changed into beautiful flat plains of long grass. The homes seem so tightly built that they are almost seaworthy. I found the Cape Cod style architecture very inspiring. I rode to a grocery store and stocked up. Then continued on to Hyannis, the home of J.F.K.

I went into a public swimming pool and met a gal that had this marvelous dark tan. For all her beauty, she was dingy and looked at me like I was crazy, when I asked her, "how are you?" She hadn't talked to a Midwesterner before and probably thought I sounded stupid.

This was my first time riding around a round a bout, and got caught in the rotary not knowing my exit. There was a 'traffic interplacer' and got so confused I had to ask a woman for directions. Finally, I found the J.F.K memorial Park, where I cooked, showered, and then met a couple from Boston. I rode into town that night and saw so many tourists. It was a pretty harbor at the memorial where they had a quote by J.F.K., which read, "Believe it is important, that our country sail, than lie still in the harbor." I pitched my tent and stayed in a clearing in some brush at the memorial as some rain fell.

## Monday Sept. 5

It was labor day I rode into Hyannis and made a breakfast. Took side roads and saw the house J.F.K., lived in. It is not so extravagant a house. The view was inspiring though. The neighborhood was small townish and quiet. A good place for contemplation. Again I had to ride over a large bridge in 'Buzzard Bay." This one wasn't bad and the traffic went around me. But I pushed hard to get to the crown and then coasted down the other side at a good speed. The traffic was thick on other side for miles. I enjoyed this immensely. I'd drive by the cars saying, "Let's here it for the bicycle." And I hollered at RVs "Next time bring your house." It was all in good fun. I passed everyone. The day grew exceptionally hot. I kept up a good pace, even though it was hilly. My cycling took me into Rhode Island where I stopped to watch a gal swimming. Stopped by a beach and saw a guy get the cold shoulder from a girl in a bikini. The continuum goes on.

### *A vacation drive into the Sierras was the turning point*

*In the mid summer of 1982, I took a weeks vacation and drove the Hotel Gordini up into the Sierra mountains to make some watercolor paintings in the Yosemite Valley. Yosemite was such a spectacular setting. The canyon walls stand like a fortress with cascading waterfalls and glorious fauna below. It was the perfect place to have mystical things happen. One evening I walked into a meadow as stars blazed overhead. At night Yosemite takes on a different character. It is as if the rock cliffs become a council of gods looking down upon you. The rock shapes are overpowering and one is immediately humbled. That night, I carried my sleeping bag into the forest and found a fine place to recline. A large rock was behind me and a fine stand of pines stood in front as I dozed off and dreamed.*

*I fell asleep and had a dream of zipping over streets busy with traffic and crowds of people. Below was a black asphalt highway and with such speed I felt as if on a collision course, but each time I nearly missed obstacles and kept on going. I was seeing new sights and my life felt totally free. It was a thrilling view of the world in this dream. Then suddenly I became aware that something was coming near me and was threatening me. I tried to awake but the sleep was so deep. Then as if by fearful chance the thing came so near myself that it breathed a nostril blow upon my face. I realized it wasn't a dream; it was real! I leaped up with a fright and it took all my might to scream out "Ahh!" My voice pierced the darkness and I listened to an animal running away. It was so close that leaves scattered into the air, some of which landed on my sleeping bag. My heart pounded and I listened to the sound of the fleeing animal as it crashed through the woods. I grabbed my flashlight and shone it, but saw nothing. I knew that it was a deer, for I have hunted them and know how they sound when they run. Then, it was almost as if a voice was speaking and I had this astounding presence. It filled my whole being with one amorphous idea. I sat up to look at the stars and a crescent moon thru the pines. "I will bicycle around the world," I said aloud. The thought of such a journey sent my mind racing with excitement and the rest of the night was such that I barely could fall back asleep. A bicycle trip around the world was imprinted upon my future and now it's beginning was in the making!*

*The next few days were a joy and I didn't mind telling anybody I'd met about my future plans. In fact on a hike up to the top of Yosemite Falls I met a high school classmate, Jim, walking down after his climb up the mountain. We talked and shook hands and I told him of my plans. But just as things were starting to go right, I had a real dilema happen. It was on the return trip to Santa Barbara where I parked at 11,000 feet on Toulomne Pass and was turning the car around. I heard a loud bang and the cars front end dropped down There was a guy directly in front of me who was shaking his hands like a football umpire does when the kicker misses a field goal and he said, "Stop-stop you have got big troubles. My car broke a ball joint and the front axle shaft tore out of the transmission. It sent oil and parts rolling across the parking lot. After a scurry trying to figure whether I should call a wrecker or not, I went to work reassembling the front end back into place with the help of wire from an old fenceline. Later that day as I headed across the 110 degree temps of the Mojave desert I noticed my temperature gauge was real hot. The waterpump belt had blown and I was 40 miles away from the next town without a replacement. Using a little ingenuity I rigged up the alternator belt to also drive the waterpump which was good enough to get me back to Santa Barbara and the Tilton Hilton. All these occurances seemed as if trials to test my conviction of riding a bicycle around the world. But they were also tests of my mechanical skills, though I no longer dwelled upon them, they were valuable.*

## Arrival in Newport Rhode Island

I rode across the Tiverton and enjoyed the view of sailboats, people, water and this old arch. The streets got bad and bumpy. I rode into Newport at 4:30pm. Stopped at grocery store and a couple took cuts in front of me. We struck up a conversation and I met Steve and Lana. They invited me too a barbecue. I came down to their house, an old place and showered. Met other good people. Stewart, Linda, Emily and I shared stories. As the night progressed and after a delicious meal, Steve fell asleep on the couch. His friends put shaving cream on him and put his hand in hot water. He woke up got mad and stormed off. Everyone thought he was pissed off. He returned later and all these people thought he would kill them. We were going to go out to the pubs. Everyone had there window soaped and air let of their tires. Steve had got his revenge. We went to a disco place. I danced one song and had to get out of there. It was too loud and annoying. Slept on the couch. Stewart looked like Kirk Douglas-his hands sprung wide open.

## Tuesday Sept 6

I awoke and packed the bike and then I woke up Steve who was sleeping soundly, but bounded to his feet when I awoke him. "Hey have a good trip." He said and he came outside he told me, "People are he same world over, they work five days a week, go out Friday night with friends, on Saturday night with lovers. You'll meet lots of good people, they're out there." We shook hand and I was off in the fog, stopping for breakfast on the dockside of yogurt and fruit and juice. Saw mansions, and an old Viking fort looked interesting. It was said to have been built long ago by Vikings with charcoal bricks found on the islands.

## Planning for a world bicycle trip

*Now I was making wonderful new plans for a world bicycle adventure! I would plan to leave on this bicycle trip in the summer of 1983. This would give me plenty of time to get things arranged. Back at Browne things were changing with great alarm. Our company was sold to a Minnesota company named MCT. Therefore our company was now called MCT/BROWNE. Except for some new employees, there were no other changes except for Mary becoming more domineering in the drafting department. She must have felt her position was threatened by me and so was now pushing her weight around. She became more overbearing even with John, who was the other draftsman in our department.*

*Mary would give us assignments that we'd have great difficulty accomplishing in her time frame. Then she'd rag at us for not doing things the way she wanted them done even though we'd get the job done right if she'd leave us be. Since she was working only part time, she just wasn't around enough to know when sudden demands came up. The engineers would come in and tell us to revise something and since Mary wasn't there we had to do it without informing her. In addition, she had double standards. She would scold us for talking to other employees, yet we caught her many times just sitting around talking to her boyfriend Bob, the chief engineer. She would scold us for making phone calls, while she would spend time chit chatting on the phone. As a form of rebellion, I got myself a pair of headphones and started listening to Bob Dylan music. My favorite tune became "Idiot Wind," which is a song off the <u>Blood on the Tracks</u> album. With this music in my ears, I could tune her out and began to look more and more forward to the day that I would be leaving on my bike trip just to get her out of my life.*

## Catching a ride over a bridge

I rode up to Newport Bridge and had to thumb a ride as it was not lawful to bicycle across. The first car that came was a pickup with a Samoan family. They stopped I threw my bike in the back and inside I met the most gorgeous young gal. We went over the big bridge. It was exhilarating. Then over the end was even more treacherous. Riding in a car really blows me away with the speed. I am becoming more withdrawn away from society's ways. Starting my own new ways. Rode down the road past many colonial scenes, which a man was out painting on the roadside. I saw a cute girl on roadside and said, "hi." She kind of, sort of, maybe said, "Hi,"??? Well I saw this nice beach full of bathing beauties. Stopped for a look and she walked past me. So I wheeled down and said, "Hi again." We struck up an interesting talk. Sherry turned to be a wonderful, pretty, young lady who was 16, tan and looked a lot like Lauren Hutton. She wanted to be a model. I took a photo of her by my bike. We talked for an hour and a half and then I headed on. I was somewhat depressed I had not pursued her, but then, what could I do?

There were more big bridges to cross the many bays along the coast and this time I rode over them. They were scary fast rides. I rode into New London and found a park to stay at. I met a cool x-Vietnam Vet on the beach and we talked of life. He had many stories about the government whore house, bathing with the V.C. and he said, "War is a young mans adventure and an old mans recollection." I walked up to my tent and almost stepped on a skunk. Threw rocks at it. The ranger came by and he, "Relocated," me in the night.

**Wednesday Sept 7**

I ate blueberry cakes for breakfast. Started to read a book Steve gave me called, "A Walk across America," by Peter Jenkins. The ranger came by and offered me a cup of coffee but I kindly, "Refused," his offer. #$%%%★★(. This was nice country, though the wind bothered me. I saw school kids on the road, and stopped for an O.J. and then a woman showed me cold water. My bike was taking a beating on the rough glass strewn roads. I must get asked three times at each time I stop. "Where you from?" "Ah-California," "Aren't you tired? How you getting back? Oh my god don't you get lonely. Wish I was in your shoes. Good luck." Two girls at 'Friendly' store were fun, they got so excited one asked me if she could come along.

I rode hard and long today. Three to four hours at a stretch. Went about 100 miles and as stopped in Norwalk and was trying to make it to Stamford for my mail drop. But the day wore on and the miles were long. While sitting at a grocery store a drunk looking guy came by with the usual questions. I treated him somewhat rudely and spurted how much I hated big cities and he defended his hometown and said he liked it here. I asked him of a place to stay and he knew none so we split up but both of us walked into the same grocery store. On a back isle he came down the isle and said hello again. During our conversation, he offered me his hospitality for a place to stay the night and I accepted. His name was Art and Atlanta was his girlfriend from England. Once back outside, they threw my stuff into his truck. They lived in a small house in a very busy neighborhood. I cooked up supper in his backyard on a picnic table. We talked for a long while with O.J. and smoked and I got cleaned up in the shower. It was another lucky encounter with one heck of a nice person. We had plenty to talk about as he was into fishing, backpacking, canoeing and cycling. He's a carpenter by trade, but he had roommate problems. Her name was Joan and she was brooding.

## Thursday Sept 8

I awoke and hurriedly got my stuff ready as Art had to go to work. In my hurry, I forgot my nice aqua colored shirt. I pedaled into Stamford seeking the post office for my mail drop. What followed was a frustrating but humorous search for that post office. I asked a gas station attendant and he said, "Stay on #1 and you can't miss it." I then asked a black woman and she said, "Go back one mile, take a left, look for a restaurant called "Doubles" and it's on the right. I followed there advice but still could not find it, so I went into a Police Station and flagged down a cop who had a very Brooklyn accent. He pointed and said, "Go down that one way (against traffic) and then at the third light take a right and you'll be there." So I did like he said and ended up nowhere. I saw this smart looking guy and asked him but he couldn't tell me where it was either. Disgusted, I ambled about on my own hoping to find it by instinct.! I saw a scroungey looking dude walking the street and asked him, "Do you know where the main post office is?" He gave me the general direction by pointing and saying, "It's that-a-way." So I finally went that-a-way and still not finding it asked another black woman who said, "It's down to "Doubles" turn right and it's down that street. The whole time she was motioning left so I asked. "You mean turn left?" And she said. "Oh, yah, that's what I mean." So I took her advice and I did find it. There was a lesson to be learned here. Black women can't tell right from left, and people in general can't give good directions.

I picked up my gorp that mother had sent to me, also the latest news from home. I excitedly sat down and ate handfuls of the foodstuff on the front steps of the Post Office. It is always the best when it comes from home.

### *Ellen*

*I was going out occasionally with a Santa Barbara girl named Ellen now and then, and though I liked her very much, our relationship was purely as friends. I did not feel she was holding me back from going, yet somewhere within me was a feeling that was saying forget about the trip and go for the gal. She was very nice, albeit deceptively sweet and innocent, until one day I saw her drive by sitting arm in arm with another guy. I realized my chances were slim of getting to know her in a deeper relationship. Even more perplexing a situation occurred because of my feelings for Ellen. I'd set a goal to complete my journey in nine months. Perhaps this was in the hope that the time and distance would make her heart fonder for me once I returned.*

*Now, problems started to arise when the police caught on to my living in the Tilton Hilton, because in Santa Barbara it was against the law. I paid one $25 ticket for a summons, and that discouraged me from wanting to pay for more. One Saturday I pulled the Tilton Hilton over to Goleta and tried parking it there for the night. At around nine o'clock in the evening the sheriff showed up and told me, "Move it or else I'll give you a ticket." I shifted to a different location and again the police hassled me. This became more of a nuisance. Several times the police pulled up and knocked on the door when I was inside. One time the police knocked on my door just as I was taking a crap into a plastic bag. Lucky for me they must have figured nobody was home and then they left.*

## Riding into Manhatten with Ralph

Continuing on, I went 10 miles down the road and met a cyclist named Ralph. "I'm riding to Manhattan," he said to me. "Mind if I tag along," I said. With the busy traffic inches away from us we pedaled along and talked about our lives. He worked at the United Nations Building, was married and had a daughter.

We rode into the Bronx. It was like entering a war zone. I stopped to ask for water and met a local black guy, somewhat high sprung but kind enough to give us directions. We stopped to buy fresh fruit, pears and drink. I saw scenes I had only seen in movies. People drinking water from fire hydrants. People laying on filthy sidewalks. Buildings burned. Cars overturned with everything ripped off the car. Some cars were nice, new ones, flashy ones, with loud music. Litter was strewn everywhere. I was so appalled at the sights. People had distant expressions set into a backdrop that looked more like sights from hell. Trash was stacked up. Music was blaring from every window as laundry hung out on the sash. Glass was on the streets, there were huge potholes and more black people with hungry looks, distant stares.

We crossed over a polluted river, thick as oil, into Manhattan. There were Police cars and people everywhere like flies on shit. Big buildings, some of which were real pretty were the foreground to giant skyscrapers touching the clouds. How things suddenly had changed compared to the Bronx. The buildings were attractive and the crowds a higher class. I pedaled along Central Park and then entered the park. It was pretty nice considering all the stories I'd heard about people being murdered or mugged. I especially liked the statues of Disney like characters intermixed with big trees, fountains and ponds.

### Ken

*In February of 1983, a guy I worked with named Ken Anderson invited me to move the Tilton Hilton over to his house. He said I could park the camper on his driveway until I left for my travels. The house was his late grandmothers, so he was living there until the estate was sold. Living there turned out to be of great asset toward helping me prepare for the world trip, in addition to adding many funny experiences. Ken loved to party. He would drink margaritas like it was soda pop. He had this German shepard dog that would dig holes in his yard. Ken would get pretty upset at the dog and he'd scold it on many occasions and then refill the holes. One Saturday afternoon Ken started drinking around noon. I soon heard Ken screaming at the dog for digging holes. This time the dog had dug a five foot long trench. Ken went inside his house and he came out with a .357 pistol and started to shoot at the dog. He chased the dog around my camper several times popping off shots. Lucky for the dog and for me, Ken was a bad shot. Ken gave the dog to Jo Beth, who also worked at Browne and already had three other dogs.*

*I had it pretty comfortably now with running water in my place and electicity. I did not feel the need to be so secretive about having my lights on at night as I did when I was out on the streets.*

## Pedaling up to Rockefeller Square

Farther down Manhattan Avenue I saw large crowds gathered at Rockefeller Square watching mimes and comedians. There was a gold statue, which someone said was Phoenix. I had someone take my photo in front of it. A black man came up and he was stoned or something and he said, "Where'd you come from man? Damn. All the way from California on that? Damn." At one point they must have made me the joke as everyone stopped and turned to look at me. I shyly moved on. Farther down the busy main street were ornate and attractive churches with hot dogs and cotton candy sales people on the corner. I stopped often to soak in the sights and spectacles. All the while Ralph stayed behind me, giving me information and taking photo's almost like a guardian angel. Then we shook hands and he split at a side street.

I continued down to the end of Manhattan to ask about riding to Liberty Isle, to visit the Statue of Liberty. But they wouldn't let me bring the bike on the ferry.

### *Spring of 1983*

*I started to plan more for the bike trip. I made lists and started shopping around for a bicycle. I also wrote letters to many companies in hopes they would sponsor me or help me with discounts.*

*I started to get some responses back from hopeful sponsors. I'd written to National Geographic, Coleman, Eureka Tents, Kangaroo Bags, Schwinn, Raleigh, Slumberjack and Aspenlite pannier company. Only Kangaroo Bags offered me a 15% reduction on thier prices if I came to there factory and picked up the bags. Needless to say I was a bit disappointed in the lack of help from sponsors.*

*In mid May all of the employees at MCT/BROWNE were suddenly gathered together for a surprise announcement. We were told the company would be closed down in six months. They said some of the personnel would be transferred to Minnesota if they wished to stay with the company. Those who wanted to terminate would be given a severance pay.*

*I kept my bike trip a secret at work until early June. Then I went in and told Jay, my manager that I would be leaving at the end of the month. He told me I was entitled to a* *severance pay. It was like a godsend for me because it would give me an additional $700. Now my date of departure was set for July 1, 1983. The word spread quickly about my proposed world tour and I was besieged with heckling and nay saying. For most of my fellow workers this idea seemed far fetched and foolhardy. I was constantly being asked, "What if this happens and what if that?" I did not have an answer for all the problems that might occur, and though their talk was annoying, my excitement drowned it out.*

## Riding in the streets of Manhatten

I went to a bank called Manhattan Trust and was reluctantly assisted by many snobs. I called my California bank from their phone. It didn't sound very encouraging that my funds could be sent here. They didn't trust me probably because I looked like a slob. They said my I. D. was not enough. I tried the Republic Bank of New York and the lady there was the biggest bitch of all. She wanted to know who I was staying with in the area. I told her I was staying at Mary's and then she asked me the phone number. When I gave it to her she dialed the number and then handed me the phone. I stumbled to introduce myself to Mary's mother and to describe the situation but it was very clumsy and unnatural. The bank lady sensed this. She then talked a bit to Mary's mother but I do not know what was said. She told me, "We cannot do a money transfer with you," and swiveled her chair around. I left there damn pissed. It was one bummer after another. I ambled down streets feeling very bummed out.

Then I headed across the Brooklyn Bridge. It was a beautiful structure. I lifted my bike up many steps and jaunted over old planks and then down more steps into Brooklyn. There I stopped and asked some firemen at a fire hall for directions. These guys got a real kick out of me. "You came all the way from California on that bike? You want to go where? Are you crazy?" said a jolly fireman. I called Mary and she invited me to stay at her place. She told me to call her once I arrived in North Bellmore. I headed east along busy streets not realizing how far it was to get there. My map was so inadequate. The streets were poorly marked and confusing. I asked many people for directions. At one point I must have traveled ten miles the wrong way before seeing sail boats and then had to turn around. The roads were treacherous and people drove like maniacs. Finally I arrived in North Bellmore in the dark. I was exhausted. I called Mary and she told me to stay put and that she would come pick me up. I was lucky she did as the grid work of streets was confusing. I followed her to her house. At her house I met her father, Richard and her mother Liz and her younger sister. Later I called mom and arranged for a Western Union money transfer.

### *Buying a world traveling bike*

*Things were really happening fast now. On June 2nd, I bought my bicycle from a bike shop called Murdochs in Goleta. The bike I'd chosen seemed perfect for the task at hand. It was called a Schwinn Voyager and it cost $525 after a $50 discount. What a beautiful bike to see all shiny and new with its metallic blue paint job and 15 speeds mounted upon a light weight chrome moly frame complete with quick release wheels. When I went for the first ride it struck me that this felt like much harder work than expected in order to make it go. "Maybe I'm in over my head?" I said to myself. Did I expect this to be nearly effortless?*

*I was trying desperately to receive my pilot's license before my bike trips date of departure. In the evening I'd go flying with my instructor, Will, who said, "You're ready at any time to take your license check ride." But now the weather was cloudy and foggy everyday and so I had to wait it out. The delays were frustrating as I was eager to stay on schedule. I was studying hard in the evenings and Mary was getting on my nerves at work. She liked attention so much that she would do things to distract me and I just ignored her and that ticked her off. To add to that annoyance there was this feeling of loosing everything to the wants of others. For example, one night Ken came over to the Tilton Hilton in the evening to tell me he needed lots of money. He was pretty drunk albeit, but he was also pretty demanding. I played along with his state of mind and told him I'd only $600 to my name and after hearing that he left. This was a hectic time in my life and each day that passed brought me closer to the thought that I was on the verge of collapse.*

*Finally I received my pilots license on Friday June 3rd. On the next day I took the bicycle and went riding for a couple of hours. It worked well but I had a very sore butt afterward. I then went to the office and saw Mary and she said, "Congratulations" for my pilots license achievement in a most sarcastic voice and then said; "You mean he didn't flunck you or anything?" She struck me as so vain. At that moment I felt she was the rudest individual I ever met.*

*Ken wanted to celebrate with me so we went to a James Dean movie. 'Rebel with a Cause.' This was a good movie and it got me to thinking about Mary and how she gets my goat up. It is so petty to let others bother you that I wondered why she did that to me. Perhaps within herself is unhappiness and she was taking it out on me. Could it be that my free spirited attitude made her feel envy?*

*On Friday June 10th I flew aboard a DC-9 to Duluth after a three hour flight from Los Angeles to partake in my older sisters wedding. My first impressions of Duluth was one of amazement as to how green everything was. The next day Nancy was married in my parent's back yard and I was honored to be the best man. The grand event was held under blossoming apple trees. We had a wonderful reception and much celebration afterward.*

*I discussed the aspect of my bike tour with all of my relatives as well as with my buddies Kim and Steve. Since we were having our 10th year high school graduation reunion on the third of August, I planned to be back in Duluth after riding the bicycle from California. They thought it was a grand way to kick off the world bike tour and that it was "a pretty wild idea." Little more was said other than good luck. As I flew back to Santa Barbara I felt nobody really believed I was going to go through with this bicycle trip. In many ways the reality was that it seemed a foolhardy idea.*

*On Tuesday I returned to work listening to more negativity from co-workers regarding my bike trips chance for success. Combined with the airlines loosing my baggage, I had a feeling that everything was turning against me while at this critical stage. It was as if the world was melting beneath my feet.*

*On Saturday June 17th I rode the bike to downtown Santa Barbara to watch the annual Summer Solstice parade and rode a total distance of 20 miles, which took me about two hours. On the following day I rode the bike out through Carpinteria and went a little ways up the winding steep road known as Casitas Pass. My kness began to hurt terribly below the knee cap. I had to turn around and go back all the way to Santa Barbara. In all it took 3 hours to go those 30 miles, so I figured ten miles an hour seemed a reliable estimate of how fast a speed I could ride the bike. With that estimate I calculated I could ride 100 miles in ten hours, which would be a good days ride. Since Duluth is about 3000 miles from here I then calculated it would take me 30 days of riding to get there.*

*The following morning of Monday June 20th I could hardly get out of bed because my knees hurt so severely. Strangely enough I tried to forget about the pain and concentrated on what to name my bike. I shall call it FRIEND and at the same time thought of the trips logo which will look like a bicycle above a globe with FRIEND written across it. In addition to my sore knees a little sadness beset me since it was my last night in the Tilton Hilton. This was kind of like losing a close buddy. I'd sold it to a young couple for $875. For nostala I went out on my motorcycle and stopped by all the places that I'd lived at in the trailer. It may seem strange, but I felt so thankful for so many good memories with the Tilton Hilton, that on that last night I played my guitar and drank champagne in the trailer as a final hurrah to this close companion.*

## At Mary's house
## Friday Sept. 9th

I slept well and awoke the morning not knowing of my whereabouts. Once oriented I got up and worked on my bike. I cleaned everything and then lubed it up. The only parts I needed were brake pads. Richard took me too the bank, then to Western Union and a bike shop. For lunch he bought me a huge submarine sandwich and challenged me to eat it. To his amazement, I did.

I had a delicious supper at Mary's of steak and corn. Later we went out to a party where Mary introduced me to Mr. Benson. He told me of his travels and how he was happy to see me doing my thing. He told me, "I'm a loner. I don't think anyone would come to my funeral-especially my friends." The party was a surprise birthday bash for 21 year old Allison. His parents were there and even his old grandma in a bed on wheels. She was delighted at all the events. Then a singing mail-o-gram arrived and this fellow sang some cleverly written lyrics. I met many nice people, ate many goodies including ice cream and cake. I met a German traveler who was hiking America. Later, Mary and I sat in the yard talking and I was massaging her back. I didn't know where I stood with her but I snuck in a kiss or two. In all it was a fun party and a hell of a ride home in a sports car with loud music.

### *The final ten days before the bike trip started*

*On June 21st, I was at work when a most unfortunate instance occurred. I was in a hurry and banged my still hurting knee on the corner of a low desk. The pain shot thru my body and immediately confined me to limp about saying no kind words. A hurt knee must be the prime phobia of all bike riders! What a terrible time to have this happen! It hurt terribly and I could hardly throw my leg over the saddle of the bike, let alone ride.*

*I was planning on sleeping in my car for the last two weeks before departure, however, Ken invited me to sleep in an extra room in his house for the duration of my stay. What a cordial guy he was. People like him are hard to find, but seem to arrive just when the chips are down.*

### To Jones Beach with Mary

After another good nights sleep I awoke to the hot morning of Sat. Sept 10th, with a slight hangover. Mary took me to a store and then we went to the bank and then to Jones Beach on the south shore of Long Island. Zillions of people were on this large beach. The day was hot and sunny and we went swimming. I jumped and frolicked in the ocean even though Mary was irritable. She said she had a headache. I read a book.

### *Final Preparations*

*I started spending money like crazy to prepare for the expedition. It takes a lot of money to go on an adventure and I was beginning to wonder if it was all worth the trouble. On Wednesnday June 22, I spent a couple hundred dollars on accessories for the bike. I was having lots of second thoughts, not so much whether to go, but rather just to beware of all the dangers. So many people were telling me to do this and do that, my mind was in a frenzy. When all this commotion got me down I'd say, "Well tough! I'm just going and that's that!" Otherwise, I think they may have won and I'd never gone. People, I felt, were trying so hard to discourage me from my dream. Of course there were those who'd say; "Go for it!"-namely Terry Cupp, John Ovrebo and Bruce Shimizu. They sensed my desire to do this venture and believed I could do it. But most were reluctant to be so optimistic and they confessed to seeing premonitions of failure along the route.*

*On Thursday June 23rd more new parts were installed on the bike. Namely the cyclometer, the tube savers and a side mirror. I enjoyed a delicious dinner at Kens place and pigged out on some chocolate mousse. It seemed of little concern what I ate because I knew that in a week I'd be burning it all off. After dinner, I went for a walk with his boys up to the top of a hill behind his house. They wanted to race down the hill and so off we ran. I ran hard for a few paces and immediately strained both knees and the pain shot through them such that I was paralyzed with agony and limped back to the house. It kept reoccurring to me how foolhardy such a venture as mine seemed. So much could go wrong because of poor planning and lack of physical preparation. Yet it would be less than honest to admit that I never felt fully prepared about anything. Questions like-what about winter and what about money were among those that people constantly asked. It had me wondering, but still I wanted to go. It was my belief that this was the time for a young man to be out there traveling, free and with adventure awaiting- that's what kept me striving.*

*I was eager to pick up my pannier bags from the Kangaroo Company factory in Ventura and then excitingly mounted the packs on the bike. Then hooked up the generator and tested the lights which worked good. Then I sat back to look at the bike which was neatly arranged with the bags and accessories and now transformed from a lightweight framed weakling to a rugged looking pack horse. I straddled the seat and felt like a soldier fully loaded with battle gear.*

*Later, that evening I had an enlightening night of conversation with Ken and Kitty about living life to it's fullest. At times like these it felt good to believe my life was being lived fully. Yet their kids were laughing and playing ball in the yard, while the sun was setting beautifully, and it was such a homey scene for me that in some ways it was something that I longed for. I now realized it was getting harder to detach myself from all the luxuries and kindness of my friends and to face the rigors of the trail and the hardy lifestyle I'd soon be immersed in.*

## Chinese Food for dinner

That evening Mary's parents invited us out to eat at Panda-Panda's Chinese Restaurant. It was for Noreen and Toms first wedding anniversary. I ate like a king, spicy food, and had several drinks. They accepted me like family. Richard was easy going, cordial, laughed easily and was generous with money. Mary was quiet, but not snotty. Her mother and sister were kind to me. Afterward Mary and I went to Noreen and Toms for a nightcap. All they did was argue. I could see their relationship was hurting. They were not problem solving. They were just arguing and getting nowhere! They talk endlessly about the South Korean 747 jet which was shot down. One minute they'd blame the Russians and the next they'd want to kill them. Then they'd blame the U.S.A. and downgrade this country. There seemed to be plenty to complain about.

## *The Final Five Days*

*On Saturday June 25th I pedaled the bike for 15 miles out to work where I designed a silkscreen T-shirt design using my logo and printed up about a dozen of them. Afterward, Bruce and I went flying above the skies of Santa Barbara and we then went to the Elephant*

*Bar to dance and shake a leg. Later, while dancing at Hobie Bakers I met a young lady named Julie, who I invited over to Ken's house for dinner tomorrow night, but she did not give me a definite answer. So I gave her the address and left it at that.*

*On Sunday the 26th I awoke sleepy eyed and hung over to another overcast morning. Drove out to Browne and printed up T-shirts and got things organized. Lots of things were needed to get ready as I planned to leave on the following Friday. Sometimes I thought it's nuts pushing myself like this. But I wanted so much so to do this trip-it was a dream to me. Maybe, I feel, I'm in a dream- yet it's not all easy going and things don't just fall in my arms, so I know its reality.*

*Around mid afternoon, Ken asked me to help him pick up a picnic table at Stephanie's mothers house. Then he asked me to go to the liquor store to pick up some margarita mix; much to my demise, as I did not want to do any drinking on this day. I had suspicion of something amiss. As I rolled into the driveway of his house there was a whole crowd of people waiting for me, to wish me farewell on my trip.*

*They had a large banner printed 'Good Luck Eric.' How astonished I was! Here was Dave the guy who always said, "the Russians are controlling the weather with cloud ships", and Bruce, the Japanese American carpenter who spoke the coolest southern Cal I've ever heard. There was Jay and his wife as well as Bob and Mary who were smiling like such a cute couple. I saw Sue and Bob, Joe Beth and Joe, Kevin, Stephanie, Terry Smith, Terry and his wife Laurie, Jacob was here and John and of course Dick. All these people were cheering me on-as if in every breath I took I would propel forward, gliding on silver wings. Now more than ever the focus of this whole adventure was coming to me-I was going! And even Julie came by, the gal I met the night before. So I felt like a knight in the days of old or a warrior making way to a battle as if I was guided on my silent mission to the land of enchantment!*

*The following morning I was late to work after last nights grand sending off. I Felt like a champion off to do battle with the men of Robin hoods band. Since this was the beginning of my last week at work, people asked me all kinds of questions. "Does your bike have a good lock?" Do you have enough money?" "It's not too late to change your mind!" All of these questions tended to irk me. I wished people would have more faith in me. It's no wonder they have no faith in themselves. Yet I discovered there were some exceptions because some people were really nice. It was on this day that I sold my motorcycle to a dear old man of 70 years of age. His name was Ernie Burton. Ernie told me many exciting stories of his younger years while out motorcycle traveling and exploring in the Baja. He said, "When you get older all you got is your memories and grandchildren." They were words of wisdom and encouragement to me.*

## September 11th, 1983

In the morning I disassembled and packed up the bike into a box. Mary and I went into New York City on a train. During most of the ride she gazed out the window, sulking in a way like that of a child. Like yesterday, she again said she didn't feel good. The scenes out the window were like a cinema to me. All the traffic, the mass of people, the contrasting buildings. We got off and walked up 5th Avenue. Mary walked fast and I made a comment at which she told me her horoscope was Sagittarius and that makes her impatient and anxious. Oh how I believed it! Yet, even though she walked fast, she was still a nice gal. At times I'd look at her and see her radiant beauty. In some ways she was like a mustang, quick to get mad or excited and always edgy. We went up to Central Park where we chatted with the park ranger and then we laid down on the lawn. I rubbed her aching back and for the moment the mustang was relaxed. We walked to the subway, then took a ride up to the top of the Empire State Building. It was an eagles nest view of this enormous city under a splendid sunset. We stopped at a bookstore for film and the checkout guy was very interested in my adventure. He said I should be on television. We again took the train home and I told Mary I would help her out in any way I could if our paths crossed. Said she would like to someday go coast to coast on a bicycle. Perhaps I inspired her.

### *A newspaper interview days before my start*

*The next day I called the Santa Barbara News Press and asked them if they would be interested in talking with me about my proposed world trip. They called me immediately and I met with a reporter and he wrote down my story. I Went to the News Press and they took a photo of me and my bike.*

*That evening I had a date with Ellen and so I brought her a FRIEND T-shirt and some roses. We went to the Timbers restaurant to eat supper and then stopped by to visit John and his new born child. We then went to the movie; "War Games," which was about a young man who bugs the Pentagons head computer and starts a war with the U.S.S.R. It was a scary possibility to think of happening and afterwards I talked to Ellen about how strange it is that we Americans have considered the Soviets our enemy when most of us have never even met one. I felt sure that if we could get to know them and they could know us we'd find out how much alike we really are. I theorized on how important I believe it is that we look at ourselves as world citizens. She listened and participated in the discussion and I realized how good she is to me. She's such a respectable young lady, with her blue eyes sparkling, and her soft murmuring voice changing from stern to sensitive. As we sat in my car in front of her house it was hard to say goodbye to her. I told her I realized our paths were going in different directions but that she was dear to me. I said goodbye and was sad when I drove back to Ken's house yet still I felt fortunate to have such a good friend as she.*

*A dream had occurred that night which startled me. I dreamed of riding my bicycle down the hill from my parents house while saying goodbye to them and to all the neighbors. I called out, "Goodbye Duluth, goodbye." It was a very sad and scary feeling, as if stepping into the unknown. I awoke alarmed and questioning this coming venture.*

## The Final Night at Mary's

Back at her house, Uncle Matty was waiting impatiently for us. "I thought you were going to have everything packed up and ready to go?" he confrontingly said to me. I apologized for not doing so and packed some more, but it was tough to get everything into the box. We ate supper, I did laundry and then around 9 p.m. sat next to Mary and watched Neil Young on TV. It was an extremely hot and humid evening, but we sat close together and had sultry eyes for the passing moment. We exchanged subtle relations, a touch, a hug but it was only slight. How I wanted to hold her and love her but the circumstance was not right. She went to bed and I took a cool shower and pondered the passing passion, then realized how I cherished her friendship more than anything. Even still I went to bed at 1am-wishing.

### *The final days at Browne*

*On Wednesday morning at work I had the feeling that things were really winding down for me. Mary assigned me generally easy jobs and I'd spend more time talking to people. Even Doug Beverly, the company president stopped by to talk to me and wished me well. There were more questions from some, while others almost implied that I was not seriously going to do this. It seemed as though some people couldn't get it into their head that I was going on this adventure! What made things hard was that Mary was a bitch all day. She bitched at John over a 15 minute phone call he made to his wife. Yet, Mary could sit and talk to her boyfriend, housemate, lover all damn day. I was convinced the woman was the most two faced, insecure lost soul I'd yet met. I drowned myself in Bob Dylan music to escape her assault. It was a relief when the workday ended. I dropped the bike off at Murdochs to have it adjusted and then purchased a pair of hiking boots and packed my clothing and equipment into plastic bags. After organizing my things I went flying with Ken.*

*The morning of Thursday June 30th dawned with the sun shining and while driving the coast highway to work the sunlight sparkled upon a curling surf. I felt excited and yet scared, but happy to be going for it. An adventure was approaching and I could feel it. With this being my last day at work I couldn't help but think about all the great people I'd met at MCT/ BROWNE and how good they'd been to me. During this last day our crew went out to lunch where I learned that Terry Cupp would be moving to San Francisco to be a truck driver. I was late returning back from lunch because of having to pick up travelers checks. I said many goodbyes to everyone. Some were envious of what I was doing while others were happy to see me do it. At times it felt as if I was standing on a pedestal. People would look at me with such concern and admiration.*

*With only one hour left at work several people came in and wanted to buy my paintings. I was convinced they must have conspired to do this as in a short time I sold the painting of Viel Falls in Yosemite to John for $60 and Mary bought the one of Half Dome for $90. Then Kenny paid me $70 for a painting of the Sierra mountains. I only had one painting left and so I gave that painting of Yosemite Falls to Jo Beth for taking care of my car. I then said a final farewell to friends and drove off from the company, leaving that fond episode to memory.*

## Leaving New York Day
## Monday Sept. 12

I didn't even recall falling asleep when the alarm buzzed me awake at 5 a.m. I showered and Liz awoke me with a cheerful, "Good morning." Mary came by and smiled as I packed the bike and baggage into Uncle Matty's car. Things happened fast. It was time to go. I found it hard to say goodbye to this fantastic family. Mary and I embraced and then we kissed with swelled eyes. We were off. Along the way we stopped by for a donut and juice. Traffic was agonizingly slow in the tunnel. I arrived at the airport about 7:30 and gave my thanks to Matt.

There was time to sit down and write postcards, then call the bank in Santa Barbara and negotiate to have mom and dad sent a check for $3200. When I called mom and dad, dad got real uptight about my money situation. He said, "Don't ask me to send money that way ever again. Never!!" He then told me it cost $70.00 to send the check my way, via Western Union.

I walked over to a gas station to ask where the post office was and they would not talk to me. So back near the terminal, I went up the steps to Air Mail and was waved away. I waited till the guy turned his back and walked into the place and told a fellow about my journey. The postman got such a kick out of it that he asked all of his buddies to come over and shake my hand for having ridden across the U.S.A on a bicycle. They teamed together to help me package up and send off my parcel even though it needed to be brought to the post office.

### *The final night of June 30th, 1983*

*I picked up my bicycle from Murdochs after work and along the way dropped off my guitar at Ellen's house. From there I went to get a haircut as well a few last minute items. As the night was getting late I packed up everything into the panniers and set the bike into the garage with everything fully loaded and ready to go. The night had such a mystical quality and yet I felt it to be a sullen occasion, scary at one moment and yet magical and nervous at the next. I went inside the house and noticed a yellow light shining from a Victorian lamp in the living room. It had such a home bound beauty that I dreaded the thought of not being near it after I'd left. My feet squeaked across the wooden floor and I snuck my way to bed as Ken was drunk and he was fighting with Kitti. I crawled into bed and laid back to listen. I could hardly sleep. So many things had happened today, so many things had happened in the last month that my mind spun out of control when I thought that it was just the beginning of this new epic. I looked forward to getting on with the journey, for then I would be of a single purpose. I felt so anxious for the night to end and I thought my brain would never stop thinking about everything over again and again that even my little prayer whispered in that bed in the corner bedroom of that house become lost as sleep ushered in its peace.*

## The final night in U.S.A. and waiting for the plane ride to England

Back in the terminal, I sat down and wrote a letter to the American Diabetes Association informing them about my travels and that I wanted to bring an awareness to my fathers struggles as a diabetic.

I took care of my tickets, showered, got a little stoned and was ready for the evening's flight. How exciting it was to see the big beautiful 747! Then we slowly boarded until every seat was occupied. It began to rain outside then it poured. The massive plane took off at 8pm and what an exciting lift off it was. The flight would be complete with food and movies on board.

# Chapter 3

# GREAT BRITAIN TOURING

**Tuesday Sept.13th**

I slept a little on the plane as we flew into sunlight on the morning. It was an economy flight, on People Express Airlines, yet, it had all the luxury of any flight I'd been on. There were movies, music and food served. It was a great deal. Seated next to me was Gillis, a young lad from London, who had stayed in the states for three months as a camp counselor. I asked him, "What's the first thing your going to do when you get home?" He replied, "Have a cup of tea."

The 747's wingtips descended through a dreary overcast and we saw England's landscape below as a pretty plaid checkerboard design that was a patchwork of greens. I had a strange feeling of fear for this foreign land, of the difficulties in cycling there and almost wished to go back home. But it disappeared as soon as we were on the ground at Gatwick International Airport, at about 8 a.m. London Time.

Once in the airport, I waited in line for a long time to have my passport checked. Afterward, I met another cyclist named Jerry at an area where we spent time putting our bikes together. Unfortunately a few bike parts were broken during the flight, but I repaired them with the help of wire.

We rode off on the crazy streets, which seemed backwards by my standards, as the traffic goes the opposite direction and it was stuffed with tiny, little cars. Yet there was a demeanor of properness, as we were meeting good, polite people.

At the bakery I ordered a roll which looked like a Danish but when I bit into it was surprised to find a spicy sausage inside. It was awful!

The people observed on that first ride seemed genuine and humble along the roadside and in the shops. Soon the rain was coming down heavily and it was quite cold compared to the previous day's heat in New York City, but I preferred the cold to the heat.

While we cycled along on a country road, we met a man walking along who was quite happy to meet us, "American chaps," as he called us. After a nice conversation, this elderly gentleman then said, "Have a bloody good time in England, after all, we are allies."

We stopped by a roadside veggie stand and bought some inexpensive food to cook for supper. We then pedaled down the road a little farther and stopped at the butcher, but he was closed, though when he saw us look in, he very politely opened the door just for us.

After buying some meat, we went to a youth hostel where I met John, who had cycled across Europe with many tales to tell. I also met Sally and Ann while eating my delicious dinner and had a very nice talk with these two Great Britain beauties. We compared our countries similarities and were amused at what we call M&M's, they call smarties, what we call french fries they call chips. What we call potato chips they call crisps. Cookies are called biscuits. We laughed and they seemed to be as interested in me as I was in them.

## Wednesday Sept 14th

This morning found me in a bunk bed in a room with many snoring men. I cooked breakfast and had to get going, but first I had to ask the innkeeper what my 'chores' were before being allowed to go. He said, "Let's see, Mr. Norland, you will be assigned to sweeping the floor." It took me awhile, as junk was here and there, I felt impatient, but finished the task and once that was done I headed out on the bike along nice country roads.

Under partly sunny skies, the air was fresh and the people were jolly.

As I neared London the traffic became very heavy, and I had many close calls. It was so troublesome to quickly learn how to ride on the left side of the road. In addition, I seemed to have a balance problem, and often swayed or stumbled.

*My thoughts drifted to my childhood days, when our mailman named Red was talking to a neighbor I overheard him say, "I can't wait to get six feet under the ground and have peace." It struck me-isn't that the way Americans live-they want to hurry up through life and and then look forward to die?*

The English people seemed slower, especially the country folks, and appeared to be enjoying life. I stopped to look at my map and immediately a man in a car stopped to help me with my maps and said he too was a cyclist. "I'm a member of the C.V.C.V.P.," he said very proudly. Whatever that was. He gave me directions and then I was off.

I stopped at Hampton Castle and toured the gardens and saw a beautiful mural on the wall called Apollo and Diana. I pedaled over colorful bridges crossing the Thames River and stopped at Tate Art Gallery to behold the artworks of many masters. There was Picasso, Cezanne, Monet, Manet and Van Gogh paintings to stand close to and examine. All of the works I had studied in art history were here. They must have written the textbooks which I studied from this place. I loved the portraits of beautiful women, in addition to "Deluge," and Turners watercolors.

My exploration of London continued passing Trafalgar Square, Westminster Abbey and seeing Big Ben, under reconstruction, and the Parliament Building. I hurriedly tried to get to Hostel Head Museum but got lost, therefore making it there too late. However, a man in the store helped me by giving me the business hours schedule.

I saw marvelous statues and beautiful buildings everywhere, while noticing London people seemed less friendly and were definitely faster drivers than those in the Suburbs.

I called Jennifer, whom I'd met in New York and she was happy I called, but said I couldn't stop by her place because she had a guest over. I called the youth hostel and reserved a bed for the night. I stopped at a grocery store and then cooked supper at the hostel where I met two girls from the U.S. and also a nice gal from Australia. Everyone was greatly concerned about getting ripped off, as stories abounded about that kind of shit happening here. It seemed a thief lurked within the hostel, so I slept with my purse at my side.

**Thursday Sept 15th**
I awoke at 7 a.m. in the bunk of the hostel and was not allowed to leave until completion of my 'chore'. This time I was appointed to kitchen duty, that is to clean the kitchen. It started as a major task of picking up dirty dishes and pots and washing them up, then drying them and putting them away. (I badly wanted to get going). I then had to tidy up the stove, the fridge and the floor. (all the while fuming at the thought that I paid to stay here, so why do I have to work?) But in half an hour I finished the task.

I purchased a Youth Hostel Card and then rode into London and bought Mary, back in New York, some chocolate sweets, which were then mailed back to her, as she asked me to do and I did with great love for her.

While at Buckingham Palace, I saw the changing of the guard and then watched them start marching down the wide street. There was an orchestra walking with them and also a few military men marched in unison. I followed close behind this procession on my fully loaded bike. What a joy it was to feel as if in the parade, waving and acting pompous to the many people lining the streets. There were a few 'rowdies' in the crowd who heckled me.

My travel around London was slow because of rain showers and heavy traffic. I stopped in Blackwater, found a grocery store and noticed beautiful girls. People here seemed nice and they were driving fancy cars.

I met a local fellow riding a bike down the road. He told me of a park I might want to sleep in for the night. So I went to Hyde Park and saw small crowds gathered around many speakers, each standing atop a heightened step, giving messages of either politics, humor or religion. The park was well kept with clumps of bushes here and there. I asked one fellow about sleeping in the park. He told me, "If the bobbies catch you they will move you on. If a beggar catches you sleeping in his bush he'll beat you up." I decided against sleeping in the park.

Reluctantly returning back to the hostel, I cooked a meal of potatoes and meatballs. I sat to eat my meal and met Jeff, a very jolly Welshman who was also wealthy and successful. I told him Americans seemed to be moving at a faster pace than the British and he agreed. We talked about success in life and he said, "Happiness is a whim of the heart that turns into reality." We talked philosophically while having a cup of tea and watching the moonrise over the city of London. He told me, "A coffin has no pockets, and a rich man is a priceless commodity." After our enjoyable conversation I went to bed and snuggled into my warm sleeping bag, happy to have met a wonderful person.

## Friday Sept 16th

Cars noisily kept racing around the parking lot throughout the night and I awoke often. Morning rain showers greeted me. I packed up, did my chore, which was to carry out the trash, and then hit the road as it rained hard and there was a cold wind. The traffic was horrible. These were busy small roads, and they drove fast. There was not always much of a shoulder to ride upon. Because of the strong headwinds, I would have to hold the handlebars with all my might each time a truck passed, as there blast of wind would sometimes knock me down. Trucks would not move over much, so I started to swerve in front of them to get there attention, and give me some room. By noon I was only 30 miles down the road. The rain finally slowed and then the winds picked up. They were so strong that I had to use my lowest gear to ride on a level plain.

I struggled against this gale, feeling frustration and impatience, but was making headway on the road to Stonehenge. On one uphill the wind was so strong that it stopped my bike and then knocked me down. Finally I began crossing Salisbury Plain and fought the wind, making the arrival all the more worthwhile when I stopped at the site of the megaliths erected in a circle.

This is a most interesting place. These huge rectangles of rock were supposedly first constructed in 2500 B.C. and the construction took 100 years to complete. That meant two or three generations of builders worked consistently to complete this task. It must have taken thousands of people to do this. They built Stonehenge on the edge of a plain, which makes it quite stunning and immediately draws attention. How and why was it built? Mysteries abound and questions arise because of its strange configuration. More than likely it was made to note the alignment of the sun at the equinox and solstice's and also as a place to worship the heavens. The massive rock shapes were very solid and one wondered how they were chiseled. It was said they were dragged all the way here from the area of Bath, about 40 miles away. There were ropes everywhere to keep spectators on paths and away from the structure. The grounds were very uneven, with treacherous holes here and there. I was excited to take a few photos, but unfortunately my camera stopped working while there. The rain fell hard, and I was soaking wet and cold, therefore after several walks around the construction had to leave.

I rode on to the town of Orchestration and found a nice little store to buy food goods. My next stop was at a campground called The Crown Inn. There was an apple tree which looked fake, but was real. It was loaded with the most delicious looking red apples. I wondered why nobody took any, and could not resist plucking a few into my pack. They were solid apples, which required chewing, but were delicious.

I went into a pub on this chilly afternoon to warm my cold body. In there, I met Andy McKickin and his gal Julie. They were newlyweds. He's Scottish and she's English. We talked alot about the U.S.A. and Great Britain, especially about the military might of our countries and past wars. We came to agree religion causes many wars, and it doesn't matter who the individuals are, whether they are holy or not they will fight over religion. We talked of the American Indian. They were more sympathetic, knowledgeable and understanding of them than most Americans are. As the sun set, an amber hue settled onto the countryside and was so pretty. We drank bitters beer and talked about life much the same as those who had lived here thousands of years ago.

## Saturday Sept. 17th

On the sunny but cool morning. I was heading west on the road to Bath and rode past a military operations area. There were all kinds of bunkers, tank courses and foxholes set up for mock combat. I saw where a tank had crossed the road and had run over a blue wool commando sweater. I thought it might be only a rag. It was stuck in the mud, soaking wet and dirty, but I pulled it out and laid it over the back of the bike.

It was a nice ride on a brilliant, sunny, but cool morning, enjoying many small towns with their red brickwork. The road cut right through these towns like a trail through the forest. I pedaled into the historic town of Bath at noon. It's been well known since Roman times for natural hot springs gurgling from the hills. I cycled those hills and again observed the rhythm of old style brick buildings. With my camera not working, I stopping into a camera shop and tried to trade in my camera. However, because the damn thing wouldn't work, they wouldn't give me a nickel for it.

Now, I needed to find a camera repair shop. I rode on to Bristol, and got turned around looking for the road to cross over the Severn River Bridge. I asked a paper delivery man how to get on the bridge and he kept saying, "Here's what you do." Then he'd talk about when he was in the British Navy and how he sailed the Great Lakes. Then he'd say again, "Here's what you do," pointing to my map. Then he'd carry on saying, "I would have had a better time if I hadn't drank so much bloody American beer." Finally he said, "Here's what you do," and he pointed me on my way.

I started across the bridge and the crosswind made for extremely difficult cycling. Half way over the long bridge I was drained of strength and the bike was leaning from this terrible crosswind and it was very hard to pedal. I feared being blown into the river. Finally I made it to the Wales side of the bridge, after a great fight and wolfed down some chocolate.

I made my way to Titern. *Along this ride I was thinking about when I was a boy and how I saw a movie called, 'A boy 10 feet tall,' and how it influenced me. That lad was very adventurous. Then there was a Saturday morning children's cartoon called Johhny Quest, whom I loved watching and his exciting escapades in foreign lands.*

I felt like the flu or a cold was coming on, dizzy and chills, yet I was still moving forward and with joy. People were very nice and the food was wholesome and good. It was fun to look in the shops. I camped in a dark woods on a tree covered hill, near a sharp curve in the road. Kind of creepy, but I was to tired to care.

## Sunday Sept. 18th

It had rained all night and was a very wet morning. I felt better after a good nights rest and coasted down into the Weyth River Valley, which was beautiful with its lush vegetation. There were round hills with nice straw-topped cottages and stone walls with hedgerows. Many nice churches were in this town. I stopped for a Coke and purchased a locally made sweet pastry bar. I regretted not going back for more. A picnic table was used at the Inn to cook eggs and to eat. The sun came out, it warmed up and the scenery was breathtaking. Everything here was so refined and not messy. I detected the people's pride and love for this countryside. I dried my gear out at a roadside Inn while the sun was still shining. People walked past me and snickered at my mess of drying camping equipment.

With my shirt off, I carried on through many nice small towns occasionally stopping at shops to pick up goods for supper. The wind was at my back and these were fun roads for pedaling. I enjoyed seeing castles along the road and listening to the people speak in their unique Welsh dialect, which I confused for Irish.

I stopped into a police station at Craven Arms and asked a bobby for directions to a caravan, (campsite). He asked where I was from. He looked on my map and pointed out Peddlers Rest. He said, "Right at the "P" on Peddlers there's a campsite, only it's called Travelers Rest." I thanked him and he said, "Cheerio." The day was a rather lonely day for me and I wished for a companion, especially for a woman. I found Travelers Rest Inn and went inside and asked the publican how much he charged for my camping there. He said, "Come in and have a drink this evening, that's all." I picked out a campsite and cooked pork sausage, sprouts, potatoes and macaroni, in addition to munching on a few handfuls of malt.

The wind was blowing hard when I stopped into the pub and had a brew. The bartender bought me one and said, "This outa help your cycling tomorrow." They were big glasses! Inside were jolly people speaking Welsh and English, well dressed and nicely mannered. When heading out for my tent I was more tired than drunk under a beautiful moonlit night.

## Monday Sept. 19th

I started the day off spinning down a busy truck-filled road. I exited and pedaled a quieter side road into Church Stretton on a beautiful morning. This was a pretty town and I especially noticed pretty girls at the street corners. I made good time with the assistance of a strong tail wind and arrived in Shrewsbury at 9:30. There I stopped at a photo shop but had no luck repairing my camera. I found another shop and they gave me an address in Liverpool where I could have the camera fixed. As I was leaving a customer asked me, "Do you need any help?" I told him my situation and he led me with his bike to a camera shop. They looked my camera over, but said they did not have the expertise and therefore called a repairman in Hanley, which is 35 miles away. I thanked them and was on my way to Hanley. It was beyond Newcastle under Lyme. In all a nice ride of approximately two and a half hours. The rain started falling, yet it was warm out as I went up and down gentle rolling hills and across plains. I kept anticipating the outrageous bill I might get to repair the camera.

Once in Hanley I asked a gal for directions, she could not tell me. I've discovered women are lousy at directions. I asked a fellow and he said, "One street down and go upstairs mid block." I walked up the narrow steps to the repair shop. The owner, Peter took the camera and said, "Come in have a seat. Care for some coffee?" I said, "Sure." He had the camera apart in no time and asked me many questions about it. Then another fellow came in and he got to work on the camera. We then talked about England, its castles, roads, traffic and etc. They gave me a delicious biscuit, which was chocolate over a graham cracker. We talked about Englands lack of supermarkets. He said, "It sounds cold to have so many of them like in America."

Soon he had the camera working. "It was full of corrosion," said the repairman. I became the spotlight, telling stories of my travels and they laughed when I said, "I've been eating like two starved hogs." When it came to paying the bill, Peter said, "There's no charge for anything, just have a grand time in England." I tipped him two pounds anyway and said farewell. Before heading out of town I stopped at a bike shop.

Later I was almost clipped off the road by a crazy van. I stopped at a roadside and asked an inspector for directions to a park. He told me of one and I then stopped by Queens Park in Crewe. It was a nice park with lots of flowers and a pond. Young kids came around and talked to me. They were wonderful, polite and jolly children. An elderly woman came and talked to me. She said, "Eeyou'll hav tah leave befoore the auld caretakah comes else eell shoo yah off." She left and just then he showed up. He ordered me to leave. I explained my situation as my supper was cooking. A gust of wind picked up and blew my box of macaroni all over the table and upon the ground. He got disgusted, pointed his finger at me and said, "Be gone by the time I come back." He certainly was an abrupt old timer. I quickly ate a great dinner but hadn't finished before he came back. As he approached I said, "Thanks for letting me finish my dinner." This time he was much kinder to me. He told me in an slight accent, "This here park was donated by the railroad over 100 years ago. I'm 73, retired when I was 65 and my philosophy is; gotta keep busy," at which he cracked a smile. He then added, "The kids keep me running-Cheerio," he said. I left and stopped by a public bath for 65 P and also cleaned my clothes and bike. Later, in the night I returned and pitched the tent.

## Tuesday Sept 20th

It was a cool night with a heavy dew on the morning. I did my typical morning routine: contacts popped in, wiggle out of the sleeping bag, shiver from the cold, then put clothes on quick. Then I stuff everything into plastic bags, take down the tent and place everything in its respective place on the bike.

I followed nice country roads to Beeston Castle. It was made in 1200 AD as a fortress to fight the Welsh. Seems as if they and the English were fighting a great deal. From the top of this high hill, was a good view of the checkerboard landscape. One of the things about this fortress, which interested me, was that they had a hand dug well which went down 300 feet.

I stopped in Chester and browsed the shops as well as old Roman memorials, an amphitheater and a wall. Clicking photos here and there, it was nice to have my camera working again. An excited security guard told me all about the proposed Castle of Chester that was never funded. I toured a local museum and learned that the Romans lived here in the 1st century AD.

It rained heavily while I pedaled in to Liverpool. On a busy street, under a rainy sky, I stopped to read my map at the roadside. The thought came to me-wouldn't it be nice if a gal would come by and invite me in for a hot cup of tea.

Just then a motorcycle pulled up and a full face helmet looked me in the face and asked me if I needed help. The face shield flipped up and I saw a fellows face and not a gals. He gave me directions and while doing so we talked and he told me he had been in the states the previous year. Gary was his name. He said, "Why don't you come stay at my house?" I was overjoyed. We went to a store, where I bought food and then went to his house. I met his "Mum" and she cooked us sweet and sour pork. It was very delicious. Gary invited me to come down to the gym, where I took a shower. I then went to his house and met a nice couple who came by to visit. She, Julie, was a very pleasant looking gal and very sociable. Her fiance Jim, was well mannered and was a skipper in the shipping industry. I met Gary's dad whose name was Eric. He was a very nice, smiling fellow. At first he was quiet, but he made me feel very welcome. We all talked up a storm. After a while they turned to me and seemed delighted to hear of my follies. When I was quiet, they enjoyed telling stories about people they knew. Not bad talk, nor gossip, but points of interest and positive commentary with humor. We stayed up until 12:30, then it was time to have a cup of tea and cookies before bed. I slept on the living room floor upon a mattress.

## Wednesday Sept. 21

It was a cold, windy and rainy morning. I was up at 8:30 and was glad to not be outside cycling. Gary's mom made us breakfast of cereal and bacon sandwiches. Gary and I went out sightseeing on his motorbike. We stopped at a huge Cathedral that was made in 1902. It was made of red sandstone and had very expensive and large stained glass windows. The building obtained some bomb damage from the Nazi's aerial bombing during WWII. Liverpool was a target since it was and still is a large shipping port with 20 miles of docks. Gary and I stopped in downtown

Liverpool and walked to the site where the Beatles started off in a club called the Cavern. Above the doorway I saw a memento to the Beatles, it was a statue of the virgin Mary with a sign which read, "Four lads who shook the world."

We then went to Penny Lane and to Strawberry Fields, a park whose name John Lennon wrote a song about. We went to a Roman catholic cathedral that Pope John Paul visited in 1982. It looked like a Gemini spacecraft and had a large, spacious interior. I thought of it not as a house of god but as a true display of wealth. Inside there was a nice painting of the Popes visit. We then went to Spekes Hall, an 18th century tudor mansion. Our personal tour guide was a 63 year old fellow who knew history like his own taste buds. He told us a story of the Child of Hale and of Queen Victoria. He could really give a good impression of what it was like to be living in that era. When the guide heard about my journey he asked me many questions and said he was delighted to hear of my mode of travel.

Back at Gary's house we pigged out on chips and goodies. Then I cleaned my bike up and we ate supper. Gray's father, Eric and I had a great talk about the U.S. and the world. We talked about racism. He's in tune to the need for a new direction. "To be open with all races and religions," he said. We rode in his car and it was the first time I'd ever been in a car with the steering wheel on the right side, and picked up Gary at Judo practice and drove to a pub called The Country Corner Inn. They bought me two pints of Bitter beer, which is a dark, rich beer served at room temperature. We all talked up a storm and had a lively conversation. Each of us had a shot of Drambuie and then wowwy my head was zinging. We stayed until they closed the bar at 10:30 and then went to a cafe and purchased some Chinese take away food. Back at the house we stayed up until midnight. I gave my thanks to all and said goodbye to Eric as he would be off to work very early.

## Thursday Sept 22nd

I awoke at 7 a.m. and ate breakfast on the nice looking day. I said my good-byes to 'mum' and to Stewart. Then Gary escorted me on his motorcycle as I pedaled my way through a maze of streets to get out of town. We made it to the outskirts about five miles and then stopped to take some photos. Gary said, "Who knows, maybe we'll meet again." It was hard to go. He was such a good person. He seemed choked up as I left after a long, firm handshake. I rode away, waving.

It was a nice day, a good day for riding. I headed north along a beautiful highway toward the town of Lancaster. At about 3pm I saw up ahead, a gal riding a bike and pulled up to her to say hi. We talked a bit and after an informal introduction I thought she gave me the nose, so I passed her by. Farther up the road, I pulled over for a snack. And as she approached I asked her, "Care to go around the world with me?" She said, "Ya! Alrighty." She stopped to catch her breath and we then went to a cafe for a cup of tea. I had orange juice like a true American! We talked a lot. Her name was Jane Elizabeth B. and she looked much like my former fellow employee, Mary. While we sat at a table having a good conversation, a fat elderly lady came over and chatted with us. She was a sweet tubby who said she was out shopping for her son and had bought him a "21 pound pen." Whatever that is. She then said, "Are you together? You look like such a sweet couple," at which we both laughed.

We went to Jane's apartment in a small village outside of Lancaster called Castle. Jane invited me over to her place for the night. How my thoughts raced at the excitement of an evening with her. We stopped at a grocery store and I bought my usual concoction of foodstuffs only more quantity. While in the store I started racing around with the shopping cart and acting silly. We went to her place and cooked a big meal. I took a hot bath and then played the guitar. We sipped on Bentinia, an Icelandic schnapps and then sat by the fireplace while I gave her a back rub. For but a moment the air was filled with erotic potential and then she abruptly said, "No, we can't do this." We were to be only friends and so it was off to bed with a cold cooker. The bed was very nice and comfortable but I had the weirdest dreams all night long.

### Friday Sept 23rd

Jane was very kind to me. She prepared a nice breakfast of crumpets and juice on the morning of We hugged and I left her apartment and rode off waving back at her while she stood outside watching my departure until I was out of sight. It was a warm day, very sunny and with a good tailwind. I stopped in a small town for some bakery and continued northward at a good pace.

At the exit for Windermere the terrain changed. The hills were yellow dry with stone walls crossing everywhere, but then changed again at Lake District, where a clear blue lake is surrounded with lovely pine covered hills. It was exciting cycling even though it was tiring from the hills. I stopped by the lake and threw some ducks a cookie. Before long I had 50 more of them, some even feeding from my hand. Further down the road, I stopped and harassed some fenced in bulls. These big fellows became very irritated and I made all kinds of trouble for them. Suddenly a rider on a horse came barreling along and shouted at me, so I pedaled off. The rider pushed his steed hard to catch me, but I poured on the coal. I imagined being chased by a Black Knight with a long lance. I cut corners, pedaled hard and flew down country roads to finally escape him.

Safe from my pursuer, I tackled steep hills up to Troutbeck which is made up of golden hills and a rugged, rocky countryside. There were sheep crossing the road. As I rose to the top of a hill I heard hounds barking and braying.

On an overlook, there were men looking with binoculars, wearing Sherlock Holmes style of clothing, leaning against stone walls and others standing. I looked off in the distance and saw that a foxhound hunt was on! The hounds dashed across terrain that was so rough and hilly it was amazing to see their fast pace. Up and over rock ledges and briars they went. I could see the fox outsmart them and dart away up over a ridge and soon the hounds had lost the scent and brayed as if they were crying.

I climbed up a steep, snaking blacktop road to Kreakstone Pass. There was not a cloud in the sky. A weathered looking fellow said to me, "Where you from?" I responded, "Southern California." He said, "Aye, your used to this heat ah?" I replied, "You betcha," He was right, it was hot and dry out. Then I went down the back side of this mountain on a steep slope with a 20% grade. I had to use my brakes constantly. The wheels got hot. The road twisted and dropped, threatening to send me over its edge. I maneuvered and leaned like a road racer until finally reaching level ground. I rode along at a good clip, making it into Carlisle at 5:3pm and sat near a old Roman gateway to eat before camping that night in the city park.

## Saturday Sept 24th

Being that I was low on money, I hung around town to wait for the banks to open. At 9:30am I took care of my finances and then rode out past Hadrian's Wall to see the fragmented layers of blocks that Romans had constructed nearly two thousand years ago. I broke a spoke near a bus stop. The wheel went out of true, making the bike unrideable. It rained and turned cold. It took me a half hour to repair the problem.

With half the day gone I'd only traveled five miles. I searched around the shops for a map of Scotland in Gretna, then entered Scotland and arrived in Dumfries at 4:30pm. I asked around for a clothing shop as I was looking for a raincoat made of Gortex. I found them much to expensive and had wasted even more time. I then headed for a campground but it cost f2.50 so I cooked dinner at a picnic table and then traveled nice country roads at dusk. I teased a bull and was thrilled watching it get pissed off. Further along, a fellow on the roadside said, "Hi yank!" I don't know how he knew I was an American. It was dark when I found a school in the town of Altrieiz with a grass-covered yard. I set up my tent and got inside while seeing my breath flare out toward a nice moon. Suddenly a kid came by my tent and stuck his head in the flap. Without him seeing me, I said, "Hi" and he jolted back and screamed aloud, "Yah gave me a fright!"

**Sunday Sept. 25th**

It was a cold morning. For the first time I pulled on the commando sweater and was thankful I'd found it. I put on a sweatshirt, jacket and winter gloves. Even while pedaling I still had cold hands and feet. My appetite was incredible as for breakfast I ate half of a large rhubarb pie, a full quart of juice and stopped for an ice cream cone. I noticed people in Scotland had a different way of gesturing hello. Rather than nod their head up or down like Americans or the English, here they twist they're head to the side like we do when we say, "Oh my god?" I tried to do it back to them but hadn't yet mastered it. People were hard to understand as they speak quickly and cram words together.

Just before lunch I passed a tractor on the inside and nearly got clipped by his big tires when he pulled over. For lunch, I ate a peanut butter sandwich, a jelly roll, five cookies and two dinner rolls. While pedaling along the country roads I saw many delicious black berries and so stopped and picked a bagful. I arrived in Kilmarnock and called mom and dad. It was amazing how good our connection was. They sounded sleepy, dad especially. Mom was very interested in my journey but dad was not. He did not say much to me. I wasn't too happy after our talk and wondered why dad was like that.

With the cool weather I found it necessary to stop occasionally and rub my hands for warmth. At one stop I talked to a nice Scottish couple on the roadside. They told me what to expect on the road ahead. I coasted down some excellent hills into the city of Glasgow. While riding along a busy city street I saw an old woman stumble and fall upon the sidewalk. I stopped and quickly picked her up. "My glasses came off-can you find them?" she asked me while I held her up. I reached over and picked them up and handed them to her. I brushed her off and she had a small cut on her chin, but seemed all right though shaken. She said to me many times, "Your a very kind lad, thank you so much, thank you, thank you so very much."

Behind the city of Glasgow I could see the mountains. I looked around town for a gortex jacket but the shops were closed. I rode across a big bridge and then began the long ascent up into those mountains. At the south end of Loc Lomond I found a picnic site near the lake and complete with facilities. For supper I prepared a huge concoction of spaghetti with cabbage, green peppers, eggs, pastry and berries for dessert. I also drank one quart of milk, ate one cookie, several handfulls of nuts and was afterward still somewhat hungry.

## Monday Sept. 26th

I had a damp evening, got up early, ate some breakfast and rode up along the side of Loc Lomond on the drizzly morning of. I bought a fruit pie at the store. It was made from raisins. I ate half of it, while thinking, "My god, I'm the incredible eating machine." I stopped at a wayside to enjoy the view of the Loc and a big tour bus drove up. Amongst the many passengers, I met a man from Santa Barbara. Amazingly enough, he had read the newspaper article written about me back in June. He said he would much rather travel my way than by sitting, "In that darned bus." We shook hands and I took off. I felt great after that. Somehow my suffering was worth it. I sang out and thought promisingly of my journey.

The euphoria was short lived as soon I was tackling large hills, up and down, up, then down and it started to rain. I crossed the spacious Scottish Highlands and saw wild rams running about. While stopped for lunch in Turntou the sky started to brighten. Then I had to go up an agonizingly steep grade against strong headwinds and more pelting rain. While crossing the flats I was tossed down on the road by strong crosswinds and headwinds. Many times I'd loose control and have to lay the bike down. The wind would send waves across the golden grasses and I could see them coming so would brace myself and duck down to take the blow. The sun popped out briefly and oh how wonderful were the rainbows and the beauty of the surrounding cliffs.

I met two Frenchmen cycling and we spoke little english, but communicated our camaraderie. Finally it was downhill into Glen Coe. The wind was so strong that I had to use the lowest gear and pedal like mad just to go down a steep hill! I crossed Glencoe Bridge and was so tired that I had to rest. There were blueberries, they call them brambles, along the roadside and I picked a handful, then rode into Fort William at 5:30pm, just as the shops were closing. With some food, I pedaled hard to the youth hostel at Glen Nevis. It was a welcome sight on this cold, wet day. I showered and was extremely tired but cooked myself an excellent large dinner. I met two Aussies who informed me that America had lost the cup race to Australia. I also enjoyed a nice visit with a gal who had been to Poland and told me about her experience. Bedtime was at 11:30pm.

## Tuesday Sept. 27th

I slept in late, until 8 a.m., and did my disgusting chore of shaking out rugs before riding off in the rain. A mile down the road I stopped by a shop and bought some pastries. It seems I just cant get full as I would eat like a horse. I loved to eat pastries and sweets as they satisfied my hunger. I pedaled merrily along the shore of Loch Lochy and it started to clear a little. The Loch was pretty and had the look of a fiord.

I crossed a hill or two and arrived at Loch Ness and pulled over for a bite to eat and to drink the water from Loch Ness. It tasted good and there was nice weather with the sun shining over the beautiful blue waters. I stopped at a little store and talked to the woman owner about the Loch Ness monster and she said, "Oh I believe in it because I saw it from my hotel with 30 other people." She stepped closer to me and looked over her reading glasses then added. "Most of us who live along the loch have spotted Nessie. She is there and we all believe in her."

I continued on and stopped by the ruins of Uruquart Castle, located on the western shore of Loc Ness. A woman came up and asked me, "Have you seen the monster?" "Yes," I replied pointing out over the loch as a British Air Force cargo plane was flying low over the waters, She squinted to see it. I then replied, "I have seen the monster and it is we." She shrugged her shoulders and rolled her eyes.

In town I saw a museum dedicated to the Loch Ness Monster. It was too expensive for me to enter so I looked in from the outside by peeping in the windows. On a nice green lawn overlooking the loch, I found a picnic table and cooked my dinner. I finished eating and it started to rain so I rode down beside the loch and found a spot to camp right beside the waters. In the twilight, I sat out on a rock watching the loch for a ripple, a sign of a monster, but to no avail, until darkness set in at 9 p.m.

## Wednesday Sept. 28th

Admittedly, it was a little scary laying in the tent next to Loch Ness. I heard the sound of a wave, but it was no different than any other wave, and went to sleep.

There was a heavy drizzle. Along the ride toward Inverness I recalled my thoughts last evening while sleeping in my little tent next to Loch Ness. I could not help but think of some big serpent lifting itself out of the water and biting into my tent, perhaps dragging me to the icy depths. I'd slept very lightly all night. How my imagination runs wild!

Once in Inverness, which is at latitude 58degrees north, I stopped into a grocery store and bought a jar of lemon marmalade and a loaf of bread. Half of it was eaten before heading up a long hill heading east out of town. I thought of and was singing a song called, "I guess I jumped the gun." The wind started blowing strong and it rained hard and was the hardest going yet. In my lowest gear at this slow, agonizing pace, it took every bit of energy to keep me on course. Trucks would go by and blow me off the road. I cursed them and the wind, while crying out, "Why me?" I wanted to go home.

My sugar rush from eating all that marmalade finally subsided after pedaling over a few more hills and made way into Carrbridge at noontime, and there ate lunch. Heading onward up into the Grampian Mountains for the hilltop village of Tomintoul, I was greeted by more strong winds that brought me almost to a stalemate. My packs nearly ripped off the bike, I had to pedal hard and lay low to the winds just to go downhill. On one uphill a truck pulled alongside me to pass and I heard some humming as it went by. It was full of people waving and cheering me on! The countryside was pretty, but hard to enjoy from my vantage.

At one point a big bull stood on my side of the road and looked as though he'd charge me. I made a cat like sound- "Meow," and he took off kicking down the road, then crashed into a fence, tearing it down and dragging some of it while running off into a field. A bus behind me honked and everyone waved and was laughing at the sight as they passed.

At 4 p.m., with the afternoon sun illuminating everything, I cycled down the main street of Tomintoul. The town overlooked valleys of farmland on either side. I saw a shop with a sign, which read, <u>Woodcarver</u> and was curious. Inside, I met the woodcarver whose name was Don and he told me about his trade. "I use the finest elder to carve, the scraps end up in the woodstove," he said in a heavily accented voice. When I asked him about making ends meet he said, "Well I don't pay rent because my father dates and takes out the landlady." He asked me, "Where have you been in Scotland?" I told him, "I went to Loch Ness." He said, "Did cha see the Loch Ness monster." "No," I replied. "Well I have," he told me, pausing while I looked curiously at him for an explanation. "She's my wife," he said adding, "I'm married to the Loch Ness monster!" At which we both broke out in laughter. Don invited me to stop by the pub and meet him later in the evening for a salute.

I found the local youth hostel and checked in as the only visitor along with the warden. I cleaned up the bike, ate and then went out to the Whitehead Hotel Pub. I met the woodcarver, Don, and he bought me two pints of beer and a shot of Scotch. We played pool and talked and padded the butts of gals. Don said, "You know here in Scotland we value our sheepdogs," continuing, "when the weather gets cold they sleep with the wife and we men sleep out in the dog house." I pedaled back to the hostel a sure bet for a D.W.I. back in the states and speeded like a racer on the streets of Tomintoul.

## Thursday Sept 29<sup>th</sup>

My room at the youth hostel was like sleeping in a refrigerator as it was a very cold night. I packed quickly and shivered on the morning. When I stepped into the wardens room it was comfortably heated but mine surely was not. "Thought that would sober you up," said the warden. I ate, did my chore of sweeping and said goodbye to the warden who was closing the place up and leaving for Spain on Sunday.

To step outside on a cold, rainy morning and have to straddle a bicycle seat, isn't without knowing ones fate. You will be wet, and cold and saddle sore. It was a rainy ride up, up and up into terrible weather on the road to Aberdeen. I uumphed it up steep grades into terrible wind, cold and freezing rain. I saw another biker pass the other way and only managed to say to him, "Hey!" It was horrible out, but I did not get off and walk once. Up through heavy fog and down steep descents, only to go right back up again on the other side. At one point the wind was so strong I had to crouch as low as possible and pedal hard to go downhill. Suddenly a flying grouse came from my right side and whizzed past my face to disappear on the left side in the fog. I made it to the top of a pass which had snow on the ground and there saw abandoned ski lifts and other equipment. My hands were frozen and gloves soaked so I had to stop and light my camp stove in the gentlemen's toilet. After warming up a little, it was all downhill from there, as I descended out of the Grampian Mountains, passing gushing streams and changing terrain. I was tired and weak, and drove like a drunk.

After thawing out and eating lunch, I stopped at historic Drum Castle which was started in the 1200's to ward off English attacks. I hiked to the top of the tower and passed through huge doors, perhaps opened for many a knight. Of interest was how they fought back in those days. There were many secret doors near the entry to the castle. One was where boiling hot oil could be dumped on the intruders. Then there were slits, where a spear could be thrust into an enemy from many an angle.

My arrival in Aberdeen was greeted by the weirdest looks from local people. They thought my helmet, which they called a hat, was hysterical. "Why yah wearing sucha strange thing on yer head?" said one fellow. "Looks like a milking bowl," he commented. I ignored the criticism and bought hoards of food and then cooked it in a park. It was a cold night and I was so tired that I slept soundly until morning.

## Friday Sept. 30th

The ship harbor was my first stop on the morning. I went around to many ships asking if any were going to Denmark or Holland. One had left the day before, I discovered. The Cooke Shipping Agents told me to go and check with their ship captains. All five of these tough characters said none were going to where I wanted to go. I had to go back and forth all morning in this dreary yard. A ship called Pioneer was a hopeful but it turned out to be a false alarm, as it was not even in port. I decided to head south for Edinburgh and try again there. Before leaving town, I had to fulfill a promise I'd made in the Grampian Mountains, after all my cycling, to take myself out to dinner. I went to a little cafe and ordered, sweet and sour chicken, 'chips' and ice cream for dessert.

Heading south out of Aberdeen, I fought a steady crosswind, coming off the North Sea, which later turned to a tailwind. Along the route were large fields with long roads leading to the ruins of ancient castles overlooking the blue sea. I pedaled into Aibroath and went down into town and saw cute girls with tight pants. Supper was cooked at a beach shelter and decided to stay there for the night. As the night progressed, a cold, salty wind blew and I had to move myself about the shelter to shield from the annoying sea spray. As the night progressed it became worse. I wrapped my tent around my sleeping bag to protect from the salty spray.

## Saturday Oct. 1st,

I started off with a good breakfast and then pedaled into rain and strong headwinds all morning. Poor time was made against the inclement conditions, which were compounded with my low moral and high hunger. While crossing Dunder Bridge the winds were very bad and the rain pelleted me. At lunchtime I found shelter and an old beggar came by and tried to talk to me but his head was all screwed up or else he was drunk. It was that kind of a day.

I pedaled on, continuing my fight against dumping rains and the wind became even stronger. Though my legs and feet were soaking wet, my upper body was dry and warm. When fighting against such conditions for duration it makes one feel tough and battle hardened. At the same time there is a tendency to become weary and careless. Half way across the Forth Road Bridge, which enters into Edinburgh, the rain stopped but not the wind. I fought on until making way into the city at 4:30pm.

Edinburgh, pronounced Ed-in-brow, has a castle high atop a hill in the city center and this gives it an old, medieval look. I bought a bag full of food and pedaled a mile or so to a park and cooked up sweet and sour pork. My appetite was enormous and it was a delicious meal, after which I was not full.

Some kids were playing in the park and they came over to see me. I was nice to them. They played and climbed on the picnic table while I finished eating. I was concerned they would steal from me, and pulled my handlebar bag closer. One of the little bastards urinated on the table, splattering onto me and I jumped up and chased them all off.

I pedaled back into Edinburgh and went down to the harbor and talked to many men on the boats about going to Europe, but none were going to Holland. One captain told me he would be going there in five months. Two whores were very friendly with me and we walked arm in arm but I was not interested in their expensive services. Nearby, a Christian ship called the Logos was being readied for a voyage to Holland in one month and would afterward go to South Africa. I talked to a few people on board and they preached to me about the Holy Spirit and the voyages of St. Paul.

I headed back into town and saw many people out strolling on the arcade and eating cotton candy. I met two American girls who were students there. In all, I felt like a hermit, unfit for this scene. I pedaled back to the park and set up my tent. A black lab came barking at me, but left when I made cat like sounds. It rained hard during the night.

## Sunday Oct. 2nd

I rode into town and looked around a bit in the morning at the intriguing castle on the hill. I pedaled up to the parking lot and looked out over the city. I pondered how cities make me sick, because they're all so much the same, geometric blocks where people seem so isolated. I felt the country folk were so much happier in outlook. They seem so pleasant, closer to nature, closer to the heart.

I headed south out of Edinburgh, and it's little sea of homes, into gusting head winds and more hard riding. The Cheviot Hills on the border of England and Scotland presented a major challenge mostly because of the wind, the cold rain and the long grade. This 'hill' was like a wedge that reached for the sky. Finally at the top, I met a nice couple that called me a "Pleasant lad." Why not, I was half frozen.

I could sense autumn in the air and noticed ducks migrating and leaves changing color. I cycled through fine woods which reminded me of the story of Robin Hood. There were large oaks and no brush. It was a nice ride, on good roads and arrived in Plonketon which is 8 miles from Newcastle at supper time. Dinner was cooked at a park in town. While out looking around the town in the evening, I got a chuckle from kids saying things like, "That a bowl on yer head?" and "He's packed all his mammies dishes," and "Thar goes a turtle past him!" They really were comical and I didn't feel offended. I cleaned up at a park and went to a pub for one beer. I slept in my tent behind a big apartment complex on a thick carpet of grass, near an athletic field.

## Monday Oct. 3rd

After a restful nights sleep I arose to the morning and looked outside my tent. There stood a man with a beret who said, "Did you sleep well?" "Yes," I responded, thinking I was going to get bitched out. "Yah know yah gave the landlady a fright," he said, adding. "She was out walking the dog and heard you snoring. She was ready to call the police." He paused as I apologized. Then he said, "Care for a cup of tea?" Catching me by surprise. "Please," I said. While I packed, he brought me a delicious cup of tea and half a pack of these delicious chocolate covered biscuits called Digestive. "Leave the tray on the step when you go and good cycling," he said walking away.

I made way into Newcastle where I inquired if any boats were going to Europe but none were. I was assured that in the city of Hull I would find a ferry which went regularly across the channel. Before leaving town I met some nice ladies in the mall and was therefore heart warmed by the sweetness of these English gals.

Just south of town I had a close call at a narrow bridge. Two trucks were coming toward me across the bridge. One was passing the other just as I approached the abutment. Neither truck was letting up and I had no where to go so I slammed on my brakes and tossed my bike over a rail to the side of the road as the trucks zoomed by, inches from me.

On that stretch of road, the trucks were aggravating and I was blown off the pavement often by their wind blasts. I made poor time against heavy headwinds. I was feeling tired and felt as if catching a slight cold. My stop for the night was made in the town of Thirsk where I found a nice grass area across from a cemetery and pitched the tent there.

## Tuesday Oct. 4th

The first couple of hours I had a very nice ride as the roads were flat and there was little wind. I stopped at a bakery and stocked up on fruit cakes. They were good to taste, but made me gassy, and I was tooting like a train all the way into York at 10 a.m.

York has an ancient feel. Old block walls made with medieval designs circumvent the city. I crossed under a gateway to enter the city. Somebody told me they were put up as protection from dreaded European wolves. At a street corner I met a couple from the U.S. and we talked a long while. It was good therapy for me to talk to them, as I needed to regain my speaking of native tongue. "Will you have a TV documentary?" the woman asked me. I did not know. They wished me good luck and I continued touring the old city with its citadel walls and arched gates. I went to an art gallery and visited a beautiful church with an old Roman foundation. Everything was very pretty and ornate.

Upon my leaving York the head winds increased and I had a very difficult time riding. The passing trucks would constantly batter me like a soccer ball. It was exhausting and maddening cycling. The winds became so strong, it was as if I was not going to make it to Hull. A truck pulled up behind me at a light and as we pulled away he moved over and tried to push me off the road. I was so pissed off I flipped him the bird for a long while. Tired, and feeling sickly, I pulled into Hull and found my way to the North Sea Ferries. A large ferry boat which was made to carry cars in the hull was named fittingly enough Norland. "That's my name," I said to the receptionist. "Well you'll have to wait for two days for her to set sail," she said. I could not buy a ticket until the morning she sailed.

I headed into downtown and on the street met 83 year old Bernard Dennison. He was a wonderful, sharp, cool man. He invited me down to the pub. "We could talk all night long," he joshed. I declined so as not to spread my cold. But we talked alot and one thing he kept saying was, "We sure do love you Americans!" He told me he would still ride a bike he said if his last one hadn't been ripped off. I toured the street and stopped for some English popcorn which is sugar coated! I cooked dinner near a duck pond and at dark pitched my night in East Park, anticipating tommorrow getting things ready, myself, my bike and then off to Rotterdam, Europe and more pedaling and discovering good people.

## Wednesday Oct. 5th

Quivering in my tent, I awoke the morning feeling terribly ill. My stomach wrenched with the flu, my body ached, my head spun and I was completely stuffed up and nauseated. I slept in late, until 8am, at my camp in a grassy park and then got up and struggled to pack things away. I grunted and groaned while pedaling the bike to a little store in Hull and bought a container of orange juice. Outside on the front step I sat, to drink it down and was definitely looking pale when a fortyish man came by and asked me, "Do you need help?" I said, "No I'll be alright." He responded, "Are you ill?" I said, "Well, yes, I've been up in Scotland and it was a bit cold and damp." He then said, "You can go to my place if you'd like. Here's the key." But I thankfully declined, stubborn as I am. I had to be able to care for myself. But it was nice of him to offer.

I bought some cold medicine and agonizingly did my laundry at a laundromat, feeling very dizzy. I went to a real big bath house where I sweated it out in a very hot bath. I laid there for so long, getting hot and even delirious. Afterward, I was dressed and sat down and leaned against a pop machine and fell asleep with my mouth wide open at the entry to the bath house.

Upon awakening, I felt better and went to search for a replacement tent pole. I stopped into a guitar shop and talked to the owner and he told me of a fiberglass factory. I pedaled over there bringing a sample of my tent pole and they helped me make a replacement.

After a visit to a grocery store, I cooked a good dinner back at the park. Several guys from a local soccer team stopped by to chat. After dessert I went to a pub where some kids attempted to rip me off. One of them diverted my attention while the other tried to reach into my handlebar bag. I got so mad at them, they ran off.

I went into the pub for a beer and brought in my bike. The bartender did not mind. Inside I met Dan, a school instructor and talked to a gal named Kim, who's mind was miles away. One beer later I rode back to the park and camped again on the grass under a starry sky. I took some cold medicine and hopped into the sleeping bag.

## Thursday Oct. 6th

I slept well into the morning feeling much better. Went to a bakery and bought a large apple pie which cost 25p or about 50 cents. Ate half of it. Went to a locksmith who made me an extra key for the bike lock and then rode into Hull to purchase a tire at a bike shop. Upon exiting, I met an elderly man of 80 years old who was still riding his bike. He was so cool, he could hear well and converse fluidly. We laughed about all the spokes missing from his bike. He gave me two pieces of candy and said, "Cheerio."

# THE WHEELS OF FRIEND

I made my way to the ship-docks and then down to the ship where I received an info packet on the 'Norland' and would send it home to my parents once in Holland. I cleaned up the bike and then entered the large ship via a drive-in-entry for cars and trucks. I met Kees, who took a picture of me while the ship was leaving the port. It was a tight fit getting this big ship through the locks. The Norland had spent some time as a troop ship in the Falklands and narrowly survived a missile attack. Kees and I ate dinner together. I really pigged out as the food was wholesome and plentiful. People were starring at me and giggling, probably wondering where I was fitting all that food. I couldn't believe how much I ate. I went back for seconds, thirds and fourths!

Kees, pronounced Case, told me about his captain's job on a north sea oil rig. He was a swell man from Holland who could speak many languages. He went to bed at 9:30pm after losing some money, playing black jack.

I went up to the bar and drank a couple of beers. As I eyed up some beautiful teenage girls on the dance floor, some other girls came over and starred at me. I got a little self-conscious when one of them took a picture of me. I went out for a walk on the deck and these girls came out and followed me. I met the cutest one, Helga, who was 18 and from Germany. They were nice girls to chat with and they followed me everywhere. I liked this, but I was puzzled, as they put me on the spot, since they didn't speak much English. I kept talking to them even though I questioned how much they understood what was said. We stayed up late, until 2am, and played thumb fights and drank scotch. A German guy who had his headphones on playing loud music had me listen for a moment to his mind-rattling rock and roll. I later went to sleep on the floor listening to the ship rock and bang and could also hear the German's headphones clanging like a blacksmith.

# Chapter 4

## ARRIVAL IN EUROPE

**Friday Oct. 7th**

Breakfast was enjoyed with my German lady friends and they wrote down their address, so I gave them mine. We stepped out on the deck and could see Europe. Soon we were in Holland and the ship came up to the dock. Before I said goodbye, Helga said sweetly, "Please come see me or write to me." I told her I would.

I took my bike through customs and pedaled off onto European soil. Holland had bike paths, some of which were cobblestone and others were paved. Some were marked with signs but most were not. I made way into the manufacturing city of Rotterdam and went through town trying to figure my way without a map. I stopped at a bank and exchanged fifty dollars for 150 gildas. I ate at a McDonald's and then rode over to the post office and posted to mom and dad. While coming out of the post office I saw a crowd gather as the Queen of Holland (Beatrix?) drove up and stepped out of a limousine and walk into a building. She was a nice looking woman.

The people in Rotterdam looked attractive, they were well kept and there were plenty of young and cute girls. The language was very different however, almost like German or like the crazy words from a Dr. Seuss book. Words like telefoon, city centruum and acadamish come to mind.

The kids laughed at me, not a giggle, but outright laughter when they pointed at me or ridiculed me. It was my helmet again, just like in Britain, which they thought was hilarious.

Once, as I was waiting in a line, I turned around to see this guy making a joke of my funny head. He got embarrassed and shut up. Admittedly I was pissed and was glad to get going out of town.

The bike paths out of Rotterdam were nice but they were poorly marked and more then once I went the wrong way. The rain began falling as I said screw this and cut across the grass and made it to a Spar Store to buy groceries. With my goods, I then rode off in a heavy downpour. I tried to stay on the bike path, but it seemed to be taking me in circles. Finally, a decent looking camping spot was found under a small arched bridge over a canal and thus I set up the tent. I cooked supper and ate while watching spiders dangling from the ceiling. Once night fell, I got into my tent and saw a large rat come bounding right up to my tent. I hissed like a cat and that shooed him off.

## Saturday Oct. 8th

In the morning I was awakened to the sound of a car passing nearby and then saw some fishermen unloading a boat. Even though I was just a few feet away in my tent, they never saw me. Once they left, I packed up and took off down good roads until seeing a bakery. I didn't even know how to say good morning or hello in Dutch. At the bakery the clerk tried to talk to me but I was speechless. It was hard because other people were around and I felt shy. They looked at me kind of queer and were smirking and gesturing. I pointed to what I wanted and held out my hand with all my money. The lady took what she needed and gave me change. She then said something like, "Foofing feefin foofen." After that I thought about Dutch people as ignorant and kind of like they're followers and not individuals. But really it was my fault for not knowing some simple phrases of their language.

The bike trails were very slow going because they'd zig zag all over. I said to heck with them and went down a highway, but was immediately beeped at and told to get off the road by motorists. As the crow flies it probably was only 15 miles to Amsterdam, but via the bike trails I must have gone 50. I arrived in the big city at 11:30am and enjoyed its curving streets and canals. I saw a street named J.F.K. and a boat with the same namesake, in addition to his portrait in a couple of places. I found my way over several canals and then went to a museum where I met two U.S. girls who told me, "This is the Rembrandt museum." I locked up my bike and a security guard told me to bring all my stuff inside or else it could be stolen. He said he would personally watch my bike. How nice of him!

The Rembrandt paintings and sketches were awesome. They were so life-like that I felt I could almost talk to the Dutch Masters. His paintings feature dark backgrounds behind the subject painted with warm colors and soft lines. It leaves one with a very strong impression of how great these artists of the region were once seeing this museum.

I then walked down to the Van Gogh exhibit. The story of his life was told and it's full of tragedy. He began painting at 28 years of age. His first works were basic flower pots and still life's, yet he puts this amazing emotion into each work. Rich, saturated colors and heavy executions of paint add to the mystery of Van Gogh cutting one ear off and then finally taking his life. Van Gogh's paintings are best studied by standing twenty feet away. I thought, wow, if I had one of his paintings in my house it would be like having a psycho case for a roomate. There were many portraits and landscapes, moving and brilliant, everything in motion but unfortunately they did not have 'Starry Night,' which is my favorite.

I rode into the city centrum and looked around but made way out of town as I was fed up with big cities. My progress was slow because of the poor markings on the bike paths. It got late and the stores closed. I became so lost in an apartment maze that it took two hours of frustrating riding in circles to finally get through. Lucky for me I saw a grocery store on wheels pass by. It was a school bus size vehicle offering groceries for sale. I headed after it, down a distant street and then pedaled like mad to chase it down. They stopped for me and I shopped inside where there was a full selection of meat, vegetables and cooler goods like in any mini market. With a bag full of food, I found an overpass to camp under, cooked dinner and again it started pouring rain.

About 3am the rain came down so hard it sounded like a waterfall. Even though I was in the tent and under the bridge I was getting wet. Lightning flashed, thunder kaboomed and the winds blew so strong that my legs and the tent were lifted up and rolled right over my head, putting me in a very uncomfortable 'U' shaped position. I forced my legs back down, but for a long while the wind kept them lifted one foot above the ground. I had to hold the tent together with my hands, legs and arms. It had to be either a thunderstorm or a tornado blowing past, as it roared like a jet engine. Perhaps the shape of the overpass amplified the situation. The winds buffeted side to side and the tent sounded like a flag in the wind, yet it held up well, considering the conditions. When the storm passed and my feet finally touched the ground, I was surprised, as underneath the tent was a pile of sticks. That was some storm!

## Sunday Oct 9th

I awoke and rode back into the maze of bike paths, avoiding downed limbs and saw many pheasants flying and running around. I finally got out of the maze and rode through a couple of small villages. Since the shops were closed on Sundays I stopped at a gas station and bought some cookies and candy. This guy, who was about my age, came by and said something like, "Lost foofen faaf feefen?" I told him "Me English." He again spoke in Dutch as I became flustered. He chuckled and then spoke out in excellent English. "My name is Peter," he said. We talked awhile and he offered me bread and milk. I said, "No thanks," though I really was hungry, but I guess I still wanted things to go my way. We rode along and Peter was so kind that I finally accepted when he offered me a sandwich and coffee at his apartment.

I went to his flat and met his roomate, who's name was Yelle. We talked in depth about our countries differences, about old Holland, Russia and about nuclear war. They were students and were so interested in discussion. They made me a meal and I kept on eating while we talked. When I told Peter about all the young kids laughing at my helmet he told me there was a children's song in Holland, which made fun of a guy wearing a funny hat and riding a bike. I stayed at his house until 2pm, we exchanged address's and then we said goodbye.

I headed down the road, with some food they'd given me and was happy to have met such kind people. I vowed to myself to repay Peter some day. A few miles later, I picked a few big red delicious apples from an apple orchard.

Later in the afternoon, I entered the town of Arnheim the site of some horrendous fighting during WWII. Some American tanks and cannons were memorialized in a park. I coasted down to the bridge called Foster Bridge or; "A bridge too Far" and rode across the span seeing visible signs of battle such as poc marks, nics from bullets and bombs. At the middle of the bridge I turned around, seeing the wide river and came back to read a plaque that commemorates the fight. A Panzer division, attacking the greatly outnumbered Airborne British Army and American troops, shot up the defenders. They made a gallant stand and held the bridge, but then lost it, only to have to fight for it back. I reflected how it must have been and it made me feel quiet and sad, with reverence for the dead. There are new buildings constructed in place of ruins and life goes on, but the memory of war is everywhere.

I continued onward to the town of Weeks and bought a supper of sausage, french fries and drank down a 'chocomile.' After a ride of a couple miles, I found a good spot to camp in a grove of pine trees across the street from a pub and with train tracks close by.

## Monday Oct 10th

It was a drizzly morning when I packed up. I rode along and listened to the radio play English and American songs. Again the kids laughed at my 'hat' or me but I smiled back at them. I had a good tailwind and wanted to take advantage of it but I also wanted a souvenir. I looked at many shops for an emblem from Holland to sew on my pannier packs. I arrived in Enshede at 1pm and bought bread and finally found an emblem at 3pm. With two hours riding time lost to shopping I was angry that I did not buy it at earlier opportunities.

I arrived at the border of Germany at 4pm and was greeted by a very poised customs agent who was extremely courteous. I noticed the nice roads in Germany compared to Holland. The countryside looked like Minnesota. The kidding about my helmet in Holland bugged me so badly that when a German kid laughed in my face I gave him the middle finger. Usually I laughed back, but that one got to me.

I camped and cooked under a highway bridge. There was a church across the river, which had a tall steeple with a bell that bonged nicely on the hour but it became more annoying as the night progressed. By eleven o' clock it was bonging so long that my ears rung. At midnight I plugged my ears and sang a song. The bridge acted like a sound amplifier. It rang every hour all night long until morning. I wondered, does the preacher stay up all night or what?

## Tuesday Oct. 11<sup>th</sup>

Made my way eastward from Osnabrock in the early morning and had a good tailwind. The day started off nice and I was treated with the sight of low flying F-4 Phantom jets flying overhead. The sky had big cumulus clouds, and there was warm sunshine and farmland, which were enjoyable sights. I tried to say hello to the people, "Vee gates," I'd say and they seemed friendly enough. I stopped into a bank and exchanged some money. In the bank I asked the teller for Francs and she said emphatically, "Ah voo vont Marcs?" "Oh, Yes" I said adding. "Goot, goot." I liked the little shops in town and walked my bike in the city center where no cars were allowed. I saw a McDonald's and it was like a miniature version of those in the U.S. I stopped at a store and bought some snacks, in addition to a loaf of hard, sweet bread, called christollen, or Christmas bread.

My culture shock was exuded as I found it hard to figure out the money and the language was so unnerving to attempt to speak. The German girls looked real cute and that made it worthwhile. I made way out of town and got lost, taking several wrong turns and discovered my map was useless. I zig zagged town to town and would buy groceries when I found a store. It took me twenty minutes to wait in line at the butcher and then order a sausage, as I was timid with my attempts to speak German. People looked at me weird with my helmet on and the kids would laugh but I was eating well.

The day got late and it was difficult to find a campsite. I pedaled along in the dark, passing fences or low ground and it seemed nothing looked suitable to camp. Suddenly a big rainstorm hit just before I sought shelter under a bridge. The rain and wind pelted down and I huddled in a puddle of mud trying to stay warm. Shortly thereafter it cleared up and the stars shone while I rode into a dark park. My narrow tires became mired in muck and slipped my way back to firm ground. While riding along the bikepath, I was tired and hungry and found a lighted tunnel and stopped to cook supper. I was setting a pan on the stove and had my back turned as some joker who laughed and screeched his bike to a stop nearly ran into me with his big bike. I jumped back and shouted, "Ahh!" in a shocked voice. The big brute, red headed, fat bellied German spoke to me but I was so pissed I responded in English. His little friend who was sitting on the crossbar said, "He cannot speak English but we are wondering what you are doing here?" I told him I was traveling around the world. "On a farrot?" He responded with surprise. "A what?" I said. "Oh a bicycle-you are traveling on a bicycle?" he said looking surprised. The big red headed guy said something and the little fellow interpreted, "My friend wants to invite you to stay the night at his house." "Ok." I said as the big guy smiled and responded, "Ok."

We talked along the way and I felt they were sincere so I continued along with the invitation. I arrived at his house and carried my bike in the back door and then went up a flight of stairs to the second story where we entered the bedroom of the big German. He had a couch along one wall and a bed on the other. The big fellow's name was Kahn and the little guy's name was Tomas. Kahn would talk German to me and Tomas interpreted, "My friend asks if you like Reagan." I said to Tomas, "I think he is a good speaker but he is too quick to use bombs as diplomacy." Tomas made a sad face and said, "Kahn said he NO likes Reagan." Then I looked at the big guy and said, "What do you think of your chancellor Kohl." In typical German Kahn said, "I like him because he is our leader." We talked more of politics and I thought I'd better not say something to offend him. I could sense, that my staying in his house was kind of a shaky situation. Though

I trusted the big guy, he had a stern edge. Tomas left to go home and then I was there on my own with Kahn.

Kahn said something to me, which I could not understand. He then spoke louder as if I could not hear. He became flustered, looking at me as if I was an idiot. I knew that this would not work unless we could communicate. I pulled out my Berlitz book, Let's talk German, and searched for the word. "Food," he said. "Ah food, goot, goot," I responded. He shook his head in a yes and smiled then went out of the room. I heard him downstairs talking to his mother and he came back upstairs with bowls of hot stew and bread. We sat to eat and it was very delicious. I offered to share some of my christollen with him but he brought some other cake up instead.

We tried to talk politics some more and could only josh while saying "Reagan," or put thumbs up when saying Kennedy. Then for a moment I could not understand him and again he got flustered. I saw a car magazine and looked at a Corvette. "Das is un goot auto," I said pointing at the familiar car. Kahn agreed enthusiastically and he pointed out a car he liked - a classic 57 Chevy. We both put thumbs up and paged excitely through this catalog of classic cars, pointing out those, which we liked. I would look in the Berlitz book to interpret words like fast, powerful, engine, this went on for well over an hour. It seemed like we were friends. Then he put the magazine away and said, "Sloffen!" (Sleep) I did not quite know what to think. He pulled out a pistol and showed me his bullets and then said, "You steal?" while holding a bullet to my head. "Nign," I said adding, "Nign steal." Kahn responded, "Goot," and he put the gun under his pillow. I laid out my sleeping bag on his couch and got in. He sat in bed and turned on the radio. "Elick good music," he said turning up the volume on a Beach Boy's song. "Yah goot, goot," I said. "Goodenaght," we said to each other. He turned off the radio and snored like a bear.

## Wednesday Oct. 12th

In the morning we both stirred at about the same time and Kahn said, "Elick goot sloffen"? At which I returned to him, "Yah goot sloffen, vu goot sloffen Kahn?" "Yah," he said. We got up and I packed but he said some things to me which I could not understand. We called Tomas and Tomas told me that Kahn wondered if I needed help finding my way out of Bunde. I told him, "Tell Kahn I can find my way and tell him I am very thankful for his kindness and yours." As a gift I gave Kahn a business card from a nightclub in California, which he really liked when he saw it the night before. I thanked him and we departed with a handshake and I was on my way.

My experience with the big brute turned out alright though we had little in common and could barely communicate. From Bunde I rode eastward on a nice day and soon got lost, zig zagging, then asked a gas station man for directions. He helped me but I screwed up and went 5 kilometers beyond my turnoff at which I swore out loud, "Fucking Highmees!" Almost from knowhere a fellow appeared and he helped me. I ate my words.

I pleasantly rode into Hanover at 1pm and saw many nice looking, blonde haired girls. The city was intriguing and among the more unusual sights were sex shoppes, though I do not check out what services they offered. I stopped into a mall area to eat christollen and when leaving the bench forgot my water bottle by accident. I rode around town exploring and visiting the tourist bureau. I met a guy outside of the bureau and we talked about the road to Berlin. Suddenly I realized I lost my water bottle. Was it stolen? I backtracked and rode to the bench and there it was, undisturbed, one hour after I left it.

The mall had many entertainers playing guitars and singing songs. There were also people walking with advertising signs sandwiched around them. I rode along and saw several cute young girls and slapped one gal on the butt. They giggled and laughed at me. If I'd done that to a gal back in the states she would curse at me.

I rode down the autobahn and got honked at immediately by angry drivers. Took the first exit off the autobahn and pedaled along a road where I met a gal who was hiking and wearing a daypack. She gave me directions and told me the way to go, which I soon discovered was the wrong way and I turned around, before going to far. I went merrily along until finding a bridge over a canal that looked suitable to camp under. As trucks rumbled overhead and long barges made way up the river I cooked my supper. There were many signs posted along the canal which bore a nuclear radiation like symbol and said, 'Achtung!' Though I could not read them, when I translated the text I realized it was a warning not to drink nor swim in the water as it was toxic. While I sat down to eat supper a wayward mouse came darting along and then leaped toward my plate but I batted it away. I set my tent and a mouse tried to get in. The place was full of mice! It started raining but I was well sheltered and kept constant company by mice wriggling under the tent.

## Thursday Oct. 13th

Considering the long-barge-ships that passed in the night, the strong winds and the traffic, I slept well, and happily woke up. All night long the wind and rain howled out of the south yet my spot was comfy and sheltered.

I rode into a hail of wet weather and after a few miles could see the stacks of a nuclear plant upstream of my nights camp, therefore I was glad to not have touched that water. I made good time into Braunshweig as the skies were clearing at 11:30am and went into a grocery store to browse then walked out, stopped to ponder and then went back into the store to buy some food. While inside I met this tall German fellow whom was very articulate. He spoke excellent English and wanted me to buy one of everything that he liked. "This is an excellent bread and you would like this fine variety of cheese," he'd recommended me. Stubbornly I got what I liked but we talked and then went out to a lovely fountain in the city center. With the sun shining, we sat there while I shared my bread and cheese. His name was Knut Von Frankenstien and he said, "I am a descendant of the author of the monster Frankenstien." I did not know what he meant, but it sounded funny. He then invited me to smoke marijuana as he said it was legal in public and so he rolled one up.

We smoked a dubbee right there at that fountain which had Martin Luther on it and I got very loaded and we talked up a storm. We started laughing as the electricity flowed between us. He reminded me so much like my old friend Morris. While he talked he would say silly things to passing people like, "Go over there, achtung." We talked briefly about politics, about Berlin, travel and life. Knut said he was a specialist at travel and he told me of his ability to take in the life of leisure at the expense of others. "You know, I find a woman who has lots of money and wants to see the Riviera or Paris." After half an hour, I finally had to go and so did he. So we shook hands firmly and then parted with a smile.

While riding toward the border of East Germany I was going through some S turns and a huge army tank came at me and then zipped past going around those curves like a sports car. It must have been going at least 50 mph. I got lost and rode my bike up onto the autobahn and the first vehicle which came along was a truck and the guy got all pissed off, beeping his horn and bitching me out. So I said, "Sprechen zee English?" He got flustered and split. I stood there in the road and a guy on a bicycle on a side road started hollering at me in German. "How do I get to Helmstead?" I shouted. Amazingly he could speak English and he told me the way.

I rode into Helmstead, the border town to East Germany at 2pm. Cleaned up and talked to the border guard. The guards gave me a visa. They said I would not be allowed to ride my bike to Berlin and would have to "tramp" with a sign that says, "Need ride to Berlin."

I made a sign and after standing there for one hour a VW van came up and I talked to the driver and he said, "Ok I will try to fit your bike inside and we can go to Berlin." I took it apart and we were off. His name was Torsten. He was a German from Hamburg. His friend was Thomas who was from Berlin. We had to go through customs and follow many gates, fences, armed guards, large barbwire walls of 15 feet and past a goddy Russian tank memorial. It was a shock to see all these sights. The place looked like a prison camp. The guard said, "Zee American will pay 5 Marcs." He then said, "Zee black car will pass you and zee next one will wait while you follow zee black car." Everything was very strict and orderly. The guards had guns, machine pistols and uniforms that looked like those which the Nazi's wore. I'll never forget the cold long stare and death look on that last guard's face as he looked at me-the American. He waved us on into East Germany.

While heading east on the autobahn we could see the farmland was not as good as West Germanys. Shabby old tractors worked the fields, houses looked run down. We went off the autobahn, which was against the law and forbidden, and went down a rough road before stopping into a restaurant. It was like a scene out of the 1920's. Everything had the same shabby, gray look. I was told by my German friends not to talk to anybody. The waitress was chunky and snotty, the food looked like it was slapped on the plate with a trowel. It was bland, cardboard tasting and tough to swallow even as hungry as I was.

Back on the road to Berlin, I got into a heated talk with Thorsten about the U.S. He criticized it as being an aggressive nation and that Reagan was a warlord. I tried to explain, the way I saw things. He continued his complaining. I finally said, "Do you remember the Marshall Plan or how about all the American's who died fighting the Nazi's. How many Germans have died helping America? How much money has America spent rebuilding Germany? It seems like everytime we help a country, they love us at first and then after a few years they say, get lost we don't need you anymore. WELL MAYBE THE U.S. SHOULD JUST SAY THE FUCK WITH HELPING OTHER COUNTRIES." Silence within the van, was accompanied only by the purring engine. This Americans point of view was well understood.

The Berlin border was worse than the previous one at Helmstead. There were more gates, barbed wire fences and long corridors with armed guards. Finally we passed through the gauntlet and entered into Berlin. Wow what a city! It was like New York City at night with all its lights and vastness. Thorsten dropped Thomas off, then went to the house of a friend whose name was Klements. I met Klements, a blond haired man of 38 years with John Denver like glasses. He showed us around town and once he found out that I was a private pilot we had something in common and talked unceasingly about flying. We went out and stopped at a nightclub and drank Dortmands beer, of which I bought several rounds. Back at Klements house we stay up until 1:30 looking at slides and home movies of flying. He was a great guy and his pictures were a welcome distraction from my routine of cycling.

## Friday Oct. 14th

Klements and his wife cooked us breakfast in the morning and it was wonderful to take a shower and eat a good breakfast. We men went touring about the town and I lent Thorsten 10 Marcs, which was about 20 dollars. I knew I'd never see the money again. He needed it and he did help me out by getting me to Berlin and staying with Klements. We visited an airplane exhibit that was not very good and then again talked much about flying. We went back to Klements to eat lunch and then said goodbye to our hosts.

Thorsten and I went to the Reichstag which was the headquarters for Hitlers 3rd Reich. Though it was pockmarked, it amazingly survived all of the bombing of Berlin. Behind it stood the Berlin Wall with its many guard towers on the other side. There was a lot of graffiti on the approximately 20 foot high wall with its rounded top. "It's their fucking wall." said Thorsten. The structure was ominous, secretive and frightening in several ways. I could see some of the death zone on the other side where they laid land mines and barbed wire. Snipers were strategically set up in their outposts for effective cross fire and deterrent from escape. We went along the wall all the way to Checkpoint Charley and then went into a museum, which was full of pictures of escapes from behind the Iron Curtain.

Torsten told me he had to go, so he dropped me off on a sidestreet. He needed more money but I told him I couldn't give anymore. We departed with some hesitation as he felt for my situation and I for his, but I said goodbye and he drove of.

It was 5:30pm and darkening outside as I headed down the streets on my own again. The shops closed early and I barely found enough food for supper. I curiously followed a protest march against nuclear arms along the wall, watching demonstrators carry torches, talking through loud speakers and blowing whistles. The East Germans must have heard this, they must have been listening, how could they help but not hear this racket? What did they think? I met a fellow from Denmark and he told me, "The East Germans are prisoners in their own country." Around 11pm I went to a park near the Berlin wall and pitched my tent, hoping for a good nights rest.

## Saturday Oct. 15

I did sleep good in the park and awoke to the sound of rain pattering against the tent in the morning. In a rebellious mood, I went over to the Berlin wall and pissed my name onto it. Then I went a bit further and sat down at a picnic table to eat breakfast. I laid out my sleeping bag and other stuff on a park bench and people looked at me like I was nuts. I headed over to Checkpoint Charley where I asked a U.S. Army guard what the cost was to go over to East Berlin. He said it was about 30 marcs. I didn't feel like paying that much and besides, the guard said it wasn't worth going over there anyway. "The place is a dump and why give your money to them?" He said. He made me feel like a traitor if I did go over there. So I turned around and went sight seeing in Berlin, but I couldn't get the thought of visiting a Soviet block country out of my mind.

I met some U.S. girls in the tourist information center and talked to them for awhile. I then went back to Checkpoint Charley and then rode along the wall thinking how it disgusted me to see that wall. I felt like I didn't want anything to do with East Berlin. Yet it held a mystique. The East German soldiers standing in their towers and people on the west side looking at them. It's a strange fascination. I couldn't see how people could live over there. The death zone is 100 yards wide and there are land mines and barbed wires everywhere. It is all intended to hold people in, yet they say it is to keep us out. They are held captive like animals or are we the animals who are kept from going in?

I met a Berliner named Ronald on a street corner and he invited me too a Turkish restaurant. He could speak reasonably good english and we talked about Berlin. I had never tried donnar kabob, a Turkish staple, and found the food was very good. The atmosphere was laid back and we talked up a storm. Ronald was a student at the university. We went to a study hall and he introduced me to Ulf, an art student in Berlin and together we walked to a pub. We had a marvelous talk about politics, girls, money and travel. Germans seem to be good listeners. They also are very obedient. It annoys me in a way. People constantly tell me when I break a rule.

"You cannot do this or do that," they'd say to me. We went to Ulfs apartment and discussed art. It was late and I was tired and slept on the same bed as Ronald but in my sleeping bag. We laid there and talked about life in Berlin. He told me how it is common to hear gunshots in the night, coming from East Berlin. "They are always trying to escape, but are shot by the guards." He said to me, "In East Berlin, "Some of the people liked having communism because then the government takes care of them, they don't worry about money, there is little crime and a sort of peace of mind because you can't have to much of anything. It is a nice place to go for a quiet walk in a park." We listened to a cassette of soothing Brecht music before falling asleep.

## Sunday the 16th of October

Both of us slept in until 8:30. After coffee I said my thanks and goodbye to Ronald. I pedaled back to Checkpoint Charley and talked a while to an MP. I thought about going into East Berlin. I was very indecisive, as one side of me said go and the other said don't. I had come this far and it was Russian occupied, which was one of my goals. I sat and deliberated many times. Finally I thought I didn't want to go there. I wouldn't pay 30 marcs and to hell with them–I'm leaving!

I rode clear across town, heading for the road back to West Germany, passing many windsurfers on a lake, and went all the way to the highway leaving Berlin. I sat at the border and again deliberated. It was tearing me to pieces. I had come too far to pass this up. I had to go back and see East Berlin! Yes I would go to East Berlin! So I rode back into the city as the leaves were falling and the weather was blustery.

I went back up to the wall and was walking along when I noticed an East German guard in a tower watching me intently. He'd take his binoculars and follow me. I stopped and stared back. He stared at me. It was a stand off-side against side. Looking at each other. I waved in a friendly but considerate manner and the guard immediately responded by giving me a thumb down gesture. He chuckled to his comrade. I stood there only for a moment with a very stern face. It took all I could to stay put and not flip him off with the middle finger. I looked at him and then turned and walked away. I imagined him shooting me in the back.

    I stopped at the park and got ready to cook dinner but unfortunately my matches were soaking wet from the rain. I looked up the word for matches in my German translation book and saw that it was 'strikenholfern.' Finally I found a guy walking in the park and asked him, "Kernen helfern zee wit strikenholfern?" He responded in English, "Will a lighter do?" I borrowed his lighter and started cooking. People came by and stopped to stare at me. Wow, this was strange. I felt like I was on exhibit. I shouted aloud, "Here you see exhibit 'A'-this is a wild man cooking in a park." They frowned and left.

    After supper I went into the city to sit and write under a lamppost. Many people were walking past, including cute chicks, ignoring me. I felt as if I was a slob. It started to rain and I set my tent up on the damp leaves at the same place in the park.

### Monday Oct. 17<sup>th</sup>

The morning was cool but not raining and there was a decided feel of fall in the air. Leaves were starting to drop. I headed down to Checkpoint Charley. And left the bike at the U.S. headquarters. The M.P. again seemed to talk down my going into East Berlin. I was adamant and so into the first gate I went. I had to stand there until a guard was ready to let me in. Then he took my pass and told me which way to go. Another man walked in and he was going the same way as me. "Hello," I said. "You are American?" He asked me. "Yes, and are you?" "Yes." he said. His name was Todd Norbitz and he was on assignment for NBC news doing a report on anti U.S. demonstrations, especially the Pershing 2 missile in Europe. Like me, he also decided to experience East Berlin. We went through all the hassles like filling out a declaration and then they searched me. They charged me 5 marcs for the visa and then asked for 25 marcs to exchange into East German money. They had so many gates that it was easy to get screwed up and have a guard get mad at you. Finally my accomplice and I stood between the Iron Curtain and the West. Todd said, "Well this is it. We are now between the U.S. and the U.S.S.R. We are people without a country." Then going behind the Iron Curtain we went, walking along, past shabby buildings and heroic pictures of Carl Marx and Lenin. They looked more like gods than idealists.

    We walked down to Brandenburg gate and looked out toward West Berlin. It looked busy. We took a side street to see things differently and stopped at a shop to buy some baked goods.

They were yuk. Everything was old and stale and not very good. I ate about half of mine and tossed it. There were many pretty and nice old buildings that were pock marked from bombing during the war. In Marx plaza we saw the most magnificent statue of the sea king Nautilis.

"I've seen enough and have to get going," said Todd. He gave me some of his East German money and we separated. He didn't spend much time there. I wondered if that's par for a newsman's viewpoint on a place.

I walked deeper into the city and stopped at a grocery store to see what they were like. There was not a good selection. It was worse than the shops in Mexico. The bookstores had many books on Karl Marx and Lenin but not much else. Every shop had pictures of Marx, and they were to be revered.

I walked up to a busy intersection, of which two streets met side by side at main street. There was an island in the middle. I stood with the crowd, waiting to cross both streets and saw that the light on the other side was green, so I continued on past the people. I heard them gasp and look at me like-oh my god, he's a lawbreaker! I made it to the island and then saw the red light at the island, though the other side was still green. A policeman, who was dressed just like a Gestapo SS soldier, with a luger pistol, saw me do this and he made a little fuss. But the people tattle tailed on me, by pointing at me and telling the cop. It was as if the people wanted to appease the policeman. I understood my mistake and stopped and waited. Then the island light turned green and the other side was green, so I walked across and the cop blew his whistle and walked over to me doing the goose step. The people continued pointing at me. The cop started to shout, "Das nichit is goot, das is forbodden." I think he was going to write a ticket. "I don't speak German." I said. He said, "Document!" I gave him my passport and he checked it thoroughly. He tried to interrogate me, but I didn't understand him. Then he bitched me out, with his bad breath. He pointed at the lights and got all bent out of shape. I acted dumb and he finally let me go. This was my first taste of police control in a communist country.

Later in the morning I stopped at a store and all the produce sucked. The fruit jars looked home canned and were scuzzy. Everything was dirty and the food looked moldy. There was no selection and the lighting in the store was horrible. A dirty butcher hacked away at a chunk of meat with a huge clever on a filthy table.

I took a trolley ride toward the outskirts of East Berlin and stood next to a bunch of East German soldiers who were dressed like Nazis in W.W.II. The trolley went deep into the city and then out into the outskirts. People riding on board seemed nice enough. A young couple giggled and ate hot dogs on rolls, like we would a delicacy, and they seemed happy. I went out quite a ways until the trolley line ended. I started to walk back and stopped at many shops on the way. People looked at me and laughed. They thought my handbag was humorous.

The 25 marcs, which I had in East German money had to be spent, else they would take it from me when returning to West Berlin. Therefore, I decided to buy food to take with me.

I saw a better looking grocery store and selected some canned food in my arms. A group of store workers came over to me, and blocked my way. I thought that maybe they were inspectors because they walked around in a group. They came up to me and said a whole bunch of German and pointed to my canned goods. I told them, "Yah, yah" and thought that would shake them off. They continued on speaking and so I said, "Sprechen zee English?" They conferred and one of them said, "Cart" and he pointed at this silly little shopping cart like everyone else was pushing around. "Nighn, nighn," I said not wanting a stupid rickety cart and went about my way. They gave me a dirty look and shoved a cart up to me and took my cans and put them in the cart. You've got to do like everyone else in East Berlin, or otherwise your a threat.

I walked to a cafe and saw people eating hot dogs like they were prime rib! They used forks and knives to cut them. I wanted to tell them to try putting some ketchup on them but there didn't seem to be any. I ate a fair meal of goulash at a restaurant and then went to a museum of art, where there were etchings and paintings by the famous German artist Albrect Durer. It actually was an exquisite exhibit of works from the 1500's.

At one intersection I saw a group of school children walking along the sidewalk and a policeman waving them to come towards him and cross the street. The schoolteacher led the kids out onto the road and the kids started across, but suddenly a car came and had to swerve and slam on its brakes. The kids ran back to the curb and the cop came barreling up to the schoolteacher and I thought he was going to hit her. He bitched her out something terrible. She talked back to him and showed that it was he who had told her to cross. I knew she was right and that he was way out of line. I wanted to say something, but he really reprimanded her and she all of a sudden almost fell to her knees for forgiveness. Like a dog creeping up to its angry master, she smiled and walked off head held low in shame with the kids. It was his fault, but I could see that the policeman's word here was the voice of authority.

I had enough of this shit. I wanted to leave but had to spend all my money or else they would take it away from me. I hunted around for a food shop but all I could find were bookstores with Marx-Lenin posters. A supermarket in the nicest part of town near customs was there to impress foreigners. They had better quality but still everything was half ass. There were no prices on items. No peanuts for instance. The local people couldn't afford to shop there. The clerks and shelf stockers walked around in white hats and cloaks and looked like they didn't give a damn. "I'm getting out of here," I said to myself.

I past all the scrubby looking shops as these dumb little 'peoples cars' that all look the same and sound like tin cans zipped here and there. I went through customs and had to wait and wait. One guy who wanted to enter East Berlin was turned back because he carried West Berlin postcards. Finally I walked across the no mans land and returned to the U.S. customs and said outloud to the U.S. guards; "That place sucks." They all laughed and agreed. A woman guard said, "Everyone in the U.S., should go there to see how good we've got it back home."

I suddenly started to notice the immediate difference that one day in East Berlin made to me. I felt like I just released from prison. The shops in West Berlin were so colorful. Wow, my eyes were like a black and white TV that suddenly became colored. The people here looked so alive. I was naturally high- on a freedom high. I rode down the street fired up and glad as hell to be an American. Wow, the girls looked great, their clothes were so fine, their smiling faces, the cars so beautiful. It all hit me so strong that the west is truly so much better! Wow was I fired up.

While pedaling merrily along for the border I met a judge riding a bike who spoke English and we talked and pedaled. I told him that I had just left East Berlin and how ecstatic I was feeling at the moment. He said he escaped from East Berlin in the late 1950's. He was very glad to not live there anymore. He said his friend does and that he wished to escape. When I told the judge that someday I wanted to write a book about my travels he asked me to please send him a copy.

I rode down to the border where there were many 'tramps' waiting for a ride. One guy said,

"You cannot get a ride with a bike." I said, "Yes I will." Another fellow came by and said the same thing. I told him the same. Then a car pulled up and these young people said, "You are heading our way. Put your bike up on the top rack." I met Stephen, Benita and Rudy. Wow was I happy. We drove off as those other 'tramps' gave me a dirtly look.

Rudy was ugly, but very sincere while Benita was a beautiful brunette. We sped along in a VW car and went through customs. I had to pay the border guards another transit fee of 5 marcs. The guards asked them a few questions, and then let my German friends off without a hassle, but wanted to look at my passport. The guard had such a steelic face, he looked exactly like a Nazi. He looked at me, and I at him, East against West, he could have machine gunned me with his icy look. He asked some questions, said something derogatory about Americans and handed me back the passport and we were waved on, past more guards, tanks, barbed wire and soldiers.

We rode on down the autobahn and they talked about Americans. Stephen said, "East Berlin is not that bad." I didn't argue because I needed a ride. But he was WRONG-WRONG-WRONG! We stopped at a rest place and they handed me a couple of beers while we worked to repair a broken fan belt on their car. I chipped in money for a new belt. We got along just fine and they seemed to like me. Once back in West Germany they dropped me off in Helmstedt and wished me the very best. I was surprised when Benita gave me a nice little hug. She reminded me so much of Molly. I had a glow as I found my way to a park and camped the night by a pond with geese.

## Tuesday Oct. 18th

My alarm clock of honking geese awoke me early and I stopped by the shops and was again in awe of it all. There is something about seeing shops stuffed with produce and merchandise that make a person feel dazzled. A fellow at the bank who liked my adventurous spirit, proudly padded my shoulder. After exchanging some money I attacked strong headwinds. Little kids laughed their heads off at me but I didn't care. I felt happy. While passing through a village I slowed, but did not stop for a stop sign and was scolded by a very angry resident. In a small town a guy offered me food and a shower, but I thanked him and kept going. After eating lunch in Schladen I fought winds that were real bad. Once I was blown off the road by the wind. The landscape was mainly farmland divided by rows of trees. Behind the town of Goslar could be seen the mountains of the Black Forest. I was helped a great deal by a guy in Seesen who gave me directions to a park where I stayed for the night. For supper, I opened a can of Russian flieshcops, a kind of hamburger, and heated it up on my stove. While I ate in the park, it was getting colder and the way the leaves were falling winter would soon be here. My tent was set up on a round hill and there was a tendency for me to roll to either one side or the other. I dozed off thinking of the many nice people I'd met on this day.

## Wednesday Oct. 19th

Had a good nights sleep in the spooky park and arose to the misty morning and packed up and the clouds burst a sudden torment of rain. I headed south but soon the Polizei pulled up beside me and told me I was going the wrong way. They gave me the right directions. Seems I was heading for the autobahn and that's a no-no for bicycle riders. Much of the morning was made up of fighting against strong headwinds and riding in the rain over long, rolling hills, past red barns and the through woods.

The highlight of the morning was when I met an old timer going the opposite way on his three speed bike. He was a colorful old guy with a red face and some of his fat belly stuck out from popped buttons. The bike was completely packed with suitcases and luggage. He had an extra tire atop his luggage which was fastened to the bike by a bungeechord. We greeted each other in German and he seemed to know I couldn't speak the language. I told him I was an American from California. "Ha," he said adding, "Beautiful." He told me he was going to Bohn. We looked at my map and he gestured that there were many hills up ahead for me to tackle. I pulled out a handful of candy and stuffed it into his pack before saying, "Offveederzain-goodbye."

In Gottingen a guy tried to tell me what picture I should take of an architecturally interesting building. I was adamant and wouldn't let him waste my film. He ended up taking a picture of me. Before I headed off, he and his wife said, "Happy Journey," to me. The weather was cold and I made it into Kassel and bought some groceries then continued onward, feeling like I needed to make more distance, riding in the dark.

My generator hummed and the little headlight and taillight provided illumination. I got lost and took a road that led me onto the autobahn. I pedaled hurriedly along and the cars were beeping at me and the trucks would lay on their horns and swerve at me. They all flashed their lights at me. Obviously I should not have been there, but they sure made a big fuss so I took the next exit. I was coasting down the ramp and approaching a stop sign when a car suddenly went past me and pulled in front of me to make a road block. I saw that it was not a police car so I went around it. The driver hopped out and shouted German obscenities at me. I said, "Sprechen zee English?" He continued swearing in a forceful manner. I repeated myself and he said rather softly. "Yes-I-can-speak-English." Then he bellered, "You cannot ride on the autobahn!" I responded, "But my map is confusing and I am somewhat lost." He barked back, "You cannot ride on the autobahn, it is very dangerous!" His eyes bulged out and he looked like a mad Hitler. He sped off. I wanted to tell him the only thing dangerous was drivers like himself swinging at me and beeping their horns. I rode on into the night asking people how to get to the next town. I stopped at a picnic table and cooked a supper of Russian goulash, then rode another hour. It was a cool fall night with no wind, the moon shining and nice roads. I found a nice park, pitched the tent and was completely exhausted.

**Thursday Oct. 20th**

On the partly cloudy morning I rode on from the town of Borken and ate an entire loaf of christollen bread for breakfast. I was like a shark in a feeding frenzy. Each bite made me want even more until I'd eaten it all.]

While waiting at a red light I saw a pedestrian who could have crossed, as there was no oncoming traffic. Instead he opted to wait for the signal to change. I went through the red light and he shouted at me. Hey humans make mistakes! German people sure like to obey their rules. I couldn't help but think it's almost to the extent of being neurotic.

I rode into Marburg, which was a nice little town with a big castle on the hillside. I watched an anti-nuclear demonstration and they blocked the road with signs and protesters. I believe the Russians must not be allowed into this land and if it takes nuclear weapons to threaten them then do it. At the same time communications must be opened up between the superpowers.

After Marburg I saw a good apple tree on the roadside and stopped to picked some of them.

I filled my hat with red apples while some sheep and a cow came strolling over. I fed some to the sheep but when I tried to toss an apple to the cow, I bonked it on the head and it went wild and was bronking like a crazy stallion across the pasture. I laughed up a storm and drivers going past looked at me like I were nuts.

This part of Central Germany has open countryside with little villages that have the church always in the center of town. It is similar to my grandparent's farmland. One church I saw looked like a Spanish mission.

I stopped at a store and bought another loaf of christollen bread which also had 'perspillen' (filling) in the center. It was so good that I ate half of it at one setting. It was cold out around noontime when I rode into Friedberg, a beautiful town with a wonderful castle surrounded by a molt. There were many stores to window shop and I saw many U.S. soldiers strutting here and there. I ate lunch on an outdoors-church bench and for dessert finished off my second loaf of christollen.

There, I met a young German fellow who was trying not to go into the military service. He said it was mandatory for all German men to spend two years in the service. We had a good talk about warfare as an unfortunate means to resolve differences and came to the conclusion that the world needs to communicate, not threaten one another. He said, "East Germany is very Nazi like. The Russians have not helped that country prosper. Instead they have robbed it." I agreed with him and we shook on it.

I rode on into the afternoon and stopped at a store to buy another loaf of christollen. At a schoolyard, I made supper of a can of Russian fleishcops and for dessert ate nearly half of my third christollen. Each loaf had about 3000 calories, which meant I had eaten 7500 calories of the stuff. Even after eating all that, I was still hungry. I pedaled on into the night, my generator whirring, crank spinning and tires whining on the pavement. Stopped at a pub and had a beer then again hit the road. It was a nice night, somewhat cloudy and I could see the distant glow of Frankfurt. I got tired several miles outside of Frankfurt and nearly fell off the bike from exhaustion so I stopped in an automobile wayside rest area to camp. I ate nearly all the rest of the christollen, brushed my teeth and hit the hay.

At 1:30am I was awakened by someone saying, "Hallo, hallo, hallo, it's the policee." I thought it was a dream. He repeated it again and I asked, "Sprechen zee English?" The policeman responded, "Please come out and auctung-ah-pay attention-I have a weapon!" I opened the tent flap and saw what looked like a 45 pistol aimed at me. "Passport," he demanded. I said, "Yes sir," and handed him my passport. This seemed like a dream. He looked it over and then lectured me, "Free camping is not allowed in Germany. You must stay at a designated campground." Then the officer said, "Like in America, in Germany your bike can be stolen or maybe your tent, or perhaps you can loose your life. This time we will let you stay here."

They parked their car not far away and I could hear them talking on the radio. Fortunately they were compassionate police, as I was so tired, not wanting to move, though I could hardly fall asleep with the police car running nearby. Finally they left, but I didn't sleep very well after thinking about what he told me.

## Friday Oct. 21st

It was a beautiful, sunny morning when I hit the road to Frankfurt. The traffic was bad but I blotted it out, thinking about last night. I could see the cops silhoutte, holding that pistol in the moonlight, his face was dark. It was kind of eeerie.

I entered the city of Frankfurt and found it to be a lovely city with many fountains. It reminded me of London. There were nice old buildings and many new ones. Everywhere one could see pockmarks on buildings from the WWII bombing. While heading out of town on this nice day I listened to U.S. News on the radio and they talked of the presidential election for 1984. Reagan was favored over Mondale. I made up my own song and was joyfully singing, "I'm heading for the Chans Elysee."

About 20 miles out of Frankfurt I arrived in Mannheim and excitedly stopped to call Helga, whom I'd met on the ferry. When I pulled out the address I discovered they lived in Frankfurt. I tried to call but could not figure out how much money to put in the phone. Disappointed I felt weird and somewhat depressed. I headed for Worms feeling lost and sullen. I spent some time looking for a toilet and instead used the woods. I was so bummed out, but the forest soothed me and I collected myself.

Worms is a pretty little town that is located on the western bank of the Rhine River. I went past the old walls that have stood since the 12th century and made way to a park to eat. Some kids came over and they talked to me while watching my every move. They really laughed when I snapped a bottle cap into the air with my thumb. I met two U.S. girls and they were pleasant. Under the Rhine River Bridge was a campsite and there I met an Italian family. The young boy was so helpful and very outgoing. He tried to help me with setting up my tent, taking out my sleeping bag and locking up my bike. I got such a kick out of him and his dog. In the evening his family sang songs and roasted marshmallows by a fire. I felt like I was back in the middle ages, like serfs looking up at the lords castle.

## Saturday Oct. 22nd

Another beautiful day though it was cold and a heavy frost covered the ground. I headed south out of Worms, picking juicy and delicious grapes along the roadside, while passing through many towns that my dad must have liberated during WWII. Towns like Neustadt and Landau. Now, they all looked like nice towns with small, cool looking, cozy churches with high steeples. I recalled how my father told me the first thing they did when liberating a town was to blow up the church steeple. That was where the observers and snipers were. One could hardly tell there had ever been a war in this area as no scars were apparent.

What a great day to pass through the town of Bad Begzabern, with the Rhine Valley on one side and the Vosges Mountains on the other. There were many castles with kids playing outside and people out shopping. I picked a few clumps of purple grapes growing along the roadside and my, how they were delicious.

# Chapter 5

## INTO FRANCE

After lunch I crossed the border into France at Wissembourg. This is a town where dad saw action during the war. I made a blunder by exchanging my money at a store rather than at a bank. They gave me a lousy exchange rate. The border guards were polite and easy going.

Just after entering France, a grouse like bird flew across the road and hit the windshield of an oncoming car. A puff of feathers flew into the air and the driver swerved and nearly hit me.

The road 'S' turned through some woodlands and I headed into a beautiful sunset while entering the town of Hageneau. The yellow facades of stucco buildings glowed with deceptive warmth in the cold air.

I ate more Russian food for dinner in a park while some kids came by and played tag. This French town was nice but I was feeling weird. Along with the bike having gear trouble, I thought about my finances and wondered how far I could go before going broke. It must have been the loneliness and the monotony in addition to the point I was at in my travels which made me feel so blue. I had a long road ahead, Paris, Marseilles and who knows what after that. It would be hard going but I was determined to keep up the faith.

### Sunday Oct 23rd

A clear and cold moonlit night passed and I slept very well in a ball field. It was cold out in the morning and I cobbled down my last German christollen with persurfillung for breakfast. Last night I finished off all of my Russian food and now looked forward to eating fresh food again.

On this chilly and foggy morning I entered the city of Strassbourg and went directly to the curious looking chapel of Notre Dame Cathedral. Strassbourg is a nice town with narrow streets and many sculptures, but this cathedral is truly amazing. Since it was Sunday morning I was treated to a symphony of beautiful bells playing in rich accord. The many facets and nodes of the steeple of this monastery creates quite a rich sound that is deep and clear with a resonance that

I haven't noticed in other churches. While looking about I met an American fellow named Eric Youngberg from San Jose who said he came to Strassbourg by ship all the way from Rotterdam and that he would spend the winter in Europe.

I headed southwest, into more small towns that my father liberated, like Barr and then Selestat. These were places that he lost buddies, I felt for them, having sacrificed so much. At a store, I bought some goodies and wow, French prices seemed high. They were three times as much as those in Germany. I then turned west and headed up into the Vosges Mountains along the steep road to St. Die, pronounced Saint Dee. I recalled my fathers stories of WWII and thought about the men and the tanks and the battle of the bulge. He recalled marching down a road and seeing a dead GI laying on his pack.

While going up that road a WWII era jeep went by and I tried to imagine what it must have been like during the war. Up I pedaled into St. Marie Aux Mines, but that was only the start of the steep grade. There was a tunnel up there for cars, but since I could not use the tunnel, I struggled and sweated my way to the top of the mountain pass. Finally I got to the 'col' at sunset. It was 773 meters high or about 4000 feet. What a view it was from up on top, where there was a memorial to the French soldiers killed in 1940 trying to fight off invading Germans. I could see the road descending below, toward St. Die.

I went down, like a descending rocket around sweeping curves. My sweaty body was soon numb and freezing cold. My muscles tensed up. Some parts of the road were cobblestone and the corners were tricky to go around without flying over a thousand foot embankment.

I made it into St. Die at dusk. It was a nice old town and very special to think about my dad being here 40 years ago. I ate in the town park and saw a memorial that was partially disassembled but was dedicated to the allies who liberated St. Die in November of 1944. I met 3 Frenchman who were older than my fathers age and they told me of the big fight in this town. They would point to the distant hills and say, "Germans de la vu." I told them my father was here and there eyes bulged in amazement and they shook my hand with gratitude.

I found a park with a lighted toilet and sat to record these events in my diary. My appetite was incredible and I finished off just about every morsel of food I had. I wrote down, "I could eat a dozen sundaes right now."

I laid there in my tent, thinking how it would be to be in a war zone. To hear explosions. To be afraid. To think of the horrors of handing out death or receiving it. I shivered myself into the thankfulness that I was not there.

## Monday Oct. 24th

It was another cold night with a heavy frost on my tent. This seemed a good indication that I'd best be heading south. I rode around St. Die in the wee morning hours just trying to warm up and to find a shop that was open. It was very cold riding. I stopped at a Supermarche and then hit heavy fog on the road to Nancy. It was a real cold fog, it stung my face. The roads were absolutely fogged in. I could have ran into a train and would not have seen it till it was before my nose. The traffic crawled.

I arrived in Nancy around 1pm and by then the fog had burned off. Like many of the towns in France, it has beautifully ornate churches, interesting fountains with statues and many honors to the Mort-de-France. (They died for France). I stopped to dry my tent out on a railing and crapped behind one of those memorials.

While passing through Nancy I recalled how my father had spent a week or two in the army hospital here in February of 1945. He had been knocked unconscious from an exploding German mortar round. Supposedly what happened was he was out back of a barn taking a crap, and the sergeant was standing in the front doorway of the barn. The shell landed right there, killing him and injuring others as well as my dad.

I then went up a long steep uphill after leaving the city. Miles later I rode into Vord and shopped at the stores but the prices looked outrageous. I couldn't make up my mind at one shop and the shop owner became annoyed. The food was so different, for instance the bread seemed old and hard.

I finally bought some food and went down by a big canal to cook it. As people walked past me, I stirred the meat and potatoes and kept my hands warm. I gobbled down a big cinnamon roll cake for dessert which was complimented with a chorus of church bells. As darkness prevailed, the air was like a refrigerator and I could see my breath. I wished someone would look out of their window and invite me into their home. Though many people walked past, no one said hi or offered to help me, unlike in Germany. I camped on a hilltop overlooking the town in which I'd felt so invisible.

**Tuesday Oct. 25th**

When I opened the tent up in the morning the fog was so thick I could hardly see ten feet. The tent was white with frost. I rode on feeling like I was in a deep freeze because of the cold. I thought alot about deer hunting. I sure loved my hunting friends and wished to join them. I've had many good hunting experiences to recount, but mostly it was the fellowship with them and with my dad that I enjoyed.

The trucks on this road to Paris were bad and I had to go off the road because they couldn't see me. The damn French roads had no shoulders and more than once I was driven off into the ditch. My bike was having trouble as the big gear on the crank was stripping. I would look in Paris for a replacement. I swung through St. Diziel, a nice town with a Venus on the fountain. Many of these little towns were very nice.

Again the trucks were so treacherous as they would roar up and expect me to get off the road. Since the road had such a high drop down off the shoulder, a couple of times I almost ruined my bike falling down the steep ledge. There were many close calls, it was the hairiest riding yet.

I bought groceries in Sezanne and headed out of town. At dusk, I jumped a fence, raided an apple tree and then rode on in the dark. With the night to contend with, I had many narrow escapes from those terrible French trucks. They had yellow headlights, which I don't think helped the drivers see me very well. They would blind me when they approached. One time a huge truck passed just inches from me at over 50 mph yet he could have easily swerved around me.

I stopped in Corpeneau and ate canned French sauer kraut and wieners along with a beer. It was getting cold out again when I decided to continue on as Paris was only 100 kilometers or 60 miles away. I headed west on this highway and started to feel a churning in my stomach. My guts wrenched and I had to find a place to crap quickly. I found a little building and opened the door and went inside. There was a trough in the middle of the building with some running water and a walkway that went down one side and then around the other side. I could see where others had made a deposit, so I let go a gusher into the steaming element. For a while I was nauseated and repeated my dispensing while setting up the tent in this sewage house. I spent my night trading off between either crapping or sleeping.

## Wednesday Oct. 26th

Without getting caught, I made it out of my 'toilet home' for the night and then hit the road on the fair morning. The trucks were again real bad, yet I rode consistently until the outskirts of Paris but then my energy seemed drained in addition to the bike gears annoying slippage. I stopped at a supermarche and bought some orange juice and goodies and afterward felt better.

While riding into Paris, I thought at first that it was like Los Angeles with all the traffic, but then the sights became truly spectacular. Everywhere there were lovely fountains, and magnificent sculptures. I rode past the Louvre and then headed down the Champs Elysee. There were many shops and people filling the sidewalks.

I rode up to the Arche-de-Triump and wanted to take my bike underneath to crown my achievement, but a cop kicked me out. I turned around and started to leave then thought about it for a moment. "Hey! I've come too far!" I said to myself. So I went up to the cop and said, "Uno momento! Je sui come from California dan la bicyclette!" But that just got him all that much hotter. "Out, out, out," he said while clapping his hands. All these people watched as I made a fantastic display of being pissed off. I peered at him and stood there. Then slowly I ambled away.

I spent some time exploring the city and found my way to the Eiffel Tower. What a wonderful construction it was and there was even a restaurant up on top. Underneath the tower was a long park where the Parisian children were so fantastic. They looked at me so carefully and then cheered me on. I went to many bike shops and located the bike parts I needed and tried to come to grips that the price would be 200 francs. To cheer myself up I bought a loaf of christollen and cooked supper on a bench alongside the big roundabout facing the Arch de Triump.

There was no place to relieve myself so I went to a hotel and asked to use their toilet. "Ou ey la toilet?" I said. The guy kept saying "Hah?" So after further butchering of the French language

I finally put my hands to my crotch and made a pissing sound. He said, "It's only for le hotel guests," I said, "Oui, oui, please can I use it?" He let me and I dashed in and did my thing.

The night was still young enough to walk the bike along the Champs Elysee and then pedal halfway across the city to Park de la Bologna where I found a woods with tall grass to pitch my tent.

## Thursday Oct. 22nd

I slept well and on the morning made my way into the city and went to the poste office to search through the yellow pages and look up baths and laundry. I found a bathhouse with a swimming pool and then went to the laundromat. After everything was cleaned up I went to the bank and exchanged 7.65 francs to 1 dollar. Went to the bike shop and bought a new crank sprocket and a new chain. A Frenchman at one bike shop helped me dearly with assistance on repairing my bike. I met Chris, a friendly American who'd been staying in Europe all summer and he helped translate for me.

Cycling around the city of Paris was a joy, always wonderful sights to see, people to watch and the smells of bread. I stopped at the markets and the streets were crazy with wild drivers and people. I found a store with christollen after a hearty search. I got all turned around and finally asked someone for directions. I made my way to the Eiffel Tower and found a fantastic overlook too cook dinner and enjoy the beautiful view of Paris. The city was well lit and this was a first class seat to eat my cuisine of sausage and potatoes. Many tourists walked past and I met two pretty girls from Paris. They spoke acceptable English and together with my French we managed to learn each others names. I drank a big bottle of beer and got a little squirrelly, so it was an exciting ride back to the park where I discovered there were many hookers doing business along the drive in the park. They would stand along the road in skimpy outfits and nice looking cars would drive past and check them out.

## Friday Oct. 28th

On the early morning hours around 4am, I could hear a prostitute coughing while she walked through the tall grass in the Park De Bologne. I also smelled her cigarette. She walked directly toward me and then tripped over my tent pole. "Ayeah," she gasped while saying a few curse words. She picked up and went on, never really knowing what she had stumbled over.

At 6:30 I headed off and went on a wild shopping spree to find my hometown friend, Jim Kennedy an ice pick. I made it to a shop but it didn't open until 11pm. I found another place and they had the pick for 306 francs. I bargained and got it down to 258 francs and in shipping would be an additional 120 francs. The shop owner said he would ship it. I didn't know if I could trust them to ship it. So I made a big stink and went to the Poste to see how much it would cost for me to ship it. The Poste said a much cheaper price and they were very angry with Vieux Camping for telling me such an expensive amount. The Poste even called them and told them off. When I went back to Vieux camping, I let them know they'd better ship it or I'd be back to see them. (Even though I knew I never would). I paid them the money and it was in their hands. It was such a hassle I would never shop overseas for anybody again.

I bought a mess of post cards and mailed them to everyone. Most of the day was spent doing all this running around for others, so once finished, I took off and did some exploring. I made it into one part of the city that had hookers on every doorstep and at every corner. They were good looking women. When walking past them they would show their legs or even a little boob. I was surprised how young some of the prostitutes were. One told me she was 16.

I was shopping around the city for christollen. I loved the stuff so much that it was like an addiction. This time I didn't find any and I was irritated when I went to the Arch-de-Triumph bench for supper. It was drizzling while I I cooked. People stared at me and I thought-bugger off. Suddenly I heard someone say, "Hello I am too a cyclist." Then this guy came up behind me and was short and squirrely but pleasant. "Me from Spain," he said tugging up on his drooping pants. "Hello, I am American," I returned. His name was Michael. We talked and I asked him where his bicycle was. He said, "Over there." I asked him, "Did you lock it?" He responded, "No, no." He left to go get it and then came running back. "Me cycle is gone away!" he said in a panic. I went with him feeling sorry for the guy because I thought his bike was probably stolen. We looked where he said he left it and then went further down the street and there it was. He had forgotten where he put it.

He was kind of a funny Spaniard fellow. He ran like Pepe in the movie with his pants hanging down. I couldn't help but feel kind of sorry for him. We went on a bike tour of Paris and rode all over the place. He got all fired up when he saw a cute girl. "Caacow-phew!" he'd say and then whistle. As he did not have a tent we went to the park and I invited him to sleep in my tent. We had a good talk outside of the tent while sitting in the woods. He said, "You are a good teacher," while playing around with a flashlight. A police car went past and he shined his light at the car. I quickly said not to do that and pushed his arm down. He did not understand why I did it.

Once again I heard the coughing prostitute coming our way at about 4am, swishing through the grass, crunching twigs and spitting. This time she walked past without tripping but I smelled her lilac perfume and acrid cigarette smoke.

## Saturday Oct 29th

We had both slept good and awoke, then went down to the Arch de Triump where I asked Michael to take a picture of me with the historic arch behind. To do this we had to stand in busy traffic. Each time I was ready Pepe could not get the camera to work. Everytime I tried the camera it worked fine. We tried this five or six times. Poor Pepe got so puzzled. "Why not work?" he said. He took pictures of my shoes and of his hands and a couple of crooked ones with the arch and me.

We rode over to the Louvre and looked at all the great art works. These master paintings were impressive. Some of them were huge.

We saw the beautiful Mona Lisa and I took a photo which had myself in it to the left of the famous lady. There were so many art works to see by Leonardo and I was interested, but Pepe got tired and bored. He sat down on a bench and dozed off while I looked at Renaissance paintings.

We went into the city. Pepe was so slow I'd have to wait at every light for him to catch up. Many times I thought I'd lost him. He had no map so I'd wait or go back for him. We stopped and ate burgers at a restaurant. After lunch we headed south out of Paris on the road to Etampes. I had a bad bulge on my tire and had to stop and repair it.

We rode for a couple of hours and found a place to cook our dinner and set camp. Pepe said he would not camp at that spot, so after some confusion we found an acceptable sleeping spot by the ruins of a castle. We laid in the tent talking about our countries and he said, "Spain is a modern country." But I had noticed the things he had were not very modern. I felt for him and tested not his pride.

## Sunday Oct 30th

We awoke to a cold, clear morning. Pepe said he did not want to get out of bed as he was too cold. It was no wonder he was cold as his bag was very thin. We went down to a fork in the road where we would separate. He was going west and I was heading east. I gave him an American nickel and he quickly dug out a Spanish peso. We exchanged good wishes and while departing I said, "Goodbye conquistador." He waved and pedaled away standing up, with his pants hanging low, and his rear showing. In all he was a wonderful companion for those two days.

I had good tailwinds and took small roads on the route to Cosne. I watched men hunting for grouse or pheasants in the golden fields. My thoughts flashed back to hunting with my dad. I missed my friends and hunting season so much. Then I thought about Pepe, laughed at his antics and remembered how nice it was to meet him.

I had beautiful weather and stopped to eat some French bread that was 3 feet long. It tasted pretty good, except for the hard crusts, which cut my gums. I stored several of the breads alongside my packs and they looked like missiles. I made way to Cosne and there cooked supper by a road with little traffic and lovely woods. It was a fantastic day, one I'd cherish in my travels in France.

## Monday Oct. 31st

The day dawned as a drizzly morning as I progressed down the road and over many hills. I was thinking about home more often. I thought about girlfriends and the good times I had with them. I thought about hunting. The more I thought about everything the more I was convinced that I should go home. So what was I doing here? My original plan was to be doing exactly what I am doing. Feeling homesick and sorry for myself was not why I came here. My thoughts become compounded with more peril when it started to rain. I stopped in Nevers for lunch and ate under the awning of a supermarche during a pouring rain. I had one beer and thought what the heck and then pedaled onward for Digoin. The rain has a way of contesting self-pity and I had to concentrate on maintaining control of the bike rather than thinking about my problems.

Finally I pulled into Digoin at 6pm entirely soaking wet and found a bus stop to sit down in and dry off. I cooked supper and with my Coleman stove dried everything out, especially my gloves. It really felt cold out when I pedaled down to a shop and bought a menthe-flavored drink from a pop machine. I cycled back to the bus stop and set up my tent inside.

## Tuesday Nov. 1st

I didn't sleep very well because I kept thinking the police would come and escort me away. Considering the conditions outside, the bus stop wasn't too bad a spot to sleep. I packed up in the morning and it was warmer out but still very crummy weather. After some deliberation and because the shops were closed, I headed for Macon and rode uphill into more drizzle. This day is called All Saints Day, a national holiday in France. I noticed people were all dressed up and carrying flowers and baskets into cemeteries. People performed short ceremonies near the gravestones of their relatives. The French cemeteries looked fully packed with gravestones.

I started a long climb up into the mountains as the tires swished in the rain and I thought about home. The rain let up and it began to brighten when I rose to the top of this pass and herd a rush of wind, then saw a blaze of orange flash past. It was a French bullet train that zipped past in speeds exceeding 120 mph.

It was all down hill from there. I coasted along thinking a lot about home again. Once again I was homesick. I sang little songs to keep me from thinking about it. The weather was warmer on this side of the mountain and I picked some delicious purple grapes. I rode into Macon and stopped at a gas station to buy some treats and came back outside and sat on the curb to eat lots of french bread with jam.

I rode on for the city of Lyon with a good tailwind and arrived in the city at 5:30pm as it was getting dark. I then stopped at a little shop to buy a green pepper. When I returned to my bike, I was thinking about ripping off some potatoes that were stacked nearby outside, but I didn't do it. I pedaled to a place suitable to cook dinner and there found my hat and gloves were missing from my handlebar bag. I believed someone must have ripped me off when I dashed into the shop. I rode back to the shop but it was closed. The entire affair bummed me out. I wasn't in a very stable state of mind after that. It really made me want to go home. Now I'd have to buy a new pair of gloves and a hat which meant more expense. Perhaps this was a good lesson for me to learn. Just when I was thinking about stealing, someone stole from me. Hard to believe I was ripped off on All Saints Day, one of the holiest days in France. I recalled my dad telling me that Lyon was known for its thieves and robbers during the second world war. I pedaled clear across the city for nearly three miles to find a park, where I pitched my tent behind a small evergreen tree.

I had very confusing dreams all night long. They were the kind where everything went wrong. Bicycle wheels crumbled, food was burning and a guy was going to rob me in my sleep. I suddenly awoke and listened intently outside of my tent for any sound.

When the morning of Wed. Nov. 2nd arrived I pedaled into Lyon but did not stay as I was disgusted with being ripped off. I headed out of the city and down the road as the skys cleared. I swung into a supermarche and bought a fruit de raison pie and a jar of peach jam. I was hungry and ate all the pie and almost an entire loaf of French bread. I didn't feel very good after all that sugar. The long routine of cycling would burn it off.

A considerate fellow at a bike shop gave me a tire patch at no charge when I stopped to fix a bulging tire. I headed south wearing only a t-shirt as it was a nice day and skirted along the Rhone River which was rather wide at this point. I enjoyed watching teams of rowing boats compete.

In the town of Vienne I shopped for new gloves. Couldn't find what I was looking for and everyone in the shops looked at me queer and suspiciously. Admittedly, I looked like hell. I was very undecisive and was going back to one shop when then they locked their doors from noon until 2pm. It was the damn French siesta!

I rode on, going down some very fast hills and entered the town of Valence shortly after 2pm. There was a flea market happening where I bought a pair of leather mittens for 55 Francs, which is about 8 dollars. I also bought a package of figs.

From there it was a short pedal over to a supermarche to buy groceries. I noticed a park and went in to cook myself a meal of rice and eggs. When I pedaled back to the entrance I found the gate closed and locked. I was locked in! I cycled to the back of the park and found a way out through the fence. Went into town and sat in a square to drink a beer and to play my harmonica. A lady was walking by and she sat down to listen to my ad-lib performance. She kindly applauded when I finished. I went back into the park and had the whole place to myself to camp for the night.

## Thursday Nov. 3rd

People were jogging past my tent and by the time I got up in the morning, the gate was unlocked. I had a foggy morning to contend with while riding. I got lost because of the contrary road signs and concluded that the French could make a straight road crooked. My rear tire was very bumpy and it demanded constant attention. I constantly felt confused for much of the day and thought this was a turning point in my journey. Every little mishap, or thought turned to homesickness and I got this feeling that I wanted to say the hell with this bicycle travel.

What good was I doing traveling this way? Where was I going? Why was I putting myself through all this hardship? These thoughts made me want to quit and go home. A couple of times I lost energy in my body and coasted to a stop. I looked around then continued but it was very agonizing.

I thought things over. It wouldn't do me much good to continue with a negative frame of mind. Should I go home or not? I voted no. What am I going to do to resolve this conflict? I decided to start working on my problem. I would keep reminding myself to get into this experience. To enjoy it and try to learn. Though ever muscle ached and my butt was sore and my head was burned out, I felt the need to continue.

My next problem was what I called, "The glory day of it all." I kept thinking about that wonderful day when I was finishing my trip and a crowd of cheering fans would be there waving me in. But I knew if I continued relishing that thought it wouldn't help me now. I would be living in the future, and might miss out on what was happening now. So I vowed to phase that thought out of my thinking. I had to believe in every step, every pedal, as an experience that ultimately lead me to some kind of bliss.

I made good time even though I stopped often to collect myself. A French child acted as a catalyst to get me rather fired me up. It happened at a stop light. I looked to my side and saw a little girl sitting in the car. She looked at me so intently with her beautiful brown eyes. When another car pulled up beside me, she got behind the steering wheel and acted out driving the car just like her momma might do. It was a precious moment.

I rode into Avignon, a fairy tale looking town that looked like Disneyland. There was a guitar player singing on the street corner and he had a dog, which carried around a hat. The dog would come up and stick the hat in your crotch, which was to irresistible not to place a tip.

While watching this singer, I met a fellow and a young gal and he informed me that Avignon was the Popes headquarters in the 14th century. He told me it was called the Palais de Pope and was made as a medieval palace. So I went up to the palace and had a look around. It was beautiful. I met the fellow again and we chatted. He told me he was English and that his niece was French. He told me some more about this area and I again said so long and then went off to cook dinner by a lovely, half-finished bridge, which is called the Pont de Pape. It should have passed over the Rhone River but they never completed it. "The Pope was sent back to Rome," I was told as the reason.

I went back into the city and for the third time met this fellow and his niece. We went for tea and I learned his name was Bruce Hyatt and his niece was Juliet. We were talking and sipping on tea for a good ten minutes when I looked at her. I did a double take. Again and again I looked into her eyes and noticed just how pretty she was. It was as if she transformed from a frog into a princess right before me! She was so lovely and so charming that it was as if I fell in love with her. We talked about other cultures and global understanding and about the French, the Germans, the English and Americans. We laughed and smiled and when she spoke, her French accent made her English words sound beautiful.

Bruce, Juliet and I walked across the cobblestone street, past the wrought iron streetlamps, to a shop, which served hot chocolate. We became immersed into a great talk about so many things especially art, music and religion. All was well, I felt close to Juliet, until Bruce asked me what I thought about Jesus. When I told him that I didn't think Jesus was god he challenged me. It seemed I offended him as he then wanted to leave, and besides he said, it was late. We adjourned by exchanging addresses and shaking hands. Even when I touched Juliet's hand my heart skipped and words came not.

While pedaling away into the night, I felt bad about my big mouth talking about religion. "I should just shut the hell up," I said out loud. I rode down and pitched my tent in a campground, which cost 12 francs.

## Friday Nov. 4th

My sleep was good and I anticipated the morning. After a good long hot shower and cleaning my clothes and trimming my beard, I looked forward to seeing Juliet again. I thought about her and afterward looked for her all around Avignon, but she and Bruce were gone. I sought her in vain, she was nowhere. My heart sunk, I felt crushed.

While leaving town, I was feeling heartache, then joy when they drove past me and I saw Juliet give a long wave while she was looking back at me-until she was gone.

Again I thought more about home, especially with deer hunting starting tomorrow. I enjoyed thinking back about hunting and recalled pictures in my mind of many fantastic memories from all those years past. I wondered if my dad would go and whether the guys would talk about me. I did miss them so much. They were like my brothers in many ways.

It warmed up beautifully and I could smell the Mediterranean Sea. The weather was very comfy and I rode into a slight headwind with my shirt off. The scenery was rocky hills, dotted here and there with pine trees. While pedaling up long grades I saw the hill behind the town of Aux de Province which Cezanne had made famous in his numerous paintings. It has a spectacular shape. I saw all kinds beautiful girls in town and with the warm weather, wow they were fine. I ate in a park but a ranger made me move because he had to lock up the gate.

I met a girl from Germany who was a student. She told me she would be in Florence, Italy in one week. We talked awhile and I knew I needed to be around people. I could have sat there and talked all night. This must have been the reason why I was hanging around towns at night. The days were agonizing work and isolation, so I enjoyed the chance to meet people. I thought how wonderful it would be to have a relationship with a woman.

As I rode out of town I met two young ladies. One was from the U.S. and the other from Germany. They were students and we talked awhile and I rather wished they would invite me into their house. I continued along a dark road looking for a camping spot and found a good field behind a building with a ship by it. The freeway was on one side and a road on the other so it was noisy.

## Saturday Nov. 5<sup>th</sup>

The morning started off foggy and warm. About 10am the fog began to burn off and I was greeted with this spectacular view of a jagged mountain. It reminded me so much of the California Sierras. I snitched some excellent grapes from a vineyard and sucked them down while the weather warmed to tee-shirt temperatures. I stopped into a small town and stocked up on groceries as it's a Saturday and no shops will be open tomorrow. People in the store stared at me.

It was good riding and nice weather when I swung into Fujal and looked at an ancient Roman Coliseum that was larger than the one in Rome. After a few more miles, I had my first sight of the Mediterranean Sea. What a lovely sight it was. I could see some rocky islands and the clear, blue-green water. Palm trees lined the beach and reminded me so much like Santa Barbara. I rode through the town of San Tropha and then followed along the beach into the city of San Raphael and explored. There were many tourists wandering around there. I cooked my meal by a beach wall and afterward wandered about the shops at night. I met an Italian couple and she spoke un-petite English, but we actually carried on a conversation very well by improvising. From our talk I determined the value of Italian money. We even talked about Beirut. They were very nice people and even though we shared a basic conversation it was lovely. I slept that night by a restaurant that was closed. I awoke around midnight after having a vivid dream and thinking I heard my friend Kim.

## Sunday Nov. 6th

Slept very well and awoke feeling kind of sticky from the ocean air. I rode into town and bought a stick of bread, then pulled over and ate it alongside the scenic roadside. Oh it was marvelous to see the blue sky and sea with its many little coves and rocky cliffs. The water was clear and blue green. I rode along the coastline and saw many bike riders going by. Along the way there was a monument to the U.S. Army 36th Infantry. This was beachhead for the second assault phase during the invasion of Europe. According to the sign they suffered heavy losses.

I rode through Cannes and stopped at a market for fruit and bread. There were some topless women sunbathers walking along the beach. What a surprise that was to see in public! I saw some guys trying to sell necklaces and they came up to me and were a nuisance. I rode along, soaking in the ocean air and taking in the beautiful scenery while entering Nice. I could see why the French Riviera is so exclusively acclaimed. The hills around the city were covered with white houses. The beaches were rocky buttes with lovely sand in between. I saw many tourists in Nice and while pedaling past they all stared at me. I met two English women by a sundial and had a short chat. I looked around town but wasn't to impressed, yet enjoyed passing cars that were caught in traffic.

I headed up the big hill behind the city and had no problem going up, didn't get winded nor feel the least bit tired. I was getting into great physical shape for cycling. I rode up to the top of Mont Blone, which overlooked Monte Carlo and Nice. There's a fort at the top. I did a little exploring around it and noticed a person up in the fort so I figured there must be a way in. There was no entrance, but a cable, hung from about 50 feet below a window. That was the way up. As I started up a head popped out above me. "Bonjour," I said. And "Bonjour," two young women said back. I said, "Ascent?" She said, "Oui." So I climbed on up and met these two gals who were cute and excited to be in an illegal place. There was also one guy up there. We went up on the deck to enjoy the marvelous view. Soon another guy, the other girl's boyfriend, climbed up with a light. We went on a tour of the old fort, laughing and flirting. I'd pinch the girls on the butt. They'd giggle. We saw many dimly lit and dreary rooms. The whole place was very prison like. An old well was on the bottom floor and I pondered how they got water up there. We ran about like fools saying things like "Police" and laughing. It was getting dark out so I said, "Auvoir" to my friends. It was tricky climbing down the cable.

I rode down a short ways to a picnic area and selected a table to cook dinner. Two elderly guys played there game of "Boiles," with heavy iron balls. After dinner I again wanted to tour Nice so I coasted all the way down into the city and looked around for a bit, then pedaled all the way back up the long hill. I spent the night in the park where it was illegal to camp, but I hid myself in the woods. Around midnight some partygoers came by and stayed up all night long making such a racket that it disturbed my sleep.

**Monday Nov. 7th**

I pulled up my tent stakes and ate breakfast then coasted at about 50-mph downhill into Nice. The city was sleepy at this hour and blanketed in light fog. I went over to the waterfront and then progressed eastward along the coast highway. I stopped at a store and this elderly Frenchman came by and felt my bike up. He was so interested in it I couldn't believe it. He asked me, "Parly vous Francais," I said back, "Une petite, jes sui American." He then spoke in broken english and told me of his friend who lived in Chicago that was a cycling champion. He told me he really liked my bike. Then he asked me where I was going. When I told him I was going around the world he rolled his eyes toward the sky, raised his hands to his head and shook my hand repeatedly while patting me on the back. "Tour de la monde, oh my, vous are une magnific American!" He said.

I continued on up and down the big grades along the coast passing the exquisite homes in Ville de France' and then enjoying the rugged coastline as blue skies prevailed. The road into Monaco had many 'S' turns, one of which, was where Princess Grace had met her end.

I pulled into Monaco and entered the red walled palace where Princess Grace lived. It was a small fortress with many armed guards present. Yet even with all the security, I was surprised how easily I moved around. Monoco has many large buildings and beautiful ships in the harbor. I continued on and knew that I would soon be crossing the border into Italy. I thought about the French people and how very few acts of kindness I had experienced from them.

I stopped at the Oceanographic Institute and a French fellow came by and asked me where I was from. He told me had once toured Europe by bike. I asked how the institute was and he said, "You must see it." So I went in and looked up the price which was 30 francs and thought it was to expensive. When I came back out he was so insistent that I go through the museum that he bought me a ticket. We shook hands and he said, "Au Revoir." I couldn't believe this kind act. He didn't even stick around to see me go in.

I went through the institute and saw many interesting articles of under the ocean discovery. They had formaldehyde samples of most every species of ocean fish. There were many colossal bone structures of whales. They had an octopus of over 30 feet length. I watched a Jacques Cousteau film and saw the aquariums filled with wonderful, colorful fish. It all made me think how varied life is on this planet.

When I came outside the wind was howling and it was very hard riding over the hills and against the wind. I stopped at the Italian border and exchanged some money. 10,000 Italian lires equaled 6 dollars. You literally stuffed your wallet with Italian money to buy something. I had a nice greeting at the border by the customs agents. They were joking and liked my mode of transportation. I even met a fellow from Canada and chatted with him.

# CHAPTER 6

# THE ITALIAN CAMPAIGN

After leaving the border the weather turned sour. I could see that because of the rugged terrain it was very poor for camping. Off in the distance could be seen snow on the Alps. In the town of Ventimiglia I bought an Italian phrase book and then continued on to San Remo. Upon my arrival I went to a supermarcono and then headed to a soccer field to cook dinner. The wind howled and it started to sprinkle a bit. I rode into town and noticed that the bricks on the streets were probably as old as the U.S. Constitution. Everything looked old, I humorously imagined this was a Hollywood set. But it is the real thing.

I sat down at a fountain in the City Square drinking my bottle of Italian wine. I decided to move over and sit down at a bench. I lifted the bike over a large curb and thought, 'this sure is a nice little town,' when suddenly, "Tah boom!"–I thought I'd been shot. Well, there was my bottle of wine all over the sidewalk. It was shot. I cleaned it up and went over to sit down. A fellow came by and talked to me. He said he had toured around Spain on a bike. He invited me to stay at his house for the night. I thought, wow, I spent two weeks in France and nobody ever offered me a place to stay with them. Now on my first night in Italy, this happens. That says something about the French.

"But first," said Mercurio, "We go swimming!" I met some of his guy friends and some cute girls. We put my bike in his Ford van and went to the pool. The Italians were so expressive. A normal talk to them looked like a big argument to us. I enjoyed these fiesty women. I swam awhile in the pool but the water was cold and I was tired. The shower was warm so I lay down in there. After cleaning up Mercurio introduced me to a couple more of his friends and then to the mother of Maria. Mother was very curious about me. She asked, "What is wrong with you?" I asked why. She told Mercurio who translated to me, "Why else would you travel alone and away from your momma and papa if something wasn't wrong with you." We laughed while sitting in a cafe drinking Coke. They asked me many questions. One of which was if I was a student. I told them I studied art. "Aaaha Ha" said Mercurio adding. "We go to an artist village."

So we all piled into the van, Maria, Julia and momma, and drove up a rough, winding road to an artists village which was actually an abandoned town that had been ruined by an earthquake in the 1850's. Back in 1960 'hippie' artists inhabited it. They lived and worked in interesting old buildings. Inside we met the artists who were painters, sculptors and poets. They lived in messy quarters, sleeping not far from their canvas. We went back to San Remo and everyone wished me good luck.

Mercurio drove his big van through the small streets with remarkable precision. I cringed that he might get it stuck between buildings. To get up to his flat, I had to carry the bike and gear up about 100 steps. This was a small narrow village. Mercurios flat was simple but nice. Inside, I played the guitar while he cooked us a delicious and simple dish of garlic and pasta. We drank wine and ate his tasty cooking at midnight.

He then made a bed for me and he wished me good luck on my journey. I laid in the bed, listening to the people talking and laughing across the street, in disbelief at how fantastic this day had been, because of the acts of kindness many friends had given me. I felt a new kind of love inside and fell sweetly into gentle slumber.

**Tuesday Nov. 8th**

I heard Mercurio leave at 6am and he very considerately did not awaken me. I listened to the sounds of the neighborhood, people talking with passion, cooking smells, laughing, flapping sheets and walking on the cobblestone street below. I got up at 7am, left him a thank you note and slipped out to the beautiful day. I stopped at a market and bought some bread. Then rode along the coast, stopping frequently to look at the view. The wind picked up and that made it hard going. The girls in Italy looked very cute. I'd wink at all of them. It seemed each time that I stopped, I'd meet someone. The Italians were much warmer than the French. I headed onward for Savona along a wooded section of road. As I pedaled along a fellow came up along side of me. We talked and it turned out he was from Boston. John was his name. He was in a hurry. "Reagan just invaded Grenada." he said. "What the hell is going on?" I said. "What is Reagan doing?" He informed me of the latest news, that Grenada was taken over by communists and the U.S. military was intervening. We talked as miles zipped away.

I told him that my plans were to head for Greece, Israel and Egypt and he told me he was considering going home soon. He had a girlfriend that he could not bear to be away from any longer. Originally he was going to travel around the world. Now he felt it wasn't worth continuing. He had seen enough.

We stopped in the town of Savona for groceries. John was fluent in Italian and it was fun to see him talk with these people. We rode past a Soviet ship being unloaded by cranes. The hammer and sickle on the ship funnel seemed an ominous reminder of the Soviets might. Along our ride we talked much about our bike travels and what's happening in the world. Then we saw a nice little park and found a picnic table to cook our dinner. While we cooked and ate, people looked in disbelief at the two of us slobs.

We chowed down, drank wine and talked up a storm. John was very homesick, probably more than me. He was riding with a friend named Dave, but they split up two days before because they got on each others nerves. It was interesting to hear his story, and to tell mine. Now he was happy to be on his own and looked forward to going home in December. I thought about my own adventure and how much further I was going and how little I knew about where I was going except that I was still going to try and go around the world. We pedaled up a dark road and found a grassy field to lay out our sleeping bags for the night under a clear, starry sky.

## Wednesday Nov. 9th

We awoke at 7am with heavy frost on our sleeping bags. I looked at John and mimicked a popular Navy recruitment television commercial. I said, "The Mediteranean-to port, Sicily-to Starboard, Africa-and your in command- the Navy it's more than a job, it's a fuck job!" He laughed hard and so did I,

We packed up and pedaled down to a cafe where we sipped on steaming cappuccino. They made it on the spot with thick coffee and blended, steaming, whipped milk. It was very good. Then we headed down the road, talking and oblivious to the loud traffic and thick exhaust. We came to a fork in the road and John said, "Ooops-this is where I make a left turn." Since I was heading right, we shook hands and wished each other good luck without ever stopping our bikes and separated on our different ways. I was a little sad afterward, for the companionship was enjoyable and entertaining.

It warmed up and I stripped off some clothes while tackling big hills on this sunny and beautiful day. I made it into Genova around 11am. A city bus almost crunched me at a corner. I had to lift and jump the bike off the road onto the sidewalk. I flipped him off. Genova was a big, stinky industrial port city that was crummy looking. I rode on through town while my rear tire bumping was getting worse. I stopped for lunch in a nice little town and went in and came out of a store just in time as they closed the doors at 12:30.

I pedaled down to the beach, shirtless and sat down to eat my bread, jam, cheese, chocolate and a coke. This guy rode up on a moped and spoke Italian to me. He got off his bike and pointed at my jam. Then he grabbed my jam and asked, "Francais marmalade?" "Si" I responded. He said something else but I couldn't comprehend it. Then he took a spoonful of jam and put it on his palm and gulped it down. He said, "Goodbye," got on his moped and took off. Bizzarre.

I rode on and had to change my rear tire as it was to bumpy. I entered a nice town but found the stores were all closed on Wednesday afternoons. As it was getting late, my belly ached with hunger and I went into a small restaurant. I sat down and nobody could speak english. It took some effort, but I ordered a pepperoni pizza. They had a big clay oven, which burned wood. All of the pizza was made from scratch. When they brought it to me, I was surprised to find it was covered with red and green hot peppers, but not a piece of pepperoni. Considering the spicy-hot red peppers it was very good. I had a beer, a chocolate bar and yogurt. The night was spent near the beach, by a nice retaining wall right next to a walkway that was hidden from view.

## Thursday Nov.10th

In the morning I found a co-op that was open and bought some bread, figs and cheese. After leaving town, the road began to go up and up and up into the mountains. Then it went down real fast and it got real cold. To warm up I was singing Bob Dylan's song, 'Tangled up in Blue' and people would stop and stare at me.

There was time to figure out that my expenses were coming to about 8-10,000 lire per day. That was 4 to 6 dollars. Some thrilling downhills were enjoyed prior to entering the village of La Spezia at lunchtime.

I rode onward after lunch and was rocket propelled from eating so many figs. Pitty the poor soul who might follow to close.

In the port town of Lerui, there was a fort with huge walls that were steeply angled. A fort like that must have seen battles from pirates or other invaders.

Continuing on this scenic section of road, I saw beautiful snow capped mountains to the east, behind the town of Carrerra. The area is renowned for its excellent white marble which Michelangelo preferred. I saw a cute girl on the beach and she had this ultra serious look and I winked at her. She winked back and beamed a great smile. All I could say was "chow," she said likewise.

I toured around town and went out on the large pier. The sun was setting into the sea in an orange fireball bringing an end to a nice day of cycling. I didn't travel too many miles, about 50 or 60, but then it was hard riding. Something which stuck with me for much of the day was the dream I had last night about Ellen. In the dream she brought me some treats. I thought about this dream all day. I've come to realize she is probably deep into a relationship by now and perhaps I'll never date her again. I often felt my heart was reserved just for her, but I didn't want to hang onto that sacred ground any longer. I did want to keep her as a close friend, but for now, I was setting her free. I would be free, easy and willing to meet any of the ladies of this world! I only needed to convince myself of this new decision.

**Friday Nov. 11<sup>th</sup>**

My night was spent on the porch of a small beach hut. I could hear the surf crash all night long. Someone walked by and I awoke but otherwise there was no trouble. I rode on in the morning hours and was heading for Pisa. It was a nice, flat ride with a good tailwind. I rode hard and fast until I could start to see the leaning tower above the tree tops. A cathedral dome could be seen also.

I went through a mighty wall around the city and entered Pisa. There it was-The Leaning Tower of Pisa. I laughed aloud as it was so comical. You'd swear it would fall over. Yet, it was so beautiful, like a multi stacked wedding cake. While taking photo's I met an American couple that was stationed in Italy named Ken and Debbie. They took several pictures of me. We had a talk about my journey and theirs as well. Ken invited me to call him when I arrived in Brindisi.

I went up the marble steps into the leaning tower. It was a walk back into the ages. Built in 1175, it took 90 years to complete. Galileo performed his gravitation experiments from the top. It gave a fantastic view of the city and I while up there, I met two U.S. guys. Meeting other Americans was such a positive experience. We always open up so much. There is more comradery abroad, than is ever experienced back in the states. We are more interested in one another's welfare. While coming down the steps of the leaning tower one must hang on dearly to handrails as the floors are extremely slippery. In addition, there are no railings on several floors. I heard stories of tourists who fell to their death.

The doors on the cathedral are intricately designed reliefs telling Biblical stories. While studying them I met a German fellow. He was trying to open a bottle of beer but had no bottle opener. I showed him that the pedal of my bike worked nicely for this purpose. He rewarded me with the first large gulp of his strong beer.

I was on the road again, heading for Florence singing aloud while passing through narrow streets. I felt charged up at first. Singing boisterously. Then I started thinking about my relationships with women. Why wasn't I married or why was I in this period I was in? It occurred to me that I was heartbroken many times as a youth. First there was Barbara Gehring, at the age of 5 I loved her, but at 6 she moved away. Then there was Lonnie DeMaria, same story, only that was age 8. Then there was Kathy Bergman. I could remember seeing her for the first time, crying in my fourth grade class. She had just moved into our neighborhood from Two Harbors and it was her first day starting at my school. She was in 5th grade, but I was in 4th. We shared a split classroom. I fell in love with her that very first day. We were goo-goo eyed for each other even as teenagers. She teased me, pushed me, probed me to see if I'd really chase her. Because I was an introvert, I didn't. I did not know how. Then she met Dave. About one year later I went to their wedding. At her wedding she told me, "I just couldn't wait for you Eric." I was crushed.

When I was in my early twenties, there was Keely. She was a gorgeous boxom blonde. I just fell for her like a ton of bricks. But after awhile I learned how she was moody and there were so many other guys in her life. Later there was Molly. I loved them all. Thinking of them helped pass the miles away.

I pieced together this puzzle that I had never fully solved. Halfway around the world, here in Italy, I figured out that my past loves had all left me. It was not always because of my own doing. Though I did let them slide away. It was because of circumstances or because I was too sensitive.

I believed this is why I tended to shy away from a relationship. I always got hurt. I was vulnerable. I figured out a new plan entitled; 'It doesn't matter that I get hurt, but rather that I learn a little and get to know another person even minutely along the way.'

The day got late and darkness crept in at 5pm. I was riding hard on bad roads full of bumps and with many trucks. I pushed on. It occurred to me how good my physical shape was. I'd ridden most of the day and was going hard even around 6pm when I made way into Firenze(Florence). I stopped at a co-op and headed for a park on the river edge. I was sitting down and eating a delicious pork chop and potato dinner when many men came by and looked me over. Then they'd go into the woods. Then some women came by, looked at me, then went into the woods with the men. I figured out that I was sitting where the whores usually do their business. I saw a couple of whores come happily along, until seeing me, then they darted away.

While exploring around town I was impressed by the amazing architecture of this city. It was so beautiful that I became turned around and searched along the streets trying to figure out where I was. I went past a store and inside saw the girl I'd met one week before in Aux in Provence. Unfortunately she was with a guy, but I waited for her to come out. She looked at me and I said, "Hello." She looked at me but didn't recognize me and then it sunk home. "You are the American I met in Aux in Provence!" She got all excited and we talked joyously. She was a pretty gal. Her escort was an Italian fellow and he gave me directions to a park. I went up there and spent the night on an overlook of Florence.

**Saturday Nov. 12th**
Somewhat of a strange night as I was out in the open and had thoughts of someone ripping me off. It was a sunny but misty morning I rode down to the public overlook of Florence. They call it the Piazzez de Michelagelio. I was standing there and this fellow walked up to me and spoke Italian. I did fine acting like I understood, but he went on and I got flustered. He looked at me like I was a dummy. Then he said, "Just kidding-I'm from the states-are you?" We talked for an hour about the city, the Italians, our country and more. His name was Glenn and he was from Virginia. Most of all on his mind were women. He'd tried all the techniques to pick up European women. He was discouraged after taking 100 names and addresses. He was going to start to do what a Greek recently told him to do. "In one hour you should get her name, a kiss, a hug, go to bed, make love, if not go on to the next girl." Glenn was good company for that hour of discussion and he motivated me.

I pedaled down to a park and took a bath at an outdoor sink and washed my clothing in the public washroom. The sun was warm and I hung everything out to dry on a children's gymnasium.

I went into Florence and explored a church called the Duomo. It was a beautiful dome shaped church designed by Michelangelo.

Late in the afternoon, I went about the town looking at various sights and then found a little square where I sat down on my helmet and looked at my map. A young woman came by and asked me if I wanted to go to the youth hostel. I said, "No thanks." We talked a while. She asked me, "Want to go for coffee?"

We went to a sidewalk cafe and though I ended up buying the coffee, she was the one who was picking me up! We went walking and talking around the town, stopping at a pizza parlor by the Ponte de Vecchio. Her name was Fredriche, she was 21 and from Germany.

Early in the evening, I bought a bottle of wine and we found a seat in a church yard and sipped the wine and talked about Florence. It was a pleasant evening, people were ambling past, our conversation flowed. After a while the wine got to us and we kissed as people walked by and watched. Then she said she had to go quickly to catch the last bus of the evening to the youth hostel. I walked her to the bus and she was off. It was a bummer to see her go. While riding back to the park I was slightly drunk and bumped into a pedestrian who was also drunk. I helped pick him up while apologizing profusely. I found a good spot to camp in a park and slid into the tent listening to the sounds of a carnival that was happening not to far away.

### Sunday Nov. 13th

Church bells rang in the morning and I rode down to the Uffizzi gallery and met Frederiche at the doorway. I was glad she remembered my rendezvous plan from the night before. We went into the Uffizzi and saw some beautiful paintings by Buotecello, Michelangelo, Leonardo and Cauracass. I especially liked the two Rembrandts side by side. One was of him at the age of 28 and the other at 55. It was an interesting perspective. We saw up close the sculpture, 'Pieta' by Michelangelo. It was a beautiful rendition of Mary holding Christ in her arms after the crucifixion. Part of it was unfinished which gave it the look of emerging out of stone. All of them were wonderful, but it was a huge place and we got burned out walking, even though we moved quite rapidly.

We walked to this courtyard by a church and sat down to eat some food. A group of Italian boys were there playing with a frisbee. They didn't know how to throw it. I went over and threw the frisbee and they grabbed it from each other playing tug of war with it. They were hysterical clowns not unlike the Marx brothers. A fellow came by and asked me about my bike. He was so amazed at it. Then all these young boys came over. They huddled around me and we joshed and talked. It was hard to understand them. They were just funny, laughing, goofy boys. 'Riche' enjoyed this sight from her bench. When I sat down by her she said, "I want to spend the night with you."

We walked up to Fort Belvedere and sat there and talked about art. She said she wanted to paint Florence. I said it would be difficult because the architecture offers so much geometry that it is hard to be expressive. She was interested so I went on about art as an emotional message. That TV programs and movies, are what paintings were in the past. I rambled on about art as a release of the human psyche, but had to stop. I had noticed how Germans listen so intently that sometimes they seem in a trance. I need not entrance this lady with my gibberish.

We went down to the Ponte de Vecchio and sat down to watch the people. There were no cars allowed, only people filled the streets! Oh it was great. I love cites that are people oriented. Cars make cities horrible, because they compete with humans. We found a place to eat after much confusion looking. I had a good but tiny dinner of Lasagna. We relaxed and watched people walk past my bike. It was like my baby. They stopped and stared at it. It was like it was a work of art. We walked to the park and set up my tent. We necked in the woods and then slid into the tent. Her hips were so big we could just barely get into the sleeping bag. It was nice to be with a woman after so long. Real nice. In her stern German way, she laid down the law, there would be no intercourse.

After much tangling during the night and after much embracing of one another I was ready to be a single man again. She moved all night long and it was cold. I got very little sleep as her big hips kept the sleeping bag from being zipped up and it was chilly.

In the early morning darkness, I heard a "ziiipp" like sound and being curious when I looked outside the tent, the ground was all white with snow. The sound was the snow sliding off the tent.

## Monday Nov.14th

When the morning dawned we packed our stuff outside in the snow and walked to the bus stop. After a long kiss we said good bye, waving and smiling sadly. I rode on through Florence stopping at several stores to munch, as I was hungry! My short relationship with Riche was good. We both needed each other in this way, at this time. It was a mutual agreement.

I headed up many long hills and was several miles outside the city where I passed a U.S. Military cemetery and memorial. I rode up to the memorial passing thousands of grave markers. A huge wall told the story of WWII. There were over 5,000 names of men missing in action. Over 25,000 graves were in this one graveyard. It was a moving monument to the men who died in this foreign country. I read an inscription, which said, "They died in the height of the battle, at the height of their lives, so that freedom could continue." I felt the patriotism for U.S.A. I felt for their suffering. I felt like crying. I felt proud of my father and in my nation.

I continued on into the medieval city of Sienna. It was a very charming city with a large courtyard and the most gorgeous church I've yet been too. The interior was ornate and covered in gold. It was like a true place for angels. Beautiful, ornate paintings and sculptures were everywhere. The dome was elegant and it was decorated with gold-inlaid stars. The floor was a mixture of marble patterns and mosaics. If heaven favors churches then this is the ultimate church. Upon stepping outside, I met an American named Shawn and he was burned out on youth hostels and trains. I told him what it was like bicycling in Europe and he enjoyed my tales.

I left the tourist city of Sienna and headed south on the road to Rome. I pedaled along a nice highway, until it started to get dark, around 5pm, and turned into San Lorenzo de Meste, a small town on a hill off the road about a mile. Hunger pains were calling as I rode into the old town.

There was one little store in this town. I went inside and this charming old woman watched me as I shopped. She only spoke Italian. I bought some meat that was like salt pork, along with potatoes, peppers and onions. When I brought my basket of goods up to the counter and handed her the money to pay, she took my money and my arm and escorted me out of the store. I didn't understand. She turned the light out, locked the door and we went across the street to a pub. She motioned and told me to sit down. I thought, 'What's going on, aren't you going to sell me my goods?' I sat at this round table with three old men whose faces were illuminated by a single light bulb hanging over the middle of the round table. There faces were all droopy and wrinkled and their eyes were bloodshot, with each eye seemingly independent of the other, like a chameleons. They looked exactly like a famous drawing by Leonardo Da Vinci, called, 'Old men'. One of them spoke in Italian and asked me where I was from. I said, "America." "Ahh," they responded tilting heads back and nodding. They leaned forward as if interested. I said, "California." They lit up like a candle. "California, belle! Belle!-Reagan-Reagan!" I did not want to take sides so I just nodded. Then one toothless man said, "Reagan goot." I said, "Reagan Ok!" They laughed and said, "Ok! Ha. Ha." Then one old man said, "Reagan-Roosky!" and he butted his fists against each other and shook his head in a no-no-no fashion. I understood what he meant. He knew of the conflict of superpowers.

I suddenly realized my bike was not locked outside, and made a gesture to them of putting my fingers together like a chain and suggested that my bike would be stolen outside because I did not lock it. "Na, na, no steal," they reassured me.

This young fellow walked into the pub. The store lady pointed to the guy and herself and said "Mamma." He was her son. He was very kind to me They escorted me to the back of the shop. "Ariva Derci," said the old men in unison and we shook hands.

I had no clue what was going on, but I was given royal treatment by the shopkeeper son. He then explained in a very broken englishly-Italian that his momma had to close the store so she could bring me more change for the 10,000 lire bill that I handed her. (this was the equivalent of about $6 US) I then was asked all kinds of things by this man. He asked me if I came all the way from California on a bicyclette? "Yes," I acknowledged. Oh he shook his head as if I was a madman. "Amerikan, Amerikan," he said holding his hands in a prayerful way. (Did he really think I crossed the Atlantic on a bike?)We shook hands heartily and I went off into this little town and cooked my dinner on a side street. People walked by and said, "Chow!" as I ate in a comfortable place with a nice view. It was a delicious meal and a fine setting, though getting cold out.

For a little town, it had so many good qualities. Children playing and laughing, old men and people moving briskly about. It had all the charm a town could ever have, except nobody could speak english and I no Italian. I found a good place to pitch my tent half a mile outside of the town.

## Tuesday Nov. 15th

In the morning, I made my way down the road to Grossetto. The wind was at my back. Though the road was mountainous, I made good time even going uphill. A tailwind made quite a difference. It was a sunny, but cold morning. I wore a down ski jacket and mittens. I thought about my trip. How long a road I had ahead of me. How would I get around Lebanon? How will I get to India? I thought about mom and dad. I must call them soon, for I sensed some worry and knew mother would appreciate it with Thanksgiving coming soon. I made it into Grossetto at 11am, asked some people where the co-op was, then bought groceries and loaded them on the bike. This had to be done now for it was difficult to find a shop after siesta.

I rode on and saw the Mediterranean Sea again. Darkness came at 4:30 as I rode into a small Italian town, built on a high knob as usual. I was quite tired as I pedaled through town. All these people along the road and on the sidewalk stopped to stare. Many of them laughed. I found a spot to cook my supper of peppers, potatoes, onion and pork chops as they walked past.

I thought about these supposedly very religious people with their cities built around the church, yet questioned what they practiced as religion. No one offered me a helping hand.

I played a little game of bike tag with some children who were running around the town. I had the feeling they knew something about Americans. I rode down to the ocean as the moon was shining and found a restaurant that was closed. It had a deck which looked great to sleep on.

I awoke to see clouds rapidly covering the full moon. Then heard the pitter patter of rain begin. The roof had a drain that dropped the water onto the deck near to where I was sleeping. The sound of the water splatter was annoying but I dozed off but soon awoke to see the water creeping up towards me in a big puddle. I got up and it was cold out. I took some planks from a painter's scaffold and made myself a raised bed in case the water kept rising. Then I took a plank and leaned it against the waterspout at an angle, to allow the water to run down the plank and off the deck. There was no more noise from the drain even though the rain poured. I slept the night like a baby and when morning arrived, it was still raining as I packed up, while avoiding the deep puddle of water under my planks.

## Wednesday Nov. 16th

I rode south in the rain, against a wet and cold headwind. Each time a truck went passed, I was drenched by the spray. The truck wind would almost topple me. It only lasted about a second in time, but it's intense and happens in this manner. When the truck is coming up from behind, there is at first a pushing sensation, then as it comes up alongside there is a terrific suction toward the side of the truck, adding to the danger are the big spinning tires. As the truck passes there is a blast of air shoving me toward the ditch, followed by a tow rope jerk back in the direction of the truck. Finally there are a few seconds of 'surfing' in the trucks wake. To counter balance all of these effects is very tiring, and it caused me to tighten up and brace each time a truck passed. Added to the fact that some of the trucks gave little room, it was a dangerous liaison. Thus the sequence is repeated each time a truck goes by; pushing-suction- shoving-jerking-surfing.

As I was fighting against a headwind, the approaching trucks would hit me with a mighty blast of wind comparable to getting whacked with a big wet rug. It was a real kick in the face, one that would take the breath away. I was not afraid of the trucks, just annoyed at them and besides it was exhausting work.

At noon I stopped in Civitavekchia and bought groceries. The stores were closed on Wednesday afternoons so I stocked up. While packing up the bike, people asked me if I was Dutch. "American," I would say. A day's worth of food added extra weight to the bike. I rode on thinking about when I returned to the states and how I wanted a brass band playing at the finish line. I'd ride up to the finish line with my hands raised like bike racers do. My parents would be there cheering.

This was not a fun day because the wind was so annoying that it caused great struggle, but I pushed on for Roma. I rode up and over several hills as the traffic became more intense. The highway had kilometer markers every kilometer and at my pace it was a strain each time passing them. They went by slowly; 30k-20k-10k, 5k, then finally I could see the Vatican. Wow, it was an impressive sight. I was so pooped I could hardly take in the views.

I went into the courtyard of the Vatican, through the most magnificent pillars and columns I've ever seen and stopped to eat some chocolate. I looked up at the church facade and then entered St. Peters Cathedral. I followed along with a guided tour and was in awe of the interior of this super church. Michelangelo designed much of it with the assistance of Bernini. It is a most spectacular building construction. The arches are colossal, the sculptures, each one a master piece are so huge yet so free they leap to life. I was in awe of the place.

I visited the tomb of St. Peter, who was crucified upside down at this very sight. I viewed the Pieta by Michelangelo, a sculpture that was broken apart by a madman from Australia who came with a hammer and hit it 13 times. I listened to the tour guide tell about Rome and Michelangelo. He said, "The Vatican is a gift by a man, Michelangelo, to all of mankind. It is all of humanities who own these achievements. They belong to all of you." He then concluded with, "I am finished with my tour and I will walk with you out of the church and I will walk home, for I live across the street from the Pope."

Afterward, I went down to a park and cooked supper. It was a mmm good meal of meat and potatoes. I then toured my way to another park on one of Romes seven hills and found a place to camp near some trees. What a great place to sleep, high on a hill above Rome.

## Thursday Nov. 17th

I arose early the morning and packed things up to avoid the hassles with the carabinerri. Coasted down to this monument at the entrance to the park and sat down to eat and write in my journal. I walked over to this monument which looked like a tree carved from stone. This fellow walked by and said something in Italian and I just said, "What is it?" I knew he was referring to the monument, but I did not know that he could speak English. I was surprised when he said, "It's a monument to the men who died on the hill in the battle of 1867. There were 300 who died there. They have 300 olive trees planted for the dead." This man told me he was French but he lived in Rome. He had done a lot of traveling in his past and he perused me on all the places he'd been. "I've been to Los Angeles, Spokane, Chicago, Florida as well as trout fishing in the Rockies and horseback riding in Montana," he commented. We talked about my plans and he listened intently. I told him people seemed happier in the country than the city folk. This brought out a frustration in him. He told me, "I also love the country but what can I do to pay for my children's needs? It isn't fair to live out there, and let them be in poverty. This is why I live in the city." When he calmed down he told me some places to visit in Rome.

I went down the busy streets and the rain began, just as I found an interesting church and sought shelter under an overhang when it began to pour. Inside, I bought some postcards and filled them out, then toured the church. It contained a tomb with the bones of John the Baptist. Seeing relics of the Christian religion was instilling into me a little more persuasive proof of Jesus existence. It deepened my curiosity of the Biblical stories because here was physical evidence-or were they fraudulent bones?

I sped down to the Coliseum and toured around that magnificent structure noting that the construction was not that much different than our modern buildings. A sign said gladiators fought each other to death in the arena. They also had chariot races, foot races, music, assemblies and mock battles with boats. There was a special place where the emperor sat and would either put his thumb up or down to judge the contestant. Many rooms could be seen under the floor of the coliseum where bulls were starved so they would fight more ferociously. I rode into old Rome and saw the tile roofed buildings. It was raining hard when I headed up to the Vatican. The police said, "It's impossible for you to leave your bike here." I told them I'd done it the night before so it wasn't impossible-just probably intolerable. Again he said, "No it's impossible." I was so mad I left.

I tried to find a supermarket. They were all closed, as THURSDAY was there CLOSING day. I got all pissed off riding in the rain and cursing the Italians for their stupid kind of system. As I pedaled along on the rough roads I ran over a piece of glass. Inspection revealed a long cut on my new tire. I found a pizzeria and sat under an awning, mad and bummed out, though the pizza was delicious. The sidewalk was choked with evening shoppers and many nice looking gals but I was exhausted and pedaled through the city and up to the park on one of the seven hills and pitched my tent in miserable weather, on wet ground and under a dripping tree. To make things worse I had to go do a big job. I clambered back out and ducked behind a tree when suddenly a car came by just as I let go. I was swinging around that tree, pants still down by the knees, trying to hide, as there lights shined until it passed by. It didn't look like they saw me. I went to bed at 8:30pm.

## Friday Nov. 18th.

I awoke to another drizzly morning and sped down to the Standa supermarket. Already, I was getting to know Rome better and finding it easier to get around. I rushed into the store and bought some goodies, especially filberts were cheap and so were figs. I went to a couple bookstores looking to trade my Italian to English book but none had it. I went to the Vatican and then entered the line for the Chapel. People stood there in line and watched me lug all this wet gear up a long spiral stairway. I paid 5000 lire to get in. The guys at the cloakroom were amazed I'd ridden all the way from Rotterdam. I went into the bathroom and stripped down to wash up. Man, I felt great after that, even though again putting on my stinky clothes. With the cloakroom attendant watching my stuff, there was no need to worry about it being stolen, I was free! While walking through many corridors and into the museum, the suspense was building to see Michelangelos great masterpiece. There were many excellent statues, sculptures and murals along the route. I went through what seemed like endless hallways and then at last entered a ochre lit room, the Sistine Chapel, filled with whispering people.

Everywhere one looks, this room is painted upon. I looked up and could see the magnificent Last Judgement by Michelangelo. The ceiling tells the story of the Old Testament. It's difficult to see everything because one must kink their neck to look up, but every one of the huge figures is proportionately superb. Their expressions so much capture the essence of each scene. The Last Judgement is confusing. Hell is easy to see, but is there a heaven depicted? Michelangelo is implying two roads for mankind to follow-that one can either be judged to go to hell or to go with Christ. I found Christ to look uncomfortable, like he is getting up from a squat. Not to take anything away, for it is a monumental work of art. I felt in awe once again of mankind.

I returned to the Vatican for a second look and again it impressed me so much. It was so gorgeous inside, so magnificent and inspiring. To me it's like walking into a canyon with a strong wind blowing, but one can't hear or feel it. It was so warm inside for such a big building, and I saw no heaters.

I pedaled down the roads of Rome to see if I could ride to an overlook of the city, but got flustered in the rain and the horrible roads. I visited the Pantheon and like they say, 'The rain never hits the floor though the hole in the roof.' I met two Swiss girls in front of the Pantheon and they were friendly and one was very cute. We talked about the city and what it was like staying in a hotel or pensiones.

I hoofed it back to the Standa supermarket and parked my bike in front of a large window, believing it would be more secure. Went in and rushed around to buy my food because I was always worried about my bike. When I came out what a shock to see it was gone! Rapidly my heart skipped and I looked frantically around then-there it was-down the sidewalk, laying up against a tree. The cable lock was wound around the axle so tight that it broke the spokes. I was pissed. The guy in the store did it because he said he did not like it up against the window. I did not say a thing to him but gave a dirty look. I went down by the castle and cooked supper when the caribineri came by and checked my identification. I dried my things out on a railing and drank a beer then went up to my hilltop camp. The full moon was out and it was cold. This time a motorcycle came by as I climbed into the tent though he did not see me.

## Saturday Nov. 19th

It was a sunny morning in Rome when my head popped out from the tent. I spun down to the gate entrance and saw some cats sitting on the monument. Fed them bread and again met my French friend. He said, "Don't go to Turkey as it's bloody cold." We wished each other well and I went down to the Coliseum to take a few photos. There I met a fellow from India who was jittery and repeated four times to me, "You ah must go to Delhi, find big church and see the view. Eat (he held his hand to his mouth) sleep (with his hands beside his head)-at no charge." He took some photos of me though I wondered if he even got me in the photo.

I rode through Rome on a rather quiet morning enjoying the magnificent sights one last time. Then I pierced past the south wall around the city which looked like it had been blown up.

It was good riding weather along the way to the town of Anzio. The steep walls along the beach are reknowned for the beach head by allied troops during the second world war. Occasionally there was some building wreckage, but one could hardly tell there had ever been terrible battles.

It was a lovely day, the ocean was beautiful and I stopped to clean my bike and repair a broken spoke. Every car that passed would honk their horns at me and it was annoying. In every town I pedaled through, the people would stare at me. They dropped whatever they were doing. Most of the time people would say insults or ridicule but I just ignored a lot of them. I caused many near accidents because of people looking at me, and not looking at what they were doing.

I rode past a bar which had U.S. rock music playing and people sitting outside on a deck. I yelled, "American Rock and Roll-alright!" The people looked at me very confused. I rode into Scudabia and shopped around. Came out of a market and this big, husky, fisherman came up to me and asked in Italian where I was from. "America," I said. "California," I added. He almost flipped and smiled, then started to pat me on the back. "Italia belle? Si?" he said. "Si" I said. Some boys came over and one of them spoke a little English. I told them where I'd been, how long, how far. Then some more people came over. One guy spoke very good English. He and all these others were so impressed at me to have come so far. They interpreted to this fisherman and he said, "Italia girl mucho cha cha," and he put his fingers together into an intercourse fashion, then said, "Good-si?" I responded, "Si," and everybody in this crowd laughed. Then he asked me where I was staying. He invited me to sleep in a big car with him. He said, "No quonto,(no charge) no steal." I made a face like 'oh-sure' and gestured the intercourse fingers to him just as a joke. The crowd around me just roared. I laughed hard and so did the fisherman. We embraced an arm around each other. It was hilarious. I didn't take his offer because I wanted to travel on, 'oh-sure!'

I ate an early supper at a park and then continued south down the road. Ahead I saw a fellow riding a bike with a girl sitting on his handlebars. I pulled up alongside and asked them for directions. He kindly confirmed that I was on the correct road. The young woman was extraordinarily beautiful with the wind blowing her long black hair and exposing her olive skin. She had dark eyes, her teeth were white, her lips full and though appearing very shy she was radiant with countenance. For the rest of the evening I kept imagining her on my handlebars.

I continued on into the night with the wind howling and the ocean laping at the beach. Looking for a place to camp was no fun in the night. I finally pedaled into Terrachino and found a spot to sleep behind a closed restaurant.

## Sunday Nov. 20th

During the night a bug bit me or stung me on the belly and it hurt like all hell. There were many bugs in my sleeping bag. When morning came, a woman who was picking flowers walked right past me as I looked out of my tent. She never saw me. I was excited while packing things up because on this day I would call my parents. I thought about all the things I would ask them. I knew they were worried about me so I wanted to comfort them. It was another fine day as I pedaled along figuring the time difference was 7 hours. I would wait until 2 or 3pm to call home. Except for meeting a nice looking girl by the beach, seeing a long Roman aqueduct and exploring a 2000 year old Roman amphitheater, it was an uneventful morning.

I started to look for a phone around 2pm and at 2:30 I found one. It was beside the highway and had no door. The traffic was bad so I took a plywood panel off a truck and improvised to make a door. The caretaker of the truck wasn't too happy. I tried to figure the phone out and put money in but it wouldn't work. 'The system here sucks,' I thought while asking a fellow in a shop for help. He said, "You cannot call the U.S." I tried again and finally reached an operator. They couldn't hear me and it was such a bad connection that I had to try another phone. I pedaled down the road as the traffic got incredibly congested. I passed so many phone boxes because they would have been useless for a long distance call with the traffic being so noisy. I found a hotel-bar and walked in and asked the man at the desk if I could use the phone. "Quonto?" I said. He said, "No quonto." So I got through to the operator who connected me with U.S. and then I heard dad say, "Hello?" "Hello dad," I said. I could just barely hear him. "Where are you?" he said. "Italy, near Naples." I responded. He said something and I couldn't comprehend it. The connection was horrible. I asked him how he was. I think he said. "Ok." Then I asked him about deer hunting, "Did you go?" I said. "Yes" he said, "We got four." I could understand that, but he said something else and it was unintelligible. "Say again," I said. He tried but still I could not hear it. "Is mom there?" I asked. "Yes," he said and I heard him say. "Donna, Donna it's Eric." *Then these people in the hotel started to swarm around me. This one guy looked mad.* "Mom?" I said. "Hello Eric," she said in her lovely way. I heard that and, "How are you?" "Fine and you," I returned. "I'm ok," she said. *These people got noisy and started pointing at me.* I tried to ignore them, "Mom I'm ok but I can't hardly hear you." She asked how was my bike. I said, "It's ok but my tires have been a problem." She said something else. I asked her to repeat. I think she said, "Justin is getting married next month." I didn't know to whom. I couldn't hear her. *This guy wanted the phone. I told him "Statis Union long distance." He seemed amazed -his eyes bulged out. The people talked like crazy.* "Mom I can't talk much longer. I have to go. I'll be in Greece in one week. I love you. Good bye." She said something but I couldn't hear it except it was like "Ok goodbye, take care." Then I hung up.

The bartender was pissed. "State Uniti?" he said. "Quonto, quonto 25,000 lire," he demanded scribbling on a note. I said. "No quonto, I call collect." "No, no" he cried. "25,000 lire." I told him, "collect," again and he burst into rabid Italian with the other people in the place in support. They all beamed at me like I was some kind of rich kid. "How long you talk." he said. I told him 5 minutes. Then he called information and they said 6 minutues and he scribbled some figures. "16,000 lire, you must pay," he demanded. "No, no quonto," I said. I was in a jam. I became outraged and bellered at him. "Why did you let me use that damn phone in the first place?" He was taken back by my anger as was everyone else. I guess I was pissed. They saw it. I went outside to a pay phone by the traffic and I finally got through to the operator. I could barely hear him. It was like hanging from a thread. Finally he told me I should not pay anything because it was a collect call. So he was going to hang up but I begged him to tell that to the bartender. So I ran in and got the bartender and he came out and listened to the operator. The bartender said, "Me sorry," to me. I was relieved. I held out my hand to shake his but instead he demanded 100 lire. I paid him the money and stormed out shouting, "Alright, alright, I made it."

I headed down the road and could not say a word as in all that confusion I'd lost my voice. I rode in heavy traffic while it became colder and I was tired. Made it to Paulozzio and cooked dinner by a church and camped there for the night.

## Monday Nov. 21st

With a good nights sleep after that crazy day, I headed into Naples in the morning. It was the worst looking city I'd been to yet. There was garbage everywhere and the streets were terrible. The entire city was like the Bronx. Laundry hung from every window in the city. Down near the waterfront there was an old fortress guarding the seaport which a big star shaped blemish on its side from an exploding shell. There were many shops but I avoided stopping at them for fear of being ripped off. I stopped to buy apples and was so fearful my stuff would be stolen that I hung onto the bike at every moment. I continued along cobblestone streets that were so rough they just about vibrated my fillings out.

Heading out of Naples and on the road to Pompei, every car that passed would beep at me. I got mad and flipped a guy off right in his face. It was so annoying. They beeped religiously, without any provocation on my part.

I saw the ruins of Pompei but could not go into the actual disaster area because it was closed. I did ride around and look over the walls to see an overhead view of the city which was buried in volcanic ash since the disaster in 70 A.D. I saw Mount Vesuvius looming in the distance behind

Pompei. It started to drizzle and I gingerly rode over the rough cobblestone streets, for they were slippery as ice.

The road headed east and began an ascent up into higher country. I was passed by an old man, who was riding on his bike going uphill, my he was in good shape! I stayed behind him and we raced along. Then I passed him and said, "Chow-arrive derce." About one hundred feet in front of him, I was rounding a bend and heard this clanging and crashing sound. I turned around to see him skidding down the road. I went back and helped pick him up. I thought it was my fault, but he let me know it was not. I gestured to him and asked, "Are you ok?" My hand embracing his shoulder. "O-K," he responded as he started to burst out into laughter. He asked me where I was from and I said, "America." He was so happy. "Grazzee, Americano, grazzee, arriva derci," he said while mounting his bike and continuing on. We rode together a short ways and then he headed off to the left.

I went into a store and these people gathered around me and stared as I walked in. I said. "Ok?" while pointing to my bike. "Ok," said the shop owner. He asked me where I was from. "America-California," I said, "California belle," he added. He stood up and announced too everyone who I was as I walked through the store. They all stared at me in the isles. I only bought some yogurt. They wanted to see my U.S. money but all I had was lire. They gave me a deal on my yogurt and the storekeeper said, "You good friend." I said, "Grazzee, arrive derci," and was off.

In the rain I head up the road to Avilleno and on a hillside saw a new house under construction. I lifted the bike over a high chain and then crossed a skinny boardwalk to sneak into the house and get out of the weather. The house had a nice view and many rooms littered with plaster and concrete. Darkness came quickly and I listened for fear of someone catching me. I was very thirsty and found a bottle of water in the building and drank much of it. I fell asleep thinking about heading into the Appenines and hoping it would not snow. It was that anticipation, knowing I would be going into some hard riding ahead, that made me nervous.

## Tuesday Nov. 22nd

The night had passed and I'd slept rather well in my own 'home' for the first time in a long time. It was drizzling as I departed. In one fell swoop, I had to lift my bike with all of its gear, up over a barbed wire fence. I slipped while lifting it over the fence and ended on the road in a very awkward position with the bike on top of me. If a car had come along I would surely have been in trouble as I was trapped under my bike. My back hurt after that.

It was a hard uphill all the way to Montemarino. The wind blew against me and the fog was thick. This disappointed me because I wanted to see the mountains. In town I stopped for 'aqua' and noticed a group of men peering at me from a bar window. To them I must have looked like a very young and crazy kid. I had a good downhill into a valley and then started a long pedal back up again over bad roads of gravel until Lioni. The mountain people were generally friendly, curious and I noticed some very tiny women. The trucks were still beeping madly at me as well as the cars. In some sections it was fairly flat riding for awhile then the road turned bad and was often times mucky. Adding to the miserable roads was the drizzly and cold weather.

I passed through little hilltop villages, some of which were in shambles from earthquakes. I asked a guy on a street corner if I was on the right road to Melfi. "Si," he told me along with some other jibberish long enough to gather a crowd of gawkers who rushed over to look at me. They were always friendly and extremely inquisitive.

I went up a long, hard, steep grade, as it became dark. My light quit working while coming down a steep grade. A spoke went "bonk" and broke, sending my wheel out of balance as I rode into Melfi. I stopped at an 'alimentaris' and bought food. Went to a park and cooked and then found a hillside to camp on with goats baaahing nearby.

## Wednesday Nov. 23rd

Frost covered my tent on the cold, clear and sunny morning. A cold front had passed in the night and the wind came howling out of the northwest. I packed up everything with frozen fingers and went to a park to dry the tent and fix the bike. While laying out the tent and things to dry, a couple of old men watched me. A fellow invited me to warm by his fire. I did and said, "Chow," to some old men gossiping. Then I proceeded to clean the bike and fix the spoke.

I had to take the rear hub off and used the park bench to hold the special tool. This in turn wrecked the bench. "Me scuzi," I said. They shrugged as if not to care. About 20 people, most of whom were students and old men watched me do the job with silence and curiosity. "Tah dah!" I said when finished. They all seemed bummed that I was done. One boy came over and spoke english with me and then an older boy came along and knowing that I was an American told me that he had been to England. "I'm American," I said. He thought they were the same country. The old men joshed and one guy sang some WWII songs about Americans. He laughed hard at me and I ignored and smirked back.

While walking the bike away from the group, a young man talked to me and invited me as his guest for the day. I declined his offer but we talked about the arms and nuclear problems in the world. He had made a button depicting an image of Christ, which said, "get out" to nuclear arms as he did to the money changers and traders in the market in front of the temple. I talked with others also and shook some hands. Eager to go, I said farewell and they all cheered me on.

Zipping down and cycling up many hills was the routine on this gorgeous day and I had thoughts about the good people I'd met, since leaving Santa Barbara. I thought about me, the independent man, the traveler. I enjoyed my image as an adventurous young man, yet, I wondered how much I really was into this thing. But the key was that I was trying this adventure. I knew I was not a real risk taker, there are others who will hang it all out on a limb. I enjoyed these periods of Johnny Quest lifestyle for now.

To the east, I observed the Adriatic Sea and made way downhill into Barletta where the sight of pretty girls was welcomed. A storekeeper graciously gave me a free bottle of Olio di Oliva (olive oil). I cooked supper at a park overlooking the ocean and myy latest eating craze was trying to replicate the pasta that Mercurio made for me back in San Remo. There was a beautiful orange moon rising over the Adriatic Sea in the direction of Greece. "Soon I'll be there," I said. I listened to Voice of America and all sorts of jibberish from Yugoslavian radio.

While looking for a place to sleep for the night, a fisherman motioned me to this changing room, beach house. He whistled and gestured with his hands in a sleeping position. He even cut apart a wire fence to help me enter. I thanked him, he walked away and I curled up in a corner of the room.

## Thursday Nov. 24th

I didn't sleep well because the ocean threatened to overrun me as it was so noisy. I had a sore stomach and pedaled along thinking I'd take my time and set camp around 2pm as it was Thanksgiving Day. I stopped at several towns along the way, stocking up on provisions. The day was cool and overcast.

Around 2pm I was riding along the relatively flat terrain with the Adriatic Sea to my left, a good tailwind and was looking for a place to sneak in for the night. Suddenly I turned around to see two cyclists right behind me and a face said, "Hi, where you from?" I was so hungry for conversation that I almost fell off the bike. We kept our pace and talked up a storm for almost two hours. I didn't remember pedaling at all. It was all fun.

I met Dan and Marc, brothers from Seattle who had ridden from Minneapolis to Washington D.C. They also had ridden across Europe and were heading for Brindisi. We talked about our journeys and compared similarities.

With the ship not leaving from Brindisi for another two days, we had time to waste. We pulled off the main road and pedaled up to this archeological spot which had an old concrete building nearby. We sought shelter there from the wind behind the building and cooked our dinners. I had pasta with pepperoni and they had macaroni so we shared each others cuisine. It was a grand Thanksgiving Day feast.

We sat there talking away when a guy came up and asked us to leave. We did, but came back after he took some photos and left. Then the caribineri came along and talked to us but they let us stay. My voicebox was tired of talking, but not of the company Dan and Marc brought. We put up our tents in the dark and the polizia came along for a second time. Later, I awoke in the night thinking I heard someone say, "On la bicyclette?" I thought I saw a flashlight but perhaps it was just a dream. What was the significance of this strange spot we had selected to camp on? Could it actually have been a military spy station?

Marc, the younger brother and Dan, the Fran Tarkenton look alike, and I packed up after chowing down on bread and figs for breakfast on Friday Nov. 25th. I had real bad farts from the figs. I smelled like hell. Even I couldn't stand it. I looked like hell also. My hair was long, greasy and dirty. I hadn't a real bath in so long. It was hard to enjoy being near others because I was self conscious of my putrid condition. I respected others who may have 'smelled me' and purposely kept my distance.

We rode hard until 11:30am, when we pedaled into Brindisi. I searched around for ferry information and then we went to a park and met Terry an American and sat down to eat and plan a hotel search. Along came Ken and Debbie, the couple I'd met in Pisa and Florence. They sat down and we talked about our amazing reunion of Americans. Ken and Debbie asked me out to dinner at what they called a real Italian restaurant. Marc and I did a hotel search. We found a place for 9000 lire and moved in. I took two long showers and was so dirty that it blackened the floor of the tub and left a dark ring. Then when I shampoed my hair it looked like black water. After that I washed my clothes and hung them on chairs, then fired up my stove to dry them, for they were soaked. Dan disagreed with me doing that, but I assured him I would be responsible. I trimmed my beard and went for a hair cut. The barber was very good and used extra care to do my style. I felt so much like a wierdo subject for him to work on. I could understand his timidness, but I sensed my own strangeness. He'd cut the hair of mostly dark, curly haired heads, not stringy blondes like me.

I went running along with Marc, Terry and Dan to meet Ken and Debbie at the column, marking the beginning of the Appenine way, an old Roman road which went from Brindisi to Rome. The night was cool and clear. We walked to the restaurant and sat down. Ken was a dentist in the Air Force. Debbie was an electronic technician. We talked about the threat they felt being in the military. We talked about the Italians and their lifestyles.

We were often intimate in our own reasons for doing what we did. Terry wanted to act. Dan wanted to have a stable job. Marc was quiet but very observant. Ken wanted to somehow realize he'd spent 10 years in the Air Force for the reason that he never saw why he should leave. He had acted once and enjoyed doing it, but now he liked his work because it paid well. He also liked Debbie, who was never agreeing with him. Deb wanted to get training to learn her trade. Our little dinner party sounded like a soap opera.

We drank four litres of wine. I felt the liquor lighten my head and slipped on many words especially "expressive," of which they all laughed at me. We ate squids, snails and octopus. Ordinarily I would never eat them, but this time was an exception. Our meals included pasta, and dandelion stem salad, an Italian delicacy especially with vinegar and oil. It was an adventurous and excellent feast. We stayed at the restaurant until 11pm and eventually had to go our own ways. We realized that our meeting was somehow meant to be and wished each other well. Ken insisted on paying the bill. His generosity was almost fatherly to us.

We walked back to our hotel room talking and joking around. I was excited about tomorrow and my boat ride to Greece. As I laid in a clean bed, in a hotel room, the first one of my journey in five months, I realized how wonderful these last days in Italy had been and how great the people I'd met were.

**Saturday Nov. 26th**

Just outside our hotel room, noise filled the streets of Brindisi at 4am. I didn't sleep much all night and surely couldn't sleep through that racket. I had been having a slight amount of insomnia and wondered why. The other guys were still snoring when I showered and hit the streets early to buy my ticket and breakfast at the grocery store. My ticket on the Libre Lines cost 35 lire. The boat would leave at noon, so I rushed around to get organized. I was waiting outside of customs, drying my laundry, at the square at 11am and met a Greek fellow from Athens whose name was Tasos. He spoke real good English. He'd been in Rome trying to get a job on a cargo ship. In a very Americanized accent he said, "Go for it," to Dan and Marc and shook their hands.

We all went through customs and got on board the ship after carrying the bikes up about 100 stairs. It was an absolutely gorgeous day. If I was to rate it, this was a perfect 10. I was excited about the boat ride, probably because of the change of pace. With my wet laundry hanging on the deck rails, the ship set sail at 12:30. Several boisterous Germans were doing some heavy drinking. I went into the lounge and found it was interesting to watch U.S. TV programs, like Welcome Back Kotter, that was dubbed over in Italian. Then they played a John Wayne movie and he spoke in a Greek accent. It didn't sound anything like his 'real' voice.

Tasos and I talked up a storm, we got along just great. We played harmonica together and ate together. The day was so excellent. I was so happy. The sun was warm, the scenery beautiful.

The ocean was calm. Our German friends, one I called Von Frankenstein offered us a drink of rum and coke. Tasos and I drank while singing songs and playing the harmonica. He knew more U.S. songs then I did. I met a gal from Israel and we talked. There was also a Frenchman and a Swiss fellow who was quiet speaking. I met a German who was in his 30's who had an old bike which he claimed he was going to ride around Africa. The bike had fat tires, was a one speed, very old and very heavy. The drinking Germans passed out on the deck as the sun was setting. Oh this was a wonderful boat ride!

With my little stove I cooked my supper on deck and let Tasos and the Israeli gal use it also. Though she was attractive, she felt strong about being anti U.S., therefore I was reserved with her. Dan and Marc were traveling first class in their own rooms so I never did see them. The Germans from Berlin were crashed out in the bathroom. A while later they were back, awake and drinking some more. They were hilarious. I laughed everytime Von Frankenstien said his favorite saying of, "Bloody fucking bastards." He had no front teeth, a bowie knife and wore black leathers. He was a rough looking fellow, but mostly show.

I went to the front room to write in seclusion but they all swarmed around me and wanted to read my diary. We pitched in for a bottle of port wine and drank until 1am. Frankenstein repeatedly sang a verse from the Doors song- "Show me the way to the next whiskey bar." He said if he had a chance to meet President Reagan he would say, "Mr. Reagan-dis one is for you-burrrapp," he would imitate a machine gun. "Burrappp, burrapp," he would imitate a machine gun and smile with his toothless grin. While that was going on, the other Germans kept hugging everyone and over in the corner a Quebec man made out with the Israeli gal. It was funny being on this love boat, a splash of craziness. Tasos and I went out at night for a breather and saw the brilliant stars over the Adriatic Sea as the ship plowed through the sparkling water. I watched a Vincent Price movie until 1:30am and then retired to sleep on the floor, with my head under a chair, in case Von Frankenstein stepped on me.

# THE GREEK ODYSSEY

**Sunday Nov. 27th**

Tasos was asleep when I stepped out on the deck and looked over the bow of the ship at the rising sun above Greece. Tall, greenish-purple mountains were crowned with fluffy white clouds. We docked at the pier in Patras at 7am, admist a jumble of confusion with long lines waiting to disembark. The Greek Customs and Immigration was a joke, for they only glancingly looked at my passport and baggage. I said goodbye to Tasos and other friends, then straddled the bike seat and pedaled away.

A hangover was clouding my thinking while going into the city where I sat down to eat Italian bread with cheese. Heading south on this nice sunny morning should have been a pleasure, but after such a good time on the boat ride it was hard to get back into the swing of cycling. The wind picked up, the sky darkened and it became cool in addition to the road getting steadily worse. I bumped along. On the brighter side, the Greek people seemed friendly. It took time to get acquainted, to know how to say hello, to nod the head or wave. The initiation phase of learning Greek culture was a happenstance adjustment.

After lunch, the road was gravel at times and I bounded along cussing, but then a couple of fellows with dark hair and mustaches greeted me on the roadside with two big apples and offered a coffee drink. Thanking them for the treats, I rode on as it began to sprinkle. I pedaled into Pirgos and it rained hard. An exploration of the shops was commenced to find food but it was a small town and was difficult to locate familiar cuisine, even to find a chocolate bar. The old fashioned glass-storefront-shops closed at 5:30pm and I just barely got any food to cook. In the pouring rain, I found a vacant building with a veranda on the backside and lifted the bike up there for the night. Supper was cooked there and nobody saw me while laying out the sleeping bag and dozing off to sleep at 7:30pm during a light rain.

## Monday Nov. 28th

It rained hard in the predawn hours of the morning. I was very fortunate to have found the veranda as it was high and dry. While sitting down to record this information into my journal a mouse jumped over a wall and ran up my pants leg but I kicked at him and he flew out, then turned around and ran off.

I could not read the Greek writing and had trouble locating a store. It was trial and error or window shopping which informed me where to stop at a store and buy supplies. I was greeted kindly by many english-speaking people. One new food source to enjoy was a chocolate spread to be 'buttered' on top of bread. After filling myself with the concoction I headed for Olympia, the ancient city where the Olympic games originated. There was a good tailwind to help make a speedy time but I felt tired with a sore stomach that I believed to be an ulcer. I stopped to rest and it rained very hard so waiting out the storm was spent indoors checking out the souvenir shops. Of interest was the Greek pottery, which was burnished earthenware with black and white motifs from ancient Greek history.

To enter the site of the ancient city of Olympia and see the magnificent columns in ruin was humbling. One large building had columns that were four feet in diameter and appeared to have been wrecked by vandals or earthquake, or blown up, because the columns laid like fallen dominos. The entire place was once very romantic, with white marble fountains, baths, arenas, grass-covered playing fields and elegant trees. I could only imagine just how beautiful it would have been to be here in its heyday.

Riding on for the coast, the weather turned horrible. First it was gail force winds and then a hard rain like that of a monsoon. At one point a river was gushing down the road and I dutifully pedaled through it with soaked feet and body aching from the dampness. The day flew past, the sky darkened early and while pedaling along the coast, looking for a place to seek shelter, I observed the waves on the ocean were tremendous. Passing several opportune looking vacant buildings frustrated me, but then I saw one and quickly carried the bike up to the second floor.

I had to be very quiet, as the house next door was occupied and when they let their dog out now and then, it sensed danger and whimpered or barked at me. But always the owner let it back in unalarmed at my presence. I found a windowless room with a bedspring, a table and a seat. With supper cooking and all my wet clothes hanging near the stove I quietly dried them and reveled in my safe surroundings. The rain continued to pour, the wind howled and later the stars appeared very bright against the dark sky.

**Tuesday Nov. 29th**
Roosters, with the craziest sounding crowing I've ever heard announced the clear, cool morning. A woman was coming in and out of the house next to mine and she was going about her chores as I sneakingly packed up. Everytime a car or truck would pass, I'd do some packing to mask my noise. Waiting for the right moment I went down the steps hoping she wasn't looking and then dashed off pedaling into the new day, entirely unoticed.

The people in this area of the Pelopennese were very pleasant. Many would say, "Yasoo," which meant hello or "Kalimehra," which was good morning. If not a verbal hello they always waved. The trucks however were not as cooperative and they didn't pull over very much either. I headed southeast for Kalamanta across a plain and noticed the mountains ahead were getting bigger and bigger. From oceanside to mountaintop they must rise 4,000 feet. In Kalamanta I bought some food and stopped to snack, then headed south. The skies were partly cloudy as I huffed and puffed up the long climb of switchbacks into the mountains. On one corner there was a beautiful girl sitting on a rock, enjoying the view and smoking a cigarette. I said, "Hello," and she said the same then added, "How are you?" I responded, "Fine but tired," then I continued on and regretted not stopping to talk with her. I was timid of what the girls were like in this new culture. Would I break some social moraas? What would I talk to her about, would she embarrass me? Oh how I wanted to go back and meet her, but procrastinated and pedaled on.

The day was getting late when crowning the hilltop and looking out over the most fantastic scenery yet. There were little towns with medieval style churches or castles and rugged countryside adjacent to blue waters and winding roads with friendly, warm people. They appeared hearty as I saw them carrying huge loads of wood or water pails on their backs. Lots of donkeys were being used to burden the load.

A tourist shop up on that mountaintop had a variety of foods and I bought an ice cream bar and said hello to the dark haired maiden with friendly features. Satisfied to have met my first Greek girl, there was a long downhill rapidly returning me to the coast where a stop was made in Karadamill, a beautiful, quaint oceanside village. The campground was closed so I holed up in the local schoolyard. Found a reasonable roof overhang to get under and cooked supper. Some kitty cats came over for left overs and petting. Aside from them, my only company was a bottle of wine made at a local vinyard. I laid out my bedroll on a terazzle floor and sleep came quick.

The sudden flash and crack of a thunderstorm awakened me in the night as a hell of a wind and rainstorm came in. I scrambled to prepare for the onslought when the high winds and blowing rain hit. I covered my sleeping bag with plastic, which kept blowing away, requiring me to jump up and retrieve it. The rain was falling horizontal as I tried to make a windbreak with boxes. I'd count the distance the lightning was from the sound and judged how fast the storm came. It took 15 minutes to travel 10 miles. Finally after an hour of this it was over and though I didn't get too wet, my sleep was hardly restful.

## Wednesday Nov 30th

Sitting in the schoolyard, writing in my journal, and along came a busload of students, whom all tried to speak their English on me with "hallos," "gooda morna" and "howa ara youa?" I smiled and said goodbye then rode up a long, steep grade out of Karadamill. I met a French couple taking photographs who said it was all uphill from there-and true to their word it was-but it was worth it. The towns were quaint and extremely picturesque. The rugged coastline and rapid rise in altitude added a charm I've yet experienced. The people were hard at work picking olives, bags of which lined the roadside. I tried one and it was horrible, for an olive needs a long time to be pickled to make it edible. Borros would go by laden with olive bags and other items. It was like traveling back in time. This could easily have been 500 or 1000 years ago as these people had few modern conveniences. There were many shepherds with goats and snow on one of the mountain peaks to add to the enchantment. The churches, most of which were of Byzantine style blended cute and harmonious with the landscape. There were huge rock boulders as big as a house dotting the fields. I saw many Christian monks walking the roads and noticed what looked like a huge rock on a mountain ledge with a doorway and shutters. Upon closer inspection it was only willow branches that gave it the illusion. But the idea of living in a rock grasped me as enchanting.

I found this section of the world to be the best I've come to yet. The waters were aqua green. I stopped in to a village to ask for "nea do"(water) and saw women with large dark skirts. A girl with dark features and a colorfull dress gave me drinking water. I headed up into the pass and then begin a long and steep descent to Githias. Once again I returned to the sea and it was just so beautiful to overlook this aqua bay and see little fish swim along the shoreline. A temple or a castle on an island reflected on the calm waters of the blue sea.

I stopped to eat bread and jelly as a busload of tourists walked by at this gorgeous vista. Then a dark cloud moved overhead, everybody took off and it rained. I headed north in a somber mood, as paradise was now miserable, adding to my search for a place to camp. It was a hard uphill battle along steep switchbacks, past muddy terrain and open to the wind with occasional rain. Then it began to clear and the scenery was again breathtaking. To the west rose tall mountains covered with powdered sugar. I continued on until entering the city of Sparti. This is the home of the spartan soldier. I thought of Sparticus the movie.

While passing through the city, I discovered an apartment under construction and stayed clear of it until night came. I cooked my supper by the statue of a bold Spartan soldier, complete with shield and sword. Then I returned to the apartment and snuck into it as a storm dumped rain and hail. Inside, the place was full of plaster dust everywhere. I quietly tried to sweep a spot and laid down some newspapers. Coughing from the dust.

## Thursday Dec. 1st

With the dawning of the morning there was cause for celebration as this marked the beginning of my 6th month of my journey. It was a cold but sunny morning. I got out of my apartment and started to ride for Tripoli. It was all uphill for a long ways. The mountains had more snow on them, then yesterday. During hard long climbs I tried to think about something else in order to get my mind off the torture. It's never a very easy thing going up these grades. The bike tended to become difficult to control if power was not continuous. So on this morning I thought about my friends and relations back home. I thought how I'd like to relish the moment of my return flight to U.S.A. I wanted to believe it would be ecstasy.

Suddenly I heard bells ringing, in a beautiful chorus of sounds. Like Swahili tribesmen making music. As I rounded a curve I saw a herd of goats hoarding the entire road and heading for me. Their bells chimed to the beat of their footsteps. The shepherd lead them along like a school of children going to a museum. When they saw me they panicked but the shepherd soothed them with his whistle. I noticed a large area of pebbly deposits on the highway at the spot where they first saw me. As I receded, I continued to hear their beautiful chimes.

Later as I navigated a corner I heard a jet plane. I looked to my right and down in the canyon and saw a fighter jet coming up the slope turning and twisting his way up the landscape and heading right for me! I stopped and watched this British fighter jet buzz over my head. Then another one came behind him and I was treated to a grand show of modern aircraft. I stopped at the summit and ate some bread by a small temple. The sky rapidly darkened. I continued on and raided an apple tree before finally making it to Tripoli in the rain.

I went into a supermarket, bought some Campbells soup and cooked right outside as it rained. It was a very good lunch but people looked at me queerly.

The road to Nafplio was rough and filled with a slurry of mud. There was a drizzly rain that pestured me while progressing up into the mountains over, rocky, rugged hills, the tops of which were covered in fog. Far below I saw a train quietly chugging around the mountain corners. I entered the fog and then began one of the most exciting downhill descents yet, in zero, zero visibility. Little warning was given which way the road would turn next. There were many steep drops and sharp corners. It was a long and a thrilling reentry until at last I leveled off and saw the ocean. The pedaling commenced in warm but rainy weather all the way to Nafplio.

Nafplio was a cute town with a palace and a colossal fortress built to withstand a mighty attack. I stopped at a shop to by a beer and in the darkness looked for a place to get out of the rain. I saw a vacant building with the gate open and rode by to check out a car that was parked in front. Two guys came out of the building and left in the car. I quickly went in and leaned my bike against a wall, then walked upstairs and checked around. One room had an opening looking out over the city and was suitable to sleep the night. I cooked supper and enjoyed the town view and looking down on my new neighbors.

After supper, a further exploration of the building lead me to the discovery of a tall, wet marijuana plant with big buds, leaning in a corner downstairs. Those fellows must have been hiding it here. I panicked thinking what would happen if the authorities instigated me with that plant. I thought it was best to get packed up and leave, but it was raining out and getting late. I would hope for the best.

My bedroll was laid out on a dusty floor and my eyelids were getting heavy when I heard a buzz sound come from my beard. It was a short sound like that of a miniscule bug that could leap quickly from one area to the next. Then I would feel a bite and scratch the area. The pesty flea bugged me all night. Surely I smelled like hell and that enticed the little hitchhiker. It all combined to make me think this place was iffy.

## Friday Dec 2nd

A windy, rainy morning and I quietly packed up my things and ate a bite. Then I glanced outside to see if all was clear. I carried my bike down the steep stairway and up to a fence. My eyes bulged and heartbeat skipped a beat, when I saw a police car sitting right there with two officers holding a radio in their hand. I hesitated, then admitted my fate, opened the gate, wheeled my bike out like I knew what I was doing, locked the gate and pedaled off. The policemen looked at me, then at each other, and shrugged. I quickly ducked down an alley and behind some buildings. Wow was that close. With those pot plants and me being a vagrant, that could have landed me in the slammer.

I laid low for a while and then explored around the town. Went up to the Xenia palace and then hiked up the 891 steps to the fortress. Within were many chambers to get out of the wind and rain. Looking west into a nice harbor I could see a gun emplacement on an island. While pondering the construction of the two-foot-thick-walls, I wondered why they went to such lengths to build such a fortress? Obviously they had something to protect here. My conclusion was that it was the Greek navy that was stationed here. If an enemy could sack the fort then the navy was there's. No wonder it was made to be such an invincible place.

I returned down into town and bought a souvlaki, which is a Greek taco-like food made of shishkabobs wrapped around a pancake like skin, that is filled with sour cream and raw onions. It was delicious and a welcome addition to my bland diet. I took my time looking around town, enjoying being a tourist and then left around noon with a police car following me for a mile or so.

The road went north and I passed through the village of Argo, then headed up into the mountains with a terrific tailwind pushing me. The wind became treacherous in the narrow canyons and would buffet me back and forth. Finally I could see the ancient city of Korinthos. While going downhill toward the city my bike started to wobble and lose control. I hit the brakes and stopped to discover a flat rear tire. I walked the bike down to a gas station and used their air pump to help repair the flat. Darkness was setting as I was several miles outside the city, when I saw a pretty young gal walking down the road wiggling her butt. I gave her a tap on the rear and then turned around and we both exchanged smiles.

It rained steadily as I toured the narrow streets of Korinthos and passed several possible vacant homes. Went down into the city square and looked around but was tired and in need of shelter. For a frustrating hour I inspected possibilities but approved none. When one feels exhausted, and it is late and raining and there is no place to stop, then the world becomes a lonely place. Everyone is snuggled and warm in there lit homes except you. You could just as well be on the moon.

Finally I found a vacant house under construction and slipped inside. This place had fresh plaster and a beautiful terazzo floor. I cooked supper of macaroni and cheese with green peppers. Wolfed it down. Then I snuggled into this small room trying to be careful not to shine my flashlight so somebody might see it. I laid down in my sleeping bag and that pesty flea returned at midnight to bother me again. I smelled like fucking hell and tried to ignore it.

## Saturday Dec. 3rd

Got up and hit the road early on and then ate a nice breakfast at the waterfront in Korinth. I didn't see many joggers running around this city in the morning. A few miles after leaving the city I went over a bridge high above the Corinth Canal that was dug into 300 feet of solid rock. It was a crucial link to the sea through the land bridge between Greece and the Pelopenaise. I took my time riding along because of a stomachache and generally not feeling well. This increasing pain lulled my appetite. I cruised through small villages and stopped for a bite to eat at lunchtime.

There were huge ships, many of them oil tankers at anchor on this inland sea called the Saronic Gulf. It was like a ghost yard for ships. They were rusty or weathered and with odd names like Oddeso and Annassis. The terrain became rugged and the wind picked up to make matters worse. I noticed a storm was approaching with lightning and rain behind me about 10 miles. It was a race against the storm! A theme I have often acquired in my personal experiences. All energy was used to outrun the fury, but to no avail it rained holy hell on me. Often it was hard and then harder until finally I stopped at a bus stop and retreated from the deluge. Two Greek men came dashing in for shelter and sat with me. They asked me if I liked Reagan. It was a joking matter actually. They made fat stomachs and pulled on their wallets. "Reagan," they said. I made a U.S.S.R. symbol on the dirt and pointed at it and put a slash through it. Then I said, "U.S.A.-U.S.S.R.," and banged my head to the wall. They got a kick out of that.

It rained hard for an hour, then slowed and I continued onward for Athens, feeling real tired. The rain had flooded the road and I was drenched from passing through these puddles. After struggling up a long hill and feeling bone weary I was rewarded with the sight of Athens off in the easterly distance. Once entering the outskirts, I stopped at a phone and called Tasos. We talked and he told me to get closer to his house and then to call him back. Many more miles passed until riding into Athens and seeing the Acropolis, which I skirted around, reveling in the amazing sight. Continuing on, looking for Taso's house, I was very tired but found my way by asking people directions throughout the progression. In the pouring rain I finally found his apartment building.

I buzzed his apartment and he came down to the gate and greeted me warmly. I was a wreck. He gave me food and his mother gave me much assistance. I was soon in a hot bath. Weary, but feeling better, they really got a kick out of my pitiful state.

We went out to a local square after I met two of Taso's friends. At a pub I had an interesting but difficult talk with Taso's cousin, Lambros. He was very anti American. He wanted to kill Americans, because so many came to his country and told him how great the U.S. was. I understood his frustration and talked to him with my outmost patience on the subject. It was a touchy situation. He had such anti American views that my insensitivity would only destroy any relationship. So I listened to him. He did most of the talking. After awhile we had resolved that people from U.S.A. have definitely a fat ego, but so does everyone else and so we moved on to other issues. How can we resolve this difference of opinion and work together? We talked as people of one world and one planet. We communicated. I finally felt at ease with him, then we talked rabidly about everything under the sun. Before long we were laughing like good friends. It was a good feeling for me.

We went to a disco but I didn't think I could make it another minute, as I was so tired. Things perked up when I met a couple of girls. I asked a girl if she wanted to dance. She said, "I don't speak english." I said, "But you do speak good english." And she gave me the nose treatment. I was quite bummed out by that, but overcame this rejection and danced with another gal whose name was Mia. She was a cute looking lady. We danced up a storm. She had a nice figure and was pretty. Of interest was that she wore black gloves. George had a curly haired Spartan look. I also met a cute curly haired girl by the name of Liana, she had a very gentle disposition. I told her she would be a good wife. She glowed after I said that.

After dancing, we all went to a restaurant that served 'putha' a soup that everyone said I should try, but would regret eating. We had a great time laughing and eating this 'putha.' I felt great because I had my arm around Mia and she also sat on my lap. Another friend of Tasos whom I met was Apostolis. He was a tall, lanky Greek who was friendly and provided much humor. Peter told me he lived in California in Inglewood for a year and was an aircraft A&P. They were all such wonderful people and seemed a close, happy bunch. We stayed up till 5am driving around and laughing at the homosexuals lining the side streets. They would tease them by driving up and enticing them, then saying something derogatory and we'd buzz off. We went back to Taso's house and I slept on a cot, which they had laid out on the floor.

## Sunday Dec. 4th

After such a late night we slept in until 1:30 in the afternoon Taso's had a Bob Dylan tape, which he played. Then we got up and ate some food. It was a lazy, recuperative day doing almost nothing. I told Taso's I could not stay up late at night like that. I had to get up early to get things done. This disappointed him because he really enjoyed staying up all-night and sleeping in late. We went over our plans, his wanting to go to the U.S. to become a pilot and I wanting to stay a week in Athens and then head on.

I met Taso's father, a quite fellow who spoke little English but was an intelligent scientist. I also met Kelly, Tasos sister. She was about 25 years old and a graduate of the University of Illinois in Chicago with a master of physics degree. She spoke excellent English and was very intelligent. She reminded me of Ellen. We talked about my trip and she couldn't really see what I got out of 'self torture' by riding a bike. We all joined in a good discussion at suppertime while eating a great meal of baked lamb, onions and potatoes.

Tasos and I went to Mia's house with Apostolis and others. We watched the movie Fame and then went out to the square. There we ate souvlaki and went back to Mia's and watched a Kirk Douglas movie called, "Paths of Glory." It was an anti war movie that showed how the leaders can screw up the system and then pass the blame onto someone else in order to escape their own reputation unharmed. Tasos took me back to his home early as I wished and then he went back out.

At about 5am I awoke and had to take a piss. I bumped my way through Taso's house and finally found the bathroom. I used a toilet that looked more like a urinal and once finished couldn't find the lever to flush. I looked about the bathroom and the only thing resembling a flushing mechanism was this cord hanging from the ceiling. I pulled on the cord and it rang an alarm with a horrible noise throughout the entire apartment complex. I knew I'd screwed up immediately, and started to get out of there but was met by Taso's father and mother. I heard the family saying, "Ok, Ok, it's Ok." Tasos got up and looked at me very groggy and couldn't understand my dilemma, until I told him what I'd done. He had to go into the bathroom and dip his hand into the pee and pull the plug. That was the flushing method. I felt terrible about the incident. The phone rang and someone from the medical service knocked on the apartment door before things once again calmed down. It was all very embarrassing.

## Monday Dec. 5th

At 8am I arose and Kelly gave me hot milk and biscuits for breakfast. She was a very helpful person and was cautious of me, yet charming. I headed off on my bike into Athens and went to the U.S. embassy. It didn't look like a very rosy place to hang around. What a hassle to go past all the guards and even by my being an American they kind of treated me like shit. They did provide some information on places to go for vaccinations and visas. I looked up in a book information for health requirements in countries I would be traveling to.

I pedaled over to a free clinic and was given cholera shot in addition to one anti-malaria pill. While riding through town in search of the post office a gracious bike rider led me there. I checked to see if a package was waiting for me via the poste restante. It was not. Back and forth I went trying to decide what I needed and what was available at the local bike shops.

It rained hard, making the busy streets very treacherous. I locked the bike up and went window-shopping but it was a nuisance walking the sidewalks getting bumped by hoards of people. I went back through town and found my way to Tasos place. His mom had cooked us a nice meal of leftovers. I bought some nuts and a pineapple and gave them to her as a gift. Mama was so kind. She helped me repair a zipper and was very interested in me. She laughed at my actions. She called me Elah or Elicka. It was nice to be around her motherly touch.

Tasos and I went to the square after dinner and I felt very comfortable with the group. We met a couple of new girls who were cute. We sat around in Athenias pub and I became the center of attention as they showed space shuttle pictures on TV and they knew I was an American. We decided to go to a movie. It was crazy getting there for they drove fast and often were lost. The movie was called Querelle. It was a movie about homosexuals on a ship. While walking down the street we played football with my rolled up jacket. Returning to Tasos house was late, when we went to sleep it was about 2am.

## Tuesday Dec 6th

I went up to the Egyptian embassy at Athens and applied for a visa. I visited several bike shops in town and bought two extra tires. One for $5 and the other for $4. A travel service informed me about taking a boat to Turkey. "There are none," they said. They were very reluctant to help me, even to talk about Turkey. The relations between the two countries was bad.

I met two Americans. One told me many horror stories of India. He told me he carried five water jugs with him but still got sick. "Sometimes ah fart and your glad it's just a fart, other times yah fart and it runs down your leg. They call that dis-entry," he said to me.

Loud obnoxious Americans were in all the little shops at the Plaka and in general they are arrogant and rather rushed or insensitive to the Greeks. I found myself shying away from some of these countrymen. I'm drawn to others, those who were travelers and especially to any cute girls.

Back at Tasos house, he was not home but Kelly was, and we talked alot about the fast lane in the U.S. She did not like the rushed lifestyle of Americans, while I hurried about to do my laundry and quickly filled out my diary. Kelly and I ate together and had a good talk about the difference between communism and capitalism. We agreed it was a silly thing to fight over especially when we had such quantities of weapons aimed at each other. We talked of the differences and amazing similarities between the super powers. I came to realize that communists are a threat to those individuals who desire great wealth and single-handed power. No wonder on the frontiers between superpowers there is conflict. No wonder the communist threat is so great to capitalists. They wouldn't make much money and would have to be equal in rank with everyone else.

Tasos and I walked up to Apostolis house and sang wildly in the tiny streets. We bought a bottle of wine and sat at Apostolis, listening to great records and clowning around. Peter came over and then we met Nicholas who said he would treat us at a pub. It was his "name" day (birthday) and therefore he would treat. On his birthday he invited all his friends to celebrate and also pays the bill. We toasted him many times with Ouzo, the preferred drink of the Greeks. Since it is nearly 80 proof it becomes a drunken party after awhile. We then went to a restaurant and ate like pigs. Mia came along with other friends and joined in. We all had a great time. The Greeks are sociable, festive people. I was beginning to feel accepted in with this communion and this group. It intrigued me so much to have this happen. I didn't want to leave. We went too a few places to enjoy one another's company. I was experiencing this little piece of the puzzle of Athens that is so minute, yet is creating in me a fondness for this city. I enjoyed the laughs we had even though so many times I couldn't understand what they said. I talked with Tasos late into the night about my leaving and somehow felt he too sensed it was getting harder for me to leave.

## Wed. Dec. 7th

In the morning I went to the India embassy and found out that it would require a one month wait to get a visa. I took an application and then went scurrying around the city. A stop was made to take another pill for malaria and then I went to browse the pottery shops, as I love the works so much. I ate lunch up by the Acropolis and then went to the Egyptian embassy to get my visa to Egypt.

On a bike ride through the traffic of Athens, I was proud of my sturdy bike and it was fun racing in and out of traffic with no panniers. I rode down to Pireas and found out the price of taking a boat to Rhodes. Then I returned to Tasos house. Somewhat nervously I rang the bell and said, "Hello it's Eric." Now I could sense my nervousness and they could sense it also. I was becoming a burden to their household. This was always a barrier to break through when meeting new people or staying with relatives, but this occasion was different. I was only a visitor who was supposed to leave by now. I was interested in this family and liked them much, but that did not mean free food and board.

Kelly helped me with supper. I talked to her but felt not at ease. She told me, "Make yourself comfortable." I had the kitchen to myself and cooked supper. Tasos came home at 7pm and Mama took him into a back room and talked to him about me. Now I felt the time to move out was approaching. I didn't like being in the position I was in. The shakedown was in progress.

Kelly invited me to a film called 'Joy,' and when we came back Tasos took me aside and explained the situation. "My momma says you would be more comfortable if you would stay at Apostolis house. Is that alright with you?" It was alright with me because I sensed some pressure from mamma and Kelly. I thanked them very much and we went to Apostolis late in the evening. I talked with the tall Greek while he fixed my bed. He was kind and generous to invite me to stay and to eat anything in the house. This act of kindness was something I never wanted to forget. His tongue became tied after speaking so much English that he couldn't take it anymore. He spat a rapid volley of Greek in his big Zorba like voice and said to me, "Eric, why you don't speak Greek?" It was hilarious.

## Thursday Dec. 8th

The phone rang in the morning and I answered it. A Greek speaking woman tried to figure out who I was and what was going on. She could not speak English and I could speak no Greek so it was very frustrating to relate to her.

I worked on my bike, cleaned it and the side bags then sewed on patches from the many countries I'd visited. I went to Tasos house for dinner and his mama cooked up a great feast of meatballs and cauliflower. We ate some walnuts and had pineapple. I could get along better with mama now and we could communicate better. Kelly invited me too a tavern with a jazz band. We went there by taxi, the music was good and I truly enjoyed a good conversation with her. She's very knowledgeable about the world and so it was nice to talk about the things we've experienced and still want to do. I caught myself bragging about my past. This is something I tend to do with women who I believe are misjudging me. We went back to the square and then she went home.

I met Mia, Apostolis and Tasos and we walked to a Greek movie. I held hands with Mia and we seemed close. We afterward went into the city and ate some sweet whipped cream on top of peaches. Then we went to this beautiful overlook of the city and I climbed to the top of a rock. It was a great view and suddenly a bolt of lightning flashed. "Oh, please Eric, come down to me because the storm is coming!" I had a nice looking girl to embrace me when I got down.

On the drive in the car, Mia sat on my lap and the driver tried to hit every bump because they figured I was getting a rise. I was. We laughed and clowned like kids. It was fun. Reaching behind the seat and grabbing a leg, they'd whack me on the head and teach me Greek words. They laughed when I pronounced them. We went past all the hookers and homosexuals and Tasos kidded with them. It was interesting to see their humanness even though they worked such an ugly business. In the pouring rain we rode around clowning and I was happy to be with Mia as she was cuddly and good to me in her own special way.

## Friday Dec. 9th

Slept great and got up at 9am. Went to the Indian embassy and turned in the visa application. It cost only two photos and 10 drachmas. After a long search I purchased contact lenses solution and then went down to the bike shop and purchased a 6-cog gearwheel by Suntour for $13.

This would convert my bike to an 18 speed. The guys at the shop put the thing on my rear hub for me. It worked well and the low-end gearing was phenomenal. I spent the day, sight seeing and shopping for pottery. My art training helped here as I became very selective in the search and finally selected an oil lamp. I met two U.S. girls who had toured Europe by rail and we talked quite awhile about the things we saw. They said the present Reagan administration is to militaristic and that the Europeans are down on the U.S. because of it.

The main reason for getting lost on the way back to Apostolis was because I was eating a bag full of Greek cookies and riding. Actually Athens is easy to get around because no matter where you are you can look up and see the Acropolis to tell which way to go.

Tasos, Apostolis and I rode on a little motorcycle to the square. We met two girls and I became reserved as I wanted to let Apostolis and Tasos talk to them. This perturbed Apostolis and Tasos. They said, "Why you don't meet these girls?" After some prodding and kidding I opened up but the girls left. George and Liana took me too a tavern that is located in the corner of some ancient ruins. Though we could not speak fluently we cheered it up and ate some exotic Greek foods. Liana looked very pretty and commented to me that she would never go to the U.S. because there is so much crime. She heard that's the way it is. Lhourgo (George) wanted to go to see Disneyland. He was kind to me. We drank two pitchers of wine and agreed to try and see one another again in the future. They treated me so well and Ehanna said, "We want to please you." They did that and more.

Tely gave me a ride home on his cycle and we talked awhile about many things as he can intellectualize very well. He talks about the earth and the environment and has ideas how Americans live as we discuss this. As I lay in bed I thought how great these people were to let me in on their lives so warmly and so generously. I felt sadness I could not let them know how much I loved them for helping me. I must never forget the many acts of kindness and return the favor.

**Saturday Dec. 10th**

The morning sun came over the flat rooftops and illuminated the deck of outside of Apostolis apartment. Most of the buildings had decks up on top. One house had several cages with chickens clucking and roosters cawing.

I cleaned out the kitchen and did the dishes on this sunny morn and opened the doors up and let the sun in. A record was playing Pink Floyd when this small boy wandered into the room and stood in front of me. I was a little hostile to this intrusion but he made comical jests and I entertained him by playing the mouth organ. He enjoyed this and did the same with it. He was a natural at clowning and I loved this kind of stuff. He put on a motorcycle helmet and raced about. When the music played a firing squad drill, he went along with it and fell over dead at the sound of shots. I took some pictures of him runny around with this hippie wig on his head and beads. He was quite a contrast from a hardened, apathetic LA kid. This little guy was great fun at kidding around and adlibbing.

Later, I was cleaning the floor when a man dressed in a sailor's suit walked in and stood before me with a queer look. I handed him a note that Apostolis had written explaining who I was and he understood. He was Apostolis cousin, named George, a sailor in the Greek navy who was visiting for a few days. He made me a coffee drink and though we didn't say a word to each other for about an hour, the silence was not hostile. When Apostolis returned he kiddingly called George, "the communist from up north." He lived near Yugoslavia.

Apostolis and I went to the bike shop and picked up his bicycle. We then raced to the top of the parking lot for the Acropolis. We walked up into this grand facade of human history and observed the ruins of the Parthenon and enjoyed the beauty of it all. What a pity it was in ruins. I had so many questions on my mind about this place and Apostolis gave me a few insights in regards to its history, but his english was difficult to comprehend. We clowned around a bit and took photos. One thing I found interesting were the pottery fragments scattered everywhere around the site. They were easy to pick up and take if one wanted to do so. I thought that it was unfortunate they did not collect those pieces for posterity. The museum held many artifacts from this monument which looked like the shards we saw laying about.

Once again we raced about the city. It was fun to have someone like Apostolis who was energetic and boisterous in comparison to my being reserved. We stopped at a cafe and I bought dinner of BBQ chops. Excitement grew as Apostolis and I raced in his car to the bus station to pick up his girl friend. He drove like a maniac. We were like wild fools as he pumped me up with excitement while rounding corners on two wheels. Effie his girl, Maria his cousin and a boy from Volos hopped into the small car and we came back to Apostolis. We bought some Ouzo and souvlaki and had a party.

Now I was getting used to the Greek people leaving me out of the conversation until the time was right to break it to them I couldn't speak a stitch of Greek. But it was a downer not being able to talk with them. I felt dumb. Eugerou(George) and I were chummy, joking about all kinds of crazy things especially as the ouzo got lower in the bottle. He liked it when I spoke certain Greek words. I learned he was in the navy and made only 500 drachmas a month. That's about $5. He was very kind and jolly. I went with Tasos and Eurgeo and Ehanna too her house and we drank more ouzo. Peter came over. Tasos and Eurgeo wrestled and Eurgeo turned his knee. He cried out in pain. We had to drive about 10 miles to bring him to the emergency room. The hospital was terrible, dirty, disorganized and the staff smoked cigarettes. The place was shabby and ill equipped. The doctor put out his cigarette and gave Eurgeos leg a twist back and forth as he hollered in pain. They took x-rays. The doctor asked Tasos to take his pants off because he wanted to give him an injection. He forgot who it was he was working on! The hospital was horrible and I thought how dreadful it would be to be ill and have to go to one here.

Even at 2am we ate pizza at Eurgeos parents house as they nurtured their injured son. His folks were much the same as any elderly American parents. They were most interested in me and very hospitable even at this late hour. Tasos and I looked at Eurgeos private photos of Liana in the nude, on a beach on the island of Mikonos. "She is a beautiful Greek woman isn't she," said Tasos, rolling his eyes.

## Sunday Dec. 11th

I slept good on the floor and then snuck out to go into the city. While passing the Presidential Palace I noticed the guards were changing and this was an impressive sight. From their little hut they took a big slow step forward with their clown boots and then did a routine with their rifles. Then they stepped backwards in big steps. A new guard came out taking big forward steps and then he stepped backwards and falls back into the hut.

I went into mobs of Sunday shoppers at the flea market, in fact all the city streets were packed with people. I looked at guitars and wished to buy one but for the expense. Went up to the Acropolis and explored around there as it was a nice sunny day. I decided to spend the next week or two in Athens since things were going well.

When I returned to Apostolis flat, they were having a party. Mia came over and a boyfriend of hers named Mikos came also. He was a rich boy with a hot Lancia car. We went to some bars and raced about the city. Mikos wore thick glasses and was very chummy but his driving was so crazy. He flashed his lights constantly and since he's cross-eyed badly he looked a tart bit like he couldn't see for shit. He beat the hell out of his car, squealing out in all the gears. He had trouble concentrating on the road while putting his hand on Mias lap and turning the wheel, flashing the lights and shifting. We nearly crashed many times and once drove down a sidewalk. For once I became rather fed up with Mia and her crazy boyfriend and I said something like, "He's a fucking crazy driver." They all got bummed out at me for some reason. They could sense my unusual mood I guess.

We stopped and ate at the putha place and then returned to Apostolis where I laughed myself to sleep as Eurgeo and I made obscene noises and the girls got bummed. I awoke late and heard Eurgeo and Liana making love and it sounded like he was killing her. Have these Greeks no timidness while others are listening?

## THE WHEELS OF FRIEND

**Monday Dec. 12th**

The morning was spent busily cleaning and tidying up the place. Then I talked Greek with Apostolis girlfriend and friends. They helped me out a lot with the words. I went into the city and shopped around for a guitar but Apostolis told me he had a friend who said I could use his. I planned to go out and sing in public, for I wanted to test my abilities and gain some experience. I again went and watched the changing of the guards, especially preferred was when they backed up into their guardhouses with a big step and then fall back into the hut. How they did this without hitting their heads I don't know.

There were always thoughts of uncertainty, if it was the right thing for me to be sticking around Athens for so long. But I thought of it as a golden opportunity to take advantage of and this gave me new insights into relating with other cultures. When I came back to the house and met Apostolis he proceeded to teach me some Greek. I was a little funny about doing this and didn't feel good about it but tried to repeat the words, though had trouble remembering them. He went out and I walked up to a hilltop with a great view of the Acropolis and the ocean. How many others have walked up here and stood on these paths? Perhaps Socrates or perhaps the Apostle Paul.

Back at the apartment, After super, I cooked a good supper of meat and potatoes, sat and played the harmonica. then took a hot bath. I walked down to the square and met up with the gang. We went to a great movie called "Sophies Choice."

I rode with Apostolis and Mia in Miltos car and again he drove like an absolute madman to the disco. We were racing down the road at about 100 mph and he went round a curve and threw the car into a skid that nearly lost all control and sent us into a streetlamp. He grabbed the steering wheel and was spinning it like a hula-hoop. If not for the Lancias good handling qualities we would surely have rolled over. I was damned if I wanted to die in a car wreck in this foreign country because of the idiotic driving of this stupid ass. I put a firm hand on Miltos arm and said over again and again, "Take it easy," but of course he didn't understand me. I got so unnerved by his shitty driving that I bellered, "Hey Heema," which means 'sick.' Then Mia screamed at him and told him off. He lay on the brakes and the car skidded to a stop. We all nearly went through the windshield. Miltos bitched about something. If he could have spoke or understood english I would have bitched him out scrooge royal. He took us home and was bummed out. He handed me a flower and acted smart like he was daring me. I was so pissed when I got out of the car I slammed a gate going up to Apostolis place and this nieghbor came out and gave me a dirty look. "Kalinicta," I said to him and quietly closed the gate.

**Tuesday Dec 13th**

Went into the city and bought a roll of film and then checked at the poste restante to see if I had a letter from Jolane. I looked at guitars, then bought some powder-sugar-coated-cookies and came to the apartment to write. Went to the square and met Mia. We hung around each other all night, but now I didn't feel right about her. We walked home that night and I didn't talk to her at all. I felt like she didn't want to talk any English. So I was kind of bummed by this. She went home and as I walked past a store I saw a little puppy inside sleeping on a couch. He was so adorable. I whistled and he looked at me with sleepy eyes. I felt a friendship return to my world, as he wagged his tail and look at me with a cute puppy face.

## Wednesday Dec 14th

Taso's was still asleep at noon as I awoke him. Eurgeo came over and we went driving around to the spots where all the young people hang out. I played my harmonica and we did nothing but sit around all day. This annoyed me to no end. I like to do activities and all these Greeks want to do is sit around. I met Apostolis at the souvlaki joint and we ate and then went over to Lambros house. Lambros was an honor guard at the palace. He showed us photos of himself doing duty. He had the shoes and the hat of a guard for us to inspect. He said the worst thing about being an honor guard was the boredom of having to stand so long. He had the best sound system I've ever heard in a long time. He had many U.S. records and it was interesting to hear the Greeks sing along and mistake or misinterpret the words.

I was getting bored of sitting around and so Maria and I walked home together. We drank a beer in a small park and talked of life. She taught students to speak English so she spoke it well. She had strong anti-U.S. views. Yet I sensed how much she would like to go to the U.S. pursue her dreams. That is what America means to all these people, the land of possible dreams.

As I walked home I went past a bakery shop with a door open and a platter full of the delicious powdered Christmas cookies. I went in and said, "hello." No one answered so I looked about and grabbed a hand full of cookies and darted off.

## Thursday Dec 15

In the morning I went to the U.S. embassy and talked to them about getting a visa for Tasos. They had a long waiting line of people for visas. The flag was at half-mast. I asked them why and they told me it was because the U.S. embassy in Kuwait was bombed. I rode toward the Ominia thinking how difficult it was to understand what my country was doing. Certainly we were more involved in world affairs than I thought. There are U.S. servicemen and officials everywhere and the locals do not seem to appreciate it.

I went to see Taso's and was also going to see the girls at the square. We went to Georges and then took the car and drove around. I met two cute girls at the square across from the school. Ones name was Ania and she was very lovely. Then I met Barbara at a shop as I was out walking. She was a sure '10.' Later I met Tina at the platia. She was from Manhattan and a sure babe. Then we all went to the Acri and I met a gal named Kelly. Kelly was so adorable I melted staring at her. She was a playboy bunny for sure. The great thing about meeting all of these girls was that they let me talk to them. They weren't as quick to get rid of me as U.S. girls were. They were all polite. I felt happy and excited as we sat around the Acri and then went out to eat some food well after midnight. I was tiring of these late night hours.

## Friday Dec. 16th

I slept late and George called me and we went to the bank and then down to the beach. Tempest, his German shepherd came also and George and I skipped stones and he tried hard to communicate with me. He was so expressive and very kind. His facial gestures alone told the story without the words.

We went to the platia and he bought me some pastry with cheese inside and they were delicious. We went to Tasos house and then to the platia. I wanted to go see Barbara and ask her out. So George, Tasos and I went and I said hello to Barbara and she looked surprised when she saw me and then showed little interest in me. I said hello and found out she knew my friends very well. I asked her to go out on a date with me. It was awkward, as I also acted interested in the clothing. She said she couldn't. I asked her if she was married and she said yes. She said she had a child also. I felt so numbed by this after she had winked at me the day before. I said goodbye and walked away to rejoin Tasos and George. Tasos told me the story.

He said he had dated Barbara for awhile and that they were very much in love. "She gave you a line to tell you no in her own way," said Tasos. This bummed me out. Why didn't Tasos forewarn me of her? Did he want to see me get rejected? We went to the platia and again sat around. I became so bored and bummed out that I went and laid down in the car. Then George and Tasos came over and were very concerned about me. I told them I was bored and they seemed pissed off about the whole thing. They wanted to cheer me up so we drove around to the guitar shops, but they were all closed. We went to the Acri and Marina (the pretty girl) Harra, Marie and Kelly were sitting around me and all teased me. I hustled Kelly then bounced back and forth between these girls. It was a heavenly experience but I ended up walking home alone as usual. Back at the house Apostolis was sickly and laid on the sofa shaking.

## Saturday Dec. 17th

Apostolis was very sick, and seemed almost the total reverse of his usual jovial self. He was sleeping with the TV on all night and well into the morning. I could tell he was in misery and gave him some soup to help him out. Maria and Mimi came over and we nursed Apostolis to health. He was a fallen comrade and everyone loved him so much when they heard he was sick that they phoned for hours. I sat around much of the day and then had to get out and ride to the shops to get some exercise.

When I returned we all saw an amazing recovery in Apostolis. He went with us to the platia and everyone cheered and applauded him when he walked in. We then went out dancing to the Beachallow. I was depressed from all my lady troubles and needed a drink. Bought a bottle of Ouzo and gulped it down. I then out danced everyone at the disco! Apostolis, Marina and I shook our legs and were the life of the disco. George invited me to the house of a friend who had a guitar that I could use. We all piled into the car and went there. I came back to our place and played a little and then everyone demanded a performance by me. I couldn't remember any songs. I did manage a couple and everyone seemed happy and wanted more. I played one so poorly I had to stop. Apostolis said, "Eric when you play guitar and sing my balls ache." I knew where I stood and put it away although Liana kept asking me, "Play songs you've never done."

## Sunday Dec 18th

I started off with my writing down lyrics from Apostolis record covers and practicing the guitar until my fingertips hurt. I thought my voice sounded better than ever. The day sped by and after supper everyone came over and brought with ouzo and wine. We had a party complete with girls, guitars and all was wild. I played a Dylan song called Knockin on Heavens Door and everyone applauded. They really listened to me singing and afterward we were all fired up. We drank Ouzo and soon I was quite drunk. We had a water fight and I recall hugging the girls and chasing them around. When everyone wanted to go to the platia, I resisted by crazily running down the street. They wanted me to get in the car but I ran away like a lunatic. I ran up on top of the two-story apartment and danced with my feet on the edge of the building. I wanted to jump on top of the car below, but they all shouted at me to come down. I came to my senses and went down by them and they chased me around the block but I hid in the bushes until they left and then returned to the apartment to go to sleep. I was awakened at 3am by Tasos, who was very concerned of my welfare.

## Monday Dec. 19th

Awoke at 5am on the wicked morning and couldn't sleep. I wasn't well. My head pounded and my guts hurt terribly. Apostolis brought me some food and I wolfed it down. I was hung over and exhausted but unable to sleep. Ouzo is nasty stuff, I vowed to never drink it again. A little bit makes one feel great but a little bit more is like being drugged. I played guitar for much of the day and then went to the platia with the gang. We sat at the Acri and I met Kelly. We talked awhile. Apostolis told me some of the things I'd done and I was totally unaware of it. "You were singing and dancing on the roof top near the edge. You are a big lover as we all saw you kissing and fondling Mia. Then you teased my girlfriend and tickled her."

## Tuesday Dec 20th

Still a lingering hangover fogged my thinking. I biked into the city and had rediscovered just how beautiful a city Athens was. The Acropolis looked so stunning in the sunlight and all the old ruins filled the air with mystique. According to old records, the red tile roofs of the plaka, had been unchanged since the time of Christ. I watched the changing of the guards, stopped at some shops and then came back to the apartment and wrote down many old songs to add to my guitar playing repertoire.

It was getting tired of going to the platia every evening and I started to feel an eagerness to continue on with my journey. Yet, I was drawn to my Greek friends, for they were so warm and so kind. I felt captivated to them and planned to stay through Christmas. My voice was cracking and sounded badly as I caught a chest cold. Apostolis seemed pissed at me about something, I didn't know what. We all went to the Acri and the platia in the evening and sat in our assigned seats. Everyone was talking to someone, but I was getting antsy from this routine. A Greek fellow who I did not know started to tell me all Californians were fags and he further insulted me by saying that all Americans were rich and lazy. I calmly told him it wasn't so and I felt like belting him but instead was very diplomatic and a good ambassador. I couldn't take sitting in the platia and was so bored that we went to a Greek movie and though I couldn't understand a thing, I liked the women. It brought light to my lusting for a Greek woman, for they are so gorgeous and erotic, if only I could understand them better.

## Wednesday Dec 21st

I did some exercise and took a hot bath on a beautiful morning. My body felt weak and I had a cold so I sat around and played the guitar. Maria brought over some delicious cookies and then Apostolis came home early and I played some songs for him. I guess he wanted more 'aching in his balls.' I then went with him to where he worked and we washed windows. After a couple of hours he was so thankful he took me to the supermarket and he bought items on impulse.

Whatever looked good or whatever I thought looked good he bought it. This reminded me of my father, he too would be very giving and appreciative after I did some work for him.

Maria, the fat but cute gal, called and said she wanted to come over and talk to me. Apostolis said to me, "When she comes here, you no play guitar, no sing, no talk-just fuck." He left and I laughed thinking about what he said. Maria came in and spilled her feelings to me and we talked about what she needed to solve her dilemma. She needed a job. Her skills were mostly secretarial but she had other interests such as teaching english. She didn't care about what she did for all she wanted was money. "I'll do anything for some money," she said sighing. This made me back off from her. Was she a prostitute? If I did any hanky-panky with her she would want money from me. Trying hard to not flirt with her, we played a game of tag and then she looked at her watch and had to go. She left feeling better and said, "Bye friend."

I didn't feel like going out this evening but since cousin George wanted the place for himself to screw a girl, I would have to. Apostolis said, "Since Eric no do it with the girl then maybe my cousin will." Then he seemed to get mad and said, "This is no bordello, no hotel with white spattered walls, my cousin no shares girls with me, he's a communist." Maria and I roared laughing at Apostolis. We went to the platia and then to the Acri where I met a girl from the U.S. who talked only about sex. She said if a guy couldn't keep it up for 5 times he wasn't worth it. She was to obnoxious for me. We left at midnight and went to the beach with Mia. Ate yogurt with honey and nuts. It was fun with Apostolis driving and Tasos, Mia and I in the back seat teasing her.

## Thursday Dec. 22nd,

The morning was spent playing guitar and washing Apostolis clothes in the bathtub. One feels the obligation to perform some work in order to justify staying in the house. This would be a big day for me to try busking, or playing guitar and singing songs on the sidewalks of Athens. I went into the city feeling very nervous and like backing out of this foolish idea. The site chosen was in the Plaka, in front of the Monasteraki. What a nerve wracking experience to set up, with people looking at me, and my knowing that I had never done anything like this before. I started to strum away on the guitar. It was a very noisy spot and so they could hardly hear me. I started singing, but it was like singing beside a jackhammer. Some people stopped and listened, they even applauded. In the excitement I could only recall 5 songs and so played them again and again. My voice went bad, almost hoarse. It was a most difficult thing for me to do, to stand there and be looked at like an idiot, but it was a good experience. My bowl had a few bills, but mostly coins. After twenty minutes I packed up and tried a couple other places.

Back at the apartment I found out that Tasos would be leaving on a ship on Sunday. He would not be going with us skiing up in the mountains as we planned. It was very disappointing news. We went to the platia and I sat there alone and then walked over to see Barbara. She was outside, near a display of dresses. I talked to her awhile. She was so beautiful. I tried to make a date with her but she said she could not because she had a boyfriend. She told me to come back on Tuesday.

I went back to the platia to meet with Marina and Harra, then Tasos came by to join us. He had tears in his eyes. I pulled him to me and told him I wished he would not go work on the ship. He almost cried when I said, "I will feel all alone without you in Athens." We were both so moved by the thought of our separation that we were like brothers. I truly realized that in this entire world there are those individuals you can communicate with so well, even though you've not known them very long.

We went to Apostolis and we sang together, "Country Roads." Tasos said, "That song was for you." I felt so moved by this dedication. Later we watched a movie about JFK.

## Friday Dec. 23rd

My voice sounded real bad. Along with hoarseness, a cold had moved in. My head was stuffed and my lungs full of flem. Tasos came over and we sat around. Then I went with Apostolis and George to several shops, buying items to get the car ready for the trip to the mountains. We installed new tires for snow and the car was tuned. We met two friends from England driving a Porsche. Then the news filtered in that we would not be going to the mountains because Tasos wasn't going. We would have a party instead. We all went out to eat, but since I already ate, I would join them for company. Actually this was done for economic reasons. I was trying to save money by not going out to eat.

We went to this restaurant and I was talked into joining the feast of chops, potatoes and wine. It was a happy occasion with "Ruebaackee music" playing. Tasos was very sad at times but yet lively and celebrative. I sat by Liana and she explained to me these foods, one of which was 'mooseaacka.' While we sat there, a gnat kept pesturing me. We cheered each glass of wine by repeating, "Hamass." Then we were all shook up when we each had to fork out 700 dracmas for the meal. Marina was weeping and kissing her dracmas goodbye. We went back to the platia and I went the Acri before going home a little poorer.

## Saturday Dec. 24th

My good friends came early and said, "This day is your day." I didn't understand what they meant by that and was somewhat perturbed as I was sitting there practicing hard for this days street performance. Then Apostolis, Tasos and George came in and handed me a big package. I had no idea what it was until opening it up not believing my eyes. It was a guitar! A six string steel acoustic that was personally signed by all my friends from Greece. A sticker inside the guitar said, "To accompany you on your long journey, your friends from Greece-George, Liana, Apostolis, Hara, Tassoo, Marina, Petrakis, Maya, Mimis and Maria." It wasn't something I expected and was very thankful. They certainly had generous hearts I could not conceive.

Once a sling was attached to the shiny new guitar I went into the city and set up at my spot by the monasteraki. I started to play as people walked by. My voice was harsh and as ragged as a torn sheet. Someone came along and dropped some coins into the handbag on my bike. Then another person put some in there. People stopped to look and listen or watch. I laid out a plate with a Christmas card on it and a few coins. This gave them a place to put there offering. In two hours I had 850 dracmas and was wailing out songs with more enthusiasm than ever. People came up and requested songs. A girl asked for 'Imagine' by John Lennon and though I knew the words couldn't play the guitar and muffed it up. She kind of liked it.

On that Christmas Eve as I pedaled toward home I felt something so wonderful happening to me. It felt as though I'd been touched by a thousand hands messaging my temples. I was uplifted!

Back at the apartment we watched "Scrooge" a cartooned version on TV while getting the place ready for a party. We decorated the room with Christmas ornaments and even had a one branch Christmas tree. We went to buy liquor and Liana and I went running down the street holding hands as a bus was coming at us. We drank champagne and sat around waiting for everyone to arrive. Apostolis danced about with his glass and a red stocking cap on. More and more people showed up and the party began. Later, Christmas gifts were passed about, then people got drunk. They drank ouzo in shot glasses. I happened to be near Maria as she passed out in my arms. Then it was George. Then Tasos. Then Apostolis. I was catching them as they fell. Fortunately I didn't drink much, for nobody would have caught them. It wasn't until well after midnight when everyone left.

**Sunday Dec. 25th**

Apostolis, Effie, Liana and I slept on the floor under a bundle of blankets. Apostolis made love with his girlfriend Effie, and at one point I shone a flashlight on him and he sat up exposing his erection. Liana and I rolled about laughing until our tummys ached. Liana looked so lovely and was so sweet. She kept asking me to tell her stories. I told her many and she would translate them into Greek to tell Apostolis while he was making it with Effie. He had no shame and bore away into the girl while we lay there.

Christmas day was spent cleaning the house, for my god it was a mess. There was broken glass outside on the deck. Cigarette butts were laying all about. We went to see Marina at Lambros house. He gave me a Christmas gift. Then I went to Tasos house and sat with mama and we exchanged greetings and talked in our simple way. I knew a few words of Greek and she some English. "Chronia Pala, Merry Christmas Erica," she said to me. She wept as she added, "Taso go." She kept wondering how my mama took it with me gone at Christmas time. I told her, "Mama sad," and she cried more.

I met papa and said, "Chronia pala." We ate a delicious dinner of lamb and potatoes. Papa said, "You should eat more Russian salad so maybe you Americans could like the Russians more." I told him I liked Russians and wished I could meet more of them." Kelly and I played cards. Pano, a young boy joined us. The meal was wholesome and deliciously prepared. I ate sugar coated cookies after a pudding dessert. Kelly and I had an intense talk about science and the future. How technology would free our lives of physical hardship but would not make us happier.

After thanking Tasos's family for treating me to a wonderful Christmas, I walked back on Christmas night to Apostolis house. My thoughts were thankful for having such a unique experience as this. To spend this special day in another country and with these heartful people. How lucky I was.

Liana, Apostolis, Effie and I went to the movie, Flashdance. I could sense my longing to return to more adventure on the bike as the movie inspired those thoughts. Liana and I sat at a sidewalk cafe and she said, "Eric we are going to the disco, come on lets go." I said, "I don't want to go." She pulled on my arm saying, "Come on let's go." I pulled away and said, "I am like a bull." She was pulling on me and insisting until they dropped me off in front of the apartment.

## Monday Dec. 26th

I awoke early and went for a long bike ride into the city and pedaled to the tops of many hills in Athens. I sat to read a paper at the monastery overlooking the city on a sunny, warm, beautiful day. Back at the apartment around mid day I watched the classic movie version of "A Christmas Carol," with Alistair Simm. We were all uplifted when he sang at the end, "I like life, life likes me, I like life like it ought to be." Apostolis mimicked this and danced around with a broomstick.

We went to Georges house where he and Liana cooked a great meal of lambchops and potatoes with salad. I helped Liana do the dishes. We were getting closer. She was so kind and beautiful. I enjoyed being with her so much. We watched a musical TV program with Marina, Harra and her 80 year old Granny who was very happy to meet an American. We went to Thomas house and I sat next to Liana the whole night and we held hands while watching a Charlie Chaplin movie. I enjoyed this much and felt warmth in my heart for her.

## Tuesday Dec. 27th

In the morning I went into the city and bought a new string for the guitar in addition to a harmonica holder. I went back to the apartment and practiced some more songs. Then Liana came over and I sat with her and we talked and there were some strong vibes between us. I played some songs for her and she listened intently to them. We watched TV and throughout I had my arm around her constantly. She was so honest when I told her I had much heart for her. I stood up and was going to make popcorn but she stopped me at the door and said, "No you don't go," and she took me by the hand back to the couch. This touched me so, but I was bewildered what to do next. She only wanted me to be near her, not to do things. I took a bath and sang in there while she made supper. We afterward went to Lambros house and played cards with them. He let me copy some lyrics from his record album covers and Liana got concerned while I did this and said, "You are acting funny, come here with me." We clowned around all night playing cards until going home late.

## Wednesday Dec 28th

I was preparing my reputoir of songs for performing in the city. Liana called and said she felt, "No good," because of me. She thought I didn't like her. I said, "No way, I do like you." She said I was different from one minute to the next. I told her about the ways of courting in the U.S. I added that though I liked her very much she was still George's girlfriend I didn't want to make a problem with him. She said," I will never call you again." I said, "I do not mind if you do call me," but she said goodbye.

I went to the city center feeling perturbed about my relationship with Liana. When I arrived at my usual busking spot in front of the monasteraki there was a lady selling flowers. The "Bastos" cops also were all about so I went to a spot by the parliament and started to play some songs. "Hey Mr. Tamborine Man," was my favorite especially accompanied with the harmonica. People helped inspire me by dropping tips into my plate. One guy came over and put some coins in and then he listened. He told me that no one could understand me because I spoke and sang English songs. I told him, "It's ok I don't care." He left and then I met a couple of guys from the U.S. and told them I was going to India and they asked me if I'd be going through Spain along the way. "Spain's that way to the west," I said pointing. "I'm not going that way, I'm going that-ah-way to the east," pointing to the east. "Oh I remember," he said. He tipped me a few coins. Then the guy complaining about the wrong song came back and asked me if I knew the notes of a guitar. I told him and he said thanks. These were but a sample of the weirdoes I put up with to perform in the streets.

Went to another spot that was quieter and many people tipped me and listened to my songs. After counting 850 drachmas, I delightedly went back to my place and cooked supper for Maria. I didn't try to talk as much with her and Apostolis because I felt it was too much trouble and besides it was hard to intellectualize when we used only a 5 word vocabulary. A song of my own creation was bouncing around and I wrote it down. All the words were Greek, and the melody my own interpretation of what a Greek song sounds like. I played it to Liana and she laughed. Apostolis said jokingly, "Me like it but your singing give me pain in the balls." I was requested to sing it to my friends many times.

Kelly called me and we went to a bar. We talked much about very heavy subjects most of which revolved around how and where we are going with our lives. I discovered she had failed to get a Ph.D. in the states. A goal she was working on but said she didn't quite make. To me it sounded like she quit trying because of a failed relationship with an American guy, although she mentioned she could not adjust to the American lifestyle. When I told her that my philosophy is, "A person can do anything they want to do," she disagreed and said it takes god given talent. I disagreed and felt that was her first problem. I tried as hard as I could to comfort her because she was very unsettled. Her temper boils over quickly and she was angry about the discussion. We then talked about Tasos and her mother, who, much like herself, was once a poet. She recited to me a verse or two and I thought it was very moving.

When I came back into the apartment Apostolis told me, "If you want you can stay here until summer." I was taken aback by such an offer. He added, "You no have to pay rent and if you want you can come work with me to make some money."

Liana came over and so did Maria. I later cooked supper for Maria and then we went out as usual to the usual places. This time I suggested a movie or a walk by the Acropolis. Instead we went to Liana's house and watched her sew a sheet for Lambro. I felt like a tag-along more than ever before. It was difficult for me to speak out. I'm not the kind who likes to make waves, so I went along with the routine, but it was difficult to hang in there, to be kind, and to still let them know the problem was I didn't like staying up so late into the night.

## Thursday Dec 29th

Early in the morning I went across the street from the apartment to the pastry shop and then down to the corner and bought some yogurt, apples and oranges. I would dice them up, mix them with yogurt and add sugar for breakfast. I played guitar and drank coffee until I was nauseated and saw flashes of light. Not being much of a coffee drinker, this new taste sensation has symptoms yet to discover.

I pedaled down to the platia and bought a few things while scouting to see Barbara, but she was not there. I returned to the house and prepared my things for we were taking a journey up to Thessalonki today. Maria came over and packed Apostolis clothing and then we spent the next 5 hours sitting around waiting for everyone to get themselves organized. They'd be so damned mixed up it was like an Abbott and Costello movie. Apostoli would go to the platia to meet Mimi and then Mimi would come walking in. Liana and George came over and tried to get me to go to the Acri but they did not understand that everyone would soon be coming here. Maria and the others went to the platia and I stubbornly stayed put. At 11am everyone suddenly appeared at Apostolis house and we quickly left at 11:30.

Mimis car carried Sophie and myself in the Mini Cooper. Miltos, the crazy driver drove his Lancia with Mia, Marina and Apostolis on board. We drove along stopping frequently. First we stopped for gas, second for a stretch, third when the cops gave Miltos a speeding ticket, fourth for engine problems which I fixed by reconnecting a spark plug cap wire. After that I dosed off and awoke at a rocky place with a footbridge spanning a river. We got out and ran around like little kids.

We stopped at a church, which had huge candles as big around as our arms could reach, and played catch with them. Then we passed snow-covered mountains and came down into Thessaloniki at 8:30pm. I met Apostolis father, who was a fisherman with only one arm, though he shook hands with each of us.

## Friday Dec. 29th

We drove to Apostolis village, about 30kilometers from Thessaloniki, where I met his mother and sister. I quietly emerged as the stranger from faraway who could not speak Greek. Apostolis made a scene of me by asking me to say something in Greek. I did say "Kalimehra" and "poss bye." Then he prodded me to speak some more so I called Apostolis "millaka" and papa didn't appreciate that very much with his grandson and family at hand.

We went for a walk and clowned around in a park, all acting as one big happy group. A nice hotel in Thessaloniki was where Miltos got himself and Mia a room. He obviously had more money than I thought, for it was an expensive place and very plush.

Everyone wanted to sleep except Miltos and I, so I said I'd go with him to the city or to a beach. He drove like crazy with one hand out the window, the other waving in the car, a leg to steer with, while dividing his attention between me and the road. The stereo was blasting and he would stop and ask people directions to a favorite beach he had in mind. He would tell people that I was a photographer from U.S.A. We went through many hair raising situations. He missed a turn and so pulled on the parking brake and spun the car around at 60 mph. We went around corners skidding and on two wheels. He'd hit bumps so hard it would bottom the vehicle out and jam the gearshift.

In under one hour we had traveled 80 kilometers upon narrow, twisting roads. We went to a hotel that was closed down and walked down to the beach. Miltos brought his suitcase and pulled out his towel, swimsuit and sunglasses then laid in the cold sun. He went swimming and was frolicking in the cold sea as I played my harmonica. He came out and had me wipe suntan lotion on his back. He acted real strange and admittedly I was concerned, so I'd tucked my buck knife into my sock.

On the drive back to the village he was very angry because he could not find a restaurant. To channel his anger he drove like a mad man, swerving in front of oncoming cars because it scared me. I told him to slow down, but he drove 100 mph around blind corners in the wrong lane. He was doing all kinds of idiotic driving and I shouted at him to slow down. He slammed on the brakes, pulled over and sat on the roadside, sulking. Finally we made it back to the village even though his shift linkage broke and he had to drive it in fourth gear. I told Apostolis that Miltos was a crazy idiot and that his driving sucked. I would not crawl under his car to repair the shift linkage so Apostolis went with Miltos into the city to find a rental car.

I slept awhile and ate supper. Then we went to the city and they took me into a gay bar. One faggot kept looking at me and I was very uncomfortable. I was glad to leave and we went to a disco, though I didn't want to stay because it stunk in there. At midnight we returned home to sleep.

## Saturday Dec 31st

Being that today was the final day of this most interesting year, which could be looked back on as filled with fantastic growth and accomplishment, extreme termoil and daily testing, I looked forward to the New Years eve party. We all went down to the ship of Apostolis father. He gave me a tour and then his father came on board and also showed us around the ship. The immensity of the nets amazed me. On the pier, we exchanged the guitar and sang songs. It was beautiful with the sea and the sun for the view was breathtaking. Apostolis came along and we scurried to the airport. Then we went into Thessaloniki and up to this mountain overlook where Mia got into a fight with Miltos because he had stopped for a man who was walking across the street. Mia didn't like to wait and said he should have gone around. They argued like fighting cats. Sophie got a little bitchy also. It seems women cannot take much stress without their emotions blowing up-but then again look at Miltos.

We left and Miltos went bananas. He would drive like a mad man. Mia screamed and hollered, even punched him. We slid to a stop on the road and Mia got out and ran crying to the other car. I rode with Miltos a little ways and then Apostolis changed with me. We went to the hotel and Miltos exploded. He and Mia had a fight. Miltos grabbed all his things and was leaving. He came back in and threw lamps and dishes around the room. We went back to the village and sat at a patisierre. Apostolis showed up mad and emotional. This all seemed like one helluva soap opera to me.

We went back to Apostolis fathers house while a friend of Apostolis named Stratus took us on a back roads tour of slutty hotels. Then we went to a friends house and Apostolis came in and broke down crying with emotion. He told us his uncle had died at home. I had just taken a photograph of him a few hours before. Apostolis said to me, "Eric, you have photo of him just before he dead. You get me that photo, ok?" I assured him that I would do that.

We all sat at Georges house and everything became mixed up, no one could solve the problem. They were so disorganized in this dilema and I did not have a clue as to what was going on.

We were shuttled to another party and there was something strange about it because these people were very leery of me; the American. They would offer me food, but only at arms length and spoke about me with their hands covering their mouths. I had a feeling I wasn't all to welcome.

We went back to Georges house and I set my watch alarm to ring at midnight. We drank ouzo, and ate big pretzels. This was a very warm household and George and his wife were very kind. We played a card game called 31 and I won all but one hand. At precisely midnight Georges watch and mine chimed exactly even though they had not been previously syncronized. The lights in the house were all turned off, candles were lit, the doors opened and the water facets turned on. Everyone hugged each other and wished, "Chronia Pola." I kissed all the girls. The lights were then turned on and a large, round, baked bread cake with an embossed; "1984," was brought out. Beginning with the eldest, the cake was blessed and then cut and served. Somewhere in the cake there was hidden a good luck surprise. Grandma was the oldest and given the first piece. Six of the pieces of cake were passed out. Sophie and I were the lucky ones to recieve a 20 dracmas coin inside our piece. We ate delicious cookies and sang a happy New Year song similar to ours.

After our New Years celebration we went to this nightclub that played bazooky music and broke dishes. They must have broke a thousand dishes on the floor. They would do a little ceremony and dance, then out came a stack of dishes which were abruptly busted on the dance floor. People would dance right over them. We stayed there until 4am, but frankly I'd run out of things to say. Sophie and I went out to the car because it was so loud and smokey inside. After that ear ringing, smoke ingested experience I vowed to not to go to anymore discos. I had tolerated this late night activity long enough and would soon have to leave. We went to a sister of Apostolis to drop the girls off to sleep. Then Apostolis and I went back to his fathers house and without speaking a word we went to our beds. I felt so abused on this day, being scurried about like a dog on a leash. Yet it was a tender New Year beginning and I would have to be prepared for greater tribulations.

# HAPPY NEW YEAR 1984

### Sunday the first day of the New Year 1984

Bazooki music and breaking dishes clanged in my ears after our Thessaloniki nightclub outing, upon awakening at noon. Everyone else slept for another hour and then we somberly went to Apostolis sisters house to drink thick coffee and look at photo albums. Katherine, his niece, was very pretty and at 17 had already acquired such brightness as all beautiful young Greek women have. We ate a very delicious lamb dinner and then Marina and I went for a walk to meet Apostolis. We were walking down the road when I saw him and the others drive away. I had to run like crazy to catch them. We then went on a cross-country tour of the village and drove over the worst damn roads one could imagine. I played guitar on the seaside as the sunset. Sophie was very bitchy to me and acted very cold after I touched her. These Greek women are unequivocally temperamental.

We went to a patisierre and I asked Sophie if all was ok. She snapped at me but after awhile we came more or less to terms and were friends again. We moved to a pub and Apostolis called a friend named Jimmy. There we sat for quite awhile waiting. I met Effie the lady friend of Apostolis, and she bought me a drink. Apostolis came along and shuttled us away. By now I dreaded to see him because he always wanted to go, go, go- go-nowhere.

I was told we had no house to stay in for the night because Apostolis relatives had arrived for his uncle's funeral. I said I would stay in a vacant house I had observed. They thought that I was being ridiculous and sort of joshed at me. I had my sleeping bag and I wanted to be alone. Everyone grabbed me and said, "Come, lets go to the disco." But I was stubborn and suffering from sleep deprivation so I refused to go. They left while I sat in Jimmy's house talking to Agea, the dark beautiful woman who Apostolis called 'the Funny Girl.' She was very different, talkative, intuitive rather like a gypsy. She would open her eyes real wide and talk excitedly about her fantastic ideas. We talked for another two hours in our broken English. I really liked Agea, for she was an individual, a free thinker and a 'funny girl'.

She understood when I said I was getting tired and at 10:30pm I went outside walking along the smoke-smelling streets of Thessaloniki, strumming my guitar and singing. The night was cool and clear. I met George, Apostolis brother in law, on the street and he told me he wanted to go to the U.S.A and wanted to come visit me. I welcomed him.

I went into the vacant house. It even had running water! Slept the night rather well despite the continuous whooping of some party goers at 3 and 4 in the morning. Also a man singing Greek songs came drunkenly up to the front door at 5am, tried to open it and then left. I think he came to the wrong house.

## Monday Jan. 2nd

After a decent nights sleep in the unoccupied house, I spent the morning eating cheese filled pastry and playing my guitar by the seashore. It was around noon, when I knocked on the door and awoke Apostolis. In the interim, I drank way to much Greek coffee, which was thick and very powerful. It gave me the jitters.

We all went to a local pub, then went with a fellow named Marcos to the shores of the Aegean Sea to visit a lighthouse where there was also a Nazi WWII bunker and pillbox. There was a tiny slit in the pillbox that I slid through and explored this German fortress. I could tell by the design that it would be very difficult to attack. Every corridor was protected by another. I played my guitar inside the bunker and fittingly sang Blowin in the Wind.

It was a beautiful, sunny day and we all were in good spirits in part to the going home of Miltos the night before. We went down to a nice section of beach looking out over the Aegean Sea. Stratos was there along with a friend who was a scuba diver. We walked along the beach skipping rocks and feeling the cold water on our feet. The girls stripped down, put on long t-shirts and then ran into the refreshing water. I followed suit and we frolicked in the cold water. Sophie sure looked nice soaking wet with her dark hair flung back and her shirt clinging to her voluptuous figure.

The scuba diver surfaced with several large octopus in addition to an ancient oil lamp, which he kept. They cleaned the octopus and then beat it on a rock to kill the arms which moved continuously after separation from the main body. As the creature died the color changed from a dark purple to a pale white. They roasted the octopus on a stick over an open fire while I sang songs. I tried some of the meat and it tasted good but was rubbery.

It was near sunset on this picturesque setting, when we loaded back into the cars and headed back to the village. We said goodbye to Apostolis family. I shook the hand of Apostolis' father and he told me through an interpreter, "I wish I could have done more for you." I was very thankful for all he had done. We took a bus into the city and went up to Stratos apartment. He showed us a porno movie while everybody took turns bathing and changing clothes. We went into Thessaloniki and saw the movie Tootsie, then returned to the apartment and I fell asleep until the rest of the gang arrived.

For the return trip to Athens we took a taxi and were packed inside of it like sardines. At times it was unbearably uncomfortable. Apostolis, Mia, Marina and I were in the back seat. I'd say whose leg is this? Apostolis would say "Mine." And whose is this, Mia would say, "Mine." A little later Marina said, "Phew who did that?" Everyone in unison said, "Apostolis." I slept a little leaning against Mia and she against Apostolis and so on. We arrived in Athens at 9pm.

## Tuesday Jan. 3rd

Athens had a distinct sound and smell in the morning. It was a day of regrouping and collecting thoughts. The day started off with the usual concoction of fruit and yogurt. Marina and Apostolis had hit it off on the trip to Thessaloniki and she spent the night with him. They were a nice couple, he being very feisty and spontaneous and she even tempered and patient. She was a school teacher after all. We all accomplished a great deal of cleaning in the apartment and I took a nap after they went out for the afternoon.

I sat around playing the guitar until heading into the city at 5:30pm and played music by the Monasteraki where I made about 300 dracmas, enough to enjoy a nice meal from a curbside souvlaki stand. While there, I met a nice Greek girl and talked to her awhile. She was pleasing to look at and had a considerate disposition.

I pedaled back to the house and went with the group to the platia and then to the Acri. I talked to Tina, the pretty U.S. girl. Apostolis and I laughed away the night talking about her. She knew all the worst Greek swear words and would repeat them, yet she was grossed out when I told her I liked to sleep on dirt. He told me a story called Five times the Bigger. It went like this.

There was an American sitting down to dine with a Greek. The Greek man said how do you like my new car? The American said, "You call that a car, Look at my car, it is five times the bigger than yours." The Greek man felt offended. Then the Greek man said, "How do you like this photo of my home? The American man looked at it and said, "You call that a home, my home is five times the bigger than your Greek home. The Greek man felt offended. Then the Greek man showed the American a photo of the tallest building in Greece. The American said, "You call that a tall building, in America our tallest building is five times the bigger!" Then the Greek man said, "how do you like Greek food?" The American said, "You call that the food? Our American food is five times the bigger than Greek food." "Oh yeah?" said the Greek. "Everything I tell you about Greece you say America is five times the bigger-well here take this." At which point the Greek man shoves a huge sea crab into the American mans underpants and says, "Now you can tell everyone in America that your crabs are five times the bigger!"

## Wednesday Jan. 4th

I went into the city, shortly after the noon hour, after eating a late breakfast of yogurt and fruit in addition to cheese filled pastry. I played music by the monasteraki and put on a good show, then went over by the palace near a fountain. I tended to look for spots that were somewhat noisy because of my self-consciousness of performing and most of all stagefright. I made pretty good money at the later spot as many people came by and gave me 100 dracmas at a time. A cute couple of girls came along and I talked with them. They asked me to play a song. I sang Danny's Song and was proud of my performance. I really digged it when a girl watched me sing. She was very nice to me afterward and tenderly shook my hand.

I went happily along, after that busking session and bought a paper, then went to a church and sat to read the U.S. News. I was reading about the Grizzlies in Yellowstone and saw two cute girls walk by. I could tell they were girls that I wanted to meet. I hungrily talked with them about who they were and they asked me to play some songs. So I played a couple. They enjoyed this immensely and I got nervous, but I played a couple more. We talked about my journey and they were very interested in it. I liked Karen, for she reminded me very much of Ellen. I also liked her friend Ronnie because she was such a lively, bubbly U.S. girl. They were both students at Gettysburg University.

I went with them to their apartment and met some of their friends. Then I went with the girls into the city and we ate at a souvlaki restaurant. We had much to talk about, but started off soaking wet as a waiter blew a cork from his champagne bottle all over us.

I was tending to like Karen, who was nicknamed 'fox', because she was more on the level. We went to an outdoor bar on the street side and I played some songs. I played a Greek song and we laughed so hard as people walked by and when they heard my song looked on in amazement. One man asked me if I knew what "Capsurrees" meant. I said lovesick. He said, "Worse."

I went with the girls' back to their hotel and made a date to see them tomorrow at 5pm. I kept thinking about the coincidence between Karen's looks and Ellen's and how much alike they acted. I liked Karen and thought much for her while sitting around playing my guitar into the night, trying to learn some new songs. Apostolis and Marina were close this evening, laying on the couch and constantly hugging. It was very enjoyable to see them together.

## Thursday Jan. 5th

I awoke at 9:30am and practiced some songs, then satisfied my craving by eating fruit n yogurt and cheese rolls. From eating this kind of food, I could feel a gain of weight.

I went into the city and played guitar for one hour at the monasteraki during which a busload of people went past, inside of which I saw Karen and Ronnie. An American girl leaned out the window and shouted, "Somebody up front wants you." I waved with my foot as I kept playing. It was my worst performance yet. I couldn't sing nor recall songs. I was requested to play 'Imagine' for a girl and she said it wasn't very good. I went to the Parliament square to try my luck playing on the steps and met a bloody-nutty-Englishman who talked to me while I played and shouted in my ear. I gave another terrible performance and decided to call it quits.

I pedaled over to the girl's hotel and upon seeing them said, "Hello American girls." They were somewhat leery of me at first and with good reason. How else would they judge a fellow whom they'd just seen singing in the streets of Athens? Ronnie was kind enough to give me a hair cut and when they saw how I blushed because they teased me, they knew all was well, and that I was a typical American boy. I liked these girls so much because we could communicate and besides they were good fun.

We walked to Apostolis and they were like chickens leaving the roost. They had no street sense and became more and more leery of me in proportion to the distance we went from the city center. I thought they would turn back at any time. We walked past little shops and local people and they saw how different it was from in the city. They made comments such as, "This is neat." We walked up the steps to Apostolis apartment and went into the house.

I introduced Apostolis and Marina to my new friends. The girls had no idea how to treat and talk to my Greek hosts. In many ways they offended them by asking too complicated questions for them to understand in english. At first Apostolis and Marina could not understand them.

Karen and Ronnie laughed at my simple english speaking techniques, I used to communicate with them. I served Greek coffee and they liked it.

Thomas, the Greek man with a Mini Cooper, gave us a ride up to the Monastery on top of the hill and it was so much fun going up to the top. We clowned like crazies and had the best time. I loved every minute of it. I got to hold the girls and was close to them. We tickled and played and hugged and were romantic. We drove to the platia and they met many of the gang that hangs out there. The girls were in delight to feel the center of attention. They really enjoyed talking with the Greek people but they probably over did it, as the Greeks looked tired.

While walking down to the Acri, Karen told me she thought people here didn't seem driven by success like in the U.S. We went to a James Bond movie and though it was not very good, I did like holding Karen and felt something strong for her. Afterward we went running down the street, dancing and going crazy on a delightful evening. In the car we kissed and she said she liked me. Ronnie argued with Thomas and he became mad at her because she intimidated him about his driving and he lashed out speaking Greek to her. We dropped the girls off at the hotel and I enjoyed a nice, long kiss with Karen. I told her I would see her tomorrow at 5 in the afternoon.

When I laid in bed that night I pondered if maybe she would change her mind about seeing me or was I just overcautious, that this was all to good to be true.

## Friday Jan. 6th

I was so excited about meeting my new friends in Athens I didn't sleep very well. It was a holiday called 'Gods Day' in Greece. The occasion is marked by the church priest throwing a cruxifix into the water and divers attempting to retrieve it before it was pulled up with a cloth rope. I sat in the house and watched TV with Apostolis and Thomas. I was longing for the company of the U.S. girls. The gang came over and we watched a Greek comedy on the tube that was funny even though I couldn't understand the dialogue. Everybody was smoking so much that I got annoyed, stormed out the door coughing and leaving it open because it was so smoky inside. This alarmed my friends and they thought I had something wrong with me. I told Apostolis it was nothing, but perhaps it was.

I went into the city and up to the room of the girls. Karen arranged with her friends that she and I could go out to dinner alone. I met some more of her friends from the U.S and they seemed cynical and acted snotty to Karen. Their behavior shocked me in some ways.

We walked arm in arm to the restaurant. We ordered our dinner and drank Coca-cola. Unlike my last month with the Greeks, we could talk about anything and we were so much on the level. She reminded me so much of Ellen and yet was different in many other ways. I felt a growing fondness for her. She had eyes that melted me. She looked so intensely at me. We enjoyed talking about personal experiences. We went back to the hotel and got close on the bed while everyone was gone and had a very intimate talk. Karen and I leveled about our limits, what we could and couldn't do. There would be no promises, no saying I love you and no sex. Period!

We met Ronnie and I talked to her and Karen into walking to the platia to meet the gang. I laughed at their friend, Jessica, a Pennsylvania girl who enjoyed the Athens bar life.

Ronnie and Karen and I walked down to the platia singing songs along the way and holding arms and dancing. We were so light and crazy and we didn't have a care even though it was raining a little. The girls kept asking me if I was lost. We went into the platia and sat down outside. I called

Apostolis on the telephone but he was not home. We met Sykees and talked to the Greeks. We walked over to the Acri and met Apostolis. We thought we could get a ride to the city but none was available. So we walked in the rain. Our feet were tired. We clowned around and sang and talked. We made it to the hotel and necked on the steps. I came to really appreciate her beauty. She had something about her I really liked. She and I both felt it. We were talking about everything in our hearts. I kept telling her how I liked her beauty. We embraced so long so much. It was a most difficult night to go home. I slept alone in the apartment this night.

**Saturday Jan. 7th**

Karen called me at noon, and I told her I'd see her at 2. I took a bath and afterward did my laundry in the tub. Then I rode excitedly and ever jolly through the streets of Athens to her hotel. She said, "Come on up," when I pressed the intercom. She was sitting on the bed alone and beautiful. I asked her how she was and embraced her. We then went for a walk in the city, holding hands or arm in arm. We were both feeling good. Went to a pastry shop, then to a coffee shop at the city square. We sat by a Toaluse LaTrect painting while enjoying the sounds and sights of Athens. We were so close. Kissing and embracing, talking and laughing. She ate a cream pastry and I an apple pie. We realized our time was short and this added to the strange kind of passion we felt. We went on a hike up to The Church of St. George, located on the very high Lycabetus Hill, stopping often to kiss and look at one another. One time she got mad at me because she said I undid her bra. We kissed on busy sidewalks or on little streets. She told me about her life and I about mine. At the top we were filled with romance at this beautiful spot. We felt the clock ticking away on our lives, for she would be flying back tomorrow. With time running out, we got closer and closer.

We went into a church and were frozen together in some kind of mesmerized togetherness. We took photos. She told me about her mom and I about my dad. We went back to the hotel. The gang she was traveling with was very arrogant and I sensed Karen's reputation was questioned by all when they saw me.

I met more American people. Ronnie went to a bar. Karen told me that Ronnie really liked me and was jealous that I was with her. We went to the bar and Ronnie came with us to eat at the Delphi. We clowned and Ronnie was silly with drink. We laughed and kidded. I turned red telling jokes. I embraced both girls and told them I loved them. We went crazy when Ronnie sang Oscar Mier Wiener in German. Ronnie was great.

We went back to the hotel and sang some songs. Karen and I took an elevator to the top floor and necked. We were both hot and yet we both were withdrawn. We were like kids. Went back to the room and Karen started packing. She got huffy when I tickled her armpit and we wrestled. She was a tough girl. After that she said she wasn't feeling well and said it was her period and Ronnie yawned. I thought they wanted to get rid of me. So I said I would go. Karen got upset at this. She blocked me at the door. She wanted to know what was wrong with me. I told her that I thought they wanted me to leave and with her sociology skills she brought me back to her arms. I felt like going home. She hung on to me. We went to a janitors closet and sat on the floor. Then we got real close, hugging, embracing, necking and becoming amorous. It was horrible. I wanted more from her than she wanted to give. I cooled down and then she changed her mind and wanted me. We could not get our physiologies to agree. We both cried as we felt the time was near for us to say goodbye. We went back to her room and went into her bed where I enjoyed holding her. She told me, "Don't touch my tits because it hurts," adding, "My boobs aren't worth a damn." There I was, longing for sex, but not being allowed to touch her above, for it hurt, or below for her period was in progress.

The alarm rang at 5:30 and we dressed. At the doorway we agreed to see each other again-someday. We embraced and held each other close. "Fox, I like you," I kept saying. She said, "Eric, I like you." We said our good-byes and I started to walk away down the hall and she exclaimed, "Oh no!" She ran to me and came crying into my arms. I wanted to burst into tears. We hugged one last time, wiping the tears from each other's eyes.

I pedaled home and stopped to sit by the church where we'd met and I almost cried. The rest of the ride home was a quiet one with extreme depression.

## Sunday Jan. 8th

There was a deep emptiness feeling throughout the day. To have rapidly fallen into a spell of love and then to accept that she was gone wasn't making things happy for me. I bathed and used the water to wash clothes, then Apostolis came in and asked me what was wrong. "I am capsurres," I told him. "You have big lovesickness?" he asked. "Yes," I said, "The American girl did this to you?." "Yes," I responded. He turned away and said, "American girl is malacka!"

I went into the city and rode past the places we had been together only hours before. Now they were empty places. My heart was gone. My body was nothing, nothing but ugly.

I played a couple of songs at the monasteraki and two girls listened to me. It helped to pull me out of the doldrums. Afterward I took a tour of the city on my bike, past Fox's hotel, again feeling like crying and ever so lonely. I knew she felt the same. We agreed to not let this affair hurt us too bad. We both knew that it could happen. I kept seeing her eyes and hearing her voice. She was engraved in my soul. At the gardens I played many songs and then went back to the square, past the places we sat happily together. This was a blue day, a day of withdrawals. I felt so much for her. Now it was all over.

I sat dazed on the steps in the garden and was feeling numb and without any hope. I stopped at Traders shop and counted my money and the Iranian man who owned the shop seemed sympathetic with me and took all my coins in exchange for paper bills. I was very sad riding home. It was like a slash is in my heart. Later in the evening I went to the movie Airplane 2 with George and Liana.

## Monday Jan. 9th

I Went to the city on the afternoon and was so sad to go past those places that I shared so many memories with Karen. Ghosts were everywhere of her and I was experiencing the blues. There was a hill in the city with a statue of Delphi which I hiked up on to. It offers a beautiful view of Athens and is a pretty place. The ancient Greeks had removed giant blocks of rock from the hill and also left graffiti from over the ages. My hike continued down into the plaka where I explored many interesting shops and loved the small streets. Two U.S. girls were walking along and we talked but I was feeling down even though they wanted to talk. I wasn't up to chasing after them but admit to have felt better after talking to them.

Back at the apartment, I cooked a fine meal of pork chops and raw fried potatoes for Apostolis.

It was a mellow evening of playing guitar and eating popcorn. Mia called and we chatted but she did not come over. I watched a good movie on TV while changing the tire and chain on my bike. Maria came over and loafed around.

## Tuesday Jan. 10th

The supermarket was my first morning stop to buy some food for Apostolis. I cleaned up the bike and the saddle bags, and then sorted things out. I felt sad about leaving Athens but knew it would come soon.

I pedaled into the city and mailed a package to mom and dad and then bought a lamp to give to Apostolis as a gift. I played guitar at the monasteraki and at the height of my performance a string broke. I then played guitar at Center Park and made about 400 drachmas. I felt good about my performance and more confident. While taking a break I sat to write a post card to Ellen. Though everything I told her was very generic, I realized that what had occurred with Karen was because I thought she reminded me of Ellen. In the end I knew they were two very different people, but it was as if Karen reminded me enough of Ellen, that it was as if Ellen had been with me in Athens.

I again rode past those places I was with Karen and the deep sadness was still dispersing. While over at Omonia a funny man at the newsstand entertained me with his crazy expressions. At least I was laughing again. I played guitar nearby and was singing loudly when a bastos came along and told me to leave while motioning with his stick.

Back at the apartment Apostolis and his cousin George were conversing in a great, heated debate. I cooked them supper and then went to the Acri with Apostolis on his motorcycle. I borrowed his cycle and drove into the city to make a circuit of all the sights where memories were spent with Karen. It was a lonely as hell experience, but was good fun riding the cycle. I came back to the Acri, picked up Apostolis and we returned to his pad and watched a western movie on TV. I told Apostolis I would be leaving in two days. He didn't believe me and said, "We will see."

Around midnight I was jumping around like a jumping bean from a bug attacking me in the night. First it was buzzing in my beard and then moved down to my armpits. I could hear the little flea buzz whenever he leaped.

## Wednesday Jan. 11th

Awoke early on the morning of and went to the pastry store where the shop owner warmly greeted me as, "The bike rider from California." It was a nice feeling to be recognized.

Back at the apartment I played guitar and ate food while getting bags ready for more travel. I was feeling scared about leaving my friends and returning to the outdoors. I rather dreaded it, but then again, I was getting soft, my belly was flabby, my hands tender, my face boyish.

Apostolis came home and I told him, "Tomorrow I will go." Maria came over and they talked and when they looked at me I saw tears in their eyes. They seemed to leave me out because of what I told them. Apostolis told me, "I am talking to Maria about her weight problem." He grabbed her on the rear and laid it on the line, "She's got a big ass." After that Apostolis didn't want to speak to me. He used Maria as his interpreter. She told me they would go to a Greek play tonight. I packed my bags.

"Come let's go," said Apostolis, "We go out to eat at Johnnys." I went with them and we ate mouzaka while talking about all of our adventures over the past month. I rode with Apostolis on his scooter to the Acri and we talked about my leaving and seemed confused about why I was leaving now. I agreed to meet him at his house at 11:30pm to talk more about it.

I said goodbye to Peter and Tely, then gave Maria a ride to Mimis and said goodbye to him. I then took Maria to her home, called mama Tasos and wished her farewell in Greek. Went to Apostolis house at 10pm but he was not there. George and Liana came over, they dragged me away. We went to Liana's and I was asked to write down a song for them. It was hard for them to understand why I wanted to go back to Apostolis apartment. Not wanting to be rude, we then went to a souvlaki place and to the plaka and up to the Acropolis. It was a beautiful night with stars shining. We sat on a big block and talked. This was what I always wanted to do with my Greek friends. I didn't care for those bars, discos and coffee houses. I later said a tearful goodbye to them with a big hug and a kiss for Liana. No doubt she is a good woman, with a very kind heart. Apostolis was sleeping when I crept back into the apartment at 2am.

I awoke at 5am with Apostolis stumbling around preparing for work. He said, "Eric you are a big malakas. Why you no meet me last night?" I told him I screwed up going out with George and Iliana and missed him. "Oh well," he said waving his arm at me. I told him how thankful I was for all his kindness and rose to embrace him. We hugged and he tugged on the back of my hair and I padded him on the back. It was over fast and then he was gone.

## Thursday Jan. 12th

I fell back into a deep sleep and at 8am arose to the morning, and showered, then ate a feast of cheese filled pastry as well as fruit 'n' yogurt. With all my things packed up, I then made a big bowl of popcorn to leave for Apostolis. I also cleaned his place real well. God I was sentimental and cried out to his little apartment- "goodbye," as I locked the door behind me.

The bike was real heavy. At 10am I was riding the beast for Pireas, the seaport, and it was strange to be back on the bike. I became lost and for a few moments panicked. It was all coming back to me; the wind, the noise, the physical exertion, the chuckholes and the sore rear. I bought my ticket aboard the ferry to the Greek island of Rhodes. Went shopping and bought four souvlakis and a bag of fruit. Played guitar on a street corner and was graciously given 300 drachmas by many kind passersby's. On the boat they charged me 300 dracmas to bring aboard the bike, so it all evened out. I got excited as the boat left the dock. Reading the newspaper and walking around occupied my time. I thought so much about my friends back in Athens. I played guitar on the deck and watched a Kirk Douglas movie with him playing the part of Mat Morgan. It was odd to hear his voice dubbed over in Greek.

The seas were rough and the weather inclimate. I didn't see anyone I wanted to talk to, except a gal who was about 16 years old. God what a lonesome boat ride, added to the fact that I was leaving my good friends. There was a fight on the ship around 9pm. It was over quick and everyone dispersed. I laid back and fell asleep on a seat at 10:30pm after watching Turkish TV news. At around 2am the ship docked at the island of Samos and several new people came on board.

## Friday Jan. 13th

The conductor or porter gave me a kick on the feet as I slept on the chair cushions. It was 7am, I popped my contacts in and looked outside to see that it was raining. Turkey was visible on the left side and the Greek isle of Rhodes on the right. I was restless and went up on the top deck to look at how hostile Turkey looked. It appeared to be very mountainous and eerie. The ship swung around to dock in Rhodes just as my watch alarm rang at 9am.

I got off the ship and had that lost feeling hit me. Went pedaling about the town and bought a map, then to the tourist bureau, then to the bank. Rhodes was a very quaint town with old castles, a palace and high walls that are very medieval. The narrow little streets of cobblestone were also very old and rough to cycle upon.

I slowly headed out of town and got back into the rigors of cycling. It started to rain and was very cold. It hailed as I stopped at a bus shelter to change into warmer clothes. Then it poured a real hard rain. I went back out into the windy rain and struggled. I almost cried. I wanted to go back to Athens. I wanted to go home. I hated this and bellered aloud; "What the hell am I doing this for? What the hell is wrong with me?" I stopped for a very long minute, shaking, distraught, nearly broken. Then I moved on.

I pedaled along the south shore, heading west, as the rain came in sheets and I sought shelter again as it poured. The day wasn't going very well, but the miles slowly slipped away. I was as sad as I had ever been, and was really feeling low down. It was utter agony. There were some big hills to cross over and while nearing a scenic overlook the sky cleared enough to reveal an aqua blue cove near a village. What a pretty place! It was called Lindos, a very old, snuggly little village situated with a fortress on one side and the sea on the other. It was gorgeous. I went down into the village and scouted for a place to stay. There were no free places to sneak into for the night so I got a room in a pensione for 4 dollars. It was a nice place with a good view.

I walked down and ate at a busy pub where I met a U.S. couple. The fellow was interesting and had traveled a great deal. He was kind of a sadist. He laughed hard about, "Shaking hands with a starfish," and then he told me about the, "Lebonese greasy cocksuckers with machine guns." He had malaria once, while in Turkey, though overall he told me he liked the Turks very much. I hiked around the village under a full moon that was very bright. What a great place this was.

## Saturday Jan. 14th

Up at 8:30am I hiked around the village after taking a cold shower, as they had no hot water. Down near the seashore, I walked up to the hilltop fortress which was made in Roman times and was rebuilt in the 11th century. From the top one can look to the west and can see a small circular bay where it is believed that St. Paul landed. It was scenic and intriguing. I contemplated staying longer at Lindos, but decided I must get going.

I made way for the western part of the island over roads that went from poor to bad. I then turned right and went up a zig zagging road that climbed up and over a saddle in the mountains, which on a map resemble the backbone of this island. The road turned to gravel. On one uphill section I met a man walking with a shotgun and said, "Yassoo" to him. He acknowledged and I hoped he would not shoot me in the back. Weary after the steep ascent, I finally got off the bike after 10 miles of climbing. The road went up into Sienna, a nice village. I stopped at a junction to Egnamo, which offered a scenic view. Then it was downhill all the way to the north side of the island and a town called Kritina. I went into a store. Bought some goods and came out and glided all the way to the ocean.

I set camp behind a tavern after getting permission from the owner. Cooked and ate supper and there I discovered my water bottle was missing. After dinner, I searched for it and rode up to the junction of Egnamo, about 6 miles up the steep grade. A dog followed me half ways and with his tongue dragging, gave up. I arrived at the junction but found no water bottle. Perhaps somebody stole it in the village or else it had bounced out. Something like this would be hard to replace in this country. It was an enjoyable glide back down to the ocean in the moonlight. That dog chased after me all the way back to the campsite.

## Sunday Jan. 15th

When I awoke in the morning, and stuck my head out of the tent to go pee, I instantly got a big lick on the face from that dog. He wanted to get into the tent and I get out, so we playfully wrestled. I rode slowly along in the sunshine and stopped at ancient Kamiros to explore the ruins. There was a nice overlook of the site and I sat there to play guitar on the hillside. I contemplated whether I could take this friendly dog with me around the world. I met some Greek boys who were studying to be teachers and enjoyed talking with them and they offered to take the dog back to it's rightful owner.

I stopped beside the runway at the airport to watch a plane take off. It occurred to me just how close I am to heading back home, if I really had to. I could be back in the States in one day.

There was a soccer game in progress on the northside of the island, where a short amount of time was spent watching. It was that kind of day, a liesurely pace on a nice, sunny day. I had traveled around the island and pedaled back into the town of Rhodes and up to the top of a hill, which had the ruins of a fantastic old Greek stadium. The vista from this vantage point was a wonderful way to look down on Rhodes and across the Straits of Marmaris toward Turkey.

I zipped down to town and checked into a pensione called Steve, which cost 500 drachmas to stay for one night. Then rode around town sightseeing and went into the ancient palace and reveled at the beautiful tile floors. Later, I explored the city at night and since there were no big street lights it was dark and very enchanting. I was feeling lonely and found myself singing the song Ramblin Man in a tunnel and enjoyed the acoustics.

The night was again interrupted as I was tossing and turning from that distracting flea living in my beard. I also had butterflies and great anticipation of going to Turkey.

## Monday Jan. 16th,

I went into town and discovered the ship for Turkey would be leaving at 11:30am. I went back to the pensione and packed my things and jammed on the guitar. I stopped at a restaurant and stocked up on souvlaki and then hurried to the port but the ship was not there. I'd busted my ass to get there and nowhere was the ship to be seen. Sat down and met two women from Canada and enjoyed talking with these travelers. Then I talked to a fellow from the U.S and he told me some bad news about going east to Turkey and going on to Israel. He really painted a horrific picture of what laid ahead.

Just then a small ship came around the point and pulled up to port. It was our ride. I boarded and the American guy told me, "Better tie the bike down or you'll loose it overboard." Then he added, "Everyone will be sick, it's going to be a bad ride." What a pessimist he was. Why I sat next to him I'll never know. He went on to tell me the roads in Turkey were real bad and then continued with a horror story of two Dutch cyclists. They had pedaled 1000 miles over rough roads all the way down to the part of Turkey that is north of Cyprus. Then they caught a ship across to the Turkish part of Cyprus but were not allowed entry into Greece because of the border conflict. Northern Cyprus is under Turkish control and the southern half is Greek. They aren't communicating. "Whatever you do don't go to northern Cyprus," he said to me continuing with the story, "Those Dutch cyclists had to come back to Turkey, pedal back 1000 miles to Istanbul and then got thrown into prison because their visa's were expired. There still there and that happened a year ago!"

I sat by that U.S. guy, who was very arrogant and boisterous, and began to feel misgivings about my journey. Then I wondered about him. I wasn't convinced he was from the U.S as he had a British accent. It was a bouncy ride and people were getting sick. I exchanged some money with him on the boat and later would learn this was a mistake as the he jipped me out of about $15.

I moved around the ship and met two white gals who were identical twins and came from South Africa. They talked a long time to me and asked me to play guitar. I played on the top deck while the ship was entering the fiords of Turkey. It was calm water and nice scenery. I sang Danny's Song to them and they liked that. I couldn't stop laughing when a string broke and went "boing." Then I continued with songs like Rosie, Country Roads, Mozambique and finished off with Light my Fire. They all seemed to enjoy my repertoire.

We arrived in Marmaris, Turkey and went through customs, which was a little more than a man touching my packs. I pedaled on roads that were very bad, past poor housing and filthy looking places. The people seemed good enough, though not as finely dressed as the Greeks. I sought out a pensione and discovered a language barrier, as few spoke english. I found out that many Turks spoke German. A young fellow came up and told me he had a pensione available for 300 lire. I went with him, looked at it and liked it. His name was Nail, a young Turk who spoke good English and lived in the house with his mother. It was a simple room without a shower but a wash basin with running water.

I then walked back into the village and met an Aussie couple. We ate an excellent homemade pizza for 420 lire or about $1.50.

About 9pm it became very stormy out, complete with thunder and lightning. The lights went out. Nail came by with a candle and we sat to play guitar. "You sing songs pretty good," he said to me. "Want a beer?" I said, "Please." He came back with a cold beer and we shared it, while the rain pounded on the roof and the windows leaked water onto the floor.

# Chapter 9

## THE TURKISH ROAD

**Tuesday Jan 17th**

The Turkish wind was howling in a sinister way when I looked out the window of my Marmaris pensione. The sky was partly cloudy and judging by the way the trees were leaning, the wind was coming out of the northwest, the direction I would be heading. My bike was packed and everything was ready, but when I went downstairs to say goodbye to Nail, he instead handed me a bill for an additional 150 lire for last nights beer. I paid him thankfully, as the amount did not seem unreasonable.

I coasted down to the patiserrie and bought several apple filled tarts, then hit the road, soon wishing that I'd bought more of those tasty treats. The road inclined out of Marmaris, providing a nice view, bustling with business, people pushing carts and small boats nestled in the port warming up to a new day. I was very weary of what I would find on the trek up ahead.

The road was paved with sharp, fist sized stones embedded in the asphalt. It was rough on my small bicycle tires. I passed through a forest of pine trees and enjoyed the sight, thinking to myself, maybe this ride wasn't going to be as bad as I expected. The road then went through a little village and I freewheeled downhill into a gorge called Gokova Isk. The road flattened out and headed straight as an arrow across The Plain of Marmara, a treeless landscape except for uniformly planted deciduous trees lining the roadside for two miles. The wind picked up and it was getting colder even though I was exercising vigorously on the pedals. Halfway across, the wind became extremely strong from a mountain wave rolling down upon me from the higher terrain.

I started up a long series of switchbacks, which afforded a view of the road I'd just traveled as well as the Agean Sea visible in a large bay off to the southeast. The steep grade made cycling difficult enough, but compounded with this was the howling wind. It was very treacherous indeed. When I crested the top of the pass. I was nearly knocked backward. It had taken me two hours of pedaling up the switchbacks to finally make it this far and now I was blown to a standstill. It was a very cold wind and real strong. With the use of my lowest gear, I crept along. A bus approached toward me and went past and I was blown off the road and onto the shoulder. I let the bus know my unhappiness with a clenched fist, but vowed instead, to hopefully someday revenge that hill by coasting down it and hailing victorious obscenities.

I stopped to eat in the cold wind and watched a crew of men working on the roof of a house. They stared at me, while I at them. Off in the distance were spectacular snow covered mountains. I continued on and pedaled over another mountain pass and entered a snowstorm. It was very cold and the road became slippery. I stopped and dug out more clothing and prepared for the worst. Against the blowing snow on a treeless plain, I saw some homes in the distance, with rooftops covered in snow and longed to be inside. I saw people out walking in the snow and pitied them, in the cold, at such a slow pace, but then my situation wasn't much worse. I was slipping and sliding and feeling a sense of dread. On one downhill run, it took all my abilities to keep the bike from crashing. My bike just wasn't made for this.

After crawling at a snails pace against the raw elements, I finally made it into the pastel looking city of Mugla at 3:30pm. There was a downtown 'otel' which offered a shared room for 250 lire, which equaled about 75 cents. It had large single pain windows painted light green and had no heat, but still it was a relief to get out of the elements.

At 6 p.m. the wind was howling and it was real cold when I walked through town to find a place to eat supper. It was like a walk back in time. There were dinky, little shops for cobblers, seamsmen, barbers, repairmen, men playing cards and men huddled around a pot belly stove just like they did in my grandfathers era. It was really interesting. The smell of burning coal permeated the air. I ate cooked lamb at a restaurant and it cost about $1.20 for a tasty meal that was very filling. I went to a movie called Belmondo, but it was actually Rambo starring Sylvester Stallone. The Turks in the theater enjoyed it and cheered each time Belmondo blew something up.

Afterward while walking down the street I met two Turks who were very friendly, though they could not speak much english. Back in the otel lobby everyone was sitting around a little cast iron stove. I went to bed in my refrigerated room. There was a knock on the door at 12:30am and a Turk told me something but I did not understand him. We resorted to sign language and finally I understand that he was telling me I would have a roommate. The Turk came in, said a prayer, took his bed and shut off the light.

In the predawn hour I was suddenly awakened by the craziest, monotonous wailing. About three words were carried on in a changing, melodically long chant that sounded like the music which Gregorian monks make. It went on and on and then finally it stopped. I couldn't tell if it was a man singing or if it was a recording.

## Wednesday Jan 18th

I fell back asleep and arose at 8:30am to pack up while the sun was shining on the morning of. The windows were all frosted up as the yellow sun illuminated them. Outside there was a steady wind blowing and it was very cold. I was suddenly flung into a Minnesota winter!

I bundled up and headed through town trying to stay upright on the snow. There was ice on the road and I skidded along while heading for Aydin, which was 120 kilometers away. One of the nice things about the ice on the road was that it filled the big potholes so I didn't have to swerve around them. Only trouble was they were slippery and nearly cost me many a crash on the pavement. There were long slippery uphills and very cautious downhills throughout the morning.

I went down the road past men hauling huge loads on little carts. Many women had huge bundles of sticks on their backs, just like that which is seen on a Led Zeppelin record album cover called Zojo.

The road passed through rocky chasms, past roaring rivers overlooked by snow capped mountains. There were big rocks and many shepherds sitting along the road watching their herds. I zipped downhill at a blazing speed and then made way into the town of Cine at 12:30pm for lunch of cheese and bread.

I was eager to travel the 37 Kilos to the small city of Aydin. Along that route were enjoyed the sights of lumbering big camels walking down the road behind many women dressed very tightly wrapped in colorful garments. They had shrouds to cover there faces.

As the afternoon sun melted most of the snow, I traversed across a good flat valley and then made way into Aydin. Searched around for a otel and became somewhat annoyed by people heckling me from all sides with, "Hello, hello." At one otel I stopped and many boys gathered around me to stare. I stopped at a pop- shop and again people swarmed around me. They were not pushy or unruly, merely curious and friendly. I met a Turk who said he was from an area near the Black Sea. He advised me where to look for a otel. I then went there and got a room for 300 lire, which was about $1.Cleaned up and went hiking around town and ate donar kabob, while again enjoying the novel sights of peasants engaged in labor, students walking with books, the elderly and children.

Went back to the otel to eat yogurt and to play my guitar. While sitting on the bed, there was a knock on my door and the police entered and asked me for my passport. They checked my bags and found nothing. Then they said, "Sorry" and left. Probably the man at the front desk called them to come check me out.

At around 8pm I had a craving for sugar to sprinkle on my yogurt and went out shopping and had a funny experience trying to get through to the store clerk what I wanted. When I said "sugar" to him it did not mean a thing to him. I tried to gesture putting sugar in tea, or on cereal but he didn't know what I wanted. I then found salt and tried to gest that it was similar to sugar, but of a different taste. A crowd started to develop and they watched my antics. I then made a sound like that which bees make and gestured to him eating thick honey. "Honey," I said, "Buzzzz." "Ahh," he said and showed me a jar of honey. Then I tied together honey and salt and he finally figured out what I wanted. He led me to where the sugar was. We cheered and shook hands and the crowd sighed. My god he was a good sport about it.

## Thursday Jan. 19th

It was a sunny but cold morning when I left the city and cycled along. The road was flat and not difficult, but it was busy with many trucks. I noticed many weathered looking women carrying huge bundles of twigs on their backs. They appeared bent over but strong under such a load. I passed a carload of girls and they said hello. "Chow," I shouted. I passed many people sitting along the road. They all said, "Hello, hello, hello." I was getting annoyed by all these hello sayers and therefore did not always say hello back to them. I met some young, pretty, teenage girls at an outdoor water facet and they informed me that I had a big mountain up ahead to go over. Indeed I later climbed up a steep grade but it wasn't too bad. Then it was a long downhill all the way to Selcuk. I entered the town and saw an old fortress on a hill. I met a fellow by this sandwich stand and he told me, "You have a big mountain to cross over to get to Izmer." I told him, "I can cross any mountain," in a rather cocky voice. "I think you cannot," he responded. He offered me to join him for tea but I was eager to get going-and to prove him wrong.

 The long valleys and expansive stretches of open road were hard cycling and the wind was a nuisance. It was a nice day though a little cold. I wished to go faster, to get somewhere and sit down, to be lazy, but I had many miles to go. Inching along, I thought about the sun. My god it is a miraculous thing. To think of all the years it has been working. To think of all the goodness it has brought to this planet and all of the people who have felt the suns warmth and enjoyed its light. Suddenly a bus blew its horn and flew past me nearly knocking me over. I made a fist and then flipped up the middle finger. I became angry at the sight of buses for they were dangerous because of their crazy drivers.

 The road worsened, and to make matters worse, people along the roadside joshed at me. They shouted or made gestures like, "What's this," or "What do you want?" Little kids would stare or some would run after me. I dodged people pulling carts or wagons going down the road. They all put much muscle into their hard work.

 I had traveled 125 kilometers from Aydin and then the road turned to gravel that was made of big stones. The dust was horrible and I for a few tense moments I was blinded. My contact lenses hurt as if my eyes were stuck with pins. I cursed at a bunch of workmen who were standing on the road as they watched me pass. They all laughed. Once, when a big truck passed me I almost crashed onto the road, after hitting a large boulder, but saved it. I was always thankful for my years of experience at racing dirt bikes.

 I arrived in the city of Izmer and saw many people filling the streets. I searched for a otel and annoyed the managers because I wanted a good price for a room. Many otel workers stood on the sidewalk saying, "Come here-come here." Finally I found a room for 300 lire. It was located on the rooftop and about the size of a woodshed. It had no heat, no water, only a bed, a table, a door and a key. What I liked was, I had a viranda and could look over the rooftop and see the people walking on the street below. I told the man at the desk that I would carry my bike up to my room. "Me Tarzan," I said. He was amazed at my strength as I carried it up four flights of stairs. "Tarzan," he later called me adding, ""Good boy."

I laid down to relax, but the bed had a funny sag that made me feel like sleeping in a hammock. I changed clothes and headed out to the streets of Izmer to eat supper. "Hello Tarzan," the man at the desk said as I walk proudly past him, strutting like a confident American and then tripped over a big boulder in the street. He laughed like crazy at me. One must watch where they walk in the streets of Turkey, or so I was learning.

At a greasy little restaurant, I ate a plate of slop and then went back to the room and took my camera apart because it had stopped working. I had meager tools for the job and was up until 1:30am, trying to reassemble the little tiny springs and screws into the shutter speed selector mechanism. Before going to sleep, I sat down on my bed and strummed on the guitar, but my neighbor knocked on the wall and said, "Shhh."

### Friday Jan 20th

I slept in until 8am and then started working on the camera. By 10am I'd really screwed it up. Only the "B" setting worked. I almost threw the camera away but curbed this anger and went into the city to find a camera shop. I looked at new cameras, but the selection was poor. At one small photo processing shop I met a fellow named Murhat. He was a student of economics at the University of Izmer. He tinkered with the camera and tried new batteries but it would not work. He took me on a tour of other camera stores and even to a camera repair shop. Judging from their response they could not fix the thing. So I looked at new cameras but the selection was terrible. A good single lense reflex camera was priced way out of sight. I went back to the repair shop but could not communicate with the repairman. So I went back to Murhat and had him write me a note. I went back to the repair shop and gave the note and my camera to the repairman. He pointed to Monday on a calendar to say that then it would be ready.

I went window shopping and bumped into Murhat who told me that he had talked to the repairman over the telephone and that they had discussed the camera's problem. We walked the busy market streets and talked. He invited me to join him for a cup of tea after 7pm. He was a very kind Turk and very good at conversation. I went back to my otel room and cleaned up.

I met Murhat and his friend Alsap at 7:10 pm and we took a ship across the bay to the other side of Izmer. There were broad sidewalks on this side and they were paved with large bricks and a long retaining wall near the ocean. We went to a cafe and talked about my journey. They were all ears and enjoyed hearing where I'd been and what transpired. Then they taught me some Turkish words and laughed at how I pronounced them. We played simple games such as thumb fighting and tic tac toe, which was one they never had heard of. Murat showed me a contest whereby they wrap a paper napkin over a glass and then place a coin in the middle. By using a hot cigarette, each contestant has to burn a hole into the parameter of the coin until it finally falls into the glass. Murhat lost when the coin plunked into his drink. I thought he did it on purpose.

We talked about God and about religion. I was very nieve about Islam, though they did not press the point nor evangelize. We talked about movies and how exaggerated they were in comparison to the way things happen in real life. When I asked them about the movie, Midnight Express, they told me it was forbidden in Turkey. No wonder, for it portrayed a pretty cruel and harsh prison life for drug traffickers.

We drank lots of coffee and all the while Murhat was very courteous and paid for everything. We then went back across the bay on an old ship that resounded with a steady clunky-clunky sound. Everything on board the ship was like what they had in the U.S. over 50 years ago.

We went into an area called Dolmus and visited a cafe. We ate chicken dinner at the restaurant and Murat paid for everything. For dessert I tried yogurt with sliced cucumber in it. Though it was different to my palate, it was tasty. We talked of the nuclear weapon proliferation in the world and each of us was well aware of the dangers if a nuclear war was to occur. None of us wanted to see such a thing happen. It was essential to resolve differences rather than resort to warfare. We continued our talk while they walked me to my otel and then we wished each other a goodnight.

## Saturday Jan. 21st

In the morning I went to the photo shop early in the day to meet with Murat. Then I came back to my otel and re-organized. I returned to his shop at 2 'o' clock and Emre was there. We always shook hands when meeting and the greeting was long and talkative. I went with Emre, who could only speak a little English, to visit a mosque. I wanted to see one and amazing as this may sound, he had never been in one. Though he was raised in this Moslem enclave he had not grasped the faith. We peeked in the door and then took off our shoes. Two women were bowing and praying toward a wall and they looked like they were jazzercising. Emre grabbed me and wanted to leave. He looked sheepish and hurriedly put on his shoes and we then left. I think he was unnerved being inside a mosque and felt embarrassed staring at the occupants. We went outside and down many steps to the sidewalk. All the while I wanted to go back in the mosque and see more.

We went to a few shops and I talked Emre into going back to the mosque. We were an odd couple. He would whistle and swing his big handbag while I would look at everything. I tried to ask him what things were by using sign language. We went back to the mosque and again took off our shoes and went inside.

I watched the worshippers pray and listened to their chants while they were down on their knees with their heads bowing, then upright and again bowing. A priest came in and sang in addition to giving a sermon. All the worshippers joined hands and turned their heads in unison at certain keynotes. A fellow named John got up and came over and said hello. For some reason he was very excited to meet me. "Come pray to Allah," he said adding. "I have a big surprise for you." He explained to me that the mosque was 600 years old and that it still had the original Arabic writing on it. He told me that there was a hole under the mosque, in fact the foundation was shaped like a "Dome".

We then went to an art gallery with John, who, after his prayers to Allah said he felt, "Clean and in touch with God." He informed me that Moslems must follow a prayer schedule of five times a day. "It is very good for the soul," said John. At the gallery I drank a bit to much tea and got so dizzy I felt like I was on board a ship. John then parted our company and Emre and I walked down the streets.

We had the fortune of meeting some attractive Turkish girls. They had olive skin and dark eyes with dark hair but since they couldn't say a stitch of English I could not talk with them. There was freshness to their expressions, a mysterious dark beauty and they were very friendly.

Emre and I went back to the photoshop and sat with Murat and his friends. More friends came in and we played backgammon and drank Raki liquor which is the same as Ouzo. "Every Saturday night we do this," said Murat adding, "We all get together and talk business and about life."

I went with he and his friends to a small shop and sat with all these Turkish fellows about the same age as myself. I shook all of their hands and though they looked at me discerningly, they were very cordial. They smoked a lot and the place was thick with smoke that burned my eyes. We went clowning down the street to a bus station but as I had my bike with, we decided to take a dolmusi. I stuck my arm out the window and held onto the bike as it rode on top of the roof of an old 1959 Chevrolet wagon. "I will be soon be drunk," said Murat. We got off at a place called Pizza Ben and jokingly repeated the word "Siz," which means me or you in Turk.

Inside the western style pub, we drank beers and told jokes. Emre told a good one by using only his fingers. He gestured a couple of lovers walking and then a peeping Tom watching them from behind some bushes. As the couple became more amorous and began making love, the peeping Tom was getting a hard-on and then knocked over the bushes. This sent the lovers scurrying.

Several soldiers joined our table and one who was from Ankara asked us, "How many Greeks does it take to put in a light bulb?" He then responded, "Six. One to hold the light bulb and five guys to turn the one holding the bulb." I laughed because I had heard that same joke told in Greece and they made fun of the Turks.

I told them a joke called Olga. The story starts off with an elderly couple of farmers who are named Henry and Olga. Each time the well aged Olga called Henry she squiggled her little finger. He let this go on for fifty years and finally he got up the gawl to ask her. "How come each time you call my name you wiggle your little finger?" Olga then returned, "Because it reminds me of your little pecker." Henry puffed up and became real mad and then responded, "Oh yeah?" Then he held each of his index fingers on either side of his mouth and opened it real wide to suggest her crotch and let out a beller- "OLGA!" My Turkish friends burst out in laughter and fell back on their chairs. They rolled on the floor and continued laughing for several minutes. I mean they really laughed hard! Everyone in the bar looked at us and they too laughed!

We talked up a storm, ate a delicious pizza and spaghetti dinner that had a special hot pepper with raw meat that was wrapped in lettuce leaves. It was real hot! For dessert I had a sweet cake similar to baklava. One man spoke French and wanted me to go home with him, but I refused, as he wasn't to cool. I played harmonica for them and they loved it and also showed them a pantomime, which Apostles often told. It is called, The Fisherman.

The pantomime is all done without saying a word. It starts off as if I am a fisherman casting off of the beach and then waiting for the fish to bite. He checks his line often and reels it in to check for fish. Then he again casts it out. While he stands there waiting for the fish to bite he lets go a fart. Then he feels his tummy and decides he must take a crap. So he looks around and since nobody is around he squats and poops out a masterpiece. All the while he is holding his rod with his left hand and checking for fish. He wiped his rear with tissue using his right hand and wouldn't you know it just after he had wiped, a fish tugged wildly on his rod. The fisherman held fast to the rod with his left hand and since he had the crap paper on his right he could not reel it in. He looked around in a panic and then stuffed the crap filled toilet tissue into his mouth and joyfully reeled in the fish.

After the laughter had quieted down I shook hands with my raucous Turkish friends and stood up to bid them a good night. It was late and even though they wanted to give me a ride back to the otel, I insisted to ride the bike back. I had only a vague idea how to get there. But by using auto-pilot, my trusty steed and I zipped through the city on the rough streets while breathing in the thick coal smoke and was drunk enough not to mind. I managed to find my way back to the otel, "hallow Tarzan" said the desk man I dashed up to the top floor and happily curled into bed.

## Sunday Jan. 22$^{nd}$

Slept in until 10am trying to rid myself of a hangover but to no avail, it would be a day of suffering. I cleaned up and went to the shops to buy some food. The bakery things were especially nice, but after chowing down I felt like I ate too much.

I lazed around and played guitar while a young hotel boy leaned in my doorway and listened to me. Then the cleaning man came in and talked Turk to me. I could only guess what he was saying. I went along with it and smiled. Then I blew it when I compared myself, whom I called Tarzan, to Allah. "Allah-Tarzan strong." I said while beating my chest like King Kong. He looked at me like I'd broken a commandment. I then said, "Tarzan dead and with Allah in heaven." I intended to say Tarzan was dead and in Gods hands but he got all pissed at me and pointed his finger and said, "Tisk, tisk, tisk."

I went to city on the bike, into a park and through the slums, then up to a castle on a hilltop. Children followed me through the fortress. They touched my bike. They were good kids. I met a fellow on the castle top. He told me of the city. Izmer was called Smyrnia in older days. He asked me to write to him of everyplace I go.

From there it was a zip downhill to visit the market place, which was busy with people. I bought a candy bag full of filberts for .25 cents. When the police came down the streets, the street hawkers would do a tist-tist-tist signal and the hawkers would run for cover. Returning to the otel, I played guitar and slept a few hours like a lazy bum.

As it approached dinner time, the street down below had the usual noises. A man at a restaurant bangs his keys against a window to get the attention of people walking by. Loud carts, bottles rattling, boys selling their huge, thick pretzels. There were Moslem chants, and shouting sellers. It was a journey back in time just to listen to these sounds.

I went to eat and had sish kabob and pop and salad for 355 lire which is about $1.10. I pedaled over to see Murat at 8pm, but he didn't show up. This triggers an emotional drop for me. I felt like I needed someone. I felt sorry for myself. Started to go back to past years. Thought of Kathy B., the neighbor gal whom I loved. My broken heart when she got married. My parents good attention to me, but lack of love. I think what my family must think of me, of all these years running away and not settling down, of any steady girlfriends. They must think I'm queer. I realize there are reasons, which are so deep, so hard to unravel. I wanted to see a woman. I wanted someone to talk with.

I almost went into a strip show, but instead bought a beer and went to the otel to write post cards. It was better to do this than to go off the deep end. There was a knock on my door. "Murat", the man said pointing downstairs. Excited, I went down and greeted Murat. With tea we went upstairs to my room and talked and talked and played a few songs with the guitar. I felt he was a very good friend. He told me the reason he was late was because he had a traffic problem. So he hunted down my otel. We ate fruit and talked of music and of his romances. We were up until 12:30am and then he had to go. It was a very tiring day and I felt good to go to sleep. The old man next door came to tell me "shh-shh." I guess he didn't know good guitar and singing when he heard it!

## Monday Jan 23rd

On this partly cloudy and cool morning, I sat around the room eating and playing guitar. Then I went to the tourist bureau and asked about the condition of the roads to Istanbul. They told me the roads were paved albeit difficult for cycling. I then went to several camera shops to see what is available. Then I cycled over to see Murat. We shook hands and as always he greeted me warmly. We chatted but he became busy with customers so I went to see if my camera was ready, but the repairman wasn't around. At lunchtime, Murat and I went to a cafe and the repairman was their eating and drinking Raki with his friends. I could tell by his facial expression and tone of voice that the upcoming news wasn't going to be good. Turks have a way of telling what they are thinking. They lift their eyebrows, close their eyes and droop their mouths to say no. "Your camera could not be repaired," Murat told me. "The repairman says you are partially to blame because you took it apart." I swallowed the fact with a great deal of sadness for this meant I would have to buy a new camera.

After lunch, I went to a U.S. Military PX store located on the outskirts of Izmer but it was closed. I talked to an American soldier who was black and he told me it would soon open. A few minutes later, I walked into the PX and saw all this fantastic U.S. food, clothing, cameras, tapes, magazines, etc. My god it was like I was back home again! There was cereal, soup, candy bars and even chips! I saw a camera I liked but did not buy it because I had not yet shopped around. I then cycled across town and went to several camera shops and then went back to Murats before going on to the otel.

Ate a good meal across the street from the otel. I like the food there, for it was inexpensive and yet delicious donnar kabob with potatoes. I went over to Murats shop and we took a bus to a small cafe and sat back to drink coffee and talk about our love lives. Murat had some great love stories. He once loved a French girl whom he had met while in school in Izmer. After a year she went back to France and she would write to him consistently every three days. She came to visit him and they had a wonderful time. She wanted him to go back to France but he did not want to go. They had a climatic separation in the Istanbul airport. She demanded he come with her and he could not possibly go. She held up the plane pleading with him but there was little he could do because he didn't have the money anyway. That was the last he saw of her.

He once fell in love with two sisters who were twins and he could not tell them apart. He said Turkmen will die of a broken heart if a girl leaves them. As for his latest love, whom he was engaged with, and to be married in April, he met his fiance on a bus, but she was not that interested in him. He dated her but she didn't love him, though he loved her and after a rocky courtship she eventually turned around and fell in love with him.

I felt so much heart in all of Murats stories. He was the greatest storyteller of love affairs that I had met. We walked all the way back to the shop and it was great to have a friend like Murat. We were close friends and we communicated well. I felt a tremendous fondness for the kindness that Murat gives. For me it was a symbol of his extreme faith, heartfulness and generosity.

## Tuesday Jan. 24th

I awoke many times in the night to pee. Didn't know exactly why, but it was probably from drinking all the coffee. The nights sleep was also interrupted with the sounds of cats fighting in the night. Rain was falling on the morning I went to buy some goodies and visited Murat at his shop at 10:30am. We packaged the camera for return shipment to my parents house in the U.S. Then I thanked him for all his help and went to the PTT. At the PTT they told me I must go 400 meters down the street and around the corner to have the package wrapped in linen. So I dashed down there and was rushed as I planned to meet Murat at 11:am.

Back at the PTT they hassled me. They wanted me to undue the package for inspection. So I took it apart with a knife in disgust. Then they sat around and questioned my intentions for sending this camera. I acted very patient, but really I wanted to scream and swear at them. One guy came and told me it was possible to ship it, but it would cost 3000 lire ($15). "You must use a wooden box that costs 200 lire,"(about 75c) I was told. "Ok," I said. Then the postal guy talked cameras with me. He told me he would fix it. "No," I told him, "It is badly broken." He jacked around and played with the scale and asked me more questions. "Will I return here?" he said. "No," I responded. "Ah we must see your passport," he said. He took it to another room and came out with more questions. "Did you buy the camera here?" he asked. "No," I said. "Then I must raise the price to 3500 lire," he announced. "Ok," I said. Then he wanted me to sign all these papers. Finally after half an hour I got out of there.

I met Murat along the street and he had missed his morning exam. He was sad. "Next year I will have another chance," he said. "How could you let this happen?" I said. "My father left me alone in the store and I could not leave to take the exam. So I was late." I encouraged him to go talk to them to arrange another exam time. "It's impossible," he said. So we went to a cafe that had many cute girls and we talked. I told some jokes. And he told me some also. There was one about the flattened roosters on the road. Then another about the soldier's buttons popping off and killing the prostitute who faced the firing squad. Marks were all over the boyfriends face after he fell out of bed. They were all so funny. Actually I wanted to cheer Murat up. I decided to buy a camera from the U.S. Army base and pedaled the five miles out to the U.S. PX, but this time they wouldn't let me in. I tried to explain but it was useless. I talked to a soldier and asked him if I gave him the money could he buy me the camera, but he was under orders not to help civilians. I got such a bad taste of Americans after this. I waited to see if somebody else would come along. But all I saw was the inflated egos of the soldiers. They strut like they are hot shit. But they are all scared to death to leave their fleet of ships and war comrades. I felt a great deal of distaste for these arrogant cocky s.o.b's and could see why world conditions are as they are.

I took a ride to Komak and looked at cameras there. The shopkeeper was annoyed by me. He said I have looked enough. He got very inhospitable and I almost slammed the door on him. But, he had a camera I could use, thus I went to the bank and cashed in some travelers checks for lires, and went back and bought the Voightlander camera. It was not a good camera and not a good deal. But it was the best I could do here. It cost 26,750 lire (about $125) and he wouldn't go any lower on the price. He sympathized with me when I told him my problem with the other camera.

I went outside and was going to take a photo but the focus on the camera wouldn't work. Nearby, was a shop owner who was selling women's shoes and he annoyed me such that I put up my dukes and went up to him and said, "I'm gonna fucking punch you in the nose if you don't shut up!" He backed off and then said, "Come in." I flew off the handle saying, "I don't want your goddamn junk!" I was blowing off steam. The stress of this situation was wearing me thin.

I went back to the camera shop, where the shopkeeper said the camera was normal. He showed me how it worked. Pedaling back to Murats store I had time to gather my senses. He greeted me but was sad for his trouble of the exam. I told him I would see him later at 7pm.

I went to the otel in a pouring rain and got soaked. "Hallow Tarzan," said the deskman. I went up to my room and played a couple songs, then fell asleep. When I awoke, I thought it was morning. My watch said. 6:19. I thought- Murat! Oh no, I missed him. Then I looked outside and thought - god, it sure is light outside for morning. I got re-oriented again, collected myself and remembered this day and realized what time it was.

I went to Murats and locked up my bike. We walked to a cafe and ate. Murat was quieter. We then went to a sweet shop and he was still a fantastic host, describing the various kinds of pastries, but he was tired.

We went walking in the rain and were always talking and stopped at a coffee stall for a drink. He talked about how some girls are not interesting. He was again telling me of romance. I could tell he was tired. We went back to his camera shop to get my bike. We embraced. Kissed cheeks. Right first, then left. And shook hands. I told him I was so thankful for everything.

He said he was worried about me, because now I am a good friend. We departed. I pedaled back to the otel, through the dark streets, past the shops and men holding hands. I went into a night club where they had free admission but you must by a beer. They wanted 850 lire for a beer. When I heard the shitty sax player and saw few gals around, I refused the beer and left. Instead I bought a beer for 85 lire and came to my room. I unlocked the door, opened it and right away the old man in the room next door knocked on the wall, and went "shh-shh-shh." What a grump!

## Wednesday Jan. 25th

It was raining hard all night long and in the morning my room had a big puddle of water in it. I packed up my things and then played a last song on the guitar to the otel cleaning boy. "Tarzan," he said. I hauled my things down the stairs. He helped me. I thanked everyone, saying, "Merci." and, "Gule, gule." As I pedaled away on the bike, the boy hollered to me all the way down the street. "Tarzan, Tarzan, okay!"

It was sunny but wet on the streets. I asked traffic polisi for directions to Bergoma. He had to ask another man. He shooked my hand and was very kind. Each time I'd stop people would help me. I was on the road again and feeling good, but soon the road got bad as I rode in goocky mud. Everything was getting mucky. I had to be careful not to loose the whole bike in this slop. A bus would come by and splash me with mud. It started to rain, but at least I had a good tailwind.

At noon I stopped for water at a gas station. I was splattered with mud. The station attendant pointed to my bike and said "su" which must mean dirty. He brought me bottled water and cleaned my bike off with a hose. What kindness!

All along the road people would say, "Merhaba" and whistle to me, or say "hello." At times I got annoyed. The children chased along with me. Then the rain and the wind picked up. I decided to go farther up the coast for Dikili.

I was riding along thinking about my life and said out loud, "Eric-you sometimes try to confuse your life, especially when it comes to women." Just then a black cloud up ahead of me suddenly whacked a bolt of lightning to the earth and struck with a loud kaboom. It then rained hard and hailed.

Wearily I rode into Dikili and was soaking wet to the bone while bounding along the bonejarring old, bad cobblestone streets. People stared at me. I looked all around and finally found a otel for 500 lire with a good room facing the sea. It was the off season for tourists, thus the prices were down on decent rooms. I cleaned up and dried my things by my stove.

As I walked to a restaurant all the lights went out in town. I ate a good meal of a sausage like meat and a salad by candlelight. Outside it was real stormy with a hard rain and high wind coming in off of the sea. When my meal was finished, I went outside to see the stars were shining and it was so clear. I made it back to the otel just in time to get the shits. After that gut wrenching, it was enjoyable to play guitar by candlelight. I sat back and thought of Turkey as the paradise I've looked for.

## Thursday Jan. 26th

A cold night with more rain and noisy streets awakened me early. There were donkeys noisily pulling carts down the cobblestone road. It was cold in the morning and I thought, maybe I should stay here until it warmed up.

I knew I had to get going and brought my gear outside. People stood and watched me load up the bike. I felt like a celebrity. A man in the bakery said, "Reagan bad, Carter good." I ate a cheese filled pastry and then hit the road.

It was nice riding for a couple of hours. There was some serene scenery, with nice villages, flat riding and the sun shining. I enjoyed a tailwind and had time to think of snowmobile racing. Some dogs chased me and to scare them away I would pretend to throw something at them. They left me alone.

Continuing along, the clouds built up as I turned west and pedaled up some hills on a rough road. There were big stones and they were sharp. One thing I was finding out was people always cheered me on." Merhaba" they would say.

On this stretch many horses and buggies passed. I pull into Havra and a swarm of people gathered around me. I asked a man, "Choke Dac." which means "Much mountain on road?" "Ah," he suggests with his hand, not a mountain, but a slope. I bought some food,(big ring pretzels) and headed out. Up and up the road went and then desended down some quick downhills. I saw a truck on its side that had flipped over on the road. Apparently it had lost its brakes. A short distance later on a fast curve there was a hut and I passed a man and he hollered to me and waved. I said. "Fuck you asshole," and he laughed and waved while smiling. I later figured out that he said, "Come here for tea." - ooops!

Up, up the road went on a tough up hill. I made a distance of 12 miles in two hours. Up, up, up. I got tired and sore and felt road weary. The sun peeked out from behind the clouds and finally the road flattened out. I went downhill and made it to the village of Ivrini at 6:30pm.

A crowd of children chased me down the street. I stopped to ask, "Nerede otel?" A man spoke english and told me where. Children swarmed around me. Wow. "Where you from." he asked. "California, Amerika." I said. "Ohh Amerika." he told them all. They looked at me with open mouths and followed me to the otel.

I got a room for 250 lire and ate at a restaurant. It was a little more trouble here to communicate with the locals. The town had a nice mosque with many minarets(they look like missles). I got to a store and bought a Coke, when a man said to me "where are you going-can I help you?" I drank some drink and ate some goodies while watching people swarm to the mosque as a chant mystically called to them. "Jar eve ah enerum…" The Mosque looks like a giant mouth, swallowing those who enter.

## Friday January 27<sup>th</sup>

It was slow getting up this morning. People got in my way as I tried to pack the bike. They were so inquisitive. I left Ivrini with many "Gule, gule." People waving good bye. I admit to feeling a bit self-conscience. I made way for Balekisir, 35 kilometers away.

On a country road that would resemble any road in the farmlands of Central Minnesota, I passed a long driveway with a farm house at the easterly end. I saw four big dogs running down the drive in my direction. I tried to outrun them, but it was no use. They attacked me. I dismounted, shouted at them and used the bike as a shield. They were big dogs, like golden rottweilers. They worked as a team to try and get me from behind. One tried a flank attack. I grabbed a stick and kept him away, while using the bike to keep the others away. I swung the bike and all the gear, this way and that like it was a rag doll. I saw there teeth and snarling snouts. They barked viciously and I shouted aggressively. Then the owner stepped out from his barn and bitched at them and they all ran off.

I crossed some hills and then made it into Baleksir. Many men lined the road and constantly I was harrassed. They stared at, and made fun of me. Every truck would honk there horn at me. It got a little old after awhile.

I stopped into a sweet shop and tasted some delicious pastery that had a sweet filling inside. I was hungry! "Var U fromme-Deutshe?" A man asked me. "No- I'm American from California." He told me about the road ahead. "Mountains, "he said "Very Big." He spoke little english, but some Deutsh. Admist a crowd of onlookers I headed out and waved just as I hit a big hole in the street. As usual, they laughed like crazy.

# THE WHEELS OF FRIEND

I rode through town and saw an old steam locomotive puffing along. I pulled over to take a photo. Wow it was a grand sight, straight out of the 1930's. It went past me and then while riding away a news photographer came and took my photos. He asked for my name. I showed him my map of the world and all the countries I'd visited thus far. He took many photos of me, but a big crowd gathered and created a traffic snarl. The police arrived and secured the scene. As I left, I had an escort by police motorcycles out of town! It fired me up. I felt like royalty.

There were more hills and rain until I stopped in Susurluk for a breather and was mobbed by the crowd. I asked for the next village and a man said 28 kilometers. "You will go now?" He asked with his freckle face. "Yes, now!" I said. It was 3:30pm. I headed out of town in the rain. Did I make a mistake I thought, for leaving so late. I saw a sign saying the road to Troy, and wanted to go visit the historic place, but somebody told me there was nothing to see there.

As I pedaled uphill, I saw a locomotive and raced to watch it, but more dogs attacked me. I pretended to throw rocks at them and it worked. They ran off. The locomotive stopped and then it continued with a huge steam cloud, and "puff, puff, puff," what power! The whistle blew at a high pitch. Wow it was like going back 80 years in time. As it passed I drank a Coke and readied to take a photo. I stepped onto the road to take this picture and a truck stopped for me and waited as I took it. I was inspired by his kindness.

I headed on across a flat highland and saw many sheep along the roadside. There was a cold wind and I huddled low against it, but heard a "Yah-who," holler and turned to see a shepherd. Wow what a wild man he looked like. I took a photo of him. He wore two different shoes. I greeted him, "Murhaba!" He returned with a smile, but did not have many teeth, only one big one. He wore ragged clothes. "Burr," I said. "Hayir," he cried out. He must have had good circulation, as his coat was opened to reveal his chest and undergarments.

I pedaled on into the cold wind and made it to Mustafakemelpasa and went to look for a otel. Some men escorted me to one and they said it was 350 lires, then he jacked it up to 800 lires. I think they did this when they found out I was an American. I went to another otel and they asked 500 lire, another asked 400 for a room. I decided on the one for 400 to save money.

I wanted to bring my bike up to my room, but they made a big stink that I could not and for 15 minutes they argued. I said nothing. Then they were trying to decide where to put it, so I showed them some ideas. Then they grabbed my bike and manhandled it. I got pissed and said,

"Get back–back." I took my bike and things to the next hotel for 500 lire. They had no troubles with my putting the bike in my room, but people looked at me like I was crazy for doing so.

I took a cold shower and ate rice and stew. Then I played the guitar and three Turks knocked on my door and came into my room. We exchanged conversation by piecing together words from our language differences. They invited me to sit by a pot belly stove. So I went with them and it was good fun, playing music for them and talking basically about the nuclear weapons threat. "Peace," I said. "USSR-USA," I said shaking my two hands. The two Turks understood and we embraced before going off to bed.

## Saturday January 28th

It was real slow moving this morning because of the cruddy weather. It was cold when I headed out on fairly flat roads, destined for Bursa. I didn't feel well however, it was like my body and mind was depressed. I kept pedaling and found my energy output was ok, though, I tried not to think about anything. My mind was constantly thinking of songs and of dreams of getting home or going south or getting quickly to Istanbul. I was thinking too much. It was such slow going and windy and there were long hills.

I stopped at a gas station and a man with a deformed face watched me eating outside. I felt for this poor man. Sure, I was having some hardship, but it was nothing compared to his. Another man came up to me and he invited me in but I wanted to move on, and thanked him.

I continued in a northeast direction and made it into Bursa at 2pm. There was snow on 8,000 foot Mt. Uladag, which is also called Mt. Olympus, like that in Greece. I was annoyed by trucks and thought these truckers must have had one hand on the steering wheel and the other on their dicks, blowing their horns. They've got nothing else to do so when they get beside me except blow there loud fucking air horns. God it hurt my ears. Then their wind blast hit me like a slap in the face. And I smelled their god-damn-awful exhaust, some were diesels, some were not. There were no mufflers on many of these trucks.

I headed for Gemlick on a long, long uphill. Why don't I take more photos? I wondered to myself. It takes time to do so. On one long uphill I was in the lowest gear. What a struggle. Finally after 40 minutes I made it to the top and then zing, I went down the other side. Whoopy. I was happy. Feet dangling, I waved crazily to everybody. "Blow your horns." I cried to everyone and every truck while ringing my Mickey Mouse bell. It was a long dowhill and oh so great.

I made it into Gemlick. There was a big mountain on one side. Gemlick is in a cove and on the Sea of Marmara. If the road goes over that mountain, then tomorrows ride will be a killer.

I found a otel room for 400 lire, ate and walked about the town. It was nice to see a good-looking Turkish girl. If only I could go up and talk to her. It was fun playing with the kids who were balancing pretzels on their heads. They can tie their shoes and jump and spin around and I even saw a kid climb over an 8 foot fence with one big platter on his head. Another kid walked with a platter on his head and read a book in a strong wind.

I walked the sidewalks and looked in the windows of men's clubs as they sat and talked while smoking long pipes. It was so much like a Norman Rockwell painting. They were very collective and lazy. I strolled past a berber (barber) and saw a man getting a shave with a long blade at 8:30pm this Saturday night. There were five other men in the room watching him. I walked about for awhile and came back and saw the same man still getting a shave 15 minutes later. They sure like to take their time. In the hotel room on this cold night I listened to some twangy music that sounded like a record player playing bent records.

## Sunday January 29th

I left Gemlich on the cold, overcast morning, and could see snow on the mountains and thought about the hard road ahead. Fortunately it was not a hard climb up this grade to Orhangzi, but my bike sounded like hell, as I think the chain is wearing out. Everything is gritty and dirty. I wrote down a song called, "Daddy come Home," and worked on the melody. It was about a soldier going to Beirut and never coming back.

The road climbed and up I pedaled. Then it was a nice downhill all the way to Yalova. I could see the ferry just arriving and had to hurry to catch it. I bought a big container of yogurt and a ticket on the ferry for 300 lire. Everyone stared at me. Once on the ship I found my yogurt had opened up and dumped inside the handlebar pack. Ok, I spooned it up and mixed apples, tangeringes and sugar as people stand behind me watching.

Many people asked me where I was from. Shoe shine boys asked me if I needed a shine. There was a lovely looking dark girl inside with the most beautiful lips.

I sat outside and ate my yogurt and drank a Coke as people looked at me pitifully. My attitude was tough shit. I went inside the cabin to share glances with this cute gal. Now I really felt if only I could talk to her, that would make me happy. She was with her mom. I was too shy. We arrived on the other side of the bay and I pedaled off toward Istanbul at about 4pm. There was a steep hill and then a freeway to travel down. It was dusty and the traffic congested, with many people walking on the road. Many houses that I passed looked like a disorganized mess. The yards were in poor shape. I could see up ahead the city of Istanbul and the grand bridge crossing the Bosphorus.

I rode on into Uskadar, which lies across the straight from Istanbul. My body was weary from the hard traveling, but I maintained a pace as the sun was setting and coasted to a stop near a policeman who guarded the Bridge Over the Bosphorus. I intended to ride across that bridge. "Yok," (No) he told me. I filled him in where I came from. "Marmaris," I said. He was so amazed he called all his buddies over. The Aziz came, they were some kind of special police and and then the city police. None could speak english. I wanted to ride across the bridge and thus would say, "Bicyclette Besiktas," which means 'bicycle to the other side.' "Hayin,"(can't do) he said. I gave him my pooped-warn-out-look and he said, "moment." I waited impatiently and pondered what they would do if I just started riding across.

Then a truck pulled up and they said, "come," my fate had been chosen. We loaded the bike into it and they took drove me across. The Turks in the truck kept padding me on the shoulders. "EEE," they would say, "Marmaris, ok!" as we crossed near the midpoint of the bridge that connected Europe with Asia.

We arrived at the Istanbul side and they didn't want any of my money for the ride. I unloaded and pedaled into the city and right away noticed how the people here heckled me. They would constantly say in english- "Hello." Everytime I'd stop someone would say, "Where you from? Want to buy something?" I got so sick of this and the bad roads in the city as well as the dust and smoke. It was annoying. I looked around and found the least expensive otel was for 650 lire, and I had to share a room. A very pleasant english speaking Turkish girl helped me out. I was shown the room. There was a man inside the room who looked sick, laying on the bed. So I said, "No want this room if man is sick." They assured me, "No sick, no sick, only tired." They told me he was a taksi driver who worked all night long "Ok, I'll take it," I said.

From the otel, I walked around looking for a bathouse and a young Turk showed me a dome shaped Turkish bathhouse. I went in, was shown a changing room and slipped into a towel. From there, I entered the steaming hot room with its hot floor and many men washing up near pools of water and faucets. There was a large, hot slab of marble for people to lay on. I washed up and laid on one slab of rock, but god it was too hot to stay on it for long. I noticed that others were getting a massage, but it was expensive, and already I was overheating. I jumped into cold water and saw flashes of light in my eyes. Then I washed up next to some boys and right away they knew I was a tourist and made ridicule of some english words, "Ok, hallow, bye bye." "Very funny," I said, and they laughed like crazy. When I stepped out of the steam room a man wiped me down real fast with towels and then tightly wrapped them around my head and body. "Sit," he ordered. I sat back and got a heat rush and it's a nice, pleasant 'high' to come back down and return to utter relaxation.

I went walking around the coal-burning-smell of Istanbul and stopped for a beer after feeling great. There was a donar kabob restaurant, which hit the spot, and I went back to my room after walking around Istanbul.

I fell asleep at 10:30pm. Then at midnight there was a knock on the door. "Passport," the man said adding, "Police." I dug out my passport and gave it to him. I asked for his police badge. "No, me-downstairs police." He took my passport.

I heard the police asking another room to open the door and when they didn't they rammed it open to enter. In other rooms they would ring the phone before entering. After a couple of hours I was worried about my passport and went downstairs to ask politely for it back. They said it was ok until morning. I got kind of mad and they gave it back.

When the taxi driver came home I was awake. He said a long prayer to Allah. Then he took deep breaths. He had a respiratory problem. He would wheeze and cough. It sounded like he had no lungs. He would rattle candy in his mouth. When he slept he snored and talked and wheezed so horribly. I put my pillow over my head. Didn't sleep well at all that entire night.

## Monday January 30th

I went into the city on the morning and bought a big, flat sweet roll and then rode up the streets of Istanbul, past some nice fountains and cute girls walking. I saw the Aziz by an Ataturk memorial. More Aziz were there. Everywhere I went people harassed me by saying; "English, Duetshman, Allman, Hello, ha, ha, ha." I didn't understand why they did that to me.

I rode up to the Sulieman Mosque and had a look inside. It was so fantastic and lovely. The echo inside was great. Huge columns came from Egypt and the beautiful carpet was Persian. I met two U.S. people with a guide and they invited me to come along and I learned more about the mosque and Moslems. It was originally made in 1550 during the Ottoman Empire and the architect made over 80 Mosques. I learned of smoke dispensers that they put into the ceiling and made ink from the oil lamp smoke. It was rumoured that there was a Christian church on this site prior to being a mosque.

The Moslems pray five times a day. They begin the daily prayer ritual one half hour before sunrise, then again at noon, at 4pm, at sunset and finally one hour after sunset.

I went to the University of Istanbul and then past giant pillars from Egypt from the third century A.D. Many street sellers were trying to sell me trinkets. I went into the Blue Mosque escorted by a young man. It was being worked on, with scaffolding here and there, but was still very beautiful. This was a Christian Church, built around 400AD, prior to being a mosque. It was called St. Sophia., named after the patron saint Sophia which meant wisdom. Though one can easily see the Arabic letters here and there, you can also see the older Christian symbols underneath. It seemed to me kind of cheeky for the Moslems to do this to a church. They were only being resourceful.

This escort of mine tried to get me to go to his fathers carpet shop but I wasn't interested, and he went his way.

I went into the royal palace and saw displayed many gems and valuable artifacts among which are supposed to be the bones of Jesus apostle, St. John and possibly those of John the Baptist. There were also rich crowns and diamond necklaces in addition to decorated guns. While in the museum I saw a cute girl, and she said hello to me in French. I turned red and my blushing scared her away, I guess.

I went back to my otel and packed up my things. Then I took off for the ferry ride across the Bosporous and stopped at a food stall in the Turkish Bazaar. There, I bought what looked like a McFish burger and fries, but instead it was a local food called an octopus sandwich. It tasted ok, but never again.

Went across the Bosporous to Uscadar and looked for a otel with a couple of Turks who said they knew where there was a good place. They took me to this otel and they wanted twice the money as the night before. I was learning that the Turks tell you once the price and that's it. If you are hesitant to decide they get annoyed. So I said, "Yok," which means "there is not, or no can do." And we went to another place. A crowd gathered around as an English speaking man intervened and confused matters. He said this is the only place you can stay, so I got antsy and said, "Ok, merci." I took off as they all stood there and watched me go. I don't like people to decide for me and the Turks try to mother me until I get pissed.

So I went to a couple of otels and finally found a room for 500 Turkish Lire, but had to share it with two other men. I stored my bike in a garage and went in and laid down with a hat over my head. I was very tired.

Into my room walked a fellow who said, "Hello." I shook his hand and met Slayeman, a very kind Turk. He did not speak much english but enough. We went to eat. He told me he was working on a harbor patrol ship. He was a good fellow, very well mannered and dressed impeccably and was understandable. I wanted some filberts and he helped me at the shop.

We walked to the Bosporous and enjoyed a grand view of Istanbul. We then went back to the otel and talked to some other men and together drank a beer. Then I met Ersin, a local fellow who wanted to go out. We walked to a pub. Ersin had a bug against Americans. He disliked Reagan and thought badly of America. We engaged in a heated discussion and he wanted to know why the U.S. was in Beirut and why in El Salvador and in South America. He got annoyed when I said, "They cause Americans to build defenses to stop war." He snapped at me; "Who is they?" I responded, "The Soviets," continuing, "especially because (they) socialists can't work with countries that have a democracy like that in the U.S. We have free trade, open borders, and they have to contain people."

We talked of the differences between our countries and that the U.S tries to promote trade between other countries, "it is for money that is for sure, but trade is a good thing. And the Soviets don't want to trade with the U.S. That is the problem," I said. Well I told him in the U.S.A., you can be as free to speak and do as you please. You can do anything. Any job. (Now I was getting fired up on my partriotism.) I said, "It's not easy. You must go to school and work hard but you can even be the president or an astronaut if you want to work for it. This interested Ersin so very much. "Turkey does not offer many opportunities," he said.

Slayeman was sitting there making peace symbols to get my attention. Ersin got really excited about the potential to do anything. "In Turkey it is not possible." I responded- "And this is why so many people dislike the U.S. It is because they are envious that they don't have what the U.S. has to offer. Therefore they hate America." We shook hands and came to an understanding. He told me, "I think all Americans are like you. Very good men and very proud-now I like Americans too much." He begged for me to stay until summer to be with him. I said, "No, I must go tomorrow." "But then stay here for one week," he said. "No, I cannot." Slayeman was so considerate and so patient. He acted like a mediator.

I was thinking of my friends in Athens and how they all wanted me to stay longer. But I felt the need to keep moving, else I'll run out of time and money and my goal will never be. So we went to the otel, shook hands and exchanged address's. "Please write me, please." Said Ersin. He looked almost like he was Chinese. He told me his ancestors were from mid Asia. Back in the hotel room I played guitar for Slayeman. He was excited about this. It was nice to have someone as good a friend as him. We talked till 1am.

## Tuesday Jan 31

Slayemans alarm went off at 7:45 as it sounded like a 1930's vintage alarm clock. I awoke and he said, "Good travels Eric." I said, "You are good Turkey man Slayeman." He said, "Tessakh Ederin," (good luck) and I responded, "Thanks." I got up and went to the city. Bought post cards and some good almond cookies.

Went back to the otel trying to decide if I should leave Istanbul. I just didn't feel like getting stuck here for a long time. I needed to head south, a winter storm was threatening and so I packed up. I would take a bus back to Izmer.

The bellboy played my guitar. Then I sang for him and he liked that. He wanted to help me. He ran around doing things for me. I pedaled down to the bus terminal. The sun was shining. Many men said, "Izmer, Izmer." I shopped around and got the Turks pissed as I selected a bus and finally picked one to Izmer. I paid 1300 TL which is about $4 for a 300 mile bus ride. I unpacked my bike as a crowd looked on in amazement. They couldn't believe how I disassembled that bike. I was having fun with this one Turk man who kept saying "American-American" and was hugging me. He thought I was nuts.

The bus pulled up at 1pm and we packed the bike on top and were off. I had time to think and to see the roads that I had ridden my bike upon from a new perspective. I was amazed at the hills I had ridden my bike over. In fact, I found this bus ride providing an entirely new perspective to seeing the countryside. It looked uncyclable, but I knew I had done it.

We stopped at Izmit and I had eye games with a gal on another bus. I ate lots of junk food on the bus and went down roads that I had pedaled over. I sat next to a soldier and he dozed off, but then suddenly awoke in the dark and panicked that he thought he had missed his stop. But it was ok.

I thought about my life on the road. It was a good life, I felt. I was proud to be doing this. I tried to think of what to do when I got back to the states and still drew a blank mind to think of doing a real job. Guess I wanted to just be me, to have a woman and a family.

The bus climbed up over many passes and it was cold and windy. I thought of the hardships I had on these passes and hear the bus groan and slow down. I saw why I was so pooped out. But there was always the other side, to go down. We made many stops on this trip. The bus would even stop for people on the road who needed a ride.

Finally, after seven hours of travel we arrived in Izmer. I unpacked my things and pedaled off to the otel, where it was nice to be greeted warmly, and though I got my same room back, they raised the price to 400 TL.(Turkish Lire) "Tarzan," they said, as I carried my bike up the 100 steps to my room. It was good to be back home, I thought, to be in familiar country and with friends.

## Wednesday February 1st

This day marked the beginning of my 8th month of travel. I slept like hell in this poorly supported bed. I felt like a banana after last night. I cleaned up my bike and got tuned up for the road. I discovered the poor thing was showing many scars from the rough roads it had gone down. I shopped around much of the day for a can of oil. They didn't have any chain lube or sprays here, so I ended up buying sewing machine lube. I washed clothes and played guitar.

Back at the otel, I was visited by several of the employees. They asked me to play guitar for them, so I played a few songs. After a couple of songs, I lose interest because they can't understand the words, and they know I'm a bad singer. But they are good listeners.

I went to Murats photo store. He was there and we had a warm reunion. He gave me a package of photos he had taken a week before. He asked me of my journey to Istanbul and I filled him in on the highlights. I told him how everyman was coming up to me and asking where I was from. And how I got annoyed and started to tell them I was a Soviet, "A Roosky," and then they left me alone. Murat was down because he had an exam and felt he did poorly. Emra would study for an exam tomorrow. So I had the night to myself.

I went to the restaurant across the street and ate doner kabob. They sliced off the delicious strips of roast lamb, which was broiled on an upright stick that rotated to cook it evenly. I walked around digging all the people out on the streets. There was a little mellower atmosphere in Izmer compared to the aggression in Istanbul.

I returned to the otel and played a little guitar, but the old man next door got pissed and came over to do his "Tist, tist, tist" to me. I discovered that he can't talk. So I picked up my guitar and went to a vacant room and there played. A busboy came in to listen. Then the old man reappeared and once again went, "Tist, tist," to me. I stood up and said, "Tist, tist, tist" back at him and strummed a few chords loudly. He started waving his finger at me. The busboy and I laughed at this and I stopped playing.

I headed out for a walk and met a shoe shine boy. He polished my shoes and told me what was happening in Izmer. He wanted some American smokes so I agreed to try and buy some from the PX.

So I pedaled to the PX and they refused me. What was worse was the way they treated me. I was happy to speak to a fellow American but you'd think this guy had fear of me or something. I saw other Americans. They were so cocky and arrogant. No wonder I think people of other countries have some bitter words in regards to Americans, especially those in the military. Anyhow I guess they have a job to do, and they're not out exploiting themselves or the military property. So be it.

Tomorrow starts a new journal. This one is of my journey through Europe to Asia. I feel it all hasn't been absorbed. All the things I've seen and done. I also felt the learning was just beginning and from now it should get more interesting.

## Thursday Feb. 2, 1984

It was a cool, foggy, smoky morning that was witnessed outside the window of my dinky penthouse on the rooftop of this cheap 'otel' in Izmer. I looked over the balcony, down to the streets below where things were rather quiet. Lazily I was getting up and organizing, while listening intently to The Voice of America informing of the latest world events. The major news was about the primary importance was President Reagan's re-election campaign. They said, "The fireworks have begun to announce his campaign." The radio made it sound like he would win easily over Mondale.

A walk was made into the city to look for another diary, as my first one was nearly full. It was discovered once again that Turkey really had a poor selection of good commercial items. The best diary to be found was of the poorest standard yet. It probably wouldn't make it long without tearing apart, but it was all that was available. Many shop owners showed me what they had in their old fashioned stores. You'd have to believe that either nobody uses diaries in this country or else, they write scantly, as one can only put about five words on the wide lines they have. Looking for a diary in Turkey was probably just like looking for a toilet here and discovering-hey they don't use toilet paper! The little water container and your bare hand seem to me the only method. One learns to be a little leery of shaking hands with a Turk, especially one who has just stepped out of the biffy.

## THE WHEELS OF FRIEND

I pedaled the bike over to the post office, an old factory looking place, with the smell of mothballs. They said it would be 850 Turkish Lire (TL) to mail the old diary back home. Then I went back to the otel and filled out an envelope. Then went back to the PTT and this time they said it would be 1300 lire. Another option was the 460 TL package, which was very slow freight via slow train and ship. It was on my mind whether it would make it there at all. I opted for this because of the price.

I returned to the otel and repaired the broken liner in my helmet. As the glue set, I played the guitar and got so thoroughly disgusted with my squeaking-ball-bearing-sounding voice, especially when, this young Turkish busboy flung my door wide open and listened to me with an awkward smile. Mine was not a performance, it was a work in progress, as this was the practice of some new songs, yet he applauded.

It was after lunch when I pedaled down to see Murat. He readily embraced me and held my hand. We always have such warm meetings. From there, I walked down along the shops to do some girl watching. The women here have rather beautiful features. They have dark hair and dark eyes, dark olive skin and nice curves accentuated with shapely, slender builds.

I asked at the INFORMATION shop if a ship would be going to Rhodes from Bodiun or Marmaris and they said, "It's impossible." I responded, "But I came over from Rhodes to Marmaris on a ship." He said. "No, it's impossible." "Okay," I said and left in a huff.

Back at Murat's, I shook the hands of all my friends, Aydin and his cousin, then Murat, whom I cheek kissed. Murat and I walked to a place to eat doner kabob. We talked about women and loves of the past. Murat enjoyed discussing his romance. He comes across as a real romantic, and loves to tell about the women he has loved. He told me he would be married in April and his wife to be was also very nice.

I asked him if it was true that their was a legal house of prostitution in Izmer and he said, "Yes, come on I'll take your there, you must see it."

We took a dolmuce (taxi) to this gate. In we went and it was like a shopping center of little 'shops' or apartments lining the streets within this compound. One can 'window shop' and see the girls in their panties. It was ok to shop all you wanted, there was no pressure. We went to all the shops. Many of the girls were fat and ugly. Some were rather nice. It cost about 1000 TL or about $3.00 for a lady. One very attractive young gal looked like she was a Hawaiian. She was very shapely. The guys encouraged my meeting her, but this bashful side of myself and some kind of fear of disease gripped me. The three of us had a good time though, just looking at these girls as they enticed us, but we were just looking.

We went back on the dolmuce to my bike and there talked with the caretaker of the building within which Murats store is located. He was plastered, drunk. He told us he was normal and that he could do anything. He said he had drank since he was 12 years old and was 60 years old now. He said he was once a cop and showed us a photo. "I drink anything," he said. "Money is to drink," he would say. He now lives alone, though he has been married four times and has six children. He told us he had a good heart when he was drunk. I told Murat, "tell him I wish I was his age, or he was mine, so we could get drunk together." The old man grabbed me and said, "Never mind the age-come on let's drink!!" "No thanks," I said emphatically.

Now it was just Murat and I walking down the night streets of Izmer. We exchanged goodbyes. We will see each other again and wished each other good luck. Finally a cheek kiss, as Turkish men do, and I told him I would always wish the best for him. "I worry for you," he said.

## Friday Feb. 3, 1984

I packed up my things and wrote 'Tarzan slept here,' on the bed board and coat rack. Went out on the street, bought some baked goodies and filberts and returned to the room to play a couple of songs. I listened to V.O.A. and then took the bike downstairs.

The faces looked longer on everybody. I shook hands with both cleaning ladies. Then with the otel manager and my friend the busboy. "Tarzan okay," he said. "Mersi," I told them and "gule, gule," which meant good luck. I rode off from that memorable otel. Went up and out of the city and through about five kilometers of rough, dusty road. I was out on the road again and it felt good!

At noon I stopped to eat lunch near a spring. It was a nice sunny day. There was a good smell in the air. I headed into Selcuk and saw a guy I had seen two week before.

I took a long side road which lead me down to the legendary, ancient city of Epheses. As soon as I got off the bike a man tried to sell me some ancient coins. I wanted them, but just couldn't spend the money for them. I learned that Epheuses was an important port city in its heyday. The ships would come right up to the base of the city. It was located on a hillside, facing the sea. Over time, the sea retreated, heavy silting occurred and malaria ended this great city. But during its time it was a lovely place. I could see this in the workmanship of the buildings and the walls. They were both colossal and ornate. One wall was made of massive, perfectly chiseled blocks that were so finely placed, that even today, one could not slip a piece of paper between the blocks. The Celsias library was so gorgeous. This library once contained the noblest works of the ancient world. It was here that scholars gathered to learn and to teach. The ruins were very interesting to see, especially the Temple of Diana, the quality of craftsmanship impeccable. There were many symbols on the walls here and there that I could not decipher with these untrained eyes.

It was a warm day and pleasantly enjoyed, while wearing only a T-shirt. I saw a beautiful peacock painting inside what was once a rich family's house that was very ornate. Overlooking the ancient harbor, is a large amphitheater that was impressive. I stood on the stage and looked up at the 'audience' of empty seats and wondered who else stood here. Then I hiked to the highest seat and again wondered what it must have been like to see and hear some great performances and speakers.

I ambled along the marble road which the apostle Paul had walked two thousand years ago. He had visited this port city several times and preached against Artemis and the worship of Greek gods. It was here that Paul spoke out against a man named Demitrius, who made Artemis statues. Other historic figures also visited Epheuses, namely Alexander the Great, Marc Anthony and Cleopatra. It was awe inspiring to think that they too walked or rode up these marble streets.

It was late in the afternoon when I hit the road for Kusadasi and was very concerned about my front wheel as it seemed the bearing was getting bad. I found a pensione and the clerk held up five fingers but said it cost 400 TL for a night. I compromised with him and took it for 450. I went to a poorly lit restaurant, which had picnic tables and there ate a most delicious Turkish style pizza. I talked with a Turk from Van on the far eastern side of Turkey and he was so helpful.

This is a nice town and very scenic. I walked around the town and the dark streets were dirty and full of things to trip over. As I've learned in Turkey, pick up your feet and watch out.

## Saturday Feb. 4th

I left Kusadisi on a sunny but hazy morning. Went up and over some big hills, and the road became very bumpy. I sympathized with my bike and tried to maneuver to miss bad rough spots. The smell was so grand on this morning. There was a combination of sea odor and fresh green grass. It brings so many thoughts to mind. I thought of the memories we all have of odors. Now that's an interesting sense to use artistically. Smelling art!

I kept thinking of California, as the landscape here reminded me so much of it. I was brushing my teeth while coasting down a long hill and passed some people whom looked at me like I was nuts! Two dogs chased me while cresting the top of a long up hill. I poured on the coal to get my speed up and swerved at one dog. After a swift kick, they all left. Now I felt more confident about how to deal with dogs. Let them know you'll swat them and they'll stay away. I would raise my arm as if holding an imaginary stick and pretended to be ready to hit them. If they got to close I would stop, jump off and use my bike as a barrier.

While riding into Sohe a 20 kilometer footrace was going on and many runners were filling the streets. I had been passing many of them while heading into town. Then, while making my way past many spectators they cheered to me in gest, and yet it was a marvelous spectacle. I was heading for the finish line when a policeman flagged me off the course and around a detour.

It was getting hot out when I stopped and drank a Coke. Took water from a faucet but it tasted bad. I discover this is lake water and it is alkali. I'd have to go a little farther without good water.

This was a beautiful day. The people were always so kind and it was beautiful here. Turkey was growing so warmly on me.

I saw the ruins of ancient buildings in a town called Euroca. Wow how could people make such massive buildings back then, and to carve out a column with such precision. At 3:30pm, I cruised into Milas, a quaint little town with white stuccos on a hillside, and hurried into the market to buy some goods. Then I decided to ride another 50k's today and hit the road for Bodrum. I pedaled out of Milas and felt confused, thus stopped to eat a bite on the roadside and thought about this. "No, I won't go to Bodrum today, maybe I'll wait till tomorrow," I said aloud. So I pedaled back into town. A young guy said, "Where you from." I told him and he said, "Can I help you?" He took me to some otels, where I got a room for 300TL.

I settled in, cleaned up my bike chain and discovered some bad news. The crank bearing was real loose and nearly falling out. I tried to tighten it but did not have the right tool. I was very glad to not have continued to Bodrum. I decided that tomorrow I would instead take a different fork in the road and go to Mugla. I walked into town and ate some stew and bought some munchies. Went back to the otel to play guitar and wondered why this place smelled like a cattle barn. While lying in the sleeping bag upon the bed, I listened to the Jami (mosque) chants.

## Sunday Feb. 5th

Awoke to the sound of an old man coughing and spitting. I could hear the snag hit the floor. After munching on some cake it was time to look again at the crank and to figure out a way of repairing it. I took the bike outside, on this cold morning and men gathered around to watch me tighten it down.

This quaint little town was tightly packed with houses on a hillside. I loaded up my bike and coasted down the narrow streets and they were steep and fast. I rounded a corner where a man was walking down the middle of the street. There appeared to be a wet spot and beyond it some bumps. I swerved to miss the bumps and missed them fine, but the wet spot was actually ice and WHAM! I went down skidding on my side. It was the first time I'd crashed on this bike. Geeze it went down hard. I skidded for awhile on my sidebags and ripped my pants and scun my knees. The man looked at me uncaringly, and didn't say a thing. I sat down and sewed my pants back up. I checked over the bike, it was ok and then left town.

The road climbed up, up and up, out of Milas on a long uphill. I made it to the top and then there was more uphill. I didn't mind these long grades as I was in good physical shape. My greatest concern was about my equipment. My poor bike. I could feel it dying underneath me. I saw some spectacular scenery, the Agean Sea and rocky points, and it was another sunny day. The girls were dressed pretty and people seemed so cheerful. The kids and men whistled to me. I felt a parch in my lungs and wondered about those coughing men this morning. Maybe I caught something from them.

Along the road to Mugla, I stopped to look at an open pit mine. Then continued and outside of Yatagan stopped for a break. Two guys came over to talk to me. One man told me he saw my photo in The Gazette of Turkish newspaper while I was in Belisar. It told of my travels for seven months. Said I went into Yugoslavia and Bulgaria but I knew that was not true. I shook their hands and left just as the wind picked up.

I went uphill again, return onto some familiar roads and made it back into Mugla at 2:30pm. It was so much different now to return to a place that I had been before. I felt a sense of reunion. My attitude of this country was so much better. I now felt good about being in Mugla. For one thing it was not bitter cold like the last time. For another it seemed as if it had a hometown feeling. I checked into the same otel and got the same room for 300 lire. I cleaned up the bike and fixed a tire, then went around town to find air for pumping up a tire. I asked two boys, and five came to help me. We all went together to some shop that had an air hose sticking out of it. They were very helpful lads.

Found a great place to eat doner and salad and for only 225 TL. At the otel I played guitar and noticed how bad the bed smelled. My lungs hurt. I wished I could listen to some U.S. news, but the radio could not receive. I couldn't learn a thing of what's happening. I went to the theater where it was a double feature tonight for 90TL. That's about 35cents. Obsession and Flying Higher were the movies. They were both filled with pretty girls. During the first movie the man next to me played with beads and it so annoyed me and I had to tell him to "Yok." He did stop after that. Upon returning to the otel I saw all of the men huddled around a stove as I walked in. They stopped talking and greeted me and I them. I went to my room and sneakingly exchanged my bed cover with that from a bed in another room.

## Monday Feb. 6th

Dreamy eyed I awoke and looked at the beautiful calendar girl on the wall, an unusual site in a Moslem country. It felt like there was a cold was in my lungs. I packed up my bike and hit the trail heading south for Marmaris. Now I was thinking how reversed my opinion was of this country after meeting such great folks as I had. I could look at the scenery and feel love. Not the same cold place as three weeks before. Up and up I climbed and I knew that big downhill that I fought so hard to pedal up, was coming ahead. A van went by and the guy asked me if I wanted a ride down the hill. It was the first time that this had happened to me in Turkey, and with this nice downhill coming up, I just flagged him away. At the top of that huge downhill I pulled over for a photo. He was there with his van and asked if I'd like a ride to Marmaris. "No way," I told him. Not wanting to miss this thrilling downhill. "I've been waiting to go down this hill for three weeks." He took my photo.

I went freewheeling down this grade, which dropped from 670 meter (2000 feet) to sea level. Wowwy. I waved my feet when cars went past the other way and could pass cars that were going my way! I enjoyed the sensation of soaring downhill, as it was so thrilling. It is amazing that the big load on my bike goes quite well. It has no instability, no shimmy or poor control. The wind was the only thing to be careful of. I was using my front brake to help me around corners and after 15 minutes of glory reached the bottom and made the turnoff to Marmaris.

I headed across the flats and through this beautiful corridor of large eucalyptus trees. Then climbed up into the highland and went through a village where a boy threw a ball to me as I passed. I caught it and threw it backwards, up over my head, then turned around to see him catch it behind me!

I continued on to Marmaris on this gorgeous day enjoying the good smells and felt so good. It was like coming home. I went up some big hills and was sweating heavily. Then coasted down into Marmaris at about 1pm. It was a fantastic view of the pretty town, nestled in the rocky cove next to the blue sea.

I stopped at a bike shop and met a Turk from Ankara working at a store next to the shop. He helped me talk to the bike repairman, who would tighten the crank. I went to check on a boat heading for Rhodes and learned it would be leaving in two days. So I went back to the shop and the repairman had tightened my crank bearing and said, "Ok." He charged me about 200 TL or approximately 75cents. I was thankful but felt it may only be a temporary fix. More importantly, I saw how he tightened the part and from now on could do it myself.

I went into town to shop for a otel. Nail was not around. I sat by the beach to play guitar. A guy came along who spoke no english. He wanted me to sing so I sang some songs. Before long about five other Turkish guys were also listening. Then one guy named Onur picked up the guitar and played the best rendition of the Led Zeppelin song- Stairway to Heaven that I had ever heard. I enjoyed their company, and one fellow named Silfoni spoke good english that almost sounded like he was a Australian. He bought us some beers and I got silly. We sat there until 6:30 and then I went and got a otel for 539 TL. It was kind of steep, by my standards, but cheap in reality as this was the off season. There were three beds in the room and it was in a good location. It even had windows, a toilet and a shower.

I went back to meet friends. Silfoni bought me some soup and a pizza meal. He wanted me to stay in his room at the otel but I wanted my things to be safe so I insisted not. Onur played guitar and had a musicians flare. We went to the sea side with all the other boys and messed around for the night singing and laughing. I met Silfoni as I walked home to the otel and he insisted to buy me a Coke and a cake, but before doing so he climbed a flag pole and dangled like a pirate on a mast. We drank and ate and I can't say how much I felt for this kind of generosity. I didn't know his motive but was touched by his kindness.

### Tuesday Feb. 7th

There was a pesty mosquito biting me during the night. My head was stuffed up from a cold. The village was quiet except for the sound of people walking about and the mosque chant before daylight. I took a cold shower. BRRR I shivered. Then I washed clothes and went to use my stove to heat water and it would no longer work. It was clogged. So I took it apart and then went off to the bike shop and asked them to blow it out the orifice of air. We had no luck.

I went to another place and while going through the streets wrote down a song by Firefall called, 'Just Remember I love you,' for Onur and met him at noon at the Ataturk statue. He showed me how to play Stairway to Heaven. We traded songs and I sang him mine.

I went to the otel to take the stove apart and then went about town asking where I could get it serviced. I met my friend Silfoni at a store near the bike shop. He helped me locate a repairman. The repairman went to work on the part. He had to cut it open and then clean out all the crud, which accumulated inside a pipe. It was thoroughly plugged. I couldn't believe how good this man was at repairing this piece. He used a hack saw to cut it and a torch to braze it back together, and it didn't leak. I paid him 400 TL., then went back to the otel to get it working. After some adjusting my stove was again kicking out heat. I felt sleepy and kicked back for an hour of siesta. How nice and peaceful Marmaris was.

I walked with my guitar to meet Silfoni who had his bag all packed up. He would be heading back to Istanbul. He missed his woman he said. He dragged me over and bought me a beer. Then I sang him half a song and he had to go. I felt a question in my mind about him. He was so kind to me and kept waving to me as he left. I couldn't put it all together, but he was so kind to me. I wouldn't forget this.

I got a little tipsy from the beer and a fellow named Windsurfer and I went walking and talking to girls. I met three gals from England. They were delighted to hear of my adventures. I met two gals from the U.S. and I said I was Tarzan and she said she was Jane. She was a bitch. The Turks felt so embarrassed by these rude U.S. girls. I went to the otel and then back to eat a great meal at a restaurant. It was a hot hamburger like meat with bread rolls and cheese inside.

I met Windsurfer and we chased the U.S. girls but they were "tired." So we went to sit. Met Onur and we played songs. He annoyed me by continually asking me if I knew a song. "No," I'd say. "You don't know it why?" He would ask. "Okay, yes," I would say. "Then could you play it for me?" "No," I'd say, "I don't know it." "Uggghh?" he would say.

### Wednesday Feb. 8th

I lazily slept in until 9:30am and then got up and made an effort not to go down and munch out. I met the U.S. girl from Georgia and chatted with her awhile. She is a student in Israel. I felt so enlightened to speak with an english speaking person. I got carried away and overtalked. There came a point when she realized I was starving for conversation, and that she could give no more.

There was an old fortress in town that I explored and inside found some iron cannon balls. While walking I met Ali and we chummed about and met four girls from Ankara. They were students. One spoke excellent english, the others were ok, but a little hard to understand. We went to a cafe and I felt awkward as Ali pretended he was an Australian and not a Turk. He knew they would not talk to him if they found out he was a Turk. The girls got suspicious, but we held to the story. The girls said that Turkey was a place of many old customs. "Girls are just beginning to be given freedom. Our religion and family play a big part in our lives," said the girl named Aiysha. They were shy and held close together like minnows. They got scared when Ali said, "Let's go another place." He played the part of an Aussie well. He was an ex-windsurfer champion of Turkey. He was Mr. Cool in Marmaris. People seemed to give way to him, but the girls caught on. "You are Turkey man, aren't you," they asked. He admitted he was, but didn't care, until they said, "we have to go."

We strutted about the streets and people would stop to look as he did his far out little dances. He really knew his moves. We went to his place, which was a two-room adobe with rug walls. There was a little kitchen and bathroom. He gave me some food, that was a rice and veggie combination and said, "Hope you like it." I did.

We went in the rain to town and met Onur. We were sitting there thumb fighting and I was bored. They do this sitting around stuff all day so it's nothing. I returned to the otel and slept until 6pm and then went out and ate my final good Turk meal. I got some donar and brought some buns from the bakery and made myself a burger. The other guys in the restaurant thought I was nutty and they laughed at me.

Ali's friend met me at the theatre and he bought my way to see the movie Star Trek. I met other friends inside. We ate nuts and had gum, then watched the movie. About halfway through the movie the film started dissolving and then it melted. That was it. I said so long afterward to Ali and others. They were so kind to me and I knew them so little but they gave me so much. At the otel I packed my things and went to bed.

## Thursday Feb. 9th

As the sun rose, I heard the crazy man of Marmaris outside laughing and crying with his mommy-goat like sounds. He gave this town an atmosphere. I heard the mosque give a chant and got packed up as the sun rose on. I headed down to the ship at 9am, stopping at shops to buy munchies. I especially liked the apple turnovers at this little bakery.

I met a German traveler and a Japanese and we talked a bit. There was also a German sailor who had been traveling the globe for the past 11 years. He had a story from everywhere. I was told I had to pay in advance for my ticket. They also wanted to have additional money for my bike to go on the ship. Since I was out of Turkish money I offered them Greek money. They gave me Turkish money in return. "No I don't want any Turkey money," I said, not wanting to get stuck with it. "I'm going to Greece." They went to find change and I went for another turnover. When I returned they had my change.

I boarded the ship and dropped sugar-coated turnovers on the floor and on a desk top. The ships mate rolled his eyes at me. I then went to pick them up and spilled a Turks cup of tea on my money. I picked the money up and it flippered, splattering tea on the Turk. Through all of this they sat solemly looking at me and I got more nervous. I said goodbye to a young Turk who waited by the dock, and kept he telling me to write to him. The Turk sat and watched me go and was waving the whole time and looking sad. This kind of devotion I have not even felt with my best of friends.

The ship was leaving Marmaris and heading past the rocky inlet toward Rhodes. On board, I met a Canadian couple, and talked excitedly. Good God I was fired up to get back to Rhodes! I played guitar with a German and we exchanged accompaniment of drum and harp. He played well. The crossing to Rhodes was rough. I felt queasy. Playing guitar kept my mind off of it. The Japanese man was hanging over the railing heaving with the waves. I had to go outside for air a few times.

Rhodes has a dark look from the sea. It appears distinctly medieval in character, until the boat docked, then again looked Greek. We walked about to find information for a ship to Cyprus and then went looking for a pensione. I knew my way around and we stopped and joked at a cafe sipping on coffee. We all shared our travel adventures. The Japanese man had been through Europe on a bike. "Eeit wasa too defficout in veenter," he said. The German had done much trekking in many countries and he really dug talking of India. "It's a crazy place," he said. We walked about and found a pensione for 300 dracma each. The place was full of ants. We went back into the city to look around and while doing so it struck me that 40 years ago the three of us were enemies but today we can be good friends. The mutual respect of our past seemed to somehow intensify this bond.

We returned to the pensione and talked about the world arms crisis. "The U.S. is to blame for alot of the problem," said the German adding, "And if anything should happen they are really much like Hitler." The Japanese was quiet through this. We got along well though and agreed there is definitely a lack of communication between many countries.

We went to eat Sovlaki and realized in the midst of our conversation that I did not know their names. I said, "Sorry I didn't get yet your names." "Gunther is mine," said the German. "Takai is mine," said the Japanese. We went back shopping for a jug of wine. Amazingly we decided on one without much debate. We headed to the pensione and sipped and talked. It was an intense talk about the U.S., while stumbling over sauced words. I felt I blew away my lips and said to damn much. We were all tongue tied and retired at about 10:30.

## Friday Feb. 10th

God almighty I could hardly sleep at all this night. I was all wound up and my head cold was like a stuffed pepper. I had to get up two or three time to shit or piss. The pain of a bad stomach ache hung in through the night. There were bugs in this place, and come morning, I discovered about 50 dead ants I'd squashed in the night. I took a hot shower and then we went to the city and bought our tickets to our respective destinations. Gunther would got to Crete. Takai to Athens. myself to Cyprus. I was again struck by the thought of our past enemies and present friends. We went to the harbor and took photos. Then I went to a few shops and back to the ship. I had to lift the bike up onto the ship as the loading ramp lifted in the waves. Then I had to go back to Greek customs for a stamp. Again had to lift the bike up onto the ramp.

On board I met two Quebec travelers. One who had been traveling for 8 months. The man at the customs asked me if I'd ever been to Israel. "No," I said. "Any packages to Israel," he asked. "No," I answered.

It was a rough sea on this day as the ship pulled away from Rhodes. My goodbye was very sentimental. I liked this place. We passed under the spot, where I was told stood the Colossus of Rhodes, a huge sculpture of a bronzed Helios, large enough for ships to drive under. It was one of the seven wonders of the world.

As Rhodes was receding behind the ship, I met Risa on the deck. She was from New York. We talked up a storm. She was traveling solo. She was dark haired and quiet, yet a rugged trekker. She had been all through Europe and said she had "hit" Morrocco. Her stories of adventure were good and rather manly. She said she had appendicitis in Paris, opened up her trousers, slipped down her panties and showed me her scar. I nearly saw her pubic hair, my mind spun.

I played guitar as the boat rocked. A long black haired white fellow with negroid features came along and asked me if he could play the guitar. I said sure. He played quite well. It was a mellow sound, but fine. He came and sat by us and talked. He looked part African and part Chinese. We exchanged songs. I joked with Risa and discovered she's had a good character. Richard P. was the Australian, who played a nice sounding song on my guitar. We ate together. And I could tell he had a liking for Risa. I did also. He and I got along so well. We talked into the night by the warmth of the engine smokestacks where it was comfy. He and I got into a good talk about the world. The nuclear problem and how if effects all of us. He too said that he could not visualize such a holocaust occurring and desired not to be a part of it. The Mediterranean Sea was rough and the stars shining with a half moon. We retired around 11pm, sleeping upon a bench, on the deck of the swaying ship.

## Sat Feb, 11

Got up and could see Cyprus off to our left side. We were all happy. I felt good to be just a tourist on Cyprus. When the ship came into port Risa, Richard and I joked alot about things we saw on the island. A Soviet ship was in port. We thought we might meet Soviet tourists. "Ha, ha." I carried my bike down onto Cyprus and went on my bike through customs and into the city of Limassol. I pedaled out to a section of beach, where I put on shorts, splashed in the sea and enjoyed the sunshine. I went to a bank and discovered prices were expensive here. Asked the Greeks about the history of this place as they drove on the left side of the road and use pounds for money. They had a British influence in the past. I went into town and explored. Discovered a market place and bought pita bread and all kinds of vegetable fillings for it. The city wasn't very nice. They drove cars very 'Greek like' with people rolling through stops signs. I returned down to the beach and made a sandwich with a French Canadian guy who told me how stuff the pita bread with fillings. It was a good day of sun.

On the return trip back to port, I rode up to a Soviet ship. There was a fellow out painting the outside of the ship. It was a fairly nice ship. "Hello," I said. He turned to me and smiled then said, "Hallo." I aimed my open hand toward him and asked, "Soviet?" Then I pointed toward myself and said, "American." He responded with, "Ah, American." "Soviet tourista ship," he said pointing at his ship. "Good," I said feeling that he understood. "Bicyclette tourist," I told him pointing to my bike and then pulling out a world map, pointing to the places I'd been. He came down off the ladder and looked the map over. He thought that was something that I'd been traveling on a bike and he told his pals and they all grinned when he said, "American tourist of the world." "Madam?" he asked me while pointing to my ring finger. "No," I replied. "You?" I asked him. "Yaw, duo children." He wanted to know how old I was. I discovered he knew english numbers. "2-8," I said. He also was 2-8 and so was his comrade. We hit it off right. Now we were friends. We laughed. He said, "Moscow?" to me and patted my bike handlebars. (He was wondering if I'd been to Moscow.) "No visa," I said, waving my head with a disgusted look. "Los Angeles?" I said pointing to him. "No visa." he replied. "Olympics," I said. He did not understand. "You Olypmics?" I said and gestured hockey. "Olympicsky?" I said adding a Russian intonation to the word. "Yah, yah," he said something to his comrades and we laughed. They imitated hockey motions and said, "Olympisicksy," while we all must have been recalling that big miracle game between the U.S. and Russia. I greeted them goodbye and shook their hands. Our hands held firm and for a split second there was a longing, a longing for a peace, for an opening, a better connection between America and Russia. When I rode off, there were many observers watching me from beside and on that ship. I felt a warm glow, as if this journeys goal had finally come to fruition, the dream long hoped for arrived– to meet Russians with my bike -FRIEND.

Before boarding the ship, I met two Canadian cyclists who had been ripped off while in Athens. They admitted to leaving there stuff un watched and therefore lost gear and money. Back on the ship I talked to Richard who was very close now with Risa. Richard had a bumm leg but it in no way impeded his ability to get along. He was soft spoken and courteous. We ate together. I bought him an apple and orange. I felt good to see and talk with Risa. The ship left port at about 8pm in the dark. We were a happy bunch. Singing songs and talking. We were good pals. I could tell Richard and I both liked Risa and we knew we were helpless. We again had a good talk about the future of mankind, the past of men and our littleness in this somehow orderly world. I spent my last dracmas on a beer. At about 10pm we heard fighter jets swoop over the ship. Someone said, there was trouble in Beirut.

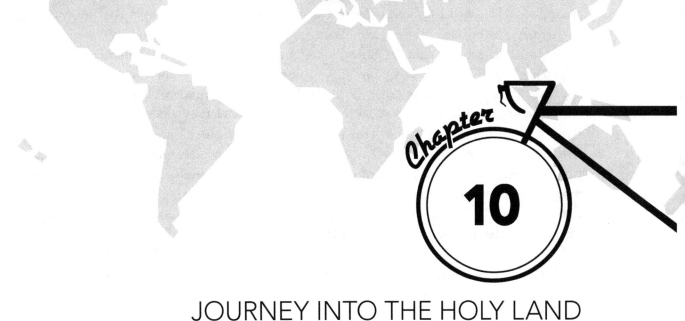

# JOURNEY INTO THE HOLY LAND

**Sunday Feb. 12**

I didn't sleep so well cause I was anxious or scared or something. I took a piss at 5am over the deck. It was warm out. I could see Israel. There were concrete bunkers out in the harbor and frequent sightings of gunboats, zipping here and there. We arrived in the port of Haifa at 8am. We sat up on the top deck feeling the goodbyes. We were making assumptions about this warlike country. Gunboats pulled up alongside. There were shore guns, machine gun nests and canon bunkers while entering the port of Haifa.

I got organized and went through customs, said goodbye to Risa. Kissed her on the cheeks. Goodbye to Richard. I ambled up into the city and found a bank. Exchanged my money. People seemed nice and a little slower pace. I rode through the city and pedaled my way heading east out of town. Put on my riding shorts and a t-shirt. It was warm out. I headed for Nazareth. Went up some grassy hills that were sometimes heavily wooded with trees. The trucks were especially bad, they did not give much leeway. The road had no shoulder. I rode with another biker, a young man, who rode like hell to pass me. He was on a one speed bike. We both agonized our way up a long hill. Then downhill we went flat out. We raced again and groaned up a long hill. I passed him and stayed up ahead of him but occasionally we closed ranks and exchanged hello and Ok and said, "phew," while wipping our brows. I said goodbye to him as he exited and he greeted me farewell. The scenery was beautiful. Rolling green hills and there was a good smell in the air. I crested a long hill while making way into Nazareth and heard rocks zing past my bike. One hit my spokes with a clang. I saw the little kids ahead of me run behind some cover. They were to blame. Then more rocks came from behind and to my right side. The kids opened fire on me with big rocks and many came close or crashed against my bike and spokes. I hollered at them and they laughed and continued until a man intervened and bitched at them. By this time I had passed.

I entered Nazareth and its little streets, thinking to myself, fuck this place. Then after pedaling around, decided, well I came this far so I explored the city and wouldn't you know it I met Richard. We talked up a storm. He'd been here an hour or so. We ate and then went trucking through the little streets with the gutters in the middle. I pushed my bike up the hills. Children helped push me also. They really push. They came running beside me for a long while. One Israeli boy insisted only he would push me. We went all over the town and this kid fought anybody else who tried to push. Finally he tires. I went to the hospice and left my bike. Richard and I went to Basilica of the Annunciation. It had the ruins of an old church underneath it. Mary had an angel visit her here. We enjoyed this church and watched a wedding precession come into the church. Israel girls sure were cute. We hiked up to the top of a hill above the city and enjoyed hiking through these quaint streets. There were children's voices everywhere. We met people. We made it to the top and I felt for Richards bum leg. How he got it I didn't ask. At the top was a grand view of this charming place. "I'll bet ol Jesus sat up here many a time," I said. "I think you're right," said Richard. We found a market and got a good bunch of veggies for $1 or 100 shukels. We hiked down to the hospice and cooked a great meal of food. Met other people and we had food left over, so I offered it to the other people at the next table. They were very gracious as the shops were closed now. We talked with a Dutch couple. The hospice was so lovely and the price was 300 sheckels a night. We played guitar a while in the nuns chamber and the place had great acoustics. I let a fart and the sound would amplify twice as loud in sound. So Richard and I exchanged a few volleys and both giggled like mischievous schoolboys. I think this would be a nice place to stay. It was so quiet here I couldn't forget it. The night was peacefull.

## Monday Feb. 13

Richard and I awoke and went through the narrow steep streets of Nazareth. I bought some food to take along with me to Tel Aviv. Richard wanted to buy a comb but dealing with the Arabs was too much hassle for him. They started out high in price and you must bargain them down. I packed up and we said goodbye. At about 9:30 I was heading down the steep mountain road from Nazareth. It was a nice village. I thought about Mary's trek to the south. Perhaps they went along this same route. The wind blew hard as I hit the plain of Megiddo. I fought that wind hard. It's so demoralizing when this happens. I went up some long grades and it was hard going with that wind. Then it started to get cold and foggy and soon rained. I headed toward the coast and the wind continued. I rode on all day and made it into Tel Aviv as darkness set in. I had seen many army tanks go past on trucks. God they were big tanks. Saw many soldiers on the road. They were pointing for a ride rather than thumbing as we do in the states. I motioned to one 'fingerhiker' to sit on my handlebars and he laughed. In Tel Aviv I found the youth hostel. It was 700 sheckels and I didn't feel like paying that much. Met a guy outside and he told me of a cheaper place. The manager came out and bitched him out for telling me. I went into the city in winter jacket and sweater, but with shorts on. I went to the market. Bought food and met other travelers. Went under a bridge in the city and cooked supper as it rained. The prices here were high so I had to budget. I went about cooking and eating and the weather cleared. I pedaled several miles to a park out of the city and camped there. A fellow told me not to because I'd get ripped off. I thought it was worth trying. I was at the park watching rats run around the grass. It was a beautiful night, with lovely cyprus trees in the moonlight. I got tired, set up my tent and went to sleep at 10:30.

## Tues. Feb. 14

Up with the dawn and I recalled getting up in the night as a cat was making noise in a trash can and I thought he was in my bags. I went into the city all the way to Jaffa(Yaffa). It was a sunny but cool morning. People didn't josh at me like in Turkey. The streets were nice and I saw that the IBM Building was beautiful. The girls looked pretty here. I asked a bike rider where a bike shop was. On the other side of town he told me. So I pedaled back there and found it and bought a chain. He didn't have derailler parts so I went to another bike shop and they didn't have any either. So I was told to go back to the other side of town. The man wanted to tell me exactly every turn and street on how to get there. I told him to just show me on the map where it was. He kept doing this," Goa down here, turna left, etc." I got so annoyed but finally he told me and I sped off as he was shouting, "Turn left on the ..." I found the other bike shops and these guys wouldn't help me. They'd try and sell me the wrong part. Some would talk to me. "No I don't have that they'd say." I'd say, "Do you have a water bottle?" They would say, "No," even if one was on the counter. So finally I got a little more demanding and figured it was my only hope to buy an entire derailler. This guy at a shop finally helped me out. He gave me a price cut he claimed. So I did buy one for about 2000 sheckels. But I felt so mad at these people as they left me stoned cold alone.

I hit the road for Jerusalem at 1 to 1:30pm. A good tailwind was blowing and now it was warm. I hit the hills and god it was hard going. They were steep going up and fast going down. I got a little weary at about 3pm, felt like collapsing off the bike. Had to ration my water. It was so agonizing at times as the kilos went by slow and my feet hurt real bad. I went over more hills then rounded some steep rugged hills and saw some buildings on top. At the top I had to go over another hill. Then it was down into the old city. I stopped to ask a gorgeous, dark, big eyed, shapely, stylish, beautiful woman for directions. What a goddess she was! Perked up, I came through the main gate (Jaffa Gate) very tired and thirsty. I saw a stand selling fresh orange juice and gulped down the glass. Met a fellow who told me where a youth hostel was. I went to a couple others then to the one he told me of. 200 Sheckels a night. I carried my bike up the steps. Met Dave from Anaheim Cal and we talked alot about Israel and forestry and the environment. He was really into working with nature. He was living in a Kabutz in Dorot and invited me. I met Doug also, who was from Anaheim. We talked about East Berlin quite alot. They were interested in my story. We went to a small cafe after I took a cold shower. We hiked down the narrow covered steets. Wow what a cool night, with a full moon, stars and being here in Jerusalem! We ate salad and fries, also some tasty bread. Talked about so many journeys we'd been along. This was perhaps the most exciting part of traveling. Meeting other people who were on a similar experience of visiting foreign places as you are. I walked along the streets and saw the Chamber of Holocaust (Zion Gate) and noticed the outer wall was riddled with bullet marks. I talked with Dave about his long hike down to the Dead Sea. He seemed prepared. But he was a little apprehensive.

## Wed Feb. 15

Awoke at 6am with Dave and he munched and drank down some water. We shook hands and greeted each other. He left as the mosques were blasting there prayers. I laid in my cozy bed and thought how good it was not to ride the bike today. I got up and stuffed my things into a cupboard. Nailed it shut and locked my bike to the bed. Then I set up a couple of booby trap noise makers if someone tried to rip me off. I went through the streets early on this clear, cold sunny morning. It was interesting to think that it hasn't changed very much from the days of Jesus. I bought some bread and was so hungry. I headed for tourist information and met Richard on the way. He and I talked about our past days and then went along to the old city. We went to the starting point of Jesus crucifixion. We were outside of Lions Gate, (Stephens Gate) and went into a church where Jesus was condemned. Walking along the Via Delorosa, we saw the numbered sections of his cross-carrying route to where he was crucified. It is an uphill hike to the Holy Sepulchre where Jesus was crucified, buried and resurrected. In the church is the most beautiful of stone work. I went into the tomb of Jesus. Richard and I were both impressed by the beauty and mystified by the events that took place here so long ago and how it so greatly changed the world. I thought it looked like Richard was tiring of hiking at my pace so I optioned to split up and to meet him later at the hostel. We sat outside the chamber of the holocaust and the bright sunshine made us both gidy and I threw a rock at a lizard and hit him on the head. He squirmed around, "By god!" Richard said, "You knocked him a good one." Then this Arab came by and tried to sell me some post cards and I said, "See you," and he said, "On the moon."

I hiked up to Al Aqsa mosque and entered to visit the rock where Abraham nearly sacrificed his son Isaac. Then I went to the Jewish sector and then to the Wailing Wall. This was a most interesting place of sacred worship for the Jews where people chant they're prayers and bob heads to the wall. It was the sound of so many people into they're ceremonies that intrigued me. I noticed the wall had a dirty level from people touching it. A fellow tourist wanted his wife to take a picture of him by these chanters and she made a big stink and they argued. Oh tourists can be cranky!

I walked up to the Mount of Olives and saw many tombs on the rocky slope. There was a wonderous Russian Orthodox church. I sat up there and pondered about Jerusalem. It was a gorgeous view. The gold mosque. The enormous wall surrounding the city, the stories of Jesus. I recalled back a couple months before when I saw the newest Bob Dylan album cover of Infidels and remembered this is the view he put with himself on the album cover.

Walked through Lions Gate and was intrigued by the monstrous doors. I moved the big door a bit and this Arab fellow in a white robe shouted at me about touching the door. "Hey what you do with door?" He said to me continuing, "Who tell you to touch door?" "Jesus tells me," I said, responding back while walking away from him. "No can Jesus say OK to touch the door," he said. I rebounded, "Yes, Jesus say close the door." "You talk to Jesus?" he shouted. "Yes Jesus talks to me," I said. "Jesus is dead, nobody talks to Jesus! You crazy if you talk to Jesus!" he argued, then said, "No touch the door!" I walked away and he went on and on about something. The important thing from this experience is how quick witted are the Arabs, how fiery they are and how playfully they use language.

I walked up into the new city and went to the market place and stocked up on food. Prices were not cheap. Went back to the hostel and an old man wanted me to move from the upstairs to the downstairs. I told him I didn't like that idea. I mixed up some food and wrote in my journal. Richard came along and we ate together. We went to a pub and again chowed down. I smuggled a sandwich in my bag. We really felt like getting pissed(drunk). I said, "Let's split a beer." It was so expensive. We gulped half a beer and went to the wailing wall. We both got a little silly. Noticed paper stuffed into the wall. Richard said, "It's rather peaceful standing here facing the wall. We mimicked what the Jews do against the wall. I thought the wall was somehow intriguing me, by its massive construction, but Richard thought it was full of sacred ghosts, and that is it. We went back to the 'ranch' and had a cup of tea still feeling a little giddy. We were good friends now. We could talk about anything and I felt he understood me and vice a versa.

## Thursday Feb. 16

We got up at about 6:30am and packed up. Richard helped me carry all my things down the steps. We went by Davids Tower and ate some goodies. Then we agreed to meet in En Gedi, a little village along the Dead Sea. He seemed like he was down about something. But I was eager to see the Dead Sea. We shook and he said, "I wish I was on a push bike." I said, "It has it's good moments." I knew I had a good down hill ahead, which was something to look forward too.

I headed east out of Jerusalem and the terrain turned dry and barren. The road follows a dry and heavily eroded canyon and it is a long downhill ride all the way to the Dead Sea. It looked like rugged countryside, a wilderness area without food or water. I pondered Christ's walk in this desert. The farther down I went, the warmer it became. At the bottom, there was an unmarked intersection and I toiled which way to go. Along came a couple of Englishmen who said Jericho was nice. So I turned north and pedaled to Jericho to see the old legendary city. It looked like just a clump of dirt and archaeological trenches. While there, a U.S. tourist bus pulled up and out hopped some guys with big radios and 'I love U.S.A'. shirts on. They talked with me and wondered if I was out to set a world record on the TV show, "That's Incredible." I noticed the native people seemed very friendly here.

After looking at the mud of Jericho, I turned around and headed south and rode along the

Dead Sea, where the air felt warm. Occasionally military jets would fly low overhead. With Jordan on the east side of this inland sea, this was a tense part of Israel. The canyon walls on my right were quite rugged and colorful. This was where the Dead Sea Scrolls were found. I read a roadside sign warning against swimming in the sea and to be off the beach after dark. I crested some hills and felt good to have nice weather. I rolled into the beach at En Gedi and to my delight met Richard. "Wow you didn't take long," he said. We were glad to be together again and looked into camping and food. We thought the town of En Gedi was further down the road and Richard hiked a ways down the road. I said I would ride up ahead to look for the town, as supplies were needed, but found out there was no town so I wheeled back to tell him. To see him walking I couldn't help but feel pity for him. His one leg seemed like a club. He stood out as he carried a pack and hobbled down the road. The locals all stared at him with astonishment. I told him there was no town of En Gedi, just the beach site. But there was a Quabutz (Kibbutz) and I pedaled up to see them, but they wouldn't let me in. So I went back and met Richard and we picked a campsite on the beach.

I went for a swim in the Dead Sea and the water was rather cool. Wow what an experience it was to swim in that salty water. The buoyancy was just amazing. I could lay back and float as if I had a raft under me. I must say the water was terribly salty, but it was great fun to swim in. Under the hot sun I met this girl from Uraguay who was a real fox. She came swimming along with me, but we could not communicate, as she spoke Spanish. Richard felt reserved and I attributed it to his leg. He didn't want to swim. "Float on over to Jordan and get a stamp on your hand," he told me jokingly. We showered and I washed his back off of sand. We went to the store and bought a load of food for a good price. Richard was very interested in skimping on money so we got along good. We cooked a good meal and enjoyed a brilliant sunset and the ominous full moon rising. We played a little guitar. An Israeli fellow joined us. A man invited us all over to his fire. I met some other travelers and a girl from Germany and Norway. I played a couple of songs of my own writing and received favorable response. I talked to two Israelis soldiers. One just got out of the service while the other was still in. They didn't like the Army. We traded the guitar around and a couple different hands played their songs. One girl I met was from Vancouver B.C.

We were all forewarned about thieves that come along in the night and as one Israeli Arab who was rather humorous said, "They can take the sox off your feet without awakening you." He said, "Zoe, zoe like co, co, go Oh, Oh," and I said make "Goo Goo." We all got a kick out this word play.

I was annoyed by the thought of thieves ripping me off and so secured my things inside the tent. A tall blonde girl from Norway invited me to go for a swim, but I was concerned about leaving my articles, and sadly decided against it.

## Friday Feb 17

The sun kissed the edge of a Jordan mountain as we awoke this morning. It was a good night of sleep, even though I slept with one eye open in case a knife blade slipped into my tent. I talked with Richard about going on to Beer Sheva. He wanted to spend more time here. So I walked over to greet the Vancouver gal and we talked about the border crossing into Egypt. She warned me that they will want me to exchange lots of money at a bad rate, they might not even give me a visa. I helped get her campfire started and an Israeli gal pointed out some places on the map and I joked with them. I again said good travels to Richard and felt that emptiness beginning when I separate from new friends. We agreed to leave a message at the Poste Restante in Cairo, last names first. I was off and I saw Richard hobble down the rocky beach. I felt for him. I headed down the road. Enjoying this warm morning but feeling sorry not to spend more time in EnGedi. My money was low and I didn't want to exchange more. So it was best to keep moving. I dreaded to think of my mountain climb ahead. "It's not impossible," keeps coming to my mind. I wheeled into New Zorae, about 10:30am. I had seen other hikers on the road. Also heard sonic booms as many times military jets flew over. I went into a store and could have ripped it off but my conscience told me don't steal. So I found the lady and ended up buying some biscuits for about $2.50. Wow it was expensive.

The lakeshore terrain turned decidedly dry, next to the blue-green sea, with white salt flats. There were strange salt formations on the south end of the Dead Sea, not unlike those from the stories of Lots wife being turned to stone.

Just past the ancient city of Masada, I saw a couple at a campground who looked so much like my friends John and Jolane. I went up excitedly to greet them, only to discover, when I got close enough, that it was not them. It bummed me out.

I headed up the steep long grade and the going was tough but my pace steady. The view behind me of the Dead Sea was fantastic. Not many cars passed, I thought of songs and women and getting to the top of the mountain. I passed sea level and then went up and up and into a desert. At noon I arrived in Arad and stopped into a supermarket for supplies. I bought lots of food, though it was very expensive. Today the stores closed early, and were not open on Saturday, so I had to hurry. I met a girl from Steamboat Springs, Colorado. I was given an ice cold water refilling in my canteens from a friendly Israeli shop worker and then left town and headed down across fairly flat roads occasioned with some hills.

Made good time getting to Beer Sheva where I met a man on a bike and he told me where there was a hostel. I went to the hostel but it was 800 Sheckels a night so I said no thanks. Went to the city and bought one potato, one onion, a green pepper for 100 sheckels or one dollar. I bought a falafa at a stand and stuffed it myself with everything. The clerk got a kick out of that. I bought some sweets and headed out of town, but soon saw a forested recreation center and asked a guy where a camping place was and he pointed down the road. So I went there and there was nothing. I returned and asked another guy and he told me to go back to the other side of town. I asked about the woods right here and he said, "You have tent?" "Yes," I said. "OK, yes you find tables and water-its ok down there." So I wheeled down a terribly rutted road to find an excellent camping area. I had it all to myself. I pulled up to a table and cooked dinner as the sun set. I ate a hot falafa and saw a tower like structure with a hut that was high up on top of the stilts. I climbed up into it along with the bike and set up a camp inside. Played a little guitar and felt lonely. With the stars and moon shining overhead, you'd think I'd be in bliss, but was not. I retired to sleep early at 9pm.

**Saturday Feb. 18**

The night was uneventful, except for one person who walked underneath but did not see me, and the day announced itself cool and sunny. I climbed out of my tree house after a good sleep and hit the road with a good tailwind. Made good time to the Dorot intersection. I sat and wrote in my diary until a fellow came along and asked me where I was going. I responded, "To Cairo." He opened his eyes wide and leapt back. "Drink a little water," he said. I pedaled up to the Quibutz in Dorot. All the shops were closed as it was Saturday, a holy day in Israel. I saw two cute girls walking down the road. While entering into Dorot gate there was a fellow named Dave from California. He pointed me in the proper direction. I went down some roads and met another couple who told me where to find Dave from New York. So I pedaled a short distance and saw Doug out talking to a gal. He saw me riding up and said, "Ha! I don't believe it. You came!" He forgot my name but I was soon introduced to everyone. Dave was sleeping. I said, "I have to see if Dave is alive after his hike to the Dead Sea." When he opened his eyes he looked at me and said, "Elijah, I don't believe it." I took a hot shower and we went to the dining room and I gorged myself on meatballs, salad and drank Coke. Mmmm. Then we went to the club house and ate all kinds of snacks. Pastry like cookies and orange drink. I met all these friendly people. Then I got a tour by Dave around the Quibutz. We talked about the lifestyle. "We make about $20 per month but they take out $2 for tax so we end up making about $18. But everything on a quibutz is free. Food, shelter and medical," he said.

Dave told me all about his adventurous hike to the Dead Sea. He had a difficult time descending the final way. A fellow quibutzer told him to never do it again. We went into the chicken house where Dave works. He showed me his job of picking up eggs for many hours each day. No wonder he is a bit strange. He is kind, but different. He picked up a chicken and it went wild on him. We went back to the tennis court and met some friends. The girls were nice. Collins from South Africa was kind of crazy. A Japanese fellow was cool.

We went to a house and I played some songs on the guitar. They applauded. The Japanese fellow played some also. We had a grand time. Played until supper time. Then we went to eat and I again gorged myself on salad and potatoes. I talked at the dinner table to Ceasar from Brazil, who spoke five languages. He was a lawyer by trade, and had been traveling two years. Each person that I talked to had an experience of travels. Each told of how long and how far they'd gone.

We all went back to the 'volunteers hut' and I met an English gal. Dave and I had a heart to heart talk. He told me he didn't like drinking and merry going and he liked Christianity and was content with his lifestyle. He wanted to do something for God and Israel, but there were little problems, like pushy people and odd habits. He started to make so many excuses that I realized he was lacking in self confidence. I wondered if this was his L.A. upbringing was coming out. There was a party for Doug going on and everyone wanted me to join them so I said to Dave,

"I think youv'e found you're mission in god with Israel's problems." He told me he wanted to do something about it.

I went to crazy Collins place and everyone insisted I play a song so I played Tangled Up In Blue by Dylan. It roused everyone. We drank wine and they did some songs of there own. They sang the Israeli patriot song, Ava Naglia. Everyone clapped and sang and we had such a good time. The Japanese fellow broke a string on my guitar. He said, "I give you a new one in Japan. I played my own song, "Turning the world Blue" and the guy from Holland liked it. I was invited to stay the night at Collins. We talked as we laid in our beds. He said the best part of quibutz life is the people. He said he had met more good people in four months than ever. I said, "it is too bad travelers weren't running the world." We chatted about our countries and then got quiet.

# Chapter 11

# THE LAND OF SAND...EGYPT

**Sunday Feb. 19th**

I awoke to hear the head quibutzer open Collins door and ask who I was. "A friend," he said adding. "He staying the night leaving today." "I hope so," said the lady. "Clean this place up, out and in," she said slamming the door. I went to breakfast and again ate very good food and much of it. Went on a tour of the quibutz with Doug, Collins and Robin. We went into the foundry and saw how they make molds and pour molten metal into them. Went to see auto lathes and machinists working. There was even a carrot-canning factory. It was all part of life on a quibutz. Then I had the feeling I shouldn't leech off these people anymore. Most of them at breakfast told me to stay. And I met Sophie, what a babe from Canada. But I felt the need to move only because it hurts more to go when you make good friends. The landlady came by and tried to tell me I couldn't make it to Egypt on a bike. So I got pissed and told her, "they told me I'd never ride across U.S.A but I did that." Finally she said, "be careful and send me a post card from Japan." "Ok, what is your name," I asked. "Mariana," she said adding, "that would be nice."

I gave all my best to everybody and they gave me a royal sendoff with applause. I got down the road aways and realized I really wanted to stay there. I wanted to go back, call home and kick back, I liked everyone so much. I felt very sad and heartbroken as I pedaled to the Israeli/Egyptian border. The wind blew hard against me. I made slow time. The day was nice though. I passed lizards sunning and enjoyed the changing landscape. I passed two soldiers holding big guns and joked with them. Then at the border I saw them and they helped me through to ride across the "no mans land" between the two countries. I passed more soldiers with big rifles and helmets. The Egyptian soldiers dressed different than the Israeli. It felt tense, I wanted to go faster and get out of there.

I went through Israeli customs and paid 920 sheckels. Damn! That was an expensive exit fee. Then I went through a maze of obstacles and entered into Egyptian customs.

The man at the customs wanted me to exchange $150 for Egyptian money at a very bad rate. I knew it would be better to wait until seeing a bank. I pleaded with him and the guy at the bank exchange said he would accept $100 if it was ok with the captain. I went back to the agent who wanted me to go back and exchange the full $150. I told him I felt it was too dangerous to carry alot of cash while riding my bike. He was adamant, "Go back, go back." He said. Then he saw my guitar. He looked at it and said, "Do you like John Denver?" I said, "Yes." "Can you play a song for me?" "Yes," I said adding, "But my guitar is missing one string." "Oh please," he pleaded. I got out the guitar and just started to sing Country Roads, when a large group of travelers came up behind me. "Fine, fine," the captain said and waved his head and said, "You can go." We shook hands and he said, "It's ok, welcome to my country." I went through customs and I paid $2.50 pounds Egyptian for entry. The exchange rate was 81 pounds to $100. In all, I probably saved $50 because of that John Denver song.

I pedaled down the road and the wind was bad. The countryside was so shabby. It was like going from USA to Mexico. I stopped and bought some goodies and kids crowded around me. I went on down the road as the day got late. As dusk was falling, I found a hidden green patch of grass by a railroad track, which was no longer in use. People were ambling across the desert. I cooked supper as a guy pounded on railroad ties. He needed wood to burn and was taking apart the ties. I finished eating and was relaxing while looking up at the constellation of Orion. A young guy came along in the darkness. He came up to me and sat and talked english to me. His name was Suley. He was a student in Cairo. He was very kind. He told me of Egypt and I told him of the U.S. We laughed about buying a woman, which he says he must do. He stayed with me for two hours. Then he ambled on into the night. I set up the tent and crawled in under the light of beautiful stars. There was no light pollution here. I put everything into my tent for protection from thieves. Once inside, I listened to the radio. What a day it had been!

**Monday Feb. 20**

Got up with the sun and packed up. People were out walking the desert already. I went down the highway feeling hungry and thirsty and wheeled into El Arish. I went right through town and didn't even see the center. I stopped and asked at a hotel, "Where is El Arish," They told me to go back. The guy at the hotel wanted my name and address. I went back on bad roads and found the town. I asked many people for Mr. Mustafe Baker. They finally told me where to find him. His name had been given to me by a guy yesterday. It turns out he is the governor of the Sinai. As I went through this dive of a town, I bought two delicious little danish-apple tarts. They were the very best tasting that I ever had. I thought, oh this is gonna be great, I'll be eating these all over Egypt, but never found them again. I then met the aides of Mr. Baker. They escorted me along and offered me tea and told me to wait. I was given a cheap map of the Sinai. I told them where I was from. Then they said, "follow us." I was escorted back to the main road. A guy got me some water, waved goodbye and I pedaled on. Strange.

There was a dry head wind as I entered the sandy desert of the Sinai. At every place people would say hello to me. Kids would run out to the road. Some of them I ignored, because it was treacherous riding, hitting a hole would ruin my bike.

On this dry stretch of road, under the hot mid day sun, I met a biker couple from England. We stopped and talked of our travels. I pried them for knowledge about Egypt. It was so good to meet somebody else. This was a rare place for it. I felt a lack of confidence about Egypt, but they were nice enough to brief me. We traded maps. They gave me a great map of Egypt and the Sinai. I then moved on.

I saw some kids on the road and rang the bell at them. This one kid hit my bike with a rock. I turned around and picked up a big rock and chased him. He ran like hell. I swore at him and tossed the rock away. I then went into town and bought a coke. While there, some kids hung from the neck of my guitar and I hollered at them. I rode on into the late afternoon sun and could see only sand in all direction. At times the highway was covered with sand. My thin tires would not go through it. I had to walk the bike. On one section of roadside I saw a snake side-winding through the sand.

I looked for places to camp the night. The day wore thin and I continued down the road and spotted a vacant house. I pushed the bike through the deep sand for about 500 feet and snuck in and cleared some smelly shits off the floor. I cooked dinner and set up my tent and listened to the BBC. The stars were spectacular and I mushed up an orange in a cup with water and sugar and enjoyed the tasty treat.

## Tuesday Feb. 21

With an early start to the day, I struggled to push the bike back through the deep sand and finally again headed south down the road, past sand dunes and occasional palm trees. The road was good. I was stopped by some students, who greeted me good morning and asked me my country and my name. I said, "shalom," to many people and waved. It was very dry here, and thus was careful to ration the water. I saw an old timer riding a camel and he hopped off to drink water from a pail some one had left on the desert. In the far off distance to the west, I could see a ship that looked like it was abandoned in the desert. It looked like a mirage, but it was in fact upon the Suez Canal. A couple of bike riders (Arabs) came along with me and they really put it all to keep up to my pace.

I started to see many blown up tanks and others that were apparently in operation along the roads. There were also many soldiers. All along the road were signs saying 'no photos.' I learned this debris was from the 1967 through 76 Arab/Israeli war. I saw some tanks blown to pieces. Many times I was stopped by soldiers. Some just wanted to shake my hand. Others to confer with me. "No photos," they warned me. I really did want to take photos of this debris. I continued to El Kantara and noticed everything in this town was blown up. I stopped for a Coke and a sweet breakfast of apple danish. I went down a ways and saw the blue ribbon of the Suez and a ferry that was crossing the canal. A ship followed me along the canal. The ships name was "Welcome." I went to the ferry and bought a ride across the canal, which looked aqua blue and quite stark against the desert landscape. On the other side I weaseled some good water from a cafe by pretending to buy some biscuits. He seemed shocked, when I left, as one must pay for water here.

I rode on with a good tailwind and saw a bad car accident. People here drive like crazy fools. They were alive, but bloody and an ambulance soon arrived. There were very green eucalyptus trees, on this side of the Suez Canal and very lush, green vegetation and many strawberry plantations. I bought a few of the tasty berries, and thought, I will enjoy eating more of these while in Egypt, but never found them again. I rode a little farther and soon entered a flat, barren desert.

A truck went by and laid on the horn. I shook my head at him in disgust. The road was getting busier with traffic. Miles went past and then the truck driver stopped to check his tires. I passed by him and rang my bell the whole time. He laughed and got to jumping around. A little while later, when he passed me again he blew every horn he had and stuck his Arab head out the window laughing.

I thought about this barren land and wondered how people can live here. The day wore on and I was making 20 kilometers per hour. I calculated I could make it to Cairo at 7pm, but it would be hell considering the amount of traffic and getting lost, so I decided to camp the night. Finally 35 kilometers from Cairo, I found an old house and pulled in quickly to hide. There was no roof and a surprisingly cold wind blew. I cleaned the floor of feces, cooked a dinner and rationed my water. I set the tent up and it was difficult with the wind blowing.

After dinner I stood back to look at the stars and pondered what an Israeli had said to me. "You like to be alone I think." I thought aloud to myself, "Yes, I do like to be alone. But I don't know why." I stood at this wall with a window cut out. As there was no roof on this house, I could see through the window out into the world. And above I could see some stars. I thought how much my life is like this room. I thought how I feel trapped in a world with walls and only small openings to see out of. Why? I traced it back to my childhood. I was a protected child. My father always was so steady and so right in his ways. My mother would tell me-push me-leave little private room for me. I had sisters that I had good fun with but kept a certain distance from. And I tied it all together with my certain lack of love, a real open love. The guidance in love from my parents left me the feeling of being unwanted. But just that extra touch is what I wanted. And so I was living in a world of searching for love. And I understand why I took art up. It was to try and explain to my family this feeling I had about my emotions and I see why I often painted lonely figures or searching icons. But I admit to not doing anything to help the problem. I felt it wasn't my job. I wasn't head of the family. And I did so many things on my own because I guess that way nobody could deny me of my own achievements, which meant so much to me. I didn't want to be handed down anything.

So I got this terrific rush of feelings about my life and this room and thus I decided I would go ahead with life. That I have been searching and learning and now I would continue to take my own steps. I watched far off an approaching train and it neared and then it thundered past and I felt the walls crumble down and like a metaphor of my own struggles was therefore uplifted from my past onto a new road to the future.

## Wednesday Feb. 22

I slept good but felt so dirty and was eager to make it to Cairo. I pedaled down the road and went past many people waiting for a bus. I saw how dirty everyplace is. Then I went past the airport and I came into the city. The streets sucked. There were huge, dirty potholes. Everything looked dinjy and run down, even the people looked disheveled. People were hanging from the sides and rear of moving buses. I continued on and found my way to a telegram station. I had no map of Cairo so I asked for directions to the tourist information center. A fellow helped me go in the right direction. I saw many traffic jams. There was broken glass on the road. People were crawling everywhere in downtown Cairo. A car slammed against a tree. More glass was on the road. I weaved in and out of cars. It was mayhem. Finally I found a place for a Coke and ate. I found a tourist bureau and was given a map. I pedaled to the Post Office to see if Richard had left a message. There was none. I looked for a hotel and met a fellow on the street who told me where a cheap hotel was. A crowd gathered around to look at me, to stare. I felt like an astronaut. I checked out with a travel agency the price of a plane ticket to India or Greece. It was very expensive.

Before riding off, I was talking to a friendly Arab when a couple of chicks walked past and we talked. They were from the U.S. We stood there and talked for about one hour and then they led me to a sweet shop. They told me of the hotel where they were staying. I ate sweet baklava like goodies with them. They were good, friendly, honest chicks and having a ball in crazy Cairo. There names were Suzy and Debbie.

I went my own way and searched for a hotel. After a long search I couldn't find anything so I went to Suzy and Debbies hotel and get a room for 225 pounds a night. I washed my clothes. I met my roommates, a couple from New Zealand and Australia. They'd been traveling for 4 years. We talked of travels. Wearing my still wet sweater, I headed into the city to eat dinner. Found a place to eat for one pound. It was a good salad and lasagna. I then went on a munching spree and bought a strawberry drink and nuts. Then I walked around to see all these people who so often say hello and welcome. I went back to the hotel to sleep.

## Thursday Feb. 2

It was a very sleepless night and one filled with crazy fleas and mosquito's bugging me. I got up early and wrote in my diary and ate a breakfast of bread and jelly with cheese. I talked awhile with a fellow named Donald from New Zealand. He told me of his five years of traveling. He had a son in California and now he was a world traveler as well. I asked him about having a student card and he told me what a help they are for getting discounts. I asked where I could find one and he told me he had an old one which was of no use to him. So I offered to buy it but he gave it to me instead. So I spent the day running down to some shops to buy pencils and erasers to forge my student card. I went to some travel places and found the cost of flying to Bombay or to Greece. I asked so many people questions of where I could go and for how much. I went to the India embassy and they said one day for a visa. I went to the Saudi Arabia embassy and they told me I could not ride a bike in their country. Travel was open only for business transit and Muslims. So I said screw it.

Back at the hotel I worked on my I.D and finished it about 3pm and showed it to others and it looked ok. I had to go to a travel agent to use a typewriter and made a mistake and went back. I had to go to a stationary store and this girl just didn't want to help me. She would act sickly. I would see what I needed and she just didn't help me. I did not know why. So I asked another man and he to was reluctant. So I reached across and got my hand on this pencil and looked at it. They got all pissed. I guess you cannot look at things here, you must buy them. I looked it over and finally bought it. They have such a screwed up organization. I had to pay for it at another counter. Everywhere in this crazy city people ridiculed me as I pedaled or walked by. Comments that were slandish hellos and "Whas yer name?" were common. It was very annoying. I had to go to a photo shop and waited so long in line.

Back at the hotel I talked with Debbie and Bill. We went to their favorite cafe and ate a good meal for only 75 peastas. Then Debbie went back and Bill and I hiked into many back roads of the city. We discovered tent markets and bazaar's. There is a huge meat market, complete with the heads of cattle which for sale. Eeech. Do they really eat the brains and tongue of cows? We went down this alley and some guy said, "Hubbly, bubbly? You want hubbly bubbly?" So we followed him through some curtains and then into this room where some guys were tokin on a big water pipe with hashish in a pipe. A fellow would take hot coals and pour it on the hashish. Bill toked on the pipe and said, "Heh, it's hashish alright." So we agreed to pay 1 pound for a few hits. We then went our way and bought a beer at a food stall. We quickly downed it and met some Egyptian men who offered to escort us along to the Cairo Hilton. We definitely got a good buzz from the libations. An enjoyable talk was had with our Egyptian friends. They were good fellows, who were clean and courteous.

We all stopped to watch workmen dropping a crane bucket into a hole that must have been 200 feet deep. It was a sloppy muck. They said it was a new building under construction, possibly the new Cairo museum.

Bill and I went into the Hilton and our Egyptian friends split. We went upstair and watched the casino gamblers. Bill tried his luck but lost five dollars. It was a Las Vegas like atmosphere, a place to waste money, which was too precious to me. A drink was about $7. Rumour was that showgirls were there, but we got cheap and left.

We went back down the streets and while walking back, got hassled occasionally by Arabs. We both felt more hostile and pissed off here in Cairo and wondered why.

## Friday Feb. 24

I had terribly annoying dreams of murder and blood. I think the tension in the city caused it. Debbie also said she had bad dreams. Many people complained of stomach sickness from the food. But I think it's from nerves. I ate breakfast and went out to find the streets rather mellow and so I talked awhile to a couple from the states.

I went down to the city center and passed through toward Giza and the great pyramids. Again I felt this aggression and ridicule towards me as a 'bicycling white tourist.' I headed down the road in the morning sun and was enjoying a blasting tailwind. I rode with an Egyptian biker who gave it his all, as he had to pass me. After awhile he tired at my steady pace and fell back.

I was looking for a market and suddenly saw the pyramid of Cheops and it startled me so. I knew what they all looked like but this first impression just grabbed me like I awoke from a dream. It has a perfect geometric shape. I cycled for some time to get closer to the pyramid. It

grew more impressive, the nearer I became. There is a feeling of greatness, as if you are entering greatness, like I felt when as a child, seeing my grandfather lying in his casket. I toured around the colossal great pyramid and viewed the 3 ton rocks and their size didn't surprise me so much as the tremendous number of them. I was impressed with the granite slabs that covered the pyramid but now were mostly gone except for the bottom sides. I went up by Mankeen pyramid and then down by Chechran.

I was confronted by a Arab camel driver, who was so persistent and pesterous to me to go for a ride on his camel. At first I thought to tell him to buzz off, but then I felt a desire to ride with him, though not to do this touristy cliche. Finally I did agree to pay him 1 pound, with the assurance that nothing would be stolen from my bike, which was locked near a truck. The camel driver had the huge beast kneel down and I stepped up on its shoulder and swung a leg over the hump and sat upon him. The driver did the same and sat behind me. Then the camel stood up, he gave some simple commands and we started off ambling toward the Sphinx. I was amazed at the strength of these beasts and at their agility to traverse rough ground. We went down some hard trails with slippery sand on rocks of marble and down steps and this camel was velvety smooth. My guide gave me a little history and said all of this was and still is a sacred place, a temple for the after life.

The guide dismounted and took a photo of me on the camel, with the Great Pyramid in the background nestled under my hand. We went back up the steps and he got the camel to run and my god the creatures can really move over sand. He said they can go 40 days without food or water, and that they live up to 25 years of age. I paid the kind guide a little extra for the great ride and headed back to the Sphinx.

At the Sphinx, I met an Egyptian man who wanted to come to the U.S.A. and seemed sad about living in Egypt. "It is so hard to make a good life here," he said. He took my photo and I think he wanted money or something from me.

I pedaled back to the museum and used my fake I.D. to get half price off the admission. I was fascinated with the grand tombs carved from black marble and some of white marble. One had markings on it of men that looked like they had space helmets with antennas. No other tomb I saw had these. They were so finely carved and painted that it was remarkable.

I viewed King Tut's gold mask and had to go back to look at it many times, as I loved that work of art. It was just incredibly beautiful. The chariots and tombs of gold are fantastic. I started to get the impression that everything in the museum dealt with the after life. I sensed everything was focused in that one aim. To send the dead into the next world with all their 'earthly goods' so they could be helped along on the journey. They had this one aim, to go to heaven. I felt this wasn't so beneficial to Egyptian society because it is kind of a waste of talent and resource to put something so valuable into a tomb and to know that you will never see it again. Of course they intended for it to be seen, by God in the next world. They're goal was internal life. But did they get it? Well in some ways this is the new world that now looks at these works from the far distant past. Yes, I think they knew something of the secret to eternal life, and though they didn't want the same old world to awaken to and for us to take they're riches, but we realize how valuable these works are that they left for us in the museums. They are a kind of time capsule. It's almost as if we are 'the heaven' that they sought after.

I went back to the hotel and played guitar with my friends from Holland, France and Brazil. I went to supper with Debbie and Bill and ate lasagna. The people on the streets of Cairo just seem so rude at times. They ridicule us and harass us. I said goodbye to Bill and Debbie and went into the city for goodies and along the way met a fellow from Lebanon whose name was Murat. He spoke good english and told me about his country. He said, "Our country is a battle ground for U.S.S.R. and the U.S.A." He felt that the war will go on until all the Lebanese are dead, on the losing side because they feel so strong about their religion and beliefs. He said friends come out of Lebanon and go to Cairo and they are very nervous. I was given a strawberry treat by Murat and met a talk hungry Canadian and we all chatted but I had to go. I ended our meeting with handshakes and left the two of them talking.

I returned to the hotel and met a fellow in my room who had the most hard luck tale I've yet to hear. His boat was stolen from Rhodes. It was taken to Marmaris and then set adrift and was picked up in Beirut where the Israeli Navy supposedly ripped off everything he owned. They gave the boat back with a hole in the hull. He spent two months chasing after it. He said he had to get rid of it and sold it to a security guard for almost nothing. It was hand built in 1971. There was something about this fellow I didn't like and yet felt for him and his dilemma.

## Saturday Feb. 25

I got up and went to write a letter to send to Liana in Athens in hopes to compare the price of air flights from Athens to Bombay. Also I bought some cupcakes, returned to the hotel and packed my things while talking with friends at breakfast. I got a tip on a place to get U.S. cash from traveler's checks. Ordinarily the banks will only give Egyptian pounds in exchange for travelers checks. It was more valuable to get U.S. dollars.

I discovered that my bike had a reflector ripped off and the light in back was gone as well. Also the lock bag was partially removed. I got my things together, packed up and prepped the bike while a crowd watched. I pedaled away at 10am, through Cairo and went through town. I stopped at an American Express Office and cashed a travelers checks for cash. They gave me a receipt for this, but I found out a receipt is useless to show the customs officials this document. It is all part of the beauracracy to try and take more money from the tourists for Egypt.

# THE WHEELS OF FRIEND

I paid a guard 10 p for watching my bike. He didn't seem very happy with that since it's equal to 10 cents. Oh well.

I pedaled down along the Nile. Everyone beeped at me and said hello. Each time I'd turn they'd laugh at me and I'd always hit a chuckhole or run over glass, so I thought from now on I won't look at these hecklers anymore. I stopped to ask people directions. They're only interest was to ask me the value of my bike and where I was from. They had trouble reading a map. I went into a small town with my helmet on, short pants and sunglasses and people just swarmed about me. I ignored them and was very stern. I continued on and went over some of the worst roads I'd ever been on. It was huge, sharp gravel. I thought about these people and why they act the way they do. They screamed at me and would do anything to get my attention. Whistles. car horns, truck horns, shouting hello and hey-mister! I figure they did it because they wanted something. Maybe attention? Maybe they felt they wanted recognition because they were jealous of us western people who come in on shiny bicycles and have cameras and always have lots of money. They probably wanted what we have and they just didn't see Egyptian people with these things and so they were perplexed between envy and aggression.

I rode into Beni Seuf and asked a fellow if he spoke english. "Yes," he said. I asked him where is a hotel. He took me to one and they wanted too much money. So we went into this town and was like a zoo of people. They all made crazy faces and run up to me and the little kids went bananas. My guide told the kids to go away. We looked at another and another hotel. Finally we found one for 250 paestas. Then my friend asked me if I wanted to stay with him. I said, "Yes." So we went walking to his place. I told him I was hungry so he showed me a cheap place with good lasagna and spicy sandwiches. After wolfing down my food, which he paid for, we walked about town and everyone stared and anytime I stopped I was mobbed. My friend's name was Khalid, he was a student of law. We talked of Islamic laws, thieves had there hands cut off. He repeated several times to me that he was a good Muslim. He took me walking all over the town and all the while I was walking my heavily loaded bicycle. It was very tiring. It was much easier to ride it, than walk it. He wanted to find a taxi, but one wasn't to be found. Then we went to his cousin's house. While sitting on the front step Khalid asked me, "Now what do you want to do?" I couldn't understand this guy. He had invited me to stay at his house but for some reason had not taken me there and now that it was late, about 10pm, he was dumping me. "I want to find a hotel," I explained. "Ok, we go find a hotel," he said standing up and waving me on.

Before we could check into the hotel Khalid said we had to register my name with the police. We went to a police station and waited and waited. Then went to another police station and waited. It was very annoying. The police officer wanted my passport, which I handed him, at which he commenced to interrogate me where I was from, where I had been. He held my passport and threatened to keep it for the night, but I refused. Finally I was given it back and Khalid led me to a cheap hotel. It was a real dive. A shit hotel! The rooms were divided with eighth inch hardboard walls. Bugs were everywhere. There was a train station just behind my room. I was exhausted, it would have to make do. I played a song for Khalid on the guitar and at 11pm we went walking back out to town for some sweet goodies which Khalid called Arabian specialties. He then had to go home and we parted with a handshake. I was dumbfounded why he mislead me into saying I could stay at his home. Someone had said something to him, undoubtedly.

Back at the hotel I entered my room, which was no bigger than a couple of toilet stalls, while a train hissed away for the next 45 minutes. I used tissues as earplugs, but could not sleep, until it left. It was very hot and dry this evening and my sleeping bag is to hot, adding to the discomfort.

## Sunday Feb. 26

The men in the room next to mine were talking away and snoring at 4am and I finally had enough and said, "Shhh," at which they laughed. It was hard to sleep with trains pulling up every hour. I got up at 7 and headed down the street and bought a sandwich and tried to eat it but a crowd developed around me, so I pedaled on. I felt like I had an ulcer in my stomach. I headed south on a good road on this sunny morning, past stucco buildings ablaze in the morning light. All along the road people would come running to me to say hello or goodbye or something silly and unintelligable. If I didn't say anything they threw rocks at me. I discovered it was dangerous to say hello to them as I always seemed to hit a hole or a truck just missed me. One must watch the road intently, or else risk crashing the bike.

By midmorning I didn't care for these people anymore, so I tried ignoring all of them. I wouldn't even look at the fuckers! I stopped for lunch and a crowd of boys gathered around me to watch me eat. One came over and got smart and I pushed him away. Then they all backed off and just watched me. They seemed so stupid in there pajamas. And they were filthy dirty. I continued on and had several near misses with big trucks. Every car beeped its horn madly even if the road was clear. People walked out in front of me. I hit the brakes and shouted at them. It was madness! I pulled into Dairut for dinner and couldn't find a restaurant. No place had any appearance to a cafe. A boy helped me along as a crowd followed. I pulled my bike right into the cafe. I tried to look to see what food they had cooking but none was displayed. This guy came over and said, "Come, come," and he grabbed me by the arm as I wanted to go another direction he pulled on me and I slammed my fist into his chest and said, "Get away!" He backed off and I went and sat down. These people all stared at me. Outside of the window, they stared in. An english speaking man came over and said, "Can I help you?" "Yes," I said. "I want food." He said, "You can have salad and meat and bread." So I said, "Yes I want salad and meat and bread." So they brought me this big stewed steak that I didn't want because it was too large and I saw everyone else eating a stew. "I want this," I said pointing at food on someone's plate. They couldn't understand me so I ate my salad, paid and split.

I continued down the road and found some thick palm trees along the west bank of the Nile River, to duck into. It looked like a good place to camp, but soon some Arab guys came down and offered me cigarettes. Also they wanted to know where I was from and to see my passport. They looked my things over. I grabbed my knife, but never let them see that I had it ready. I was tired of Arabs and couldn't even talk to these fucking people anymore. Trying my best to be cognitive yet get rid of them, they finally left as it began to darken. I set up my tent and in the process I was impaled in the leg with a barb from the many thorns cast about the grounds. I went down the embankment and washed a few things in the Nile River and splashed water on my face and myself. Finally there was peace, yet I was concerned someone would return in the night to rip me off.

About 2am I listened to what sounded like a pack of wolves or dogs running on the other side of the Nile River during the night. It was a haunting, howling sound that moved southward and would fade then brighten in intensity as they seemed to be moving in on a kill. One yip, yip, yeew was followed by dog barks. Could they be hyenas? I was glad they didn't come my way.

## Monday Feb. 27th,

At first light, I cleaned up the bike and then headed down the road. Right from the start I got the crazy people running up to me again. It was almost like a bad dream, except I laughed at how nutty this was. I felt stronger now about ignoring them. I was chased by some dogs, but used the water bottle to spray them, while shouting at them until they retreated.

It was a cool, sunny morning with a wind to my back. I saw a couple of wrecked cars on the roadside. Some were smashed very bad. I rode into Asyit and met a German fellow who taught classes at the local university here. We talked about my predicament and he told me where we could go for some great pastry at a shop. I sat with him for a moment or two during which I filled up on baklava and sweets. Mmmm.

I headed out and rode on this horribly shitty bumpy road. I felt sorry for my bike. I'd been informed by a German traveler that the east Nile road was better than the west, so I thought maybe I could get a boat across. I stopped in a village to ask someone this but they didn't understand me. An English speaking man then greeted me. "Hello, how are you, can I help you?" A crowd gathered around as he kept repeating those words. That was all of the english that he knew how to speak. He too couldn't understand me. I took off my San Francisco hooded jersey and lashed it under a couple of straps. As I was leaving some kids tugged on my guitar and I gave them dirty looks.

I rode onward down this fucking road, weaving to avoid potholes and huge cracks. It was so rough, that at times I felt like I was on a motocross course. The only good thing was the tailwind. Kids all along the way ran up to me and threw rocks and were little assholes. "Goodbye," they'd say and I ignored them. I got about 20 kilometers down the road and stopped to check my battered gear and discovered my San Francisco jersey that Aunt Marion had given me was gone. It was either grabbed back in town or a bump had loosened it. I looked back down the road and felt this tremendous loss. I had a strong wind to fight if I went back as well as that horrible road. So I started back and these kids came out from nowhere to mob me. I was mourning my loss and trying to decide what to do. If it fell off, I was sure someone quickly grabbed it immediately. This kid came over shouting, "Hello, hello," and he grabbed my only other sweater and pulled on it. I got so pissed I threw the bike down and chased him. All the other kids scrammed. I chased him through some trees. He was to fast. I threw a big rock at him, hitting the water along side. Then when I came back to my bike all the others threw rocks at me. I returned fire, headed on feeling bummed.

About two hours later I saw up ahead, a big Pepsi billboard with a couple of camels walking in front of it and felt like stopping to take a photo. I then heard cars beeping behind me and looked behind to see two cars careening down the road side by side going madly out of control. I got to the side of the road as they went past me banging doors and then one truck went skidding. I saw a cloud of dust, heard screeching then saw the truck dart just behind the Pepsi sign and miss the camels by inches. It slid side ways and went backwards into the canal. Splash! I picked up my pace as the truck quickly sank with 3 people on board. I rode over to help. A village on the other side went bananas. Kids came pouring out of schools or homes and ran to look at me and they hassled me! "Look at and help, those people, that is what you should be doing, not looking at me-you bloody buggers!" Two guys inside the truck popped out and swam to the opposite shore just as the truck sank. I wasn't sure if everyone was out of the vehicle and wanted to help the swimmers out of the canal and was concerned if anyone was still inside the vehicle. But this mob and these kids kept hassling me. I was concerned about turning my back on my bike and equipment. I thought there was nothing I could do except shout, Finally I saw some men arguing on the opposite side of the canal and all three men appeared safe.

I rode on as everybody looked at me rather then the men arguing on the canal side. A van followed me and he too hassled me. They looked so stupid inside the vehicle grinning and saying things I could not understand.

I rode several miles and then ducked into a little park area. This looked like a nice place to camp. No sooner had I sat, when some Arabs came up and invited me to join them at their table. They invited me to have a beer and I accepted. One Arab was especially good to me and we all talked about politics. They liked Anwar Sadat. Then I went to use the mens room and this kind Arab followed me into the toilet and while we peed at the urinal he offered to make love with me. "I want vedy much to make love with you," he said. "No thanks," I replied, adding, "I love the woman and not the man." He leaned closer and said, "But I vedy much love you. I love the man." This caught me off guard. My reply was, "I no love men." He nodded his head and said, "Ok, ok vedy well." We went back outside as if nothing ever happened and he and his friends and I continued our talk. I set up my tent a good distance away from the building in which they were staying, but all these men came over and watched me construct my little tent. Later, when it was dark, one guy came out, laid down a bedroll and slept alongside my tent.

## Tuesday Feb. 28

A cold wind blew in during the night and I got a stiff neck from the breeze against me. The Arab who had slept beside may tent had left during the night. I packed up my things as the Arabs gathered around and watched me loading the bike. I shook there hands and must say they were very kind, albeit somewhat kinky, but nonetheless trusting to me.

I headed south, down the rough pavement on a sunny warm morning. Both tires had big rippled open seams with bulges of inner tube peering through. I had to fix the tire and therefore pulled into a small town and found an air hose. The guy tried to blow air into my tire with just hissing air hose, there was no nozzle, and he was flustered as to why that wouldn't work. I had to kindly wave him away and proceeded to change my back tire in addition to installing a four inch long piece of tire, which I carried in my repair kit, to secure the bad spot. A crowd gathered around to watch my every move. To them this must have been better than cinema. I filled up the tire with air and all was well. I realized the importance of always watching my possessions when I went into crowds like this, or else things disappeared.

I pedaled down the road. The landscape was changing. There were more palm trees and tall grass. I saw men working on their fields of crops. Two oxen pulled a plow. Fires smoldered in brick houses. Everywhere people said, "Hello," from the fields. The valley had high cliffs colored of red and tan dirt. There was a dry looking, formidable landscape just behind the lush green vegetation near the Nile River. I didn't feel very enthusiastic and was in a depressed state. I couldn't quite understand why, except for the loss of some articles and the general dislike I felt for these people. They all ambled along at a camels pace in their pajamas. I couldn't help but feel they didn't give a damn about work. They were probably hard workers, but had a lack of motivation and education. I thought the valley would have a fantastic crop yield and manufacturing potential, if the right people made it happen.

I came to a crossing of the Nile and beheld some very beautiful scenery. I made a wrong turn and went several miles out of my way. I returned and crossed a bridge with donkey and camel, etc. I rode on and the road got poor. Big cracks would jolt my body each time I crossed them. I felt like this was similar to riding the whoop-dees in a motocross. I came into a village feeling bone dry and downed a warm Pepsi. I ate pita bread with sweet jam. I learned that if you don't agree on a price with these guys they'll take you for as much as they can get. Especially if you just hand them a pound. They won't give any change back. I had no shirt on and the kids chased me down the road. I ditched them but was quite amazed at how strong they rode, upon one speed bikes.

I continued on from the village of Qena with 60 kilometers to go until the city of Luxor. The road was good. The kilo's seemed like miles. I felt weary. Kids wanted backshesh from me and threatened to throw rocks. I pulled out my stick and threatened them back. They threw rocks anyhow. I watched the sun sink. The flies were bad. I made the last 3 kilo's to Luxor, feeling weary and not very well. I was tired but something else bothered me. I rode into town. What a crazy mess, with dust and horses. But what a joy to see white tourists! I was flagged down by a guy who said he had a room in a hotel for 1.50 pounds. So I followed him and got a room. I took a badly needed shower, then went into town and bought dinner. I met friends that I'd met in Cairo and I ate with a Holland man. I felt like hell walking around. I was weak and tired. I went with a German girl later on to find her something to eat as she was ill all day. I set my tent up on a cot in my room and used mosquito netting to sleep under.

## Wednesday Feb. 29

I didn't know it was a leap year? I slept until 7am and then went into the town and to the ferry that crosses the Nile. I met a couple from Switzerland who were interested in my journey. I hadn't really thought about all I'd been through. We waited one hour for a ferry to go across the Nile. It cost 15peastas. At the other side some Arab men walked out on the path and stopped to chat.

They blocked my way and I made a loud beep sound like that of a truck and they jumped clear. I glanced over my shoulder and noticed that the Swiss couple saw this and they were laughing.

I headed up to the monuments toward the Valley of the Kings. First I stopped and gazed in awe at two statues called The Colossus. They were immense and finely carved, yet seemed out of place, sitting in a pasture. I bought tickets to four places. Went to see the valley of the Queens. It was no good. Ramesseuna was most impressive with the mammoth columns and heads of pharoahs toppled here and there. The art work was intriguing. Looked like the Sistine Chapel. I went to a temple and it wasn't very good.

A long, dry uphill ride was progressed under a hot sun toward the Valley of the Kings. It was a rocky valley I strode up into while buses of tourists spewed past. At least my bike was light, as I carried no luggage. Finally arriving at the parking area, I was about to lock my bike when an elderly Egyptian man told me I didn't have to lock my bike. "No lock here, no Egypt man steal," he said. I replied, "Oh, no, Egypt man steal." He said, "No say that! Europe man steal." I recanted, "Every Egypt man a thief." He got so pissed about it, but I stood my ground and meant it and felt strongly that they have taking money and possessions on their minds like an obsession. I locked the bike and went walking up the entrance to The Valley of the Kings. The day was getting hot. I locked the bike to a pole.

There were many tombs to visit and I went into as many tombs as possible as these were very intriguing. They were bored into solid rock some as far as 120 meters (350feet). It was a wonder how they did make these chambers. There were hieroglyphics everywhere upon the walls and ceilings. Why, I tried to imagine did they do this? This art work was very nice. Perhaps some of the oldest paintings I'd ever seen. The figures were always from a side view and didn't use depth perception techniques. I went into so many chambers. Some were rather elaborate, with spacious, big rooms. In one, I talked to a girl from California and she said they did this because they believed that in order to go to the next life you must be in one piece and have your possessions with you. So they made deep chambers with trick anti-chambers and some dead ends. Often there were deep chasms, which separated the chambers. The hieroglyphs told of offerings to the gods of the lives of these Pharaohs. I learned that work on a Pharoahs tomb began as soon as a king or queen took the thrown. I studied the work at the entrance to Sedi the Seconds tomb. There was a plaster inset relief of the Pharoah which was so clearly done. The toes were very realistic.

During my visits to these tombs, guards, who wanted baksheesh, often harassed me. They would tell me a few things and expect money. I didn't pay any of them. I was getting so tired of climbing up and down these chambers as it was so hot and stuffy down in them.

I went into King Tuts tomb. It was very small, but so well hidden that it wasn't for 3000 years until it was discovered. The people of that era had tremendous talents. They had beautiful art. They must have had quite a civilization. By doing their tombs they left a time capsule for other generations to observe how they lived.

When I returned to my bike I discovered that a bungee strap and a tailight cover were stolen. I told this one Egyptian guy and he said, "Not my problem." I told him, "All Egypt men are thieves." He raised his hand like he was going to hit me. I said, "Egypt man only want to steal and to have money." I poked him with my finger. He got all pissed. And he and his pal said, "You are a bad man. You steal and no good man." So I rode away saying, "Egypt man go to hell." I was pissed off.

I rode downhill from the Valley of the Kings and across the plain to the ferry where a guy wanted to sell drugs to me. The ferry operator tried to rip me off of 25paestas. I went across with all these people and I was feeling no love at all for them. However, there was a young Egyptian woman on the ferry boat ride, who was exceedingly beautiful. She looked like the drawings I had seen of ancient Egyptian women. Her eyes were almond shaped, her lips full and her bodily features trim, yet swollen with lovely curves.

I hadn't a chance to meet her and was regretting this while pedaling into town while also thinking that I must now shop for a bungee strap to tie down my pack. I went back to the hotel and stopped to buy a section of tire for my bad front tire. I wasn't getting any help from anyone at the bike shops. They just shut me out. I fixed the tire myself and had to hunt around for an air nozzle. All these Arabs would try and blow air into the tire with just an air hose. I met two guys from England and told them of my hotel. I brought them to the hotel and the managers got all happy toward me. They shook my hand and thanked me for bringing them business.

We went out to eat a dinner of falafa and fried potatoes. I started to feel a little sickly after eating two big sweets. We went to Luxor temple and then tried to bargain with men for souveigners. He went from 50 pounds down to 5 pounds. I offered him one pound but he wouldn't take it. I split up with the English fellows and while passing through a market was harassed and approached by an Egyptian man who grabbed me and I gave him a shove. Then I went to all these shops to look for a bongee. A fellow at one shop escorted me a couple of blocks to a place that sold them. He didn't want any backshesh for his kind act. I was thankful. For every 10 bad men you meet one good man.

The Egyptian men are fun to joke with. We kidded about momma, papa, brother, sister while walking down the street. I went back to the hotel feeling rather sickly. I sat with the English boys and my ears started to ring. I felt as if I was getting ill and went to bed at 10:30, feeling very tired and aching all over.

## Thursday March 1

Today marked the beginning of the 9th month of my travels. I started this day off in horrible shape. I felt so ill. I was very weak. My head felt swelled and dizzy. My body ached all over. The manager of the hotel banged on my door several times and I had to pay him for another days stay. I slept off and on all morning and then into the afternoon until 1:30. I had dreams of all kinds. I was flat out, like a sheet on the bed. I couldn't even move. My body went through cold spells and hot flashes. It was horrible.

I finally got outside at 2 and pedaled over to Karnak temple. Didn't go in because the admission fee seemed excessive. So I walked around the place. I climbed a small wall and a woman came out screaming, "Baksheesh! Baksheesh! Policee!" I slowly ambled along. Then some boys pestered me for baksheesh. They threw rocks at me. I climbed a hill and stood looking at the temple. It was just a lot of ruins. But one archway, or facade was so beautifully done. I think it would be difficult to build even today. It faces to the southeast and the hieroglyphs are exactly the same on each side. So precisely the same that it is a wonder how they did this. The top cap rocks were mammoth. I was told they raised the dust to place them there and it was done about the time of Alexander the Great. This boy came over and wanted to know where I was from, what was my name etc. Then some other boys came over and he threw rocks at them to shoo them from me. He hit one boy in the nose with a rock. A furious rock fight started. I just moved along. This guy came over and tried to get my watch or some baksheesh and I told him, "Go away." I wasn't feeling well.

I walked over and bought an ice cream and sat by the Nile. There was peace for a few moments. I returned to the hotel and slept until 5:30. When I awoke, I met an English man, who gave me aspirin and diarrhea medicine. I took some and felt better one hour later.

I went out and ate. And then thought of making a souvenir of Luxor. I bought some crayons. And got some paper and rode over to Luxor temple. I thought I could make a "paper embossed replica" of the hieroglyphs. I rode up and this Egyptian man came over and started to tell me about the great arch. He was beginning to grab me to lead me around and he asked me how much my bike cost. I said, "I will not sell you my watch, nor my bike and I will not give you any baksheesh. So please go away!" He got erect and raised his hand and said, "I don't want any baksheesh and I don't want to have your bicycle. I am a student of Egyptian history and I want to tell you so you can learn of Egypt. I studied many years and I have many good friends and ..." I interrupted him and said, "If I had a medal I would put it on you!" He again got mad and said, "I don't want a medal. I want to tell you of Egyptian men, for they are very good men." I said, "I have had much trouble from Egyptian men. Some steal from me. Others give me insult and many throw rocks at me. But most of all they do not treat me with respect." "Why should Egypt man give you respect?" he asked. Your country was living in the trees when Egypt was building great pyramids and civilizations." I retorted, "And now do they do this?" He came back with, "Yes! But in Egypt you will find some very bad people-they are the new tribes and you will meet many good people. They are the Egyptians." I told him I was sorry to cause trouble with him, but I said everyday people come to me and want money or my bike or they steal from me. "For this I was not happy to see." He nodded in approval and said, "I am also not happy for this, and Egypt has had many bad governments and the people were not treated good but I hope they will become better."

So we came to terms and he told me more about the hieroglyphs and then the police came and said we must leave. I left but came back and tried to rub my paper on the hieroglyph but I couldn't do it cause of cars going by.

I went back to the hotel and had a roommate this evening. He was from Karachi in West Pakistan. He was also a tourist. He told me he was in Sudan, and said there was a ship I could take to Saudi Arabia and from there get to Karachi. "Sudan not good, no go," he said to me adding. "No cafe, no water, no taxi." He wanted to talk all night but I got tired and dizzy.

So there was a way around Saudi Arabia, but whether or not it was for my bike travels was the big question.

## Friday March 2

I got all packed and slipped out of town at 8am. I rode along heading south, on the east side of the Nile, away from the villages and into sand dune countryside. I was taking it easy at a slow pace. At 11am I stopped for water and a snack of oranges. The day was hot and this dry looking landscape added to it. I felt a little achy. People would say, "Hello," but aren't so aggressive. My thirst was unquenchable. At 1 I had a cold Pepsi and man did it hit the spot! Water just doesn't satisfy my thirst. Especially hot water. At 2pm I stopped to drink two Pepsis. Then I rode on and again got so thirsty. I tried to suckle water to keep my mouth moist. I was so thirsty I stopped at 3:30 and bought 1 more Pepsi. There was no food available. This Pepsi was hot, uck! I continued on and stopped to ask a villager directions and he bought me another Pepsi. I filled up my canteen with Pepsi and sucked on it while riding along. I started to have caffeine flashes. My body temperature soared and dropped. The sun was getting lower and dreading to drink any of the water I bought one more Pepsi and some wafers at a shop. Hot Pepsi was again served. "Eeuck!" I said to the proprietor. "No electric," said the store owner. "Cold water?" he said to me. My eyes lit up to the sound of cold. "Ah, ok!" They brought me some clear cold water and I gulped it down regardless of what was in it. I headed down the road. My head was zinging from drinking 6 Pepsis. Looking for a place to camp. Many kids were on the roadside. Some rocks fly. "Baksheesh!" They cried. Some play soccer on the road. I finally found a section of trees and went into them to make camp and eat bread and oranges for supper. I spent time thinking of what I would do back in the U.S. when I got home. I felt my way to go was into a political role and wonder if my responsibility would be strong enough. Orion was high in the sky. Polaris low.

## Saturday March 3

With only 50 kilometers to go I got up early and recalled the drumbeats I heard and chanting of last night. They were truly Africana style. I wheeled my bike through the sand and then down the road. I had motocross like bad roads all the way to Aswan. They were rough enough to knock tooth fillings out.

My thirst built up tremendously and I rode into town and looked for something to drink and met Debbie and Bill. They rafted four days from Luxor on the Nile. I went and bought some grub and cold fresh water and then went to a park to eat. A fellow Egyptian man came over and wanted to sell me a boat ticket and I just cried out, "Go away!" He said, "You go away. This is my village!"

The Nile has some islands at Luxor to speed the waters along and the islands are covered with trees. I went to find the Continental Hotel and looked at some rooms. I got a room facing the Nile for 70 paestas a night. I met an Italian guy in the lobby. I thought he was an Arab and we talked and he asked to play my guitar. So he came with a friend to my room. His name was Franco and his German friend was Thomas. They told me they had been in the Sudan for four weeks. They rolled a big joint and we smoked it. Franco played some rhythamic riffs so cleanly so cooly and I got totally absorbed in this style of play. He was just picking the strings but his fingers seemed magical the way he molded them to the guitar. Thomas played the harp. A & D & F scale. As they played I couldn't help but get into their story of travel. They had been riding on top of trains and camping in the hot desert sun. They were both dark right down to their toes. They were both young men and they were not tourists but rather they were like men hewned from logs and weathered into character by the hard road they followed. They put on a good performance of harp and guitar.

I met my roomates from Belgium. I played a couple of songs both letdowns after previous performers. I took a boat across to Elaphantine Island and walked about. Very nice trees and quaint village. Big rocks like in Minnesota. The water look so tempting to go for a swim in. But a little voice inside my head told me that dangers lurked in these waters. I took a rowboat across the Nile and enjoyed this. I went into the city and ate lasagna and was going for ice cream when

I met Faulkner and he said to me, "Are you a cyclist?" We talked about cycling in Egypt as he too had come from Cairo. He treated me to ice cream and I told him of my disagreements about the Egyptians. He offered to me a water bottle as mine had sprung a leak. So I agreed to meet him at 7 on Monday at Continental Hotel. I came back to my room and again met Franco and Thomas and they came and played and we smoked. I played my song "Turning the World Blue," and felt it was my best performance yet. We stayed up until 12 or 1am and talked of our travels. I had a hard time going to sleep as it was so noisy.

## Sunday March 2nd

I slept bad and felt like shit in the morning. Went into the market and bought some honey and bread. I rode my bike to see the Aswan high damn. I met resistance almost immediately as I was directed down the wrong road to go on. Then I was helped to the right road. I again came to a fork and asked a traffic policeman and he told me the wrong way to go. I was helped by a child. Then I rode down some busy streets full of students and they wouldn't move to the side to give way to me. It was sort of a dare. I would have to just go straight and hope they would move. Kids on bikes came along and started teasing with me. One grabbed my bike and was pulling on the back rack. He was off to my left rear side. His other friend intended to cut me off to my right front. They cried out, "Backshesh!" and I said, "No backshesh!" and then wound up my leg like a donkey and kicked this guy to my rear hard and he banged into my bike and went down with a nasty crash. Saw he was OK in mirror and continued on not feeling bad about what I did. I rode over the old dam and then up across some desert to the entrance to the new dam. Paid one pound to cross the Aswan Dam. I saw a nice memorial of Egypt-Soviet cooperation in dam building. I slowly went across the dam and got a good look at it. I stopped in for a cold pepsi and could see the 12 turbine exits. I went to the train station and met Belgium roomates and we took a 3rd class train, boxcars with seats, back to to Aswan. That was quite fun I thought. It is rikkedy and I was getting a real kick out of this low budget travel. The Arabs would smile at us as we stared back. The conductor over charged us and my Belgium friend got mad and said, "That's not fair," he went and argued with the conductor as the train swayed to and fro and then he came back and said he would go to the police. The conductor came along and said, "if you go to police me will charge you 65 p for the bicycle." It was blackmail!

I showered and went out to eat at the fish place close by and then I went walking about. I came back and played some guitar and met a German from next door. He came over and we played guitar. We smoked some Sudan grass. He told of his journey into Sudan and seeing the monkeys. He told of riding the trains and I must say his story of hanging on for 2 kilometers until the police stopped the train, was hair raising. He said they traveled four days on top of trains. Then I got tired about midnight and more friends came over. They partied until one or two. I again slept like shit. This night I had to get up and shit like a bowl of mucky cereal. I felt horrible.

## Monday March 3rd

I went to the other side of the river on this hot day. I sat beside the Nile on some big rocks as faluckas went sailing past. "No swim," said one Arab man to me. "Crocodiles," he added. They said not to swim in the river because of bacteria, but not because of the crocs. I explored awhile around the island and came walking into a "no entry museum" place. The day was getting short and this was the quickest way so I proceeded. I snuck past an archaelogist and a sleeping guard. Then I came to the gate and had to back track up and over some ruins to get around it. I would have had to pay 1 pound otherwise. I took a boat across and really noticed the faces of the Egyptian men. I recalled the ancient drawings and carvings and I could see resemblance's between those and today's people. They aren't real black and they have clean attractive faces. Either way the tribes are mixed and the Egyptians are made up of many breeds.

I went to the hotel and sat about writing and playing guitar. I had a knock on the door and in walked Faulkner the friend from Germany. He remembered and brought me a new water bottle. We went to eat at a place he knew of. I was so sluggish and weary feeling. We had an excellent talk about Egypt as it turned out he had done much studying and was writing a book on Aswan. We discussed dressing according to their standards as he claimed they accepted you quicker then. I said they might as well learn the rest of the world is different. We met some other travelers and talked. I found him to be very much into Egypt. We split and I went along and met Deb and Bill from New Zealand. We sat and talked about their adventures. A rat jumped onto Bills face as he slept on a fulucka. We had a good time talking about all these happenings. Again I met Faulkner. We all had to split and I went to the hotel and slept. My Belgium friends were there and we talked awhile.

## Tuesday March 6

Karen, the Belgium girl felt ill. I slept good for once and I used earplugs which helped. I was out on the balcony eating and I saw Cezar from the kibutz, walking along down below. "Cezar," I cried out. "Cezar." He said, "Hello," and searched around until he finally saw me and waved me to come down. I went down and met him and Sophia once again. They went to the swimming pool. I rode to see the unfinished 3,500 year old obelisk and I didn't even know that's what these things were called. Quite impressive to see the work they had to do to get the rock out. They cut slots in rock and put wood in with water and let it sit. The wood expanded and it cracked. This thing was mammoth and over 1000 tons. The engineering of such a feat was evident. I went to the hotel with swimming pool and could not get in so I talked with Cezar and Sophia awhile. "Death by the Nile," a murder mystery written by Agatha Christi was filmed in the old Cataract Hotel. We talked quite awhile and Cezar proved to be an excellent communicator and his two years of travels and work in other countries was intriging.

I went to the hotel and walked to the ferry. Went across the river to the other side and started a 2k walk to the mosque along the banks of the Nile. The sun was super hot as well as the sand. I saw fish in the water and birds sitting on rocks. I hiked up to the mosque and had a look inside. The view was spectacular. I hiked a distance across barren desert and came to San Simeon church. It was a Christian refuge. I hiked back down to the Nile. Tried to get a hand by tourists to a lift to the other side. Then I talked to an Arab boat owner and they vary in price from 5pounds to 2pounds to 75 paestas to 50p depending on how far I walk away from them and not act interested. I thought of lifting a small boat but it was locked. I hiked back to the ferry. And I got into the ferry with a whole bunch of black cloacked women. They looked at me bare shirted and shorts and giggled. They even seemed upset. A child laughed at me. I kept cool through it all and made it to the opposite side of the river. Some women had beauty and others were very weathered looking.

I hiked up to the restaurant and met a gal from Texas while we ate kabob. I went into the market and headed for the hotel. I shopped a bit for a King Tut painting which I wanted to buy. I came to the hotel and met a gal from England, named Sue. I talked with her for awhile. She said she would split with her roomate and needed a roomate and wanted to come in with me. I said sure. We talked awhile and I went up and felt great and wrote a song called, "Traces of love." Goes to show me that this little sense of female relationship fired me up. I understood how much I needed someone. I met her again and also my new roomate Jean Pierre from Paris. He studied architecture and we talked awhile and I said I'd like to be an "Artist conception," trade man and this interested me. I did feel I would like this. We had tea awhile with Sue and Chritina. And I went out and bargained with an Arab on a painting. Got him down to 6pounds but didn't buy it. I went to sleep with ear plugs.

**Wednesday March 7th**

I hiked around the town searching for a papyrus painting and all the prices were high in the morning and no one would bargain at that early hour. The guy of the night before got down to 7pounds but not 6. So I came back to the hotel and sat about and I took the ferry across to Hotel Oberic to sneak into the hotel. Sue told me, "Act like you own the place." I made it in and sat down and took off my shoes and sox and shirt and started to write. A fellow came over and said, "You stay here 3pounds." I looked at him and said, "Iam guest." He said, "Which room you in?" "In 17," I said. "No," he said. So I thought I'd try 117 at which he said, "You have key?" I said, "Yes." I dug into my sac fumbling for a imaginary key, then said, "My father have key." He looked sternly at me and said, "You must show me key!" I said, "Okay, I talk to my father." So I got out of there and went out to the garden and sat and wrote and it was a good place. I went back across to the other side. Bought a papyrus King Tut painting for 6pounds and then went to eat and I sat with the snobby fag hotel clerk who wouldn't talk with me. I hiked up to the room and took a shower of cold water. BRRRR. Then I met Sue and some friends and we sat on the balcony talking. It was a delightful sunset. Then I saw Richard and the Aussie who I'd tramped with so much in Cairo. I threw some orange peelings on him and said, "Hey Richard you old dog." He cheered back to me so then he came up and joined me and we were happy to be together. And we talked for quite awhile and then we hiked across town to his hotel and had a good talk of our travels. He seemed tired and weary and we talked more and then I went back to the hotel I met the friends Sue, Jean Pierre, and a cute French girl with her boyfriend named Mani. They asked me to go along on a late night fulucka ride. I agreed and we walked across town. And the tow french men talked and Jean Pierre ran into a parking sign. I guess I felt a tad alienated by language. We got to the fulucca and it turned out to be a brandy drinking, hashish smoking in port boat ride. A fellow named Foo Foo was a boat captain and was very funny. He got me speaking Arab and I don't know what I was saying but they sure laughed. The Arab who offered us the ride only wanted to get it on with the French girl. He tried everything to hustle her. The two frenchmen jabbered like women.

**Thursday March 8**

I met Richard and we went to eat a bit in the market. Then we went to the train station but he was so pokey that it took us awhile to get there. When we did the train was gone to see the High Dam. So we hiked back and played guitar. Just as fun. Singing on the balcony of Hotel Continental

Aswan, the most centrally located dive that somehow has character. I went with Sue to the pool and she said she would treat me. The price was up 3pounds per person from day before 2 pounds. Fucking Arabs! We sat back and chatted. I sensed she was a woman who was feeling good about her new position and was an interesting compassionate person as well. The day got real hot. We dove into the pool waters many times. Then I read a paper and she met a rich Frenchman and they talked. This guy was a travel guide for 11 years. He had an opinion of everyplace. But only as a big wheel tourist. Sights, foods, fine hotels was his way to travel. He warned me of India and Nepal and Thailand. It was a sweltering day. We toured through old cataract hotel and it was so Africanis styled. I enjoyed the whirling fans, fine woodwork and plaster embrodieriy.

Went to the hotel and met Richard and we went into the market and ate ice cream. God it was hot. No breeze. We went to a small cafe and ate with French girls. We had a salad and orange juice and water and a meat that was spicy. God it was hot out. I went back to the hotel feeling weary and bought a ice cream and got to the hotel and crashed out on my bed. I was just pooped out. I slept so well until Richard came in at 10:30 and Sue also. I felt a bit ill and Sue came in and we had quite a conversation about traveling life. It was so hot and stuffy. We kidded about getting up at 3:30 with the Egyptian camel drops. Then we had a good bye kiss and I met my Icelandic roommate. A hearty looking fellow. Only shorts and on top of bed we dozed off. I had these terrible dreams of trying to find rocks in the desert of the same shape, and had only a little time to do it. But this dream went on and on. I was just boiling hot and I felt terrible. I got up at 3:30am and squirted shit and then bent forward and barfed out my guts. I went back to lay down but soon got up and did it again. This happened for the rest of the night. I felt so sick my head spun, I could hardly walk, not think, nor talk. I slept hard finally, like I was exhausted.

**Friday March 9**

In the morning I couldn't move because I was so tired and sick inside that it hurt to do anything. Richard said he was also ill. We took some medicine and I saw sparkles every time I stood up and my balance went all to hell. I was so sick at 8 in the morning that my guts wrenched and I staggered my way to the toilet in just the nick of time. I passed Richard on the way back. We laid in bed moaning. Then we slept until 10 am. Richard and I moaned and couldn't cope with this illness. We drank some cold water and it was so good. But I just shit it out like stepping on a plastic bottle filled with water. At noon we still couldn't move. "Hey Richard, do you think we should try and get up?" I would ask. "Yes, mate, I think we should." We would both try and could not get up. Then the hotel manager came in and hasteled us about either checking out or staying an extra day. "Can't you see were sick?" We told him we would leave before 2pm. "I'm sorry to see you sick," he said closing the door. At 1:30 we finally decided to try and get up because we had to pack and catch a train back to Cairo at 4:30. It took all the energy I had just to get up. Then I'd have to lay down to get my strength back. I'd sit up do one thing and sit down. My head hurt and spun and I had no energy. I was so sick. I would help Richard with something. He would help me. Our moral support to one another helped. I had so many things to do. Pack tent, pack bags, put my guitar into case was almost unbearable. My mind was step by step for each move. Then I'd sit. Finally at 2:45 I laid back and slept from exhaustion. Richard woke me at 3pm and said, "Come on you can't sleep you'll miss the train." So we carried on and had to sluggishly take things down the steps to the first floor. Fast moves were impossible. I packed up the bike and paid 320 pounds for the six days of staying and then pedaled off very slowly.

I made it to the train station alright but had to sit down right away. Richard came we both were in a daze. I started to sweat very heavily. I could feel a fever. I laid down on train station seats. I saw everyone boarding train and it took all my might to get up and thanks to Richard moved my bike on the train. The man in the train said, "No bicycle." Then he added, "You pay 5 pounds." "Bull!" I said mustering the strength. I put the bike on the train and my bags also. Then I was hastled by the train porter. "Five pounds," he said. I said no and went to sit down. He demanded 5pounds or no bike on train. I said, "Ok 2pounds." He said, "Three," and I tried to get him down to two but felt so ill I again was hardly able to move. So I gave him 3pounds. We got a seat in the cooler car and the train started to roll. Later a ticket guy came along and said, "You must pay two pounds for the bicycle." I was startled. "No I already paid three," I said. The chief conductor looked seriously at me and said, "To what man you pay?" I told him my story but he couldn't understand me. So we got another guy and then we went looking at all the porters. The chief conductor would ask, "Is this the man?" "No," I'd say. "This man?" "No." The man I learned was a porter at the station. Not on the train. But he was with a guy who was on the train. This guy denied even knowing another guy. We argued so much about this. In the end they made me pay 1.50pound for the bicycle. The train went on and it gradually got full. Richard and I got bounced around all over the train. Finally we found our own seats and slept at midnight. Richard was getting all mad at the Arabs. He pushed one big guy who stepped on his foot. He called out to another guy, "Go fuck yourself." The Arab smiled back because he didn't understand english, however another Arab who understood said, "I can listen to what you say, and it is not nice." This fellow was funny. He was a big Arab who was thin but tall and with a very deep voice. He had no front teeth. He said to a french girl. "Did you enjoy in Aswan?" "NO!" she belted back at him. He continued unscathed. "Ah-can you drink the beer?" "NO!" she again said. He added. "Do you want to drink the beer? I can drink 12 beers! I have eyes to see and legs to walk to find more the beer." His dialect was very interesting and whats more is that the French girl did drink a beer with him. We all grew to like this Arab.

## Saturday March 10

This overweight man who was hot leaned against me and bounced into me as the train swayed. I would elbow him many times to move him. I think he would have continued to do this had I not told him and pushed him over very assertively one time. I slept with one eye open much of the time, trying to watch my purse, and baggage.

Daylight came as the train swayed and clanged in unison with the Moslem chants on the train. People neeled where they sat and bowed to pray to Allah.

We went into villages where the train would stop and many people piled on board. Bedouin pajama boys. One guy leaned against my bike chain and dirtied his jamies. The train finally arrived in Cairo and we waited for the train to clear before unloading. The porter insisted on helping me get my bike out and he was so forceful with it and I tried to get him to slow down. He banged the bike through the train doors. We went outside. I carried out my things and found my side mirror was shattered, the fenders bent, and the derailleur rendered unusable. He manhandled the thing so impatiently. I wired things together and rode to the Select Hotel. Richard and I got a room. Still moving slow. We sat in the room and then went to sample some goodies. We went to travel agents. I split and went to the poste. We ate lousy pizza. Back to the hotel I laid back and talked to my new roommate. Richard came and we went along to get a bite to eat. Richard said he got a ticket to Athens and wanted to spend his Egyptian money. "Let's eat good tonight," he said. So we went down the sidewalk slowly and he bought some clothes. Then he got real slow. He was feeling ill, or down about something. We asked two Arabs for directions to a restaurant and they told us. But we stopped to deliberate. We both looked like hell-dirty and slow moving, feeling sickly. We went to this Chinese restaurant and these two Arabs came along and said, "Do you want some money?" "Ha?" Richard and I said in unison. "Here," he said handing us some money, "Go eat good food." He gave me 5 pounds. I refused it. But he said, "Go eat good food." So we shook there hands and said, "Shokran," and we went into the Chinese place and Richard was down for some reason. But he was a bit cramped and yet I felt he was down for another reason. We ate a good meal of Chinese cuisine. Then we went and had a strawberry drink and then went to the hotel.

We talked awhile about why we travel. He felt lost doing this. I said it was to learn of our world and of ourselves. And for me it was my personal goal of a bike trip. He said, "Of all the things I have tried in my life, I have never finished one of them to completion." I could see the frustration on his face. "Now I want to go home and forget about traveling, another non accomplishment in my life," said Richard. We discussed how important finishing something was. His music was so fine that I thought he was a success.

**Sunday March 11**

Richard was off early at 7:30 and we said farewell. We would try to meet in Greece. I ate breakfast. Went to the India embassey and applied for a visa. Then I went shopping to several ticket agents for an airline to either India or back to Greece. I went to the post office with hopes that I received a letter from Liana telling me of airline prices to India. But no letter was there. I heard different stories of bank receipt. Student card. Two places told me Ok. I had a compound problem. First, the student I.D.'s validity and second at the bank receipt. 3. Should I gamble and black market change cash and if airlines demands bank receipt would I loose? So I was up against some odds. I went back to the hotel at 1pm and met Alan who offered to change money. I asked him if I could change money on the condition he would change it back if my ticket attempt failed. He and I had a hell of a talk about life. For a 19 year old he was a good communicator. We talked of Egyptian life and he said Egyptians interbreed within the family. He claimed this was the reason for often craziness and lack of direction. We talked of God and space and other life. Then Mark came in and a Canadian also and he talked quiet and it annoyed me. He agreed to exchange with me and we did so. I told him about my bike trip and had to make frequent trips to John as Aswan (ass-swan) called.

I met Ho at the dining room of our hostel and we went to dinner. Ho was from Hong Kong and he was traveling in Egypt.Kong and he was traveling in Egypt. We were walking down a dusty alley and talked and discovered we were a great trio. Here was a man from Hong Kong, a Canadian and an American each seeing Cairo as an "Opposite than our world kind of city." We ate at a place I found in the alleys of old Cairo. "The food doesn't look to much good," said Ho. "Welcome to Cairo," we said in unison. After a meal of spaghetti like stuff and great conversation with my new found friends, we took a jaunt around the city. Our walk included stops at the Cairo Hilton, the hashish alleys and construction in the big mud hole. Then we went back to the hotel. I sat and wrote and met Franco, who was looking for a room. I helped him out and got him in. I talked with an Arab at the table who said god was in him and he loved the church and he asked me what my religion was. I said, "No religion." I talked to Franco awhile and met a girl from Germany. We all agreed on the Arabs rudeness in this part of the world. Ass-swan called again and again to me. Franco asked me whats this? And he had a lump on his abdomen. "A hernia I think," was my comment. He said, "I think it is an amoeba living in me. I drank some bad water in the Sudan." He stopped to twirl his hands and then said, "Oh shit, I want to go home healthy."

## Monday March 12

I awoke in a sweat, a fever, a lousy feeling in my belly. With a full schedule of activities I ate breakfast and headed to a bike shop, then was told I could come back at 5 for a bike box. I went to several other bike shops but they wouldn't help me. One place a cute gal talked to me. I could see such beauty in some Egyptian women. I stopped and got an offer to pick up a bike box. I went to the India embassy and recieved my India visa. The tension grew as I went back through the streets to Olympic Airlines. My heart was pounding as I pulled up. A man asked me, "How much," for my bike and I said, "Why you ask?" He continued and I said, "This bike no good," pointing to the bad tire. I don't like telling them the amount of value of my bike as I could see desire in their eyes.

I went in to the airline office and a big fellow said, "Can I help you?" "No," I said. "I want the other woman to help me," I said in a tactical move. So I sat back and she came in 15 minutes. I waited a bit more and she seemed to not be in a good mood like the day before. 'Oh boy,' I thought. "I want a ticket to Athens. Do you have an opening still for Wednesday?" She searched her computer and said yes. I gave her my fake I.D. and my receipt from the bank as well as my passport. She inspected each. Then she wrote the ticket down. All was ok. Then she held the student I.D. in her hand and leaned back and said in Arabic to another gal, who then took it up the steps. I was shitin asswan. You pay here she said. I stalled. Ready to get screamed at or questioned. Slowly I ambled over and paid. I heard a big argument up the stairs. Oh no, I thought, regretting this. I'll be hauled off to jail for forgery. The gal came down the steps with some others and they walked to me and I felt an edge cutting me in two. Then this trio split and I was handed my I.D. and I saw her give ticket lady a photo copy. "Thank you," she said. I can't recall saying thanks but I do remember this laugh going from my toes to me crown.

EEEEeeeee I went outside and felt a rush of relief. I rode off to change some dollars. Then I was happy and riding down the street the wrong way and a guy came running across the street right toward me. I saw him and he saw me. I also saw a car coming but he didn't. I stopped and left room for the guy to run in front of me. But he stopped and looked at me as I gestured to him to move mister move. WHAM! the car hit him and he flew into me and then went face first onto the pavement. The taxi didn't swerve. The taxi driver did a Oh no not again look. I attended to the injured man but a crowd gathered and he spit blood. He was in shock and then I heard, "Hello Eric, how are you? How long have you been in Aswan?" I looked and it was Sue from England and I said there's been an accident and she said, "Maybe we can meet for dinner?" As I held the mans head up I said, "But, but, I eat cheap." "Oh yah," she responded adding, "Well listen-." But I interrupted, "No I've got to get out of here," as the police were gathering around. "I'll see you Sue." She looked puzzled but smiling as I rode off this time in flow with the traffic. The man was ok.

I went back to the hotel dropped off the bike and then went up to room to tell Marc and Alan all was ok and I found out they left at morning. So I went to the poste office and met an Aussie and we shuffled through lines trying to figure this disorganization. We went to a shop and I ordered a drink and he ordered some food and he said he was divorced and was into traveling and his life had changed. We came to agree traveling buys you time to yourself and time to think. Because in business you don't think for yourself but for business. And I said I had to go to learn of my self and my world and then maybe I could be ready for marrying. We are funneled from the start and it's a continuous push to succeed, but traveling can break that up. We ate and talked and though we'd just met it felt like we were old friends. He asked me to help pay a bit and I did. We split. I went to the bike shop and waited there for the Arab to get me a box. One guy said 5 minutes and other worker said he didn't like Americans. "Egypt number one, "he said and gestured with a single finger. I waited and helped the friendly Arab with a few moving projects. Then finally I got the angry Arab to bring the box. I rigged a strap to carry it and was ready to head off. The Arab that didn't like me because I was an American asked for some baksheesh. "Fuck you," I said smiling. He did not understand what I said.

I went to the hotel and the elevator man stopped me from bringing the bike up the elevator. So I carried it up 8 floors of stairs. I walked over to eat at a glass front restaurant and had good cold french fries, shit macaroni and blah salad. The drink was good and tasted rather like prune juice. I then went to the alley and found a money trader and exchanged a few dollars into Egyptian money. Then I went to the hotel and talked and played guitar with Franco. He told me it was not a hernia that he had but an infection in his foot.

I had quite a day today. I walked into the city and saw many police lining the street. I asked someone what was happening and they said that Egyptian President Muburak and Greek President Pompouslaus were having dinner and they were going to pass by shortly. So I sat and waited and soon the motorcade passed and I saw the Egyptian president and other dignitaries. The crowd went wild with enthusiastic cheering. Security wasn't so tight. I could see Muburak very clearly and the motorcade moved at a peoples pace.

**Tuesday March 13**

Franco coughed real bad during the night and I doubted I could sleep through it, as I knew I would probably catch his illness also. In the morning I felt a dryness in my mouth and throat. I scampered down to a sweet shop and ate three rolls. Then I met a Belgium couple. I led them to a croissant shop and we said our goodbyes. I went to a bazaar market and discovered places in Cairo I didn't know of. I got a good drink for 5p. I bought tape. The crowd was heavy and the buses overflowed. The trains and cars and black and white Egyptians shopped and hollered and donkeys pulled carts and old men spat and this was Cairo.

I packed up my bags and showered and hauled my bike and box down the elevator. The elevator man caught me at the bottom and he bitched and moaned and I just ignored him. I met Bill and Debbie and bid them farewell. I packed up my bike, said a few fleeting words to another American who said, "Iran's borders are open to U.S. tourists." I didn't say goodbye to Franco and

I didn't feel the need to. Our time was spent together and no I didn't feel like another good bye. I went riding down the streets with my overloaded bike and big box strapped over my shoulder. It was tough to ride like this. People kidded me and they had every right to. I weaved and flowed with the traffic. Stopped and bought a big jar of strawberries. Made my way and often the wind or a car caught the box and almost sent me spinning. I slowly made it to the airport. Once there, I walked the bike inside the terminal. Some people said, "You sleep at airport? Ok. Ok," so I looked around and took the bike apart. I put it all in the box and then ate some sandwiches. Didn't have much to do at the airport so I sat and played guitar and some boys came over and told me to play disco. I played some blues and they got wild. Others came to listen. They were all good sports to play music too as they didn't have a a real sensitive ear and they got off on any kind of beat.

When I visited the toilet, the guy inside always wanted backshesh. I made a little camp in the corner of the air terminal and took out my sleeping bag and slept in such a way that my body purposefully blocked my stuff to prevent thieves from ripping me off. The place was noisy all night but I managed a little shuteye. Earplugs were were the secret, they were an essential item to sleep here.

# LEAVING EGYPT AND RETURNING TO GREECE

### Wednesday March 14

My alarm sounded at 6am and I bounded to my feet and shoveled down some goodies and then pushed my bike box and a bag through Egyptian customs. I was surprised to not have anything opened up and inspected by the agents.(Not that I had anything to hide.) I was excited to be flying and traveling and so I nervously went through tickets. They took my bike box and my luggage and didn't charge me for the bike. I was surprised at the number of shaggy, 'pajama men' who were flying on my plane. They looked like they had no money, but I knew better than to be so easily fooled.

With some extra Egyptian money to spend, I sat and ate a roll and a drink and talked to a German fellow who was happy to leave Egypt. I went to spend a few last paestas and I couldn't find a good item to buy when I noticed my flight gate of people empty out and into a bus. I hurried and just caught my bus ride out to the plane.

We walked up into the nice plane. I was fired up to be again traveling by plane. The Greek stewardesses were such a welcome sight. I sat down and overheard this talkative old gal who was so happy to be leaving Egypt. She had nothing good to say. She was so harassed by the Arabs.

The plane took off and I watched the Nile Delta and the coastline disappear beneath us. Then, over the Mediterranean we ate breakfast, which was the best meal I'd had in weeks. I talked to the lady sitting next to me and said she lived luxuriously in Egypt and still found it offending. I told her of my voyage and she said, "I couldn't see anybody doing that-taking a trip in Egypt by a bicycle.

After a couple of hours, we landed in Athens amidst a layer of fog. It was very cool out. I went through customs. They had me open the box to see the bike. I was feeling this cultural shock already. It was a release of stress to not have the Arabs hounding me. I could see more pretty girls and a cleaner environment. It took some time to reassemble the bike and then pedal off to the city. A strong wind blew against me, but I made good progress from the airport toward the city, despite carrying the box and pedaling uphill to get to Apostles house. It was a good feeling to see the neighborhood. I felt like I was back home. I met the downstairs lady and said, "Yasso," to her. She told me Apostles was working. At least I knew that he was still here. I went to a shop and got some food. The food here looked so appealing.

I returned and sat outside on Apostles deck for only 5 minutes when he bounded up the steps. "Oh my god-Eric!" he said, "How are you!" I was quiet but smiled. He said, "Me in a big hurry, come back soon." He ran off. It did not take him long to run an errand, and then he came back and we shook and embraced. "Apostles!" I shouted adding, "Good to see you! Me themaste?" (Do you remember me?) "Ney, ney, ney," he said. "Like a pain here," he laughingly said while grabbing his rear. He showed me his newly redecorated apartment and it was very nice. He said, "I and Marina are all the time together and in love." "Good," I acknowledged. "I am happy for you." He called Liana and she didn't believe it was me. He handed me the phone and I said hello to her, but I didn't understand her Greek. "That is you Eric!" she said. And so I passed the test.

I went about unpacking and Apostles commented, "You are to much thin. You no eat?" I said, "Egypt food no good. Arabs no good also." "Yah, yah, yah, you to much very right," he said. I went with him to Marinas house and she cooked a great bunch of potatoes and salad and gave me a cold beer. I eagerly ate. We then went to a friend of Marinas who was a potter and we each ate a piece of cake. The potter had beautiful pots of cobalt blue. We went to Lianas and she gave me a kiss and I was happy to see her. "Oh," she said, "You are too much thin." I went into her place and we listened to music. Then Apostles came and brought ice cream cake. Liana showed me the letter she wrote to me, but I didn't receive it in Cairo. We went to Apostles house and Liana and I talked, but only for a little while as I felt a timidness come upon me. I took a hot shower. We then went to eat souvlaki and drank a beer. From there we went to the Acri where I met Mia and the others. We talked but after awhile I felt alone because I am different from this group. It didn't matter, because I was with friends. We went home and slept at 2am and I was eager to call mom and dad in the morning.

**Thursday March 15**

I got up at 6am and started working the phone over to try and get through to the states for information. I tried many combinations of numbers and talked to information and they told me numbers that no one answered. I kept getting a please hold voice in Greek and the time sped by. Finally at 7 I got through and the phone rang and I heard dad. We talked awhile and mom also. It was 11pm in Duluth. They told me they were on vacation. They said I could expect some mail in New Delhi. I was trying to get as much out of all this phone conversation in this short time. But to remember important items and to converse requires effort for me. It was so grand to hear that they are good and healthy and everyone else was also. I ended our discussion telling them of my intentions to go to India and Thailand and head back to the U.S. in the summer.

I laid back upon the bed, thinking of them and then slept until 11am. I awoke to a gastrointestinal pain and then ran to the bathroom. My old buddy from Aswan was calling again.

A neighbor boy came by to visit with me. His mom came as well and asked to use the phone. I bought some goodies to eat. The little boy, whose name is Leftedi, got rough with me and I bounded about with him on my back. I went to sit him down and he pulled me over backwards on top of him and WACK went his head under my weight against a concrete floor. He cried but was alright as he rubbed his head.

I pedaled a distance into the city to a travel agent and they said it would cost $298, for an airline ticket that would fly from Athens to Bombay to Rangoon to Bangkok. That was a good price. I went into the city and really felt the rush of it coming to me in comparison to Cairo. It was so much cleaner and saner here. Everywhere I was feeling and seeing this difference.

Back at Apostles apartment, I was quite comfy just sitting back, playing guitar and then cooked some dinner for Apostles, but he didn't care for it, so I ate it alone. Liana and George came over and they brought Puzzler, there dog, who had a haircut and he now looked like a naked rat. We went to a movie starring John Travolta called Staying Alive and I paid for everyone. At 2am we went to sleep.

## Friday March 16

I was up at 8:15am and I ate and played guitar and then went to the city. I bought an airline ticket to Bombay, Rangoon and Bangkok for $298. I was not sure if it was all good because it went too smoothly. I said that to the Greek lady. "Something is wrong because this is working to well." "This isn't Cairo," she said ironically, then adding, "This is Greece."

I shopped at some bike shops for tires and other things. I had some thoughts as I pedaled through the streets about my travels and I reminded myself this is what I make of it. I asked myself if the going has been hard enough and I only can say I wish I would get into more binds and stay a little longer in places that are not so comfortable and just try to take it all in. Sometimes, as in Istanbul and along the Nile, I just move on and go, go, go. For India I don't want this, but more so, I want to keep moving and still get into it all. I had this need for an affair and wished I could meet a gal in this next week before going on to India, which will be on Sat the 24th.

I pedaled up to the Parliament Square at 7pm and waited to see if Richard from Australia would rendezvous with me as we planned. I sat there pondering and hoping my good pal would make it. I was there until 8pm and really looked forward to seeing him. But he did not show. So I went down to this restaurant and ate and drank a beer. I was a little down and I felt bummed not to meet him. I ate a souvlake and then went biking around the city and looked for something to do. I felt lonely and wished I could talk to someone. So I went through the plaka and then back to Apostles, where I met him, Marina and Liana. We sat and talked over a beer and George came over. He soon had Liana in the sack and then Apostles and Marina slept together and once again I was the lone wolf, as the sounds of lovemaking caroled the corridor.

## Saturday March 17

The alarm sounded at 5am and the phone rang and George got up and he has the biggest mouth in the morning. God he was loud and rammy. He shook me and said, "Teeagenneee," his craziness and mild disorder gave me a chuckle. They all had a big job to do today and it sounded like they were eager to get going to it. I got up and went to the shop and got some breakfast and then sat about playing guitar and watching TV all day long. It was a lazy day and I enjoyed these American movies (Westerns and WW2). I ate supper and then Apostles and Marina came over and we went down to the Acri, where I met pretty Kelly again and chatted with her.

I talked to many people about my travels and especially of interest were the comments my Greek friends had to say about Turkey. Greeks have a great amount of distaste for Turks. I could not convince them that it really was OK over there. They told me that a dispute which occurred between Greece and Turkey in the last year or so has made the countries relationship icy. Supposedly, a Turkish ship strayed into Greek waters and the Greeks arrested the crew. This tit for tat exchange has gone on for eons. As I sat with the girls and kidded them a bit, I really felt like there is a little bit of a follower in me, but also there is a conversationalist, a reporter, trying to unearth the story. I talked to a fellow about Egypt, and he thought wild people were moving in and upsetting the Egyptians.

Apostles and I took a cab home and along the way talked a little bit about our lives. He said he was happy with Marina. It felt like we were in a Bogurt movie, riding in that cab, with the lights flashing in our eyes.

Apostles went off to see Marina, and I went out for a walk, but not before I had to wire rig the door as I had no key. Later that night I came back and stuck a wire under the door and hooked the latch wire and then pulled it to release the catch. This was tricky in the dark, but I did manage to get it open.

## Sunday March 18th

The alarm rang and the phone rang and I was the only one who got up to answer the annoying noise. I shook George and then he stirred and once again like a storm cloud he burst with boisterous talk and activity this morning. He teased with me and I played along with it but it really was annoying. I slept until 10am and made some breakfast and really enjoyed just the quiet and the good food. I'm into mixing yogurt with fresh fruit or just fresh fruit blended in a mixer.

I went to the city in hopes of visiting the Acropolis and the museum, but found they were all closed. So I went up by the observatory and found a good place by this ancient rock wall and wrote a song about my bike and I. Down below, the Acropolis looked nice, accented under the mid day sunshine with a pinkish-orange color that I found very beautiful.

I went down through the woods to the Acropolis and sat back on a bench to watch the girls walk by. One gal came and sat by me. We talked and she was French and from Paris. Her name was Odela. She was traveling in Turkey and so we talked about that. An Aussie joined us and we talked about cycling and our travels. It was interesting to hear their plans and of their countries. They were interested in my tales. This is the fun part of being a traveler and I found it an educational tool as well. The Aussie left and I sat with the French girl.

We walked to another place and enjoyed the view of Athens. I noticed she had similar thoughts as me. I would be just about ready to suggest tea or coffee and she would offer it to me. Also, when I was thinking we should move, she'd say it at the same time as me. We walked through the city. I found Odela very easy going and flexible. We found a cafe and had coffee and we ordered the same drinks. I said would you like to go for a good walk and she said, "yes to the top of the monastery." That was just what I was suggesting. We hiked up and sat back. Then we went to a park and sat and talked. We played soccer ball and then walked to a restaurant. The lighting was amber and it felt so romantic. Our conversation was simple and carefree, frequently laughing.

We again walked up by the Acropolis, in the dark with the lights shining on the Acropolis.

While sitting on a bench as the moon rose and the stars shone I said, "I've never kissed a French girl from Paris. Can I?" We kissed a long one and embraced. Our breaths were hard and in unison. Then things got deeper from there. Her hand moved over my belt and then moved below. We found a place in the trees to vent our passions beneath the ancient monument. We giggled and moaned as people strolled along the Acropolis sidewalk, below us, hidden by trees as our caressing went wild.

I knew this girl thought like me. She needed this companionship just like I needed it. Nobody got hurt, nor was there any risk, we played it safe, no entry was made. We walked back to the busy street arm in arm. I told her she made my day and I would wish her the best and we parted feeling on the same wavelength with no strings attached.

I pedaled joyfully to Apostles where he and Marina were watching TV. I told Apostles about my activity and he told Marina, and god they laughed. "In the trees!" He then asked me about who is to be the next president – "What time the new president?" he said. I said, "November," and Marina laughed, but couldn't understand what he meant. But I understood the cryptic message and what he meant, though our 'presidents' were not currently standing at attention.

## Monday March 19

I was up early and went to the corner baker and he made me a fresh hot cheese filled pastry. There I met an english speaking Greek who told me about his stay in Boston. I made it to the fruit shop and then to a yogurt shop and stopped to buy a couple of eggs. Back at the apartment, I cooked a good breakfast and then rode down to the bike shop by the Platia, where I went to see Barbara. She is a pretty girl who works nearby. But she is a little mysterious to me, like an old girlfriend. I talked with her quite awhile. I couldn't put us together so came back to the apartment and cleaned all my stuff and my bike and did some laundry. It started to rain hard outside. Apostles came over, the phone rang all day long. I was told Apostles father was coming to Athens on an airplane. I cooked supper and enjoyed a little peace of mind as I ate. Then came Apostles into the apartment like a storm cloud and he slept and then we went to pick up Marina. He drove real fast. We went to a port where Apostles said his papa had sent him some fish. We passed a prison where the Greek president of 8 years ago was imprisoned. Apostles and Marina are so nice and good together. She has such peace to her and Apostles has such character. We waited at the port and I slept awhile in the car, then a truck came and we got the fish. We then went back home to sleep.

## Tuesday March 20

I made a good breakfast and then went to the city to buy some bike parts. There was a couple at the shop who were also biking around Greece. I talked to them for a long time and saw them off. Much deliberation was done on whether I should buy new tires and a chain. The tires the bike shop sold were not good tires. It cost $4 for a chain. I went to the city and met a Canadian gal. She wanted a souvenir. I took her to a pot shop and she bought a lamp that I wanted to buy two months ago. We had a nice talk. She was from Edmonton, and her name was Wendy. She works at A & Ad records. "How do you like the latest Bob Dylan album, "I asked her. She said, "I thought it was great."

I came back to Apostles place and stopped into a shop to buy a mirror and Sikes came by and gave me cake as he bought a new car. I sat about and wrote much in my journal. Marina came over and cleaned. I cooked a good meal of fish and chips and salad. Apostle joined me and cooked fresh shrimp and squid. I had never tried this before and I must say it was good. I went to the barbershop with Apostles and he spoke to the barber and told him to take care of me. I was given a nice trim by this barber, who wore thick glasses like those of Ray Orbison. He worked intently and seemed to put it all that he could to give this *American*a a stylish haircut apart from his normal business man haircut. He even blow dried my hair. He told me that his daughter was in San Francisco. He put lots of cologne on my face. I thought his scissors would surely trim my ears off. He left me with wings on my hair so I had to ask him to take a few extra swipes to cut them off.

I met George and Liana and Minos and we went to the Acri. We went to eat souvlaki and gayly strolled and kidded. I came back to the apartment and watched a western movie.

## Wednesday March 21

I have this routine in the morning, of going to the baker, and then to get some yogurt, and then return home to eat. I did some laundry and cleaned my bike derailleur. Apostles jacket needed repair and I sewed it up and then I tried to write down some songs, before making a run down to the supermarket. The girl in the store wanted to know where I was from and how I could afford my travels. I tried to tell her I saved money in the bank but she continued to be intrigued by that asking me that question only and I got annoyed.

I sat around all day eating popcorn and blending fruit drinks. God I was a pig. Marina came over and I sang one of my songs to her and she said it was good. Many people were calling on the phone and I got so annoyed because they would talk louder to me. "I don't speak Greek," I would say. They would shout at me as if the Greek would make sense with more volume.

Minas came by and asked why I sat in the house all day. Apostle said the same thing to me. I tried to explain that after all my travels and moving all the time that now it was nice to stop and collect myself. But really I think it's a nervous problem because of going to India and my apprehension. I cooked supper then Marina came over and I played a Pink Floyd record and copied a song. I drank a beer as Apostles and Marina played lovingly on the couch. Later I talked to Apostle and I said, "Why you don't marry Marina and make family because you is good father and Marina good mommy." He smiled and responded, "Yes I like that very much." Then he thought and said, "Why? Marina maybe no like me." "No, no, she like you too much." I said. He gave me his big Greek hug and said, "Eric you is full of bullshit."

Before going to be, he told me some Greek words to use on the telephone.

## Thursday March 22

I had to get up many times in the night to take a whiz. Beer! I was treated to fresh hot cheese filled pastry and mixed a yogurt shake with oranges for breakfast. While it rained outside, I wrapped a mail package and then took off for the city. I was annoyed as my bike slipped out of gear, and the tire is bad in the rear. So I went to the post office, dodging cars and pedestrians. The buses are a big problem here. At the post they told me it would cost $6 to mail my package. I said it's too much. They asked me, "What's inside." I told them souvenirs. They said if I opened it up and showed them what is inside the price would be $2.50. So I opened one end and they said ok, $2.50. I then closed it up and mailed it. But I still don't understand their price system.

I then went to the bike shop and bought a tire. "You're going to bike in India?" The man at the store said, "You crazy?" It was $4.50 for the tire. I went through the Plaka and the Monasteraki and looked at shops for a flashlight, then came back and looked at the supermarket for some munchies. I went back to Apostles in the rain. Then went to the supermarket later and bought a light and other things and they undercharged me. Thanks! I peddled to a shop for seasoning for my spaghetti, this guy tried to sell me noodles, and cheese and this annoyed me. I bought only the seasoning. Went back to the apartment and cooked the spaghetti but Apostles brought me mousaka. Marina then came over. I took a ride to the store for popcorn. A big dog came after me, then another dog chased also. I kicked the big dog square in the jaw. God he got pissed! I kicked him again. And I had to use the bike to keep him away from me. I belted him hard with the back tire. And I wanted to murder this damn dog. He kept coming at me. The other dog went behind me. I kicked him also, and had the big dog back off and I was going to squash him with my bike. This man came running along and he bitched at me to get back. I think they were his dogs. I then continued on and he kicked the dog as I walked away. Wheew.

I bought some popcorn and then went back and cooked it. Sat around playing guitar and watching TV with Apostles and Marina. Talked to a gal named Julie on the phone. Ate popcorn and played guitar until sleepy.

**Friday March 23**

Apostles slept in a tad too late and George burst in to the apartment and started screaming at him to get up and it was quite humorous as Apostle is quite reserved and George just keeps yelping. I got up at 9am and chowed down on my usual yogurt and fruit blended concoction in addition to a cheese filled pastry. I wrote down a few things. Sent post cards to friends and relatives from the Olympics. Leftedes, the neighbor boy, came over and he wanted to play. He got rough and I recalled the day before when he did the same thing and got hurt and went off crying, so I tried to be easy with him but he got rough and I pushed him to the floor and he banged his head and cried. I soothed him with a massage and he later gave me a hug and a kiss. He is a good kid and a very good communicator for a young lad. I took my new tire, and did a few adjustments to my bike. The gears seem to slip. I went down to the city center and went to the post and ticket office but they said come back at 5pm. I went to a gas station and installed my new tire onto the rim upon the sidewalk and people walked by and didn't bug me like in Egypt. I then went to Apostles place and his cousin named George, (the communist) came and he had a stereo cassette. I worked on a few songs and now have written about 6 songs of my own. Apostles came in and ate. I went to the city, picked up my airline, and then went to the Plaka to the shops where I bought a little gift for Apostles. It is a dish with Apollo on it.

It was so charming in the plaka at this late afternoon hour as the sun was setting and a red glow filled the shops with a warm relaxed atmosphere. I went to the supermarket and I felt a passion for the Greeks. They are rather to themselves and busy doers but also they have a life style that is romantic.

Back home, I cooked a meal of potatoes and spaghetti and the phone rang continuously so either I, George or the sleeping Apostles would answer it. Any time I answered it they laughed at my lack of understanding Greek. We sat and watched a music video on TV. I was beating on my homemade bongo and George was smoking cigarettes and Apostles started to throw this ball around. We got kind of wild. He kicked it and landed on his back. I threw the ball up and kicked it and it went straight to a vase and the vase fell and burst into pieces. That was my moment to give Apostles the dish I'd purchased for him. "Oh why no you have to give me this," he said. But I insisted. We got cleaned up. Hurrah and Marina came over. Then we went to the Acri and I met Demitri and also Petrakis and Mimi and I talked to everyone. Demitri and I had a good talk about Greece. He speaks great english. Apostles bought me a drink. I sense the comradery of my group of friends. We got to the city and ate strawberries and cream. Minos told me, "Remember God is always watching you, so give him your very best." And also, "There's no place like home." He told me he wanted to do like me and travel the globe. We clowned around. George would burp and say, "Mooscow." We rode in the car and saw the postes (transvestites) lining the streets. My friends loved to laugh at them.

Returning back to Apostles place I told him, "so many thanks for all you have done for me". But it didn't come out right. I felt scared in a way or maybe a little down because I know it won't be a picnic in India so maybe the parties over.

## Saturday March 24

The alarm rang at 4am and George got up and I shook hands with him. "Addie yasso," he said wishing me good luck. Then at 6am George and Liana got up and Apostle slept later and George started to bitch and he pestered me and hugged me and breathed all over me. Then they were off and I hugged them, but again I didn't say it right. "Thank you Apostles," I said sincerely. He was kind of weeping and said, "You too much good for me." We hugged and shook hands and he was off.

I slept in till 8am and then ate and got organized. Took a bath and listened to U.S. news on the radio. I heard of a disturbance in India where 100 were dead and 3000 were injured. *Great!* Just when I'm going there.

Leftedes came pounding on the door. I went out and swung him around. Then I went back in and closed the door. He pounded on it and I opened it and he had set a booby trap of boards which fell in against me.

I went to the shops, came back and then Marina came over. I packed up my few last things and she said, "I can't believe you will go. I think I will see you again this afternoon." So we hugged and I thanked her some more. Then, I was off.

I took my load and my box and went down the busy streets. I went through the traffic riding with one hand on the handlebars and the other holding the bike box. I had some close calls but did make good time in getting to the airport. I packed the bike up and sat to write in the journal. If only I knew what the next country was like and understood it, maybe I would feel better before going there.

I waited at the ticket counter for my seat pass and they started to talk about my big bike box. The man behind the desk said he would have to charge me $40 for this. I thought I might persuade him to let me by without paying be jokingly using my newly learned Greek words to get a laugh out of him. Just as Apostles had taught me, I said, "Thenpeedrawzee," rather arrogantly. He perked up and took a step back to repeat to a fellow ticket agent what I had just said. They lifted their eyebrows at me and shrugged there shoulders. "Thenpeedrawzee?" I overheard him say to the other. Then he wrote down the amount I would be charged. "Hey wait a minute, are you really going to charge me $40?" I asked. "Yes," he said matter of factly and adding, "You said you did not give a damn so here it is." Me and my big mouth! I thought 'thenpeedrawzee' meant something like the French word 'cest le vee' or 'such is life.' Now I was out $40. My coffers were not bottomless and now here goes more money out the window because of my thoughtless use of the Greek language. I was bummed.

I met Avril an Indian fellow, at the waiting area. We went hurriedly before the flight. I was nervous as we entered the big DC10 plane. I sat next to a cute dark skinned girl. The plane taxied along and roared off at about 5pm. I talked to the girl named Silva from Malaysia. She was interested in my trip, and I was in her life. She had a very English accent and lived in London. We talked alot about life. She was going home to vacation. I was traveling around the world. Avril was going to India to see his girlfriend.

After about an hour had passed, we ate a good meal and then in the inky blackness outside, watched some very curious flashes of light down on the ground to the north of our planes location. I was told we were over the Persian Gulf. It was either a lightning storm or else shelling from artillery while we were skirting around Iran. The Iraq-Iran war was going on, we were told.

Avril laughed and talked rapidly as he was anxious to get to India and to be with his lady. I dozed off a short while and the time zones changed quickly. At 1am Athens time, the plane landed, which was 4am Bombay time. Even as the plane taxied I could tell the air was hot and sticky. As we disembarked down the ramp, it was very hot and sticky and I was tired. We went through customs hectically and I had to fill out some forms for all of my possessions and there value. Many dark skinned, colorfully dressed people were sitting about. They peered at me with dark eyes. I felt like Egypt was drifting through me again.

# Chapter 13

# INDIA EXPERIENCE

**Sunday March 25**

There was an odor to India, like that of an old house. I unloaded the bike from the bike box and laid all my stuff out on the sidewalk, in a corner. I had to keep the people away from my stuff. A wall was behind me, while the bike was upside down nearest to the crowd, acting like a barricade and everything else was laid out in between. The derailleur had been broken in transit, probably it was banged while being loaded or unloaded from the baggage department on the flight from Athens. I tried to repair it as mosquitoes swarmed about and a big rat hopped past me, but it had been broken in half. Luckily I had purchased a back up derailleur in Gaza, Israel, and thus installed it onto the frame. I realized how fortunate it was that I bought that, while at the time it seemed like a lot of money to spend. Complementing my reassembly of the bike outside on the sidewalk were many dark skinned people with dark eyes watching my every move.

Already, at this early hour, 5:30am, I was sweating profusely from the stifling heat. Night was giving way to day, as the sky lightened in the east and soon the red sun peeked over the horizon. A tall dark Indian security guard loomed over me. "She's really heating up," he said in a tumbling accent, as a big drop of sweat fell from my temple. He was right. It was unbearably hot at 6am. I had everything loaded up onto the bike, but was perplexed with what to do with the bike box. I thought that it might be difficult for me to find another bike box, therefore stored it in a facility at the airport. It would cost a small amount of money for them to hold it for the next three months.

The roads leaving the airport were shabby at first and heavily littered with trash. The sight of dark skinned people lining the streets as they roamed to and fro could be seen for as far as the eye could see. My bicycle pedaling progress was slow, while stopping often to ask people for directions. Near the ruins of a building, with pieces of red clay pots littering the roadside, I asked a woman dressed in a silky red sari for directions. She spoke softly and told me to stay on the road and then turn left. Another person I asked was a man dressed in white pajamas and he said I must take the main route into Bombay. The smell everywhere was fecal. There was debris scattered all about and crumbling buildings of red brick atop reddish dirt. Then there were wonderful little motifs to remind me that I was in India. Sandscript signs, brass urns, whiffs of incense, the bikeshaws, the roofs of buildings with temple like eves.

Headway was made onto the busy streets of Bombay, into traffic jams, hectic roundabouts and eventually past tall buildings and vacant beaches. The sun was hot, it was muggy, but fortunately there was a slight breeze. I pedaled along very busy streets, wading through a river of humanity, past a train station and headed for the ocean near the Gateway to India. This arched monument was a leftover by Queen Victoria and the British. It was once a gathering place for royalty, now with many beggars gathered nearby holding there skinny fingers and palms outstretched, to seek money from tourists.

I went along a side street and asked a tourist where a cheap hotel was but then an Indian fellow, skinny as a toothpick said, "I'm sick, but follow me." He helped lead me to a hotel where I found a room. I gave him 10 rupees for his effort. He gave me a long face and whined, perhaps because of the meagerness of my offering. The hotel was like a large locker room and smelled about the same. It cost 25 rupees or $2.50 to share a room. Each 'room' was a six foot cubicle, one of about twenty, with walls made of a thin hardboard and going up about six feet, leaving another two feet or more to the ceiling. You could hear the person in the cubicle next to you and even the one on the far side of the room. It all blended into a hum of noise, like that within a chicken coup. The ceiling had a few fans twirling, so everyone felt a little breeze, although it was still very hot in there. My roomate sat atop his bed, in a yoga position and didn't look very well. He gave me a key to a lock on the door. I tucked my non-important belongings under the bed and headed out.

Before pedaling around town like a lost fool, I bought a map and then went back to the hotel to sleep. After a short nap I went out walking, but very slowly, as it was so hot outside. A cafe, which seemed inexpensive served me hot rice and chicken. It was not very good food. I then went walking around and bought a pineapple and some bread, munching while continuing to walk around.

As the sun was setting, I walked over to Gateway to India and watched with interest the cleverness of a little Indian girl who was a beggar working the hoards of tourists. She was about 3 years old and had a very high pitched voice. Her english, however was excellent. Her tactic to get money was to walk up and grab hold of your pants leg and say, "Please sir, my mommy is very sick and I need your help to make her better." She was very persistent and would not give up until she got some money. I could not resist her story and gave her a couple of rupees. She said, "thank you sir," and then went on her way. She would do the same to the next tourist and the next. Then she would empty her cup into the bag of an adult who would quickly come up to her. There were also several European beggars also seeking handouts from the tourists. I was told they were drug addicts who had become hooked while in India and now were stranded without enough money to go back home.

I went back to the hotel and saw that my roommate was high on some kind of drug trip. He sat on the bed, in a lotus position, with his eyes rolled back into his head. His shirt was off and his skin appeared lumpy. He was very pale and there were tracks up on his arms. As I reclined for my sleep he looked at me and started to converse. He said he was from France and had been in India for 14 months. It was his 7$^{th}$ time here. He offered me a smoke on his pipe but I declined.

I fell asleep and awoke at midnight, hearing and seeing my roomate smoking 'brown sugar'- hashish? and he was so loaded he talked to himself and laughed, then cried, then jerked his head like he had bugs flying inside his brain. All night long I could hear him smoke and go through this madness. He wasn't the only one, other people made so much noise it was difficult to sleep. Their radios were blaring at 2am. I got up and asked the manager to please tell them to shut them off. This didn't win me any favors with him nor with the hotel guests. They argued and bitched when he told them to turn off the radios. Bugs bit me so badly that I put some OFF bugspray on. I was so tired that I actually slept ok despite the noise, the heat and my drugged out roomate.

## Monday March 26

First thing in the morning I went to the Salvation Army across the street and asked for a room. I got one and transferred my stuff over there. I then went to the city tourist office for maps and information.

I needed to get some anti-malaria drugs and anti-dysentery capsules. First I had to go to the hospital and get a prescription. After some searching on my bike, I found the hospital on a busy narrow street, with New Orleans style buildings. Inside it was looking like a disaster zone. The halls of the hospital were lined with injured, bleeding, moaning, sickly people waiting for treatment. They looked so pathetic, I wondered why no help was given to them. It seems in India one has to wait their turn until an opening comes. After much commotion, a very nice doctor, who was interested in my journey, helped me. He was very relaxed and casual as we walked past all the patients. I thought that was strange that I should pass all these needy people and that the doctor should seem so jovial passing them. We went into his office, which had a very nice rolltop desk and he wrote up my prescription. Then he escorted me past the old, the dying, the sick and the injured and with a smile watched me pedal off on my bike.

The road was absolute madness, with cars, buses, bikes and shuttle bikes clogging the streets from curb to curb. I felt like I was running the rapids of a river canyon. In some ways it was exhilarating, like being in a race, with all the noise and people lining the streets. Then some nut in a truck became irritated and accelerated ahead into the crowd, until everyone did the splits and got the hell out of his way.

I headed for the business district, where a chemist could fill out my prescription in the case of malaria. I made my way through the helter-skelter streets toward downtown, past a cricket game in progress. This area of Bombay was a more 'green' section with parks. It was interesting to watch the lanky Indian pitcher run toward the batter in a very flamboyant style. His arms cranked the ball around and around and his legs skipped to and fro and then he let loose the speeding ball. The wicker stood nonchalantly and then clanked it on his bat and the ball bounded into the field, but the players only watched it with interest, and did not run as they would in baseball. I thought what a strange game this is.

The streets of the business district of downtown were near the Indian Ocean, and they were calm despite a dust storm blasting sand everywhere. I found the chemist and he filled my prescription. The container said, 4 anti-malaria tablets, one per day, 2 after 6 hours. I also bought pills in case I became sick from dysentery. There were two different kinds of pills. One was to help bind up the bowls to prevent dehydration and cramps and the second was to kill the bacteria. I put them in my pack hoping to never use them.

Returning to the hotel it was noon, and a good lunch was to be had at the Salvation Army cafeteria. I went to the airlines to ask about my flight itinerary through Dacca and Rangoon. I met Shawn, from Ireland and we talked of our journeys. He was back packing around India and found it "excitingly frustrating."

I washed and packed up, then went for a walk with a fellow from New Zealand. The streets were packed with Indian people and white tourists. We went down by Gateway to India, looking out on the murky waters of Bombay Bay, where small boats seemed to be floating in scum. Haggard drug sellers and tenacious beggars bugged us. I turned the game on these people. "Baksheesh, baksheesh, please give me rupees," I said in an annoying and pushy way to them with an open hand. It was a cruel thing to do. But one becomes numbed by the multitudes. They then left us alone.

At a small restaurant with the wonderful smell of Indian cuisine, we ate a good meal of curry potatoes and meat that was not very spicy. There, we talked about travels over a cup of tea. I was debating whether to leave my guitar in storage at the hotel. If I was to strap it on my bike and bring it with me as I traveled around India, I would be afraid of damaging it or having it stolen. The Salvation Army seemed a good place to store things.

Back at the hotel I talked to a hairless, clean shaven and friendly fellow from England. He looked like a brute but was casual and pleasant. I got into my bunk and found it hard to sleep because of all the traffic noise and people talking outside. There was a blend of craziness in the sounds of beeping horns and, people shouting in undecipherable languages. I used my earplugs and sanity returned.

## Tuesday March 27

Almost to my regret the morning came. It was warm at dawn. I decided to leave my guitar in storage at .50 rupee per day. It seemed ok. I ate with a fellow from Reno who smiled nervously

## THE WHEELS OF FRIEND

and said he had lost his job. Now he traveled. He said he had ridden a bike in some parts of the world, but then his knees hurt and his bike was stolen in Ireland. I returned to my bunk to get my bags. The skinhead Englishman was just getting up and went to the washroom. Suddenly he came back saying his wallet was missing and he was in a panic. "I've been ripped off," he cried. "Me money was here around me neck." I helped him retrace his steps and then search his bags. I discovered his wallet hanging from his bed post. "Here it is," I said. His eyes rolled back, "Oh thanks a million blowck, I put it there last night and forgot all about the bloody thing." He was a nice young fellow and lucky that nobody had stolen it.

I packed up the bike just outside of the Salvation Army on this sunny morning and noticed that the seat was ripped from a cat during the night that thought it was a good fabric to work his claws. I met one Indian guy who said, "Where you going?" "Delhi," I responded. "Humph, good luck," he said and shook my hand.

I was off through the streets of Bombay, feeling the weight of the bike. It was heavy, but ok once in motion. I felt as if I was heading into the wilderness, fear invaded my system, still I pedaled north and made it past the airport and was almost wishing I would turn around and leave India. A deep sense of dread took over and a desire to quit rather than beginning to cross this great unknown.??? Oh how this was confusing. I almost wanted to pack up and go home and to say, ok I cycled in India.

I continued on heading north out of the big city. There was a man on the roadside selling bread off display racks he'd built onto his bicycle frame. I went right passed him and then thought maybe I should go back. I did and bought a loaf of bread from him.

Frequently it was necessary to stop and ask for directions and whenever I did, people poured around me. They looked at my hairy legs. I pedaled past many poor people along the road. Human shit was on the roadside and everywhere it stunk. I started to leave the city although it extended for many miles. When I stopped for a cold drink at 11am people just stared at me. They laughed at me and I laughed back. This one guy left madly because I did that. They played with my bike and I shouted at them, not to.

The road went up some hills. It was really getting hot out and there was a stiff wind. The terrain was a certain brownish-red color and the trees were a vivid green.

I stopped at 1pm at a fruit drink stand and again people stared at me and at the bike.

They came running to encircle me. It was a little unnerving for this Minnesota boy.

I walked away and they still came to me and stared. How rude!

The asphalt road was sticky from the heat. My narrow tires made a slush'y sound while I stood up and beared down on the pedals to climb up a twisting grade 25 miles north of Bombay. Goo'ey clumps of tar plugged the fender's, dragging the bike to a stop. I had to stop often to use a stick and peel off the sticky tar. The sun's heat was so intense that my watch burned against my wrist. Before taking it off, I noticed the time was 2: 15 P.M., the hottest period of the day. My handlebar thermometer said the temperature was around 115 degrees. The road was nearly empty of traffic. Most of the drivers sought refuge under trucks or beneath a shade tree. An occasional water buffalo would amble across the road and judging by their slow gait, they too were suffering from the heat. I could not escape the inferno, rising higher and higher; I felt my own blood would boil over, as I pedaled into a heat mirage.

I continued onward and realized that I had drunk too much water. My belly hurt, because it was so hot and my mouth so dry. For some reason my thirst was not satisfied. I longed for a Coke. I felt tired from the heat and had to stop often. One time was to eat some fruit at a nice cool spot under a tree.

I continue on, but then the bikes derailleur broke apart. I pulled over by a morgue or a temple and repaired it. Many people stopped and came to look at me. While repairing the bike a couple came up to light incense at the base of the temple.

I made my way up an interesting hillside. There were big rock formations that looked mesa like. This brought back reminders of familiar countryside. It made me think of someplace I'd been to back in America. I went through a forest of nice green trees. It was like being in Minnesota. It even cooled down. Wow I felt better. The traffic decreased and for a short while I was euphoric. Then I passed through that zone and was back into red dirt, and scattered trees, the bliss had left. A motorbike passed with the rider wearing a Bell helmet.

I swung into a restaurant and got two drinks. These seemed like nice people. They gave me some space and did not stare. I continued down the road and enjoyed that it was much cooler at 6pm. I made it to a cafe 20 kilometers away as it got dark. The big trucks at this hour were hair raising, as they did not turn their lights on until it was really dark. I ate a delicious meal called Masala Dosa, a taco like food that was spicy hot. It was so hot, that I drank a lot of tea. People stared at me and chuckled. I had to pull the bike right into the café, because people were mobbing it.

After a filling meal, my belly rumbled and I continued on my way looking for a camping place. The road was very treacherous, and my choice was made quickly into a open field, under a power line. It was a good spot. Close enough to still see the highway. I got into my tent and watched the trucks going past, flashing there lights at each other and blowing their shrill sounding horns. It was an enjoyable cinema, then "snap!!" my tent pole broke and the tent fell in on me. I had to get outside and use my flashlight to figure out how to fix it. I repaired the broken tent pole by using a leftover spoke and some black tape to reinforce the break.

## Wednesday March 28

It was a hot and sticky night, but then toward morning became cold and yet still sticky. I tossed and turned all night. There was so much truck noise. I got up before sunrise and pedaled up the road to a café, where I ate a great omelet. I met an Indian fellow who'd lived in North Carolina for 3 years. He showed me some Indian onion rings and fried potatoes, but I did not buy them. I was off. This was a good time to ride. It was cool and pleasant and peaceful. I passed many other bike riders. They all ride a black bike, that looks very heavy and solid and have only a single speed. This was pretty country, where there are sometimes nice groves of forests interspersed with dry land. The trucks became my main hazard. They would blast there shrill horns and blow by belching out black smoke that smelled bad.

I pedaled until 1pm then stopped for a cold drink at a well. I started thinking about being done with all this traveling and settling down in Duluth, and having a home and a family and a cold ice box with cold water and water melon and ice cream. Wouldn't it be nice to have some peace to my life. Then it was time to pedal onward along a sticky asphalt road.

I stopped at a pump for a drink. Water seemed available along my route by just finding these pumps. I had no stomach problems as yet. I continued on, under a frying sun, in the stifling heat and went 10 more miles and at this next drink stop a guy said, "Where do you go?" I said to Delhi. He said, "Ah do you speak Hindi or Gange?" "No, I speak only english." He said, "I don't speak english," and walked away. Am I in France?

I went a little farther down the road, crossed over a bridge and suddenly the rear rack cracked loose and all my gear went down and hit the road. It had broke clean off. I found some bolts in my pack and then took wire from a nearby fence to repair it.

I was fighting the heat of the day and stopped into one roadside stall where they gave me a lemonade drink. Then I drowned my head and body in cool water at a roadside pump. This was the only way to cool down. It did not take long in this arid air, until I was perfectly dry.

I saw a bad truck accident (one of many) and god were they smashed. I saw any people swimming in dirty water in a ditch. I stopped for a drink and wet myself off and an India guy talked to me. He bought me a drink. My feelings were better toward the people, here in India. They didn't say too much. They just stared at the bike and me. They really were blown away by me. I wish it wasn't so. I'd rather not have this kind of 'rock star' reception.

I went on, pedaling northward across a delta plain and looked for a cafe. Trucks drove me right off the road. They did not tolerate swerving around bikes. They just blew the horn and expected me to jump off the asphalt onto the rough shoulder. There were some close calls.

I asked many people where a café was. It appeared there was one here but it was not to be found. I pedaled on, enjoying the sunset and continued on into the dark and then finally found a cafe.

I ordered an omelet, potatoes and bread. Enjoyed a cold drink during the meal and had a lassi (buffalo milk, rose water, sugar and crushed ice,)for desert. It all cost 200 rupees which was about $2. I felt it was kind of expensive. Roadside truck stops were a little more pricey. People stared at me and a crowd sat to watch me eat. From all directions they watched me. The waiter spoke good english.

I headed away from the crowd, entering into the cricket sounding darkness and annoying truck traffic. I went about an hour north and saw a truck burning off of the roadside. That was where I ducked off into a field to camp.

## Thursday March 29

I awoke at 3:38am and dozed off occasionally, smelly something awful and felt like I wished morning would never come. This India bike riding was giving me anxiety. But morning came and I got up and started packing. I thought something smelled during the night and wasn't sure if it was me or if there was some trash nearby. In the morning light I discovered what it was. I had set my tent up on a place where people took a shit! Now the tent smelled and I attempted to wipe it off, only making things worse.

As I pushed the bike out to the road, I saw an Indian fellow dressed in a white outfit walking out toward the site I had just left. He carried in his hand a little clay pot with water to wipe his rear. This was probably his shit on my tent.

I pedaled up the road and found a cafe. Went to the toilet and got stranded there without toilet paper. I waddled to get water, as this was the custom. Then I washed myself with soap and water.

While I ate an omelet for breakfast, everyone watched me. Now, I felt I was getting used to this.

I headed down the road against a steady headwind. A truck narrowly missed me, I dove off the road and cursed. It made more sense to dare the truckers to let me stay on the road. The shoulders were very rough and would damage my tires. Yesterday I sewed up a tire with dental floss and now I saw a seam was tearing in another area. I would have to stay on the asphalt as much as possible. They would blow their horns at me like crazy, and I'd wave them around me.

I stopped for a drink and biscuits called Glucose. Everyone just stared at me stern faced. I laughed and would say hello. "Smile!" I said. There was no reaction. I belched. And they stood back. For that moment, I felt they were like cattle. Just staring at me.

Pedaling northward, I made it to a toll booth. Dosed myself with water, soaking everything wet. Even my towel was wet, head cap, etc, all draped over my wet body. I headed out across dry countryside on this hot day. It was real hot, but I was comfy inside my wet caccoon. It dried fast. Again I stopped after 10k and dosed myself with the same method. At the pump, I met an Indian man who was British and was living in India. He was a kind fellow.

I moved on against a hard, hot wind and rough road. Trucks were my major annoyance. One truck stopped me and the driver offered me a ride and some water. I thanked him but refused. I continued pedaling on to another roadside pump and again dosed myself with water, but this time had a bloody nose. There was probably some medical reason for this. Now I wondered if I was drinking too much water.

I rode on and many times dosed to stay cool. I saw a temperature readout on the side of a bank that read 44 degress celsius, which calculated to 110 Fahrenheit. I stopped for melon and discovered that ice cold water melons were real good. It was so hot out and yet I passed women working on the roads. They cracked rock into gravel and carried baskets of rock on their heads. I asked a fellow where a restaurant was and he told me 10k. Asked another fellow and he said 4k. Asked another guy and he said, "There is no restaurant." Shaking his head side to side like it was a spring.

I was so pooped and hot I went into a business to ask a fellow. He gave me cold water. He said, "In two kilometers you will find a cafe." Then I asked another fellow and he said, "Yes in 2ks." Then I met a guy on the road and he pointed where to turn off. I did so and noticed that his pointing finger wasn't pointing straight, rather just waving a index finger in the general direction.

I found the restaurant and went inside feeling very tired. People gathered around my bike and began touching the brakes, pulling on levers, ringing the bell. I was too tired to care. It was dark in this restaurant. They had booths, with naugahyde seat covers, like the U.S. did back in the 1960's. I ordered some food and it took awhile to arrive. I ate this very hot, spicy dahl, rice, chili and potatoes and it was washed down with hot tea! It was so damned hot in that restaurant and I was eating this hot food and all these people gathered around to watch me eat. There body heat made it even hotter. I was sweating profusely and ready to pass out. "Could you please turn the fan on?" I asked the owner. She turned it on but seemed surprised at my request. Did they really think it wasn't hot enough in there to turn on the fan? Then the power went out and they brought me a candle. I was overheated and had to go. I paid my bill after some discussion on the price.

I went on up the road to camp on the roadside in a field. It was still fucking hot at 10pm.

## Friday March 30

I made good effort to get going early and was on the road at 6:30am. The trucks were many, and they blew their horns constantly on this stretch of highway. I rode for about two hours then pulled into a cafe for breakfast. Inside, I met a couple from Gujarat. They helped me order an omelette and cream filled pastry. We talked. They were very kind. He was in the army. When I told them of my route, they said I had missed Baroda, which was too bad as it was according to them a very nice city. I was thankful to have their help in ordering food and her offers of staying with them. This Indian hospitality seemed wonderful.

I left the restaurant, headed out under the blazing sun, and was aglow with good feelings, when a truck came up on my rear. He blew his shrill horn expecting me to jump off of the road. There was a deep drop off the shoulder and embankment. I waved for him to go around. He blew his shrill horn. I shouted, "turn your fucking steering wheel and go around me." The big truck came right up alongside of me and suddenly whack! Something hit my helmet, spinning it sideways on my head. At first I thought it was a swat from an arm, but then as the truck passed I saw the passenger pull his leg in. I careened down into the ditch, holding the bike upright and came to a frightful stop. I vowed to slash his tires if I caught him. He had run me off the road on purpose, as he had the entire road. There was no traffic.

My head hurt from the jolt, when I stopped for cold Soyso and water. While doing so, some guys played with the gear levers on the bike. I hollered at them. When I pedaled off, clang went the gears. It took some adjusting of the gear shift to bring it back to normal.

I stopped to take a picture of 5 women walking alongside of the road, holding jugs of water on their heads. They were so elegantly dressed in their Indian saris, and adorned with jewelry. This was classic India apparel. I snapped several shots then realized I'd left the lens cap on. They wanted baksheesh for another photo. I quickly took off, stopped, turned around for a photo of them and left.

It was really heating up at 11am when I stopped for water. This was the start of dunking myself at wells on this day. I had learned, that the heat could be tolerated ok via this way. I thought about Duluth, about winter and about good water. I thought about having a business there. Maybe it could be a World Sandwich Restaurant.

There was a hot headwind. It was like standing in front of a blower from a furnace. Everytime I stopped, I was mobbed by people. I made it into Ahmemdebad and stopped for a drink and was again mobbed. I had two glasses of lassi that were ice cold. That was damn good. I could feel it coat my stomach and leave a cool, soothing glow inside my belly. The shop owner graciously gave me a good deal on the 2$^{nd}$ cup. But when you watch them make these things it is a wonder more sickness doesn't come. They take a block of ice, chip off some pieces, stick them into an inner tube, pulverize them with a hammer and then dump the ingredients of sugar, buffalo milk, rose water and ice together.

I rode through this busy and congested city. There was an excellent statue of Ghandi in the middle of a street intersection. I wanted to stop and take a photo of it but the mobs of people and the horrendous traffic hindered this. I asked directions on how to get out of town. I could see this was a developing town, with lots of new construction going on. But the methods of building are archaic, as they use human power for most everything.

I stopped to have a cold soft drink called Limca and was mobbed by children. They touched me and giggled. They especially marveled at my hairy arms and legs, "Like a monkey," I overheard one say.

I made headway under this roaring heat and after many miles pedaled down the damn nicest road ever in all my travels. There were trees lining this beautiful stretch of road. It was so incredibly hot that each pedal was as efficient as possible to save energy. I felt like I was in a psychedelic dream from the intense heat. I stopped by a water pump and cooled off as kids played naked under it.

This royal road continued until I made it into Ghandinigar. This city was in an early form of development. It was named after Mahatma Ghandi, the great spiritual leader from India. I found a hostel that was a rather elegant old building with single rooms and shared bathrooms. It was a cool place and cheap, only 50 cents a night; with an International Youth Hostel Card. The room even had embroidered white curtains, that blew in with the hot wind and a little balcony overlooked a green area to the west. It was a nice place to kick back and come down from all the stress of India.

I took a shower and then went to a restaurant, where the owner told me to park my bike on the street. "No way," I told him. He did not understand why, but soon did, as a crowd gathered around the bike. He kindly let me park it up by the front window where I could watch it. He also appointed someone to use a stick and drive people away from my bike and from staring at me. I ordered masala dosa but he persuaded me to try umbagar. So I got umbagar, a pizza like food and a bowl of hot soup. He told me of another good Bhanjia (restaurant) and I went there to eat with him. He turned out to be the owner of the restaurant. He was 31 years old and his name was Struddah. We talked much about Ghandi and India. He warned me of looters and violent people. We had a good discussion of Indian food, of the currys and of the dahls. This was a good, kind man. I had ice cream, for desert, drank two sodas and he paid the bill. The restaurant was called Struddah Dining Hall and it was located near the Youth Hostel. I'll remember the kindness of this most gracious host.

I went to buy some goodies. The people got kind of crazy near the theater. They mobbed me. I returned to the hostel and worked on my bike. I sewed up a tear in my pants and nurtured my aching, very sore ass.

## Saturday March 3

The fan annoyed me at 3:30am, so I got up and turned it off. Then a cool breeze came in from the balconey door. I dozed off and slept nice until 6am. I wanted to stay, but realized the length of my journey and therefore got underway. While pedaling down these nice roads and leaving Ghandinigar, I thought what a peaceful place and cheap. There was a touch of Ghandi in that youthful city. I was sad to leave, almost felt like going back and staying a week.

But, I rode on into Humatnagar as it was getting hot. I put on my wet wraps at 11am. Within 15 miles, I was nearly dry. While in town, I asked for lassi. Here I was given an ice cream lassi with fruit and nuts. People just swarmed around me. Men tried to keep them away. Then the police came with sticks. People just swarmed around me. The police got rifles and looked like they intended to use them to protect me from these wild people. These people just looked at me so lustfully. Like a leopard eyeing his kill. They got to my bike and touched everything. Yet there was a peace to them, they were not violent. It was just the momentum of the crowd that caused a pushing feeling.

I was trying to move through this big mob of people and said aloud, "My god, you people are like flies on shit!" This white turbined elderly man with big front teeth said, "And who is the shit? It is you!" I did not think anyone could speak english in this crowd. I was wrong. Finally I was off and the crowd ran behind me.

I went a few more miles and again stopped for a dose of water at a well and a man said, "You are air conditioned." I felt good riding now. I went 10k's and cooled off again. Today there was a good tailwind. I sailed down the road and made it to Seljmet at 2pm. There was a circular Hindu temple with elephants carved onto the front that was worth visiting. The temple was carved from a dark rock and was around 1000 years old. Many finely carved figures of men and elephants in battle, adorned the exterior. It was hot and stuffy inside the dark temple. There were many figures of gods or goddesses that I did not relate to. I knew too little to understand this place.

I dosed my body again at 3:30pm and headed for the hills under a blazing sun. Up I climbed on bumpy, shitty roads. I had seen peacocks today and monkeys but now it was dry-desert like countryside. The road twisted up a grade, and with this heat it was challenging to keep the energy going. I pedaled past a few rambler style houses that were good enough for use in the U.S.A., if they were tidied up. They were the bungalow style homes, and India was where the word originated.

Women here wore nice, colorful outfits. I headed for a village in the dark to get a cool drink. I arrived in the dark after tackling these rough roads. Feeling tired, I sat and drank a lassi as a crowd gathered. They asked me many questions. "What country you are from?" "How you come here?" "Why you come here?" I got flustered with all this madness and took off through town.

I rode along a sticky pavement toward the Rajastan border and stopped into a little restaurant and ordered some dahl, rice and chippadee. The food was delivered and a big crowd of people gathered to watch me eat. They filled the doorway to the restaurant. I was dipping the chippadee into the dahl with my left hand. "You must stop!" said a plump man in a white robe. I looked at him puzzled. "You must stop, you are making us sick!" he demanded. I said, "what it the matter?" He said, "You cannot eat with your left hand. You are making us sick. You must not eat with your left hand in India!" "Ok," I said, putting my left hand to my side and eating with my right. I ate a good meal and wondered about not being able to eat with my left hand. "Left hand is for dirty business," the man told me.

After my meal, I stopped at the market place, where they wanted 20ruppees for an apple. This seemed expensive so I shopped around and this crowd followed me. It was hot and I was tired and I was pestered and they pushed me until I just said, "Get me out of here." I took off as people seemed to chase me and heckle me all the way out of town.

I went a few miles down the road and found a place to camp. I was washing off my body with water from my water bottle, when a man came along. I had heard two men talking and a dog barking previously. This man came along as I was standing there naked after my 'bath.' He looked at me as I covered myself. I said, "All India cycle tourist." "Ok," he said. We shook hands. He pointed to his house. "Ok," I said. He said something else. I said goodnight and we again shook hands. It was a nice place to be as darkness set in. There was a good field of stars shining overhead and peace returning to me.

## Sunday April 1

This date marked 10 months of travel. I slept good until 3:30am. Then it was so, so. A rock was pushing under my back. I got up and going at 6:30. There were rough roads to pedal down and more hills followed. I tackled them under the early morning sun. I stopped to eat at a café that was made for tourists. They didn't have anything nourishing to eat but did have snack like foods. I crossed the street and ate at a food stand where they offered a fresh orange drink along with spicy hot papado, which are batter dipped potatoes and onions fried in boiling hot oil. While I was eating, a man tampered with my bike. He grabbed the gearshift and worked it over several times. I warned him to stop it and go away, but when he did not I got up and slapped his hand. He left but his friends stayed and continued to tease me.

With indigestion, I pedaled on my way as it was getting hot and hotter. I soaked myself under a well pump at 10am. It felt good to be riding along after wetting down. To my delight good water was to be found at these pumps. I stopped often to wet myself. Sometimes local people pumped the well handle when I washed under the spigot.

It was slow going because of the hard hills and rough roads. Winds were strong. It must be a harsh landscape and environment to live in. I toughed it out through the heat and dry air. At one point I shouted aloud to myself, "Why do I do this? Just keep going!" I rode into Udaipur at 1pm and saw a very ornate palace near a lake.

At the famous Lake Palace there was no one who could watch my bike. I locked it up to a sign as people stared at me. Up on the second floor of the palace, I met a man by the name of Craig Betos Canteera from Lake Arrowhead, California. He had a video camera and he interviewed me for a few minutes. We talked and he advised me to go to China.

After looking around the ornately white Lake Palace, and seeing all of the grandeur from the days of the maharajah, I met an India man who was from Jaipur. We talked about India and I learned that he worked for General Electric. He was a sales engineer. I went with him into the city. He and I had dinner and he bought me masala dosa. He had sold an X-ray machine the day before and was happy. We ate a good dinner. But I had to keep watching my bike. This annoyed my new friend and he kept saying, "Nobody will touch it." But I was cautious and kept going outside for a look. I saw two guys working over my tire pump. I starred at them and they left. India people understand punishment or guilt. I returned to eat with Mr. O.D. Sharma and again while we were eating I looked often at my bike.

I looked again and suddenly saw that my bike was gone! I dashed through a crowd of people and went outside and saw a little girl dragging my bike away. I ran up to catch her and she got scared. The bike fell into her arms and upon her and was slowly crushing her. The weight was too much but she was managing to keep it off her. I grabbed the bike before it fell completely on her and she ran off and ducked into a doorway along the corridor of shops.

I returned my bike and again sat with O.D. Sharma and we talked much about everything. He invited me to his home. After our dinner he rode with me on his bike to a sweet shop and we had a nice snack. He then told me it would not be possible for me to come to his home. He really helped me so much, and was very kind. I asked him if it was ok to touch the cows on the street. He said, "The cow is like to touch your mothers feet. Yes you can touch the cow and it will bring you life." So I touched the cow and as I rode off. I told him, "Touch the cow." And as he looked at me with acknowledgment. I passed another cow and gently touched that one. He was smiling at me and we waved goodbye.

I stopped for a cool drink and met some tourists. They said I should stay here in this city for awhile, as it was a nice place. So I took it easy and thought ok, I'll stay. I found they're from U.K., and enjoyed seeing them argue for a bit. I followed them out to Hotel Keerteel, which was rather like a farmhouse in the country, about two miles from downtown Udaipur. The manager said I could pitch my tent and camp outside of the house. It cost two rupees per night. I stored my belongings and went back to the city. Riding again past the palace, I toured the nice streets and markets of this city.

I met an attractive, young, Indian lady who was very friendly and seemed interested in me. She was about 19 years of age and a student in town, although she was not from Udaipur. We had a cool soft drink together and talked. I then gave her a lift on my bike to the entryway of her apartment house. During the ride, she sat on my crossbar, with her dark thin legs, covered by a long dress, off to one side. She was very relaxed and we talked quaintly and laughed. I was amazed at her balance and poise as the streets were rough and it could not have been a very comfortable position. People looked at us in a startled fashion as we went past. I then said goodbye to her without even getting her name nor address. It was a short lived, but memorable and exciting meeting.

As the sun set, I returned on paved roads to Hotel Keerteel out in the country. I met more traveling people at the hotel. There was an English girl who was weary of Indian men from the many encounters she had experienced. This 'hotel' was a quiet place, there were some who sat quietly and read. I showered and relaxed, drank a soda and in the dark met other traveling people. There was an Englishman staying there, named Ron, who was apparently senile.

## Monday April 2

I awoke at 3:30am as a mad rooster would crow, but it did not sound like the roosters back home. I don't think that rooster knew the time. He would not shut up. Off and on I slept until 6am. I cleaned up my bike and found the wheel bearing on the front end was getting loose. A breakdown here would end my bicycle journey.

I ordered breakfast in the hotel, which was more like an apartment house and talked to Ron. We ate and then I met a German. I noticed the French girl was pretty, but she ignored me. The English girl said I was doing it right. Ron said I was mad. "Just remember," he said, "a shroud has no pockets." He then paused and finished, "a rich man's a priceless commodity."

I pedaled off after breakfast and was feeling good to have met these other travelers. I wanted to stay longer at the place. In fact it crossed my mind that I might just stay here for the duration of my visit to India. But reality set in, and it was time to get going.

I went pedaling the one or two miles back into town and bought a sweet cake and then some bread rolls and headed out of Udaipur. With the water bottles filled up, the journey continued down some shitty roads. Then up, up I climbed across valleys and over hills with good smells in the air. People seemed kind here today. There was not much traffic. I rode with an Indian biker. We raced along for 10K's on his Hero bike he stayed with me. He invited me to stop for a soda but I had to go on.

On my way to Kthdarwara, I went past many Jain temples. One was made in 741 A.D. Monkeys climbed upon them. I didn't go in because of the kids outside and my bike was at risk. A temple in the valley was a clever way to wall in from the outside world. There were gates at both ends. Upon entering the village of Kthdarwara, I got some food and then looked for ice cream. The Indians laughed at my searching. I forgot how to say ice cream in Hindi. It was another moment of frustration. I headed out of town.

In Rathmansu, I stopped into a tourist bungalow and relaxed to drink a limca. It was a good lunch and then was time to head off. The head wind was strong and the road turned continuously into the wind. I felt cool today, as it was not as hot as the previous days. Still I wet toweled myself and rode along until 3:30pm and then pulled over to wash. My map showed a distance of 20 miles or so to the next town, so I thought it best to eat now.

A fellow offered me a soda and some food, so I went into his little hut. It was a small cafe, restaurant, hotel, but it looked mostly like a hut. He wanted to know what I wanted to eat and I told him dahl. He said ok. I thought he had it was all ready to serve. He got busy preparing the food. First he had to get the clay oven up to temperature. He used a hand accordion like blower to get the oven up to temperature. I wondered what I'd gotten myself into, but knew that I had a barren section of road ahead and would not find provisions for many miles.

He made me a bread like stuff called bongee. He cooked it there in his clay oven. Then he gave me some spicy dahl sauce with potatoes etc. I ate and drank a pop. We talked a little as he knew some english. He was an alright guy. He laughed and clowned and helped me. It was good food, very spicy and I ate three breads and lots of pani.(water) Others came and sat around me. He told me he was a papa and had one son. I paid him and we wished each other well. When I was outside a kid wanted some money and stuck his hand in my face, "You no Ghandi." I said. He ran off to tell his mom. Wonder what she said. I gave another kid some candy and he was happy.

I rode off in the late afternoon sun, heading down a long hill and was thinking if I would get sick from that spicy food. I could see the road rising upwards into a 'little mountain' and felt reluctance. I began the long hillclimb and got into a rhythm of cycling and recalled how girls in my class thought that the only thing on the mind of us guys was to lay them. They were right! They were always scared of me, I thought. This labeling of a guy can leave him with a complex. It now seemed all those years of feminine pursuit was such a waste of energy.

I stopped at a water pump and a girl pumped water for me. I then pumped for others. Soon there were 10 guys who I pumped for as if they were the sheep of my shepherding!

As the sun was setting behind some small mountains, I stopped at a roadside shop and bought some goodies, then continued on downhill on a bad road that was narrow and rough. It was hotter down here in this flat valley and more humid. I quickly exited the road and carried my bike up a rocky formation for about 300 feet. There, I found a place to camp. Thinking, nobody saw me, I quietly found a spot near a single tree, with sand underneath. Suddenly an old man came over the rocks and spoke to me with a little english. He told me he was in World War II in North Africa, including Libya and Tunis fighting against the Germans. He made a machine gunner like gesture to explain what his duty was. I told him my father also was in the war. He pointed thumbs up and we shook. He seemed interested in camels, church's, tent's, America and my touring India. We could communicate, although it was difficult at times. Two other men came and I talked to them as well. They told me that there were tigers here. I said, "Me not afraid of tigers. Me hit tigers with rock." The men stood back shaking there white turbined heads and spoke in a jutting accent. "No. Tiger is very bad. Very big. He can kill you." "I will be ok, I like tigers." I said. The old man told me he would sleep beside my tent with his axe at the ready, in case a tiger came. I told him that wasn't necessary. "No, no, me ok." I said. He then pointed down the hill and to the village and told me he would be at his house if I needed help. They left. I laid in my tent in the dark listening and thinking to myself, "What was that? What's that noise?"

I dozed off and then at about 1am, I heard a very loud chirping sound that might have been a monkey outside. Then I heard something scratching, clawing its way up the tree that overhangs my tent. It sounded just like a house cat scratching up a tree. It was like a nightmare. I was so scared I could not move. I could not scream. I knew something was out there. Finally I jumped and said, "Ahh," and the thing scrambled off like a rushing wind.

Not much time had transpired when I heard women and children in the village scream in the night. They banged on pots and pans and men shouted. It came from down in one area and then moved to other areas of the village. This was getting very frightening. Then things calmed down.

## Tuesday April 3

I slept with one eye open all night as I was quite aware of my setting. I got up feeling groggy. I did not feel very well. I packed up the bike and noticed at the base of the tree near my tent, a large impression of an animals track. Now I do not know what a tigers track looks like, but this was certainly as large as my hand. I pushed the bike down the hillside and to the road. The old man was walking up the highway. "Tiger," he said pointing his axe in the direction of the village. "You ok?" he asked me. "Yes, ok." I said. He smiled and I smiled and we gestured an anjali and I headed onward along the bumpy road.

My energy was low. I stopped into a cafe and asked for an omelet, but they had nothing but tea and many pajama men stirring and sipping. I continued on and was tired and a little down. I came into a village and asked another restaurant for an omelet but they didn't help me. I got a Limca, which was ice cold and a couple of bakery goods, then sat to feast. These boys asked me, "From what country are you?" I answered and they said, "I want money from your country." I ignored them. An old witch doctor looking fellow sat by me. He had red paint on his face and lots of jewels. He too wanted money. I was tired and the heat was getting to me. People stared and some laughed. I drank another Limca and flicked the bottle cap with my thumb over my head. They seemed amazed. I picked up another bottle cap and flicked it at a spittoon and ding it hit it. They all laughed. So I did a few more tricks and they watched me like I was on stage. I got up and the crowd came running to me. The witch doctor or beggar wanted money. I showed him how to flick a bottle cap and say, "Rupees, ruppees." He put his stick in front of me and I kicked it away and went on my way.

I went into a market and bought some apples and the crowd came again. People started fucking with my gear shift levers. I got pissed and just backed the bike over there feet. I continued on.

At about 1pm, the sun was high overhead, but there were some large trees lining the road. I was just south of a very congested city and this Indian fellow rode up beside me and said. "I want to talk to you," in a very loud voice. He continued and said, "You are from Europe and I must talk to you! I am a very poor Indian man. I am a school teacher. You must ride slower as I want to talk to you," he shouted. I looked at his glasses which were purple and said, "I am from U.S.A." He said, "All U.S. people have very much money. Indian man have no money. Only good heart." I acknowledged him and said, "I am thirsty. Do you know where I can find a Limca?" "Yes," he said. "I also want Limca, you will buy me Limca. I am a poor Indian man. You are from America. We will drink Limca! I like Limca very much, yes you will buy me Limca!."

He took me into town and we toured what he said were one of the three famous cinemas in town and famous market place. We stopped and had a Limca. I paid. But I was so hot and I was so tired and thirsty yet, even after the limca. He insisted I didn't have to watch my bike, but I ignored him. People did respect it here. I talked a little and then drank an ice cold Lassi. While doing this, I met a young fellow who was the same age as I. (28) We shook hands on it. All were amazed at my wristwatch.

I took off against a strong rear quarter wind and made slow time. At one stop a guy came over and started touching the levers on my bike. I hollered at him and he jumped back. I don't like it when they mess with it.

I went into Ajmer as the traffic was heavy. People harassed me saying, "Hello, ha, ha, pssstt." I found the Tourist Bungalow and talked to some guys from the bureau. They were amazed that I came from Bombay. I got a room and met a woman in the room who was bitchy. She then talked my arm and legs off. She's fed up with crazy Indian people. I relaxed, showered, and went out to eat. Found a restaurant and had chicken curry. I went into the city, with it's old, small streets.

Upon returning to my room I slept with the fan going and then watched the TV and learned about Raki Shamar who was the first Indian astronaut to go into space aboard a Russian rocket. I watched the Russian rocket lift off and then saw the Soviet-India press conference and listened as the cosmonaut talked. It was very intriguing, this kind of coverage, as we in U.S.A. never see this attention to detail on how the Russian system works. Also I could see that the cosmonauts have a lot of camaraderie.

## Wednesday April 4

Feeling good in the morning after a decent night's rest. I worked on my bike and then pedaled into the city. There was an Indian kid, who was riding a bike alongside with me, but he kept cutting me off on the road and laughing. At one point he ran into me, making me stop and plant my foot, to keep myself from crashing. He took off on his bike, and I chased him and grabbed for him and he fell down. He wasn't hurt and I correctingly kicked him in the rear and also upon his back tire and said, "that's for cutting me off!" I didn't much care to do this, but my anger had to vent and he deserved it.

I felt a strangeness here, Ajmer seemed unlike other India cities I'd been to in India. I felt like I was back in Egypt. I noticed it last night as well, when I went through the small streets lined with shitting and pissing beggars There were cows and pigs and people selling goods as well as people laying on the road.

As I walked my bike through the marketplace on this morning, I saw an old man who was lying on the pavement, completely naked and with flies covering him, especially swarming around his crotch. No one seemed concerned. People walked around him like he was invisible. "Why doesn't somebody do something for this man?" I said. Soon a crowd gathered around me. Then the police came, dressed in white uniforms and white pith helmets. They shooed all of us away. I got out of there because everyone was so crazy. One Indian guy said, "Be careful the people are hoolagans."

I went to the bank and then to the hotel and packed up my stuff. The hotel owner kindly allowed me to store my bike and gear behind the counter. I cracked open a fresh coconut and drank the milk, then went to the bus station and bought a ticket to go to Pushkar.

The bus left Ajmer station and from the start I knew this would be a wild ride to this scenic resort, in the mountains, beside a lake. This driver was a lead food, a swerving dare devil. He stopped at nothing that he could not go around. I sat in the far back of the bus. We went up and over tight winding, rocky hills on a narrow, paved road and then descended down into Pushkar. Wow what a rush. I'd read about people being killed when buses went off 1000 foot cliffs and now I could see how it happens. We hit some bumps and all the heads went up a foot, as people were lifted off their seats. The bus driver constantly blew his shrill horn at other vehicles, pedestrians and bike riders. It amazed me how people jumped out of the way of the careening bus at just the last minute. People in India live this maniacal way and are more conditioned to this than we from the west.

Arriving safely, and a few prayers lighter, we made it into Pushkar where I met a fellow named Roody from Holland. We walked around this quiet city next to a clear lake and found a place to sit and enjoy some chipadee with dahl.

I asked a young lady from Belgium about the sights here and she almost puked in my face. The 'India bug' had hit her and she was very sick. There were many western travelers here who were sick.

We went walking through the city, sampling many foods and drinks and talking of our world travels. At an ancient carved rock temple I saw a beautiful 2000 year old small statue that was made of black stone. It was one of the many Hindu gods. A man wanted baksheesh, and Roody gave him 10p and he joshed and gave it back. It wasn't enough money, I guess.

I went down by the greenish waters of the lake and was told that some big fish, like carp lived in the waters as well as a few crocodiles. There was a yearly festival held here, where people came from all around and bathed in the waters, much to the delight of feeding fish and crocodiles.

There were many beggars in Pushkar, they came in all types of men, women, and children. The noblest thing Roody and I discussed was, "If this were our system we would try like hell to make it better. These people don't."

We walked back toward the bus stop where we met a Danish girl. "Is there a difference between Dutch and Danish?" I asked. Roody said, "There language is strange." We laughed and she bellered back, "Ours is? Your is!" I broke it up by saying english was strange. Roody went to his hotel.

I walked with the girl and it was nice to have her company in this pleasant place. The afternoon was more relaxing, by the water chatting, then we took the bus back to Ajmer and to the hotel. This driver was much saner than the madman who brought us to Pushkar. We went over the mountains, marveling at the rugged terrain. I was disappointed in myself for not biking this route, then again glad to not be on this bad stretch of road. We chuckled at the cows lining the streets, interspersed with people and sometimes cows and people created a mosaic like all were cattle here. We disembarked and then went to drink a lassi. The Danish girl went her way and I mine. At the hotel, I got a room and the crazy Indian manager lady went around and turned the lights out on the Indian roomates.

Over these past days I had made an observation here. I had felt as if I was back in Egypt and there was a plausible explanation. I learned that many immigrants came here yearly from Egypt. This was a predominantly Muslim community and thus I was feeling a similar attitude as Egypt. It was interesting to note how this religious difference can vary in disposition from the Hindu part of India.

## Thursday April 5

I got up and packed my bike up at 6am. Back on the road, pedaling out of Ajmer and feeling good at 6:45. I was really feeling good, and in the heat was shirtless. It was just perfect weather. Not a cloud in the sky. I looked for a place to eat but all they had was shit food. I ate a coconut which was good, and then an orange. I felt great and then the road roughness started to slow me a bit.

On one long stretch of road I saw cars going around a couple of rocks and a sac on the road. To my surprise I saw the arm of a dead man under the sac. He was obviously hit by a car. I went a way's farther and then stopped, turned around and thought this would make an interesting photo. So I went back getting the camera ready. I got to the dead man, stopped, aimed the camera and a policeman with a stick came running out and shouted at me, "No, no!" I said to him, "Can't you move this man off of the road?" The Indian policeman said, "No, he is dead! Now go!" I turned around to leave and probably missed the best shot ever as he was shooing me away. I could have clicked and run, instead I continued on and took one photo of this sorrowful scene from farther away.

At 11am I was still shirtless, hungry and especially thirsty. I looked in vain for someplace with omelet's or potatoes or something firm beside this mushy stewy shit. Finally I saw a place with rolls and soda, so I carried my bike into the cafe. I bought a pop and a roll. People came in and started to look at my bike. One guy knelt down and appeared to be jamming everything on the bike he could find. He pulled the front derailleur at a bad angle. I got up and said, "Hey! Don't touch!" I l saw no response from him, he seemed intent to tear it off the bike, so I kicked him in the ass. He got up and looked like he wanted to fight. He grabbed the bike. I pushed him away three feet and said again, "Don't touch!" I pushed him again saying, "Don't touch." He was looking rather savage and we stood in a face off like two dogs fighting. Some kids laughed and egged him on. I felt confident I'd put him down. He backed off. Then he stood looking at me and the bike. What is this possessive desire that they have to touch my things? That is to say, why do they touch other peoples things, let alone in such an aggressive manner?

As I crested a rock-covered hill, a dark skinned young man who wore no shoes ran beside me on the side of the road. The rocks along that roadside were very sharp, they would easily have cut most feet wide open. I was amazed how this man could run over this difficult terrain. Surely he should have had hurting feet. Then he ran down the pavement, which in the heat of the midday sun was extremely hot. It was almost gooey. How he did not burn his feet I can only wonder. This gave me an insight into the incredible adaptability of the human being. Our feet have greater resilience to the elements, if conditioned.

I rode on and got tired and stopped to relax. It seemed everytime I stopped to relax, I was harassed. I rode into a village and said, "Rham, rham. Tata, tata," to a guy and he went nuts weaving about me on his bike. I couldn't stop in the village as he was so annoying. I continued on feeling as if my nerves were back on edge. I continued heading north, over some hills and then stopped at a roadside stall and drank one more pop, and refilled my canteens with water.

The day was really heating up and I stopped into many villages to wash off and get wet. People always asked me questions and children would pull on my bike. I gave them a fist and sad don't touch. They all withdrew.

The miles were hard won, then finally I found my way through a maze of traffic and humanity going into the red walled city of Jaipur. I searched around and found Mr. Sharma at the General Electric office. I peeked my head into the door and asked for him. We shook hands. He told me he was leaving to Bombay tomorrow for business. So he could not give me a tour of the city. We talked about it and he told me to meet him at Teej Hotel at 6:30pm, so I said ok. It was 4:30 and it took me until 5pm to find a place to stay. There was a Frenchman who commented on my tan and wondered how I got it. When I told him I had cycled from Bombay, he thought I was awesome. I showered and relaxed. Then fell asleep. Awoke at 6:28 and jumped on my bike and raced to the Teej Hotel thinking of my excuse to tell Mr.Sharma. I got there at 6:34 and waited. This older Indian guy came along and he started jamming the deraileur mechanism on my bike back and forth. "Don't touch!" I bellered. I said it loudly and stood up to push him off. Then he acted like he knew it all and told his friends all about my bike and was pointing with his foot at me. Do they have no respect for others property? Isn't that taught here in India?

I was thinking about how these people must not have many toys as children because they have no concern over the care of things. Another guy came along and started asking me about the price of my bike. And I told him, "If you want a bike like this why don't you get one from Japan. They've got millions of them and they're not that far from here." He told me my bike was not practical in India. His bike was one year old and it was a wreck. I told him so. And he said, "We people in India are very careless with our things. This is why we don't care if they go bad. Your bike is a toy," he said adding, "To us it is shiny and different. But it's no good for India."

I sat there until 7:30 waiting for Mr. Sharma, but he did not come. I went into the city of Jaipur on the well lit city streets. This was a crazy place in the night. It was full of bikes. I got punch happy and started pushing a few people. There were so many of them. There was a festival occuring. People were carrying god like images and horns and banners. I bought a large white, sweet festival cake for about 50 cents. I went back to find a veggie restaurant which offered all you can eat for 50cents. I met another Frenchman. He spoke very little english, so with my use of French and his english, we understood something. We ate an ample meal but it was not so good, without meat. I went to the hotel and it was very hot in the room. I showered before going to sleep. This was the only way to stay cool, for about a couple of hours.

## Friday April 6

In the morning, I went down to eat breakfast in the hotel café, and there met a fellow from the States. His name was Charley. He had been in India for 6 months. We talked about the attitude of people in India and some of our experiences. He felt there nature was due to the Hindu religion. They don't have the same kindness to one another that is learned in Christianity. Rather you are born into your niche or caste and there you stay. In this philosophy some are born better off than others. He was telling me how he just wanted to continue being a Christian because it was a better system.

Charley and I sat at our breakfast table, sipping tea and he told me of his Vietnam experiences. He was a helicopter pilot and was wounded twice. One bullet went under his helmet and up his scalp. He showed me the scar. He reflected about that war. One of the horrors he recalled was seeing a man who looked just like himself laying dead on the stretcher with his eyes wide open. He said he objected to flying Cobra gunships on moral grounds but he lost, and had to fly them. He said, "I knew a U.S. Army soldier who was informed by a V.C. woman, whom he was in love with, that there was going to be a mortar attack. The lieutenant pulled his G.I.'s back just as the shells landed right where they were. It was that kind of war." He then added," One memorable battle was where they dropped $500,000 dollar's worth of bombs just to kill two V.C. We lost that war because the South Vietnamese lacked the willingness to fight and the V.C. knew that and they fought even harder." Charley said ever since he left Vietnam he stripped himself of his flag. We shook hands as fellow countrymen and I thanked him as this was a most interesting talk.]

I went to the city on this sunny and clear blue sky morning and saw an exhibit of old astronomical measuring devices made by Joshua Stein in 1700. These were huge astrolabes and descending scales, which were the size of a house. Many of them had micrometer accuracy marked off in stone.

There was also a wonderful palace where I saw a huge painting that showed the British on one side and the Indians on the other watching an elephant parade. There was a lot of pride, which the Indians felt during the British period of rule. But that wore off as independence was declared.

There are many shops in Jaipur, which I searched through in hopes of finding a good restaurant but opted to buy food at the market and cook myself. I really need a good meal. I was laughed at frequently, and asked how much money is my bike worth and where do I come from, all day long. These people were giving me an ulcer. I went to the hotel, cooked some food and slept. After I awoke from this nap, I felt great and again hungry. I met Rito, my Swiss-French roomate and we went down to a restaurant. We walked the sidewalk and strutted about. The Indians whistled and ridiculed with me but I was pushing them. I'd tell them move and get with it and they seemed shy'd by my aggressive attitude. When the price was too high I'd say, "You want too much." I felt good doing this with Rito and we laughed. We both ordered mutton chow mein. It turned out to be pretty good and we enjoyed eating and talking together.

Rito had rented an Indian bike and we rode together into Jaipur. It was great to have someone along. I felt more secure and pushy. He spoke some Hindi and it helped. We ate junk food all night, like cake, lassi, ice cream, nuts, curd and milk.

We were riding down a long street full of hanging Christmas lights strung here and there, when a rickshaw bike went by. Rito sped up and grabbed a hold of it for a free ride beside the 'rickbike', which suddenly turned and this flung Rito, who went with such speed that he passed right between 2 Indian men. I thought he was a goner. There were merchants and traders jumping out of his way. It fired me up. He was such a fearless bike rider! We raced back through the streets to our hotel and talked awhile about India. He felt the people were just like children. "The Philippines was better than India," he said. I told him I felt like I was destined to get ripped off here. He thought the Philippines was worse for getting ripped off.

## Sat. April 7

Up at 6am, I ate some curd and banana, then hit the road and went through the city with lots of hissing, laughing and snickering from people. I stopped to buy something and they came right away to envelope me. This was a sort of reversal of their ludicrous laughing.

While exiting Jaipur, I could see the hill to the west, where the maharaja once lived. Nearby, I came around a bend and saw a string of elephants walking the road and looked in amazement at how they walked. From behind, an elephant walks just like a man wearing baggy pants. They are so big, so docile and gentle for such a huge creature. As I passed them I noticed their smell was not unlike that of a zoo. Of course when they crap it was like dropping a clothes basket full of manure on the pavement.

There was an amazing red wall surrounding the city of Jaipur. To think how they built such a structure is commendable to the ingenuity of Indian people.

I pedaled up and over a hill and saw a palace in amber and some more big walls. These buildings were real pretty and well fortifide. There was a strong headwind now on this coolish morning. For me it was perfect.

Each time I'd overtake a slower bike rider they would speed up and come ride alongside of me. By doing so, they created a traffic hazard to me. Sometimes I hit rocks or sometimes I had to go in the ditch, because they were beside me. These bike riders did not always talk to me. Some just wanted to escort me. The traffic was intense and this made it even more dangerous. This annoyed me when they'd try to pedal alongside of me. So generally I stopped or sped up, to get away from these other riders. There were some riders who understood this, and sometimes they stopped for me and sometimes they speed up to avoid a hazard as traffic approached.

There were many stinky trucks, blasting their horns and my eyes burned from the diesel engines. My lungs hurt also from the polluting exhaust. Many times I was forced off the road by them. It was a real bumpy road and my butt was sore. I dunked myself occasionally and at noon was riding with a wet cloth on my head and a wet towel hanging down my back. It was another thirsty day. I stopped for a Limca, on this road to New Delhi. There were some hills but generally it was flat out pedaling. I stopped now and then for a break and sat down, and typically people stopped to look at me.

I resumed and some bike riders picked up speed to catch me and tried to ride alongside with the same annoying routine. A truck came and I had to dive off of the shoulder as it passed. This one Indian guy kept doing this to me. I told him to "jow" (piss off) so it would not happen again. Then I got pissed at him and stopped quick to get behind him. He tried to come alongside of me again but I wouldn't let him. I sped up and he pedaled like all hell to stay with me. He rode along side of me and gave me a why?? look and just then a truck sped by almost wiping us both out. I told him off, but this knucklehead did not even notice it. I ignored the dumb S.O.B. He was replaced by some kids who would do the same thing to me and they would tease my straight face. They made faces to me and I said "go away!" as I didn't want them messing with me and my bike.

At about noon, I pulled into a tourist stop and enjoyed cold Rose Milk and cold water and an omelet. I mixed a banana sundae and took it easy.

I headed back onto the pavement, which was sticky and soft from the heat and saw this crazy guy riding behind in front of me on a bike. He was singing and had no hands and was all over the road. "Allah!" he cried. I rode past him. He sped up and sang to me. He put in some english words to his song. He was funny, until some traffic came. He almost crashed into me many times. He looked like he was high on something. He sang and said, "Bye, bye," to every car. He said things to people around me. He sang, "I love you, I want you," and he got a little strange, almost grabbing me. So I stopped enjoying him and ignored him. Then he got loud and obnoxious. Just a little further buddy, I thought and I'll punch him. Well I burst my anger and bitched him out. "Come on big mouth India man- talk, sing, dance-come on-go crazy, but don't bother me!" I did this rapidly to his face and boy did he ever get pissed. I also did. So he sang a little more and I just took off riding as fast as I could. He tried to catch me, and did stay with me for a few miles, but I was too fast and too strong for too long. I pedaled real hard like this for 10k's, through a green forest of nice big trees that blurred past, and then looked back to see that he was finally gone.

My progress was good despite the upsetting meeting with that crazy man. About 90k's from Delhi it was getting dark and I finally found a hay bale to camp behind, in an open field. It was an ok spot to set camp and though the road was busy with traffic and people were constantly passing, nobody knew that I was there. A cool wind blew, making it more comfortable as I laid in my tent, with the fly wide open to let the air soothe my sunburned body.

## Sunday April 8

It was a cool night and I loved it. I slept well until 5:30am and then got up, packed up the tent as the sun trickled through the eastern horizon and I left. There were lots of stinking trucks on this stretch of road. I fought a headwind and felt a little weak. I went into a tourist house and got a map of Delhi, but they had no food. It was too early to serve. I went into a little village and ordered Tonda Lassi. I made it into a banana milkshake as a big bunch of bananas cost 2 rupees and it was 2 rupees for a big lassi. This mixture was real good for my belly. People crowded around me like animals, looking at me eat and when it was time to pay, I had to open my wallet and sneakingly pull out a 100 rupee note so no one could see all of my money. I was proud of being so clever. When they gave me my change, 1 rupee note was torn so they said, "you can have it, take it ok." I took the one rupee to a cookie stand and they gave me 2 sweet cookies for it. When I turned around there was a huge crowd of people pushing in towards me. Then I motioned to them to get away, like one might do to dogs. I waved, "chello," which means 'lets go or go on.' I was again on my way.

Along the road there were many bad truck accidents. These were real pile-ups. These drivers are like children playing with knives. They don't know what they're doing. Again I was followed and escorted side my side by bike riders. I continued onward feeling a little diarrhea. I stopped at a place for a drink and met a couple of very sane, well educated New Delhi Indians. I told them, "You are different from the other Indians I've met." They said, "We do business with your country and we are educated." They asked me about the water, if I'd been sick. I said no. But after talking to them, I went to the toilet and had diarrhea. Then I felt dizzy and slow. I took my pills and continued, stopping often on this hot day.

Admist a chaos of humanity pulling all kinds of four and two wheeled contraptions down the streets, I rode into Delhi. Finally there were nice streets, and pretty buildings and trees. I passed the Ghandi memorial and it was a wonderful sculpture in bronze of this ambitious nearly naked leader of the Indian independence movement.

I met a couple from Hungary and they said they didn't like India because, "It was too dirty and corrupt." I made it into the center of the city and asked people for directions. A wonderful treat was to eat Popsicle's. Then I went to the nation's capital called Delhi Gate. There was a curious structure that was the Parliament building. It looked like a huge bunker, with a large slit for windows.

I found a youth hostel. There was a cute girl at the front desk. I relaxed in my assigned bed and fell asleep. Afterward, I pedaled again into the city and found a place to eat and over ate. I also bought a coconut. It was a warm night and I felt a little sick. I was so tired from the heat and the bicycle traveling. Then I met my Indian roommate and he offered me a drink of gin and water. We talked of travels and of our occupations and of girls. He was sort of a rebellious Indian, bucking the system. So with the fan twirling and my head also, I went to dreamland with a new friend.

**Monday April 9**

I was rather excited to eat breakfast in the youth hostel and then get to the post office to see if I had any mail from home. However, this tanned fellow with a cheerful smile came over and asked to join me for breakfast. So I obliged and found out he was from Iraq. He said there was a war going on between his country and Iran. He was glad to not be there now. He said thousands of his countrymen were killed in single attacks.

We talked about the difference between Indian and Arab countries. The Arab countries are mostly worshipers of Islam, and that India is split into Hindu, Buddhist, Moslem and Christians. We also talked about the difference between Arab countries and Europe and America. We discussed this puzzle on how religion can effect the attitude of a nation. The Hindu religion deals with many God like personas appointed for individual tasks. Moslems deal with God worship and Christianity has a man/god relationship that promotes change and concerns for other men. He said he was a Moslem and admitted that he felt his religion wasn't as good for the country and for modernization. He was a good listener and we left feeling education and religion play the major role in a countries evolution.

I went to the post office and nervously shuffled through a stack of letters. Getting to the rear of those letters I found with such happiness a letter from mom and dad. I saw the Duluth stamp and my adrenaline flowed. I held the letter close to my heart and went outside to open it, but there met another traveling cyclist. We talked of our journeys, compared stories, while at the same time I opened the envelope. Between talking to him and reading that letter, I was taken asunder by the shocking information.

Mom told me that Ellen was getting married. It stunned me, floored me, crushed me and I almost stopped reading right there and tossed the letter. I guess I had a little plan for us, and now it was never going to be true. I wanted to go home to be swept away by Ellen, but now it was over. Ellen said, "I'm sorry Eric, to be surprising you with this news. I know how you wanted me to wait for you, but this is the way things are." For so many miles I had ridden with the inspirational thought of Ellen leading me toward this effort. I always thought of her and of someday going home and being together with her. In some ways, she had escorted me, pulled me through these hard times, because I would concentrate on her, and not the difficult circumstances I was going through. Now it was as if a big part of my life was gone, there was suddenly a void, a darkness around me. Though it was a beautiful morning, with green grass and new friendships to engage, that moment of reading that letter in front of the New Delhi post office was like a visitation to hell.

Mom also told me of her uncle dying and other news and current events. But I was really down to hear of Ellen marrying. In light of the circumstance, I offered a helping hand to Gerald, the Dutch cyclist. We went to the tourist office and I saw him get mad at an Indian.

# THE WHEELS OF FRIEND

We split up and I went to the Nepalese embassy but it was closed. Then to Rail House and it was absolute madness. I wanted to check on taking a train to Simla but it seemed a hopeless mess. I went to the Thai embassy and it to was closed. I felt sick. My guts ached. I was tired and had no energy. Back to the youth hostel I went, feeling low and ready to nap.

I was locking up my bike when this tall, strong Indian fellow asked me if I'd been touring India on cycle. He then told me of his world travels where he spent two years on a cycle and covered 200,000kilometers and visited 59 countries. His name was B.V.Narayani. I told him that I had seen his photograph in the newspaper back in the early 80's in Chicago. Somebody had stolen his bike and he was pretty bummed out. But Schwinn helped him get another bike and he continued his journey. "Yes, that was me!" He said excitedly.

He now planned to go on a world tour upon a motorcycle. He invited me into the cafetaria to have lunch and bought me a great lunch with his friend and pinion rider P. Ravi. They said, "Would you like to go to a movie with us, you will pay nothing!" So the three of us loaded onto his motorcycle and we sped along the streets of Delhi and they got lost, thus asked people directions in Hindi, but the responding answer was always in english. I was surprised to hear this.

We made it to the theater. B.V. went to the manager and used his "World traveler," statement to get us three free tickets. This surprised me, how he had such nerve. As we waited in line, an Indian fellow came up and asked if he could take our photograph. He was with the press, he said. So we stood together and this strange fellow held his 'wrist watch camera' and took our photograph. He then said, "Wait a minute, let me take one more." He again aimed his watch at us, and clicked a button on the watch and it went "beep-beep" and then he thanked us and left. I did not believe him, nor in his 'camera,' but wondered a little. "Was he really a reporter?" I asked B.V. who then said, "That guy was a quack, never mind him."

The movie we saw was Grease 2. Each time someone would kiss, B.V. would cover his eyes. And each time someone would suggest sex, P. Ravi would giggle and grab for me, and innocently say, "Oh my god, I cannot look." They probably did not see movies like this very often, like we do in the U.S. The movie was full of motorcycle stunts and the guys became very excited and vocal. It was a riot being in the theater with them.

After the movie, we climbed aboard the motorcycle and B.V. went wild on the streets, imitating the movie. We flew between buses and cars and people and I was shitting bricks. "Where is your heart?" said P.Ravi. I responded, "In my boots." He said don't worry Allah is with us. I would beg the nut to slow down a little. On one curve we were going much to fast and he leaned the bike hard into the turn and the footpegs ground into the pavement, sending a shower of sparks flying behind us.

Back at the hostel we ate again but I had only bread. Then we talked into the night. The conversation was never ending, but they had to get going, I thanked them immeasurably and they were off, speeding down the streets.

I went to my room and Gerald was there so we talked. We drank a little whiskey with a couple of Indian friends. I felt a bit ill and had a case of diarrhea. In all it was a very good and exciting day, despite such depressing news.

## Tuesday April 10th

Gerald joined me at breakfast. He told me of cycling in Nepal and getting very sick. "Don't drink the water whatever you do. I got a tapeworm that was three feet long," he said. He said he took some medicine and the worm died in him and he pulled it out of his rear like a long string.

He also told me about his bike ride through Bali and Sumatra. He really liked Bali. I could tell how much he loved that island by the way his voice sounded. I hoped to someday go there as well.

I sped off to the U.S. embassy and waited in line. There were so many Indian people requesting a visa to visit the U.S. I heard each of them being turned away, or given yet another challenge in order to get the visa. Finally when it was my turn, I asked them for a reference letter to visit Thailand. They said it was unnecessary. I would not need it. But I felt good to speak with other Americans. Even to speak 'American'. I stayed in there to read voraciously a few U.S. magazines and felt like I was hanging on to a little bit of home turf being in there.

I went to get some photos made for my visa to Nepal and Thailand. Then went to the Thai embassy and applied for the visa. I went to the city and shopped for a shirt. They wanted 25 rupees. So I had time and I explored old Delhi. This was like a journey back into the real India. There were so many people in this bazaar that it felt hotter with the big crowds. I went through small stands and tents that were crowded with people. Some annoyed me by touching my bike. I bought a lock, a pair of shorts, a towel and then went looking around the Red Fort. This old structure was from the 1500's. I watched an elephant parade and then went back to the bazaar at Connaught Place and bought a shirt for 5 rupees.

I visited a fruit market along Connaught Place and turned to see this young white man ride past on a red Honda motorcycle. "Hey Gary," I said continuing, "How's it going?" He turned around and came over to me. I thought he was someone else. I thought he was Gary, from Liverpool. He looked just like him. The fellow stopped his dirt bike on the side of the street and spoke with a British accent. We talked and his name was John Taylor. He was from Nottinghamshire in England. We shared similar stories of adventure while walking around the market. I followed him to the tourist area of Delhi and then we really got into story telling while seated in a Chinese restaurant. We had a good meal and conversation of our adventures. We also talked about women. Then he took me back to the hostel on his cycle and I carried my bike with the rear wheel rolling on the pavement. We left the bike at the hostel and he took me on his motorcycle to his place. He was staying with an Indian couple. There names were Nat and Bunte Sing. John and I ate curd and drank coffee. It turned out that Nat was a motorcycle racer and he showed me the motorcycles that he raced in a Grand Prix Motocross. They were street bikes. His was a 350 R.D. of 1969 model. They made many changes to be competitive. He said the Japanese bikes were not available in India. Then I sat to talk to Nat and Bunt. I met Keeshaw a Nepalese servant, who lived with them. We talked rabidly of motocross bikes. John and I talked and drank so much coffee. It was rush hour when we rode back to the hostel on his motorcycle, dodging cows and cars and cattle(people). We talked about maybe going to Himachel together. I was surprised he said sure let's do that, and we agreed to meet tomorrow.

## Wed April 11

I ate breakfast with Gerald and we talked about his bike travels across Sumatra. He really liked the country and its people.

I then went to the Thai embassy and picked up my visa and pedaled across town to the Nepal embassy and waited in line. Inside I had to sit in a cramped room with many others. We fought for our space to fill out the two forms. Then in a most disorganized sense and in this order I was first given a receipt, then paid $11, was handed the visa and then asked what I was going to do in Nepal. I couldn't believe that this disorganized mess could work. I went to buy some bananas and headed back to the hostel.

Not long after taking a shower John arrived. We went to his place. Again I met Nat and Bunte. I was given a fine lunch and we sat together against an embroidered pillow on the floor eating dahl and chipadees. We then kicked back and talked of Britain and Indian clashes and the differences between U.S. people and British. John defended his British ways. Buntee got huffy and Nat slept. Then Buntee and I had a good conversation of art as she loved pottery. We talked about the styles of pottery in the world. She would be going to the U.S. to study pottery. I read magazines and sat about, drinking cold coffee. Nat and I talked of motocross." We ate dinner then I met an Indian fellow who had lived in Canada for 3 years. People were coming freely in this household. Later, John and I talked about our travels and the itinerary of our ride up to Manali, which is in the northwest part of India. John gave me a ride to the hostel in the dark of the Indian night, as cows sat on the roadside and the streets were mellow.

## Thursday April 12

I met a new roommate from the States. We went to breakfast together with Gerald. We were all cyclists. We shared stories and as usual exchanged information. Then B.V. Narayana came along and we were all cyclists eating together from our countries. Kevin was going back to Michigan on Saturday and he was excited to return home. "I'm going to talk to my family!" He said, as the first thing he wants to do when getting back. He had been away for 3 months. I decided to check out of here at noon. So I hurriedly got ready and B.V. offered me a ride to the Nepalese embassy with Gerald. All three of us got on his motorcycle and B.V. cranked up the old clunker screaming out of the driveway and scraped it around the turns almost hitting a car broadside. I stuck my boot out and banged it against the car. We then just missed another car before turning to the left and again scraping the foot pegs against the pavement. I screamed wildly. Gerald said frantically, "Does he always drive like this?" "Yes, worse!" I exclaimed. We went careening wildly down the streets. At the Nepalese embassy I got my passport and visa and then we went around to the banks. Gerald said he had to go his own way. I think the motorcycle riding scared him. B.V. wanted to go to the movies and it was all in Hindi and I had to do other things so he dumped me off in the city.

I shopped about. It was a good chance to go into the many shops and see the greatest selection of ivory work ever. If not for the fact that many elephants had to die to make these works, it is a beautiful medium, that the artists carve into intricate masterpieces depicting enchanting scenes of ornate patterns. I walked and took a bus but had to get off while it was still moving as I was on the wrong bus. I hitched a ride from an Indian fellow driving an under powered moped and he returned me to the hostel.

I met Kevin again and talked to him for quite awhile. When I meet a fellow countryman I tend to desire more conversation on what is happening back home. It was a hot day and I was on my way packing my bike and Kevin gave me a tube of chain lube.

I pedaled off with all of my bike loaded up and headed down the road to Nat's house. The ride went smooth though I did get lost. I rode into Nat's and nobody was there so I went to the restaurant next door and ate a pizza like food called umpusar at the restaurant. My friends returned and I asked if I could spend the night and they welcomed me wholeheartedly. They were upset that I ate at the restaurant rather than have the servant cook me some food. Oh well.

John Taylor and I cleaned his motorcycle and packed my things into a travel bag. An Indian male visitor stopped by who had just returned from 6 months in New York City. He said, "I was never disappointed for a minute while in the U.S." Nat let me test ride a nice looking 1970 CB 350 motorcycle which had some problems. I told him it needed new points, there wasn't much else I could do for it. We ate some more food and talked, then I slept on the floor. "I want you to stay in my home," said the turbined Nat. I had learned to trust the Sikhs because they were always helpful and honest. I replied, "Ok".

I met his wife and then his father and mother. I discovered that three families lived in this house. "How can you think of inviting one more person into your house?" I said. "Oh it is with honor for us to have a visitor stay at our home." he said. His head shook side to side as if his neck were made of rubber.

We talked of my travels. He was concerned about my dwindling finances. "Why is it you don't try and get some sponsorship from the Rotary International in Delhi?" he said to me in a very rapid and accented voice. He had traveled around India several years ago and had been sponsored by Rotary International. During the following days he took me around to meet the officers of Rotary, but they were against sponsoring me because I was not from India.

## Friday April 13

This being Friday the 13th it could be a superstitiously bad day to even move out of bed, but we were heading off to northern India. The bike was packed up and John took off early to get gas. He returned an hour later on an Indian bicycle to say the coil had gone dead. "It just quit. I'll have to send it home," he said knowing he'd never find a coil in Delhi. So I rode Nat's Indian bicycle and he drove a motorcycle to the station. I discovered the kill switch was faulty. We worked all morning on the ignition system but could not find the fault. So I disconnected the switch and it ran fine. We finally got underway at 1pm on this, sunny and windy day. The motorcycle was loaded heavily and we fought a headwind. God my butt was sore. We had many close calls all the way with this crazy Indian traffic. We both observed how madly these people would drive. "Look at that bloody idiot!" John would shout as we were forced off the road many a time by cars, buses and trucks. They had no lawfulness on the Indian roads. Vehicles switched lanes at will, the bigger vehicle wins the right of way, stop signs are meaningless. We dove into the ditch one time, as oncoming trucks passing each other didn't give way back into their lane. We stopped for a drink and people mobbed us with curiosity and questions. "How fast is it? How much does it cost?" Are common questions they asked us about the motorcycle. The people aren't as aggressive as they are to me on my solo travels with the bike. I felt more comfortable having another fellow with me. The people respect us more also.

We stopped for tea and then continued on into the Punjab. At a banana stand we were mobbed by people. One guy touched me much, looking for rupees.

Because of some trouble in the Punjab, there were several roadblocks that we went past before entering Chandigarh. The security people briefly looked at us and we continued on arriving in the city at dusk. We found the house we wanted to visit and it was nice. Very nice! It was like a home in Malibu. A servant came and asked us what we would like and he fixed us both ice cold coffee. Then we met a very nice Indian family. The children were well dressed and spoke excellent english and so did their mom who was attractive and nicely dressed in a sari. It struck me that I didn't think they lived like this in India. Wow. The servant cooked us a delicious meal. And he was always there to refresh our cups with whatever we wanted. He was a very nice person and made it look easy. I stayed up late into the night to read. This place was so nice I felt my impression change of India. I watched a video of motocross racing in India. I talked to John about why racing was fun. John was a very polite and careful person. He had more manners than I and yet he yearned for adventure. We shared this one common trait.

## Saturday April 14.

We were greeted with a cup of tea and a paper in the morning and ate a great breakfast with John and we both overate. Life with a servant was rather nice as he tended to always be there to help out. An invitation was given to us to stay another day and thus we decided to spend the day in Chandigarh. This city was the center of the Punjab unrest. We heard stories about the problem. The citizens of the Punjab, are mostly Sikhs, and they wanted to separate from India and have self-rule. The Sikhs were a majority and they would rather not be under Hindu control. John went to visit a friend and I slept until 1pm.

Upon John's return, we went to Happy and Pradees house. The day was extremely hot, with almost furnace like heat. We met Happy and Pradee and talked. I felt the heat. We all did. Everyone spoke good english and they were most kind and intelligent. Happy was a schoolteacher and lived in Australia for a short time. Pradee was Malaysian born and was also a teacher. He said to me, "Want to listen to some music?" He pulled out a Bob Dylan file cabinet with albums of all of his music! Wow! So, I spent the afternoon immersed in Dylan. "Like a Rolling Stone, New Infidelis. I again saw the tremendous world impact of Bob Dylan.

We ate such good food, of dark rice with peas and a stew of dahl and corn. Later, a friend arrived with a guitar. I played and sang a few songs. They said they liked it. But really I was down on my playing. We drank gin and friends arrived. I sat outside, under a full moon, with a cool breeze, playing and singing. We went to a house party and visited with these most respectable and kind people. They spoke english fluently and with such beauty, the accent soft and wonderful. These were wonderful hosts and hostess. Occasionally they would intertwine Hindi words into the english sentences. They were so happy and congenial almost as though they were British born and raised with this 'lofty air' to them. We drank and then ate Chinese like food. I never caught their names but they recalled mine. I was in awe of such wonderful, and very pretty hosts.

John and I rode through the streets of Chandigarh at midnight and were stopped by the police on the way back because of our headlight not being 1/3 rd darkened. At the house, we watched a late night movie, and with very full stomachs tried to sleep.

## Sunday April 15

I slept bad as bugs bit me. It was hot and I was restless. The overhead fan whirred all night. I was eager to get going, and got up early and prepared my things. I awoke the servant sleeping on the floor. Read the paper and drank tea and then showered. John stirred and Buntees brother came down. We sat awhile to converse. John went to Prefroms place.

I talked to Buntees brother and some of his friends came over. He really asked me many questions about what I would do when I returned to America. I felt that emptiness, once again come over me, that was an unknown for me. I always felt this because I didn't know what the heck I would do. When I told them the story about Ellen getting married they laughed at such a hard luck tale. The servant was also 28 years old. He looks like he is 30.

I played the guitar, and it was a real bad one, accentuating my poor playing skills. All morning long, I felt kind of like I'd better decide what I will do and it's stupid not to decide. Damn stupid. If I don't somebody will for me.

John came at 11:30am and I felt annoyed as he took so long. I played a song for all and they liked the Bob Dylan song- A Simple Twist of Fate. We all ate a good meal of eggs and toast. We added cream and honey on to our toast, and drank good cold coffee. We were all packed but John fiddled with his motorcycle. He was adjusting the chain. Finally at 1pm we were ready to leave.

It was another hot day as we rode off from Pradees comfortable home. This could easily pass for any neighborhood in the U.S. I was feeling a little like we were leaving too late. John and I disagreed on some things. Motorcycle speed is a lot faster than a bicycle. We rode on through the heat and then began a long slow climb up into the foothills of the Himalayas. We saw some cute girls from Bengal at one scenic rest stop and the view of them and the hills were inspiring.

There were terraced hillsides and waving fields of golden grass. We slowly continued on uphill. My butt was very sore riding on that motorbike and was continually adjusting the shifting bags. We went off onto a small road and saw some monkeys on this hilly terrain that was forested with pines. The winding road passed through more terraces and more pines. We went past a jeep with Indians in it and said hello to them. They smiled at seeing the two of us riding merrily along.

We rode into Chail, a nice little town located on a curve in the road. There really was not much to the town but a few restaurants and hotels. It was 6:30 and John said, "I'm staying here- this is nice." I wanted to look about. He went into a restaurant and ordered tea. ""Want tea?" he asked. "No thanks," I said. He joshed at me, "He's an American and they don't drink tea." In truth, I wanted to look around town to see what accommodations were available.

While John sat to drink his tea I took his motorcycle up the road. A jeep came beeping behind me. I stopped because I thought I dropped something. These Indian men wanted to meet me. Out they popped from the jeep laughing. They came up and shook my hand and poured me a drink of liquor. I said," I don't drink," and they laughed. They were very drunk. I talked to them but had to leave to their dismay. They tried to get me to stay saying, "You must relax with us!" But I went on up the hill to where there was a hilltop palace made into a hotel and resort.

The Jeep again pulled up. They all hopped out and teased with me. One guy shook my hand and then another told me he and the others wanted to fuck my ass. I dropped the drink and one Indian told me don't listen to him. "He's sore at other Indians." I said, "Never mind the world is full of the good and the bad." I left and went back to see John. We started talking when I heard a Jeep pull up. I ran out and told the guy to go away and get lost and I said to his face, "All you do is treat me like a toy." They took off and John came out laughing. "What in bloody hells going on?" he said looking puzzled. I explained it to him and he roared with laughter.

We went to the village and ate chowmein for dinner. Then we drank Indian wine, it was whiskey actually-whew, strong too.

The full moon shone overhead and it was such a lovely evening. John and I went up to the hilltop palace which had beautiful music playing from speakers along a walking path. It was enchanting Indian music complete with sitars, drums and melodic singing. The smell in the air was so scented from the trees. Everyone seemed so joyous and kind. We chatted with three fat gals under the clear moonlit sky and then walked back to our hotel in the light of the moon and slept.

## Monday April 16

For breakfast, we ate an omelet and drank tea on this cool but beautiful morning. I Was anxious to get going, I had to push John to get him moving. "Ketma Piesa," I asked the manager and we paid our bill. Chail is a quant and beautiful hilltop resort at about 5000 feet. We headed out and rode on this winding, hilly, tree lined road and stopped often to dig the scenery. After about 30 miles we stopped at a village and drank tea and made sandwiches from bread. We felt at ease as people didn't mob us. As we sat there, a truck came by and blew a tire. Kaabloom! The wheel clanged on the ground. It was comical to see the guys get out and look it over. "We didn't do it," we assured them and left to continue on our way for Simla.

While driving uphill around a left-hand corner at about 55 miles per hour, we had a truck approaching and a car on our right side trying to pass us. I could see the potential accident unfolding and banged my fist against the car. He forced us off the road. John brought the skidding motorcycle to a halt between two big rocks the size of our wheels. It was a close call.

We made headway to the hillside resort city of Simla, but not without making many wrong turns. The place looked rather slummy and we continued without stopping. I drove the motorcycle after that and we picked up a good pace. We stopped for tea, 'chai' at a stand on the roads edge. John was shown x-rays of a mans chest and the man said, "Me heart no good." He stuffed the x-ray in with his sac of potatoes.

It was very hot as we went down into a valley, which had papya trees and palms. We rode onward and the gas tank needed to be switched to reserve. John felt we could make it to Bilaspur, but just barely.

It was really hot. The wind was searing our skin. I did all I could to ride efficiently and smooth and not to waste fuel. We coasted on the downhills. John's legs cramped and we had traveled a long ways so he drove. We made it into the village just as the bike sputtered and coasted into the gas station.

We went to a juice bar and had a refreshing drink of papaya juice. I discovered that John has a few motherly antics that annoy me. He said, "Now come on put a napkin on your lap. Chin up," as we ate.

While riding along a tree lined highway we passed a couple of bicycle riders and greeted them. They appeared to be Japanese. We discovered that they were Tibetans on an all India tour. We stopped and drank tea with them. They spoke very well and decided to go our way. We found a place to cook and stopped and ate fish together, complimented with bananas and melon. We drank more tea. These young men named Danny and Tanding had been all around India. We decided to stay here, in this old gravel pit for the night. Tanding was very funny and jolly and his brother was more serious, but so kind. Danny told me of Tibet and his cause to inform people about the problems in Tibet. He felt Tibetan people weren't treated well by the Chinese. Tanding and I took the motorcycle and went to the store. We decided to ride to Bilaspur for beer and bread. We got there and shopped about as people chased us madly from shop to shop. The crowd got so crazy and big. Tanding said he felt uneasy. "These people find you very amusing to look at," he said. Tanding paid. We decided to buy beer, since John likes beer, "And so do I." said Tanding.

The bike was hard to start in the village and I kicked the 500 cc bugger many times until it fired. The crowd got crazy. They pushed right up against the motorcycle to look at us. Finally it started and we took off. I had to stop again at a small roadside egg stand later. It took time to start there as well. Then we had to ride slowly on the way back to our camping spot to prevent the breakage of our bottles of beer.

We finally got back to the camp and John was pissed. He pointed his finger at me and was threatening me by saying, "Where in mothers name have you been? I'm telling you it makes me feel like putting you in a bad way." I explained to him the perils of trying to start the bike. Tanding stepped into the fray by saying, "He's a hero. He work hard to make motor work and so many people go crazy looking at us." I was thankful Tanding stuck up for me.

It took John a few minutes to calm down, all was well between us. I started to cook supper and then my stove quit. I had to use Tandings stove. Finally we ate as darkness set in. We drank beer in the moonlight and shared many a story. This was a good meeting we had with these Tibetan guys. They were such great friends and could philosophize about life, men, money, and strife. They laughed at the humorous teasing between John and I. We each cried out and howled as we sat on thorns, as there were plenty at this site, yet we laughed and felt the life of youth. Each shared a sense of adventure in the past, present and future. The night was so right. We slept on the ground. It was a warm night and I almost wished I was bicycle traveling with these fellows.

## Tuesday April 17

In the morning, we cooked a nice breakfast of omelette and tea and sat on a rock to eat in this old gravel pit. Tanding played music on his cassette player. He was so jovial and philosophic, when he proclaimed, "one adventure ends and a new one begins." Danny told us of his Tibetan message to the press and how he would like to someday travel around the world. We joshed around, even playing catch with a ball and finally at 9am shook hands and separated our ways. They coasted away on their bikes, waving until gone.

We made our way north to Mandi and the weather was warm. Then we drove through the narrow roads in canyons and it was like Norway. John was a slow driver so when I took over, I made better time. We came into some nice scenery. I couldn't help but again reflect on life values as I feel to be a good person with friends and community is one of great value. We rolled into Kulu, a hustling, small town. The narrow streets were lined with storefronts that had balconies like those in New Orleans. We ate at a restaurant and watched the crowd gather around the motorcycle. Then we bought some food goods. As we motored up the road, it rained a bit.

We came alongside the Beas River, following a bus and it suddenly stopped. In front of the bus stood a strange creature on the road. He had bounded out of the woods and came up to us. It was a man colored all yellow with a red face and a strange crooked, forked tail. He came to us scratching and grunting. He had money in one hand. I took a photo and he made a weird pose. He ran with a hunched gait. "Didn't trust the bugger," said John. "Thought he'd pull a knife on us," he quipped. All the while we laughed at this character.

We were traveling into pine forested countryside when we entered the town of Manali. There were snow-covered mountains in the background "Yahoo," I shouted. We motored into town which was like an Alaskan gold rush village. Old wild west streets were filled with all kinds of people, Tibetans and Indians and white men. We looked for a hostel. Then we went to a tourist information center and met an Indian who told us of a hotel. We went with him and got a decent room by an apple orchard and a stream. It was only 15 rupees per night. We relaxed and then the power went out and it was dark. We walked in total darkness to town and ate Chinese food that was very good. We shopped around. "What a dump," John said. We ambled our way back, looking for our hotel, getting lost and nearly falling into the river. With no lights in town and only candles, it was like a journey back to the middle ages.

Back in our room, we would have to share the same bed. I said to John, "Let's go up the mountain pass tomorrow." "Okay!!" John acknowledged and then I said, "After that let's take a hot bath." "Okay!" he said again.

We washed up in cold water and then it was time for bed.

## Wednesday April 18

It rained all night and we both got up occasionally to go pee. John turned to me and asked for "pudding" while in his dreamy sleep. Another time he said, "She's running real fine." "You snored like a train, Yank," he said to me in the morning. We cooked a good meal in our room of omelets and toast. This was a good value at 10 rupees for the two of us.

We packed up and at 9:30 left town to head into the mountains. There was a light drizzle, but some blue sky. The road to Leh wound its way through villages of Tibetan people who were colorful and cheerful and hard working. A dog gave us a good chase up the hilly road. We climbed up into the mountains. The scenery was spectacular and changing as rapidly as the bike traversed the switchbacks. We went through road checks and then made it to the snow line. On one stretch on the way up it hailed hard. It was a rocky, wet road. I commented to John, "Every turn is a new picture." John was concerned with driving now in some snow and on the bad road. People played in the snow and the girls smiled at us. We rode in more snow. We fell down as the snow was deep and slick. We only laughed it off. The weather was cooler, but not bitter cold. We made our way up to 3320 meters and had tea at a little business that a Tibetan looking fellow operates.

The air was thinner up here and our breathing was effected. We got the ok from a policeman to head on up and we went slowly along the bad road. A bad decision could be tragic, as the road sides dropped for thousands of feet.

Soon it turned to all snow. The snowbanks were 15 feet high and they lined the road. We had a trail to follow from a Jeep. We maneuvered through the slick snow and I was amazed how well John and the Honda did. I got off and pushed a few times. Wheew-the high altitude air made my head spin. "Wow look at the mountains!" I said to John.

The world was brutal up here. Our feet were wet when we finally reached the last switchback, where the road was blocked by two four wheel drive vehicles. One had a snowplow and was blocked by a small avalanche. We could see from here the top of the pass to the northeast and noticed some trekkers, whom looked like dots going up over the pass. We were now above 13,000 feet.

This was the road to Leh. Leh is a Tibetan like village that is about 50 miles north of here. It is some very rough country to pass through in order to get there. We had been shown slides from a motorcycle journey that Preshees had made a few years ago, of this same route. He had forewarned us, that the snow can fall any time of year in the Himalaya's.

Happily we played in the snow and made a snow man. We ate a snack and then noticed the weather was changing and snow was falling harder. The fog and snow increased and soon it began to hail. We turned around and slowly went through some ruts on the way down. My feet were frozen. We were both real cold. We finally got back to the tea stall. When we got off the Honda, John and I faced each other and whacked both of our hands against each other and declared victory on Rhotang Pass. We then warmed ourselves by a fire and drank tea, both noticing how exhilarating we felt. This was a good moment and we laughed and talked and smoked a cigar each.

We coasted back down to Manali and John talked how satisfied he was and that he felt good about going through the rough conditions and making it that high up a mountain.

Back at the hotel we got a towel and soap and went to the natural hot spring, where we soaked awhile. Wow my head was spinning, but with a 'clear feeling.' We walked to town and ate again at the Chinese restaurant. I went for a walk and told John about the big dipper and he enjoyed learning of the north stars location. This was a fine place. We decided to spend one more day here hiking.

## Thursday April 19

This was a clear and sunny morning when I got up at 6:30am. I hiked into town, enjoying the mountain air and bought some supplies. We cooked a meal of French toast and omelette and really stuffed ourselves.

Deciding to take a hike, we walked through town and the mountains shone above with white capped glory against the blue sky. By midmorning, it was warm out and the altitude and heat were getting to us. We stopped in a grove of pines and rested. Then we headed on to a tea stop. We met two girls and talked to them awhile. Also we met an Indian family with a cute girl. Just as I was about to take a photo, the back of my camera popped open and exposed the film to sunlight.

John went back and I hiked on. I went along through a little village, where people looked like American Indians and up onto a good lookout of the valley, where I watched condors soar above. People worked oxen in the terrace below and I could see how hard they worked those darned creatures. They would barely do a row and then the ox would run off. They would whip the thing and bring it back.

I met some ladies carrying loads along the steep paths and passed through more villages with totems and flags waving. There was a mill for grinding seeds or corn that was run by river power on the waters edge. They had ingeniously channeled water down a sluice which turned a turbine. I hiked over big boulders, strewn by tormented rivers and again past villages of Tibetan refugees who have a facial and costume resemblance to American Indians and Eskimos. In this village I saw an old temple, beautifully crumbling down, and could not tell if it was Hindu or Buddhist. There were again many triangular flags flying here and there, and totem poles. Children were practicing their writing on clay tablets. I wound my way back to Manali feeling good to have taken a walk.

I picked up some bread, curd and cookies and walked up to the hotel where John was talking with others and to the military police. They requested our passports. John lifted his eyebrows and said jokingly, "They're looking for you mate." In fact they were only checking passports.

I made a cake for an english girl who's birthday is today, and whose party we would go to. I used bread and jam and curd covered with sliced banana and pineapple. We rushed about, getting things ready and then we went to the party. I rode on the motorcycle behind John, facing backwards to keep the cake from getting damaged. What a sight that was to the Indians. They pointed at me and laughed. It was an interesting way to travel. At the party we met other travelers. John was at home with the other english couple. We ate a cream of wheat like dish and then rice and veggie dish. "It was glorious," as John would say.

Out by the campfire on this cool night and listening to the roaring river made for an enjoyable party environment. We all talked up a storm and drank wine. There was an Israeli, French and Indian family. Our host told us, "A married man is the most happy man and also to have children is the most happy."

Happily and jokingly, John and I made our way somewhat drunkenly across the creek over two planks for a bridge. He nearly lost it and I shouted, "Give yer the gas, Sir John Taylor of Nottingham Lancashire, this ain't the Grand Canyon!" He laughed and responded, "Tis as wet though!"

## Friday April 20

I got up at 6:30am and John said, "You sure snored last night." I jokingly said to him you mumbled in your sleep these words, "Sir John Taylor of Nottingham Lancashire!" John said, "ha" and got pissed at me for saying that. "Where are you getting Nottingham Lancashire from you bloody yank? Don't you know your bloody British geography. There is only one Nottingham and only one Lanchashire, there is no bloody Nottingham Lancashire you bloody idiot!" I laughed up a storm at his outrage. He caught on and lightened up.

We cooked a good breakfast and then packed up. We paid our bill but were alarmed because they tagged on a charge of an extra 10%. We paid the amount and left Manali at 7:30am, heading downhill in the beautiful crisp valley air. We rode past some peasants, mostly Tibetans who walked the roads with their tools as they went to work. We had to be careful to avoid them. The Indian people are the most careless. Often they jump in front of the bike only missing us by inches. "Dumb bastards!" shouted John.

We stopped in Kula and John bitched at me for, "Shifting your weight around as we rode because you weren't comfy." I told him I didn't complain when he did it, and I said, "If you don't like the seat change it but don't blame me." I drove on rough roads. We stopped for tea and John blew his cool at some pestering people who surrounded us and acted like damn idiots. They stared at his motorcycle and poked on everything. "Bugger off!" John said. He had little tolerance for them.

We went on to Bilaspur where we saw some trucks that were burned on the roadside. There were four trucks farther down the road. These were trucks that were full of coal. We figured something strange had occurred. Some kind of sabatoge.

We rode on and experienced the most dangerous road yet. There were tight turns with buses hugging the lanes and trucks around each curve. I hugged close to the corners. One time I heard the beep of a bus and I rounded the curve and just missed a speeding bus. "Good job, well done," John said patting me on the back. We went along with sore butts.

This was a different route than what we came up on, through dust and along rocky roads, and it was under new construction. There were so many Tibetan laborers seated on a rock, chipping rocks to make gravel, along the banks of the roadside. Others had shovels and pics and wheelbarrows. It was a journey back to the 1890's in the U.S.

We weaseled past stuck vehicles and around dangerous curves with huge drops down to the valley below. At 2pm we crested a hill that overlooked the Chandigarh valley. Once we stopped to enjoy the vista but soon people swarmed about and kept messing with the motorcycle and saying, "How much is this and is it a self starter?" John blew up and said to them, "Bugger off I've a headache!" We cruised down to the valley, which was much warmer and had better roads.

We were back on the plain of India and upon entering Chandigarh, came up to a road block by the Indian Army and the guard with a machine gun said stop! But John wheeled past him and the guy chased us with his gun pointed at my back and we had to stop. John told the machine gun guard that we are just tourists and that they should let us through. They did and we continued on but soon another road block stopped us. They demanded we turn around but John said, "No, no, we are tourists." We again were allowed to continue on. John said, "You better take off those sun glasses of yours cause you look like a radical." I did and we approached another road block, where a bus was cleaned out of all its passengers. The police held big sticks. We tried to get past, and almost got whacked by the big sticks of the police. They shouted and demanded us to pull off.

We talked to the checkpoint officials who said, "Chandigarh is on curfew until 8am tomorrow. A shooting has occured in the city and violence was on the upswing. Nobody is allowed into the city, not even an Indian diplomat." While we were there, I saw people get whacked by the policemen with their big sticks. Even after being hit, they still didn't move to fast.

We were secretly told by a policeman to attempt to sneak into Chandigarh and that we could follow a diplomat. However, he warned us, we could be shot. Following the diplomat was nerve-racking, we did not know what to expect. He led us to a dry river bed and then he pointed the way across the sandy terrain and we decided to go for it. On the sandy bottom of the river the bike was very hard to control and John lost control and we dumped over. We were lifting up the motorcycle, when a military vehicle pulled up. They snickered as they went past us. We made it to a deserted road, and then sped along the streets under full suspense and on the look out for police or roadblocks. People looked at us suspiciously from their homes.

We finally made it to Buntees mothers and were greeted by Romeil. He warmly helped us unpack and fixed us a cold drink. We found out three people had been killed in the last two days. The city was under curfew. "Marshall Law has been declared," he said. So we would spend the night here.

In the evening I went out to meet a cute Indian neighbor gal and we chatted, though we retreated inside to escape from the taboos of her being seen talking outdoors to a single man.

A glorious cooked dinner was prepared by our wonderful host. The Indian girl told us about the dating game in this country and the troubles in the Punjab. She said young ladies can date a man, though it is not approved. The arranged marriage is still the main way that couples come together. Her family religion was Sikh and they believed that there should be an autonomous region for Sikhs from India. This is what the fighting was all about. India did not want the Punjab to separate.

We were tired after an exciting day, graciously thanked our hosts and those we'd met and we retired at 10:30.

## Saturday April 21

I slept like a baby and must say this was probably the very best of conditions for me yet in India. We had morning tea and were off on the motorcycle to see Happy and Preefron. As we rode the streets during a relaxation of the curfew we sensed the rush that people were in to getting things done in two hours. There were gas lines, food lines and many frightened looks. We were stopped by a cop, who kept his gun at the ready, but he let us go because we were tourists. He said we violated the two-up law on motorcycles.

Joining in the frantic fray, we went to a gas station and filled the gas tank and then went to Preefrons who was not home. We found Happy's school and he warmly greeted and welcomed us. We went into the school for breakfast and talked. We ate the most wonderful breakfast of toast, cold coffee, french fries, eggs and oat meal. Time flew past and we said, "Wow we'd better get going," we barely got out before curfew. We rushed back through the mazes of people and got back to Ramolas as curfew began. A civil defense siren blew.

The curfew rules ordered that people stay inside and that there was little to do but laze about and read magazines. I noticed that they had many Russian books, Lenin books and therefore learned a little about Lenin's life.

The television played a Paul Newman movie, we also listened to music on this rather cool and stormy day. God this was the life of luxury. At a snap of the fingers we had service from the servant. We ate a good lunch. What pigs John and I were! The afternoon slipped by and at 5pm we decided we better go to stay at Happy's.

The hurry, the packing, the curfew and goodbyes to Mr. Ramola took us some time but were necessary. He was a great fellow! We arrived at Happy's in one piece. Cadbury, the servant, showed us our room. We listened to some Bob Dylan music and what a selection he had. We drank a beer and talked to Happy. A storm blew in and there were big black clouds. The wind blew very hard, and it cooled off. Then the lights went out and candles appeared. We loved the suspense. The lightning flashed and the thunder clapped a really big kaboom. Soon the rain fell.

Our discussion turned to talk of old India. Happy's father was British. They had many servants. The attitude was much different then. He painted a picture in my mind of people who, "would work hard for their Sirs and were treated well in return," according to Happy who added, "The British developed this country and changed it. We had 24 servants," he said. It sounded like a golden age in India, but it wasn't theirs, "India always wants to do it on their own."

We ate a good meal and then the lights came on at about 9pm. We went to bed at 12:30am as it was now warm and the mosquitoes were out.

## Sunday April 22

Easter Sunday. Before anyone else was up, I discovered a Dylan book on Happy's shelf and devoured the pages of it. We were invited to spend the day here, and therefore agreed.

John and I were getting along just great. We kidded one another about ourselves. I called him Sir John Taylor of Notinghamshire Lancastor and he called me You Bloody Yank. We had shared some hardship and some good times. Perhaps this was our bond.

At curfew relaxation I walked into the marketplace and saw the police walking with sticks. There was a feeling of suspicion in the air.

Back at Happy's pad I played guitar and learned some new riffs. It was so great today as I didn't have to do a thing! A guitar, the sun and good company. We lazed away the day, ate a great lunch and read books. We listened to many Dylan albums.

At the afternoon curfew break I took a bicycle and rode the streets. I saw a camel walking or standing and eating weeds. The Indian bike was so heavy and slow but rode smooth. I rode for one hour, enjoying the sights and then returned and saw the camel standing in the same place.

John and I walked to the market. We saw a kid throwing rocks at a sign post and I challenged John to go a round. We picked up our rocks and I hit the sign first, "Bloody American," John said.

Upon our return to Happy's, we met Preefron at the front gate and so we had more to talk about. Soon more guests arrived. After a quick chat they had to leave before curfew returned. Preefron was a natural and reminded me of my cousin Justin. He was easy going and enjoyed talking about Dylan. We read Dirt Bike magazines. My mind was enchanted by past memories of riding dirt bikes.

As the evening progressed, we sat outside and watched the stars overhead. I saw Mars in the east. Happy was always keeping our spirits up by humour and candor. He lectured Cadbury the servant for waiting too late to buy oil for the lamp and called him a "stupid chap." Cadbury drooped. We sat about engrossed in conversation and ate a late meal, as sometimes is done in India, at 10:30pm.

Afterward, I drank a good shot of Indian whiskey. Then it was off to bed feeling full and with no pain. John was told his mom had arrived in Delhi. Happy chuckled when I said to John, "John no talking in your sleep."

## Monday April 23

"Sir John Taylor of Notinghamshire Lancastor, good morning," I greeted John. He said, "And a good morning to you, all being well." We got packed up and had tea and ate biscuits at our bedside. Then we did some loafing about and ate a good breakfast. We commented on our filling waistlines. It was a warm morning. We all sat about. A fellow Indian appeared and talked to Happy and left. "Why did he come here," said Happy adding, "I think he was sleep walking." Happy told us a story how the names are selected for the hit list, which is the murder of certain anti-Punjab independence individuals. "The leader has a servant who picks his name. He won't do the job because his man is cool. The leader throws away the slip, then says, Ok you write your name on a piece of paper and put it into the hat. Then the hit men reach into the hat and select a name. That is who they murder." He laughed like crazy at his own story. I tried to understand the Indian logic from this, but mostly the complex humor comes out and I too laughed.

Finally it got to be 11am and we have many handshakes and said goodbye and I felt so sad because this was such fun. We motored off into Chandigarh, and began heading back to Delhi.

With no curfew today, the situation was more relaxed. We went through town and past many roadblocks. Some cop wanted us to stop but he hesitated and we sped by as he shouted. We made it out of the city and soon started the traffic madness. We bolted and ducked about to escape big trucks and buses that would pass anywhere and run us off the road. We went past more road blocks and each time I would take off my glasses so they could see my blue eyes and light skin. Riding two up was still a violation.

We rode on and our butts got sore. At 2pm we stopped for petrol. There were so many near accidents on this stretch of road. There were people walking on the road, cows and goofy traffic.

Then the weather really heated up as we made our way through the crazy Delhi traffic. I feared for my life as we went through intersections of people and buses and scooters crisscrossing everywhere. Finally we hit the home stretch, not more than a block from Nat's home when I finished eating a mango and then tossed the big seed at a passing truck. Wack! It hit the truck. John was startled and he slowed down. I hit John on the back and said, "Don't stop." The truck appeared to turn around in a 'u' turn. We ditched it into a side street and John cursed at me. "You bloody yank what were you thinking, throwing that seed at a truck?" I said, "I got revenge on a truck but not on the right one."

We greeted Buntee and Johns mother and I felt like a fool. We conversed and all was well. His mother rambled on about her journey from England. She was very elite and proper. I asked Buntee if I could stay the night. She said it was fine.

We packed things up. John and his mom couldn't decide what to do. John, Nat and Buntee went somewhere, so I treated Johns mom to dinner at the restaurant. Afterward we were returned and were invited in for some treats. I couldn't figure out what's going on. Mom seemed to say she wanted to try a hotel. I asked why they don't stay here. We had a big talk about the U.S. and the road to riches. It was a good conversation and I realize again that people would love to go to the U.S. to work for the money that they can make. We talked about the U.S. policy, President Reagan, etc. I fixed a bed for myself outside and the bugs came to haul me away. John and his mom took off for a campground. I did not know what was going on. Perhaps this was because Buntee didn't want to put Johns mom up in this little house.

## Tuesday April 24

I was greeted this morning with a cup of tea and breakfast. Buntee and Cheeshawn swept the floor with a hand broom. I put together my things and headed for town. The streets were a whirl with people and cars but I enjoyed this city. I went to the post office to check on the postal restante mail but there was none for me. I inquired about mailing a package and then went to the bank. I shopped about, and looked for souvenirs. At one shop, I bought a cobra skin and then spent some time looking for a shipping company. Each person told me a new place to look. I hunted all over Delhi.

I met John and his mom and paid him $20 for petrol. I went to a film shop and bought one roll of film for $4 and told the guy of my All India Cycle tour and he gave me a second roll of film for $2. That was the magic word, I guess. I dashed about hectically buying essentials. Then I headed for the post office after I discovered the shipping company dealt only in bulk. I waited in a long line and they told me I needed a cloth cover over my package. Where do I get that? I had to pedal quickly to a tailor, who custom designed a bag for me as time ran out. I hurried back and was helped by a kind Indian. I packaged it and a fellow sewed up the bag as I filled out 6 forms. I left my tape for one minute on a table and it was stolen. I finally pasted stamps to the cloth and penned on the address. Then I waited in a long line and mailed the box. This rinky-dinky-postal system in India is full of hassles.

I headed off to find a welder to repair my camp stove. He was out on vacation. Found another place and this guy said, "here sit down well take care of it." He bought me a Limca. He asked what I needed and I explained it precisely. Something got confused as the part came back welded backwards. He took it back and returned, but then again was confused as the gas pipe was all plugged. Then they tried to do it again and it came back too short. They tried to lengthen it but the welder burned up the little pipe. The worker then tried a new attempt to rebuild it. Meanwhile I laughed it up with these jolly guys. One fellow was a cop, one was a drivers license examiner, who asked me if I wanted an India drivers license. He said, "In India there is no test needed for a drivers license. Just Baksheesh!" One guy owned an automobile body shop. So they were jolly fellows. And they kidded alot with young people walking past. They almost cruelly mistreated them. The shoe shine boys had a tough time from their sarcastic ridicule.

I supervised my part rebuilding. They screwed around. Burned holes. They didn't understand me but we finally got it back together, though I wouldn't know if the Coleman stove worked until getting back to Nats.

I headed back to Nats and on the way saw a shapely lady walking along the street and slapped her on the butt. She got pissed. I rode up and was greeted by Nat. Soon John arrived with a pizza. Ah ha!. We munched. And we talked. I found out I could not fix the stove as the welding job plugged it up. I washed up and talked to all.

Nat wanted to be an architect and I saw a fine plan for his future house, and a model also. It was an octagon shape. I saw that between he and Buntee, their talents were exceptional. I joked with John. He was a good fellow, strong headed, stubborn and finicky, but he was all right. He had his mothers ways. We then said our goodbyes and so long. We shook hands for quite awhile in a gesture I feel was bonded by our many perils. We had a great time!

They loaded up and were off. Mom was slightly unnerved by it all. Will she last? Nat said, "I don't think she will make it very far." I worked over the stove, and then retired to read dirt bike magazines and drink cold 'quash'. It was another warm night. Buntee gave me a nice pot, as a keepsake of her talents.

## Wednesday April 25

I thought of Dads birthday coming and my absence from it. I would think of him all day on the 27th. I got packed and was served a cup of tea. Then charming Buntee ordered Cheesham to make me breakfast. Nat got up and we talked of future exchanges for information on motocross. Perhaps I could write a photo and article on India motocross. He could use rules etc., by the AMA. I ate and then regretfully said goodbye to Nat and Buntee. They were one of a kind, super generous honest, intelligent hospitable folk that the world needs to take lessons from and including myself.

As I was saying goodbye, I told Buntee to stick to it for a U.S. visa and said to her, "If its easy, it ain't worth a shit any way." And Nat swayed his head and told me, "I hope you always have strong tailwinds." With that I was off and they smiled and waved and I tell you, I felt so much as they gave me what even my own family probably might not do.

I jammed down the streets of Delhi, feeling good to be back on the road. It was very warm. I had to carry the bike under a railroad gate as a line of cars honked at me. It was a nice stretch of road on the way to Agra, with a decent shoulder, and so I could talk friendly to other bike riders. At 11am I stopped to have a drink and a snack. Then I stopped at noon for lunch and drank a lassi, which soothed my upset stomach.

The heat of the day arrived and it was time to get soaking wet. It was very hot out. This was a slow pace. At another dunk I noticed something unusual happening. I was turning purple! I looked at my back and it was all red and purple colored. I wondered what was happening and then noticed that my cheap new India towel that I recently purchased was bleeding all of its colorant out and upon my body.

At a town I went to get some drink, but people only harassed me. I had to drink poor water and get by. As I rode along, I felt my stored up fat that was hanging over my riding shorts from the past two weeks of idleness. I stopped to catch my wind. Whew! I continued and was tired when I made it to Mathura, the birthplace of Lord Krishna.

I rode into the city that was jammed with rickshaws and crazy Indians who crawled about the place like ants. There were cows, pigs, shit and road-blasting-music blaring.

I saw a civilized looking guy pedaling along in a bikeshaw and rode up beside him to ask his passenger where the International Guest House was. But the large wheel of his bikeshaw cut into my back pannier and it hooked me and pulled me down. I fell right into the spinning rear wheel. My bike and gear all dropped, but I kind of held myself up against the turning bikeshaw wheel for a moment longer pending from disaster. Then I fell and quite rapidly all these people rushed to my aid. I just picked up my bike and chased the guy not noticing my arm was scraped of skin and bleeding. I saw that the bikeshaw rider was trying to ditch me. I caught him and asked his passenger where the guest house was. He told me directions and I found the hostel.

This little youth hostel was straight out of the hippie days, with flower power paintings here and there. I got a room for 80cents and washed up after relaxing for a bit. I was a tired guy. I went outside and it was a real cooker.

There was a Krishna temple here, in commemoration to his birth. Inside was a display with some life-sized mannequins that portrayed the stories of Lord Krishna. He was depicted as a blue colored playboy, playing a flute in many of them. He was generally escorted with nice looking young women. This display was a wonderful way to get an introductory idea about the story of Krishna. For others, this was a holy place, people bowed to Krishna and left gifts.

I drank a lassi and ate at a restaurant by the hostel some rather shitty India food. An Indian fellow sitting at the next table told me not to eat with my left hand and I said, "I'm not an India man." This annoyed him, but I continued. This is because they wipe their ass with the left hand.

I was chased by some cute little girls selling candy. God they were cute. I bargained with a fellow for bananas and he gave me a deal after I said I was on an all India cycle tour. I asked him his name in Hindi. He told me and I said, "Rham, rham." He swiveled his head and said, "ah cha," and we shook hands. I walked along and a sweet but devilish little girl wanted to sell me sweets and wanted backshesh, which I gave her. It was a hot night, the soul needs to feel good to sleep in this hellish heat.

## Thursday April 26

I again walked over by the Krishna temple and saw old men praying outside, seated in a yoga fashion or bowing with hands together. Inside, I again enjoyed the statues of Lord Krishna, who looked like such a jolly fellow. He was a pipe fiddler and always a ladies man. The music inside was interesting and very entrancing. It sang, "Holy, holy, Krishna," with citar and drums accompaniment. It was very magical.

I packed up my things as a crowd gathered to watch me load the bike. I pedaled through this funky town on a clear sky blue morning past other cyclists and down shit roads. I made good time along the highway and pedaled on into Agra. It heated up fast outside. I was heckled and followed and called monkey by many people. A slow riding cyclist would speed up to ride by my side or stay on my tail. I sped up and so did they. I slowed down and so did they. I switched to the other side of the road and they paced me. It was very annoying, mostly because it was dangerous and each time I'd have near misses from cars of trucks because of their foolishness. I can only say these people lack judgement or concern for others. They appear to be hypnotic.

I rode into Agra, which was busy with commerce and was really looking for a cold drink. I saw a westerner walking along through town and asked him if he knew of a hotel. He said follow me. He took me to the Bakshi House. I entered and was given a cold water and struck up a conversation with this fellow and gal whom were from Canada. I was told a room costs $5 for a night so I declined and said I'd better look elsewhere. I talked awhile longer and the madam said she wanted to see me.

We went into a light green colored office and the madam said, "You can stay here free of charge. We want you to be our guest! This is our house," she insisted. I was dumbfounded. "The colonel and I want you to stay in our house, free of charge, Ok?" Dazzled, I accepted and met the fellow behind it all. He was called the 'Colonel,' He told me he too was a cyclist in 1953 and went from Agra to Columbo. I met his mom and she was quite old and very kind. I was shown a big room and I can't believe it was pretty good. I cleaned up and kicked back. Then I went to see the Taj Mahal.

Now this wasn't any ordinary day. I pedaled the roads and eventually saw the Taj piercing the blue sky. I went to a restaurant and the Indian waiter screwed up and gave me two dishes. I accepted them and really over ate.

I then walked over to see the Taj Mahal. It was so sensual in all so many ways. I couldn't help but feel that lovelyness. One had to take it in from many angles to appreciate the Taj. From every angle it was so beautiful. One must get closer to see its riches. The marblework was intricate and so finely finished that even with closer inspection the better it was. Shoes must be taken off to go inside. I used a flashlight within to see the dazzling inlays of gems in the marble. The inside of the dome had an amazing echo and a mystique. There were two tombs sitting side by side and they were graced by a marble screen so precisely cut that a mosquito couldn't fly through. I sat inside the mausoleum for quite awhile, enjoying the architecture and the coolness. Then I explored around the outside of the place. The marble gets real hot under the Indian sun. As we were made to walk in stocking feet, the heat was nearly unbearable. I had to run between shadows. However, inside the marble floor it was cool. I thought of the story of the Taj and how it symbolized the undying love of the Maharaja for his wife. Right next to the Taj was a Mosque that was nicely made but rather imposing. I walked down along the long pond and flower garden in front of the Taj and then passed through the front gate, which framed this postcard view so gracefully, that it smiled.

While walking to the shops, which had marble work for sale, I discovered that they all wanted to sell me drugs. They said they would mail me marble with drugs hidden inside a secret chamber. I was shown how this was done and told the hefty price of doing it. The marble work is the exact and it is the same style of inlay as used on the Taj Mahal. One legend says that all of the craftsmen who made the Taj had their hands cut off. Yet, these inlays were the descendants of a long line of craftsmen handed down from the Taj construction, some 500 years ago.

I went to find a lassi and was assisted by a fellow. He helped me find a lassi stand, where I drank a great lassi and then he told me how I could make some money in Nepal. So I followed along with him and it turned out he was a salesman for a drug selling and gem selling operation. He too wanted me to carry some drug and gems in the marble work. I declined his offer. He did not smile when I left.

I pedaled back to the hotel and mixed a cold drink and relaxed. Then I was told of a great marble shop that must be seen.

I went to visit the most exquisite work ever done with inlays of agate, jade and fine carvings into marble. These were the real modern day inlay workers, the real descendants of the Taj project. I was in awe of this high quality operation. Maybe someday I'll return to buy some of these items.

I went back and sat down with the others and we ate a delicious meal. The pudding with apples in it was delicious. The colonel told us about his adventure of cycling and scootering from India to Europe in 1963. It was an amazing tale of crossing Afghanistan and Iran. He had been helped all along his journey, by many people, and told some hair-raising tales of tigers chasing him. When he finally arrived in Europe, he said life was far richer there, but he opted to come back and help his countrymen. He was a Sikh and they believe in acts of kindness.

He and the others seemed intrigued by my story. I was given a Sikh's wrist bracelet by the colonel. He said it was for good luck, "And you'll need that!"

## Friday April 27

Today was Dad's birthday and I'd planned to think of him as much as possible all day. I packed up after a very stuffy night. I was given tea and biscuits from the colonel, his wife and mother. They are very kind to me and declined any payment. "Drop us a letter," they said and the colonel brought out a special guest book that I was allowed a whole page to fill in. Finally I was off and he told me, "It was on a morning like this when I left. I wasn't frightened because I wasn't alone, there were two of us, me and God. God above me and a cycle below me. I always keep the connection open to him and on a bicycle there's no roof over me." He then said, "Happy travels." I shook his big hand and was off.

I went through Agra, over rough roads littered with trash. For a long time I pedaled past a fantastic old red fort and then went under its gate. I stopped for a cold lassi and bananas. I weaved through crazy traffic and even crazier people who gawked at and insulted me. I had one last magnificent view of the white Taj in the distance. While in the foreground there was a polluted river, garbage strewn everywhere and some of the most impoverished looking conditions and people I'd yet seen in Indian. It made me think of the cliche, that the Taj is like a pearl on the top of a pile of shit. In other respects it looks like an H.G. Wells moon rocket.

I headed east, and went buzzing through little towns assisted by a good tailwind to thank for that. There were all kinds of riders coming alongside of me. Some talked with me and others I just ignored as they spoke Hindi to me. Each wanted to know the price of my bike. "Ketma piesta?" they would ask. I stopped at 10am and enjoyed a cold lassi. Then at 11am I had two more, then at noon a 4$^{th}$. They always soothed my aching belly and thirst. I made great time and even rode fast on pretty good roads. The heat really wore on me though and I had to stop frequently to cool off. At 3pm I rode into Etarvah which was 120 k's from Agra. I decided to stop. I hunted around the town for a hotel. While stopped at a food stall, I drank two delicious lass's as a huge crowd developed. The authorities came and had to throw water at people to keep them from staring at me and playing with my bike. As I went through town throngs of people enveloped me each time I stopped. They would heckle me alot. And the traffic was horrible. I went to several hotels, all of which were poor rate. But finally I returned to the first one called the Annephaar and checked in.

I took a shower, relaxed and dozed off. After awakening, I walked to the lobby where the hotel offered free ice and chipped off a large block and made myself a cool drink, then went to town. I shopped for a drink mix and was mobbed everywhere. The people stared at me as if they were hypnotized. They loved to tease me and just push my tolerance to the limit. I slapped one kid a good one for playing with my bike. Then they stood back. I bought some things and drank one more lassi as the kids gathered around in throngs to stare. I quieted them with peaceful gestures. I returned to the hotel to find a large wedding was going to happen. Now my room was being used as a heat sink, as fans blew the heat from the big room toward my room. There was music blaring outside. It was so hot, I had to leave my door open, therefore people who were passing by would pop in and stare at me. I was given a few non alcoholic drinks and snitched some ice.

## Saturday April 28

I had a night of on and off sleep all night long. The power went on and off and so did the fan overhead. There were mosquito's biting and humming constantly. I packed up and slowly went through town on a piece of shit road. Many people heckled me, until I got back onto the highway and picked up the pace, due to a nice tailwind. I made good time all morning. At one stop for a lassi the kids came running. They liked to irritate me such that I slapped them on the arm. They see pleasure in this. While they are not aggressive, they certainly are annoying and make it known. One kid twisted my mirror and I grabbed his nose. He then backed off. I stopped for a bath at a guesthouse. It was real hot out and so the cold water was refreshing and very clear from the pump. An elderly fellow dumped a huge pail of water on my head and back. Wowwy! Each time I stopped I was watched by mobs of people. People would stop doing everything to stare at me. Even when I took a piss, they came to stare. I swear they are hypnotic. They go into a trance like state when they see a white man.

The road got bumpy and dusty and it was only one lane and I had to go slow. Many bikes followed me and they wouldn't pass me. It was annoying and often my tires hit rocks on the shoulder because of that. One guy pulled alongside of me demanding my attention and told me that the U.S. was full of stupid people. He tried to match wits with me and I just ignored the obstinate S.O.B.

As I rode along one section of road lined with trees I noticed up ahead a few people dressed in white robes and walking along barefoot, right down the middle of the road. All the cars and buses went around them. They were called Jains, a religious sect that believes in all creatures as being sacred. They are very careful not to hurt anything, not even step on an ant, but nearly caused horrendous traffic accidents and lots of anxiety from drivers.

I rode into a crossroad after breezing away many kilometers. There I drank another lassi. With lots of crushed ice. My thirst was unquenchable but lassi provided the most relief and it felt so good in the tummy. I rode on and again dunked under a pump but this time by a deep open well. The water was again clear and cool and it felt so good.

As I continued down the road I noticed that the wind had changed and was now a side wind. I looked behind me and saw a foggy like brown cloud rolling in from the west. Up ahead it was hot, with blue sky and bright sun, scattered with some clouds.

I was 50 kilometers from Kanpur when I met a 17-year-old boy riding his bike. We went along silently, as he said little. After 20k's he turned off the main road. I felt really tired. I stopped, sat down, cooled off and then continued. About 10k's from Kanpur my pace was real slow, even with a tailwind, it was as if I was drained of all my energy. It was cloudy now and getting cooler. I struggled along rough roads, full of various types of industry and then rode into Kanpur. I asked a hotel for the price of a room. At the same time this crowd followed me into the hotel. They stood so close to me, that there was no room to move. I walked up to the front desk and jokingly said, "I would like a room for me and all my friends." The clerk failed to see the humour and the rate was much to high, so I decided to leave, but was blocked from my bike by the crowd. There was a guy wearing a turbine who talked Hindi interspersed with english words to me and to the crowd and finally I gently motioned my way through the crowd to get to my bike.

Everything was ok, I was invited to tea with him. He was a Sikh and very kind. Soon another huge mob of people developed around us. We spoke and Sikhs are the most helpful people in India. I looked at him and suddenly a blast of dust blinded all of us, and there was a horrible wind. It was a sudden sandstorm! Things went flying through the air. Hats, pieces of tin, shoes, branches flew down the street. Everyone vanished. I grabbed my bike and dashed down a dust blasted street, blinded badly by flying sand. I almost couldn't see a thing and had to stop often to get out of the blast and to breathe. Signs blew over, trees bent, and I hit a traffic jam at an intersection.

The next danger was a stampede of water buffalo who almost ran over me. I didn't have to pedal, the wind blew me down the road. I weaved my way along a murderously rough stretch of road entirely 'flying on instruments.' I could not see a thing. I asked people which way it was to the railroad station and thankfully was helped by a fellow to get a hotel room and a place to store my bike. I got a room, where I sheltered from the storm, showered and relaxed.

The storm soon dispersed and I walked to the train station, which was full of people, wiping away the dust, and bought a cold coffee. The marketplace was packed with people and it had madness to it. People pushed and were mean spirited and it felt like a nut house. I then went to the city and ate curried rice and chicken. Afterward, I bought two lassis and some fruit and made my own milkshake. The people heckle me, as they watched me do this. The lights went out at about 8pm, and when they came back on half an hour later. By then the crowd had left.

I walked around looking in shop windows and made my way back to the hotel. There was such a tranquility to the streets now. Gone was the sandstorm, the madness, the aggressive frustration that was there around 6pm. Such is the pulse of India.

## Sunday April 29

The fan whirred all night long above me and I slept pretty well. I realized that today is my birthday. I'm 29 and I should be cocky as hell, as it is my golden birthday, but I just want it to go its own way and I'll see what happens. I walked over to a restaurant, got a lassi and a tea, then headed out of town amidst followers, staring people, hecklers etc.

I was crossing a large river plain and soon could see the twisting waters of the Ganges River. There was a long skinny bridge over the muddy waters of the mighty river, the spiritual waters of India. As I rode over the bridge, I could see bathers on the end of a long sandbar cleansing themselves in the sacred waters and praying in the name of their God. There were funeral pyres burning on sandbars in several other locations. The river appeared brown, the color of tea, with a greenish tint near the center. I pedaled across the long bridge and just after crossing it, out popped a couple of scantily dressed fellows with turbans who darted out on the road carrying a dead body high above them on a stretcher. The arm of the deceased dangled and flowers covered it. I hit the brakes and held my breath, in case it smelled. He was to be cremated near the sacred river. This is the final resting place for many Hindus. The parade included many women dressed in colorful saris as they wailed beneath black veil covered faces. Participants in the parade beat on drums and clashed hand cymbals.

There were lots of people riding upon the road today. I had time to think about my dad's birthday, and the wish that he celebrated it with our family. It was also on this day that Ellen's wedding was scheduled. Her wedding and my birthday, those thoughts clashed in my thoughts, as I pedaled along.

As I approached Lucknow, people who came alongside of me would speak Hindi or english and they would ask me where I was from. One guy came alongside and asked me and I just said, "America." This was happening in busy traffic. Then a thin, dark haired fellow asked me in a very excited voice, "What State is it you come from in America?" I kept my concentration on the road and replied loudly, "California." He then started to ask another question while looking at me with those big black eyes, then suddenly WHAM! He crashed into and hit another cyclist who was carrying milk. I looked back and milk was flowing and spurting every way along the road. The two riders were untangling their mess of machines and milk. They said very little in the way of heated words. I just kept going. That was the problem with my 'escort riders.'

A few miles later the same young fellow came up again beside me, but this time he didn't stop to chat with me. This was unfortunate, as I did not want this unfriendly scene, but I felt what they did was a most dangerous problem and it was happening to me all day long. I would get exhausted trying to talk to them and to prevent these mishaps. There were just so many people here and they seemed to have poor judgement. It wasn't worth wrecking my bike to speak trivial words with them.

The kilometers went by slowly. All I could think of was getting a cold drink. I went into Lucknow and stopped for directions and people laughed, stared and joshed at me. I found a cool place with lassi and drank two big glasses. There I met a guy and he asked me for my address, which I gave and then he left. I spent a few minutes repairing my bike bracket for holding a water bottle. A crowd gathered and they were entertained by my every move.

An attitude of indifference came over me because today being my birthday. I thought, what the heck, why let anyone push me around, or why not enjoy myself and treat myself to something. Though I'd just eatin, I was still hungry, and took my time to leave town. I stopped for ice cream and the clerk sold me a stale product. It was no good. I refused it and he gave me a different one. As I pulled away he demanded more money. I rode on, thinking to myself, "Hey it's my birthday."

Though I never told anybody that it was my date of birth, one kind individual came to give me a very nice gift. It was very hot as I rode along and I saw a roadside stand and pulled over for a cool drink. This short and sturdy looking Indian man would not let me pay and insisted he buy me a extra large glass of freshly squeezed sugar cane juice filled with ice. It was so delicious and hit the spot. I was refreshed for several hours and thankful for his wonderful gift. I was joined on my ride for the next few miles with the fellow who bought me the drink. We rode on to Bave Banki and people there really harassed me bad. Even he was startled and offended by his countrymen. With his help, he found me a hotel and I got a room for $1.20. We shook hands and he then went on his way.

A young boy, about 10 years of age, who's parents worked in the hotel helped me carry my things to the top floor room. The view from my room was of the flat rooftops in this dinjy city. The bathroom of my hotel room had a shower with a skylight and while I showered there I was suddenly alarmed at a thundering sound overhead and looked up but only saw a dark shadow dart away. After the shower and while relaxing, more shadows were seen and then I saw that they were monkeys hopping and running on the rooftops. Frequently they would bang on my roof and dash into their playground of rooftops.

I could tell that this town did not see many western tourists while walking out to find a place to eat. They really stared at me and gave me more harassment. I bought a big lassi. It was my birthday! I had a crowd standing to watch my every move. They must have thought of me as a puppet. I ordered them to sit down and gestured such and they did so. All about me were sitting people looking at me with interest. I talked to them but it did not take long for them to become smart-ass. Someone commented in Hindi and then they laughed and they started talking. I felt like a monkey in the zoo.

Back at the hotel I was given a block of ice and had an ice water. The young boy came up to my room with the water and he enjoyed joshing with me. He laid on his back and looked at me upside down. His eyes bore the most startling shape while in this peculiar position. They were black as open wells and his S-shaped eyes and strange smile made me think he was some kind of devil. What a way to end my birthday!

I made the mistake of sleeping in the hotel bed, under the thin blanket and at about midnight, awoke to severe bites upon my legs and sides. I could feel the little bedbugs crawling about me like a hungry animal. They bit me quickly and darted away. I rubbed some insect lotion upon the area, but they were soon back. It is a horrible feeling, to be attacked by such minute creatures. I then reached for my cookstove and poured out a little of the Coleman fuel and spread it about my body, and went back to bed. This time the bedbugs left me alone for the remainder of the night.

## Monday April 30

Today was my grandma's birthday! I packed up and struggled down the steep steps with my bike and gear to reach the street. There were puddles here and there and I recalled the tremendous thunderstorm of last night.

Admist a huge crowd of dumb looking watchers, I cleaned my chain. They were so easily amused. The crowd closed in and I had to push them away so I could move. I got a little ice from a block and bought a cold tea and was off.

Pushing against a slight headwind, the ride was enjoyed with other cyclists who played the usual games on me. They wanted to ride alongside and I wouldn't let them. They act very smart-ass so I just ignored them. Sometimes I cut them off to the other side of the road. I rode into Fiazdebad and had a lassi with bananas.

I selected a small food stall that served chipadees and dahl baht, a spicy stew made from lentils. I rolled the chipadees up like a taco to make them easier to eat. After eating five of them, gastric pains set in. I left the restaurant and made way quick, to relieve myself in the gutter of the street, in a toilet that was made of two planks and a plastic sheet. No toilet paper was available, I understood why the people here ate with only their right hands.

Slightly blue in the face, I had to settle my stomach. I searched out a food stall that sold Lassi. Whenever my stomach was upset, or if I was real hot, Lassi was the perfect remedy. They took buffalo milk and added crushed ice with sugar and then mixed it together by dumping one glass to another at arms length. Lassi was so rich in vitamins that they claim you can live off it.

I passed an area known as the Anoydan and did see many temples there. I crossed the Gorakphar River and noticed that the plain is immense and many people were bathing in a procession. There were more than five temples in this town, as this is the birthplace of Rham, the great god of the Hindu story called the Rhamayana. There was a sculpted figure of a god, that was lying in water, and many people dumped red blood looking colorant on him and themselves. It made no sense to me what they were worshiping, but I knew if they saw a Christian communion, that would make no sense of that either.

A storm blew in on me in the afternoon. The driving tailwind was just terrific. At times I did not have to pedal. Wow what a blast. It was so strong that tree fruits fell on the road and kids were running to gather them. Some rain fell. I had to stop before I fell off the bike, as I was so tired.

I rode until dark and made it into Basti where I was heckled all through town. I looked for a hotel but the pickings were slim and so was my search for food. People rode so crazy and walked so nonchalantly along. Despite repeated ringing of the bell, they would not move out of the way. I purposely rammed them to get them to move off the road. I went into a store and bought bread and butter and waited in the front of the line with money in my hand and finally I gestured to walk out if they didn't want my money. They made a fuss and accepted my payment. When I got out of the crowded store, I sat down to butter my bread as an amused crowd gathered to watch me eat. This looked so stupid, so I acted like I wanted to feed them as though they were dogs. They just laughed. Are they ever dense! Then someone caught on to my parody and backed off. "He is fooling you, treating you like a dog," said one voice in the crowd. But still, they stayed. I ate some rice and mutton and again a group watched. I went over and got a lassi and the biggest crowd yet gathered. I sat back and just enjoyed my meal at times hollering to keep them away from my bike. They came right up to my face and stared. I mimicked them and they found it so entertaining. Not the older ones, they were more discreet and they glanced a look, and then told the others to leave me alone, before walking away. Kids chased after me as I rode off.

I was nearly out of town when a man at a roadside stand offered me a drink. I sat with him and drank this Indian whiskey with the man.

I went down the road feeling the booze and found a place to camp. This was a good spot near some trees. I found a well pump and cleaned up and then went to sleep in my cozy little tent.

**Tuesday May 1**

I awoke as a mumbling Indian walked past on his morning ritual to take a shit. After packing up and hitting the road, I pedaled north, as the orange sun rose in the east and squeaked over the horizon. It was common to see many people squating in the fields and farting as I rode by. It was humorous and I nearly fell off the bike laughing when on my left side, I passed one dark skinned man in a white gotee and white turbine who was squatting and let out a long fart. Then a little farther on the right side was a woman who sounded as if she had diarrea, a squishy sound. The air was none to pleasant to say the least, but it all blended in with typical India odor.

I stopped for tea and was intently stared at by some very serious, yet curious fellows who then received my dog treatment. I was whistling and saying, "Come on boy, come here fella," all the while holding my bread out, arm stretched and then held it near the ground. He was actually going to eat it like a dog! He crept up and was bending down to eat out of my hand. Then the other Indians told him what I was doing, that this was the way a dog is treated, and that angered him and he stood up wide eyed, insulted and left. At the time I did not feel bad about this. They had rude manners and it was uncalled for. All the while I sat there, the others continued they're hypnotic like stare. I call it the hypno-stare.

I had a good tailwind and made fast time. There were some monkeys on the road, which I passed and they looked uncaringly. I met a fellow from Switzerland driving a van and he offered me a lift. "No thanks," I said. "Wouldn't want to miss any of this."

I rolled along and it was quite pleasant now except for the goofy Indians. I played a game of –'chase me if you can with them' and some were strong riders. Some would just follow my tail. I arrived in Gorakpuer at 10:30am and bought some big bananas for 4 to 10 cents. I met an Indian and he treated me to a lassi. I pedaled into town and bought another lassi and the crowd gathered so large. I offered them to sit down but they stood back. I tried to just ignore them and drink a Coca Cola, an ice cream bar and two cookies, and noticed a parade of marchers walking with Soviet flags. Then I watched in awe as some Mig combat jets flew low overhead.

I headed for the border of Nepal. The savanna like terrain now had better water under ground as I found the pumps clean enough to drink and were great to cool off under. It heated up and I cooled off lots of times. I cut off a rider who wanted to straddle me. I mimicked one guy saying "Vedy good, vedy good," and he hollered back the same. I felt irritated, because I was fighting a strong wind. This was a rough road and narrow. I stopped in a village for two lassis.

While leaving on my bike I had to push my way through the crowd. I didn't even answer the irritating S.O.B's. That's what I think they have in mind for me; IRRITATE HIM UNTIL HE CRACKS UP! So I fired back at them, "Jow, chello, jow!" I got tired and pulled off to rest. There were many more hyno-stares.

I rode on and reached Narahwa at dusk. As darkness settled in, I scouted for food to eat and people laughed and harassed me. I found a Sikh and he told me of a place to eat. It was never possible to leave my bike alone. They just went wild over that machine. I ordered an omelet and drank two lassis. Then I went through the market in search of a snack. It was very dark and I stopped to adjust and clean my electric dynometer. I rode to a tea place, had a cup of tea as a crowd developed. I never left the bike unattended.

Then I headed down the road in the dark. The dyno light was blinking but I could see the washboard bumps on the road and also used my hand held penlight. The passing trucks would blast by without their lights on, hitting me with a murderously hot blast of wind as they passed. I was often driven right off the road, by the sleepy drivers, onto the rough shoulder as the inky darkness hid boulders or crevices, ready to devour my skinny tires. All the while my eyes stayed peeled for a camping spot.

I pedaled north, on this hot night, with stars above, for about 10 miles and pulled off the road and rolled under some large oak like trees. I selected a spot in the grove of trees near an adobe house as a campsite. In the dark I was preparing to set up the tent. I leaned the bike against a tree and walked around to check the place out. My bike was about fifteen feet away when something knocked it over. A dog started to bark so I went walking swiftly back to the bike. I started to push the bike through the darkness but stumbled into a hole and fell down. The bike and gear hit with a crash. The dog barked more and came closer. When I picked the bike up I immediately saw that my front right side pannier bag was gone. I was in a panic and looked all around for it but it had disappeared. I searched the area but could not find the bag.

At about 9pm, in the inky blackness, I back-pedaled my course down the road, searching and hoping to find my lost bag, but it was gone. I cycled all 10 miles in the darkness, back to the tea stall and then turned around and pedaled back to return to the grove of trees and searched once again.

During my search, I met the owner of the property while setting up my tent and gestured to him that I wanted to sleep here. He laid some straw down for me and held a flashlight while I set up the tent. He left and I laid in my tent, under those huge trees, feeling uneasy about the whole thing.

I awoke around 3am to a drip of chilly liquid on my chest and heard the sound of birds. I wondered if a monkey took my bag. I thought about it all night. What happened to it. I believe it must be here or else it fell off on the rough road. That pannier had my cooking utensils, as well as a towel and a t-shirt saying FRIEND on it.

One humorous thought occurred to me before falling asleep. I pondered if a monkey had taken the pannier, how amusing would be the image of it stirring those pots and pans with that big silver spoon and wearing my ragged yellow t-shirt saying-FRIEND.

# CYCLING IN NEPAL

**Wednesday May 2**

As the sun peeked over the horizon, I packed up the tent and sleeping bag and attached everything to the bike as a fascinated woman looked on. I did not sleep well, as my mind was troubled because of last nights missing pannier bag. I searched the large yard, under cottonwood like trees, kicking leaves once again looking for it, as these Indian people watched with troubling curiosity at my strange jests. Without being able to speak Hindi, it would be very difficult for them to understand me. I shook my head in disbelief and mumbled, then got on the bike and left. They could not understand my strange behavior, though I tried to tell them that my bag was missing, but it was to no avail.

I hadn't pedaled more than twenty feet when my chain became jammed and raveled around the sprocket. It stopped me from going up this slight grade, and I nearly fell hard. I laid the bike down and struggled to free it. This place was truly becoming a "black hole," as though I was struggling to get out of this sinking quagmire of India, but it would not free me, not without a fight. Again the chain jammed, but I remedied the problem by using all my patience to clean it. Finally I pedaled away very bothered and perplexed. I wondered if a monkey had stolen my bag. It was hard to part with my bag, to let go of it, it was like a death, an important part of my journey.

I traveled another 10k's and arrived at the border of Nepal and there was some confusion going through the very simple border customs. I passed through and had not gone far when I stopped to enjoy some tea and donuts at a shop. I exchanged some Indian money for Nepalese and bought a colorful towel. Then, I had a cold lassi and drank it down but did not agree on the price before I paid. It was so hot, that my thirst could not wait. Because of my terrible thirsty I got screwed about the price. This guy wanted way too much money and some of his friends came in to help him argue and since I only had Indian money, we had to exchange India money to

Nepalese. What a mess! Five people got in on this discussion. I diplomatically resolved it, "One rupee equals one Napalese pound," I said, and we arrived at the right exchange rate, then finally agreed on the price. All was well, just a little more expensive than in India.

I rode onward under a bright sun and very hot conditions. A long uphill was soon commenced on the road to Pokhara. I rode up the long incline and got some water from a pump and some kids rushed to my bike. I did not know what they would do, so just in case, I kept stones tucked in my pocket. They just stood and watched me pass by. Then I went a few more miles and I suddenly felt great. The craziness of India had changed! I felt for the first time in awhile-genuine solitude. I was happy even though the steep grade was exhausting. I saw a waterfall and rushed to cool off under it but slipped on some slimy rocks and banged my helmet. Unscathed, the cool and clear water was very refreshing. God knows where it was coming from, but I drank it and bathed in it. Refreshed, I wrapped my new, wet, colorfully stripped towel around my back like a cape and pigged out on a roll that was sweet and good.

I pedaled uphill, and it got hot and I cursed at the horrid conditions. Soon my towel was bone dry. I stopped to again wet it and noticed that my body was colored like a rainbow. The towel had bled its colors onto me! My back looked like one very wild tattoo. Laughing it off, I doused again by walking right under the cool waters of a waterfall. My hill-climbing muscles were returning to life on these steep grades. I climbed up and saw the many rice paddies and little villages, which were rather poorly maintained. I again and again dunked under cool waters. Sometimes, I had to walk the bike over rough, steep, gravel roads. I toured slowly and enjoyed the beautiful contrasts of shapes on this terraced landscape. I rode up a long hill and kicked back on a cube shaped rock and fell asleep. Peace was coming to me again after so long. I had nice dreams then awoke and wondered what time it was, and where I was. I relaxed so much that I even dashed off into the trees and took a couple of craps.

As I tackled one steep grade a group of Nepalese kids ran behind me and they pushed my bike as I pedaled. They helped get me up about 2 kilometers of very steep hill. I was amazed at their strength. Then they ran behind and alongside of with me and god could they run fast for kids about 7 years old.

I swung up a slope and went through a town and after a couple of k's discovered it was 4 more kilometers uphill to a town with a cold drink. So I screwed it and turned around to go back on my course about 1 k to a little town, where I had a drink and then continued back attacking the contoured slopes.

It cooled off a bit at 3pm. Then I rounded a curve and had a view of many downhill switchbacks to a valley. I started a fast descent on some pretty good road. It was like high speed motorcycle racing. I used body english to lean around the curves and zipped down the straights. I had a sore ass, so I changed position often and would lean back when going over the bumps. I side straddled with my leg swinging out like snowmobile racers do. This was all so wonderful until on one fast section my rear rack suddenly broke loose and the tent and sleeping bag all swung backwards down to the road and dragged by their bungee chords. It sounded horrible and sparks were flying. I jammed on the brakes. Indeed it took me several hundred feet to come to a stop. Some wire was 'borrowed' from a nearby fence to mend the rack.

I continued and went downhill fast. The road flattened out after 5 ks and then again there was more down hill. This went on until 12 k's or about 6 miles had passed. I came into a town, which was made up of about five shops on a bend in the road. There were hecklers, staring Indians and the usual frustration I felt while looking for food. A kind Nepalese guy took me here and there for food and then he took me to what seemed like a families house. They had rice and vegetables, which I wondered about their purity. They rushed about and were crazy to get me food out of baskets, but I just did not like the way it looked, so I left. I went back to the tiny shops but they did not offer a great selection in fact most of the stuff was junk. I bought a couple of cheap aluminum pots, dishes and silverware. I had a mug of tea and a donut from the stall next door. The woman demanded one rupee, which I paid. The shop owners seemed annoyed by my presence, so I moved on. I had a delicious bowl of berries or cherries with curd from the shop next door for one rupee. I slowly spat out the seeds from the cherry curd. It was not a good combination. Just when you had a mouthful of curd, the seeds would choke you.

On the way out of town, I stopped for a lassi at the crazy families house and the woman poured a glass of the shittiest looking lassi yet. It even smelled sour. I said, "No thanks," but she demanded I taste it and forced it to my mouth with her hand. It was cool and sweet but the smell and taste still was not very good. I rebelled and was reluctant to drink it but she encouraged me. Then she poured me a glass of rum. She motioned for me to try it so I took a swallow. I did and it tasted good like Myers Rum. I then asked her the price. She wanted way too much for a glass. I bargained with her and paid her what she wanted, but the amount made me believe I had been ripped off. She turned her head and I took the bottle and poured a little of the rum into my lassi. She didn't see me do it. Now, that lassi seemed pretty good and I drank it down. She quickly mixed me a 2$^{nd}$ lassi and I paid her for it and then she went into the backroom. I reached again for the bottle of rum and sprinkled it upon my lassi, when suddenly she came through the curtain and caught me in the act. She hollered at me as I fumbled to put the bottle down and she demanded an extra 50 peisa. I paid her, but she was mad at me and hollered as I took off quickly.

I pedaled a little farther uphill, and stopped to buy cookies from a sharp little old lady who spoke good english and seemed very poignant. Then the road went up a long, steep incline and I pedaled all the way up it, while the sun was setting and darkness slowly filtered in. I found a spot to camp on a curve in the road. The spot was hidden from the passing traffic. It afforded me a good view of the valley below. I set up my tent and sponge bathed with a wet cloth. The bugs were bad, so I got into the tent with a candle and commenced to write in my diary. Suddenly the tent started on fire and it burned a hole in the tent netting, which had to be stuffed with tissue to keep the bugs out.

## Thursday May 3

At the crack of dawn, I ate some cookies as an orange 'Popsicle sun' rose above the terraced slopes. After a few minutes to clean the grimy chain and feeling real stiff and out of shape, I rode on, noticing that a sign said it was 85 k's to Pokhara.

I felt hot until finding a cool spring-where I cleaned and cooled off. It was a nice morning and I heard an unusual bird that sounded much like a cuckoo clock bird. I stopped into a small shop and hungrily ate boiled eggs and tea and sweets and bananas and milk all for 7 rupees or 50 cents. I went cycling off and the road passed through canyons and over gushing rivers. These were very steep drops. At times I would have thoughts, that I also don't like these people, they were like the Indians, but I realized they were more kind. They were more peaceful. The children though, were loud. They screamed hello and good bye, continuously. Then again, some of the children had a helpful instinct, and pushed me up hills. But they get out of hand a bit and I had to take fast action and shout at them. I noticed that they left behind fingerprints on the back of my bike, from their dirty hands. I again had to fix the loose rack. Up and down hills the road went, pedaling onward until I stopped for tea and sweets in a shop at noon.

I was joined in my ride by a curious Nepalese boy on his bike. He pedaled hard to stay with me. He really got amazed when I shifted my bike into low gear and breezed up a hill. He got off of his bike and ran it up the hill. He got to the top, just behind me. Then there was another boy who joined us and we started up another hill, but they crashed together because they were looking at me and not at the road. They were not hurt.

It was 15k's to Pokhara and it was all down hill. I dropped down into the warm valley but saw no big mountains in sight, albeit it was cloudy and foggy. I rode into Pokhara, saw a few shops and saw a white girl. "Where is the center of town?" I asked her. She told me in good english where and how far it was. It was so startling to see such a white woman, so big and cumbersome.

I headed off and saw many other white people and money changers. I also met a hotel room salesman, who wanted to show me a hotel. I stopped for a drink as the rain began to fall. I talked to some French people and then went to a few shops and stopped into a cafe called "Hungry Eye." There I ate vegetable chow mien and had apple pie for dessert. There, I met a gorgeous young lady named Florence who was from Pakistan. What a babe she was. She'd been living in Australia and she looked Indonesian. She told me that was a problem. "I'm Pakistany," she said. She had an interesting story of quitting her job, buying airline tickets, rushing on a plane, rushing through countries until getting here. Now she felt this slower pace was ok. She wasn't sure why she was here. I pedaled down the road after she walked away without saying goodbye.

I met a gal from Minnesota. She was a nice Finnish girl named Julie. She took me along and showed me an adequate hotel. I greeted her roommate Doreen. We talked up a storm, and it started to rain hard. I got a room and took a shower, then talked some more to the girls. The rain came down damn hard, and then the thunder neared and soon lightning struck real close and the sparks flew from an electric transformer on a pole. The lights went out. I legged it through the puddles and talked to these girls. They asked of my trip and I of theirs. They were in China, but admitted to feeling insecure in this traveling life. I talked until 11pm with Doreen, and then we had to call it a night. They said they were masseuses. Doreen told me excess cycling causes sterility. I thought about that as I laid in my hard bed.

## Friday May 4

I got up and looked out the window to see Julie and Doreen head out on a trek. I washed my clothes in a pail and then went to the market and bought some museli. I went to Hungry Eye and had a delicious omelette and tea and museli and curd for breakfast.

At the market I slipped a little clump of miniature bananas into my bag without paying for it. I later felt bad about doing this and wondered for what reason it was that I had a tendency to steal. Perhaps it was the daily expense and my lack of income, or the feeling like I would soon run out of money. Or perhaps it was that I believed that prices were too high and that they were taking advantage of tourists. Regardless, it bothered me, I did not understand why I did it, and I wished I did not do it again.

I bought a little bag of pot from a villager for .50 cents and then went exploring along the village roads. In the bright morning sun I looked over the treetops to the northwest in hopes of seeing a mountain. I could not see anything but a big white cloud. Disappointed, my eyes focused on that cloud and scanned upward until at a higher angle I saw the white peak of a mountain. It was huge! My first look at this picturesque and awesome Himalayan mountain behind the green hills just blew me away. I went further down the road and turned around and then saw another truly large mountain named Machupurna in the distance and it was even higher yet. My god it was high up and shaped like a steeple. I went into the village to inquire about buying a cooking pan and an umbrella.

I continued through many streets along very rough roads and stopped to explore a cave. A young Napalese man showed me another cave that was bigger. We hiked down into the mouth of the cave as thousands of bats went whizzing past our heads. We saw stalagmites jutting up from the ground and stalactites hanging from the ceiling. I thought, if our flashlights stopped I'd use matches. So I had them ready. Sure enough the flashlight quit and it was so dark that I could not find my hands. Finally my friend struck a match and we fixed the flashlight and saw above us, hanging like sinister monsters, hundreds of bats. We turned around and headed out. Once out of the cave we discussed money matters and my friend said he wanted some money and I told him we didn't agree upon that and he said, "Ok. I will be friend." I gave him a couple of rupees anyway.

I stopped by a tree and smoked a little hooch, and wrote in my diary. A group of kids stood nearby and I told them to sit. I watched cows fight and buffalos mooing. It started getting cloudy over the mountain. The kids became a nuisance, so I rode down to Pokhara then on to my hotel. I asked a guy if he had a map of the trekking area and he did not. His name was Chuck and he was from the U.S. We were nearly the same age. He was planning a trek. He told me of his experiences while staying in Japan. He was from Kansas and was nervous in his movements, but he was a well spoken man. We went to dinner together and met a group from North America. They were interested in my travels and were quite amazed at some of my stories. I had smoked a hit of the hooch and so got intensely fired up about my own journey. They laughed at my stories of the 'brutal children in this world'. The kids who threw rocks at me in Israel, the kids who heckled me in Egypt, the little girl who took my bike in Udaipur, and those kids who played with my bike parts. Kids can be cruel! I met a gal named Robin from Canada and she was cute and we agreed to go on a hike tomorrow morning.

It rained a bit as we hiked back to the hotel. I began to really feel strong about myself. I like what I am doing and felt good about doing it and about my journey. Chuck and I talked about politics, Reagan and Mondale and then went to bed.

## Saturday May 5. 84

I got a little ill in the night as I suspect it was bad water and the over drinking of tea. Chuck and I got dressed to go on a hike and I put together a light pack. We walked down the road to eat and Chuck said, "Do you know the route we will go," meaning a map, or a plan. I replied, "Yeah that away," pointing to the mountainous area before us. We ate a hardy breakfast and then set out as it was getting warm.

We hiked along a lake and then went past a few villages, and then crossed some terraces. A young boy, about 5, came up behind us and said, "I will be your guide." We replied, "No we no want a guide." "Turn this way to the top," he said. We hiked on and he came along again saying, "You need guide. 5 rupees, me your guide." "No thanks," I said. He said, "4 rupees." "No thanks," I said. "3 rupees." "No." "2 rupees," he said. "No." "One rupee?" "No." "Ok, me your guide for 50piesta. I good guide." He was so cute because he was climbing up over a stone wall and screaming and helping point us along the right path. We said, "Ok."

It got hotter and we were feeling the heat. Ascending a long hill. We went past workers and village people, whom were dressed brightly and beaming a happy attitude. We had a slow pace, as my legs were out of shape to hike. I reached a top point and we saw some fine young Napalese girls. They were anywhere from 6 to 16 years old. They were fun to kid with and I played it up with them. The young girls giggled in there colorful outfits. The older ones watched me closely. I tried some Hindi, asking what is your name. And they told me all their names, Rheema, Shine, Cheema, etc. I played that rhyme with them. One thing I noticed was that their rugged feet impressed me. They could walk on rocks without a problem. We sat on an overlook of Pokhara and saw a clouded dark sky covering the Himalayas. This was dissapointing as it blocked our view of the high mountains. Chuck and I ate a banana and I handed out the rest of the clump to each of the pretty girls.

A young kid came along and showed us a little hilltop cafe which served tea. Actually it was a few rocks where a gal had a pot of tea and some cups. We each had a cup of the tea. All the while as we sat beggers, kids, guides, came up to us and they all wanted rupees. "The tea not hot, girl no make fine tea," said our guide in a humorous way. He was right, we each finished our tea at that moment by dumping the remainder of it onto the ground. Just thinking of the unboiled water turned our stomachs. That is how one gets tape worms. We heard a guy walk past with western rock music blaring from a boombox. Soon more beggars appeared and we left with the little beggars chasing us. We were making good time hiking along a ridge with a good valley view of Pokhara when I said to Chuck, "I really like it here." "Me too," agreed Chuck.

We made the long hike down to town and hopped a ride on a bus. Then we hitched onto another bus to get us back to the lodge. I felt good but was disappointed riding a bus. Riding a bicycle seems to make me feel at one with the locals, that is my preferred mode of travel.

At the hotel we cleaned up and then went to eat at Bubs. It rained real hard and harder yet at 2:30pm exactly. We hustled back to take care of our duties.

Later in the afternoon, Chuck and I went to eat dinner. We tried the Hungry Eye and the dinner was not to bad. While we ate, I overheard an Indian girl talking, and she talked so much like my friend Jolane that at first I thought it was her. I then turned around and saw the gal, and made eye contact and we talked and I found out she was from Calcutta. Her name was Rheema. She asked me if I could fix her cigarette, which had broken. I used my skills to do this and while doing so, she talked to us. She was a lovely young Indian lady. I enjoyed just listening to her intonation of every word. Her accent was enchanting. We all had a smoke of hooch and then ate and had a tea while it rained so hard. I enjoyed moments like this. We were sitting under a balcony, in this great setting, with new friends and good food. It was a joy to meet these other travelers.

Later, we were given a ride back to our hotel by Reemas driver, said goodbye and hoped to meet them again. Later, Chuck and I admitted to each having a fling for Rheema.

## Sunday May 6

I slept like a bum until 7am. I showered in cold water and while outside found a huge marijuana plant. While looking up I saw the high mountain and awoke Chuck to show it to him and also the plant to him. He wore thick glasses and was asleep when he came out. Obviously he was not an outdoorsman but was eager to try. He cleaned and sewed his torn pack.

I packed and listened to the radio all morning. I got the bike in tune and found the back hub was loose. I repacked the wheel bearings and noticed that the rear tire is showing chord. I wanted to swim at 2:30pm but a thunder boomer rolled in and it rained. Chuck appeared and we discussed some trekking problems and money problems as it rained hard. When it stopped, I ran around to ask about changing money. Suddenly I felt my money was going too fast and was worried whether I would make it or not on the money I have left. I dreaded that thought, and felt I must work out the problem.

To get a trekking permit one must have a bank receipt that says they exchanged $100 at the bank for Nepalese money. I wanted to change money on the black market but when that is done, no receipt comes with it. I didn't want to cash another $100 cheque in the bank. So what would I do? I needed to economize my money, and asked more people for information about this. I decided to cash $15 at the black market, which gives me it at 18.50 rupee. I will decide in Kathmandu if I must cash at a bank to get a reciept. Maybe I will look for another way to get U.S. cash.

I went to eat with Chuck and it rained. I changed $15 and hiked back to my cheap hotel. I did some writing by candlelight as the rain fell. I liked this place as it has kind people and a nice environment. I hiked down into town and met Chuck. We went to meet a couple that traveled in Burma with him. We ate in a western style place with music and atmosphere. I had chow mien, but preferred the "Hungry Eye" to all places. It had good food and atmosphere. Then I listened to other travelers telling about their hotel hopping route around the orient and felt out of place. My hotel was mainly my little tent.

I went back to the Hungry Eye and met Jane and friends who told of their day trek adventure. I liked this place. Ordered lemon pie and shared it with others. You could walk out of here without paying the bill but no one does. This place was full of lively people. We talked of traveling and adventure.

Later Chuck walked in and said, "Look who I found." He was with Rheema and Anita, our lady friends from Calcutta. We took a place outside and though my mind was on Jane it soon switched to Rheema. We sat together and drank some beers that she bought. Her family was wealthy. We enjoyed laughter and conversation. I told stories of my travels and we discussed the wonders of the world. I listened to Rheema's articulate way of speaking and noticed her beauty. At closing time the waiters gave us candles to use so we could sit on the porch. We sat there until 11:30pm.

Rheemas driver then drove us about the town. I got close to Rheema in the back seat and learned that she was Assamese, which is in the northeast of India. She lived in Baroda and was currently a student. Her hometown was in Calcutta. We giggled and kissed and held each other close.

What she sees in me is a world traveler, what I see in her is an oriental beauty. We toured the town in the back seat of that car, and even bought more beer. I sang to them Contrary to

Ordinary, a song by Waylon Jennings. They said they loved it. We stopped by a lake and were all a little drunk. I kissed Rheema's soft 20 year old lips often.

Under a starlit night sky, Rheemas driver pulled the car over and she and I walked to a grassy place where we kissed and hugged and more. I guess bodily desires took over...but she was Indian, and going beyond touching would never be allowed. We held each other so close and I didn't want to let her go. She told me if I came to her hotel tomorrow night we could take a shower together and make passionate love. It made my head spin. We could have gone 'far' in that grassy field, but her brother got mad and came shouting out to get her. Her driver paced back and forth. We listened to Anita talking loudy and this awoke a screaming baby in a nearby hut. It was time to get out of here.

Chuck and I were dropped off at our lodge at 3:30am. It was hard to say goodbye to Rheema, though I was tired, it had to be done. We embraced and kissed, deeply.

Chuck and I laughed it up, before calling it a night.

**Monday May 7**

I awoke at 8am to a clear, sunny, morning. I saw the high mountains clear up to the top. My head was foggy when I went to town to eat. Along the way I met Chuck. He rented a bike and we went through town to see what was going on. Every turn offered a new look. Often there was a subtle, fragile, funny and innocent look at the Nepalese people who are into there wonderful little world. There were cows rolling in water, children playing, smiles and uniformed policeman.

Chuck and I stopped under a huge baroda tree to rest and talk. I rolled a jay, we had a toke and I set the film canister of hooch beside me. Some children appeared and stood beside us. They goofed around, playing with each other and talked. I then looked for my film canister and could not find it. I looked madly for it, thinking one of the kids stole it, I grabbed a kid and twisted his arm and demanded it returned. He said, "No take." By the look in his eyes, I believed him, but I thought he was lying. His friends joined in and searched for the container. They climbed a tree even to look for it. Then I realized it was here with me all the while, stuffed in my stocking. I had put it there. I embarrassingly said to Chuck, "Let's get out of here." I told him where it was and how foolish I was and that this weed was really causing me to space out.

We pedaled back to the lodge and discovered Anita with her driver. We were told where Rheema was and met with her and others and met with them at a boat rental on Lake Pokhara. Then we took a pedal boat out upon the lake and to a place called Sacrifice Island, where they still have a daily sacrifice of goats and other animals. There was a retaining wall where we dove in to the refreshing water off of some rocks at the island. I was jolly to swim, and clowned about in the water. We returned to race against the coming rainstorm across the lake. It poured on us, but did not matter.

We then went to Happy Eye and ate. Chuck and I invited them to our hotel. We went there and they sat in my room and we talked and I felt sometimes a slight lack of common interests with Rheema, but we all got along and laughed though everyone was smoking wacky tabacky. I could tell they were not comfortable here.

We then went to Rheemas hotel room and my god, it was a real plush hotel called The Chrystal. No wonder they did not feel comfortable at my cheap hotel. We had room service bring us ice coffee. Her younger brother was along with her and we could not get rid of him nor

Anita long enough to be intimate, as both of us had hoped. That plan was foiled. So, we ordered a Continental Dinner and went to eat it in the dining room. Our goodbyes were hard to take but I managed to step aside with Rheema into a side hall for a nice long kiss and embrace. I liked her alot. She invited me to come visit and stay with her in Calcutta.

The driver gave Chuck and I a fast ride to our lodge. Chuck and I then shook hands and exchanged goodbyes as I was real happy to meet him.

**Tuesday. May 8**

It was a cloudy morning in the morning, and I saw Chuck leave and said goodbye to him and saw him hike down the road. I packed and paid my hotel bill of 40 rupees for 5 nights. That was about $2 each night.

I pedaled toward the Hungry Eye for breakfast and immediately my thoughts focused on Rheema. I almost felt as if this wasn't a true happening. So happy I am, but lonely I felt. This image came to me - she was such a beautiful woman, but moreso, I had a glimpse of her personality and I liked it. I missed her so, though I cautioned myself that it may all be an infatuation. I stopped and ate a good breakfast. It started to rain. I waited a bit to see if it would stop. It did not. I was almost haunted by the good memories I had of Rheema and of this place. I almost panicked at the memories. It was everywhere. I had to get going.

I started to pack up my bike for travel, when a cow came along and stole from a veggie stand some carrots. The owner then chased away the cow. I went over to buy and pay for a bread loaf and some peanut butter, and then on the way out swiped a big cookie and put it into my pack. Why do I do this? I put on my rain coat and straddled the bike saddle and pushed off.

There was a lot of water on the road and a gray sky with showers, as my bike tires swooshed through big puddles. It was raining inside of me as well, I had the blues.

I cleared out of Pokhara and it slowly changed from a drizzle, to a fog and then out came a clear blue sky. I made good time as my new rear tire was fast. I sang my own song, "The Roving Man." I picked up the pace and zipped along feeling ok. When nobody was around, I pedaled back a side road and crapped in a field and used leaves as toilet paper.

Back on the road, the crank bearing loosened up and I stopped to repair it as hecklers, gawkers and onlookers gathered around me. I tried to fix it, but it was still loose. A little farther down the road, I stopped in town and shopped around for a pliers, the kind you'd find in most any store in the States. There were none to be found here. Finally a trucker let me use his pliers. I tightened the crank and it was better now and the knocking ended.

The road followed a valley to the east and soon the back hub loosened up. I stopped to meet another biker who was from England. We talked of our journeys while tightening my rear hub. He had visited Nepal's, South Park and saw a white Rhino. I enjoyed his tales of running up a tree. He said the ground shakes when a rhino runs past.

I passed a childrens fantasy land of people at work, Nepalese children smiling and playing and the wonderful contrasting terraces upon this sloped land. I had some hassles from the people. Mostly the children are devilish and will laugh and throw a stick or a twig at me. There was always a new face to enjoy an expression.

I climbed some big hills and the crank loosened up again. I stopped into a village and asked for some tools, but there were none. While riding past a small café, a lady waved at me to come in. I went into the kitchen to see what's cooking. I lifted the pot lid and actually it looked good and I got a fair meal. I even was given seconds on everything. This lady had a special touch and that is what counts! I really liked her, even though we could not converse.

I stepped outside and met a Nepalese fellow who told me that he knew where some tools were. While I waited for him to return, I bought six big green bananas for 2 rupees. The man returned with the tools but they were archaic. A crowd gathered and a kid slapped my derailleur with a stick. This pissed me off and I told him to get out of here.

I took off down the road, but soon stopped at the next food stall to make a dessert of milk and bananas, along with a cup of tea. This sure was good, but the locals laughed at my strange concoction!

I headed out of town and pedaled for another five hours and then found a open terrace with a grass hut and set up camp nearby. While sitting around near sunset, I saw a huge spider and did not question whether it was poisonous, instead just got away from it. There were banana trees everywhere, though the bananas were too high to grab.

I thought more about Rheema and was glad that I met her but now felt I was heartbroken that she was not here with me. I wanted to call her, or suddenly see her waving to me and come walking up saying, "There you are, I have been looking for you." I could end this crazy bike trip and go off together with her. But then reality set in. I was alone and this bike trip was my driving force.

Camping here on this muddy hillside, in a deep gorge, as darkness pervaded me, gave me some alarm, as I watched clouds roll in and cover the twinkling stars.

## Wednesday May 9

With a start I awoke around midnight as rain drops the size of melons began to fall on me. I got out and attached the fly over the tent. The rain began, hard and pounding. I saw flashes of lightning and then, Kabboom! The thunder resounded. It was a fast moving storm, with a hard rain and cool winds which smelled like the mountain air. One storm passed and then another approached. This happened three times. I could hear the river below me getting very loud. Then I slept and awoke often as it was getting damp inside my tent. I felt a puddle of water under me. It was a hard rain until morning's first light.

I got up a bit wet and looked at the river down below me, it's banks swollen with a muddy red color and gushing madly. The sky, however looked hopeful as it turned from gray to blue. I packed up and struggled in the mud to get the bike uphill and back on the road. After a couple of bananas, I headed off on the road to Kathmandu, thinking about the knocking from my crank.

Banana trees lined the road. I waited until nobody was looking and then leaned my bike against the tree. I stepped up on the seat and reached for a banana. "Ha, ha, oh, oh," said this man. He caught me in the act. He raised up his kukri as I dashed off with a clump of tiny bananas.

On a descending right hand curve, I was going fast, suddenly the bike slipped out from underneath me, and I slid on the slimmy surface and crashed hard, banging my helmet against the pavement. When I picked up the bike, this thought came to me - is this my payment for stealing a cookie and bananas from the Nepalese?

The road climbed along the valley and went down a nice, enchanting road. I saw a Nepalese guy sitting in his roadside booth look at me like- "My god! What was that!" He spun his head in shock. There were more sprinkles of rain. I coasted into a small town and looked again for some tools. A store worker gave me a monster wrench to work on my bike. I saw a trucker and asked him to borrow a wrench. He produced some tools, but none worked. Then the rear hub felt real loose, but I could do nothing to tighten it.

With my rain parka on, I continued along in the downpouring rain. While rounding a curve I felt a bump, bump, bump on the rear tire. I thought, "I didn't see that stone?." I coasted around a curve and the rear end felt skiddery and it was just as I braked to give a truck some room. Then ba-boomp, ba-boomp, the rear tire jumped. I stopped to see a huge boil or bulge on the f-ing rear tire, so I pulled over under a tree. It was really raining as I worked off the tube. I decided to put in a repair patch. As I put the tire back on the rim I heard the tube going 'ppssst'. A leak had developed and so I took it off again, repaired the leak but then the patch leaked. I repaired it and put everything together and started to pump up the tire. Then the pump broke. Now, it started to rain heavily. I mean, it went from downpour to deluge. I tried to repair the pump, but it would not work. I asked a truck driver if I could use his pump, but it would not work in my tire. It rained and I sat there weighing my options in the pouring rain. I saw a truck coming and stood out in front of it and flagged down that truck and asked, "Going to Kathmandu?" "Ok," said the driver. I was surprised because the truck took off and then stopped 50 feet away. "Come," he said. I threw the bike together and rushed up to the truck. I put it and myself in the dump box of this big dump truck which was up real high and afforded a good view. We headed east, under a constant rain and inside the box, I made a fort out of canvas and still got wet. The truck bounded slowly along. We squeezed by others on the road and I ate peanut butter sandwiches. Then we had to stop in the rain and wait for the road to clear from an accident. It was getting cold as we climbed up steep grades on this bad road, but I enjoyed the view from my lookout and kept the flap open. It was a real hard rain, but that did not hinder me from looking out from under my canvas at the scenery. The Himalayan Mountains were visible and were capped with white snow, which was accented against the pale sky. As we crested the hill it was windy like hell and I held the canvas tarp down.

We descended into Kathmandu and I got off in town and paid the driver 10 rupees for the ride. I pushed the bike down the street to a vacant shop and laid the bike down. I hiked across the street to use a bike pump. A crowd gathered and one guy was an expert at this yet he didn't know shit. I f-ked up the tube two more times. Then finally I changed to another tube, and then got the tire back working. Some kids wanted one rupee for using the air pump. I just rode off into Kathmandu.

This was a touristy looking town, with white people walking here and there and all kinds of stands selling whares or food. I went into the city, and met a fellow who told me of a hotel that he was in. I went along and shopped, then got a room for 15 rupees, which was expensive in comparison to India. I met a girl from the room next door, and some French people, whom I sat with for a cup of tea. They were also bikers of the world.

I repaired the pump by making a leather plunger and then I took a cool shower. I went back to my room, changed and then went off to eat with my new French friend. I enjoyed a new insight into Katmandu. It still had a Nepalese charm, despite all of the Indian hawkers and sellers. We shopped for a restaurant and chose to eat Tibetan. The food was good. I had "Ning," with pork and vegetable and then a slice of apple pie for dessert. I paid and then split company with my friends and then shopped around for money changers. I went along with a money changer and put my knife in my pocket, just in case. We did not make a deal, and I would shop more tomorrow.

I came back to the hotel and saw again the French people.

Katmandu is the capital city of Nepal but it is more like a walk back 400 years in time. An exotic feel permeates this simple mountain village. There are carved lions guarding temples with multi layered roofs rising high above the smoke of burning incense. Oriental and western music blare from loudspeakers along cobblestone streets lined with shops selling a variety of hand crafted items made by the Nepalese. Good restaurants abound and some cafe's even sold delicious apple pies. Upon its streets, one might see a mountain farmer dressed in multi colored shawls and carrying a long kukri knife stop to smile at passing foreigners. The Nepalese seemed to be just as amused at seeing foreigners as foreigners are to see them. Little trivial things happened that were so enlightening. A child rolled a wire wheel zig-zagging his way thru a crowded market place. A cow sat on the street basking in the sun while cars drove around it. Each night a group of locals would come out to the streets to sit and play music and entertain. If ever there was a Shangri-La this was it.

## Thursday May 10

First thing in the morning, I headed for town on my bike and met a guy who lead me to a few bike shops. Then I went to a repair shop. I ordered a tire and looked for a tool to help tighten the crank. The selection in Kathmandu shops is much better and I found the narrow, yet wide mouthed tool. I finally tightened the crank. A boss for the cycle shop heard of my trek and gave me a reflector.

The next stop was to the Burmese embassy, which had the nicest embassy people yet. They had a sense of peace in their disposition. I went to see the Royal Palace and then past many shops selling every kind of item one can imagine. I exchanged a travelers checque for cash on the black market, and got $50 dollars in U.S. cash.

Went back to the hotel and again repaired the pump, then slept for two hours. Later, I talked to the French people, drank tea, ate peanuts and had more conversation about travel. I went to the city at 6pm after smoking a jay and drinking more tea. I noticed how I felt so low key compared to India. This place has good and genuine people, they are not plastic. I went past a temple and took some photos of the ornate Hindu designs and old statues.

At a little shop I saw a kukrey, the Nepalese Army knife and bargained to buy it but the guy wanted 350 rupees and I said 100. Then 125. I played with the seller. Then I walked off and he came after me and said, "125 ok." I bought the thing and then went past other shops and found the same knife for less. What is the moral to this story? These street sellers are clever. I was bummed to have wasted more money.

I took a walk to find a restaurant called Yak and Yete, but could not find the place. I did meet other travelers, one was from Detroit. I bought an aluminum cooking pan at a shop. Then ate at a Mandarin Cafe and talked to a Swiss couple, who admired my kukree, with its big curving blade and yak horn handle.

While walking down Freak Street, I stopped to have dessert of a slice of apple pie. There, I met a very down British man. He had his passport stolen and wondered what to do next.

I hiked through the smoky streets of Kathmandu, past the ancient stone lion looking temples and muddy streets to my hotel and ate yogurt for a night cap.

There was a stairway up to the rooftop, where I went to think about my busy day and my money situation. I was thinking about trekking or cycling in Nepal. I'd love to trek, but the Trekking Permit and exchanging money is the problem. While I looked out on the dim lights over Katmandu, I thought about Rheema, and missed her so. She was a nice thought. I noticed today I paid more attention to the oriental girls of Nepal and I really liked them. They stood out from the Indians, with more Mongol like features. Maybe the altitude was getting to me?

## Friday May 11

I showered in a cold stall and packed my duds, cleaned the bike, and then paid the guy at the front desk. Filled up my water bottles and then went to a bike shop. "Come back in one hour for a new tire," said the salesman. I went to hunt for a café and got lost in these busy streets. This wasn't a big city, but one can still get lost here. I went way around town and finally found a cafe in Tamil and there ate a hearty breakfast of omelette, two pieces of toast, hash browns and brown tea. Yet, I was still hungry afterward.

I pedaled up the road and met a guy alongside of me who asked me all kinds of questions and he was a white man. I thought only Indians did this. He showed me where to sell some books and then where to find a diary shop. His name was Will, and he has been working in the south of Nepal with the Peace Corps for about a year. He was bearded and kind of skinny as he said, "Let's go to a coffee house and I'd love to talk with ya." So I went with him and we walked in and I guess I thought he would buy me a coffee but he didn't and instead he wolfed down a strudel and a coffee before my envious eyes. Then when he was finished he said, "Didn't you want a curd or something." I said, "No the price was too much for me." He responded, "Oh hey, I was gonna pay for it." Well, I was down a bit after that because of the way it all sounded, like he was going to pay. I was really getting skimpy and becoming money conscious. It bothered me.

We went through the streets asking for a diary. He said, "Boy it must be great to be cycling, it must be great." I heard this clicking sound and stopped and discovered a piece of glass in my new tire. "Yeah, it's great." I said, pulling the glass from the tire. We found a shop that had diary's for sale. I bought one and Will gave me his address and he invited me to visit him in the south of Nepal.

I left town and fixed the inner tube with a patch. There were no replacement tubes in Kathmandu. The road took me past the airport and then out of town. It was a nice day, as I headed for Bhaktapur. I felt carefree and I made up a tune called Carefree Man and sang this for many miles.

Upon arrival in Bhaktapur, I went along some shitty streets to enter a temple park, where there were beautiful temples with wood overhangs that were decorated and gold statues of praying men. Many monsterous carvings of lion like creatures were carved from stone, in front of The Golden Door. This was a new and exciting religion to unravel, though I knew not what I was looking at.

I headed for Nagrahot, and rode past some heralding villagers, who enjoyed my mode of transportation. I climbed up a steep grade as the kilos passed slowly. Many villagers chased me and giggled. I stopped for lunch and a family came over looking for money. The women and kids only approached open handed and the man stood back. I gave a rupee but took off a little disgusted with that. My arrival in Nagarhot was at 3:30pm. This was not a town, just some lodges of poor quality. I pushed the bike to the hilltop and some kids tagged along and picked some raspberries for me. I sat on top and loved the view. There were more berries to be picked and then I went back down to the lodges while trying to decide where to camp. I visited one great lodge that asked $12 per night. Then another and was greeted warmly and got a bed for 11 rupees.

I met 3 Danes and we sat outside awhile. I hiked up to the hilltop and picked a container of berries while I started thinking - hey, I should go into the berry business. I sat and smoked a few puffs off a jay as the sun set and watched the shadows and the deep orange colors of the foothills. The high Himalayan mountains appeared more and more vivid in the shadows. The women at the lodge pointed at a peak which at first I thought was a cloud. That was Mount Everest, they said. The mountains really formed a wall across the countryside and I imagined it likened to a side view of an arrowheads jagged edge. I all of a sudden thought, "I'm missing the sunset." I dashed off giggling, while clambering up a hill to see the most spectacular scene. It was like in a movie. The rays of the sun were blue and orange bands, like the fingers of a hand.

The Kathmandu valley was multi hughed with these colors, from the orange fields to a winding blue river, like the color of the sea, that snaked through the valley. I took a photo and then a plane took off and climbed into the setting sun. "That's class." I said out loud. I hiked back down to the lodge and went into a lamp lit café, where there were four people playing cards. They offered me to join them and we played a game of make a bet, high card wins, meet your quota-cards. Then we were served a Tibetan dinner, which was enjoyed by the lamp light, in this nice wood worked setting.

Afterward, I again repaired my tire pump and we talked of travel and then it was off to bed.

I would sleep in the same room as the Israeli girl. We took the mattresses off other empty beds to comfy up our hard beds. This Nepalese kid came up whom I had seen earlier and thought he was being a lot obnoxious. He put up a fuss and wanted me to put the mattresses back on the bed. So I said, "Why don't you take another bed?" But he insisted on this. So I put my mattress back and he went and squealed on us anyways.

The landlady entered and put up a fuss, about me moving the mattress. I said I would put them back in the morning. The Israeli girl insisted on having it her way, to keep the extra mattress. I tried to stick up for her, but the kid made a gesture to me I did not care for. I had my jacket hanging over my shoulder and swung at him with it and it accidentally slapped him in the face. Actually I was pissed at him because he went and squealed. So he wanted to fight me and I stood up to him as he put his fists up. I stood right up to him and said, "Let's go outside. Come on, come on." I spun him around as I passed. His mom was shouting, "No fight, no fight." Needless to say he didn't follow me outside. The landlady left and so did the kid, and we kept our double mattresses.

I talked with the Israeli girl and felt an air of confidence in myself. Nepal must have its ways of putting something feisty into me.

## Saturday May 12

I awoke at 5am to see if the view of the mountains was good but it was hazy. I awoke at 7am and had a tea and was off after paying.

Coasted down the long hill into Bhaktapur, where I then saw glimpses of a majestic high peaks in the Himalyas. Wow.

I went into Bhaktapur, thinking about cooking my own breakfast, bought some bread and then headed out of town after looking at a fine temple. The next stop was to buy some gas for my cook stove. I hunted around the market for some eggs, green peppers and onion. Before leaving, I stopped on the roadside to repair the loosening crank bearing.

I rolled into Thislalee and found a quiet park to cook and eat. Some kids, and adults watched me. I pulled out my stove and started to cook but it quit working and I could not get it going again. So, here I sat with my eggs mixed in the pan and my stove inoperable. It was plugged up and would not work. A crowd gathered. I had to watch my bike and stuff and try to fix the stove. I got so mad that I tossed the stove over my shoulder in disgust. Fortunately it landed on the grass, and not on somebody's head. One guy offered to bring me up his stove. "Ok," I said as a dog ran off with my bread. Amazingly the man returned shortly with a big cook stove. I cooked my meal and then they all left me alone to eat in peace. That was nice of them. The Indians would never have done that.

I stopped for curd and then rode northwestward destined for Tata Pani, along the Tibet border. I went down a long hill into a hot valley. As I was going slow on an uphill grade, some kids purposely got in my way to ask for money, and I gave one the boot in the rear. I then went around a curve and met a truck, but dove into a rock hard ditch and a rear spoke exploded. The wheel wobbled and went bent. I stopped to repair it but the tool stripped the adjuster. I adjusted the spokes and rode on, stopping often to repair the loosening crank.

I pedaled into a village and saw a repair shop called, P.W. Garage and pulled in to discover he had a vise. Inside, I made ingenious repairs of the wheel spoke and rear bearing as a crowd watched. They helped me out. Whew, it was a challenging repair. I rode on up a hill, past some rivers as darkness closed in. I still had 30 k's to go until the next town. I was chased by a big dog and kicked him in the jaws. Then two more gave chase and I got one with a rock. He yelped off and I hit another dog with a rock and they all left.

I headed along shitty, bone jarring roads in the dark. At one point they got so bad that I had to get off and do some bike walking. Finally there was a good stretch of road. I pedaled with my flashlight in my mouth, felt exhausted, and wondered if I would ever get to the next village. At times like this, my limits are tested. Finally I went over a black hill and saw a dim light in the distance. This was the village of Barahbise. It was a good sight. I found a hotel, probably the only one in town, for 5 rupees a night. I ordered a cup of tea and talked to a nice Tibetan man who reminded me of Wes H., and he helped me order food. I ate a good meal of Chinese food.

Returning to my room, my flashlight broke, I considered this lucky that it did not happen earlier. What a day it had been and what a way to end diary number 3.

Begin Diary Number 4. This Diary was lost in a house fire. I tried to remember the following events until Diary Number 5 starts up on July 28th.

## Sunday May 13

I awoke in a shoddy little home stay to a street sounding morning, here in Barahbise, Nepal. The road I was on is to Tato Pani, which was at the border of Nepal and Tibet. My previous nights ride was adventurous along the poor roads and with a poor light. Now, I dug into my handbag for my comb but discovered it was gone. Another weight reduction (theft) I presume. I ate some curd and tea. Then hiked around the 3 building town to buy food. I saw a pretty Nepalese girl in a shop. I passed the shops and returned to the hostel as Gurka soldiers ran past fully geared with Kukrees flapping on there breasts, they sprinted into town. The village people looked on with a sense of pride for their soldiers. I ate an omelet and curd and tea. My stomach was a bottomless pit. I unpacked some weight and left it with the hotel, then headed north on good roads for 1k and then the road turned to a rough stretch of dirt. Soon it became mud. I rode on carefully avoiding anything too sharp or too bumpy. The valley was warm but the air was crisp. I got off and pushed the bike often, over hazardous spots. This was dry countryside, with a river running down at the base of the canyon. Sometimes there were long cliffs down to the river. I stopped frequently to tighten the loose crank bearing. I hit a real bad mud section of road. Huge boulders were strewn on the road, as there were landslides here as recently as last night.

I carried the bike at bad spots, as my fenders had clogged with sticky mud. Then pedaling again, I went past many workers, some who appeared to be Chinese. They had the horrid job of breaking boulders into gravel. I watched them do it. I could see their piles of gravel. One guy had only one eye. No wonder, that kind of work would be dangerous.

I pedaled only on good road, the rough hills were too much of a risk on my equipment and had to be walked. I went down one rough stretch of road, then forded a deep stream and then another stream keeping upright and pedaling through it all and pedaling like a madman. The road workers watched and applauded me. I was thrilled by this new adventure, of going cross country on a touring bike! I was often helped by village children. They pushed me up hills. Soon I started to notice more Tibetan people. They look like Chinese, but with a darker skin, almost like American Indians. I asked people how far it was to Tata Pani, the town on the border, and they would tell me with fingers. I stopped to adjust the crank, and had to get off and push the bike more.

There were blue-gray mountains surrounded with white clouds, to be seen between the gorge. A gushing river ran down the middle of this valley.

# THE WHEELS OF FRIEND

I met a Tibetan fellow, whom I'd met at the hotel and he said I was only 2 k's from the border. He had a deep voice and eloquent speech which reminded me of Wes, my fathers good friend and hunting buddy.

I pushed the bike up gooky, mud covered roads past workers and hammers and occasional tractors helping the men work. The men banged away on rocks, turning them into blocks. It was dangerous work, as more than one was missing an eye. Some sat and beat rock against rock, to make a gravel. Such hellish work seemed uncalled for by a human being. When I passed, they really looked wide eyed at me, as if I was a savior, or a comedian, as sometimes they roared into laughter.

At one rest stop I had my foot up on a big rock and the men shouted, then one said, "Dynamite!" and I ran for cover behind a rock. Boom! Went the blast, which sent some particles of rock flying high into the sky. They splattered on the river upon return to the earth.

I saw a nice waterfall coming off a high cliff. A little while later the road was thick with mud. My bike was in the lowest gear and it took all I could to gain headway. More than once the front wheel jackknifed and bore me deep into the mud. Many Chinese looking road workers watched and they were surprised to see my progress. I pedaled hard along this muddy rut, past more workers who stepped aside to let me by. As I was nearing the end of the mud, they cheered me on and then when I finally made it to the good road, they gave me a big roar of applause. I pedaled on and lifted my hat to thank them.

The road was better in the deep canyon where I pedaled up past Tata Pani and only a few kilometers more reached a checkpoint where an armed guard stopped me. I tried to get an ok to go on, farther up the road to the Tibetan border, but he stopped me once again. This was the final checkpoint before the Nepal-Tibet border. I could see buildings on the Tibetan hillside looking rather nice. The guard told me, "River is border. There is a Chinese police post, you no can go." The man pointed to a building. So I sat on a chair and watched what happened at the border.

Many people came and went and passed through this border. Some wore Chinese blue outfits. I saw truckloads with goods come and go. Guards chased one truck and hauled back a guy, as he did not sign something. Many Tibetan men walked up the road carrying heavy packs laden with goods. These men looked taut, there skin was browned and weathered and their slanted eyes seemed frail but they must have been incredibly strong to carry such weight.

I returned down to the village and felt I did an admirable job of riding downhill through mud and ruts while the road workers heckled and cheered me. I repaired and cleaned the bike at Tata Pani. There, I met a French girl and we had tea together. After that, I went down and took a natural hot bath and showered under the hot water which was just pouring out of pipes jammed into the thermal aquifer. A cold rushing stream was next to the hot spa. All the people came here to bathe and wash. They left their clothes on and just walked under the hot water. I really enjoyed the hot bath. It was so beautiful a spot and a wonderful sensation. Someone told me that the locals come here once a month to bathe. I thought once a month? No wonder they have b.o.

I returned to the hotel and the French girl said, "That's why they call this town tata-pani, because that means hot water." We hiked around town afterward to look for a dining spot. It turned out the place next to the hotel was the best. We sat and had a candlelight meal of rice and dahl baht with potatoes and drank tea. We even were served seconds. A little Nepalese boy would wave to me using the Tibetan style of waving. He held his hand against his forehead, palm out and rather like a salute. After awhile it became second nature to do it, as everyone waved like that. I sampled some chang, which is a homemade beer that the Nepalese enjoy.

Back at the lodge I talked to the French girl for awhile. Though the evening was perfect for romance, I felt sore and sickly. She was kind enough to walk on my back. But this did not pop my vertabre, nor relieve the yucky feeling. I layed back and thought about this frontier land I was in and this shabby lodge. I could see the trees and the river through the cracks in the wall.

**Monday May 14**

Got up to a sunny morning feeling very sore and sick. I took a pill for diarrhea, and relaxed. I was definitely not well. I went to eat and had a donut and an omelet with tea. I found the Tibetan people very courteous and helpful. I took a thermal bath with women and men and they appeared wary of me. I guess I was a little down, and they sensed it. I noticed I was so thin that my pants hardly stayed on me. I thought about eating some good food. I thought about getting back to Kathmandu. I was weak. The food here stunk. The lodge was noisy from the gushing river and smelly from dirty trucks. I went back and told the host in primal talk that I wanted a ride back to Bahabise. So he understood me. I watched Tibetan headed packers pass with tremendous loads on their backs. I saw them even carry two Indian bikes in their bare feet. I shall never know such hardships as placed upon these people.

I slept and packed and got into the scenery of big green hills steep with little villages spotting the slopes. I slept. Then had a cup of tea. There were chickens running around. Smiling, happy faced Tibetans walked past toward the border.

I understood that Nepalese with a pass could go to Kodari, Tibet for a day. A truck passed and stopped but he wouldn't take my bicycle. I talked with some very nice people who were "interested in my ride."

Then another truck pulled up and he was heading south. I put the bike in the back of this dump truck. "You paesa," said the host pointing to the driver. That meant I had to pay him, for my ride. I sat in the dirty dusty bed of the dump truck from China with another Nepalese man. To keep the bike safely secured was a major task. The truck bounced severely and each shock was a real jolt to my system A little sickly still, I just hung on and watched my bags get filthy dirty. We bounded along and I started to notice the many places that I had missed. It really occurred to me that I didn't look around too hard when I came to Tatapani. What I saw now was beautiful. I saw the village people and really noticed the waterfalls and the beauty of the steep rocky and often green slopes. Sometimes a white, snow covered peak of the Himalayan mountains was seen towering above the canyon like a skyscraper. Amazingly speckled in between, on the high slopes were tiny villages. I did not see those on my ride up to Tatapani.

I also saw how much of an uphill climb I had ridden. Now it was the crank pedal I was most worried about breaking as the truck tossed and flung me and the bike about the box, from the rough road. I'd adjust the bike frequently while getting jostled like a tossed salad when I stood up. We stopped and I saw the road workers. Some wore Chinese style straw hats like the Viet Cong wore in Vietnam. Some looked like freaks.

We got a new driver, who was younger and drove faster. He went along fast and most of the road had dried a great deal from the previous day. Still, I was glad I was not riding my bike. I noticed how much scenery was revealing a place I did not see. This is yet another lesson to learn, that the hard work of riding a bike caused me to look down, and not see more around me. Was traveling on a bike going to fast? Or was I just not looking? In my case I was preoccupied with watching the road.

The truck was going way to fast and we bounced around a corner and came close to a wall of rock. I released my hand off the side of the box just as it scraped against the rocks. When I did this I was thrown to the bed and stepped on a kid's bare foot with my boots. He only moved over. What a tough Nepalese kid!

A little later we were going too fast down a rutted hill and I saw we were going to hit a rock. The truck did a donkey kick and I braced myself as we banged into the rock and rolled over it. The bike and I jumped up a good foot and even though the bike was tied to a large tire with Chinese letters on it, it was still thrown down on the bed of the dump truck. Damn crazy drivers and damn tough are these Chinese trucks!

We arrived at Barahbise and I unloaded and paid the driver. I met a Nepalese Gurka Army Captain and he was very nice. I stopped at the Tibetan lodge and got my gear. The manager said there would be no charge. I stepped outside and the truck driver said, "You want go to Deulihel, we go soon?" I thought sure what the heck and loaded all my stuff back into the truck. We again passed along bad roads that I could not believe I had ridden on a touring bike. I saw fisherman with long poles fishing the river. More passengers now boarded the truck. They all helped to hold the bike up and keep it safe. The Nepalese lend a hand, where they see a need. They are quick to react to assist others and I appreciated that consideration.

As we went down into the canyon it became hotter. We went down into a valley. Then began a long climb up to Deulihel, where the truck stopped and I got out. I unloaded my gear and paid the driver some rupees and he was off.

A crowd gathered to heckel me. "Cycle geara," they said over again, so I heckled them with the same- "Cycle geara." Then I went to clean the bike and many people just watched me. I ordered them to be quiet as they were screaming. I made them stay away from my bike by squirting them with water from my water bottle. I washed stuff slowly. A man worked the well pump and was very helpful.

I pedaled up to the park and laid out my things. Another crowd gathered. I asked them to please go away. They started to get so close to my stuff and me. Well. I felt a bit ill and irritable. So I told them, "Go!" And they did. They stood back about 15 feet away. I relaxed. They ran off with my plastic tarp. I got it back. Beggars came. I looked at the scene. I stopped into a restaurant and asked if they had pie. None. I asked for lassi. None. Then I had chowmein and curd. I felt my body was like an old bar of soap. God I was thin! My ribs were sticking out. I went back to the restaurant at 7pm and had to carry a stick as the kids were devilish. I ate fried rice and talked to some very kind people on this cool full moon night. Went back to the park to camp and it rained later.

## Tuesday May 15

It was sister Cyndi's birthday today. I got up at 4am and saw a little outline of the Himalayas. Laid back and watched the sun pop above the high peaks. It literally was like a bobber the way it jumped above the peaks. I noticed everything was damp from the dew. I had diarrhea and it took awhile to get moving.

I rode to town. Then coasted downhill for quite a distance and god I felt good just shouting along and waving. I had a good ride all the way back to Kathmandu, where I went to Patar. There, I saw festivals, as today was the Buddhas birthday. I passed temples, that were ornate and architecturally beautiful. I went on to Mandarin house and had a breakfast of pancakes, lassi and toast. Then I went to have apple pie. I walked to a garage and a fellow helped me repair my cook stove for no charge.

I went to Boude and saw the big stupa which had the Buddhas all seeing eyes painted up on the side. There were many prayer wheels along the sides of the pagoda. One must walk around the Buddha and spin the wheels and say a prayer.

Nearby, I met a German family who was interested in my adventure. They left and I sat to polish my kukri as a crowd of Nepalis watched. I met a guy who said he would polish my kukri. He did. I gave him two bananas for it. I went to Gorkana forest. While crossing a bridge a devilish kid chased me and struck my bike. He demanded rupees. I turned around and chased him. He took off. I took off my helmet and swung at him as he screamed for mercy. My strap got caught on my handlebar, else I'd have whacked him. I chased him more as he screamed for momma and really I felt angry. I could have got him but just past by him. He turned and ran off.

I went and saw monkeys and saw a spotted deer. I gave a litte beggar a banana and she shared it with her sister. I went to Swayambata temple, otherwise known as the monkey temple. But there was no safe place to park as people were festiving all over. There were many finely dressed people here and there was an order to them. This could be comparable to Easter Sunday in the mannerisms and correctness of conduct.

I passed along a horrible street back to the city and went to Peace Lodge but they had no room. There, I met the French couple again. I found a hotel along Pie Alley called the Crown

Hotel. A very eager young fellow took care of me. I got a room for 11 rupees and it was private and ok. I bathed and my hair was a dirty mess.

At the hotel, I met a pretty young Nepalese gal named Anita, who lived there.

I went along the street and heard the most preciously beautiful music. A string instrument lying flat on the ground with two bridges was played by a young boy with a hammer like device in each hand. His melodies were so intellectual, so precise and bongos and an organ accompanied. I thought of the market potential for such music. This was enchanting.

I went to a restaurant that was very westernized with music, newspapers, TV, etc. I ordered mousakka, a Greek cuisine, and sat with a delectable looking English girl. Then went for pie afterward and she showed me the Mustang Lodge. I talked to the host about trekking and yetis and Nepal. Then I ambled back on a full moon night as the street side singers played and people seemed peaceful. I tried to see if a rooftop view was available and I met Anita. She showed me a view from her home. We talked a little and she spoke only a little english. What a babe!

**Wednesday May 16**

I awoke to a sunny morning and hiked up to the square in search of fruit. The fruit was all out on display, but the sales guy wasn't around so I waited. Meanwhile, this guy tried to sell me a necklace of "Jade" for 200 rupees. I said no thanks and he followed me around. I offered him 10 rupees. He said, "Ok, two necklaces for 300." He revealed a "tigers eye" necklace which I liked. He wanted 300 rupees for the both of them. I just kept walking and bought some curd and sugar and through it all he followed me. I was interested, but was it really jade? I thought it might be. But then I said to myself, "Hey here's a good buy." So I gave him 100 rupees, ($5) for the two and then I came to my room to inspect them and ate curd with bananas. I asked around if it was jade and some shops said no and others said, "Yes it is Indian jade."

To further complicate things I thought I'd make some tea and my stove stopped working again.

So I wanted to get rid of the jade necklace, and get the stove repaired. I went to the square and looked for the guy who sold me the necklace and almost made a trade with other street hawkers. God these guys are hungry for cash. I almost traded it off. The lesson to be learned is not to deal with these hawkers. They were real sharks.

A hike was made up to the monkey village called Swayambhonath and looked around the 2000 year old structures. The Buddhas around the stuppa are almost comical, in their expressions. I saw a monkey sitting on top of one and fumbled for my camera. It was hot today, and felt like drinking always. As I hiked along, people always asked what country I was from and I got sick of answering them. I just wanted to be accepted. Hiked across this crazy, swinging bridge with old boards and I swear it was ready to crumble. These village people lived so shabbily and there were lots of beggars by the stuppa of the temple. I saw Anita and her sister Sahita and stopped to say hello to them. Neither of them could speak english very well, so, while I wished to get to know Anita, it was cut short.

I didn't even have a plan of what I was doing but I went to the square and again tried to trade off my jade necklace. I ambled around like a lost fool, but stumbled across a camping store which had the stove part I wanted, and for only 75 rupees. I ate at The Mandarin and went back to work on writing some post cards and repairing the stove. I got the stove working after much disassembly and was up until 1am working on it. I felt a little anxious now, as I really didn't want to go back to India.

## Thursday May 17

I got up on a clear, sunny morning and took a cold shower and tried the stove out and it worked just fine. I hiked into town and went to eat at The Lost Horizon, a Tibetan restaurant. I had a poached egg, toast, and tea and it was really quite affordable and good. I especially liked the friendly atmosphere. "You ain't been anywhere until you've eaten at the Lost Horizon in Katmandu," say the servants and so I agreed with them.

I returned to the street hawkers and tried to make a trade with them for my Indian Jade necklace, but they didn't want it. I shopped around and asked more storeowners if this was Indian jade. They said yes and, "It's real cheap." So I shopped about for a nice little souvenir for a special gal and found a real nice necklace for a good price. The beads and the artistry were different between shops. I returned to the hotel and everything was rather cluttered.

I saw the people walking around the temple in a counterclockwise motion and they were ringing bells and making prayers. It sounded like ding-doing-clang-bong.

I decided to make my necklace into a bracelet and earrings and I used whatever crude parts I had. Used wire for the earrings and the bracelet and actually made a pretty nice set!

I went down to a pie shop and asked how much and they said 4 rupees for a piece of pie. So I got a peach pie. Then I had some water. When it came time to pay they said it was 5 rupees. I had been in here on two previous occasions and they always said 4 rupees. So I held my ground. The man told me, "Here is one rupee back now don't come here no more!" I told him, "I don't think that was good business sense." He just said, "If you pay five rupees you can come back, if you pay 4 you don't come here anymore." I paid four and said, "You're pie just lost its flavor."

I went to the post office and got some stamps and mailed postcards. Then I asked them what the necessities were to mail a package to the U.S. They were very unhelpful and this chief postman came over and picked up my package which had my necklace and diary in it and he threw it on to the table very recklessly. I said, "Hey, you fucking jerk, why don't you stick your head in the toilet and flush it you careless cocksucker!" I then was interrupted by a clerk, "Don't say that to him he is the chief." I responded, "Well I think he's an asshole," and I stomped out.

I returned to the bike and hiked into town to deal with the street sellers. I almost traded that necklace for one lucky lama. The guy wanted it. But he also wanted rupees. I went to the market place and bought some small peaches. They were good and at a good price. It began to rain as I dashed along the crowded streets. I couldn't help but feel a personality to Katmandu. Everywhere I looked I saw people involved in there thing. I sensed they liked it here by there cheerful disposition. I went to the Jasmine Restaurant and ate a great meal of pork chowmien. There I met a German and Israeli couple whom I had met before on a ship from Italy to Greece in November of 1983. We wished each other well and they said goodbye.

While I ate, I read an article about the universe. One sentence struck me. "A star who's gravity is receding faster than the speed of light will become a black hole, hence exit the universe." The thought of an exit from the universe blew me away. This is what many great religions have considered. That there might be another universe coexisting alongside of ours, yet we might not be able to relate to it.

It was dark and at about 8pm, as I hiked down along Freak Street and all these hawkers and thugs tried to sell or change something with me. One guy said, "Want to try some good Tai stick?" "What's that?" I asked. "Good grass," he said with a smile. So I went along acting interested. We went down an alley then ducked under a blanket into a shop with a man and women. They made me feel comfortable. I saw this heavy, gooey, sticky pot and the guy rolled me a joint with it inside. I only took two puffs. Each one caused my head to spin and almost made me pass out. "Very good." I said. He told me, "Next time you buy, no sample." So I thanked him and hiked down Freak Street and it started to take effect. First I noticed I was fumbling in my pack for my eye solution and I smoothly pulled it out and dropped the drips in while I walked. I went into a pie shop and delectably ate every morsel of a chocolate pie and got off on the reflections on the plate. I listened to some great music. Now I was feeling very high. It was almost a meta-physical sensation.

I hiked to the dimly lit square and dug these dogs which were fighting. They would wrestle and it was so sportsman like. This one dog was so strong, the other dogs could not out wrestle him. He was the alpha dog. Even as these dogs played hard, they did not bite and they remained respectful. I wanted to 'meet that top dog and I went up to him and we began a great wrestling match. God he was a good dog. He played nicely, but was hard. He was a real brainy kind of dog. We played hard and then when it was time to quit, we embraced and off he went, strutting like the coolest dog on earth.

That is when I saw the cow. There was a dark cow sitting in the square! I went up to him as he kneeled, resting, chewing his cud. I slowly encircled the cow, who watched me with anticipating eyes. I tried to touch his long horn but he darned near jabbed me. He tossed his head at me each time I came close. This cow was more aptly described as a bull, since it was big and black. I came close to his head and gently touched his horn. I then carefully wrapped my hand around that horn and gently kneaded like soft clay back toward the tip. Slowly he stopped bucking. Then I petted his ear. He became quite passive. Some people stopped to look at this scene. I continued petting his ear, and could gently pull the cows head by his ear to the side. Soon his head became totally relaxed and it was on the ground and he was sleeping! I pacified a cow in Katmandu! People applauded and I overheard them say, "Look at what that guy is doing to the cow!" Who is that guy?

Then this Nepalese guy came along and said, "You like the cow?" "Yes," I said. Suddenly he kicked the cow in the ribs and it got up and it lunged at me, almost gouging me with his horn. I talked nicely to the cow and the cow once again sat on his knees and I did this scene all over again. I gently stroked its horn and then its ear. This time the cow did not lay its head down, it was wary of me.

I continued on, listened to some street music and then went back to my room. "Life is a mystery to be lived not a problem to be resolved." It said on the wall of my room. It was left by some previous traveler. I had a feeling that this night was all too good to be true. I felt a lot of life in this town and now Katmandu was grasping hold of me with this character of happiness and youth.

## Friday May 18

In the morning, I hiked about the town, once again looking for a stove part as it quit working. Breakfast was corn flakes at the Mandarin. I was continually thinking about my money problems and thought I should go to Rotary or Lions for sponsorship. But actually I was not spending that much. It was about $4 per day. It just seemed like it was so much because I was not used to seeing this many products available for so cheap.

I got on my bike and rode out to Bhudhanilkantha past celebrating Hindus with red die all over them and carrying a shrine. Here, I saw a large reclining Vishnu. There were all kinds of freaks around here. People would come up and throw flowers on Vishnu and then kiss his feet. I had beggars continuously come to me.

I rode back to Ring Road and met a U.S. man and his son on bicycles and talked to them for a bit. Then I pedaled down to Bouda and bought a Tibetan made purse or tobacco bag. A man sharpened my kukri knife. I stopped and had a chang beer like drink that I found had a very yeasty flavor. Next stop was to see a hockey game. Some little kids were very entertaining as they'd fight and play and one kid was like a mini Bob Hope. Then they started to fight and the Gorkas broke up the fighting kids. I was spotlit as I pedaled away.

I went through streets and street hawkers wanted to buy my bike. I tried to trade off my necklace combo and almost do, wanting a silver box for trade. During this, I met a former world cyclist. We chatted and then I met other westerners interested in my travels. I made it back to my pad at sundown and again the charm of Katmandu filled me with a joy and playfulness. Once again I saw the bell ringers at the temple, the smiling children, Anita's pretty face, and a glow from the setting sun that filled everything with warm reddish-brown tones.

I cleaned up and tried the stove. Then hiked back to the Jasmine Restaurant. Where I again got absorbed into the book; <u>The Universe</u>. The book was interesting, but a cute chick across the room was even more. I had a great meal and listened to some good music. Then I hiked over to the square. Along the way I passed a dummy, or retarded Nepalese man, who held a clump of marijuana like a baby holds a rattle, and grabbed a tuft of the stuff as I passed. I laid a rupee in his other hand and continued on. He did not seem to care.

I had a piece of apple pie, and then met that cute girl whom I had seen in the restaurant. She was from Ireland. I listened to a guitar-playing fellow and joined in with the harmonica. We harmonized together very well as he was playing Blowing in the Wind. The guitar was handed to me and then I played a couple of songs. I kind of got carried away with my singing and really let it out. People were laughing and I just kept on singing. When I finished they demanded more. That made me a bit nervous as I was rusty and they wanted me to sing some songs that I did not know. I calmed myself down by talking to a Boston fellow. Then the guitar returned to me and I played a couple more songs. I hiked back to the hotel, feeling, well I love Kathmandu, it's great here, but I gotta go, tomorrow unfortunately. So I treated myself to an apple strudel and headed off to bed.

## Saturday May 19

I awoke at 6am to see a bright, sunny morning. Children were outside playing. I got up and packed my things and found it was difficult to leave here. I had a small boy help me with supervising as I packed and adjusted the bike. The rear rack was badly broken. I was off, but did not go far, as I stopped at the Mandarin house and enjoyed a lassi with toast. I ate muesli and listened to some Ann Murry songs. I then pedaled to the pie shop and the guy gave me a free piece of pie for the adventure. These Katmandu people always said; "for good luck," and I cherished that last piece forever.

The street hawkers came with their lucky lammas and beads etc. I tried to make a trade with a guy, the jade for a silver box. He wanted rupees. I ambled on. Later he caught me and said; "Ok, give some rupees and I trade." "No rupees," I said. "Ok, it is a deal," he said. He said the box is good luck for you. And I almost didn't want to give off my bracelet, necklace and earings, but I did and I was gone.

I pedaled my bicycle past the place where I first saw Katmandu while in that truck. Back then the city looked foreboding and scary, now it was a wonderful, happy memory. That was ten days ago, in the cold and rain. Now it was warm and comfy. What a difference a day makes.

I was now heading back toward India, and rode up to the pass then went down, down a long hill. I stopped and bought some raspberries from a boy for one and a half rupees. I poured them into my water bottle and rode along gulping on them. I rode into the crossroads and had a Coke. Then I started an uphill climb of switchbacks that lasted from noon until 4pm. I rode steadily in the lowest gear up to an altitude of 6500 feet. I stopped often to cool off. The kids along the way were devilish. Some threw rocks at me. Some heckled. I went down from Tistang on a bad road. My rack was rattling badly again. I rode to the valley below. Then the children came from all sides in the fields, on the road they started shouting "American paestas." They chased me down the road. How did they know I was an American? I glimpsed my target- the road to Daman on top of a twisting steep road. It was 5pm when I began the ascent. I wondered if I could make it before dark. Already I was tired. And yet I figured if I can see it, then I can make it.

It was a grueling one hour climb through switchbacks and washouts until I finally arrived in Daman. I cooled off my feet in a fresh water spring and then hiked up to a lookout tower and discovered it costs 30 rupees per bed per night. I figured I would camp. I went to a tea shack. Had tea and asked if they had food. "You want rice?" Asked this guy. "Yes, I want rice, dahl baht, vegetables please." "Ok," he said, "Come back at 7." So I went to take a bath and this Nepalese guy offered his home to me as a place to sleep. His name was Keechum. I took a bath at the outdoor faucet as a little girl watched. Then I hiked on down to eat a good meal of food. I met two Indians and I swear they had a wildness or restlessness to them. There eyes get so big and they speak rapidly and it started to churn my guts so I got across the table from them.

The stars were shining and I hiked back with Keetchum to sleep in the same room and on the same bed as he. I was hoping that tomorrow would break clear so I could see the mountains one last time. I took out my contacts and Keetchum was just dazzled, even amazed by the sight. "You are taking out your eyes? He said.

## Sunday May 20

Up at 5am and Keetchum said, "No clear." I returned to sleep until 7am. Went to find something to eat. I hiked around town and discovered a guy who would make me an omelet. So I ran back to get a loaf of bread and a confused Keetchum saw me but did not understand. I returned to have my omelet and toast and tea. I went back to the house and worked on the bike. Cleaned it up and adjusted the spokes. Two kids got close to me for rupees. I climbed a plum tree for treats. Then I put them in a bag outside to ripen. I went inside and sat with Keetchum. I had a toke and admired my souvenirs of Nepal. My necklace, I discovered was broken. I tried to piece it together. I heard someone down below, outside and thought they were messing with my bike. I walked out on the porch and my tiger eyes necklace came apart and the individual stones all pattered below onto the deck and ground. I noticed two women down there. I started to pick them up as the women dashed over to search for my gems. I raced downstairs as Keetchum laughed. The women were kicking the ground around and I pushed them away. I searched to find nothing. They kept what they found. I returned upstairs and the women again looked and they obviously had found one gem as I missed one.

At about 11am, I slept a bit. After my refreshing nap, I went uphill, for a hike to a beautiful overlook of Daman and the mountains. It was a nice, cool day. Some clouds rolled over the mountain top like ghostly fingers. I then returned to the house to find it locked. I hiked into town and saw Keetchum and he treated me like I was his kid. He then had to go somewhere.

I bought some gorp like mix and went back along a trail to sit by an overlook. I sat my bag down and watched the changing patterns of light and color. I thought about being a live-in artist in Nepal, or elsewhere in the world. I could move into others homes and paint or draw their life stories or habitat. Just then, from the corner of my eye, a goat came dashing along. It ran right passed me and grabbed my handbag, which contained all my credentials, camera, passport and money and it ran off with the entire bag! It went running downhill, over a steep drop as I hollered and threw stuff and chased it for 20 feet. Then it dropped the bag. I then checked the bag over, finding everything intact, wiped off the dust from myself and the bag and then left.

I offered to buy Keetchum dinner and so we went for tea and sat. No one talked very much to me, but they talked a great deal in Nepalese about me. I tried only to relax and just enjoy their company. I rather liked the folks here. They were kind to me. A young girl cooked me noodles and tea for luck.

After our dinner, we went into someones house and got a glass of Roksi and Chang. We ate a spicy food also. Then we returned to the house and it was cool out so I put on a sweater. Keetchum cooked some food. Then we went back to eat an omelette and drank more chang, which I did not find was very flavorful here. Keetchum got a little louder with the liquor. We sang, while walking down the road.

Back at his house, we ate his meal of rice and spicy hot potatoes. Then I got tired and at 9am retired.

Keetchum seemed like he wanted something from me. He looked at me in strange ways that did not fare me well. I wondered if he was a queer, and if that was on his mind. I would have none of that. He soon lost interest, perhaps because of my foul smelling farts which fouled the air and turned him off. This went on well into the night and I had to get up at 4am with a bad case of the trots, the dreaded Nepal diarrhea.

## Monday May 21

I was up at 6am and got things packed up. Keetchum seemed even more distant, even more strange and was continually telling me he had no money. But he had a wife and kid in the village below. Why? He had a business he said. So what gives? I pushed the bike out to the street and shook hands with the sleepy Keetchum. He tried to ride my fully loaded bike but lost his balance and did not have the strength to pedal it. We laughed, and then I said, "Thank you for letting me stay in your house." He said he wanted, "Backsheesh, 20 rupees." I did not understand if he was joking or if he truly wanted it. "20 rupees give me," he said to me loosely, almost jokingly. I was rather fed up with his weirdness. He had gone from a person who acted friendly and rich to this bummed out bugger who looked desperate and cared less about me. For this reason I mounted the bike and just left him with a thank you.

I pedaled away waving, as he looked at me solemnly and others waved goodbye. I should have known that Keetchum would look at me as a possible way of getting some money, much the same as the other beggars I had passed along the way. Why did I not give him a mere 20 rupees? My justification was that he invited me in and offered me comfort, therefore I did not feel inclined to pay him. I did buy him dinner and chang last night, yet, I was getting tight with money.

There was time to think things over while climbing up a steep grade and into a evergreen forest which smelled the wonderful fragrance of pine. I pedaled up a gradual incline and then finally I made it to the top of the pass. There was the small village of Simyajang at the top. It looked like a gold rush town, or a truck stop. The morning sun was rising up over India, which was way down below. This was a busy little village, with many vehicles passing through, with plenty of food and goods available. I pulled into a teashop as children screamed and chased me. I got a couple cups of tea and a donut and a boiled egg. I paid, but the woman, had ripped me off, as she kept the change, thinking I was just another dumb tourist. I started to get a stomachache.

From Simyajang the road is all downhill until the Terrai region of Nepal. Keetchum had told me I would go down for 75 kilometers. I stopped to enjoy the interesting trees in this highland area. They appeared to be like those in a rainy climate. They had long tentacles hanging from their limbs. I also enjoyed this cool weather and dreaded returning to the heat of India down below. My stomach pains got worse. I had to stand up a lot to relieve this ache in my belly. I think Keetchums spicy potatoes were like a revenge for not giving him some baksheesh.

It was a gentle coast down the long grade and soon I was flying along at 50 mph. The road was poor and on each bump I would wince from abdominal pain. There were fast switchbacks, and my brakes were constantly on. I had concerns about my tires blowing out and whether the broken rack would again fall down.

The road passed through villages with screaming kids and I stopped for water as they gathered around. When I brushed my teeth they watched in amazement. Then I continued the long downhill run. It started to get warm and foggy. I passed another cyclist going up the hill, "You're going the wrong way," I said. He smiled and heaved into his pedals.

Racing with a truck, I cursed at the road upon hitting bump after bad bump. Finally after an ecstatic one and a half hours of coasting, I arrived down into the flatland or Terrai region of Nepal. This is where the plains of India meet the high country of Nepal. On my left side was a large park and the only one in Nepal where rare white Rhinos roamed, tigers were allowed to stalk and elephants lived in a nature reserve.

I continued to pedal south and then headed east on the terrai as I passed by a camp where many shiny booted Gorkha soldiers waved at me excitedly. Their camp was picture perfect with a mountainous Himalayan backdrop.

I rode into Hetaunda and bought some bananas and a lassi, then headed east and went over a hill on a real bad road. I was riding along absorbed in my thoughts, when I was hailed at by another cyclis; "please stop" he said. He was an Indian. "I am an All India Cyclist, who has been traveling around India 4 years and my name is K. Kannan," he said wagging his head. While we pedaled together to a tea stall he told me he was heading for Katmandu and was sponsored by the Lions. We each had two teas and biscuits and exchanged adventures and I found him proud of India and yet admitting of its disorder. His bike did not even have a bag on it. He had a waistbelt and that was it. He would always stay at homes or hotels. When he looked at my bike, loaded to the gills with tent and baggage, he was shocked at the weight. We shook hands vigorously and parted company.

I headed east along a good road that turned into the tri-highway. It was fairly flat here now, and the road had narrowed, and had only enough room for one car to meet. There was a nice forest that lined the road. Monkeys kept dashing across here and there and they were always wailing a mysterious call. I started to feel the heat of India building up, draining me of energy.

Pedaling on, I saw workers coming out of the woods to the road. They carried the tools of their trade, axes, saws and picks, over their shoulders.

I had some to take some diversions as the road was under construction. I pulled over to eat in a tea shop. They made me a dahl and rice dinner and a cup of tea. There were plenty of people gathered around and staring. As I ate, a kid tried to push my bike away, and I jumped up and grabbed my bike and could have kicked him in the head but only scared him with a mean look.

When I saw the Bagmati River with its nice looking water and grassy banks, I thought of camping nearby. It was 5pm and I hastily dashed off the road, into a clearing, with trees between me and the road. I was naked and cleaning up in the fast current of the river, when I saw two woods workers approach. I grabbed my towel and met these Nepalese men. They did not seem to care about my state of dress. I put on clothes and we relaxed and had tea. My guests had a goat following them and in my distraction it nearly chewed off my bike seat.

I talked to Mr. Rhan (Dharan) and the other guy about our lives. He told me of his position in the Hindu caste. He said because of his position, he could not get married until he was 35 years of age. He also said he must work for his father. I said, "We in the U.S. could not live like that." We talked alot under a big tree as the sun set and lamps were lit. They were amazed at my tale of traveling on a bike. They told me to be wary of tigers and then they walked home and I stayed at my camp along the riverside. It got really hot at 9pm and I was sweating in the tent, but then I awoke at 2am feeling cold and had to get into the sleeping bag.

## Tuesday May 22

It was a hot night, but one with plenty of sleep. I packed up and had an audience of local people come to sit and watch me pack up. I laughed at them, squating nearby enjoying my every move. I walked the bike back to the main road and these guys remained seated in the woods somewhat dazed at my machine and me. I rode on, as they stood up and seemed dumbfounded at what I was doing.

Running low on water, my thirst was increasing. I pedaled east and dodged many village people standing and walking on the road. I stopped for tea in one place and a crowd gathered. It was difficult to keep them from crushing my bike. Constantly they tried to move closer to me and the bike. I said, "Kateea Rupea," which means how much does this cost, and paid the man. The people looked amazed that I could speak there language.

There were more monkeys along this section of road. They darted here and there. A heavy forest of trees skirt both sides of this area and big, dry river channels. The people here seemed to be woods people. They were quiet but the children were loud.

The road continued down long stretches that soon transitioned from forest to plain. I stopped again for tea, and would have filled my water bottles but the water was bad. Later, at a pump, I found good water and cleaned up and drank like a horse! At times like this, water is the nectar of the gods.

I noticed the wind had markedly picked up and saw dust flying my way. Boom!. I was fighting a bad headwind and I struggled to bear down on the pedals. I was in my lowest gear, pedaling as hard as I could, on a flat plain. I made it into Dhalkebar and the wind was howling. I ate some curd and sweets and sat as people starred at me.

As the crowd gathered around me, a policeman, who was very strongly built, came over and he wanted to ride my bike and I let him try it. He swung his leg over, took hold of the handlebars, stepped on the pedals, pushed off and fell over. He could hardly even lift up the bike. His macho image was ruined, many village people laughed, as he tried to walk the bike to me and dropped it again. People asked me questions. One guy said, "Where do you come from?" I answered, "Earth," and he said he did not know where that was.

I sat maybe 45 minutes to see if the wind would die down, then decided that this was a cold front moving in and I'd better get going. I could feel an occasional cool breeze. I fought against that wind, sometimes it was so demoralizing. Here I was on a flat plain, as I pedaled and pedaled and only got tired, and would hardly go anywhere. I stopped often for tea to while away this monotony. The only food available was rice and dahl and this I ate, but was gawked at by people watching me eat with my hands.

I saw a maypole ceremony occurring and stopped to watch. This guy pointed at me and said, "Cycle, cycle," and all these people stopped playing their musical instruments and ended their dancing and rushed out to the road to gather around me. This one guy screamed, with his hands to his ears, like he'd seen Elvis, and these people seemed to worship me. I could not understand it. So I took off and they chased me.

Kids laughed at me as I struggled into the severe wind, trying to make headway. I stopped for tea and these kids appeared stunned when they heard I was a world traveling cyclist. It was as if the news was spreading in front of me, that I was coming through their village. People gathered along the road and moved over for me and gave me a sense of respect.

The ride progressed for many kilometers on flatland to Lahan, where a crowd gathered as I relished a cool bottle of Coke. A German woman appeared and I asked her if she knew where Sukhipur was. She did not, but a fellow told her in Hindi that it was 15 kilometers back down the road. I had passed it! Damn I got upset. The map that Will had made for me was not so great. I was feeling frustrated, when this dark fellow who had large teeth and bad breath laughed right in my face and I slapped him. He ran off.

My demeanor was uncalled for in spite of the rudeness of these Indian characters and the crisis of the moment.

I pedaled back on my route and stopped to eat at a roadside stand, where again a crowd gathered about. They came right up to me and stared. I dared each one of them by doing the same back to them and walking up to them and staring. They did not like this and turned and walked away. After a bite to eat I was back on the bike and headed down the pavement until coming to the intersection that Will had told me about. From there, I turned south and traveled a very rough and bad gravel road, all the while thinking, "What am I doing? Is this worth it? What if Will is not there?"

Finally after a bone jarring ride, I arrived in Sukhipur escorted by a mob of dirty looking, but enthusiastic youngsters. I went through the village of dirty streets and straw huts and was led to a building of concrete, which was noticeably different. I was then truly mobbed by people. It seemed to be getting out of hand when to my delight Will came waltzing through the crowd and I said, "Doctor Livingston I presume?" He said with a big smile, "I can't believe you made it here." We talked and the crowd dispersed.

I went to Wills private hut and bathed under an outdoor pump and then we sat back to talk for awhile. We then walked into town. It would be classified as an absolute dump by western standards, but to me, it had frontier qualities. We went to a restaurant (a shack like tent structure with picnic tables) and had some Roksi, an alcoholic drink, as it was a hot evening. Will truly showed his qualities as a good person, both to me and to the Indians. He was patient with them. He spoke with the people fluently in their language. He tried hard to mix with them and not stand above them. He was also good conversation for me and I enjoyed being around someone as intelligent and congenial as he. We ate dahl and rice at the 'hotel,' which was in fact a large tent like construction. I did not tire of talking to Will and we both appeared hungry for conversation. We talked of bike trips, his army days and girls soon became the gist of our discussion.

We hiked back after a sweaty supper in the hot 'hotel,' and shared a smoke of some native homegrown and sat outside to talk of life. Times like this I relish. "Hey, do you want some real honest chocolate?" said Will. "Yeh! I sure do," I said. He gave me a piece of Hersheys bar and it was ecstasy to my tastes. It was so good that never should another Hersheys bar be taken for granted. How fantastic! We talked some more and then both slept outside on a veranda, but eventually the bugs got to me as they were quite bad. I put up my tent and slept in it.

## Wed May 23

"Oh Eric, you'd better be getting up," said Will at 6. I got together my articles and we went to the hotel and met Sing. Then we hiked about 6 ks to a tea shop and ate some tarts. We then walked to a fish pond that was under construction. This was Wills big project for the Peace Corps and he told me of his role to help supervise the project. We walked around the perimeter and there were some problems he needed to discuss with the others.

Will talked about the Peace Corps mission and it appears he has a good handle on the attitude of the Peace Corp and what is expected from the project. We listened to workers talk about the fish pond project. Will spoke fluently, in the local language and was right at their level. When we hiked back to town, it was getting hot, and I saw many birds along our return route. This part of Nepal, known as the Terrai, also has a charm all of its own, as there are rice paddies, creeks, birds and scattered trees.

Back at Wills home, the concrete bunker, I washed up and then relaxed. Will and I then went to eat dahl and rice. Along the way we kidded with the children.

Another project that Will was involved in was a rice mill. We went on a tour of the "factory" which was nothing more than a brick building with a single cylinder engine that exhausted its pipe out the wall. Everytime the engine fired it went "Poof, poof." The archaic diesel one lunger did a lot of work and many belts distributed the power to turn a stone grinding wheel. A worker shoveled rice onto the path of the wheel and it was pulverized and then swept off into a bin. While we watched the wheel in progress I saw a belt come loose and shouted to Will, "Watch out." The belt snapped off a big pulley and twisted around like a snake that had been run over.

It was interesting to see what the people did here, some were sitting about but some were very busy. I watched a veterinarian work on a cow with an abscessed tooth. Ecch. He pulled it out with a large pliers.

Back at Will's place, I started to do work on my bike and sure enough all these people came over and I had to work carefully around these bungle heads who were in my way. Will kept the crowd well informed on my bike repairs. They were so nosy. They moved in so close, perhaps wanting to smell me. We finished the work and I browsed some books, and then took a bath. The people just hanged around and stared at me. They were treated well by Will. He was very tolerant. We closed the curtain, sat and shared a smoke and had a good talk. I learned that Will had done a lot of cycling in the southern states of the U.S.. We went to eat food at 9pm and the gang was there to watch. They all gossiped about me and Will. Will would chuckle at some of their presumptions. "They wonder why you do not have a wife?" said Will, adding "They also wonder why we are meeting here."

By lantern light we ate a great meal of rice, veggies, potatoes and dahl. For dessert we had a few hot sweets. It was a delicious meal. I think they cooked it especially for us. After eating this kingly meal, we were both very full. Some of these people were so rude and loud. They annoyed the hell out of me. Will said, "You have to brush it off as a cultural difference. They are curious at never seeing anyone like us."

We went back to his house and ate another Hersheys chocolate bar. This time it was not as novel as the night before, but still it was very delicious. The stars were out, as I put up my tent.

## Thursday May 24

I had a good sleep, on a cool night. In the morning, I stepped over Will who was sleeping on the front porch and I packed up my stuff. I even carried the bike over him. The wind was blowing, and I felt like staying here longer, as I found Will to be great company, but the village was rather quaint, and the traveler needs to keep going and I felt the road calling.

As we rode our bikes to the 'hotel' we were greeted by all the folks. Will talked gleefully to them. I walked with him over to the 'hotel' and we each had curd dahl and puffed rice. It was a feeling of madness that overwhelmed me as I really enjoyed Will and did not want to say goodbye, also I felt for him and all these natives that he must cope with. When I leave he will be alone with them. So as the crowd mauled us we talked. All I could see were root beer colored legs and black toes twitching closer and closer. Occasionally I pushed them back. With a shove! But Will talked to them nice. I said so long to him and we shook hands and I walked off. A few yards later the crowd raced after me and Will said, "Oh Eric! Be sure to tell any tourists, especially cyclists, to stop in, I sure enjoy it." His hunger showed for conversation and company. What a noble American he was.

To get back to the main road, I had to go back down that rough, dirt road. It was very windy, and I was fighting for control. I was concerned that my tires would be destroyed. There were sharp rocks and potholes that needed to carefully be traversed. Finally, I made it to the pavement.

Oh, what a stiff wind to fight against as I retraced that 15 kilometers I'd traveled days before. One feels as if back tracking is a waste. It is not. There can be adventures gained by doing so.

After one hour of hard pedaling, I made it to Lahan and the crazy people heckled me in the streets. I stopped into a cafe and had dahl(curd) and sweets and the guy over charged me. He said one rupee for the sugar. I said 50 paesa and he agreed but did not give me any change back so I just picked up a cookie and walked out as he hollered. I threw the cookie into a cart driver's lap as it was lousy.

The wind worsened and my pace slowed, I was in the lowest gear, on the flattest road yet and it was hard work. I noticed the women would face into the wind and the way that their eyes looked and hair swept back made them look exquisitely beautiful. Even though the pace was slow it was not an easy one for looking around as the bike took so much effort to control that I had to stay down low to keep streamlining the wind resistance. The wind became stronger and the gusts worsened. The only consolation was the occasional wind blasts that helped me stay cool. Still, I was sweating like crazy.

I stopped at noon to eat food and the people surrounded me. The calorie loss to power such a bike into the wind had developed for me a healthy appetite.

It felt good to have made some progress, and I was surprised at how far I'd ridden, despite the hardship. The mountains of Nepal got farther away. It was now a plains, scattered with big trees. I went at a snails pace, and finally I got so tired and had to dash into the woods for Delhi belly.

The road passed along a long causeway and then went over the Sahti Kosi River and it was a really big sucker. I crossed the bridge and then asked around for food. I found a little hotel, with a cafe in this crowded bunch of shops. I was given a good cup of tea and met Narang, the Nepali chief of police. I looked around town and decided to spend the night here. It was a relaxing atmosphere. I had fun teasing with the kids along the river. They kept saying "disco" to me and "shalom." These kids were as much fun as kids can be. I put my hand to my head or closed palms and they mimicked me.

I went back to the hotel in the later afternoon sun and Narang cooked me a big meal of dahl, rice, veggies and tea. I was full. I enjoyed this busy restaurant and the scene of the river. Outside the wind howled. Street peddlers walked about selling their goods. One fellow hollered "omelette" and a wild looking crazy woman poored water and called out "pani." The place had great- cold- drinking water, from the pump, so I don't know how much business she will find. This is a fun little place to stay.

Just for kicks, I thought I would look to see if I might find a camping spot, so I pedaled my bike into a field behind the hotel and went past some guys sitting on a mat. One guy hollered to me, "Hey where are you going?" He dashed toward me shouting, "Are you looking for something?" I told him, "I'm looking for a place to camp." He said, "Where are from?" I told him and he invited me to his hut. "You can sleep in a room tonight," he said and added, "Do you want a drink?" He had a servant run and get me a cold drink and then he told me. "I was in Ohio, going to school. I got a masters degree there in one year. Ha, ha, ha, it was cold there," he laughed. We shared a drink of whiskey and he was delighted to hear my story of the goat taking my bag and running down the mountain with it. "I'm the commissioner of this district," he said. We shook hands and he cried to a servant, "Get him a bed ready." He then showed me a room and it was a great mud and straw hut with lights and a mosquito net. The wind howled but I was cozy and felt no pain.

## Friday May 25

Up at 6, I was given tea. Then I said good morning to the commissioner who was feeding pigeons. I thanked him for his kindness and went to the hotel and ate breakfast. I was about to leave town when a peddler sold me a few leechey nuts or loquots. I rode on against the hardest wind yet. It was real open country, a big river plain. I fought to maintain control and had to use the lowest gear. In Inaruwa I stopped for tea and people packed around me. I pushed some off and had to keep constant watch on my bike. They were like animals, but at least obedient. I made it to Itahari with hopes of having a cold Coke but that was not available. I ate lunch as a crowd watched me. The terrain was rather nice with grassy field's backdropped by mountains and straw huts. Then I headed for the border of India. The wind was to my side for once, and I made better time. I stopped for a piss and a people crowd of people care around to watch. "This pisses me off!" I said aloud. I ate a leechey and threw the shell and seeds at them. Then I jammed through the damn crowd and headed into Biratnagar and for the border of India.

I was heading south out of a small Nepal town near Chatra in the southeast corner of the Terrai region, for the border of India on my bicycle. Off in the distance I saw an entanglement of trishaws, autos and roaming cows mixed with people walking every which way as if they were exiting a stadium concert. I rolled to a stop and ducked behind a tree to relieve myself. No sooner than I'd begun peeing a few 'spectators' dashed over to watch. Generally they didn't do this in Nepal. This was in some strange fashion my re-initiation to India.

There was a little shop, which offered a chewing gum, that tasted just like Juicy Fruit. I thought-Juicy Fruit gum in Nepal? Maybe this is originally where it comes from.

Annoyed but undaunted by the crowd that blocked the road ahead, I started ringing my bell spasmodically until I made it to the Nepal customs office at the border.

While standing there with the customs agent, black market money traders swarmed in. I had quite a selection of offers to choose from and even the customs agent egged me on to the best offer. They each offered me a better exchange rate than the next, until they started arguing with each other and I continued on.

As I entered the Nepal customs office I did not expect such a hassle. They asked me everything that was right there on the passport. "Where are you from?" "U.S.A., America," I said. "What is your name?" I told them. They looked the passport over carefully and noticed all of the countries stamps. His eye grew large. Finally, I was passed through with the Nepal exit stamp into the passport. I walked my heavily loaded bike across to the India customs, expecting the worst.

Eyes as black as coal stared at me from every direction as I leaned the bike against the India customs ofice. I shook hands with the officer and noticed an old dust covered calendar hanging from the wall. The crowd outside was gathering around the office. The agent wanted to see my passport. "Amedeekan," he said to another agent. Now he wanted to see how much money I had and an airline ticket. With the crowd looking over my shoulder, smudged against the window and hanging from tree limbs, I was a bit reluctant to let them see my money. The agent though counted it and waved it about so all eyes could see. He asked why I was coming back into India. "All India tour on cycle," I said. "Ahh chaa," he said, while looking my baggage over. He started toying with me now and asked more redundant questions. Where do you go?" Where do you stay? What will you do?" I was forewarned that this part of Bihar did not have many tourists, that I was a novelty to them.

People crowded around. There was poor crowd control. The crowd got bigger and began crushing my bike. A policeman went out to control things but he was as dazzled as were the others at the size of this crowd. As the agent inked his entry stamp into my passport, I went out to check my bike. The policeman whacked a few people with his baton, but it had little effect. One group of kids were up in a tree, looking into the window of the border guards at me. Suddenly, a tree limb snapped and three of the laughing boys crashed to the ground. My bike started to buckle from the shoving mass of humanity. I had to take immediate action. I went outside and let out a yell. "Jow, chello!!" I said. They backed off more so by the look in my eyes and the color of my red face then the yell.

I was told to have Indian money on my person and that I would have to go to the bank and change money and report it back to them. I had to push my way through the crowd. Down the busy streets I pedaled as a group of children ran screaming along behind me. I had quite a selection of money changing offers to choose from and even the customs agent helped me along to find the best offer, but I ended up changing at the bank as the whole lot seemed suspicious.

I went to the bank to change money. They asked if I had a passport. "Yes," I said. "We cannot change unless you have form." "Where is the form?" I asked. They said it was back at the customs office. "They did not give me a form," I said. Then they said very assertively, "No, we cannot change money without the form," Then I said, "Ok, I will leave and get one…" and they said, "Ok I will change your money." I was dumbfounded about the zany Indian mindset but in the end it worked out.

Returning to the customs office I showed them that I changed money, there eyes went wide when they saw the money and finally I got the stamp in my passport. I then had to gently push my way through the crowd.

I had my money and then pedaled 100 feet back into Nepal to buy some more of that Juicy Fruit bubble gum. Customs did not mind, they treated me like a hero and parted the crowds to let me pass. I flung a few sticks of that 'Juicy Fruit gum' into my mouth and while blowing bubbles entered back into India.

Heading down the busy streets, I pedaled southeast, watched by crowds of staring faces with that hypnotic gaze as a group of children ran screaming along behind me. "I'm back into the soup," I mumbled to myself.

# RETURN TO INDIA

**Saturday May 26**

The craziness of India was returning after only a few minutes had passed since crossing the border of Nepal into India at Biratnagar. People walking in front me, horns blasting, staring eyes, bicycles careening with mine, busloads of people laughing at me.

I went another 30 k's, watching the mile markers slowly pass by under the hot sun. I stopped for tea and people had such a sullen face. Then I pedaled along a small winding road, surrounded with dense jungle and many settlements. Surprisingly, people spoke more english here, in fact I was stopped by a car with customs officers who checked my documents and then shook my hand and congratulated me for, "All India Cycling."

With the bicycle as the main source of transportation in all of India one sees it is ridden by all ages. I saw an old man going the opposite direction and he looked at me as we passed and he rode right off the road into the ditch. I saw his feet raise up as he went into tall grass. Later, two young cyclists who were riding side by side ran into one another as I rode past them. None of these individuals was hurt in unfortunate comical satire.

As the afternoon heat started to tip the 40 centigrade mark I pulled off in a small town and found a roadside stand for a bite to eat and a drink. The stand wasn't full of people and I'd be able to watch my bike. I leaned the bike against the food stall and sat down so I was facing it. I then went into the kitchen, lifted up the kettle and made my own diagnoses of the food to determine if it was all right for my tastes. They don't mind if you do that.

Soon the curious were gathering to look at me, which brought more onlookers. A crowd gathered. They were rude and came right up to me and stared. I told them to sit or to stand back. Solemn, smile-less faces looked at me as if they were hungry. They just stared, with those big, coal black eyes. They crowded around my bike like it was free cake. Finally I got pissed off at them because the owner was ineffective in containing their excitement. "Jow, get away, go," I shouted and motioned for them to move on. They acted like cattle. Looking at me startled, and stepping backwards, quivering, then jumping back.

Food was served to me of dahl baht and chipadeee combinations. I took a bite and it was so hot with chile that my eyes bulged and I choked. I longed for some privacy, but these people were like pests. Quickly I downed some hot tea the color of a muddy river. The crowd went hysterical with laughter. Soon they were even more entertained by me blowing on the food and sipping tea. They started to notice my every move. As I bit into my food they seemed to bite also and when I drank they listened to my swallow. Any move, any twitch any smirk was giggled at. I thought to myself if anyone yearns to have an audience, this part of Bihar Province is the place to be for them to come. In a curious way, I rather liked the Indians again.

Finished with my performance, I paid, said, "Rham, Rham," and then moved the bike slowly through the huge crowd, gently asking people to move, which they slowly did. This was a new thing for me.

I rode out of town, down a little road that went past huts and past more village people. I was thinking, "Did I take a wrong turn?" I asked people if this was the road to Purnea. They would wave their head sideways and wave their hand down the road to suggest to me a yes. God they looked crazy.

From 2pm untill 4pm it's the hottest part of the day and I set a steady but conservative rhythm. I wore a head cloth with my helmet over it. I had no shirt but draped a towel covering my back from the intense May sun. This combination generally worked the best for maximum air flow and minimal sun exposure. I started to get hot and found a pump and wet down my clothes. I'd learned that it's important to drink before getting dehydrated and eat before becoming weak with energy loss. Also to drink and cool down before my internal thermostat overloads.

A roadblock by the customs police stopped me to check documents and baggage. "I think you are feeling very hot," said the officer as a river of sweat ran down my brow. "All India tour with cycle," I said and he allowed me to move on and even stopped traffic to clear my way. Fifteen kilometers down the road there was a fork and then a detour and then the road fizzled into a footpath past villages.

Asking someone directions was becoming a testing experience in India. With so many people walking about you'd think it would be an easy matter. This was not so. I asked a white robed fellow which way to Purnea and he only mimicked my hand motions. "Purnea?" I then asked him pointing to one way and then the other and he'd just agree either way with me. I showed him my map, and he rotated it every which way, until I knew that he was even more confused than I.

It was best to ask about five people the way, in order to get an accurate consensus whether they knew the directions and then I would decide. So I asked an influential looking man in a horse and buggy which way to Purnea and he could speak real good english. He straightened me out and told me, "Be careful where you camp as there are many poisonous snakes," I thanked him and nearly ran into a big white cow crossing the road. I heard him laugh.

About two hours later, I passed by a hut which was to the west, just across from a watery ditch. I heard a woman screaming and saw her in her sari, wearing a white head veil, inside holding a baby. Outside, on the other side of the hut, I saw a man dressed in his doti whisk away a large snake from the side of the building. The snake had a fat head, it looked like a King Cobra. It raised toward him once. He did not kill the snake, he merely brushed it away and it slithered under the hut.

At 6am I stopped to wash up. I was told where a well was but my first analysis of the water changed my mind. I'd learned how to judge water in India. First I look at it. It must be clear. There should be no specks or organic discoloration. Second test is the smell. There should be no chemical, rancid, or contaminated smell. Then I check the feel of the water. I was amazed at the different hard or softness of water. This can be a clue to the water's quality. Soft water comes from a spring or hard water from a reservoir. The last test comes only if the others pass and that is to taste it. I swish it in my mouth, but don't swallow it. There is a freshness to drinkable water that experience becomes the best judge. This water did not pass as it was a foggy color and it smelled, so I found another pump and tried that water.

Judging it was good water, I filled my water bottles. Then, since I was alone, I rapidly stripped down to my skivvies and quickly and quietly went about washing myself. Soon a few people stopped to watch me and by the time I was toweling off a crowd developed. They ran over to me like a lion rushes to his kill. I was alarmed. People gathered around as I wiped myself. Then I stared at them one on one and they backed off. There would be no denying me even this little bit of privacy. For now I was there cinema, their television, their free concert, a live one act play!.

There were people everywhere, so I decided to continue riding until nearly dark and look for someplace to pitch my tent. A brilliant orange sunset was taking place when I noticed a school yard with a temple. On the opposite side of the road was a tea stall.

I pulled up to the tea stall at twilight and sat down with four men as they quietly stared at me. I tried to talk abit to the people, and they spoke Hindi or something and I said, "I can't speak Hindi, "Ney Hindi," but they continued talking to me like I was short of hearing. They shouted to me. I spoke a few words of Hindi to them and said, "all India tour on cycle," they responded with questions of where I came from and how much did this cost as they pointed to everything I had. I always told Indians far less than the real value of my stuff. They got a real funny look in their eyes when I told them my bicycle cost six hundred dollars. That might be ten years earnings for some of them.

As it was getting dark, I waited around and drank five cups of tea and that emptied the shops supply. We started to drink boiled lemon juice with sugar., The tea stand owner asked me where I would sleep and I asked him if I could camp in the schoolyard. He said, "ahh chaa." I overpaid the man 50 paesa and he did not give me back any change, so I left it at that. He and another fellow were kind enough to show me a spot to sleep across the street and escorted me over to the area, where he said I could camp. He watched in amazement as I put up my torpedo tent. I rolled back the fly to let the air flow through it. He left me and I felt good about this nice spot to sleep. There was a small Hindu temple, with a concrete foundation and it was surrounded with a steel fence. The grass around the temple was short, as if it had been recently cut. I felt as if I'd drank to much tea.(which I did) My head had a buzzing, nervous feeling. So I stood outside of the tent and tried to relax as people passed by with their flashlights shining at me and my bike.

Then, wearing only my skivies I crawled into the tent and laid on my towel. Someone came and locked the outside fence.

Ten minutes time had passed and a young idiotic boy approached and talked Hindi loudly to me. He was shining his flashlight right into my eyes. He wanted to talk with me, so I got out of the tent and told him "Ney Hindi," but he could not understand. I showed him my things and told him where I was from. Then I thought to hell with this kid and went back to bed. A couple of people came and wanted to talk to me. They shouted and I said to them, "Goodnight, Tata, Rham, Rham," but they only continued to harass me. They left and then returned twice more and shone their light at me continuously, but soon left.

Then the same idiotic fellow came back, shined his light on me and wanted to get into my tent and lay with me, but I would not let him. He had buck teeth and real bad breath. He actually succeeded in forcing his way head first into my tent, but I pushed him back out. Though he never saw it, I had my kukri in my hand. Should I show it? Should I brandish it and warn him to leave? No I did not. I just said, "Jow, piss off, get out of here." Then the idiotic guy, whom I had seen moments before smoking hashish began shouting "Ramsees, ramsees," at the top of his lungs. He ran off.

It wasn't long when I saw people coming toward me with their flashlights. The time was ten past eleven. There were about 6 men, each carrying a shovel, or a pitchfork, a hoe or an axe They gathered around my tent talking loudly and shining lights on me. I saw a pitchfork in the bearded mans hand and a shovel in another's beside him. Others held sticks. I silently said a four-letter word to myself and gulped at my situation. This one tall bearded guy acted as the spokesperson and asked what I was doing. Those magical words I'd been saying all day, "All India tour on cycle," rang out from my lips as if my saving grace. "Passport," demanded the man. "No!" I said. I did not know who he was, whether he was a policeman or what, so I would not give it to him. I tried to be kind, but could feel a tension growing. But he was nasty. The guy who had the tea stand and who led me here told him I was an "All India Tourist." So I also tried telling him that, and in the past, saying that phrase would move mountains, but on this occasion it seemed to mean nothing. The spokesman wanted rupees and the mob mentioned rupees several times. I made gestures like I wanted to sleep, but they were indifferent and motioned for me to either give them my passport or else go.

I felt like fighting them but then in a last ditch effort to relieve the tension of this situation, I reluctantly began packing up my tent at this late hour. Strangely enough they shined a flashlight to assist my packing up my tent and gear and they monitored my progress. I put everything haphazardly onto my bike, strapped it down and then was ready to go. Someone had to run and get a key to unlock the gate. We waited. Lucky I did not make any trouble, as I never would have gotten out of there because it was a sturdy lock.

I kept thinking they'd see that I was up to no harm and they would just call this whole misunderstanding off and allow me to get some sleep. The gate flung open out toward the road. There was no moon, but plenty of stars. It was pitch black and I could not even see the road. I could tell I was heading southeast because of the star patterns. I'd decided I would go and look for another place to camp. I could hear drums beating in the distant direction that I would be heading.

In the darkness of the night I was escorted to the road by this mob yielding there pitchforks and shovels. "Where you go?" said a voice. I just motioned down the road. I kept thinking they'd see I was up to no harm and would invite me to stay. I quickly mounted my bike, took a few pedals and turned around to them and shouted, "Jow you fucking cocksuckers!" I then left. They shouted back something that I did not understand. I rode quickly, looking back only once to see there flashlights still on me, but I was pedaling hard as I was concerned about getting a spear in my back.

Something was in the air on this night. Some kind of madness. People were chanting like a bizarre cult. I passed camp fires flickering, and occasional wailing. I turned off my light as I passed a group of chanters. They were grouped around a fire and looked drunk. A dog barked and then chased me down the road. Pedaling madly, I got away from it.

The time was nearing midnight when I made way into the inky blackness upon that road. The stars shone overhead like plums. I recognized some star patterns and felt comforted by this. My generator hummed, but it was going bad and very little light shone from it. I held a penlight in one hand which was more effective. Sometimes in order for me to steer with both hands, I held the flashlight in my mouth. Even at this hour, it was very hot, and very dark, such that to run into a wall would be devastating.

Fortunately no mishaps occurred, except for hitting the occasional potholes. After five miles of pedaling in dangerous conditions, I hastily found a spot in the ditch, which looked adequate to pitch my tent. This was done with great caution as I recalled the large snake I had seen on this day, and the woman who was screaming about the snake under her house. Therefore I felt reluctance to camp here.

Inconspicuously, I pushed the bike down into the section of ditch. A big tree hung over the site and offered me concealment. I froze at the thought of meeting a snake. I looked the area over good, but frankly was too tired to care. I put up the tent, got into it, and listened to the drums beating to the south and to the east. It sounded as if they were in a trance and chanting. Then, a torturous scream pierced the night. I wondered what madness was occurring. With one eye open, I drifted into sleep. I heard crazy hollering, screaming and distant drumming. I set the tent just in time to get inside as a truck zoomed by. The headlights did not hit my tent as it passed.

At about 2am, I awoke to the sound of creaking wagon wheels and hooves plodding on the road. It grew louder. I heard music playing from the same direction. There was the melody of drums and bagpipes on the road. I heard cattle walking. I looked outside my tent and saw lanterns flickering to the northwest. Wagons were approaching! It appeared to be a team of oxen, pulling a covered wagon filled with gypsis. They had lantern lights flickering which illuminated the scene. A man led the team of oxen. I could just see the shape of one oxen heading directly for me in the ditch. I couldn't let that man see me nor let the oxen step on me. My mind whirled. I braced myself like a sailor before a storm.

The man leading the wagons didn't notice me as he walked past. I now could now see the lead team of oxen and the first of three wagons. Music blared from a violin like instrument. Bells chimed and sitars played a melody. People talk fast and loud. Their was some laughter. The second wagons team of oxen past and I could see on the sides a lamp lit the canvas and made out the silhouetted shapes of people. There was talking and men groaning, women giggling and laughing and talking. I only can speculate what was occurring by the sound.

The third wagon passed and I heard men apparently involved in gambling and men talking. Now I could see the shape of that oxen ambling toward me in the ditch. I cold feel the thud of each of its steps. I started hissing like a leaking tire. "Siss, siss." The oxen came to a complete stop just down from me and I could see its rope to the wagon go taught, "Hiss," I went, sounding like air escaping from a leaking tire. Quickly, it leaped up out of the ditch to the road, snorted and then went around me, but very close. Relieved I was, but now too worked up to sleep, I listened to the wagon train fading away and again heard the sound of the drums and chanting. I looked up at the stars and felt comforted that they were the same as always. For now they were my only grip on sanity.

What happened next seemed like a dream. There was this slithering sound in the grass beside the tent. I could feel the vibrations beside me and through the ground. Snake! I thought as I tried to awake, tried to scream but could not. I opened my eyes instantly and looked up from my puddle of sweat. Then reality set in. Facing me was a dark, elderly Indian man, with a white turbine and coal black eyes peering down at me. I greeted him, "namaste," in Hindi. He responded the same to me and he stood back to watch me come out of the tent. He sat back to watch as I packed up my gear, as the orange ball of the sun peeked over the horizon. I figured I'd get out of here quick. Before a crowd gathered. Welcome to India, I thought.

**Sunday May 27**

Today was my moms birthday, and I vowed to think of her all day. I was on the road by 6am, as it was a clear, sunny morning. The sun rose like a orange stoplight while I pedaled on past village people out in the fields taking their morning crap. It was a comical sound to hear, while passing. "Freeiiittt, fluuuurritt, flossssshhh and foomp."

I made my way into a small town. Everywhere the people looked with hostility at me. I shopped around for a place to eat and this amused them. They laughed. They played with me like a toy. One guy stepped in front of me as I rode along and I carefully pushed in the chest to prevent injury. "Ahh," he said and I heard laughter from others. Two bikes collided while the drivers watched me. Kids ran behind me.

I chose a small tea shop and put the bike into a vacant room. Immediately a crowd enveloped me. They went to look at the bike and I had to move it to a different spot, or else it would be crushed. This time I placed it between two walls. There was just enough room for the bike. This was an important thing to remember. The people get so close and I had to keep saying, "Back, back."

I ate a good breakfast of 'pancakes' and potatoes, which were spicy and all served on a banana leaf. No silverware was offered, it was all eaten with the right hand. The man made me "three feet tea". He would take one cup of tea and dump it into the other at arms length until all the sugar, milk and tea had mixed and frothed and then handed it to me. The entire meal cost me 1.50 rupee.

After my meal I truly wanted to be considerate to the crowd of Indians and tried patiently to part with my bike without incident. I straddled the cross bar, one foot on the pedal, the other walked the bike through the masses, saying "tanda baht," (thank you) and waving my arm in a gentle sweeping fashion to move them. They moved very slowly. Some stumbled, others backed up but kept looking at me, like I was a god or a politician. I gave them time, the crowd was large, but slowly I made way out from them, mounted the seat, and pedaled off. I waved to them as I left. They stood there dumbfounded.

On the outskirts of town I discovered a sweet covered bread that was tasty. Soon I was out into the countryside, riding along fields of grain and generally open country. I watched with amusement as an ox drawn cart approached with the driver sleeping. I went passed it, thinking "Now that is on autopilot!"

It started to rain and I rode with other bike riders and they often asked the dumnest questions. "You are a cyclist?" said one fellow. "No, I am a traveler." I responded. He looked puzzled. Another said, "I think you are speaking English, yes? English?" I responded, "Yes, I speak English, how are you today?" He responded, "I do not speak English, only Hindi. Can you speak Hindi." I said, "Rhamm, rhamm." He would not talk anymore to me.

I asked several country folk the way to Purnea and always they would just indicate that-a-way at forks in the road. But they wouldn't say specifically. Rather vaguely, they would brush their hands in the direction with the same kind of motion we might use to shoo away a bug. And everywhere the young people would say, "Disco!" Or they would say "World cycle." So I figured news travels fast. They somehow knew that I was an around the world cyclist. Nearly each village proved my theory as someone would point and shout, "World cycle."

At about noon, I made way into the busy industrial city of Purnea and had a lassi and tried to cool down in the hot sun. I then headed out against a hot head wind. This was a slow ride. I stopped for tea and chipadees at a hut and was feeling quite tired. The people seemed to respect that. They were shocked and so was I when I took off my sox and my feet were prunish. I dried them out, trying not to let folks see them.

It was hot and sticky with high humidity when I took off at 2pm and rode another two hours until 4pm. It was killer hot, when I pulled into a truck stop at Dal Cola for water to drink and to wash up at an outdoor pump. There were only a few truck drivers around and I saw this well pump located in the center of a parking area, nearby to where many trucks were parked. As I washed up a huge crowd soon gathered in a semi circle in front of me and they watched as I dried myself off with a towel. I noticed how solemn, expressionless and non-smiling their faces were. So I danced and made smiles and still they did not smirk. I said, "Come on smile," and gave them a big smile putting each of my index fingers at each side of my mouth. "Smile!" I ordered. There was not a smile on anyone. I then quickly turned around, pulled down my cycling shorts and underwear to reveal my bare ass at them. I mooned them! They all jumped back, extremely startled, and seemed to be terribly offended. They made a commotion. I pulled my pants back up and said, "Come on smile, Rham, Rham, Ghandi." I pointed to the sky and jumped up and down. But they still did not smile. So I just said. "You guys are losers." I threw my leg over the seat and left. I did hear some of them laugh, while others were so offended that they chased after me shouting obscenities and reached for something to throw at me.

I pedaled down a few miles and stopped into a restaurant and ate, once again being served food on a banana leaf, instead of a plate. I was getting good at eating with only my right hand.

I took the time to sit and write in my diary. This crowd came over and watched me for some time. While I was just sitting there, they were entertained by my concentration on writing. They chuckled. I met a Bengali fellow who spoke sharply and rough. I asked if I could put up my tent behind the place. This guy said, "No it is not good to sleep here because there are too many snakes." With a sneaky smile he said while jumping up, "You can stay with me, I have a bed for you." Well, I felt a little uneasy, but really needed a place to rest. I washed up and the guy watched me queerly and was smiling in strange ways. I went with him, down several roads and then up to his house. Something did not seem right to me. It wasn't even his house. I just decided, nope, I won't stay with him. "Thank you sir, I must be going," I said. "But, but, you cannot…," he said. I took off.

I headed down the road into the evening twilight and the early darkness. I went into a village and down a dirt road as it became dark. There were many Indians out walking at this hour. There was some kind of event happening nearby. An intelligent looking guy heard me asking a villager where I might find a hotel and he said, "Come." He took me to another villager who got all bent out of shape when talking about hotels. People have the craziest eyes in the twilight, eyes that are lifeless and black as coal. These guys were looking at me like cannibals. I was told that they're is a hotel farther up the road. "Nope, that's the one I just came from," I said and I just took off. I passed many more people, then when I saw a gap where there were no people, I turned off into a grove of big trees.

Being careful of where I stepped, in case of snakes, I set up a camp as fireflies danced all about. It was so dark in this grove of trees. I put the tent up and crawled inside. Soon I heard something slither past my tent. It would return several times during the night. I stayed away from that side of the tent. Then, very late, or early in the absolute darkness of morning a man walked past, but be did not see me. Stars overhead, between the trees, comforted my dozing eyes.

## Monday May 28

It was still dawn, when I was greeted with big raindrops and quickly I packed up. Then it poured down with rain. I pedaled off into a torrent. In some way, it felt kind of good. I made headway past rain soaked roads and overturned trucks and green fields with interesting shaped mud huts and then entered the town of Katihar. I stopped to buy some leeche fruits and bargained as a crowd developed. I gently pushed through the hypnotic idiots. They get so entranced and lethargic, that they would not move. It was better to be patient and let them part from my path.

All morning long the other cyclists would pull up beside me and I would either tolerate it, or when the traffic came, pull away or behind my cycling accompaniment. In one instance, this cyclist kept riding beside me. He pushed me off onto the shoulder a couple of times. Then a few cars were approaching and he damn near caused me to get killed by the passing car. He pulled up beside me again, as I told him to "jow, chello," but he did not understand. So I gave his bike a firm kick. He went wobbling off into the ditch and upended in tall grass. He got up and looked at me as I was riding away with a big WHY? on his face. I had to save myself.

I stopped at a cafe and had trouble finding a safe spot to park my bike. So I had to stand and eat as all these people (about 50) gathered and stared and started touching the bike. I pushed some away from crushing my bike. The manager hollered at them and at me to sit down. I could not. These people had no control. So I ate and the guy over charged me dearly. I tried to get his price down, but he was a jerk. So I paid and made my way through the crowd, this time like Ghandi would.

The next few miles passed along nice pathways, pedaling hard and at a good pace. All the way I reminisced about mom and had a good time recollecting events in my life. She heroically saved my younger sister by grabbing her in the front seat of the car, while we rounded a curve, in front of a shopping center, as my sister had opened the car door, and she swung out. Mom kept control of the car, with one hand on the steering wheel, while hanging on to her. Especially I liked thinking of how I enjoyed mimicking my mother by saying, "Oh mother!" and "Ish these kids these days!" She always gave me a reaction that was firm and positive, and I liked recalling that.

The miles past and I hardly noticed the frequent down pours. It was very warm out with this warm rain. I did notice my front bearing was getting worse. It rattled with every bump. I rode along the Bangladesh border and noticed these strange fruits hanging from a tree above the road and grabbed some. I discovered they were leechee fruits. The red skin was like the hide of a lizard but the inner fruit was bleached white and very soft and sweet to the taste. I picked and ate plenty of them.

I continued on as there were more sudden downpours. I felt depressed while passing so many staring eyes and people with no smiles. However, it was exciting to watch two guys cutting a palm tree with a loggers two handled saw and seeing it fall with a mighty crash. I also watched two men sawing a log into lumber with a long hand saw. The log was up on top of a rack. One man stood above the log, holding the saw handle, while the other stood below the log. Together they sawed, and the blade sliced off a long board.

English Bazaar was the name of the town where I stopped at a tourist lounge to cool off. I found a lassi stand and drank the refreshing drink. I ate dahl and chipadee at a tea shack and leaned the bike against a bench seat. These people rushed over to see me. One guy tried to grab something on my bike like it was a free for all. By complete reflex reaction I shoved his head back about four feet. He didn't hardly seem phased by that and came back for more. He talked about the bike like it was his, and he wanted to grab and damage things. I tried to eat and drink tea in peace. It was no wonder that I have indigestion.

The day became really hot and sticky. I slowed down, to pace myself, but made good progress. I was arriving at the Ganges River and pushed hard on the pedals against the wind and finally made it to the bridge. It was a huge bridge over the river. Slowly I crossed the Ganges, looking down at the enormous river below me, as armed security guards were very suspicious of my passing by. I met one of them. He motioned me to go quickly. Wow what a big river. I could see for miles the flat plain of the river. It was actually the size of a lake.

Once across the long bridge or dam I turned right and went down to the river, where I found a sandy beach, at a spot upstream of the bridge, which looked good to take a dip in the river. I went down the embankment, carrying bike and all and then crossed the sand to a bamboo pier. I worked quickly to undress as a crowd rushed to me as I stripped to my underwear and they stopped. Then I took a refreshing bath as the crowd kept a distance and laughed. I relaxed a bit in the cool refreshing water. The water was very nice and the sandy bottom beautiful to touch. When I came out I grabbed a towel and was confronted by two thin men who shouted, "Only the Hindu may bath in the Ganga. You make the water unpure because you are not a Hindu." I responded, "I am not the only unpurity to go into the Ganga. I think god would share this river with me and the Hindus." "But you are not a Hindu!" said the tall thin fellow. "Is god a Hindu?" I asked. "No, god is god," he added. "Then god told me to swim in the river," I acknowledged. I ignored his rabid rambling.

Some curious boys intervened and calmed the situation and were most interested in looking at my bike and comparing our bikes. I told them that an Indian bicycle was like a 1920's style American bicycle. They helped me push my bike up the sandy beach and over a hill. I was then escorted to a guest house that was full.

They told me to try a field hostel. I went there and it too was full, but I met some business people and they offered me tea. I sat until dark talking to them and met the hostel manager, whose name was Kalyan. He gave me a room for free, after some paper work. Then I worked on my bike. People dropped off a bundle of leechee fruit for us to eat. My host ordered a pizza like dish, which I ate fervently. It was a good meal and afterward I went to cool off in the shower and then got under my mosquito net.

Later, I talked with the fellows about the two extremes I had seen in India. From the very poor to the very rich. They agreed, that this was what India was like.

Kalyan offered me some advice. He said as I traveled India, if I went to the Public Security Bureau, they might be able to give me a free room to stay. We sat and drank whiskey n water and laughed until very late, then we called it a night.

## Tuesday May 29

I thanked my hosts and was off into pleasant country roads with rolling green hills. The roads were becoming arteries full of traffic that were headed for Calcutta.

In one stretch of road, while riding along, I could reach up high and grab a clump of leechees with my hand and then enjoy these delicious fruits.

I passed through one small village of Jangipur, that was selling little ceramic heads of Kali and Radha or various other gods or goddesses of India. They were so finely hand painted that I just had to get two of them. They were fragile and I carefully packed them into my bag, wondering how long before they were broken.

It was not always easy to find a trusting face to ask directions on these roads in India. It was sometimes an upside down experience for me. Massive crowds of people and there curious nature to suddenly do the unexpected. Once I rode up to a large Hindu temple that was intricately designed with thousands of colorful figures. I looked up at it and tried to decipher the connection between God and humans involved in everyday activity and of their unknown gods. The Hindu religion has many levels of gods. I guess they choose the god that fills the niche. I marveled at the erotic carvings of beautiful women, so curvy and enchanting in form.

A few inquisitive souls filtered over to look at me, while I looked at the temple. Dazzled by the sight I took a few photos of the temple and then of them. More people came, which collects even more people, until it became a critical mass. I turned around to a large crowd looking at my blue eyes and hairy arms. "Mr. Monkey," someone said. I felt like E.T. One fellow said, "I think you are feeling very hot today?" I said, "Yes, I'am," as a ball of sweat trickled down my brow. The heat was extreme and the crowd was getting to me. I had learned, that slow motions and peacefulness was important in India. I recalled how once a mob got out of control and the police came with sticks to beat the people away. This time, I made my way through the crowd very slowly. "Tanda bad," (Thank you) I said. I moved my way through this sea of people. I felt like Ghandi as they followed me right to the edge of town. "Bye, bye," I waved and rode off like John Wayne.

I arrived in the busy city of Berhampore at 4pm. There were bicycle riders everywhere, swarming like bees. I went to the Public Security Bureau to see if they might give me some advice on where to stay. I met a man who said if I wanted to, I could stay here in a room to sleep the night for free. They did give me some hassle though. For one thing I was limited to leave only once during my visit, and from then on, I must remain in my room. Curfew was at 10pm. It was a hot building, an old room, with a fan, and though it was free, in some ways I felt restricted from the freedoms so frequently cherished.

## Wednesday May 30

I awoke in this room full of natural woodwork and packed up. I said my thanks to the officials, paid them a little and hit the road through a very busy city.

It was a steady ride along extremely busy roads through Burdwan, Bhatpara and into Calcutta. The heat was nearly unbearable even in the early hours of the day. By noon, the asphalt road turned sticky and my tires clogged with tar. The traffic was very intense as the roads came together into Calcutta. I passed some industry, then big temples, saw a river to the east, crossed over some big bridges and weaved in and out of congested traffic all morning. The road led me right down into the heart of Calcutta.

I was in the busy city at about 3pm when I stopped at an intersection jammed with humans and vehicles, waiting for the light to change. Behind me was a motocross start of cars, trucks and trishaws. People by the hundreds filled the sidewalks and other cyclists all watched as I pedaled off. At one very busy intersection, I waited for the light to turn green. It was like the start of a motocross race. So many vehicles were reving beside me and we were all lined up and ready to go. The light turned green and I started pedaling. It was then that I was chased by a shouting Indian fellow who called out "Stop, please stop, where do you come from?" I answered him, "U.S.A." but did not stop for him, because I was tired and it was so damn hot. This kind of thing happened frequently, so why should I? But he kept running behind me and shouting to me. "Stop, stop." He ran along the sidewalk, thru masses of people and caught up to me about a block down. He then shouted something that made me hit the brakes, "Can I buy you an ice cold Coca Cola?" he said. My ears perked up and I pulled over to see who he was. He said, "Come with me. My name is Nieladri Gosh. You need a cold drink, I can see that, I will buy one for you." As promised he bought me a Coke in a bottle at a little shop, and we each gulped two of them down and talked. He was interested in my travel story and wanted to hear about it. He offered me a room to stay in for free at the YMCA, where he said he was the manager. I explained to him that I had someone that I wanted to see in Calcutta and that I would come back to the YMCA later in the day.

I spent some time going along the congested streets of Calcutta, dodging people and avoiding the streetcar rails, to find my way to the city center. I found a pay phone and called Rheemas house, they asked who I was and I was told by her sister that she was not available. I then began to search for Rheema's house. I had her address and strangely enough seemed to know where to find her home. It was almost as if I'd been there before. I made a lot of turns, asked people for directions and then pedaled up to and found her house. It was a big home like those in east Duluth. I knocked on the door and Anita answered. I greeted her and saw Chuck inside and was very surprised to see him. "Where is Rheema?" I asked. "She is not here," said Anita in a rather facetious way. "Chuck acknowledged that he had been waiting to see her for quite awhile and that she had not yet arrived. I was skeptical and did not believe them. I kept asking them if this was a joke or something. "No she is not here and she has gone to Sikkum to be with her family." "I have to get going," said Chuck. He hailed a cab as I continued to question how, when and where I might see Rheema. Alas I lost my composure and shouted upstairs. "Rheema I just want to say hello and I'd like to see you." My hosts became irritated and told me I would have to leave. By now a servant had become alarmed and wanted me to depart. I was shooed out the door as I shouted, "Rheema, Rheema," again and again even as I was backed down the walk looking up at the upstairs window. I had the feeling that she was there and had heard me. But I had to leave. It was like a scene in a movie, only this time it really hurt.

I was on a bummer while making my way back to the YMCA. Had Rheema not wanted to see me because we had become too close back in Nepal? Or was it because of Chuck? Did he woo and persuade her? Or was it because of the coincidence that both Chuck and I were interested in her and that would not look good in a higher caste Indian family? The thoughts carried me all the way as I pedaled back to the YMCA on a hot, orange colored Calcutta afternoon.

Nieladri greeted me and as promised he secured a room for me. It was a long room with a big table and a sink. He said, I could stay as long as I wanted to for free. He took me out to a place to eat and watched me wolf down some dahl, rice and curry. We ate with our right hand, in the Bengali fashion. Once back at the 'Y', I was allowed to sleep in a meeting room on a big table. It was comfortable enough, and cheap as well.

## Thursday. May 31

The night was spent upon my long table with a fan going to ease the stagnant heat. I awoke early and at 7am Nieladri came in and warmly greeted me. He was so nice to me. He was just thrilled at my around the world adventure. I went to eat breakfast with him and later met some of his friends. We played electric guitar and I sang a song but my voice sounded so bad.

They were Christians, and told me a story about the Apostle Thomas coming to India after the time of Christ. We discussed Reagan as president and the music of Bob Dylan and the Beatles. They knew so much about them that I did not know.

We were walking down a Calcutta sidewalk and my friends asked if I had tried the Indian delicacy that is called betelnut. I had seen the Indians eating this red colored nut and had wondered what the red spittle, which looks like blood, was upon the sidewalks. The young friend of Nieladris named Rajiv, bought me a betelnut and I packed it into my mouth. Soon I was crunching on the bitter nut and spitting out juices. It became unbearably spicy hot. My head started to spin and this required my sitting down on the curb, else fall over into the busy traffic on the street. I was so dizzy and ill it took great willpower to overcome this narcotic. After some time spitting and drinking a cold drink, the side effects wore off. We went to a touristy part of town and bought some Chinese food, and then had supper at the YMCA. I tried calling Rheema, and Anita, her sister answered. She told me Rheema was not here and that I should not call for her anymore.

## Friday June 1

It was another hot, muggy day in Calacutta. I went with Nieladri and his friend Ganeesh on our bicycles and we rode out to visit the Kali Temple, also called Kalighat, or as it is locally called, Kalighat Kali. It was a large temple that was constructed around 1100A.D. and had many chambers. One might think they were chambers of horror. The worship of Kali involved bloodletting. They actually do kill goats and chickens there for sacrifice to Kali. Inside were many statues of Kali, with her tongue hanging out and blood splattered everywhere. The blood was flung across the walls and figures, rather like a red colored dye, yet the drama convinced me it was blood.

We waited in a long line and then Nieladri, Ganeesh and I had our foreheads dabbed with a red smudge by a high priest. "I believe in Kali to help me," said Ganeesh with his hands in a prayful position. Nieladri would not go through the temple because he did not believe in Kali, as he was a Christian.

We stood before a statue and Ganeesh prayed. He poured his heart and soul into Kali, reminding me of Christians praying in a church. Inside the temple were many unfortunate souls with leprosy, sickness, missing limbs and disfigured. They held outstretched hands for rupees.

Our tour also took us to the Jain temple and its fine white marble work. The idea of not killing anything was especially pertinent as a few flies buzzed our faces and we refrained from slapping them. I sat in a Buddha pose on the front steps, as my friends took my photo.

Our bike ride back to the YMCA was exciting and challenging as each raced against the next in the blazing afternoon sun. The traffic was heavy as we zigzagged along, missing people and cows. These guys had single speed bikes, but they could make them go fast and drive dangerously through crowds and heavy traffic. I was amazed and nearly fearful of crashing many times with these Indian racers.

There lived a poor homeless man in front of the YMCA in a cardboard house. He had pots, bricks and blankets to make it as comfy a home as possible. I was told that the Indian authorities, "look the other way," at such a sight as he.

### Saturday June 2

Inside of the Calcutta YMCA, was given the honor of addressing a small group of young people about my travels. Nieladri provided the introduction and then I stood before the group and told my tale. I provided my insightful philosophy of friendship and world peace. They marveled at my stories and asked many questions. Then I sang them a song from a borrowed guitar. My voice was raspy but the song was my own called "Friends around the world." They applauded and it was time for questions. One fellow who had lots of questions was very hard for me to understand. I had to have Nieladri interpret for me. He wanted to know why I wanted to travel around the world. A reporter came to talk to me and took a photo. It was an interview that I would never see in print.

### Sun. June 3

I went to church in the morning with Neiladri and friends. It was a typical service, with the typical message about going to hell if one strays from the path of Christ.

In the afternoon, I went to the train station with the help of my friends and reserved a spot on board a Tuesday train back to Bombay. I had to go back to Bombay to pick up my guitar in storage. Also my airline ticket went from Bombay to Dacca.

We went over to Nieladris house as the rains began to come down in earnest. Time was spent indoors playing backgammon and drinking tea. We then went to a friend's house and played his electric guitar without an amp. They marveled at my imitations of Bob Dylan. I really think my singing stunk and thought they were easily amused.

### Monday June 4

The monsoon rains continued all day and night and the the streets were heavily flooded with water. Everywhere one looked there was mud colored water. The rainfall was very hard and occasionally thunder shook the buildings. The day was spent mostly indoors, talking and doing little projects. I went to a few shops under my umbrella.

On this night I was alone at the YMCA and was hungry so I walked outside into knee deep water. I noticed that the homeless mans house of cardboard and cloth was completely gone. I walked across the street into deep water under a pouring rain. My umbrella sheltered me until suddenly I fell down into an open sewer. Into the murky yuck I fell. It smelled awful. The umbrellas framework caught the rim side of the manhole and saved me. I shot back up, completely soaked and there was yuck hanging from me from the waist down. I brushed it off and went ahead to the shop only to find it was closed. Back at the YMCA water was dripping from the ceiling.

### Tuesday June 5

The rain continued hard all night. In the morning, there were small boats passing along on the streets of Calcutta. There were dead rats, pineapples, mangos, coconuts and crap floating along the streets. People still went outside, to work and to shop, wading along, with their saris lifted and dhoti's rolled up while traversing the mire. It was very treacherous and uncomfortable. Many people took shelter on the rooftops. I was concerned about catching the train tomorrow. My hosts assured and comforted me, that everything would be fine. We laughed and ate, played games and enjoyed our fellowship.

### Wednesday June 6

With my train leaving at 3pm, I wanted to get going early and headed for the train station. Nieladri, Ganeesh and Ranji wanted me to go with them to visit friends for lunch. We went and had a wonderful visit and lunch. Considering the rain and flooded streets I was anxious and thought it wise to get going. I had to push them a bit.

At first we were going to hire a cart and a man to carry the equipment. We tried this, strapping the bike and gear on the flatbed, but it was too difficult to push and maneuver in Calcutta's rain swollen streets. I insisted we could ride our bikes. So they helped me carry my bags as we rode them over to the train station in the deep muck. Many times we floundered. Thankfully the rain stopped, leaving overcast skies and very muggy heat. The waters were so deep that each of us carried a couple of bags over our shoulders. Some of the puddles were waist deep. Nieladri had strapped my tent and sleeping bag on the bike rack behind his seat. The traffic and pedestrians, hindered our progress, and I thought we would miss the train. Finally we made it to the train station and waited in a long line. My friends helped me get my seat ticket. It was so fortunate these friends of mine were there to help me. Firstly because the ticket sellers spoke very little english and knowing which train to catch was very confusing. Secondly because they watched my stuff from thieves, who lurked in the station like phantoms in the night.

At 10 minutes to 3pm we ran down through the station with a ticket, but found out that my train could not make it into the station because of the rain. It was about 6 kilometers from town, and we had 10 minutes to get there, through the streets of busy Calcutta. "Follow us," said Nieladri. We rode like fools along the narrow streets of Calcutta, sloshing through puddles and then headed out of the city. We took a few wrong turns and backtracked. Finally we saw the train. It was very long and was preparing to leave! We raced along, carrying my bike and bags along the railroad ties, trying to locate my passenger car. Each car was stuffed with people. Finally we found the car. Once inside, someone had taken my seat and would not give it up. My friends told the man it was my seat, they argued heatedly and finally I was given my seat. Then the train nudged ahead. "My bike!" I said, "We must get it inside here." As the train slowly moved ahead, we carried my bike and gear over railroad ties without tripping. We dragged it inside the train, but the conductor insisted it could not come inside. Ranji walked along with it beside the train outside. "Eric your bike cannot go inside the passenger car!" Nieladri then told me, "You must get a baggage ticket and put it into the baggage car." I did not want to put my bike in a baggage car for fear it would be stolen. I was adamant with the conductor about keeping it with me. My friends argued with him. They sounded like they were speaking 100 words per second. The conductor finally agreed, but still we needed a baggage ticket for the bike. So Ganeesh jumped off the slow moving train and ran back to another car to buy a ticket. He raced back up with the ticket and gave it to the conductor who then approved me to bring the bike inside. "My bike can you bring it to me?" I said to Ranji through the window. My bike was never so manhandled in all its days as it was now. Many hands grabbed it, even strange people on the train and pulled it through the window, where it was disassembled and stuffed neatly under my bed. Ranji pushed one last bag of mine through the window and now everything was inside. As the train slowly moved along these boys had performed a heroic feat. We cheered and shook hands emotionally. The Indian people on the train seemed enthralled by this camaraderie, we said goodbye again, waved, shook hands, and then the train suddenly stopped.

It was very hot inside the passenger car. The boys all came into the passenger car and shook my hand and we said long farewells. "We are friends for life. Someday I hope to see you again," I said to Nieladri. "Yes, I very much would like to be able to go around the world for god," he said. "And it would be my hope to see you again." Nieladri gave a wonderful speech to the passengers nearby that I was on an around the world bike tour and that they might help me out and be kind to me. Then the train nudged ahead. My friends helped me get meal tickets and talked to the conductor to make sure my bags were watched. My ticket was stamped and the train lurched ahead. "Goodbye my friends," I said. Nieladri said, "Goodbye Mr. Eric, you are so lucky to be seeing the world." "Goodbye, god bless ram, ram," I said with my hands in a prayerful angelee. They exited and as the train sped up, Nieladri and Ganeesh ran alongside my car waving and shouting goodbyes until the train was to fast for them to keep up. I watched them fade away still waving. It was the crescendo to my visit in Calcutta.

I sat back in my seat and smiled at the Hindu family across from me. At first they smiled back and asked a few questions. "Where you are from? How much does the bike cost? How much money you are spending?" I answered them frankly though admittedly felt an annoyance. Soon there faces became solemn and serious. They looked at me, stared at me, as if in a trance. Long stares with blank hippopotamus eyes. It would be a long train ride and it was very hot, even with the curtains blowing in the hot breeze as the train chugged westward for Bombay.

I watched the terrain carefully and questioned myself how it would be to cycle across, these hot flatlands and over dry hills. The interior of India looked dry like the terrai. There were constant streams of cars and trucks passing along the road, and people living in squalor conditions and occasionally a nice looking house. The terrain flattened out after crossing some hills. I ate supper and sat back. There was not much to do but write in the journal. I went to bed at about 10pm. The train kept clickety clacking along.

## Thursday June 7

After a restless night on the noisy train, I pulled out my earplugs and was up at about 7am, wondering if anyone could say they truly slept well on this ride. I ate breakfast and looked once again at my fellow occupants and those staring and smileless faces.

Of interest to me was watching the daily sights of India. There were car and truck accidents along the highway. People were walking everywhere, or they were sitting beside tarps or shacks. There was the busy commerce of India. All kinds of goods moving in all kinds of ways, this way and that. I saw dry plains and arid hills and everywhere out in the middle of India, and it was wretchedly hot.

The towns and cities we passed through did not look particularly interesting or scenic. This was mainly an arid land, perhaps good for growing wheat. The cities in the interior was sprawling concrete jungles as India cities are. In one city in which we stopped, the vendors frolicked to the windows selling all kinds of food and wares. They were poor looking and shabbily dressed. One had to be selective of what food one buys, as the potential for getting sick is prevalent.

After many hours of riding, the train began descending down some steep grades and through mountain passes as it neared Bombay. Then the train was back into the city of Bombay and it took a long time to go through all of this city. It finally arrived at the station around midnight.

I unloaded all of my belongings and quickly piled up bike parts and started to put them together. The train station fell quiet at around 2am. I watched the rats run on girders overhead. It was as if they were the late night shift, going to work. I decided to stay in the station and slept sitting up in my seat to protect my stuff. I was hassled by security guards, they wanted me to leave, but I ignored them in order to save a buck.

## Friday June 8

At 5:30am I pedaled sleepily along into the quiet streets of Bombay. It was wonderful to be back here. Bombay looked rather nice and well organized in comparison to other places I'd been in India. I went down to the Gateway to India as the sun rose with some peace and sanity for the moment. The beggars were not yet out, there were few moments like this in India.

I went over to the Salvation Army and got a room and a breakfast and also paid the man $7 and got back my guitar. I then took a long nap until 1pm.

I was getting reorganized in the afternoon and also had to eat with some other travelers. One of the few places I wanted to see in Bombay, was the red light district. I had been told it was really quite a sight to see these sexy Indian women along the roadside. Thus, in the early evening and darkness, I rode out to the peninsula, passing through several areas of fine homes, but never did find the place that was mentioned to me.

## Saturday June 9

It was in the later afternoon, when I headed toward the airport, bought some bike cables and brake pads along the way and mailed post cards and a package of film back home. The bike ride to the airport went past some of the poorest slums in the world. The smell was enough to sicken, the roads rough enough to loose a filling, the heat enough to nearly faint. I got my bike box out of storage at the airport and packed up the bike for airline transport and prepared for the flight to Dacca. It was evening, and with all my bike packed up, I found a place to lay down for a couple of hours to sleep.

# BANGLADESH AND BURMA WITHOUT CYCLING

**Sun June 10**

Up early, I had my stuff ready to go. The flight was boarded at about 7am. The plane took off and flew above the thin layer of clouds over the interior of India. I watched the sunrise over this amazing country and ate a wonderful breakfast on board the DC10. The plane was up for about an hour and then it landed in Dacca, Bangladesh. It was supposed to continue on to Rangoon after only a short while, but I was informed that they would continue tomorrow, because of a problem with the airplane. We would be laidover in a hotel. Hurrah!

The airline transported us in a mini bus to a hotel in the heart of downtown Dacca. Along the way, I met a Frenchman named Frank and he and I would share a hotel room. We had a glorious lunch together courtesy of the airline. Then we went out exploring the streets. This was a big, bustling city, with plenty of motorscooters and bikeshaws.

We went to a big mosque, I took off my shoes and walked right inside. Worshippers were inside praying toward the setting sun (the direction of Mecca). But a crowd of worshipping men kept looking at me and then they approached and gathered around me. One said to me, "You must leave, you are offending my god!" "What do you mean?" I queried very puzzled. "You cannot enter a mosque without covering over your legs. This is a provocation of the Koran to enter gods house like this. Now go!" I was shocked by his rudeness and hastily said, "I'm leaving, but is it not god who made my legs?" "Yes," he said. "Then what god made would not he not be happy to see?" I said it like a smart alek. "They are not to be seen! Now get out!" He said.

The bearded man with a white cap was frothing and pushing me like a farmer shoos a pig. I went at my own pace, which was not fast enough for him. When I got to where my shoes were, these fellows were very aggressive and they escorted me right down the steps away from the mosque. "Never come back!" said a short skinny little fellow with rotten teeth. I left in a huff.

Frank was surprised at my defiance. I was not well versed in how to act in Moslem countries. This had been the most extreme reaction yet. We then went to a soccer game and watched it for awhile, though I was more interested in the beautiful puffy orangish-red cumulus clouds away in the distance, than in the game.

Crossing a street in Dacca was a true challenge. The streets were stuffed with mopeds, trishaws and motorized carts of various kinds. One had to dodge them and the noise alone was paralyzing.

We returned to our hotel and noticed that there were two attractive gals in the room across from ours. They were from Germany. I got up my courage and said hello to them. They were very shy. But soon Frank and I had them in our room where we passed around a joint and rounded up a few beers. Our party consisted of telling stories. I told them the Greek fisherman story and they laughed. It lasted a couple of hours. The gals joined us at supper. We had a marvelous meal again courtesy of the airlines. It was very nice and cool in the air conditioned hotel but miserably hot and humid outside. We ate in a big dining room which was quite vacant except for us.

Our hopes for meeting these gals were dashed as they wanted to get to bed early. Frank and I joked that they were lesbians. He had much to say about those kinds because he'd seen many of them in France.

## Monday June 11

We were up early though feeling stiff from the cool air conditioning. The noise outside was rather quiet. I heard church bells ring and mosque chants. We were taxied to Dacca airport, where, Frank and I each bought a carton of cigarettes and a quart of Johnny Walker Black Scotch to bootleg in Burma. We then boarded the plane.

Soon we took off and were headed to Burma, over the Bangladesh delta where hoards of people are living in reed huts and wading in snake infested paddies. This area covered a long ways. It was incredible to see how spread out the villages were along the delta, yet some of the highest concentrations of people lived there.

It was only about a one and a half hour flight and we were on the ground in Rangoon. The next step was going through customs. The guards all seemed silly, like actors in a spaghetti western. They impounded my bike still in the box, and stuck it behind the customs desk, which was high up, the length of the room and half as high as the ceiling. They gave me a receipt and an assurance that it would be there when I returned in a week. I did not have to pay them anything.

Frank and I took a cab, with our cigarettes and Scotch into Rangoon, instead of selling it to the guards at the airport. We thought we could get a little more money in the city. We then hiked about looking for a place that might buy the stuff. We also looked for a hotel. It was possible to catch a train tomorrow to Mandalay at 5pm. So we bought tickets and then went to the YMCA and met with other travelers.

The guy at the front desk of the YMCA said he would buy our Scotch and cigarettes for a pretty good price. Frank and I thought we should check out the black market and see if we could make a little more.

We went to the city, enjoying the British colonial style of construction and influence on the buildings. Our walk took us to a market, but they did not offer us as good a price for our 'wares' as did the 'YMCA.'

There was a marvelous Buddhist Pagoda here called Shwe-dagon. It was from the 13th century. It had wonderful carved human figures guarding each of the many small pagodas that surrounded the massive temple. Everything was covered in gold. There was a high stuppa with eyes on it, much like that one in Katmandu. Everywhere were the markings and impressions of the Buddha figure. An orangish golden hue was cast upon the temple in the hot, late afternoon sun illuminating the temple to a very beautiful nirvana.

## Tuesday June 12

The day was starting off by talking to other travelers who had been on the road that we are heading toward. They gave us the highlights and Frank and I went to again ask about selling our 'goods.' We finally decided to sell our booze to the YMCA. I attempted to talk to some government officials about riding my bike in the country but they said it was illegal for foreigners to do so.

We bought some food for the train ride and boarded the 1870's vintage steam locomotive at about 4:30pm. The train slowly headed north, puffing a plume of smoke, past many scenes of despair and yet ingenuity. Poor people who lived in all kinds of squalor and conditions were to be seen from the train. There were men walking on 'water stairways' to pump water into fields and there were water buffaloes churning stone mills.

The train rattled along heading northward, perfuming us with its burning coal smell. At around midnight I watched with wonder and interest as we passed a large hilltop Buddhist stuppa that was shaped like a giant Hersheys kiss. It's foil exterior glittered in the moonlight with a bluish twinkling light as it must have been covered with handsized pieces of mirrors. It was enchanting, though the train was very bumpy and the wooden seats were as hard as those I had in my second grade elementary school.

## Wednesday June 13

Our train rocked all night and rest was attempted upon a hard seat. It came to a stop at about 7am in the morning and we were told we had about an hour to goof off, before it would again leave. Frank and I went to stretch our legs and met a Burmese Buddhist that invited us into his home for a cup of tea. The gentleman spoke elegant english and he was very interested in what was happening outside Burma. I told him of President Reagan's reelection campaign and that relations were not that good with the Soviet Union. He told us it was illegal to speak about Burma to foreigners at the risk of being shot, but then he quietly expressed his dislike for his government. We listened to his defiance, but he stopped talking, when some other Burmese people passed. He greatly feared the police, and did not want to further jeopardize himself.

The train ride to Mandalay continued as the steam locomotive chugged up the tracks. The cars were very rustic, with wooden seats like pews in a church. I would hang by one arm out the doorway between cars and catch the breeze to cool off. Frank took my photo as I hung out and looked far ahead at the chugging steamer as it rounded a long bend. We later passed through a graveyard of steam locomotives and it was something from the American wild west days.

The train arrived at Mandalay about noon. It was a dusty city, with not much to see except the locals who were to themselves.

There was a lovely temple called the Queens Palace Pagoda in Mandalay that we explored. Then we rented bicycles and pedaled the long distance along an old water moat in front of Mandalay Hill, which was the seat of power for King Mindon, in the late 1700's. Our rented bikes were typical single speed Indian bike to help us get around this sprawling, dusty town.

The evening meal was a very delicious Chinese style food which had bird eggs in it. This meal was finely prepared and enjoyed.

## Thursday June 14

We were up early and went by taxi to the Irrawaddy River and then boarded a small boat up toward Mingun. On this river tour, we visited a huge Buddhist pagoda. It was supposedly the largest Buddhist temple built in the world. The size of it was impressive, though it looked as if one side of the building had sunk inward or else it was made slightly off kilter. It was built like a step pyramid from bricks and mortar, though they looked like huge blocks the size of a small house. It supposedly had a large cast bell inside, which was the worlds second largest to that in Moscow. There were big cracks along the sides of the building from a devastating earthquake, which ended its construction before it was finished. While we were riding in the long, narrow boat it was adventurous, with a cool spray in our faces, but the suns rays and heat were intense and dried it quickly.

We went back to the hostel, packed up and boarded a small bus to Pagan. It was a bumpy road, and the bus ride was very rough for much of the afternoon. It was terrible even inside the small bus. The road was jarring and dusty, crossing many plains and then traversing jungle countryside. About half way there, we caught a ride on a Jeepney type vehicle with a tarp cover that brought us to the ancient city of Pagan. There were many old Buddhist temples on this expansive flood plain along the Irrawaddy River. It was even said that Marco Polo visited this site in the 1200's.

At Pagan the taxi brought us down a sandy road to a lovely reed house with many small huts surrounding it. Frank and I met other tourists. There were some cute gals from Europe and Canada. We ate some delicious noodles, meat and rice for dinner. It was an enjoyable setting, to be amongst so many other travelers. I shared a room with a couple of other guys. We each had our own bed and mosquito netting.

There were many personalities to engage in here. I talked to people from all ends of the globe. This little village probably had a good slice of the world coming here to visit.

## Friday June 15

The shower and toilet were outside in back of the huts, side by side. It was tricky to use either one without having a member of the opposite sex in the stall next to you. If you wanted to, you could easily look over the top of either one and see the next stall.

It just so happened that I was taking a shower and Frank was seated on the toilet next to me. I noticed down by my feet a huge bullfrog. The frog was not very quick, I picked it up and soon my inspection of him revealed his length as long as my forearm. With Frank, being a Frenchman, who some people called 'Frogs,' I thought it perfect to plop the frog over the top of the stall where it landed perfectly on Franks head and then slid down between his legs. "Ahhhh!" screamed Frank. "What is it?" I asked. "There is a- a- frog-a froggy in here!" he said. "Where is it?" I said letting out a little laugh. "There is a froggy which jumped on my head and it is so very, very big." I could not hold back my guilt much longer and let out a good laugh. "Oh it is you," said Frank. In no time at all the frog came back over the top and landed on my crotch, before hopping away. "I know it was you! You jokester!" Said Frank.

We rode bikes around Pagans dusty roads and visited many temples. There were so many of these yellow sandstone carved temples that it boggled the mind. Some of them were 1500 years old. They were at one time completely painted with a gold covering. There were some temples that looked plain, while others were towering and many were domed with a stuppa to a point. At one time there were 13,000 temples here.

On one big temple Frank and I clambered treacherously up to the top. He was a better climber then I and very brave. I tended to stay back from hanging over the precipice. Not him, he clung to the sides of a narrow ledge and shimmied around the temple.

While up high on this temple, with a view of the Irrawaddy River in the distance, as the sun was moving to the west, we had a wonderful conversation about Buddhisim and Christianity. We saw some similarities between the Buddha and Christ. The Buddha was an Indian, but he looked like an oriental in sculptures. Christ was an Armenian Jew, but he looked like a white man in the paintings. It seems that a religion changes its face as it is accepted in other countries. Frank agreed with me that Christianity's stories were probably exaggerated tales taken from actual events. But on this hot, dry sunny summer day we agreed on the importance of faith. Faith is like the breeze in our face on this hot day, it helps keep one cool.

We again marveled that Marco Polo was a visitor here when Pagan was in its heyday. The great Kublai Khan had invaded Burma and sacked the place, robbing many of it riches.

The river Irrawaddy was very dry on this day, yet Pagan was such a peaceful place, perfect for contemplation and relaxation.

## Saturday June 16th

We headed back for Rangoon via a very slow route. I pooled my money along with a couple of other travelers and we hired a taxi to Myingyan in order to catch a train that would be heading south tomorrow at the very early departure time of about 5am. We stopped in this small forested town in the late afternoon and found a decent restaurant to sit and eat and drink a beer. It was at about 10pm when we walked over to the train station and entered the empty train station and went out on the tarmac and laid out our sleeping bags on a clear star filled night. Our peaceful rest lasted until about 4am when the stationmaster came out and discovered us and made us get up. He scolded us severely and demanded some payment. He wacked me with a stick and we all moved on until someone spoke with him and he let us sit down and be left alone.

The train came at about 7am and we boarded it and headed for Rangoon. The train ride was again a look at this country under transition. With a socialist type of rule running the government, they had censorship and suppression of the press and denials of freedom of speech.

At one station, the train stopped over for a couple of hours. During this time Frank and I walked around the village. We met a very easy going and well educated Burmese man who was a monk. He was about 45 years old. He told us of the hardship of living under this present government. He told us of the denial of human rights. He also told us that he could be arrested if the authorities knew that he was telling us this. He wished we would tell the outside world about this.

It was a pleasure meeting that interesting man, and we ran back to the train and then continued the long ride back to Rangoon. When we got off the train, it seemed so modern and plush in Rangoon compared to where we had just been. Though it is a third world city it has many modern conveniences.

## Sunday June 17th

In the morning, Frank and I went on a taxi ride to visit a famous reclining Buddha called Swe Dagon. Frank and I had a nice chat with the driver. He offered to sell us a joint for 25cents and so we accepted and lit it up, then passed the thing amongst each other while driving along.

The conversation was joyous when we were dropped off at the base of a hill which had a long stairways going up it. Frank was behind me as we started up the steep stair. I was feeling high and hoofing it toward the top. The last step was taken and before me revealed a most puzzling sight. It was a tall, broad, orange, curtain which rose high above me. It reminded me of looking up from the base of a very tall movie theater curtain. I kept looking up and did not understand what I was seeing. Frank came up behind me and then I looked to my left and then upward and there, I saw the eyes of the Buddha peering at me as big as a Volkswagen. What I was standing in front of was the orange robe of the Buddha as he laid before me in a reclining position. This was an awesome sculpture, probably 60 feet long. The undersides of the bottoms of his feet had concentric circles, like fingerprints. There were circles around each of the toes, balls and heels of the feet. The feet alone were about 8 feet long. I was so dazzled by this enormous sculpture and the huge mystery surrounding the meaning of Buddhism, that it, and the dope left me entranced for the rest of the day.

Back in Rangoon, we walked to a food court in a tent complex and found a simple food stall consisting of a picnic table and a cooking wok. They cooked the Chinese style food right there and it came complete with birds eggs in the dish. It was excellent to the taste. We barely had finished eating when a sudden and very heavy rainstorm hit. It poured so hard, that waterfalls were cascading from rooftops and tarps. Suddenly a few of the tent tarps collapsed from the waters weight.

We then visited a gory meat market with all kinds of odd foods that people eat. There were snakes, monkeys, alligators for sale and all were ready to be eaten. The bazaar also had lots of silken fabric for sale and many interesting items to tempt the tourists.

## Monday June 18

Leaving Burma would turn out to be a hassle. I had to go through customs and reclaim my bike. They had stored it and moved it into another location. This took some doing to get it back. I think they wanted to claim it for themselves. After much confusion, and my being adamant, they finally came back with it. Then, when we were going through the checkout line they asked me if I had any chat (Burmese money) left. "No," I said. They let me pass, but then just as we were preparing to exit, the customs agent saw that I had some chat stuffed into my front shirt pocket. "You come with me." He said. He took the money and made me pay a $7 fine. When I went to pay the fine he saw that I had a couple more chat in my wallet and he took that as well. I almost missed the plane because of this and received a stern warning to; "Never come back to Burma again."

The plane we were flying on to Thailand was an old Boeing 707. It was slightly delayed in departure because of a thunderstorm in Bangkok. Finally, at about 5pm the plane took off. We had a bite to eat as the plane ascended up to flight level and we watched a movie.

The descent and approach to Bangkok was made in the evening darkness. It was very windy and the big plane buffeted severely. I could see the long wing flexing up and down like it was made of rubber. It looked like it would separate. The pilot flew lower and began doing a zig zag pattern at about seven thousand feet. It seemed as if he was lost. I could see the lights of villages and towns down below. In one instance, the plane swung sideways with its wings nearly pointing straight up and down from a strong wind. It was pretty scary. He leveled it off. The engines roared and then quieted then roared again. The plane sounded like a rattle trap and the roar of the jet engines was deafening. The winds buffeted the rickety jet and the wings looked loose as if they'd start flapping like those of a goose. I really think the pilot had his hands full on that final approach. Then the engines roared and we climbed up and he swung around. He did a missed approach in Bangkok. On the next try, we finally came in like a mallard duck and the plane shuddered to a stop onto the runway. We were thankfully back on the ground, and now in the country of Thailand.

# Chapter 17

# BANGKOK, THAILAND TO MALAYSIA

**Monday June 18**

I reassembled the bike outside of the Bangkok International Airport Terminal, on the sidewalk under the lights as a few onlookers marveled at all of the gear attached to that skinny frame. Everything was loaded up, including the guitar, strapped to the back, once again a part of my ensemble, making for a very full load.

    At about 10 pm I pedaled away from a small group of onlookers, into the darkness, away from the airport and toward the cities glow off another ten miles to the east, I went about one mile and was very tired and saw a large park or cemetery on the right side, which looked like a free place to sleep and pedaled in for a closer look. I was thinking of setting up my tent but noticed some young people and they saw me. I went over to them and said hello. They spoke a little english and I asked them if it was ok to sleep here. "Ok, you can sleep here," said a young man. The darkness made them look like hoodlums, though they sounded like nice young people who were kind of shy. I was probably interrupting there little party, perhaps that is why they did not want much to do with me. Amongst them was a young Thai lady, who's curvy figure I could make out in the darkness. She had a very nice voice. But, since I could not see their faces and I did not feel right about going back into the park after they knew that I was thinking of staying there, I decided to go, and pedaled toward the city.

    I pedaled down dark streets and felt so tired I nearly fell off the bike. On my left, across the street, I saw a police station and went inside. The man at the desk was not very compassionate, he wanted me to get a hotel, but I said I had little money, and was real tired. After some persuasive haggling of my predicament, he allowed me to sleep in the detectives office. I slept with my head under a desk and my feet sticking out. They checked on me occasionally, but I was so tired I slept through lots of noise and commotion.

## Tuesday June 19

It was around 6:30am when a cop kicked my feet, and said, "Morning sir." He left me a Danish roll and some coffee. I ate it, thanked them, and left.

I pedaled into Bangkok's busy morning traffic and marveled at the throngs of mopeds and buzzing machines. "Could a road hold any more vehicles at once?" I thought. There were beautiful golden temples, with curvey roofs and pagodas reaching up between the squaller and flat topped business centers. This was a busy city, it had all the earmarks of modern congestion, yet those glorious temples made it tranquil and exotic. The temple of Thonburi looked so much like a space ship. It was made in the Khmer style, a Hindu influence and marked with its white, multi tiered construction. The Royal Palace was especially beautiful with ornate roofs and golden spires surrounded by a white gate made of concrete. I spent the morning eating and looking at the boats on the canal and at the temples.

At about noon, I was in the heart of the bustling city and saw some students eating outside of a school on a picnic table and approached them. I asked them if I could buy a lunch in the school and they said yes, then I met more students and an instructor named Laci, who taught english. She invited me to an oriental lunch of chicken stirfry. As I ate, I talked more to her and the students, and she invited me to come visit them again. They had no accommodations for me to stay the night thus my search commenced toward a cheap hotel. I went down by the train station and found a hotel and checked in to it.

My room was up on the third floor, and as I was walking past the lunchroom, a familiar voice caught my attention. I backed up and looked into the room to see Frank, my friend from France, sitting in there. "Hey Frank, bonjour!" I said. "Oui, hello mon ami," responded Frank. We shook hands and sat with other travelers and soon engaged in lively discussions about places to visit in Thailand. The afternoon slipped away in shared discussions about our journeys and the real adventures we held and desired to tell of distant shores.

I went to eat with Frank as the sun was setting and we had a real spicy, yet delicious Thai meal. Afterward, we reentered the dark, muggy heat of Bangkok, and walked down a narrow street, which was surrounded with closed businesses. These lovely Thai ladies approached us and one caressed my arm and made warm advances. They had such beauty and charm. They wanted to know if we would like to 'play' and I felt shy and out of place. We walked a little farther and again these beautiful and shapely ladies came up and asked if there was anything they could do to make us happy. I had never enjoyed this kind of reception in all of my life. This was outright bliss, especially after all the hard traveling through the Mideast and India. To see women so fine and so forward and to be hugged and embrace them was making me feel kingly. I just felt wonderful and euphoric. Frank was enjoying it as well.

We went into a bar where I had a real beauty sit on my lap as Frank laughed. "This is paradise," said Frank adding in his French accent, "You can have any woman here that you want, but for a price." We laughed and listened to their proposals. We were in heaven for awhile but it was short lived. When it was time to pay for the beer, it was expensive, and the girls wanted us to buy them champagne, and everything about them was about money. We were both running low on money and began seeing our desires shrivel as our thrifty sides were showing. Messing around with these ladies would put a drain on our finances.

Our walk back to the hotel included some more ladies approaching us and we teased with them and enticed them right up to the entry to our hotel. We hugged them, but then we had to say goodnight. My economic situation was just too much on my mind to pursue what my pants craved further.

## Wednesday June 20

In the morning I looked around Bangkok for a couple of new bike tires and some other bike parts. This new culture fascinated me. It was such a break from the lunacy of India. I visited the students at the English Speaking University and agreed to come talk to them tomorrow about my journey.

I then went on a tour of a golden, pyramid shaped Buddhist Wat near the river. I also saw the emerald Buddha, which was actually made of jade at the Royal Palace. There was one exquisite Buddhist temple complex with many golden Buddhas that were especially beautiful. I kept thinking how I would like to build something like this or make a sculpture like that. Then it became very obvious, even with tremendous talent and funding, it would be extremely hard to do anything as fabulous as these temples are. I was humbled by their craftsmanship.

There were other Americans to meet, some who were on vacation in Thailand, others who were working here. "Where you headed?" asked one guy from Texas. "To Singapore," I said. "Wholly smokes!" he exclaimed, adding, "That's a long ways, were flying there tomorrow." They were amazed at my story of travel.

Near the river I ate lunch as these crazy looking long boats passed. They had car engines attached to long shafts spinning a little propeller and were hinged to the boat. To see how the pilots maneuvered these boats entertained me. They could spin them around in a circle, but always the pilot was carefully looking out where he stuck that long propeller, as it would be a lethal weapon if not placed appropriately.

The traffic in Bangkok was very noisy and smoky as mopeds and motorcycles made sitting at a red light feel like the start of a motocross race. I got right in there with them on my bike and would pretend to do a wheely and this brought out good laughs and thumbs up from the moped riders. They'd rev their engines and away they'd go at the turn of a green light.

In the dimming light of evening, Frank and I again went out to walk around the Bangkok streets. This time he met a very sweet Thai gal who was from near to Burma. We talked and she told us about the drug smugglers near the Golden Triangle. It sounded like a place to stay clear of, yet held a certain mystique. Frank stayed to talk to her, I went back and wrote down the verses of a song, "I'm a headin for the Burma Triangle, that Golden Pagoda land."

## Thursday June 21

My visit to Bangkok University was made in the morning, where I met with a class of young students. My hostess, Laci, introduced me as "Mr. Eric traveling over the world on a bike," and

I then stood up in front of the class and spoke to the group about my travels. An interpreter translated for them.

My one year journey was condensed into 20 minutes of short stories from each country. Then it was time to sing a song to them, so I chose one from the 1960's called, "Where have all the flowers gone?" The song seemed appropriate because of all the U.S. servicemen who had passed through Bangkok during the Vietnam conflict. The students clapped in rhythm to my twanging guitar and it helped put my nerves at ease and spared them from my squeaky voice. They applauded me and my bike trip, as, "Friendship makers of the world." I answered a few questions, then gave a few autographs and was soon on my way, feeling good to have done this.

A tour was made of the reclining Buddha and it was interesting to see the number of people who waved incense and left fruit before the Buddha, which literally means, "the one who woke up."

I then went to the bike shop and bought new tires for my bike. They cost $1.50 each and were made by the Thailand Bicycle Tire Company. I ate at the school and it was a very low price for a decent meal. One thing that I already noticed was that this city has so much air pollution that my lungs started to hurt.

In the evening Frank and I hit the streets of Bangkok and repeated our teasing of the ladies on the streets. After awhile it becomes ordinary, this delightful reception by these exotic lovelies. I wanted to get as much fun out of it, for as cheap as possible. We had a couple of female escorts walking with us, and both were a little drunk on Thai beer and laughed like fools. Frank jumped up and grabbed a horizontal fire escape ladder, and 'walked hand to hand' until he was dangling high above the street. Our female escorts scorned him to get down. He was in a predicament, until it slowly descended from his weight and he was low enough to let go. The ladies were not amused with our rambunctiousness.

Frank and I said our goodbyes, as he was headed for Chang Mai, in northern Thailand tomorrow.

## Friday June 22

I paid the front desk for my hotel room and packed up the bike outside of the hotel. Soon, my petals were spinning vigorously through the city and past all the rail yards, factories and outskirts of Bangkok. I was destined for Singapore, at the end of the peninsula, 1000 kilometers to the south.

After leaving the busy city I headed west under a baking tropical sun, past homes on stilts and green low swamps to be seen everywhere. I had to cross some flats of rice paddies and it was very windy. I leaned hard into the gale. For some time, I was not real sure if I was even on the right road. Then, after crossing the delta for about 50 miles, I came to an intersection that had one sign with a few numbers. I turned south, at that intersection, still not sure if I was on the right road, but I kept on going south, passing little grass huts with people watching inside color TV's. As poor as the people are here, they had enough money to buy a 20 inch TV and the way they looked engrossed, they were probably watching soap operas.

After about 20k's, I realized I was on the right road, and set a pace and could tell that there definitely was a big difference riding in Thailand than from India. There was not all the wildness and the staring eyes. They gave me more space, more privacy, but still they looked at me and I back at them. Some called out, "hello or ok." Others laughed at me passing by, covering there mouths with the palms of their hands.

A Thai greeting was the most wonderful one yet to be experienced. They put their hands together in a prayerful position, close to their face and tilt forward with a little bow and say "Sawattdeecrap."

This reception was dramatically different from the madness in India. I already felt more personal space and less of that intrusive India stare. Here, there was so much more self respect. Even the bicycle riders stayed to themselves, and did not try to come up beside me, like in India.

Traffic was also much more orderly and therefore headway was going well as I entered the small city called Kao Yoi. It was very busy city and I passed through hoping to make the next city called Phetchaburi before nightfall.

It was around sunset when I arrived in the busy city of Phetchaburi. I criss crossed the city, over some canals and searched for a hotel, but did not have much luck, and then I pedaled over to the police station and asked them if I could be allowed to sleep there for the night. They took me outside and asked me to follow them. We went down about half a block and they showed me a small one room shack, which was right in the median of the road. "You can stay there," said the sergeant in the twilight. Traffic sped past only a foot away on each side of the shack. It did not matter to me, it was free and thus I went inside that little building.

It was dusty and rather dark inside, but there was a roof over my head and it was relatively safe. Also it was the right price. I stuffed my bike into there and then went out to get a bite to eat and came back with some sweets before bedtime in my noisy little home.

As I laid in there, the thought occurred to me, what if a truck crashes through the wall? They zoomed past, shaking the sides. People also walked past, yacking and laughing as I drifted off to sleep.

## Saturday June 23

I thanked my police friends at Petchaburi for the night of 'rest'. One cop spoke a little english and said, "I hope-ah youah havah goodah travelah onah youah bikeah." Soon I was again on the road and heading south.

The green Thai jungle was everywhere interspersed with rice fields and huts scattered wherever there was high ground.

More snakes were seen along the roadside and crossing the road. There were big and little ones and I stayed away from them, not knowing which ones were poisonous. Also lizards, some of a good size ran across the pavement.

At a water stop, I filled up my water bottles from a pump and the villagers moved in closer to see me. They were very orderly and gave me the angeli greeting of Thailand. One man asked me where I was going. "To Singapore," I said. He stepped back dumb founded saying. "Singapore very far, you cannot go on bike, take bus."

I passed through a lovely town called Hua Hin and enjoyed the views of the sea. This town is 118 miles south of Bangkok.

The roads were paved with a large aggregate and therefore felt rough under my thin tires. I made good progress and enjoyed the friendly faces and saw nice looking gals in addition to rambunctious children.

I had traveled about 60 miles and at 4pm saw many young people by a school house sitting and chatting. Some of the girls were real cute. I went up and asked a guy if he knew where I could stay. "Stay here tonight," said this chubby, relaxed Thai fellow. He offered me a cold whiskey and coke and then a smoke of marijuana. We sat to talk at a picnic table next to a school. I took a puff. "Do you want this gal for tonight?" he asked me. "Sure," I said, and l looked at the pretty 18 year old Thai gal in her silky red shirt. "You like me?" she asked. "Yes," I said, not really thinking that anything would come of this. "You stay here tonight?" asked the fellow. "Yes, ok I sleep here," I replied. "Then you can enjoy her at 10 o clock. She will come looking for you. What room you in?" I dashed into the school house and saw room 210 and then went back to tell him. I was a little apprehensive about all of this but excited. "Ok room 210," he acknowledged. They departed and my thoughts were, all right, that girl was ultra fine, I got ready to meet her tonight.

I went up to the third floor of the empty concrete schoolhouse and cooked my supper on a veranda. I washed up, put some cologne on and prepared a bed, beside a teachers desk for my nights sleep. As night settled in there was a gathering of more and more people down in the courtyard. I watched from the balcony as they set up a stage. At dark, they started a presentation of dance and music. Soon the courtyard was full of people. They were dancing and singing and I listened and many people saw me, though nobody seemed to care. This must have been a high school graduation dance. I noticed that they had to pay money to get in. People were dancing and listening to the loud music. For me it was free entertainment, but it was real loud. The night wore on and several times I had to hide from security personnel. I hung around the second floor veranda until well after 10 'o' clock had passed. They even had fireworks shoot up into the sky! The young gal with the red dress never appeared, though by now she greatly entertained my thoughts. Then I remembered that I said room 210, not 310. I went to bed lonely and disgusted with myself. The bedroll was laid out behind the teachers desk and it was there that the night was slept.

## Sunday June 24th

In the morning, I quietly snuck out of the schoolhouse, as a janitor looked puzzled at me while I rolled away and headed down the road.

Not to far down the road was a Christian church that I passed as many worshippers were dressed nicely on there way to service. I kind of wished I'd stayed there for the night, to see how Christians act in this part of the world. My thoughts revolved around religion, which path to choose or what god is greater. How Buddhism offers its golden statue of a meditating man and how Christ is hanging on a cross and how we have such creative faiths in the world. Yet which one is right? The Hindus and Moslems would all love to enter this discussion, I felt like I was a neutral observer, heading into a new realm of discovery.

There were many snakes along the road on this day. They especially were active in the morning, before the sun heated up. On one fast downhill, I could not avoid a huge snake and ran over its midsection. Instinctively, I lifted my legs up high as the snakes head swung up to strike. It struck its head against my left rear pannier. For a moment, it dragged along with me, its fangs stuck to my pack, wriggling and churning. I was horrified, though kept my cool. I maintained control of the bike, keeping my leg away from the snake and it fell off.

Around midmorning I stopped to take a leak and heard a loud, peercing, screeching sound. I looked down to see near my stream, a big green snake devouring a screaming green lizard. God, there were snakes everywhere.

There were many rubber tree plantations lining both sides of the road. It took me a little while before figuring out what these ornate tree plantations were. When one looks down a row of rubber trees, they have an arch like shape. I finally stopped and walked up to a rubber tree, which was dripping a white latex into a bucket. It was kind of sticky, it smelled bad and soon dried to a film on whatever it was applied.

The afternoon heated up to around 90 degrees and was very humid so it was a problem keeping cool and drinking enough. There were fruit stands along the road and tea stalls in addition to some cool drinks. Tea was what I drank mostly, though it badly stained and clogged my water bottles.

I made way after 60 miles of jungle and took a sideroad down to Prachaup Khiri Khan. The town was located next to the Gulf of Siam and there it's known for a long stairway up to the top of a hill located on the north side of this quaint setting. I hiked up there and saw many monkeys enveloping a temple. The view from on top of this high overlook was pleasant of beaches and sea as well as enjoying the nice breeze. It was possible to see the hills of Burma off to the west, as it was only about 10 miles away.

A church was my first choice of accommodations but the door was locked. I also tried the police station but they could not help me. The railway station had some rooms but I did not want to spend any money, even thought they were very inexpensive.

I decided to camp near to the monkeys, as there was a level spot for my tent, but a fellow came along and told me it was not wise and he showed me where there was a cheap hotel. It was back at the railway station. I went in there and looked around. It was very smokey and loud in that tiny hotel room. It was also hot. I could not stand it.

I told the man at the front desk about my economic situation and he said he would watch my guitar for the night. I could pick it up in the morning. I left some things with him and took the bike and tent and went to this small park as night was falling. I put up my tent and got inside. It was a nice evening, and while I was concerned about being ripped off, I slept pretty well, listening to the train whistles blow.

## Monday June 25

As the sun rose, I pedaled down to the temple and walked up to the 412 stairs to the top of Mirror Hill, which is actually called Khao Chong Krajak, to once again see the monkeys and watch the sunrise over the ocean. The hill had a Buddhist stupa at the top. It was so peaceful in the morning. Along the side of the hill is a hole, which one can see through to the other side and thus this was how the name came to be.

I went back to the hotel, paid $.50 and picked up my guitar and stuff. My muscles were aching from the previous days ride as I mounted the bike and headed away from town to the main road about five miles westward and all uphill. This brought about some groans from me, but upon reaching the intersection, the sun was shining hot and there were pleasant green fields all around to lighten my spirit. It was about 11am, when I took off my shirt and had a bite to eat while enjoying the green beauty, which reminded me of summertime back home. I was again heading south, on a pleasant ride that skirted along the jungle and sea.

I had a good tailwind and was cruising downhill when I saw a large dog sitting like the Sphinx on the roadside. As I passed it, I could see that it was bloated and dead. Flies were buzzing around the head of the Doberman and it smelled awful. Why did somebody do this and what did it mean? There was not a very good relationship between man and dogs in many Asian countries. They think the dog is a reincarnated bad person, and a baby is a reincarnated good person. That is why they kick dogs.

While going down a long grade, my front tire began to bump. It became more frequent and then suddenly I could see a large swell appearing on the tire. I was trying to come to a stop, as a tear in the middle of the tire had split wide open and the inner tube was pushing through the bulge, as if the tire was giving birth. It looked like it was alive! I tried to stop as quick as possible, but I was going too fast. When I did finally stop, I was about to hop off the bike to let the air out and reach for the air valve, but the inner tube rapidly pushed through the opening and the tube blew apart. "Kerpaaoww!" It sounded like that of a shotgun. The bike shuttered, my ears rang. The tire was blown wide open.

I saw a group of people come running from a village to my left. Others came running up to the road screaming and shouting and wondering what had happened. A bunch of children came toward me and they all watched as I pushed the bike off of the road with the tire going 'floppity flop.' I pushed it up to near a house, where changing the tire was commenced. A very big crowd soon gathered to watch me change the tube. One little boy asked, "Hey mister, who are you?" "I am Elvis!" I said, and the kids laughed and called out, "Elvis, Elvis." Young boys were laughing and pointing at me, as the heat increased from such a crowd.

Getting the patch to stick to the tube was giving me a lot grief. "Let me help you," said a young boy. He put glue on the tube and then on the patch and then let it air dry. He blew onto the patch. Then, he stuck the two together and it made a great repair. Up until this time I was always putting the patch on with the glue wet. I'd probably patched 100 punctures <u>wrong</u> in this past years time! I gave my thanks to this little boy.

Patting a child on the head is a definite no-no in Thailand. I learned this after having a cold drink and touching a little boy. His mother gave me a real 'dirty look' and I caught on.

To point at someone is also considered bad manners. While seated, a foot must not point toward another person, else the Thai's think it is like a curse which has been placed upon them. The foot must always be aimed at a wall or else be kept flat on the ground. This is something I noticed over and again. I learned this as I sat crossing my legs, and discovered people were annoyed at my foot pointing, and thus I corrected this by not doing it anymore.

An afternoon rain shower in the jungle caused the road to become slippery. While going around a curve on a downhill, I slid and laid the bike down upon its side, hurting my rear end, more than anything else.

The afternoon heated up to around 90 degrees and was very humid so it was a problem keeping cool and drinking enough. I would sometimes find well pumps along the road which had clean water that was safe to drink.

I went over several hills and upon one was followed closely by two fellows on a single motorcycle. It was a light rain, and very warm out as I was cresting a muddy hill. They came alongside of me and said something. I looked to see the passenger holding a handbag at arms length out toward me. Either he wanted me to stop or he was aiming something. We crested the hilltop and spontaneously. I bore down on the pedals and just took off, pedaling like a madman. I blazed down the rough, sloppy, muddy road like a motocross racer. They closely followed. I flew over potholes and slid around corners and hoofed it across the flats. The motorcycle dropped back and then about a half mile later it turned off. Perhaps they thought,

"If he was that tough to catch on a bicycle, just imagine what he'd be like off of it."

It was getting late, and I had to get off the main road before dark. I came to a police roadblock and stopped to talk to them about someplace that I might be able to spend the night. They said I could sleep in the, "Little house over there." I went over there and looked into the little house. It was only about 6 x 4 feet. There was a bed with a big spider hanging from the ceiling overhead. "First you got to go," I said using a broom to move out the spider. I cleaned and inspected the room as best that I could. I ate some bananas and rice and listened to the pouring rain.

It was hot in that little house and when I opened the shutters of the only window in there, a big green snake suddenly swung off the roof and dangled in front of my face. It attempted to swing into my room. There was about two feet of snake hanging there and god knows what else was on the roof. I dodged to one side and then the other and slammed the shutters into his flickering red tongue. No sooner was I done with the snake when this big buzzing insect took off from the ceiling and wanted to get out of the house. I was damned if I would open those shutters again. "Let's have it out with the broom," I said to him and squashed it with a broom.

After that excitement, nature was calling, and thus in the pouring rain I made a mad dash in the pitch black night for the toilet. The toilet was worse than my 'little house'. The night was so dark that my flashlight worked overtime to cut through the ink. Once back at the little house I inspected every nook and cranny for guests and then laid on top of a sheet in the steamy heat. Not an hour had passed when bedbugs made me twitch and jump! I fixed them by covering my body with Ben Gay. Creeping things later awakened me in the night, yet I was so tired it did not matter. The rain fell outside so loud that it sounded like a passing jet. At least I was dry. *At least.*

## Tuesday June 26th

The rain had stopped around 3am and it became very muggy. The day dawned warm and sunny. "How- you- like- sleep- in- little- house?" said the roadblock guard smiling between steel capped teeth. "Big snake!" I said. He laughed and I thanked him and was off.

It started to rain and soon the road became a dirt track. I was riding in a slurry of mud that sprayed up on me. I had been warned to be careful in the south of Thailand as there are bandits which stop foreigners and will rob them at gunpoint.

The road was paved once again and soon my gear dried out under the midday sun, though I smelled rotten. There were many snakes along the road on this day. They would slither across the road and I swerved to avoid them and saw a few really big and long ones along the roadside. I dreaded the thought of getting a flat tire for changing it on the roadside would be unerving.

The sounds of insects was especially noticeable in Thaliland. The cicadas were loud and crickets and flying bugs. The bird sounds were just amazing. It was like being in song bird paradise.

I was feeling the heat of the day and from my effort was feeling exhausted and only eating rice and noodles the lack of energy and wishing for a restful place to sleep the night.

I had traveled at a steady pace and went around 50 miles and entered Chumphon and looked around for places to stay. There was a Buddhist temple along a busy street and I was feeling exhausted, I asked the elderly abbot if I could stay the night. He said I could. Another monk with glasses was appointed to provide help for me. Monks do not eat dinner, only one big meal before sunrise, so I stepped out for a bite to eat.

When I came back I had a sense that my escort monk did not approve of my behavior. I shrugged it off. This temple had many young men, perhaps thirty of them who were aspiring monks. They were dressed in orange robes and there heads were shaved bald. It surprised me that some of them smoked cigarettes. Inside there was a sanctuary with a glass room in the middle for quiet isolation and discussion. The escort monk invited me up to his office where he wanted to see my passport. He asked me how much money I had. I would not tell him, saying only, "Not very much money." He wanted me to show him a U.S. dollar. I showed him one. He looked at my passport but when it came to looking at my traveler's checks I dodged the issue. At one point he wanted to keep or trade me for my passport. I finally got it back from him. He acted weird and wanted more from me, but I was resistant.

I was allowed to sleep in his room but when I laid down he played loud music and then got faggoty towards me. He wanted to lay by me and put his arm over me and I did not like that. I got up and went to sleep in the 'glass room', which was made for quiet meditation. This made him very irritated. He came down and wanted money from me for staying here for the night. Then he wanted my passport. I told him, "You are a Buddhist monk and you only talk of money and sex? I think there is something wrong with you! Now get out!" I really got mad and my nostrils flared and eye bulged and he finally left. I could not sleep from then on, because one eye was kept open in case he came back. Even my buck knife was at the ready. I got up early and left after saying a hasty thanks to the head abbot, who did not know this had happened.

## Wednesday June 27

I headed down the road very disappointed in the Buddhist monks. I was very tired after a sleepless night.

The ride went well all 60 miles to Surat Thani. I strode into the city noting a canal in the middle and looked around the quaint city. I continued to the ferry dock for going to Ko Samui. I thought the ride was only about 10 kilometers to the pier where the ferry departs for Ko Sumui. I searched Surat Thani for a place to stay and considered the Buddhist temple. This was a decision not to be taken lightly. What had happened last night was a dark spot on my impression of Buddhists. Would I always feel this way toward them because of this? I decided to be fair and try again, hoping that I would not hold malice toward monks for the rest of my life.

The head abbot at the temple seemed very straightforward and sincere and he warmly welcomed me into his wishan to stay the night. I was shown my own bedroom which was made with real nice woodwork and had mosquito curtains surrounding the bed. The abbot must have caught wind of me because right away he showed me where the shower was. Afterward we had a talk about my travels, as the suns golden illuminated the room, alighting his orange rob and the bamboo curtains. He was very impressed with the journey I had been on. I needed to eat or else faint, so I walked to town and got a supper of rice with a spicy hot stir fry.

I returned to the temple and had a nice talk with the monks. "You are very brave," said one bald fellow with a strong build. "How do you find Thailand?" I answered the questions honestly,

"I like it here very much," and enlightened them with my travel experiences. They accepted me as a unique tourist. "You are not like most of them who come here," said the wise old monk.

In the evening, I sat around with the young monks and played guitar and sang. They really liked doing that. They also sang a song or two. We talked about U.S.A. and Reagan. They joked about having a drink of beer and smoking marijuana, but did not partake in it. We played a game of thumb fighting and all of the monks tried to outdo me. It was an enjoyable evening meeting with these joyful fellows.

I was so tired at 11pm and went to bed under a mosquito netting.

## Thursday June 28

I was up early to go through devotions and to eat with the monks. There was a genuineness on how they treated me. I was accepted as a unique person on a personal journey, an enriching experience and they recognized that element in me.

We all sat on the floor before the the teaching monk, who was seated in a yogic position, much like how the Buddha sits. He spoke in Thai, but interjected english words to help me understand. I heard him say, "Deep compassion" and "inner calm" and "suffering is ended when desire is no more." There was a young monk who was from California, and he seemed very educated in the Buddhist principles, a natural leader, a well poised individual. He knew all of the procedures and treated everyone well. The headmaster was also very nice and thoughtful. He was my image of a true Buddhist, honest, deep in compassion, heartful and sincere.

We were brought food, by people from the village and it was set before us. There then was a final prayer and we were allowed to eat. I had a great choice of cuisine to dine on. There was stir fry, fried rice with eggs and yogurt dishes. Ice coffee was served and we all had an enjoyable meal. They only have this one meal each day, and so it is a feast for some, but most of the monks looked lean, as if they starved themselves.

We took photos together outside, with a Buddha statue in the background. I thanked them, then I pedaled onward and it was more like 35 miles to Don Sak. There was one point on this journey when the road was full of monkeys running across it. I steered clear of them and kept on going.

I was very wary along my ride and was told by a tourist that the boat would not be leaving until noon. I had to go another 10k's to a dock. We wished each other well and I was off.

I pedaled about 10k's to the dock and got on board a boat for Ko Sumui. It was a pleasant ride across the sea of about an hour over a slightly choppy sea. Some people got sick. I disembarked at a little tin roofed village called Na Thon and shopped around to pick up a few last minute items.

I pedaled about 12 miles to get to the resort area of Lamai and looked around the beach area and searched for a hut. This was where the bike was especially handy, as I could go quickly along this large area to compare places. I found a nice little hut, for .50 cents per night called Sunset near the ocean where there protruded a large rock formation. I explored this tropical paradise, which was teeming with western tourists.

I ate coconut, which was accomplished by most tryingly knocking one off a tree by throwing a big rock. The real danger is when these objects fall. You do not want to get hit on the head by a coconut, nor by a rock. I finally got a coconut, without hurting myself, but that was only the beginning of the job. Cutting open the husk of a coconut is hard work, especially with only a pocket knife.

It was a peaceful night, enjoying the sound of the surf and strumming my guitar.

## Friday June 29

The morning was spent trying to make my own coconut candy and coconut with rice. It was not a successful cooking experience. I began to feel ill from eating too much coconut.

Lunch was enjoyed at the open-air restaurant where I ate Chinese food. I walked back to my hut, enjoying the fine sandy beach, the aqua colored sea, the graceful palms hanging toward the ocean and went snorkeling in the clear seas. It was worth spending lots of time in the water, as the tropical fish here were so beautiful. It is a fantasy world under the sea.

While I swam, what surprised me were the many Thai tourists who would walk up and pose for photos before this strange looking rock formation. My first impression of the rock was that it looked phallic. But it surprised me that these Thai's would come in by the busloads, pass by my hut and pose for a photo in front of the rock. I later learned it is called Grandfather Rock or Hin Tau in Thai. There was also nearby a grandmother rock called Hin Yau. Both relish a suggestion of virile prosperity, and the Thai's loved it.

That night I went to eat supper as the sun set and it was so pleasant. I met two gals, Judy and Claire from San Francisco and later we danced, as the music played. They both seemed interested in me. I discovered Claire a little warmer than Judy and we got along well.

Under a starlit sky, Claire and I walked the beach over to her place, which turned out to be next to mine. "I heard you singing last night," she exclaimed. In the dark of night, I led her over to point out the phallic looking rock and told her about the busloads of Thais that come to see it. She said, "I was wondering what they were looking at." We laughed at this huge erection and sat down before it, on this beautiful night, under the twinkling stars. Not long had passed before we too were embracing our youth and sharing our vigor. The rock worked!

## Saturday June 30

To think that it had been one year since my journey began. Here I was, spending the night in paradise, doing paradise things. It was the start of another beautiful day. I said goodbye for now to Claire and went out searching for coconuts, and did some more snorkeling. This was the most beautiful place to snorkel. The underwater world was alive with color and exotic fish. It was an entirely unique realm to explore.

After lunch, I was walking down the path from the restaurant to my hut and noticed Judy, was sitting on her veranda. I said hello to her. She smiled but was speechless and even said, "I can't talk too you right now." I thought that it was strange.

Later, Claire told me that Judy had eaten an omelette with magic mushrooms. That explained why she was speechless when I walked past her hut. At least she was smiling.

At the restaurant I dined with an Englishman who invited me to join him, as he ordered a big fish for supper. The waiter came waltzing out with this big baked fish laid out on the garnished plate. It looked like it was still alive. It had a red pepper in its mouth, otherwise I would have sworn it would jump off the plate and flap back into the sea. "Try the bloody thing," he would say to me adding, "it's bloody delicious." Finally I did try a morsel and he was right. It was the most delicious cooked fish I had ever had!

As I walked the beach back to my hut, I looked up at the night sky. Before me was spread out the Milky Way, like I had never seen it before. Directly above me was Sagitarius, with the stars of Centauris to the right and the Southern Cross. To the east was Cygnus and Cassiopea. It was a stunning view of the night sky. The light from the Milky Way was so bright it illuminated my palm. The stars at night were well worth seeing as the Sagittarius section of the Milky Way laid overhead and the entire band of our galaxy stretched from horizon to horizon across the sky. What a treasure to see this viewpoint of our galaxy from these the southern skies.

## Sunday July 1st

I saw my lady friend at breakfast and she told me that she had waited for me to come see her last night. I rather regretted not doing so. She told me she and her friend were leaving tomorrow. She wanted to know if I wanted to do mushrooms with her. I declined her offer.

After lunch I again met Claire and we went into her hut and enjoyed an afternoon romp. She was risqué and I was long on the trail, hungry for this, besides she had a shower in her hut, which made for a much desired bath.

I took a bike ride up to the river, as it allured my curiosity to find its source. I hiked upstream.

While hiking cautiously through the jungle a long, black creature dashed away from me. It was a giant monitor lizard. I grabbed a rock and snuck up on it, then clambered up a high boulder above the gushing stream and looked down below me. There it was, this big black lizard, with specks. He could not hear me, for the stream drowned out my noise. I thought, how glorious it would be to have the skin of such a big lizard. I carefully aimed and tossed the rock but missed. He darted off, at first leaping toward me, then running like a prancing horse in the most interesting fashion over rocks and blasting across water to disappear into the jungle. On my walk back down along the stream I had visions of being gobbled up by that lizard.

Back at the hut I met the most curious of traveler. He was full of questions about my journey. He came from Holland. I played guitar. Claire was doing mushrooms. I walked to the restaurant.

## Monday July 2$^{nd}$

When the light of the morning sun was rising high above the horizon, I decided to move to a different location and pedaled over to check out the huts at Lamai Beach. There was one cute little hut which was available with an ocean front view of the bay and the big beach. I hurried back to my hut, packed up my stuff and was ready to pedal off, when I saw Claire step outside and stretch. She said she had a memorable night of hallucinating and was now coming down off of the mushrooms. She said she did not sleep well, but she and Judy had one observation last night, "Grandpa Rock was a lot bigger when we were high on mushrooms!"

I said goodbye to Claire. I was sad to see our meeting come to an end, but we wished each other well, hugged and went our separate ways.

Rushing over to Lamai, I checked into the hut that I wanted. This was kind of a sad morning, and I was feeling a little down with Claire leaving.

The sea was very pretty, the color of aqua blue green in front of this wide shallow stretch of beach. The sun was very high at noon, and my hut was hot, so I took to the ocean and played in the sea water.

There was a bookstore on Lamai that had an outstanding collection of books to be rented for a dollar. I saw a Triston Jones book and was very desirous of reading it. I thought the price was $1 was too outrageous and so stuffed the book into my shoulder bag. I went to my hut and felt very guilty about what I did. Why do I have this tendency to steal? Where did this thievery come from? I somehow knew that everybody knew that I was dirt because I did this. I was a thief! I wanted to return the book and apologize, but did not have the guts.

The afternoon was spent reading, swimming, talking to travelers, making coconut food and lazing about. Of course it gave me the Thai Revenge as too much coconut can do.

In the evening I walked over to the restaurant and ate.

## Tuesday July 3

It was an excellent big stretch of sandy beach in front of my hut, but it was a lousy hut. There were fleas inside of it. I spent the morning trying to finish the Triston Jones book. Checkout time for my hut was at noon.

My gear was all loaded up onto the bike and I moved over to Chawang. These huts were located far from the beach, which I did not like, but the beach was pretty, with a nice view of a small island in front of the bay.

The waves would crash hard into the beach in the afternoon hours. It was invigorating water to swim in. There was a nice pounding surf which provided for some enjoyable body surfing from waves off the South China Sea.

There were gals from Sweden, Norway, Finland and Denmark staying here. I thought of them as the 'snobby' but beautiful Scandinavian girls. I had a nice discussion with the Swedish girl about my last name being Norland and that there is an area called the same in the middle part of Sweden. This is possibly where my ancestors came from.

There were many monkeys roaming around Chawang. These monkey were loads of fun.

One especially was curious of me and it would climb on my back. Then in one moment it swung from my hair and grabbed me by the balls. This hurt dearly, but was entering to some onlooker.

The monkeys had a lot of fun spinning the petals on my bike. They would grab whatever they could and run with it. I saw one grab a Frenchmens hat and run up the tree with it.

## Wednesday July 4

I was on my way to leave Ko Sumui in the late morning, but after passing the giant Big Buddha statue located on top of a bluff, surrounded with huts that were overlooking the sea, it started to rain. I had a couple of flat tires, and rode on in the rain and returned back to the pier to find the ship would not leave until tomorrow. I searched Na Thon for a cheap hotel but none caught my budget. I went over to the Catholic Church and talked to the father who was surprisingly compassionate and allowed me to stay the night for free. He was a very nice elderly fellow around 65 years old. He told me, "Not many travelers stop in anymore to ask for free lodging. They'd rather

go down and smoke there marijuana or eat mushrooms and pay for a hut." He was amazingly insightful. I stayed the night in my own room and listened to the hard rain pattering on the metal roof.

## Thursday July 5

I was offered breakfast with the father and we sat to eat French toast. He was an Irish born white man, who had come to Ko Samui 10 years earlier to help the church. It was a culture shock for him he admitted, but he always liked the Thai people and they treated him kindly. He had good things to say about the Buddhists, other than that they, 'have no god.' After an enjoyable breakfast, I thanked him and was off heading to catch the ferry.

I left in the morning, feeling the heat, pedaling south, realizing I was getting thin. It was fairly flat countryside.

I caught the ferry at about noon and it was a rough ride back and several people hung over the railing. Once back on the mainland, my pedaling commenced southward to Nakhon Si Thammarat, which was about 75 miles to the south.

While pedaling slowly through Sichon, along the busy main street, I was on the left side, heading south. I stopped at a red light and was waiting for it to turn green. Suddenly I felt this sharp pain on my left leg. I looked down and saw a small, white, one eyed dog hanging from the flesh of my leg. I kicked him off and stopped to curse at the little bugger, but the rascal lunged at me once again. I dropped the bike and chased the dastardly white mongrel while loading my yak horn slingshot with a stone. The first shot hit the creature in the rear end. It yelped and then ducked into a little factory, which was busy with workmen using machine presses and drills. The Thai employees had no idea what was going on as I chased that mongrel back and forth. It ran beside a big press and was cornered. I had the dog in my sights and it knew it! There was no escape. I was going to put out the other eye of this little mutt! I aimed, pulled back the rubber and let go a powerful shot. My rock went abruptly upward at an angle, straight toward a second story window where the manager of the company was sitting at a typewriter. "Clank!" Hit my stone against the glass. It did not break the glass window, thank god. But the manager jumped up, gave me a fist and was shouting in Thai at the top of his lungs. Then he stepped out of his office and said, "What da hell da matter you? You crazy or what?" The dog slumped as if to give a sigh of relief, then immediately shot up and ran off. The workmen all stopped what they were doing and several of them smiled while gesturing with thumbs up. One even said, "OK-Rambo!" I said, "Sorry," and turned tail like the dog did, hopped on the bike and got the hell out of there before the police came.

As I exited the city of Sichon, with my leg bleeding, from the dog bite, I thought about the Buddhist monks. What would they have thought of my actions? Would they have turned the other cheek and forgiven the dog for biting a leg? What would the Buddha have done? I hoped that they did not see me. They had congratulated me for being a peace maker of the world. Now what might they think of my actions after warring with a dog?

I headed south and then east for Naknon Si Thammarat. The day was getting late when I spotted a Buddhist temple and stopped in to ask the wise thirty-five year old monk if I might spend the night with them. "Sure, you can stay here," he said. I entered the compound and talked to several young monks. They liked my bike and were very interested in me. I was given a cold drink, and had a wash. Around 8pm several monks came into my room and we sat on the floor talking as best we could about life. It was a pretty typical conversation, "American girls are beautiful and you have free sex?" "How much money you can make in American?" After answering that I was asked to play a song on the guitar. I did Country Roads and this improved the atmosphere. We all sang and they clapped, as I strummed. I played another song and then handed the guitar to a muscular and good-looking monk. He and I got along wonderfully. Our fellowship was not conversational, since we could hardly talk to each other, moreso it was comradery, we were the same age and shared a similar spirit. It was as if we had been friends for many years. Around 11pm they had had enough and bowed to me and prayerfully gestured to me a good night. I then had the room to myself.

## Friday July 6

In the morning, it was still dark when I was awakened for alms and then food. We entered a long, narrow room and the monks all sat in a row, on a platform in typical Buddhist fashion, sitting with legs crossed. I was seated on the floor, facing them along with about twenty five other monks. Peasants walked in with food and laid it out at the monks feet until the room was filled with the aroma of Thai cooking. As the head abbot spoke and blessed the food in eloquent Thai, I looked at the many foodstuffs laid out. There were many rice like dishes, curries, fruits, but also to my surprise cinnamon rolls! God how I craved those!

All the monks were given bowls and they dished out their meals and began to eat. They had not finished eating when we spectators were allowed to take a bowl and select our dishes. It seemed strange to be selecting food from below the monks feet. It was also strange to eat supper time foods this early in the morning. My cinnamon roll was kind of a letdown, as it was made of cardamom, not what I expected.

After the monks had all devoured their only days meal, most of them were bloated and lethargic, holding their orange gowns around the belly as if to suggest they were stuffed. Yet my friends stayed with me until I left. They were fascinated with my freedom, my traveling bike and my adventurous lifestyle. "Singapore too far to go on bike," said one monk. "You get very tired. Maybe dead, I hope not"

We posed and took a photo together outside of their temple with a golden Buddha in the background. We had a very warm goodbye with our hands in prayerful postures and saying, "Sawatdeecraap."

I had not ridden to many miles when I noticed a most beautiful temple and chedi. The temple was called Wat Phra Mahathat. It was about 1000 years old. I toured the complex and was informed that the white chedi had a solid gold spire on top that weighed hundreds of pounds. There were magnificent statues of the Buddha within the temples. I was most impressed with the graceful architecture of the temple and its elegant curving roof.

The ride south took me along the coast on a fabulous sunny day that was very pleasant next to the sea. I pedaled for many miles down along a beautiful stretch of road, next to the South China Sea.

I rode along until about 4pm and saw a church. I went into the Catholic Church and asked the father, who was about 40 years of age, with dark hair and was from a European country if it was ok if I stayed the night. I went into the courtyard and asked the father if I might seek shelter there for the night. He was at first questioning me but then he said yes. I was shown a room. The father invited me to come and eat some food with him for supper. He told me he had spent time visiting in the U.S. He acted sort of fresh with me, or maybe I thought so. He was just that kind of priest, with an air of love and friendship. I stayed up in the second floor, with a very hard rain lasting most of the night.

## Saturday July 7th

I had a very nice breakfast with the father. The father gave me some kind of feeling like I was an intruder, but this could have just been his way of showing care for me. He admitted to feeling isolated here in this part of Thailand. He had been here for a couple of years. We talked about the spread of Islam in Malaysia and how he felt he was loosing the battle against converting to Christ.

I left in the morning, feeling the heat, pedaling south, realizing I was getting thin. It was fairly flat countryside.

I came to a spot where I had to catch a ferry across to Songkla. There was a wonderful mermaid sculpture along the waterfront.

I passed through the city and then continued on to Hat Yai. I thought of it as a big, polluted Thai city and chose to pass through it. I stopped to eat lunch and met some very nice young peaople. They bought me a cold drink and wanted me to stay with them. I was eager to get going, but they were so nice. We talked a long while and sipped on a cold refreshing ice coffee. even though it was getting late.

I left the big industrial city amazed at these kind hearts and continued on down the road and entered a very small town, outside of Hat Yai called Phru. There was a fire station in town and I asked the fireman if I could spend the night camping in the yard. He invited me in and though he did not speak alot of english we had a wonderful visit. I was fed supper and had a cold pop. We sat to watch television and only one emergency occurred on this evening. It happened around 2am when the alarm sounded and the men all jumped out of bed and ran off. The trucks roared to life and sped away. I was glad to be able to sleep. The men returned a couple of hours later, making some noise as they entered, then going to sleep. In all I slept on a bunkbed very soundly.

## Sunday July 8

In the morning my fireman host told me I was not far from the Malaysian border and he greeted me warmly and wished me farewell. I was very thankful for his kindness. It was a wonderful way to conclude my visit with the nice folks of Thailand.

On this overcast morning it was very humid as I progressed toward the heavily treed border of Malaysia. There was a checkpoint with Thai guards, who inspected my passport and then allowed me to enter the no mans land between these two countries. There has long been a border conflict between Malaysia and Thailand. Now this buffer zone was peaceful except for scattered sightings of troops.

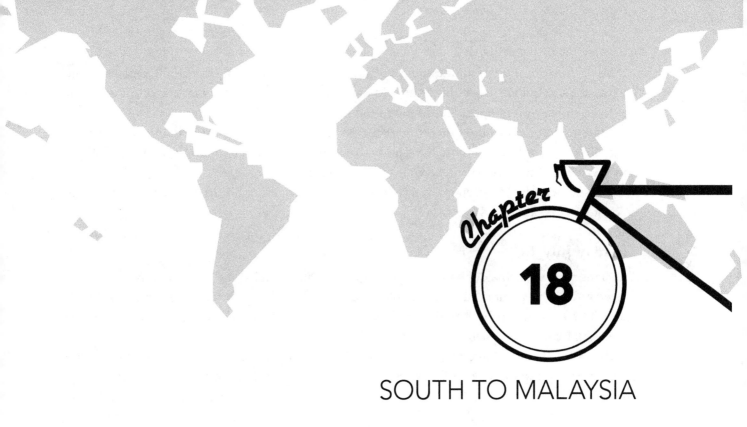

# Chapter 18

## SOUTH TO MALAYSIA

After about 5 kilometers of travel I arrived at a very informal Malaysia border. The customs agents looked slightly at my bike and stamped my passport and I was on my way. The first thing I noticed was the change of language and the observation that more people spoke english. I spent some time browsing in shops and enjoyed seeing more high tech products like walkmans and stereos.

The afternoon sun was hot and I was tired when pedaling into Alor Setar. There were a few mosques and one or two Buddhist temples. One of these Buddhist temples had a villa with many orange robed monks milling about outside. I stopped in and asked if I could stay the night. They asked for a fee, to my surprise and somewhat dismay, but it wasn't more than a quarter, and I paid it and had a small box shaped room all to my own. This was enjoyable, as I was exhausted after two nights of entertaining in addition to the hard traveling. This night I talked with the monks and we did sing a few songs but they were more disposed to be quiet. There was something about these monks that was not as genuine as the Buddhist monks in Thailand.

### Monday July 9

Up early in the morning, I went to alms with the monks and this time it was a little less formal than in Thailand. We all sat at tables and the food was on another table. The monks went first and all the guests followed with plates to help ourselves to the food.

I rode onward to Butterworth and then caught the ferry for the island of Penang. The ride took about twenty minutes. It was a lovely afternoon when I arrived in Georgetown and I cruised its busy streets looking at the obvious English influence of the store fronts and signs.

I called Steve, whom I'd met at Ko Samui and he said I could come over to his home and stay as long as I wanted to. It took me some time to find his house. The streets in Georgetown were rather oddly laid out. I had to call him again from another location. He told me how to find his place from there. It was around sunset when I finally did arrive.

My host, Steven, was a businessman and was very interested in my travels. "Come in, come in, you can stay as long as you like," he told me. I followed him on a short tour of his house. It was large and had an upstairs. He led me to the shower. I needed that.

After getting cleaned up, I met his servant, Kree, who was an elderly Buddhist. Kree saw to it that I was well fed. We all sat around and talked up a storm. Kree could not speak english, he only hovered around, to make sure we were well cared for.

I was shown a bed to sleep upon. It was Krees bed normally. I would stay in his room, while he slept near the kitchen. He insisted, it would be no other way.

## Tuesday July 10

The house was of such a design and construction that it reminded me of those in Minneapolis. Plaster walls were painted in earthy shades and trimmed with dark oak. The house was an L shape. The kitchen was built with a walkout screen porch. It was there, in a hammock where Kree would stay while I slept in his bed.

I ate a fine breakfast and then went shopping in 'Georgetown for airline tickets that would fly me from Singapore back to the states. I was told that I would need to have an airline ticket out of Singapore in order to be allowed entry into that country. It would cost me around $800 dollars, so I really had to look around for a bargain. I went from agency to agency, comparing. It took a lot of time and was frustrating. This one ticket agent would have my tickets ready in two days, and so I bought the ticket for $1100. This ticket would take me from Singapore to Hong Kong, to Seoul, to Tokyo, to Honolulu and then back to San Francisco. I thought, what am I doing? I only had $100 left. I could not go to those cities anyways, without some more money. This was real hard for me to figure out. It looked like I would just have to go home. I needed to spend some time rethinking this journey.

## Wednesday July 11

I decided to make the best of my stay on Penang by touring around the island. I told Steven and Kree my intent and packed the bike up and headed out at about 2pm.

There were some nice homes and beautiful streets, in this city. They were lined with huge trees that provided a canopy over the roads in some areas of Georgetown. This again reminded me of The Twin Cities in summer. I was hungry at around 3 o' clock but all I could find to eat was reddish colored, crappy Moslem like dishes that were covered with domed-screened fly protectors. Upon closer inspection I saw that a good many of the flies were swarming inside the dome!. "No thanks," I told the annoyed vendor dressed in white gown and cap. He must have thought I was rude to pedal off without buying his food. He shook his serving spoon at me.

I kept on pedaling and found a store that sold Ramen noodles and moon cakes and bought a couple of each. I found an undeveloped beach area on the northwest side of the island and made a little camp near the beach and the sea. I cooked my noodles and enjoyed the exotic view of palm trees hanging over the Indian Ocean.

During the night, some hell raising kids made some racket not far from me, but I was not noticed and the left me alone. A lightning storm moved in later on. It was rather frightening and yet exciting. The rain poured down.

I laid there and thought about my travels. Tomorrow, I would try an experiment. Perhaps

I could raise some money by singing on the sidewalks of Georgetown. I was mustering up my courage and thinking of the songs I would sing. It made me so nervous to think of doing this, so much that I thought it best to just go home. Yet, something said, try it, go for it...I drifted off to sleep.

## Thursday July 12

My bike ride commenced at the break of dawn, continuing the ride around the island. I passed up and over some big hills, which afforded beautiful views of the Indian Ocean. It took some hard cycling to get over these hills, but I persevered and made it up to the Snake Temple and explored its interesting sights. There were a variety of poisonous snakes there, and many Chinese temple designs, such as the dragons on the roof. This was a nice temple that was high on a hill and was finely crafted with gorgeous woodwork.

From there I went to a large Buddhist temple on a hill, that was called Kek Lok Si. This exquisite temple looked like a multi tiered white wedding cake with a gold top. I strolled around the temple, met a lovely Swedish gal who said she was spending the night there. I looked about gardens and wanted to spend the night there sleeping in a guest house or by camping, but money was my big problem and thus decided to spin back down into Georgetown.

It was all downhill to Georgetown and I enjoyed the ride. Once there, I treated myself to an ice cream cone and drank a Coke. Then at 3pm, went and picked up my airline tickets and the agency lady was very nice. Her name was Rose, and she seemed so caring.

I got up my courage and tried busking for the first time in Asia. I stood out on the sidewalk of Georgetown and played my guitar and sang about five songs. During this show, nobody gave me any money. I was so embarrassed. Some people stopped to listen. I thought I failed. I would have no chance of continuing my journey. I packed up the guitar and was visibly shaken. Yet it was a good experience for me, just to have tried it and to have dusted off the cobwebs.

I returned back to Steve's house and Kree was overjoyed to see me again. It was like we were old buddies. We had some food and tea and sat to chat. Steve was also pleased to see me again.

We laid outside on the hammocks and sipped on a beer. It was a hot evening. I was enjoying there nice company. Kree liked to joke around. Even though he could not speak english, we still communicated by making gestures. He continually wanted to help me. He would bring me anything I needed.

## Friday July 13

In the morning I packed up the bike and said goodbye to my hosts. Steve had to rush off to work. Kree was very moved by my visit. "Ok, you ok," he said. He then took the shirt off his back and gave it to me. I put it on graciously and was thankful for his gift. It was a Hawaiian style of shirt made of a silky material. I thanked him immensely and headed down to the ferry and then made the journey across to Butterworth.

My ride south was along very busy roads heading to Ipoh. There were frightening fast drivers in Malaysia. Big trucks would speed past inches from me. I had several flat tires from thorns along the road. On one stretch I got a flat tire and was changing it when a big truck sped past and knocked the bike over on top of me. I was pretty mad.

The road passed through heavily forested hills, lined with large shade trees and hills that challenged my pumping legs and then cooled me as I sped down the steep declines.

At a tourist cave I met some travelers who were so surprised that I would ride a bike in Malaysia. "You must be crazy, to be out there with those mad drivers," said a very nice looking Canadian gal to me.

I explored a Buddhist cave and temple and inside admired the many Buddhist statues. One had a basket with big red apples at the base of the Buddhas feet. I lusted for a red apple. I had not seen the likes of them since leaving Greece. I waited until nobody was around and grabbed an apple and an orange and left behind .25 sen. I felt guilty about doing this. But really, where do these fruits go from here? It was not as if the Buddha himself would eat them. Wouldn't the Buddha want to share these with a hungry world traveler? I went a few miles down the road and munched on the fabulous red, delicious apple.

I arrived in Ipoh as the sun was setting. I thought I'd just ride up to the edge of this big sprawling city and find a place to camp, but I continued into the city and was very tired. It was getting dark when I entered this small Chinese restaurant. I ordered Chinese food and there were some local fellows who were curious of me. We talked and they were very concerned with my welfare. "You can come stay with me," said Ringo Chu. I have always trusted Chinese people, and after eating followed Chu and his friends, Sam, Sonny and we went to Chu's house. He introduced me to his mom and his sister. They lived in a little apartment above a business. They were very warm people, with a generous spirit and very concerned about me. I enjoyed a shower and was given a new shirt by Chu and then spent the night on a nice bed.

## Saturday July 14

Chu and I ate a breakfast that was made of a donut like bread called 'utow' that was dipped in a sweet sauce. It was tasty and filling. He had the next two days off and invited me to stay the weekend and I accepted.

We went walking to his friends house and everyone looked at me like I was a novelty. All the friends went together to a coffee shop where we ate lunch. I could not pay for anything. They were so interested in me and very cordial. Yet they talked like joshing young friends do. They truly reminded me of my Greek friends only these were Chinese. We went on a tour of the city and all the way had many nice talks about the world. The night was fun and we had a few beers and got a little drunk. It was a joy to be with these friends.

## Sunday July 15

We went to many art shops and craft shops to look at items that are locally made. I had this feeling that Chu and his friends wanted to buy me something expensive as a gift, but I tried to avoid them from doing so. I kept them moving and was careful not to like something to much. We went to a movie and it was really funny to see Rambo speaking Chinese. Chu and I talked and I told him that we could be friends in the heart for life. This touched him and Sonny took our photo in front of a fountain with one of our hands over our heart and the other embracing each other.

## Monday July 16

It was very early and I had a very heartful goodbye to Chu and Sonny. They were delightful hosts. Chu's mother had some breakfast laid out for me and after that I was off. Ipoh became more than just another old mining town in Malaysia. It would touch me as a surprise does. I had friends here and that gave this place a face.

The road out of Ipoh climbed up a grade and then down through Kampar and Tapah. I continued along enjoying the sight of the wild looking Cameron Highlands to the east. Some of the hills reach up high in altitude. From what I was told, there were few roads and the native people were headhunters and cannibals still roamed those backwoods.

I headed south out, uphill and then along some roads lined with large and tall trees. I saw a heavily forested land, full of huge trees and it was challenging cycling up and down these steep hills. It was exciting for me and I loved seeing this part of Malaysia.

I had traveled many miles on this day and it there was an interesting site to visit. I pulled into Batu Caves and commenced looking around the large structures. There was a stairway that had 272 steps up to 'heaven' or to be 'closer' to God. I went up those stairs with little effort. There were several caves to explore. One of them, called Batu Cave was especially noteworthy. It had 272 stairs that led up to the cave. It was said that if you could go up those stairs, you would surely get to heaven. I was in such great shape that I had no trouble making it all the way without much effort, though I must say I was winded when I entered the huge cave. I felt for those along the staircase suffering, some trying to catch there breath or energy.

As the day progressed, I knew it wouldn't be a good idea to continue further into the big city of Kaulu Lampur at such a late hour. Thus I asked one of the Indians if it would be possible that I might camp in my tent somewhere for the night. He told me that he had a guest room that I could stay in for about $1. I was shown the tiny room and allowed to spend the night there. It was a most welcome respite, as the rain started to pour down.

My Indian hosts were very suspicious of me. They kept checking on me during the night. A couple of times I thought I should shout at them and then get up and leave. But I remembered what happened to me back in India in Bihar. I thought it better to be calm and just let this night of intrusion pass. The Indians stared at me just like they did in India. Smile! I thought. How similar these Indians here in Malaysia are to those back in India. Peoples characteristics must be related to their culture.

## Tuesday July 17th

I was up early and thanked my Indian hosts and then decided to hit the road. I continued on the road to Kaula Lampur.

It was early in the morning, when I headed downhill and then entered the large city. The first thing that caught my eye was a very large blue shaped mosque. I was dazzled by the blue folded roof of the National Mosque. It had a wonderful design. I could see it from far away and when getting closer, it had as much appeal.

As I rode into the bustling city, I felt like a visiting dignitary. People would look at me with such interest. Many would stop and watch as I passed. I felt like someone important, as if they were witnessing history passing by. How silly were my thoughts. They seemed to chuckle when I did an abrupt 'u' turn on a busy street to go up to a McDonalds restaurant, though, at such an early hour, I could not get a burger. I also saw the price and decided it best to pass this by.

There was one building which caught my fancy as I pedaled past. It was called the Sultan abdul Samad Building, now the Supreme Court. It had 'red onion' domes on top of spires and a clock tower. Across the street was a park, which I eyed up to see if I could stay there, but it did not look good.

I spent a few hours in the morning, looking all about the city and trying to see if I should stay longer and try to make some money busking. I decided against it. This did not look like it would work.

I searched here and there for a bicycle shop and needed a new tire. This quest took me on many streets and asking many people questions. They were nice people. Very helpful and could speak english. I finally did find a shop.

I returned to the McDonald's at about noon and they made me two Big Macs and a large order of golden fries. I was about to pay, when some fellow stepped in and bought it for me. Thanks! It was well worth the wait in the long line to bite into that Big Mac and munch those golden fries.

I looked around the city, and saw 'K.L.' as another big city and decided to get going, as my impatience demanded a return to the road. I headed south up a long hill and pedaled along in the drizzle. The road passed through the hills, lined with occasional monsterous trees. It was wonderful cycling countryside to witness. The road was very good and I made great time.

The day was getting late, I pedaled along until darkness began to set in. I was exhausted and realized it was best to quit. I was passing through a little town, which had only a few shops and a post office. The post office entryway had a large overhang and I found shelter under it from the elements. I sat there and ate my second McDonalds burger and a few fries. Even though it was several hours old it was delicious nonetheless. It was just fantastic.

It was soon dark and since nobody was around, I pitched my tent right on the porch floor, between the railings. This would give me some mosquito protection.

## Wednesday July 18

I awoke to a drizzly day and had a surprisingly good nights rest and was up early before anybody came. I packed up my gear and headed down the road to Port Dickson. I inquired about taking a ship to Sumatra, but was told it would be better from Malacca. I met some western travelers and enjoyed talking to them. They said I would meet more in Malacca.

The road followed the coastline along a twisting small road for Malacca. Again enjoyed the orange highlights of sunlight on clouds to the west, over the Straight of Malacca. I could see big oil tanker ships out on the straight. This is one of the major shipping lanes in all the world. The sight of these immense oil tankers in the distance, plying the Straight of Malacca impressed me. I could see the island of Sumatra, Indonesia far off on the western horizon, like a mirage. How I wondered what that place must be like. I dreaded the unknown, were they wild people? Was there rugged conditions and many dangers? Yet I longed to go there and be a participant in such an exotic place.

I arrived in the city of Malacca and immediately saw many western tourists. This was a joyful sight. I looked forward to talking to them.

There were many sights to see in Malacca, as this was once a Portugese and then a Dutch settlement. The Portugese first came in the year 1511 shortly before Magellans voyage around the world. Many Europeans, who made it look like any European town, settled this town. Before there arrival, it was a Malay seaport that handled much of the trade in the region. The Portugese set up a trading center, and brought in missionaries. This went on for 200 years, then the Dutch won a few battles with the Portugese, and inherited Malacca.

I rode up before a red church that was in the heart of town and had the date 1753 right on the front of it. This was a quaint little town, with a gentleness and calming atmosphere. There were ancient fortresses and canons aimed here and there. I stayed at an inexpensive hostel and took the liberty of walking the historic old streets on a dark night. It had this distinctive old world charm, like being in New England in the 1700's.

## Thursday July 19

The morning was humid and warm when my pedals propelled my wheels away from Malacca as I headed south for Johore Bahru. I followed the coast and then went uphill, until I was once again able to see the sights of distant oil tankers and puffy, orangish, white sunlit clouds over the Straits of Malacca.

The cicadas were humming and birds whooping to create a satisfying background sound over the occasional passing tourist buses. It was not until the town of Ayer Hitam that traffic really started to pick up. This was the main artery between Malaysia and Singapore and it was busy with passing vehicles. Each blew a healthy blast on the horn, one that lifted my hide and pissed me off as the day progressed.

It started to rain around 2pm and I was getting tired, but maintained a steady rhythm all the way to Johor. I had traveled around 125miles and arrived around 5pm and looked around for lodging. A Catholic Church had a kind white priest and a tall lanky Indian fellow who was the fellowship director. They both were sympathetic to my asking for a nights rest. I was led to the bath and then invited to supper.

The priest was from South Africa and had much to say about that countries problem. He was a big man, with enormous hands and a firmness in his disposition. He came across as a gentle giant, a person you respected, but could trust. He questioned me on my religious upbringing and what I had learned about religion in the world. I summed it up by saying, "The Moslems seem disorganized, like they are cluttered, almost uncaring in how they treat the world around them. The Hindus are winged out on some far off Disneyland, the Buddhists seem so relaxed, as if they haven't a care in the world and the Christians all want to bring more people into Christ." He laughed and admitted to putting up a big sign for Christ.

We talked after our dinner. Went out for a short walk into Jahore in the evening. Anticipating Singapore. I had a nice bed and slipped off into pleasant dreams.

## Friday July 20

In the morning, I was told that in order to be allowed into Singapore, I would need a haircut. The youth director was from India and he knew exactly where to take me. He led me to a fine haircutter and soon my long locks were clipped. He paid the bill, it was most kindly of him. We stopped to sit and enjoy an ice coffee, then returned to eat lunch with the priest.

Back at the church, I loaded up the bike and was watched by the father and the youth director as I pedaled away from the white church and left Jahore Baru and headed toward Singapore. I was leaving Malaysia behind and began crossing the long causeway between the countries. I had been forewarned to abide by all of the rules at the customs for Singapore, or else risk trouble.

It was a nerve-wracking ride, on this hot, sticky morning, under a blue sky and green trees everywhere, when I pedaled up to the Singapore customs station,

CPSIA information can be obtained
at www.ICGtesting.com
Printed in the USA
BVHW010216301120
594464BV00021B/712